# Taking the Constitution Seriously

## Essays on the Constitution and Constitutional Law

**Gary L. McDowell**
*Dickinson College*

**KENDALL/HUNT PUBLISHING COMPANY**
Dubuque, Iowa, USA     •     Toronto, Ontario, Canada

Copyright © 1981 by Kendall/Hunt Publishing Company

Library of Congress Catalog Card Number: 81–80943

ISBN 0–8403–2432–4

Printed in the United States of America

C   402432   01

# Contents

# Preface

In the study of the law there is no shortage of secondary literature. Scholarly journals of history, political science, jurisprudence, and sociology; national journals of opinion; and law reviews from every law school annually produce a mass of essays, reviews, and comments relating to the theory and practice of law. Yet, amidst this plenty, there is poverty. Most articles tend to concentrate on the field of "public" as opposed to "constitutional" law; and among those who write on constitutional law, essays that take the Constitution seriously are few and far between.

This is due in part to the character of the Constitution itself. In attempting to produce a document "for future generations, and not merely for the peculiar circumstances of the moment," the Founders wrote in language that would be broad enough to be lasting. To do otherwise, as Madison told Washington, would have been to create not a constitution, but a digest of laws. Interpretation is the inevitable concomitant of our limited constitution. And, since the doctrine of judicial review was firmly established by Chief Justice John Marshall in *Marbury* v. *Madison* (1803), we have looked to the judiciary, and to the Supreme Court of the United States in particular, for the authoritative exposition of the Constitution. The effect has been to replace the Constitution as the object of our study with constitutional law. We tend to accept too uncritically Charles Evans Hughes' nonjudicial *dictum* that the Constitution is only what the judges say it is.

The purpose of this volume is to attempt to put the Constitution back into the study of constitutional law. Although the essays presented here are diverse and may not take the same perspective, they are unified by a common sentiment: the Constitution matters, and to understand constitutional law we must first endeavor to understand the Constitution.

I would like to thank those who contributed to this project with their encouragement and thoughtful suggestions. In particular, I am indebted to Henry J. Abraham, David K. Nichols, David M. O'Brien, and Jeffrey Poelvoorde of the University of Virginia; Sotirios A. Barber of the University of South Florida; Joseph M. Bessette and Mary Pollingue Nichols of the Catholic University; Stanley Brubaker of Colgate University; Paul Peterson of Northern Illinois University; Ralph A. Rossum of Loyola University of Chicago; Glen E. Thurow of the University of Dallas; Peter Schultz of Allentown College; Lane Sunderland of Knox College; and Tinsley E. Yarbrough of East Carolina University. To my colleagues in the Department of Political Science at Dickinson College for creating an atmosphere of collegiality, academic rigor, and scholarly concern, I owe a special thanks. Without the good services of William McConnell, Victoria Kuhn, Mary Hatcher, Andrea Allen, Suzanne Fish, John Roberto, Dave Frees, Donna Bartenfelder, Brad Schwartz and David Raczenbek in assembling, typing, and duplicating these essays, this volume could not have appeared. The entire project was generously supported by a grant from the Faculty Committee on Research and Development of Dickinson College.

To those who have taught me about the Constitution—Henry J. Abraham, Robert Jennings Harris, and the late Herbert J. Storing—I owe that debt that can only be owed to those who teach in the true sense of the word. I shall be ever grateful to them.

Last, but never least, I must thank my best friend and most insightful critic, my wife Karla, without whom nothing would be possible.

G.L.M.
Carlisle, Pennsylvania

# Introduction: Taking the Constitution Seriously

> I entirely concur in the propriety of resorting to the sense in which the Constitution was accepted and ratified by the nation. In that sense alone it is the legitimate Constitution. And if that be not the guide in expounding it, there can be no security for a consistent and stable, more than for a faithful, exercise of its powers. If the meaning of the text be sought in the changeable meaning of the words composing it, it is evident that the shape and attributes of the government must partake of the changes to which the words and phrases of all living languages are constantly subject. What a metamorphosis would be produced in the code of law if all its phraseology were to be taken in its modern sense!
>
> *James Madison, 1824*

The study of the Constitution as the source of our political being has fallen on hard times. Not only has the place of the Constitution in the study of political parties, the presidency, and Congress been eroded, but it has also lost much of its authority in the study of constitutional law as well. As students of constitutional law, we need at least to reconsider the advice James Madison gave to Henry Lee in 1824:

> If the sense in which the Constitution was accepted and ratified by the Nation . . . be not the guide in expounding it, there can be no security for a stable [government] more than for a faithful exercise of its powers.[1]

What, exactly, was the purpose of the Constitution; and how is that purpose to be regarded in the difficult business of expounding and applying the Constitution today?

## I

The basic intention of the Framers, taking into account the permanent attributes of human nature—both its strengths and its weaknesses—was to create a government that could be safely administered by men over men. The end sought was a safe balance between governmental power and individual liberty, or, as Madison explained in *The Federalist,* to combine "the requisite stability and energy in government with the inviolable attention due to liberty and the republican form."[2] The Constitution was the magnificent product; it was understood to create an institutional arrangement whereby the political principles of the Declaration of Independence could be achieved, and the most hallowed of the Framers' objects, political liberty, would be secured.

1

The object of the Constitutional Convention in 1787, it was frequently asserted, was to draft a constitution "for future generations, and not merely for the peculiar circumstances of the moment." The Founders hoped they had devised a constitution that would "last forever" or, at the very least, one that would "last for ages."[3]

The Constitution was intended to be "paramount," "fundamental," and lasting, in order to achieve a steady and just administration of the laws.[4] By being held above the law, the Constitution would contribute to the necessary political stability by drawing unto itself that "veneration which time bestows on everything."[5] Certainly the Founders entertained no utopian notions that they had written the last work in republican constitutions; they knew the necessity of allowing for future amendments. But they also understood that the process of changing the fundamental and paramount law must be cumbersome so alterations would not be made for "light and transient causes." It would have been dangerous to render the Constitution "too mutable."[6] The Constitution was left to posterity to "improve and perpetuate."[7] The alteration of the Constitution, where necessary to meet the unforeseen exigencies of the future, was left to the people, not to their deputies alone.

This older view of the Constitution as paramount to the ordinary law and to the branches of government has become undermined to a great degree by a new judicial view of the Constitution. The latter is made up of two distinct but related lines of judicial logic: the first is that the opinions of the Supreme Court—constitutional law—have the same status as the Constitution itself; the second, that the Constitution is not bound to any particular theory and, instead of being permanent and fixed, is free to move ameobalike through history.

Between these two lines of judicial logic—the alleged supremacy of Supreme Court opinions and the notion that the meaning of the Constitution changes from one era to another—lies the fundamentally new judicial view of the Constitution—the idea of a "living Constitution." As Justice Felix Frankfurter pointed out as early as 1937, the "people have been taught to believe that when the Supreme Court speaks it is not they who speak but the Constitution, whereas, of course, in so many vital cases, it is *they* who speak and *not* the Constitution. And verily I believe," Frankfurter concluded, "that this is what the country needs most to understand."[8] The idea of a living Constitution" is, in the words of Justice Hugo Black, "an attack not only on the great value of our Constitution itself, but also on the concept of a written constitution which is to survive through the years as originally written unless changed through the amending process which the Framers wisely provided."[9] The result of the new judicial logic has been to blur the distinction between the Constitution and constitutional law.

The maintenance of the distinction between the Constitution and constitutional law, however, is of fundamental importance. The Constitution, on the one hand, is considered the supreme law of the land in that it represents the collective will of the people. It is alterable, to be sure, but only by the intricate and lengthy process of formal amendment. Constitutional law, on the other hand, is not considered as fundamental. Insofar as it is only the interpretation of the supreme will of the people by agents of the people, it is susceptible to error. The justices of the Supreme Court were no more expected to be that "philosophical race of kings wished for by Plato,"[10] than any other deputy of the people—representative, senator, or president.

The Constitution is more fundamental than constitutional law in the same sense that it is more fundamental than legislative enactments. Constitutional law and legislative enactments are, and must be, more mutable than the Constitution. To assume that constitutional law is by its nature somehow of the same status as the Constitution is to conjure up frightening conclusions about not only what Philip B. Kurland has called the "derelicts of Constitutional law,"[11] (e.g., *Dred Scott* v. *Sandford*) but, more deeply, about the necessity of maintaining certainty in the administration of a republican form of government.

To try to instill an appreciation for the distinction between the Constitution and what the judges say it is in their opinions is no mean task. Whereas one may argue against the view that many of its commands are "written in Delphic language,"[12] the Constitution is certainly not free of indeterminate language. Nor is the application of the language of the Constitution a merely mechanical process. But however indeterminate its language may be, and however much judgment may be necessary to apply its provisions, "there are large areas of clarity in constitutional language which could limit the operations of government by providing limits to the discretion of those who apply constitutional rules."[13] It is necessary, in order to restore the distinction between the Constitution and its "judicial gloss," to point out that a "coherent account of events in judicial history requires principles which transcend the cases themselves."[14] As Sotirios Barber has argued: "The meaning of the Constitution itself is one source of those principles, as are such other sources as the deeper intentions of the Framers and the needs of current generations."[15]

## II

Granting the indeterminacy of some constitutional language, the problem of interpretation and application of the Constitution remains.[16] Constitutional interpretation must begin with the document: what does the Constitution say? Most often, the provisions of the text are clear and unambiguous. There are, however, areas that lack clarity and thus demand that the Court look elsewhere for the meaning of the Constitution. The first place to look is to the Founders: what was their intention? Since we still live under basically the same document, we have an obligation to understand what it was intended to do; and what it was *not* intended to do. Yet while there is a hefty collection of writings such as *The Federalist* and James Madison's "Notes on the Federal Convention," it is not always possible to divine the Framers' intentions.

To supplement this fundamental mode of interpretation, the Court often must be creative. It may be best to approach a case on the basis of precedent or *stare decisis*; or to resort to logical reasoning (for example, John Marshall in *Marbury* v. *Madison*[17]); or perhaps even to the construction of constitutional doctrines (e.g., "clear and present danger"), which may be a combination of precedent, logic, and constitutional language. But whatever the method, it is essential that the Court never lose sight of the Constitution. It must first seek to understand the intentions of the Founders, "not because they were demigods and not because we are obligated to yield to their will or authority and to embrace their judgments uncritically . . . [but] because they did, after all, establish the constitutional order within which we live, and, as long as that order remains in force, we need to know as much about the Constitution as possible including what purposes it was designed to achieve and what evils it was intended to avert."[18] Joseph Story said it best:

In construing the Constitution of the United States, we are in the first instance, to consider, what are its nature and objects, its scope and design, as apparent from the structure of the instrument, viewed as a whole and also viewed in its component parts. Where its words are plain, clear and determinate, they require no interpretation. . . . Where the words admit of two senses, each of which is conformable to general usage, that sense is to be adopted, which without departing from the literal import of the words, best harmonizes with the nature and objects, the scope and design of the instrument.[19]

The often dry, administrative language of the Constitution is the means to achieve the noble ends of political liberty and safe republican government. In this context, the ideas of separation of powers, federalism, and even judicial review are exposed to a standard by which to evaluate the legitimacy of the claims made in their behalf. Yet this view of the Constitution as a means to higher ends has been largely abandoned in favor of the contemporary notion of a "living" constitution, a constitution whose meaning does not depend upon an underlying and unifying theory of politics, but only upon time and circumstance.

It is necessary to recover the idea that the Constitution was intended to be a permanent means, a fixed arrangement of institutions and processes that will issue in safe popular government. To the extent to which this older notion can be recovered, the result will be a Court and citizenry able and willing to look upon the Constitution as the source of our political liberty and private happiness. To that extent we will be able to heed the advice of Abraham Lincoln when he admonished that we must make the Constitution and the laws that flow therefrom the political religion of the nation if we are to contribute to the perpetuation of our political institutions and thereby to the last best hope of earth to the cause of freedom.

### Notes

1. Gaillard Hunt, ed., *The Writings of James Madison* (New York: Putnam, 1900–1910) Vol. 9, p. 191.
2. Jacob Cooke, ed., *The Federalist* (Middletown: Wesleyan University Press, 1961), No. 37, p. 233. All references are to this edition.
3. Max Farrand, ed., *Records of the Federal Convention of 1787, 4 vols.,* (New Haven: Yale University Press, 1937), I, pp. 422; 462; II, p. 125.
4. See *The Federalist,* Nos. 14, 37, 53, 63, 78.
5. *The Federalist,* No. 49, p. 340.
6. *The Federalist,* No. 43, p. 296.
7. *The Federalist,* No. 14, p. 89.
8. Max Friedman, *Roosevelt and Frankfurter: Their Correspondence, 1928–1945,* (Boston: Little, Brown, 1968), p. 383.
9. Dissenting Opinion in *Harper v. Virginia Board of Elections,* 383 US 663, 678 (1966).
10. *The Federalist,* No. 49, p. 340.
11. Philip B. Kurland, *Politics, the Constitution and the Warren Court,* (Chicago: University of Chicago Press, 1971), p. 86.
12. *Ibid.,* p. xiv.
13. Sotirios A. Barber, *The Constitution and the Delegation of Congressional Power* (Chicago: University of Chicago Press, 1974), p. 9.

14. *Ibid.*
15. *Ibid.*
16. The following section is based on Ralph A. Rossum and G. Alan Tarr, *American Constitutional Law and Interpretation* (New York: St. Martin's Press, forthcoming.)
17. 1 Cranch 137 (1803).
18. Rossum and Tarr, *American Constitutional Law and Interpretation.*
19. Joseph Story, *Commentaries on the Constitution of the United States,* 3 vols., (Boston: Hilliard, Greay, and Company, 1833), I, pp. 387–388.

# Prologue

> Many . . . differences may arise among polished nations, from the effects of climate, or from sources of fashion, that are still more unaccountable and obscure; but the principal distinctions on which we can rest, are derived from the part a people are obliged to act in their national capacity; from the objects placed in their view by the state; or from the constitution of government, which prescribing the terms of society to its subjects, has a great influence in forming their apprehensions and habits.
>
> *Adam Ferguson*

---

## The Necessity of the Constitution*

James Madison

As the weakness and wants of man naturally lead to an association of individuals, under a common authority, whereby each may have the protection of the whole against danger from without, and enjoy in safety within, the advantages of social intercourse, and an exchange of the necessaries and comforts of life: in like manner feeble communities, independent of each other, have resorted to a Union, less intimate, but with common Councils, for the common safety agst. powerful neighbors, and for the preservation of justice and peace among themselves. Ancient history furnishes examples of these confederacies, tho' with a very imperfect account, of their structure, and of the attributes and functions of the presiding Authority. There are examples of modern date also, some of them still existing, the modifications and transactions of which are sufficiently known.

It remained for the British Colonies, now United States, of North America, to add to those examples, one of a more interesting character than any of them: which led to a system without a precedent ancient or modern, a system founded on popular rights, and so combining, a federal form with the forms of individual Republics, as may enable each to supply the defects of the other and obtain the advantages of both.

Whilst the Colonies enjoyed the protection of the parent country as it was called, against foreign danger; and were secured by its superintending controul, against conflicts among themselves, they continued independent of each other, under a common, tho' limited dependence, on the parental Authority. When the growth of the offspring

*This is from a rough draft written by Madison near the end of his long life. The original title Madison gave it, "Preface to Debates in the Convention of 1787," he later crossed out. Perhaps more than any other single document, this gives us an insight into the circumstances that caused the Founders to reflect upon the necessity of an energetic yet limited constitution.

in strength and in wealth, awakened the jealousy and tempted the avidity of the parent, into schemes of usurpation and exaction, the obligation was felt by the former of uniting their counsels, and efforts to avert the impending calamity.

As early as the year 1754, indications having been given of a design in the Brittish Government to levy contributions on the Colonies, without their consent; a meeting of Colonial deputies took place at Albany, which attempted to introduce a compromising substitute that might at once satisfy the British requisitions and save their own rights from violation. The attempt had no other effect, than by bringing these rights into a more conspicuous view, to invigorate the attachment to them on one side; and to nourish the haughty encroaching spirit on the other.

In 1774. The progress made by G[reat] B[ritain] in the open assertion of her pretensions, and in the appended purpose of otherwise maintaining them by Legislative enactments and declarations had been such that the Colonies did not hesitate to assemble, by their deputies, in a formal Congress, authorized to oppose to the British innovation whatever measures might be found best adapted to the occasion; without however losing sight of an eventual reconciliation.

The dissuasive measures of that Congress, being without effect, another Congress was held in 1775, whose pacific efforts to bring about a change in the views of the other party, being equally unavailing, and the commencement of actual hostilities having at length put an end to all hope of reconciliation; The Congress finding moreover that the popular voice began to call for an entire and perpetual dissolution of the political ties which had connected them with G[reat] B[ritain], proceeded on the memorable 4th of July, 1776, to declare the 13 Colonies, independent States.

During the discussions of this solemn Act, a Committee consisting of a Member from each colony had been appointed to prepare and digest a form of Confederation, for the future management of the common interests, which had hitherto been left to the discretion of Congress, guided by the exigences of the contest, and by the known intentions or occasional instructions of the Colonial Legislatures.

It appears that as early as the 21st of July 1775, a plan entitled "Articles of Confederation and perpetual Union of the Colonies" had been sketched by Docr Franklin, The plan being on that day submitted by him to Congress; and tho' not copied into their Journals remaining on their files in his handwriting. But notwithstanding the term "perpetual" observed in the title, the articles provided expressly for the event of a return of the Colonies to a connection with G. Britain.

This sketch became a basis for the plan reported by the Come. on the 12th of July, now also remaining on the files of Congress, in the handwriting of Mr. Dickinson. The plan, tho' dated after the Declaration of Independence, was probably drawn up before that event; since the name of Colonies, and not States is used throughout the draught. The plan reported, was debated and amended from time to time till the 17th of November 1777, when it was agreed to by Congress, and proposed to the Legislatures of the States, with an explanatory and recommendatory letter. The ratifications of these by their Delegates in Congs. duly authorized took place at successive dates; but were not compleated till March 1, 1781 when Maryland who had made it a prerequisite that the vacant lands acquired from the British Crown should be a Common fund, yielded to the persuasion that a final and formal establishment of the federal Union and Govt. would make a favorable impression not only on other foreign nations, but on G[reat] B[ritain] herself.

The great difficulty experienced in so framing the fedl. system as to obtain the unanimity required for its due sanction, may be inferred from the long interval, and recurring discussions, between the commencement and completion of the work, from the changes made during its progress; from the language of Congs., when proposing it to the States, which dwelt on the impracticability of devising a system acceptable to all of them; from the reluctant assent given by some; and the various alterations proposed by others; and by a tardiness in others again which produced a special address to them from Congs. enforcing the duty of sacrificing local considerations and favorite opinions to the public safety, and the necessary harmony; nor was the assent of some of the States finally yielded without strong protests against particular articles, and a reliance on future amendments removing their objections.

It is to be recollected, no doubt, that these delays might be occasioned in some degree, by an occupation of the public Councils both general and local, with the deliberations and measures, essential to a Revolutionary struggle; But there must have been a balance for these causes, in the obvious motives to hasten the establishment of a regular and efficient Govt.; and in the tendency of the crisis to repress opinions and pretensions, which might be inflexible in another state of things.

The principle difficulties which embarrassed the progress, and retarded the completion of the plan of Confederation, may be traced to 1. the natural reluctance of the parties to a relinquishment of power; 2. a natural jealousy of its abuse in other hands than their own; 3. the rule of suffrage among parties unequal in size, but equal in sovereignty; 4. The ratio of contributions in money and troops, among parties, whose inequality in size did not correspond with that of their wealth, or of their military or free population; 5. The selection and definition of the powers, at once necessary to the federal head, and safe to the several members.

To these sources of difficulty, incident to the formation of all such confederacies, were added two others one of a temporary, the other of permanent nature. The first was the Case of the Crown lands, so called because they had been held by the British Crown, and being ungranted to individuals when, its authority ceased, were considered by the States within whose charters or asserted limits they lay, as devolving on them; whilst it was contended by the others, that being wrested from the dethroned authority by the equal exertion of all, they resulted in right and equality to the benefit of all. The lands being of vast extent and of growing value, were the occasion of much discussion and heart-burning; and proved the most obstinate of the impediments to an earlier consummation of the plan of federal Gov't. The State of Maryland was the last that acceded to it held out as already noticed till March 1, 1781 and then yielded only to the hope that by giving a Stable and authoritative character to the Confederation, a successful termination of the contest might be accelerated. The dispute was happily compromised by successive surrenders of portions of the territory by the States having exclusive claims to it, and acceptance of them by Congress.

The other source of dissatisfaction was the peculiar situation of some of the States, which having no convenient ports for foreign commerce, were subject to be taxed by their neighbors, thro whose ports, their commerce was carried on. New Jersey placed between Phila. and N. York, was likened to a cask tapped at both ends: and N. Carolina between Virga. and S. Carolina to a patient bleeding at both Arms. The Articles of Confederation provided no remedy for the complaint: which produced a strong protest on the part of N. Jersey; and never ceased to be a source of dissatisfaction and discord, until the new Constitution, superseded the old.

But the radical infirmity of "the Arts. of Confederation" was the dependence on Congs. on the voluntary and simultaneous compliance with its Requisitions, by so many independent communities, each consulting more or less its particular interests and convenience and distrusting the compliance of the others. Whilst the paper emissions of Congs. continued to circulate they were employed as a sinew of war, like gold and silver. When that ceased to be the case, the fatal defect of the political System was felt in its alarming force. The war was merely kept alive and brought to a successful conclusion by such foreign aids and temporary expedients as could be applied; a hope prevailing with many, and a wish with all, that a state of peace, and the sources of prosperity opened by it, would give to the Confederacy in practice, the efficiency which had been inferred from its theory.

The close of the war however brought no-cure for the public embarrassments. The States relieved from the pressure of foreign danger, and flushed with the enjoyment of independent and sovereign power; (instead of a diminished disposition to part with it), persevered in omissions and in measures incompatible with their relations to the Federal Govt. and with those among themselves.

Having served as a member of Congs. through the period between Marc. 1780 and the arrival of peace in 1783, I had become intimately acquainted with the public distresses and the causes of them. I had observed the successful opposition to every attempt to procure a remedy by new grants of power to Congs. I had found moreover that despair of success hung over the compromising provision for the public necessities of April 1783 which had been so elaborately planned and so impressively recommended to the States. Sympathizing, under this aspect of affairs, in the alarm of the friends of free Govt, at the threatened danger of an abortive result to the great and perhaps last experiment in its favour, I could not be insensible to the obligation to cooperate as far as I could in averting the calamity. With this view I acceded to the desire of my fellow Citizens of the Country that I should be one of its representatives in the Legislature, hoping that I might there best contribute to inculcate the critical posture to which the Revolutionary cause was reduced, and the merit of a leading agency of the State in bringing about a rescue of the Union and the blessings of liberty staked on it, from an impending catastrophe.

It required but little time after taking my seat in the House of Delegates in May, 1784 to discover that however favorable the general disposition of the State might be towards the Confederacy, the Legislature retained the aversion of its predecessors to transfers of power from the State to the Govt. of the Union; notwithstanding the urgent demands of the Federal Treasury; the glaring inadequacy of the authorized mode of supplying it, the rapid growth of anarchy in the Fedl. System, and the animosity kindled among its members by their conflicting regulations.

The temper of the Legislature and the wayward course of its proceedings may be gathered from the Journals of its Sessions in the years 1784 and 1785.

The failure however of the varied propositions in the Legislature for enlarging the powers of Congress, the continued failure of the efforts of Congs. to obtain from them the means of providing for the debts of the Revolution; and of countervailing the commercial laws of G.B., a source of much irritation and agst. which the separate efforts of the States were found worse than abortive; these Considerations with the lights thrown on the whole subject, by the free and full discussion it had undergone led to a general acquiescence in the Resoln. passed on the 21 of Jany, 1786. which proposed and invited a meeting of Deputies from all the States to insert the Resol. . . .

The resolution had been brought forward some weeks before on the failure of a proposed grant of power to Congress to collect a revenue from commerce, which had been abandoned by its friends in consequence of material alterations made in the grant by a Committee of the whole. The Resolution tho introduced by Mr. Tyler an influencial member, who having never served in Congress, had more the ear of the House than those whose services there exposed them to an imputable bias, was so little acceptable that it was not then persisted in. Being now revived by him, on the last day of the Session, and being the alternative of adjourning without any effort for the crisis in the affairs of the Union, it obtained a general vote; less however with some of its friends from a confidence in the success of the experiment than from a hope that it might prove a step to a more comprehensive and adequate provision for the wants of the Confederacy.

It happened also that Commissioners who had been appointed by Virga. and Maryd. to settle the jurisdiction on waters dividing the two States had, apart from their official reports, recommended a uniformity in the regulations of the 2 States on several subjects and particularly on those having relation to foreign trade. It appeared at the same time that Maryd. had deemed a concurrence of her neighbors Pena - and Delaware indispensable in such a case, who for like reasons would require that of their neighbors. So apt and forceable an illustration of the necessity of a uniformity throughout all the States, could not but favour the passage of a Resolution which proposed a Convention having that for its object.

The Commissioners appointed by the Legisl: and who attended the Convention were E. Randolph the Attorney of the State, St. Geo: Tucker and J[ames] M[adison]. The designation of the time and place for its meeting to be proposed and communicated to the States having been left to the Comrs; they named for the time early September and for the place the City of Annapolis avoiding the residence of Congs. and large Commercial Cities as liable to suspicions of an extraneous influence.

Altho the invited Meeting appeared to be generally favored, five States only assembled; some failing to make appointements, and some of the individuals appointed not hastening their attendance, the result in both cases being ascribed mainly, to a belief that the time had not arrived for such a political reform, as might be expected from a further experience of its necessity.

But in the interval between the proposal of the Convention and the time of its meeting such had been the advance of public opinion in the desired direction, stimulated as it had been by the effect of the contemplated object of the meeting, in turning the general attention to the Critical State of things, and in calling forth the sentiments and exertions of the most enlightened and influencial patriots, that the Convention thin as it was did not scruple to decline the limited task assigned to it, and to recommend to the States a Convention with powers adequate to the occasion; nor was it unnoticed that the commission of the N. Jersey Deputation, had extended its object to a general provision for the exigencies of the Union. A recommendation for this enlarged purpose was accordingly reported by a Come. to whom the subject had been referred. It was drafted by Col: H. and finally agreed to unanimously . . .

The recommendation was well recd. by the Legislature of Virga. which happened to be the first that acted on it, and the example of her compliance was made as conciliatory and impressive as possible. The Legislatures were unanimous or very nearly so on the occasion, and as a proof of the magnitude and solemnity attached to it, they placed Genl. W[ashington] at the head of the Deputation from the State; and as a proof of the deep interest he felt in the case he overstepped the obstacles to his acceptance of the appointment.

The act complying with the recommendation from Annapolis was in the terms following.

A resort to a General Convention to remodel the Confederacy was not a new idea. It had entered at an early date into the conversations and speculations of the most reflecting and foreseeing observers of the inadequacy of the powers allowed to Congress. In a pamphlet published in May - 81 at the Seat of Congs, Peletiah Webster an able tho' not conspicuous Citizen, after discussing the fiscal system of the U. States and suggesting among other remedial provisions one including a national Bank remarks that "The Authority of Congs. at present is very inadequate to the performance of their duties; and this indicates the necessity of their calling a Continental Convention for the express purpose of ascertaining, defining, enlarging, and limiting the duties and powers of their Constitution."

On the 1 day of Apl 1783, Col. Hamilton, in a debate in Congs. observed that: "He wished to see a general Convention take place."

He alluded probably to ["Resolutions . . . by Schuyler in the Senate . . . of New York, . . . to recommend to the States to call a general Convention.]

It does not appear however that his expectation had been fulfilled.

In a letter to J[ames] M[adison] from R. H. Lee then President of Congs. dated Novr. 26, 1784 He says" [that a general Convention is suggested by members of Congress.]

The answer of J[ames] M[adison] remarks: [Question is only as to the mode.]

In 1785 Noah Webster whose pol[itical] and other valuable writings had made him known to the public, in one of his publications of American policy brought into view the same resort for supplying the defects of the Fedl. System.

The proposed & expected Convention at Annapolis, the first of a general character that appears to have been realized, & the state of the public mind awakened by it, had attracted the particular attention of Congs. and favored the idea there of a Convention with fuller powers for amending the Confederacy.

It does not appear that in any of these cases, the reformed system was to be otherwise sanctioned than by the Legislative authy. of the States; nor whether or how far a change was to be made in the structure of the Depository of Federal powers.

The act of Virga. providing for the Convention at Philad. was succeeded by appointments from other States as their Legislatures were assembled, the appointments being selections from the most experienced and highest standing Citizens. Rh. I. was the only exception to a compliance with the recommendation from Annapolis, well known to have been swayed by an obdurate adherence to an advantage which her position gave her of taxing her neighbors thro' their consumption of imported supplies, an advantage which it was foreseen would be taken from her by a revisal of the Articles of Confederation.

As the pub[lic] mind had been ripened for a salutary Reform of the pol[itical] System in the interval between the proposal and the meeting, of Comrs. at Annapolis, the interval between the last event and the meeting of Deps. at Phila. had continued to develop more and more the necessity and the extent of a Systematic provision for the preservation and Govt. of the Union; among the ripening incidents was the Insurrection of Shays in Massts. against her Govt.; which was with difficulty suppressed, notwithstanding the influence on the insurgents of an apprehended interposition of the Fedl. troops.

At the date of the Convention, the aspect and retrospect of the pol[itical] condition of the U.S. could not but fill the pub[lic] mind with a gloom which was relieved only by a hope that so select a Body would devise an adequate remedy for the existing and prospective evils so impressively demanding it.

It was seen that the public debt rendered so sacred by the cause in which it had been incurred remained without any provision for its payment. The reiterated and elaborate efforts of Cong. to procure from the States a more adequate power to raise the means of payment had failed. The effect of the ordinary requisitions of Congress had only displayed the inefficiency of the authy. making them; none of the States having duly complied with them, some having failed altogether or nearly so; and in one instance, that of N. Jersey, a compliance was expressly refused; nor was more yielded to the expostulations of members of Congs. deputed to her Legislature than mere repeal of the law, without a compliance.

The want of authy. in Congs. to regulate Commerce had produced in Foreign nations particularly G[reat] B[ritain] a monopolizing policy injurious to the trade of the U. S. and destructive to their navigation; the imbecility and anticipated dissolution of the Confederacy extinguishg. all apprehensions of a Countervailing policy on the part of the U. States.

The same want of a general power over Commerce led to an exercise of this power separately, by the States, which not only proved abortive, but engendered rival, conflicting and angry regulations. Besides the vain attempts to supply their respective treasuries by imposts, which turned their commerce into the neighbouring ports, and to coerce a relaxation of the British monopoly of the W. Indn. navigation, which was attempted by Virga. . . . the States having ports for foreign commerce, taxed and irritated the adjoining States trading thro' them, as N.Y., Pena. Virga. and S. Carolina. Some of the States, as Connecticut, taxed imports as from Massts. higher than imports even from G[reat] B[ritain] of which Massts. complained to Virga. and doubtless to other States . . . In sundry instances of as N.Y., N.J., Pa and Maryd . . . the navigation laws treated the Citizens of other States as aliens.

In certain cases the authy. of the Confederacy was disregarded, as in violations not only of the Treaty of peace, but of Treaties with France and Holland, which were complained of to Congs.

In other cases the Fedl. authy. was violated by Treaties and wars with Indians, as by Geo: by troops, raised and kept up witht the consent of Congs. as by Massts by compacts witht. the consent of Congs. as between Pena and N. Jersey, and between Virga. and Maryd. From the Legisl: Journals of Virga., it appears that a vote to apply for a sanction of Congs. was followed by a vote agst. a communication of the Compact to Congs.

In the internal administration of the States a violation of Contracts had become familiar in the form of depreciated paper made a legal tender, of property substituted for money, of Instalment laws, and of the occlusions of the Courts of Justice; although evident that all such interferences affected the rights of other States, relatively Creditor, as well as Citizens Creditors within the State.

Among the defects which had been severely felt was that of a uniformity in cases requiring it, as laws of naturalization, bankruptcy, a Coercive authority operating on individuals and a guaranty of the internal tranquility of the States;

As a natural consequence of this distracted and disheartening condition of the Union, the Fedl. authy had ceased to be respected abroad, and dispositions shown there, particularly in G[reat] B[ritain] to take advantage of its imbecility and to speculate on its approaching downfall; at home it had lost all confidence and credit. The unstable and unjust career of the States had also forfeited the respect and confidence essential to order and good Govt., involving a general decay of confidence and credit between man and man. It was found moreover, that those least partial to popular Govt. or most distrusting of its efficacy were yielding to anticipations that from an increase of the confusion a Govt. might result more congenial with their taste or their opinions; whilst those most devoted to the principles and forms of Republics were alarmed for the cause of liberty itself, at stake in the American Experiment, and anxious for a System that would avoid the inefficacy of a mere Confederacy without passing into the opposite extreme of a Consolidated govt. It was known that there were individuals who had betrayed a bias towards Monarchy . . . and there had always been some not unfavorable to a partition of the Union into several Confederacies . . . ; either from a better chance of figuring on a Sectional Theatre, or that the Sections would require stronger Govts or by their hostile conflicts lead to a monarchical consolidation. The idea of a dismemberment had recently made its appearance in the Newspapers.

Such were the defects, the deformities, the diseases and the ominous prospects, for which the Convention were to provide a remedy, and which ought never to be overlooked in expounding and appreciating the Constitutional Charter the remedy that was provided.

As a sketch the earliest perhaps on paper of a Constitutional Govt. for the Union (organized into the regular Departments with physical means operating on individuals) to be sanctioned by the people of the States, acting in their original and sovereign character, was contained in a letter of Apl. 8, 1787 from J[ames] M[adison] to Govr. Randolph. . . .

The feature in the letter which vested in the general Authy a negative on the laws of the States, was suggested by the negative in the head of the British Empire, which prevented collisions between the parts and the whole, and between the parts themselves. It was supposed that the substitution of an elective and responsible authority for an hereditary and irresponsible one, would avoid the appearance even of a departure from the principle of Republicanism. But altho' the subject was so viewed in the Convention, and the votes on it more than once equally divided, it was finally and justly abandoned, as, apart from other objections, it was not practicable among so many States, increasing in number, and enacting, each of them, so many laws. Instead of the proposed negative, the objects of it were left as finally provided for in the Constitution.

On the arrival of the Virginia Deputies at Philada. it occurred to them that from the early and prominent part taken by that State in bringing about the Convention some initiative step might be expected from them. The Resolutions introduced by Governor Randolph were the result of a Consolidation on the subject; with an understanding that they left all the Deputies entirely open to the lights of discussion, and free to concur in any alterations or modifications which their reflections and judgments might approve. The Resolutions as the Journals show became the basis on which the proceedings of the Convention commenced, and to the developments, variations and modifications of which the plan of Govt. proposed by the Convention may be traced.

The curiosity I had felt during my researches into the History of the most distinguished Confederacies, particularly those of antiquity, and deficiency I found in the means of satisfying it more especially in what related to the process and the principles—the reasons and the anticipations, which prevailed in the formation of them, determined me to preserve as far as I could an exact account of what might pass in the Convention whilst executing its trust, with the magnitude of which I was duly impressed, as I was with the gratification promised to future curiosity by an authentic exhibition of the objects, the opinions and the reasonings from which the new System of Govt. was to receive its peculiar structure and organization. Nor was I unaware of the value of such a contribution to the fund of materials for the History of a Constitution on which would be staked the happiness of a young people great even in its infancy, and possibly the cause of Liberty throughout the world.

In pursuance of the task I had assumed I chose a seat in front of the presiding member with the other members, on my right and left hand. In this favorable position for hearing all that passed, I noted in terms legible and in abbreviations and marks intelligible to myself what was read from the Chair or spoken by the members and losing not a moment unnecessarily between the adjournment and reassembling of the Convention I was enabled to write out my daily notes during the session or within a few finishing days after its close in the extent and form preserved in my own hand on my files.

In the labor and correctness of this I was not a little aided by practice, and by a familiarity with the style and the train of observation and reasoning which characterized the principal speakers. It happened, also, that I was not absent a single day, nor more than a casual fraction of an hour in any day, so that I could not have lost a single speech, unless a very short one.

It may be proper to remark, that, with a very few exceptions, the speeches were neither furnished, nor revised, nor sanctioned, by the speakers, but written out from my notes, aided by the freshness of my recollections. A further remark may be proper, that views of the subject might occasionally be presented, in the speeches and proceedings, with a latent reference to a compromise on some middle ground, by mutual concessions. The exceptions alluded to were—first, the sketch furnished by Mr. Randolph of his speech on the introduction of his propositions, on the twenty-ninth day of May; secondly, the speech of Mr. Hamilton, who happened to call on me when putting the last hand to it, and who acknowledged its fidelity, without suggesting more than a very few verbal alterations which were made; thirdly, the speech of Gouverneur Morris on the second day of May [July] which was communicated to him on a like occasion, and who acquiesced in it without even a verbal change. The correctness of his language and the distinctness of his enunciation were particularly favorable to a reporter. The speeches of Doctor Franklin, excepting a few brief ones, were copied from the written ones read to the Convention by his colleague, Mr. Wilson, it being inconvenient to the Doctor to remain long on his feet.

Of the ability and intelligence of those who composed the Convention the debates and proceedings may be a test; as the character of the work which was the offspring of their deliberations must be tested by the experience of the future, added to that of nearly half a century which has passed.

But whatever may be the judgment pronounced on the competency of the architects of the Constitution, or whatever may be the destiny of the edifice prepared by them, I felt it a duty to express my profound and solemn conviction, derived from my intimate opportunity of observing and appreciating the views of the Convention, collectively and individually, that there never was an assembly of men, charged with a great and arduous trust, who were more pure in their motives, or more exclusively or anxiously devoted to the object committed to them, than were the members of the Federal Convention of 1787, to the object of devising and proposing a constitutional system which should best supply the defects of that which it was to replace, and best secure the permanent liberty and happiness of their country.

# The Constitution and Constitutional Law

> . . . we must never forget that it is a constitution we are expounding.
>
> *John Marshall*

## The Progress of Constitutional Theory between the Declaration of Independence and the Meeting of the Philadelphia Convention

Edward S. Corwin

Critics of Gladstone's famous aphorism on the Constitution seem often to assume that he supposed the members of the Philadelphia Convention to have emptied their minds of all experience upon their arrival in the convention city.[1] The assumption is an entirely gratuitous one. Unquestionably the problems before the Convention were suggested by the experience of its members and were not posed *ex thesi*. But the fact remains, nevertheless, that the solutions which the Convention supplied to those problems not infrequently owed far more to the theoretical prepossessions of its members than they did to tested institutions.

For Americans hardly less than for Frenchmen the period of the Constitution was "an age of rationalism," whereby is intended not a blind ignoring of the lessons of experience, but confidence in the ability of reason, working in the light of experience, to divert the unreflective course of events into beneficial channels; and in no respect was man more the master of his destiny than in that of statecraft. Surely if any man of the time may be regarded as representative of the sober, unimaginative intelligence of America, it was Washington, in whose "Circular Letter addressed to the Governors", of June 8, 1783, occurs the following passage:

> The foundation of our empire was not laid in the gloomy age of ignorance and superstition; but at an epocha when the rights of mankind were better understood and more clearly defined, than at any other period. The researches of the human mind after social happiness have been carried to a great extent; the treasures of knowledge acquired by the labors of philosophers, sages, and legislators, through a long succession of years, are laid open for our use, and their collected wisdom may be happily applied in the establishment of our forms of government. . . . At this auspicious period, the United States came into existence as a nation; and, if their citizens should not be completely free and happy, the fault will be entirely their own.[2]

Reprinted with permission from *American Historical Review*, (April 1925), pp. 511–36.

The same sense of command over the resources of political wisdom appears again and again in the debates of the Convention, in the pages of the *Federalist,* and in writings of contemporaries.[3]

Nor does the economic interpretation of history, of which one has heard much in late years, detract greatly from the significance of such facts. No one denies that the concern felt by the Fathers for the rights of property and contract contributed immensely to impart to American constitutional law its strong bias in favor of these rights from the outset, but the concession only serves to throw certain still unanswered questions into a higher relief. For, what warrant had these men for translating any of their interests as *rights;* and why did they adopt the precise means which they did to advance their interests or secure their rights—in other words, why did they choose the precise system set up by the Constitution to do the work which they put upon it? Questions of this nature are altogether incapable of answer by any theory of human motive standing by itself. As Sir Henry Maine has phrased it: "Nothing in law springs entirely from a sense of convenience. There are always certain ideas existing anteced-ently on which the sense of convenience works, and of which it can do no more than form some new combination; and to find these ideas," he adds, "is exactly the prob-lem."[4]

## I.

A colloquy which occurred between Madison and Sherman of Connecticut in the early days of the Philadelphia Convention as to its purpose affords an excellent preface to the more particular intention of this paper. "The objects of the Union," Sherman had declared, "were few," defense, domestic good order, treaties, the regu-lation of foreign commerce, revenue. Though a conspicuous omission from this enu-meration is of any mention of commerce among the states and its regulation, it was not this omission which drew Madison's fire:

> He differed from the member from Connecticut in thinking the objects mentioned to be all the principal ones that required a National Government. Those were certainly important and necessary objects; but he combined with them the necessity, of providing more effectually for the security of private rights, and the steady dispensation of Justice. Interferences with these were evils which had more perhaps than any thing else, produced this convention. Was it to be supposed that republican liberty could long exist under the abuses of it practiced in some of the States?[5]

These views were heartily chorused by other members: the faulty organization of government within the states, threatening as it did, not alone the Union, but republican government itself, furnished the Convention with a problem of transcendent, even world-wide importance.[6]

In short, the task before the Convention arose by no means exclusively from the inadequacies of the Articles of Confederation for "the exigencies of the Union"; of at least equal urgency were the questions which were thrust upon its attention by the shortcomings of the state governments for their purposes. Indeed, from the point of view of this particular study the latter phase of the Convention's task is, if anything, the more significant one, both because it brings us into contact at the outset with the most persistent problem of American constitutional law—that which has arisen from the existence of a multiplicity of local legislatures with indefinite powers; and also because it was to the solution of this phase of its problem that the Convention brought its "political science" most immediately to bear.

The singular juxtaposition in the Revolutionary state constitutions of legislative supremacy and the doctrine of natural rights need not detain us here.[7] In the words of a contemporary critic of those constitutions: Although their authors "understood perfectly the principles of liberty," yet most of them "were ignorant of the forms and combinations of power in republics."[8] Madison's protest, on the other hand, against "interferences with the steady dispensation of justice" had reference to something more subtle—to what, in fact, was far less a structural than a functional defect in these early instruments of government. That the majority of the Revolutionary constitutions recorded recognition of the principle of the separation of powers is, of course, well known.[9] What is not so generally understood is that the recognition was verbal merely, for the reason that the material terms in which it was couched still remained undefined; and that this was true in particular of "legislative power" in relation to "judicial power."

It is pertinent in this connection to compare the statement by a modern authority of what is law to-day with actual practice contemporaneous with the framing of the Constitution of the United States. "The legislature," writes Sutherland in his work on *Statutory Construction,*

> may prescribe rules of decision which will govern future cases. . . . But it has no power to administer judicial relief—it can not decide cases nor direct how existing cases or controversies shall be decided by the courts; it can not interfere by subsequent acts with final judgments of the courts. It can not set aside, annul, or modify such judgments, nor grant or order new trials, nor direct what judgment shall be entered or relief given. No declaratory act, that is, one professing to enact what the law now is or was at any past time, can affect any existing rights or controversies.[10]

Turn now to the operation of the principle of the separation of powers in a typical instance in 1787. The New Hampshire constitution of 1784 contained the declaration that "in the government of this State, the three essential powers thereof, to wit, the legislative, executive and judicial, ought to be kept as separate and independent of each other as the nature of a free government will admit or as is consistent with the chain of connection that binds the whole fabric of the constitution in one indissoluble bond of union or amity." Notwithstanding which the laws of New Hampshire for the years 1784–1792 are replete with entries showing that throughout this period the state legislature freely vacated judicial proceedings, suspended judicial actions, annulled or modified judgments, cancelled executions, reopened controversies, authorized appeals, granted exemptions from the standing law, expounded the law for pending cases, and even determined the merits of disputes.[11] Nor do such practices seem to have been more aggravated in New Hampshire than in several other states. Certainly they were widespread, and they were evidently possible in any of the states under the views then obtaining of "legislative power."[12]

Neither is the explanation of such views far to seek. Coke's fusion of what we should to-day distinguish as "legislative" and "judicial" powers in the case of the "High Court of Parliament" represented the teaching of the highest of all legal authorities before Blackstone appeared on the scene.[13] What is equally important, the Cokian doctrine corresponded exactly to the contemporary necessities of many of the colonies in the earlier days of their existence.[14] Thus, owing to the dearth not only of courts and lawyers, but even of a recognized code of law, bodies like the Massachusetts General Court had thrust upon them at first a far greater bulk of judicial and administrative work, in to-day's sense of these terms, than of lawmaking proper, while conversely such judges as existed in these early days performed administrative as well as judicial functions, very much as had been the case with the earliest itinerant judges in England. By the middle of the eighteenth century, it is true, a distinct improvement had taken place in these regards. Regularly organized systems of courts now existed in all the colonies. A bar trained in the common law was rapidly arising. Royal governors sometimes disallowed enactments interfering with the usual course of justice in the ordinary courts, on grounds anticipatory of modern doctrine.[15] Then, however, came the outbreak of the Revolution, and with it a reversion to more primitive practices and ideas, traceable in the first instance to the collapse of the royal judicial establishment, but later to the desire to take a short course with enemies of the new régime, against whom, first and last, every state in the Union appears to have enacted bills of pains and penalties of greater or less severity.[16] Furthermore, it should be observed that, owing to a popular prejudice, certain of the states—notably New York and Massachusetts—at first withheld equity powers from their courts altogether, while several others granted them but sparingly.[17] The result was fairly to compel the legislature to intervene in many instances with "special legislation," disallowing fraudulent transactions, curing defective titles, authorizing urgent sales of property, and the like.[18] Between legislation of this species and outright interferences with the remedial law itself there was often little to distinguish.

That, therefore, the vague doctrine of the separation of powers should at first have been interpreted and applied in the light of this history is not astonishing. This, as we have seen, left legislative power without definition on its side toward judicial power, except as the power of the supreme organ of the state, which meant, however, the withholding from judicial power of that which, to the modern way of thinking, is its highest attribute—to wit, power of deciding with finality. Nothing could be more instructive in this connection than some sentences from Jefferson's *Notes on Virginia,* dating from about 1781. Pointing out that the Virginia constitution of 1776 incorporated the principle of the separation of powers, Jefferson proceeds to expound this principle in a way which leaves it meaning little more than a caution against plurality of offices. "No person shall exercise the powers of more than one of them [the three departments] at the same time," are his words. But even more significant is the following passage:

If, [it runs] the legislature assumes executive and judiciary powers, no opposition is likely to be made; nor, if made, can it be effectual; because in that case they may put their proceedings into the form of an act of assembly, which will render them obligatory on the other branches. They have, accordingly, in many instances, decided rights which should have been left to judiciary controversy; and the direction of the executive, during the whole time of their session, is becoming habitual and familiar.[19]

The concept of legislative power here expressed is obviously a purely formal one: "legislative power" is any power which the legislative organ may choose to exercise by resort to the ordinary parliamentary processes.

And not less striking is the recital which Hamilton gives in *Federalist,* number 81, of certain objections by opponents of the Constitution to the powers of the Supreme Court:

> The authority of the Supreme Court of the United States, which is to be a separate and independent body, will be superior to that of the legislature. The power of construing the laws according to the *spirit* of the Constitution will enable that court to mould them into whatever shape it may think proper; especially as its decisions will not be in any manner subject to the revision or correction of the legislative body. This is as unprecedented as it is dangerous. . . . The Parliament of Great Britain, and the legislatures of the several States, can at any time rectify, by law, the exceptionable decisions of their respective courts. But the errors and usurpations of the Supreme Court of the United States will be uncontrollable and remediless.

Hamilton's answer to all this was simply that "the theory neither of the British, nor the State constitutions, authorizes the revisal of a judicial sentence by a legislative act," that "the impropriety of the thing" even in the case of the United States Constitution rested not on any distinctive provision thereof, but "on the general principles of law and reason"; that a legislature could not, "without exceeding its province . . . reverse a determination once made in a particular case," though it might "prescribe a new rule for future cases"; and that this principle applied "in all its consequences, exactly in the same manner and extent, to the State governments as to the national government."[20] This answer, for which is cited only the authority of Montesquieu, is conclusive from the standpoint of modern constitutional doctrine; but its contradiction of the views and practices which were prevalent in 1787 is manifest.

## II.

Finally, the structural and functional shortcomings of the early state constitutions played directly into the hands of both popular and doctrinal tendencies which distinctly menaced what Madison called "the security of private rights." Throughout the Revolution the Blackstonian doctrine of "legislative omnipotence" was in the ascendant. Marshall read Blackstone and so did Iredell—to what effect later developments were to make clear.[21] And even more radical doctrine was abroad. One Benjamin Hichborn's assertion, in a speech delivered in Boston in 1777, that civil liberty was "not a government by laws," but "a power existing in the people at large" "to alter or annihilate both the mode and essence of any former government" "for any cause or for no cause at all, but their own sovereign pleasure"[22] voiced an extension to the right of revolution hitherto unheard of outside the pages of Rousseau; and even so good a republican as John Adams was disturbed at manifestations of social ferment which he traced to a new spirit of equality.[23]

The sharp edge of "legislative omnipotence" did not pause with the Tories who, as enemies of the state, were perhaps beyond the pale of the Constitution. Everywhere legislative assemblies, energized by the reforming impulse of the period, were led to attempt results which, even when they lay within the proper field of lawmaking, we should to-day regard as requiring constitutional amendments to effect them. Virginia, as Bancroft writes, used her "right of original and complete legislation to abolish the privileges of primogeniture, cut off entails, forbid the slave-trade, and establish the principle of freedom in religion as the inherent and inalienable possession of spiritual beings";[24] while elsewhere the liberal forces of the hour assailed the vested interest of negro slavery more directly. Vermont, Massachusetts, and New Hampshire ridded themselves of slavery by constitutional amendment or in consequence of judicial construction of the Constitution.[25] In Pennsylvania, Rhode Island, and Connecticut, on the other hand, gradual emancipation was brought about by ordinary legislative enactment.[26] Yet the cause of reform did not have it all its own way. When a similar measure was proposed in New Jersey, it drew forth a protest on constitutional grounds which is remarkable in its anticipation of later doctrines.[27]

But it was not reform, nor even special legislation, which early affixed to the state legislature a stigma of which as an institution it has never even yet quite ridded itself.[28] The legislation just reviewed belonged for the most part to the period of the war and was the work of a society which, the Tory element apart, was politically unified and acknowledged an easily ascertainable leadership. Once, however, hostilities were past and the pressure alike of a common peril and a common enthusiasm removed, the republican lute began to show rifts. The most evident line of cleavage at first was that between seaboard and back country; but this presently became coincident to a large extent with a much more ominous division into creditors and debtors. That class of farmer-debtors which now began to align itself with the demagogues in the state legislatures, in opposition to the mercantile-creditor class, was experiencing the usual grievance of agriculturists after a war, that of shouldering the burden of the return to normalcy. But the point of view of the creditor class may not be justly ignored either. By their provincial policies with respect to commerce the state legislatures had already seriously impaired legitimate interests of this class,[29] and they now proceeded to attack what under the standing law were its unchallengeable rights. In each of the thirteen states a "rag money" party appeared, which in seven states triumphed outright, while in several others it came near doing so. Nor was payment even in paper currency always the creditor's lot, for besides rag-money measures and tender laws, or in lieu of them, statutes suspending all actions upon debts were enacted, payment of debts in kind was authorized, and even payment in land.[30]

It is a frequent maxim of policy that things must be permitted to grow worse before their betterment can be attempted to advantage. The paper-money craze at least proved serviceable in invigorating the criticism which had begun even earlier of the existing state governments. One such critic was Jefferson, who in his *Notes on Virginia* bitterly assailed the Virginia constitution of 1776 for having produced a concentration of power in the legislative assembly which answered to "precisely the definition of despotic government." Nor did it make any difference, he continued, that such powers were vested in a numerous body "chosen by ourselves"; "one hundred and seventy-three despots" were "as oppressive as one"; and "an elective despotism was not the government we fought for, but one which should not only be founded on free principles, but in which the powers of government should be so divided and balanced among several bodies of magistracy, as that no one could transcend their legal limits, without being effectually checked and restrained by the others."[31]

And this was also the point of view of the Pennsylvania Council of Censors, in their celebrated report of 1784.[32] Extending through some thirty finely printed pages, this document listed many examples, "selected," we are told, "from a multitude," of legislative violations of the state constitution and bill of rights. Several of the measures so stigmatized were of a general nature, but those for which the censors reserved their severest strictures were acts involving the rights of named parties. Thus fines had been remitted, judicially established claims disallowed, verdicts of juries set aside, the property of one given to another, defective titles secured, marriages dissolved, particular persons held in execution of debt released—and all by a species of legislative activity which had been explicitly condemned both by "the illustrious Montesquieu" and "the great Locke."

Two years later came the early volumes of John Adams's *Defence of the Constitutions,* in answer to M. Turgot's criticism that the American constitution represented "an unreasonable imitation of the usages of England." In reality the work was much less a "defence" than an exhortation to constitutional reform in other states along the lines which Massachusetts had already taken under Adams's own guidance. A new and significant note, however, appears in this work. In his earlier writings Adams had assumed with Montesquieu that the great source of danger to liberty lay in the selfishness and ambition of the governors themselves. But with the lesson of the paper-money agitation before him, he now gives warning of the danger to which republics, when they have become populous and overcrowded and the inevitable doom of poverty has appeared in their midst, are peculiarly exposed from the rise of parties. "Misarrangements now made," he writes, "will have great, extensive, and distant consequences; and we are now employed, how little soever we may think of it, in making establishments which will affect the happiness of a hundred millions of inhabitants at a time, in a period not very distant."[33]

Copies of the *Defence* reached the United States early in 1787, and were circulated among the members of the Philadelphia Convention, reviving and freshening belief in "political science" and particularly in the teachings of Montesquieu. Yet in one respect at least the idea of reform for which Adams's work stood and that which the Convention represented were poles apart. For while the former still illustrated the opinion that constitutional reform was a purely local problem, the Convention represented the triumph of the idea that reform to be effective must be national in scope and must embrace the entire American constitutional system in a single coherent programme. That such a programme could have been elaborated without the signal contribution to it of the effort for local reform is, on the other hand, altogether improbable.

### III.

It was Walter Bagehot's opinion that Americans were prone to give credit to the Constitution which was more justly due themselves. "The men of Massachusetts," he declared, "could work *any* constitution."[34] What had evidently impressed him was the American habit of supplying shortcomings in the Constitution by construction rather than outright amendment. Yet for construction to do really effective work, it must have elbow-room and a handle to take hold of; and at least the merit of having afforded these can not be denied the Constitution.

Nor were the early state constitutions entirely lacking in invitation to this American aptitude for documentary exegesis, which had its origin, one suspects, in an earlier taste for theological disposition. The executive veto, which was the practical nub of all Adams's preachments, was brought about, to be sure, through specific provision being made for it in the written constitution, and to so good purpose that it is to be found to-day in nearly every constitution in the country.[35] The other suggested remedy of critics of "the legislative vortex," on the contrary, was introduced solely by the processes of interpretation and without the slightest textual alteration being made in the constitutions involved. This was judicial review. Thus while the executive veto and judicial review have a common explanation in the political necessity which they were devised to meet, the manner in which they were respectively articulated to the American constitutional system was widely and for us most significantly divergent. The executive veto was and remains mere matter of fact without the slightest further interest for us; judicial review is both a practice and a *doctrine,* and in the latter aspect especially is of immediate interest.

As a practice judicial review made its initial appearance in independent America in 1780, in the case of Holmes v. Walton,[36] in which the supreme court of New Jersey refused to carry out an act of the legislature providing for the trial of a designated class of offenders by a jury of six, whereas, the court held, the state constitution contemplated the common-law jury of twelve. Although the opinion of the court apparently was never published, the force of the example may have been considerable. From this time on the notion crops up sporadically in other jurisdictions, at intervals of about two years, in a series of dicta and rulings which—thanks in no small part to popular misapprehension as to their precise bearing—brought the idea before the Philadelphia Convention.[37] And meantime the main premises of the *doctrine* of judicial review—the principles whereby it came to be annexed to the written constitution— had been worked out.

First and last, many and various arguments have been offered to prove that judicial review is implied in the very nature of a written constitution, some of them manifestly insufficient for the purpose; though that is not to say that they may not have assisted in securing general acceptance of the institution. "Superstitions believed are, in their effect, truths"; and it has accordingly happened more than once that the actual influence of an idea has been out of all proportion to its logical or scientific merits. These more or less spurious proofs of judicial review, however, we here pass by without further consideration, in order to come at once to what, on both historical and logical grounds, may be termed the true doctrine of judicial review. This embraces three propositions: First, that the Constitution is supreme; second, that it is law, in the sense of a rule enforceable by courts; and third, that judicial interpretations of the standing law are final, at least for the cases in the decision of which they are pronounced. Let us consider the two latter propositions somewhat further.

The claim of the Constitution to be considered *law* may rest on either one of two grounds, depending on whether "law" be regarded as an unfolding of the divine order of things or as an expression of human will—as an act of knowledge (or revelation) or an act of power.[38] Considered from the former point of view—which is that of Locke and other exponents of the law of nature—the claim of the Constitution to be obeyed is due simply to its content, to the principles which it incorporates because of their intrinsic sanctity; considered from the latter point of view—that of Hobbes and the "positive school of jurisprudence"—its claim to obedience is due to its source in a sovereign will—that of the people. Actually both views have been taken at different times, but that judicial review originally owed more to the former than to the latter conception seems fairly clear.

Of all the so-called "precedents" for judicial review antecedent to the Convention of 1787, the one which called forth the most elaborate argument on theoretical grounds and which produced the most evident impression on the membership of the Convention, was the Rhode Island case of Trevett v. Weeden,[39] which was decided early in 1786. The feature of the case which is of immediate pertinence is the argument which it evoked against the act on the part of the attorney for defendant, James Varnum. In developing the theory of a law superior to legislative enactments, Varnum appealed indifferently to the Rhode Island charter, "general principles," "invariable custom," "Magna Carta," "fundamental law," "the law of nature," "the law of God"; asserting with reference to the last, that "all men, judges included," were bound by it "in preference to any human laws." In short, Varnum, going directly back to the Cokian tradition, built his argument for judicial review on the loose connotation of the word "law" still obtaining in the eighteenth century, especially among American readers of Coke and Locke—to say nothing of the host of writers on the Law of Nations. Nor is the conduciveness of such an argument to judicial review open to conjecture. In the first place, it kept alive, even after the fires of revolution had cooled, the notion that the claim of law to obedience consists in its intrinsic excellence rather than its origin. Again, it made rational the notion of a hierarchy of laws in which the will of merely human legislators might on occasion be required to assume a subordinate place. Lastly, by the same token, it made rational the notion of judges pitting knowledge against sheer legislative self-assertion.

Contrariwise, the Blackstonian concept of legislative sovereignty was calculated to frustrate judicial review not only by attributing to the legislature an uncontrollable authority, but also by pressing forward the so-called "positive" conception of law and the differentiation of legal from moral obligation which this impels. Fortunately, in the notion of popular sovereignty the means of checkmating the notion of legislative sovereignty was available. For, once it became possible to attribute to the people at large a lawmaking, rather than a merely constituent, capacity, the Constitution exchanged its primary character as a statement of sacrosanct principles for that of the expressed will of the highest lawmaking power on earth.[40]

But to produce judicial review, the notion of the Constitution as law must be accompanied by the principle of the finality of judicial constructions of the law, which obviously rests upon a definition of the respective rôles of "legislative" and "judicial" power in relation to the standing law. In other words, judicial review raised from the other side of the line the same problem as did "legislative interferences with the dispensation of justice"; and, in fact, it can be shown that the solution of the two problems proceeded in many jurisdictions *pari passu*.[41] The whole subject is one which demands rather ample consideration.

Although the functional differentiation of the three powers of government, first hinted in Aristotle's *Politics*,[42] necessarily preceded their organic distribution to some extent, it is not essential for our purposes to trace either process further back than to Coke's repeated insistence in his *Institutes* that "the King hath wholly left matters of

Judicature according to his laws to his Judges."[43] In these words, it is not too much to say, the royal prerogative, which had long lain fallow in this respect, was thrust forever from the province of the courts. One of these same courts, on the other hand, was "the High Court of Parliament"; and Coke nowhere suggests that "the power of judicature" which he attributes to Parliament is to be distinguished from the power which Parliament ordinarily exercised in "proceeding by bill."[44] Far different is the case of Locke. His declaration that "the legislative or supreme authority cannot assume to itself a power to rule by extempory arbitrary decrees, but is bound to dispense justice and decide the rights of the subject by promulgated standing laws and known authorized judges" represents progress towards a "material" as against a merely "formal" definition of legislative power, both in the total exclusion which it effects of the legislative body from the business of judging and also in the ideal which it lays down of statute law.[45] Noteworthy, too, from the same point of view is Montesquieu's characterization of the judges as "but the mouthpieces of the law," accompanied, as it is, by the assertion that the mergence of "the judiciary power" with "the legislative" would render the judge "a legislator" vested with arbitrary power over the life and liberty of the subject.[46]

As usual, Blackstone's contribution is somewhat more difficult to assess. He adopts without qualification the views just quoted from Locke and Montesquieu, and he urges that "all laws should be made to commence *in futuro*." Yet the very illustration he furnishes of his definition of "municipal law" as "a rule . . . permanent, uniform, and universal" violates this precept radically, since it shows that in his estimation the *ex post facto* operation of a rule, however undesirable in itself, does not affect its title to be regarded as "law." Nor, in fact, does it occur to him, in assigning to Parliament power to "expound" the law, to distinguish those instances in which the exercise of this power would mark an intrusion upon judicial freedom of decision, while his sweeping attribution to Parliament of jurisdiction over "all mischiefs and grievances, operations and remedies that transcend the ordinary course of the laws"—a matter evidently to be judged of by Parliament itself—lands us again in the Cokian bog from which we set out.[47]

The differentiation of legislative and judicial power, upon which judicial review pivots, appears to have been immediately due, not to any definition of legislative *power,* but to a definition of judicial *duty* in relation to the standing law and especially to the law of decided cases. In the opening sentence of Bacon's Essay on Judicature one reads: "Judges ought to remember that their office is *'jus dicere'* and not *'jus dare'*; to interpret law, and not to make or give law"—words which have been reiterated many times as embodying the doctrine of *stare decisis*.[48] Coke employs different language, but his thought is not essentially different: "judges discern by law what is just"; the law is "the golden metwand whereby all men's causes are justly and evenly measured." He also notes the artificiality of the law's "reason and judgment," and pays full tribute to the burden of study and experience "before that a man can attain to the cognizance of it."[49] Judicial duty is thus matched with judicial aptitude—the judges are the experts of the law—or, in the words of Blackstone, its "living oracles," sworn to determine, not according to their own private judgment, "but according to the known laws and customs of the land; not delegated to pronounce a new law, but to maintain and expound the old one."[50]

In brief, it is the duty of judges to conserve the law, not to change it, a task for which their learning pre-eminently fits them. Yet a mystery remains to clear up; for how came this *duty* of subordination to the law to be transmuted into a claim of exclusive *power* in relation to it—the power of interpreting it with final force and effect? By the doctrine of the separation of powers, the outstanding prerogatives of each department are no doubt its peculiar possession; but still that does not explain why in the final apportionment of territory between the legislative and judicial departments in the United States, the function of law-interpretation fell to the latter. The fact is that we here confront *the* act of creation—or perhaps it would be better to say, act of prestidigitation—attending the elaboration of the doctrine of judicial review; and what is more, we know the authors of it—or some of them.

In his argument in the case of Trevett *v.* Weeden, Varnum put the question: "Have the judges a power to repeal, to amend, to alter, or to make new laws?" and then proceeded to answer it thus: "God forbid! In that case they would be legislators. . . . But the judiciary have the sole power of judging of laws . . . and can not admit any act of the legislatures as law against the Constitution." And to the same effect is the defense which James Iredell penned of the North Carolina supreme court's decision in Bayard *v.* Singleton,[51] while Davie, his associate in the case, was in attendance upon the Convention at Philadelphia.

> The duty of that [the judicial] department [he wrote] I conceive in all cases is to decide according to the laws of the State. It will not be denied, I suppose, that the constitution is a law of the State, as well as an act of Assembly, with this difference only, that it is the *fundamental* law, and unalterable by the legislature, which derives all its power from it. . . . The judges, therefore, must take care at their peril, that every act of Assembly they presume to enforce is warranted by the constitution, since if it is not, they act without lawful authority.

Nor is this a power which may be exercised by ministerial officers, "for if the power of judging rests with the courts their decision is final."[52]

Here are all the premises of the doctrine of judicial review either explicitly stated or clearly implied: the superiority of the Constitution to statute law—the case of the common law had still to be dealt with; its quality as law knowable by judges in their official capacity and applicable by them to cases; the exclusion of "legislative power" from the ancient field of parliamentary power in law-interpretation, except in circumstances in which the law is subject to legislative amendment. The classical version of the doctrine of judicial review in *Federalist,* number 78, improves upon the statement of these premises but adds nothing essential to them.


## IV.

We turn now to that phase of the problem which confronted the Philadelphia Convention in consequence of the insufficiencies of the government established by the Articles of Confederation. And at the outset let it be remarked that with all their defects, and serious as these were, the Articles none the less performed two services of great moment: they kept the idea of union vital during the period when the feeling of national unity was at its lowest ebb; and they accorded formal recognition that the great powers of war and foreign relations were intrinsically national in character. Those two most dramatic and interesting functions belonged to the general government from the first and became the central magnet to which other powers necessarily gravitated.

The essential defect of the Articles of Confederation, as has been so often pointed out,[53] consisted in the fact that the government established by them operated not upon the individual citizens of the United States but upon the states in their corporate capacity—that, in brief, it was not a government at all, but rather the central agency of an alliance. As a consequence, on the one hand, even the powers theoretically belonging to the Congress of the Confederation were practically unenforceable; while, on the other hand, the theoretical scope of its authority was unduly narrow. Inasmuch as taxes are collectible from individuals, Congress could not levy them; inasmuch as commerce is an affair of individuals, Congress could not regulate it; and its treaties had not at first the force of laws, since to have given them that operation would again have been to impinge upon individuals directly and not through the mediation of the state legislatures. Furthermore, the powers withheld from Congress remained with the states—which is to say, *with their legislatures*. The evil thence resulting was thus a double one. Not only was a common policy impracticable in fields where it was most evidently necessary, but also the local legislatures had it in their power to embroil both the country as a whole with foreign nations and its constituent parts with each other. So the weakness of the Confederation played directly into the hands of the chief defect of government within the states themselves—an excessive concentration of power in the hands of the legislative department.

The endeavors which were made to render the Articles of Confederation a workable instrument of government proceeded, naturally, along the two lines of amendment and construction. In theory the Articles were amendable; but owing to the requirement that amendments had to be ratified by all the states, in practice they were not so.[54] Recourse, therefore, had early to be had to the other method, and eventually with fruitful results.

Yet the possibilities of constitutional construction, too, were at the outset seriously curtailed by the transmutation of the Blackstonian teaching into the dogma of state sovereignty.[55] Fortunately, the notion of American nationality, which the early fervors of the Revolution had evoked into something like articulate expression, did not altogether lack a supporting interest. This consisted in the determination of the states with definite western boundaries to convert the territory between the Alleghenies and the Mississippi into a national domain. Their spokesman accordingly advanced the argument that the royal title to this region had devolved, in consequence of the Revolution, not upon the states with "sea-to-sea" charters, but upon the American people as a whole[56]—a premise of infinite possibilities, as soon appeared.

On the very last day of 1781 Congress passed the act incorporating the Bank of North America. Not only was there no clause of the Articles which authorized Congress to create corporations, but the second article specifically stipulated that "each State retains its sovereignty, freedom, and independence, and every power, jurisdiction, and right which is not by the Confederation expressly delegated to the United States in Congress assembled." Quite naturally, the validity of the charter was challenged, whereupon its defense was undertaken by James Wilson. The article just quoted Wilson swept aside at the outset as entirely irrelevant to the question. Inasmuch, said he, as no state could claim or exercise "any power or act of sovereignty extending over all the other States or any of them," it followed that the power to "incorporate a bank commensurate to the United States" was "not an act of sovereignty or a power . . . which by the second Article . . . must be expressly delegated to Congress in order to be possessed by that body." Congress's power, in fact, rested on other premises.

> To many purposes [he continued] the United States are to be considered as one undivided nation; and as possessed of all the rights and powers, and properties by the law of nations incident to such. Whenever an object occurs to the direction of which no particular state is competent, the management of it must of necessity belong to the United States in Congress assembled.[57]

In short, from the very fact of its exercise on a national scale a power ceased to be one claimable by a state. The reflection is suggested that if the Articles of Confederation had continued subject to this canon of construction, they might easily have come to support an even greater structure of derived powers than the Constitution of the United States does at this moment.

The question, however, upon which the permanently fruitful efforts of constitutional construction were at this time brought to bear was that of treaty enforcement; and while the story is not a new one, its full significance seems not to have been altogether appreciated. The starting-point is furnished by the complaints which the British government began lodging with Congress very shortly after the making of the peace treaty that the state legislatures were putting impediments in the way of British creditors and were renewing confiscations of Loyalist property contrary to Articles IV. and VI., respectively, of the treaty.[58]

Now it should be observed that the immediate beneficiaries of these articles were certain classes of *private persons,* whose claims, moreover, were such as would ordinarily have to be asserted against other individuals *in court.* If, therefore, it could only be assured that the state courts would accord such claims proper recognition and enforcement, the obligation of the United States as a government, under the treaty, would be performed and the complaints of the other party to the treaty must thereupon cease. But how could this be assured? The answer was suggested by the current vague connotation of the word "law" and the current endeavor to find in "judicial power" a check upon legislative power in the states.

Nor can there be any doubt as to who first formulated this solution. It was Alexander Hamilton in his argument before a municipal court in New York City in the case of Rutgers v. Waddington in 1784, practically contemporaneously with the British protests above referred to.[59] The case involved a recent enactment of the state legislature creating a right of action for trespass against Tory occupants of premises in favor of owners who had fled the city during the British possession. In his capacity as Waddington's attorney, Hamilton assailed the act as contrary to principles of the law of nations, to the treaty of peace, which he asserted implied an amnesty, and the Articles of Confederation, and as, therefore, void. Only the manuscript notes of his argument are extant, but these sufficiently indicate its bearing for our purpose:

> Congress have made a treaty [they read in part]. A breach of that would be a breach of their constitutional authority. . . . as well a County may alter the laws of the State as the State those of the Confederation. . . . While Confed. exists its cons. Autho. paramount. But how are Judges to decide? Ans.: Cons. giving Jud. Power only in prize causes in all others Judges of each State must of necessity be judges of United States. And the law of each State must adopt the laws of Congress. Though in relation to its own Citizens local laws might govern, yet in relation to foreigners those of United States must prevail. It must be conceded Leg. of one State cannot repeal law of United States. All must be construed to Stand together.[60]

There is a striking parallel between the cases of Rutgers v. Waddington and Trevett v. Weeden, and especially between the subsequent fate of Hamilton's argument in the one and Varnum's in the other. In each case the court concerned decided adversely to the party relying upon the statute before it, but did so on grounds which avoided its committing itself on the issue of judicial review. In each case, nevertheless, the exponents of Blackstonian absolutism raised loud protests in behalf of the threatened legislative authority, with the result of spreading the impression that the judges had met the issue squarely. Yet since what the judges had said hardly bore out this impression, interested attention was naturally directed in turn to the franker and more extensive claims of counsel; and while Varnum was spreading his argument broadcast as a pamphlet, Hamilton was reiterating his views in his "Letters from Phocion."[61]

Of the various repercussions from Hamilton's argument in Rutgers v. Waddington the most important is the report which John Jay—a fellow New Yorker—rendered to Congress as secretary for foreign affairs, in October, 1786, on the subject of state violations of treaties. The salient passage of this document reads as follows:

> Your secretary considers the thirteen independent sovereign states as having, by express delegation of power, formed and vested in Congress a perfect though limited sovereignty for the general and national purposes specified in the confederation. In this sovereignty they cannot severally participate (except by their delegates) or have concurrent jurisdiction. . . . When therefore a treaty is constitutionally made, ratified and published by Congress, it immediately becomes binding on the whole nation, and superadded to the laws of the land, without the intervention, consent or fiat of state legislatures.

It was therefore, Jay argued, the duty of the state judiciaries in cases between private individuals "respecting the meaning of a treaty," to give it full enforcement in harmony with "the rules and maxims established by the laws of nations for the interpretation of treaties." He accordingly recommended that Congress formally deny the right of the state legislatures to enact laws construing "a national treaty" or impeding its operation "in any manner," that it avow its opinion that all acts on the statute books repugnant to the treaty of peace should be at once repealed, and that it urge the repeal to be in general terms which would leave it with the local judiciaries to decide all cases arising under the treaty according to the intent thereof "anything in the said acts . . . to the contrary notwithstanding."[62]

The following March Congress adopted the resolutions which Jay had proposed, without a dissenting vote, and in April, within a month of the date set for the assembling of the Philadelphia Convention, transmitted them to the state legislatures, by the majority of which they were promptly complied with.[63] Nor is the theory on which such repeals were based doubtful. We find it stated in the declaration of the North Carolina supreme court in the above-mentioned case of Bayard v. Singleton, which was decided the very month that the Convention came together, that "the Articles of Confederation are a part of the law of the land unrepealable by any act of the general assembly."

From all this to Article VI. of the Constitution is manifestly only a step, though an important one. The supremacy which Jay's plan assured the national treaties is in Article VI. but part and parcel of national supremacy in all its phases; but this broader supremacy is still guaranteed by being brought to bear upon individuals, in contrast to states, through the intervention in the first instance often of the state courts. Thus the solution provided of the question of treaty enforcement, whereby the cause of national supremacy was linked with that of judicial review, clearly foreshadowed the ultimate character of the national government as a government acting upon individuals in the main rather than upon the states. Logically, national power operative through courts is a deduction from a government over individuals; chronologically, the order of ideas was the reverse.

## V.

The theory that the Articles of Confederation were for some purposes law, directly cognizable by courts, entirely transformed the character of the Confederation so far forth, and must sooner or later have suggested the idea of its entire transformation into a real government. Nor was judicial review the only possible source of such a suggestion. As Madison points out in the *Federalist*, "in cases of capture; of piracy; of the post-office; of coins, weights, and measures; of trade with the Indians; of claims under grants of land by different States; and, above all, in the case of trials by courtsmartial in the army and navy," the government of the Confederation acted immediately on individuals from the first.[64] Again, proposals which were laid at various times before the states for conferring a customs revenue on Congress, though none was ever finally ratified, served to bring the same idea before the people, as also did the proposals which never reached the states from Congress to endow the latter with "the sole and exclusive" power over foreign and interstate trade.[65]

But even earlier the suggestion of a "continental conference" for the purpose of framing a "Continental Charter" akin to Magna Carta had been propounded in that famous issue of *Common Sense* in which the signal was given for independence itself. It would be the task of such a body, wrote Paine, to fix "the number and manner of choosing members of Congress and members of assembly," and to draw "the line of business and jurisdiction between them (always remembering that our strength is continental and not provincial)." Such a charter would also secure "freedom and property to all men," and indeed, would fill the place of monarchy itself in the new state. "That we may not appear to be defective even in earthly honors, let a day be solemnly set apart for proclaiming the charter; let it be brought forth placed on the divine law, the word of God; let a crown be placed thereon, by which the world may know that so far we approve monarchy that in America the law is King."[66]

In this singular mixture of sense and fantasy, so characteristic of its author, are adumbrated a national constitutional convention, the dual plan of our federal system, a national bill of rights, and "worship of the Constitution"; and this was some months before the earliest state constitution and nearly four years before Hamilton's proposal, in his letter to Duane of September 3, 1780, of "a solid, coercive Union."[67]

But the great essential precursor to the success of all such proposals was the consolidation of a sufficient interest transcending state lines, and this was slow in forming. It was eventually brought about in three ways: first, through the abuse by the states of their powers over commerce; secondly, through the rise of the question—in which Washington was especially interested—of opening up communications with the West; thirdly, on account of the sharp fear which was aroused among property owners everywhere by the Shays Rebellion. The last was the really decisive factor. The call for a constitutional convention which had emanated from Annapolis in the autumn of 1786 was heeded by only three states, Virginia, New Jersey, Pennsylvania, and was ignored by Congress; but the call which Congress itself issued in the following February under the stimulus imparted by the uprising in Massachusetts was responded to by nine states in due course—New Hampshire being the last on account of the late date of the assembling of its legislature.[68] Testimony from private sources is to the same effect; it shows how the Massachusetts uprising completed the work of the paper-money craze in convincing men that constitutional reform had ceased to be a merely local problem.[69]

In this connection a paper prepared by Madison in April, 1787, and entitled "Vices of the Political System of the United States,"[70] becomes of great interest both for its content and because of the leading part later taken by its author in the work of the Convention. The title itself is significant: "the Political System of the United States" is *one,* and therefore the problem of its reform in all its branches is a single problem; and the argument itself bears out this prognosis. The defects of the Confederation are first considered: the failure of the states to comply with the requisitions of Congress, their encroachments on the central authority, their violations of the treaties of the United States and the Law of Nations, their trespasses on the rights of each other, their want of concert in matters of common interest, the lack of a coercive power in the government of the Confederation, the lack of a popular ratification of the Articles—all these are noted. Then in the midst of this catalogue appears a hitherto unheard-of specification: "want of guaranty to the States of their constitutions and laws against internal violence"—an obvious deduction from the Shays Rebellion.

It is, however, for the legislative evils which he finds within the states individually that Madison reserves his strongest words of condemnation. "As far as laws are necessary," he writes, "to mark with precision the duties of those who are to obey them, and to take from those who are to administer them a discretion which might be abused, their number is the price of liberty. As far as laws exceed this limit, they are a nuisance; a nuisance of the most pestilent kind." Yet "try the Codes of the several States by this test, and what a luxuriancy of legislation do they present. The short period of independency has filled as many pages as the century which preceded it." Nor was this multiplicity of laws the greatest evil—worse was their mutability, a clear mark "of vicious legislation"; and worst of all their injustice, which brought "into question the fundamental principle of republican Government, that the majority who rule in such governments are the safest Guardians both of public Good and private rights."

Indeed Madison proceeded to argue, in effect, that majority rule was more or less of a superstition. No doubt the evils just recounted were traceable in part to the individual selfishness of the representatives of the people; but their chief cause lay in a much more stubborn fact—the natural arrangement of society.

> All civilized societies [he wrote] are divided into different interests and factions, as they happen to be creditors or debtors—rich or poor—husbandmen, merchants or manufacturers—members of different religious sects—followers of different political leaders—inhabitants of different districts—owners of different kinds of property, etc., etc. In republican Government the majority however composed, ultimately give the law. Whenever therefore an apparent interest or common passion unites a majority what is to restrain them from unjust violations of the rights and interests of the minority, or of individuals?

Merely moral or persuasive remedies Madison found to be useless when addressed to political selfishness—which itself never lacks a moral excuse—nor does he once refer to the teachings of Montesquieu, for the reason, it may be surmised, that the model constitution of the Union by this test had broken down at the very moment of crisis. One device, nevertheless, remained untried: the enlargement of the geographical sphere of government. For the advantage of a large republic over a small one, Madison insisted, was this: owing, on the one hand, to the greater variety of interests scattered through it, and, on the other, to the natural barrier of distance, a dangerous coalescence of factions became much more difficult. "As a limited monarchy tempers the evils of an absolute one; so an extensive Republic meliorates the administration of a small Republic."

And how precisely was this remedy to be applied in the case of the United States? In the paper before us, Madison seems to imply the belief that the states ought to surrender all their powers to the national government, but his letters make it plain that this was not his programme. Rather, the powers of the central government should be greatly enlarged, and it should be converted into a real government, operative upon individuals and vested with all the coercive powers of government; then this enlarged and strengthened government, which on account of the territorial extent of its constituency would with difficulty fall a prey to faction, should be set as a check upon the exercise by the state governments of the considerable powers which must still remain with them. "The national government" must "have a negative in all cases whatsoever on the legislative acts of the states," he wrote, like that of the King in colonial days. This was "the least possible abridgment of the State sovereignties." "The happy effect" of such an arrangement would be "its control on the internal vicissitudes of State policy and the aggressions of interested majorities on the rights of minorities and individuals." Thus was the Balance of Power, which Montesquieu had borrowed from the stock teachings of the eighteenth-century diplomacy, to transform it into a maxim of free constitutions, projected into the midway field of federal government.

Every constitutional system gives rise, in relation to the interests of the people whom it is designed to serve, to certain characteristic and persistent problems. The most persistent problem of the American constitutional system arises from the fact that to a multitude of state legislatures are assigned many of the most important powers of government over the individual. Originally, indeed, the bias in favor of local autonomy so overweighted the American constitutional system in that direction that it broke down entirely, both within the states, where the basic rights of property and contract were seriously infringed, and throughout the nation at large, because from the central government essential powers had been withheld.

In the solution of the problems thence resulting, four important constructive ideas were successively brought forward in the years immediately preceding the Philadelphia Convention, all of them reflecting the doctrine of the separation of powers or the attendant notion of a check and balance in government. The abuses resulting from the hitherto undifferentiated character of "legislative power" were met by the idea that it was something intrinsically distinct from "judicial power," and that therefore it was exceeded when it interfered with the dispensation of justice through the ordinary courts. Then building upon this result, the finality of judicial determinations was represented as extending to the interpretation of the standing law, a proposition which, when brought into association with the notion of a higher law, yielded the initial form of the doctrine of judicial review. Meantime, the idea was being advanced that the Articles of Confederation were, in relation to acts of the local legislatures, just such a higher law, thus suggesting a sanction for the acts of the Confederation which in principle entirely transformed its character. Finally, from Madison, who from the first interested himself in every phase of the rising movement for constitutional reform both in his own state and the country at large, came the idea that the problem of providing adequate safeguards for private rights and adequate powers for a national government was one and the same problem, inasmuch as a strengthened national government could be made a make-weight against the swollen prerogatives of the state legislatures. It remained for the Constitutional Convention, however, while it accepted Madison's main idea, to apply it through the agency of judicial review. Nor can it be doubted that this determination was assisted by a growing comprehension in the Convention of the *doctrine* of judicial review.[71]

### Notes

1. See, *e.g.,* R. L. Schuyler, *Constitution of the United States,* p. 5. Professor Schuyler voices the opinion (p. 6) that "the Constitution is not to be regarded as in any true sense an original creative act of the Convention at Philadelphia, which framed it." It is interesting to oppose to this sentiment the following passage from Professor Roscoe Pound's *Interpretations of Legal History,* p. 127: "Except as an act of omnipotence, creation does not mean the making of something out of nothing. Creative activity takes materials and gives them form so that they may be put to uses for which the materials unformed are not adapted." Professor Schuyler's sweeping statement would probably be quite as near the truth if the word "not" were omitted from it.
2. *Writings,* ed. Ford, X. 254, 256.

3. See Farrand, *Records of the Federal Convention,* I. 83–84, 134–135, 137, 139, 151–152, 161, 254, 285 ff., 304 ff., 317, 356, 398ff., 426 ff., 437–438, 444–449, 451, etc. The lessons of the past, its successes and failures, are cited for the most part. The term "political science" is used by Mercer, *ibid.,* II. 284, while "the science of politics" is Hamilton's expression in *Federalist,* no. 9 (ed. Lodge). This, he says, "has undergone great improvement." The entire passage is worth perusal in this connection. See also Madison in *Federalist,* Nos. 14 and 17, and Adams's preface to his *Defence (Works,* IV. 283–298).

4. *Ancient Law* (New York, 1888), p. 226.

5. Farrand, I. 133–134.

6. *Ibid.,* I. 48, 255, 424, 525, 533, II. 285.

7. See W. C. Webster, "State Constitutions of the American Revolution," in *Annals of the American Academy of Political and Social Science,* May, 1897.

8. Niles, *Principles and Acts of the Revolution,* p. 234; from an address by Dr. Benjamin Rush delivered at Philadelphia on July 4, 1787, before members of the Convention and others. The address testifies throughout to the importance of the governmental situation in the states as a problem before the Convention.

9. See *Federalist,* no. 47.

10. Sec. 11 (second edition, ed. Lewis).

11. See *Laws of New Hampshire,* ed. Batchellor, *V. passim.* Some of the less usual items are those on pp. 21, 66, 89, 90–91, 110–111, 125–126, 130–131, 167–168, 243, 320–321, 334–335, 363, 395–396, 400–401, 404–406, 411–412, 417–418, 455–456, 485, 499, 522. The volume is crowded with acts "restoring" a defeated or defaulting party "to his law," "any usage, custom, or law to the contrary notwithstanding."

12. See the references I have collected in my *Doctrine of Judicial Review,* pp. 69–71; also Baldwin, *The American Judiciary,* ch. II.

13. McIlwain, *The High Court of Parliament and its Supremacy,* ch. III.

14. Baldwin, *op. cit.,* ch. I.

15. See, *e.g., Messages from the Governors* (of New York), ed. Lincoln, 1, 55.

16. A good summary of legislative persecution of the Loyalists appears in Van Tyne, *American Revolution,* pp. 255 ff.

17. *Two Centuries Growth of American Law,* pp. 129–133.

18. Cooley, *Constitutional Limitations,* ch. V.

19. *Writings,* Memorial ed., II. 163–164. See to the same effect Chief Justice Pendleton's words in 4 Call 5, 17 (Va., 1782).

20. In *Federalist,* no. 47, Madison also declares that "the entire legislature [*i.e.,* Parliament] can perform no judiciary act." This assertion is based on his reading of Montesquieu, but it is untrue even of Parliament to-day. Stephen, *Commentaries* (eleventh ed.), IV. 283; Pollard, *Evolution of Parliament,* p. 239.

21. Iredell's perusal of Blackstone produced an entire change in his theory of the basis of judicial review. Compare McRee, *Life and Correspondence of James Iredell,* II. 172–173; and *Calder v. Bull,* 3 Dallas 386, 398. One aspect of Marshall's thinking on the same matter is touched upon briefly in note 40, *infra.*

22. Niles, *op. cit.,* p. 47.

23. *Life and Works,* VI. 94–97; Morse, *The Federalist Party in Massachusetts.* pp. 68–69.

24. *History* (New York, 1892), V. 329.

25. Hart, *Slavery and Abolition,* p. 153. See also G. H. Moore, *Slavery in Massachusetts.*

26. Hart, *op. cit.,* p. 154.

27. Moore, *Diary of the American Revolution,* p. 362. See also *Works of Alexander Hamilton,* Constitutional ed. IV, 232.

28. This seems to have been the origin of the American distrust of legislatures, upon which Bryce comments in his *American Commonwealth,* I. 427, 451 (second ed.).

29. D. W. Brown, *The Commercial Power of Congress,* ch. II.; A. A. Giesecke, *American Commercial Legislation before 1789.*

30. McLaughlin, *The Confederation and the Constitution,* ch. IX.

31. *Writings,* Memorial ed., II. 160 ff.

32. *Proceedings relative to the calling of the Conventions of 1776 and 1790* (Harrisburg, 1825), pp. 83 ff. For a contemporary criticism of the report, see *Federalist*, no. 49.

33. *Works*, IV. 273 ff. The quotation is from p. 587.

34. *The English Constitution* (New York, 1906), p. 296.

35. F. J. Stimson, *Federal and State Constitutions*, sect. 304.

36. Austin Scott, "*Holmes v. Walton*, the New Jersey Precedent," in *Am. Hist. Rev.*, IV. 456 ff.

37. See generally my *Doctrine of Judicial Review*, pp. 71–75, and references there given.

38. Holland, *Elements of Jurisprudence*, thirteenth ed., pp. 19–21, 32–34, 41–45.

39. See note 37, above; also Varnum's contemporary pamphlet on the case. The case was the first and last case of judicial review of the sort under the old charter.

40. Compare in this connection Luther Martin's "Genuine Information," in Farrand's *Records*, III. 230, with Hamilton's argument for judicial review in *Federalist*, no. 78, and Marshall's opinion in *Marbury v. Madison*, 1 Cranch 129. The former regards political authority as a *cessio* from the people to the government which "never devolves back to them" except in events amounting to a dissolution of government. The latter regard it as a revocable *translatio* to agents by a principal who is by no means bound to act through agents.

41. See my "Basic Doctrine of American Constitutional Law," in *Michigan Law Review*, XII, 256, 260.

42. Bk. IV., ch. 14.

43. *Institutes*, IV. 70, 71; 12 *Reports* 63.

44. *Institutes*, IV. 23, 26, 36.

45. *Second Treatise on Civil Government*, ch. XI., sect. 136.

46. *Spirit of Laws* (trans. Pritchard), bk. XI., ch. 6.

47. *Commentaries*, I. 44, 46, 58, 160–161, 267, 269.

48. Broom, *Maxims* (fifth American ed.), p. 105 and citations; pp. 140–141 of the original edition.

49. See note 43, *supra*.

50. *Commentaries*, I. 69–71.

51. Martin 42.

52. McRee, *Life and Correspondence of Iredell*, II. 145–149.

53. See especially *Federalist*, no. 15.

54. McLaughlin, *op. cit.*, ch. XI.

55. Van Tyne, "Sovereignty in the American Revolution," in *Am. Hist. Rev.*, XII. 529 ff.

56. *Journals of the Continental Congress*, ed. Hunt, XVIII. 936–937; Wharton, *Revolutionary Diplomatic Correspondence*, V. 88–89; New York Historical Society, *Collections*, 1878, pp. 138–139; J. C. Welling in Am. Hist. Assoc., *Papers*, III. 167 ff.

57. *Works of James Wilson*, ed. J. D. Andrews, I. 558 ff.

58. MacDonald, *Documentary Source Book*, pp. 207–208.

59. See H. B. Dawson's pamphlet on the case; also Coxe's and Haine's well-known volumes. Hamilton had the year previous been a member of a committee of Congress which had the subject of violations of the treaty of peace under consideration. For the report of this committee, see *Journals of the American Congress* (Washington, 1823), IV. 224–225.

60. Allan McLane Hamilton, *Intimate Life of Alexander Hamilton*, pp. 457, 460–461. "Our sovereignty began by a Federal act," he asserts (p. 459).

61. See *Works*, Constitutional ed., IV. 238–240.

62. *Secret Journals of Congress* (Boston, 1821), IV. 185–287.

63. Jefferson's letter of May 29, 1792, to the British minister Hammond, gives all the facts. *Writings*, Memorial ed., XVI. 183–277.

64. *Federalist*, no. 40.

65. D. W. Brown, *op. cit.*, ch. II.

66. *Political Writings of Thomas Paine* (1835), I. 45–46.

67. *Works*, Constitutional ed., I. 213.

68. See the credentials, Elliot's *Debates*, second ed., I. 159 ff.

69. Beveridge, *Life of John Marshall*, vol. I., ch. 8.

70. *Writings*, ed. Hunt, II. 361 ff.

71. *Cf.* Farrand. II. 73–80; and *Federalist*, no. 78.

# The Declaration and the Constitution: Liberty, Democracy, and the Founders

Martin Diamond

In an address delivered in 1911, Henry Cabot Lodge, Sr., looked back wistfully to the joy with which, not long before, the country had celebrated two anniversaries: the centennial of the framing of the Constitution and, two years later, the centennial of its ratification. On both occasions, he remembered, great crowds thronged the streets, processions passed by amidst brilliant decorations and illuminations, and cannon and oratory thundered. What made the occasions so joyous, Lodge explained, was the conviction universally held by Americans of the original and continuing excellence of their Constitution: "Through all the rejoicings of those days . . . ran one unbroken strain of praise of the instrument and of gratitude to the men" whose wisdom had devised it. During those happy centennial celebrations, "every one agreed with Gladstone's famous declaration, that the Constitution of the United States was the greatest political instrument ever struck off on a single occasion by the minds of men."

But in words that speak to our own condition, Lodge then reflected with sorrow on the way all had changed so soon. The vast mass of the American people, he said, still believe in their Constitution, but now they "look and listen, bewildered and confused," as the air is "rent with harsh voices of criticism and attack." On every side, they begin to hear opinion leaders, as we would call them now, who raise a "discordant outcry" against that which the people "have always reverenced and held in honor." Some "excellent persons" attack the Constitution out of an innocent but misguided hope for human improvement by the easy means of constitutional alterations. Others attack the Constitution out of darker motives and even greater folly: "Every one who is in distress, or in debt, or discontented . . . every reformer of other people's misdeeds . . . every raw demagogue, every noisy agitator . . . all such people now lift their hands to tear down or remake the Constitution." All such calling into question of the country's fundamental political principles and institutions presented "a situation of utmost gravity." "Beside the question of the maintenance or destruction of the Constitution of the United States," Lodge solemnly concluded, "all other questions of law and policies sink into utter insignificance."

Now, as we celebrate another great national anniversary, the Bicentennial of the American Revolution, the situation would seem to be graver still. The "discordant outcry" of 1911, which Lodge thought threatened our constitutional felicity then, has grown in the course of 60 years from a few "harsh voices" out of tune with the country's constitutional reverence into a majority of intellectual voices, the conventional wisdom of those who give academic and intellectual opinion to the nation. Moreover, not only has Lodge's minority become our majority, but the then sketchy, somewhat confused, and inconsistent theoretical foundations of his discordant minority have been transformed into a formidable and comprehensive account of the founding of the republic. It is a disquieting account which, quite apart from all other possible causes of political distress, has itself the logical tendency to make impossible the kind of constitutional contentment that so marked the nation's first centennials. And it is upon the basis of this disquieting account that generations of American students have now received their instruction as to "what really happened" at the founding.

### The Nature of American Democracy

Lodge's defense of the traditional understanding of the Constitution was in answer to Populist and Progressive demands for the democratization of the Constitution, and thus of the American political order, through such means as the initiative, the referendum, and the recall. During a generation of Populist and Progressive attacks on the ugly plutocratic tendencies of the turn of the century, these democratizing demands had brought steadily to the fore—as usually happens in American political debate—the question of the meaning and intention of the Constitution. The question took an historical form but—again, as is usually the case—had ultimately a philosophical and political significance: Was the Constitution originally democratic, only to have been perverted in later years, or was it simply undemocratic from the outset? The larger significance of the question, so formulated, is this: It assumes that *the* comprehensive political question is the extent to which things measure up to the requirements of the democratic form of government; democracy becomes the *summum bonum,* the complete good against which all else is judged.

It was around such an assumption concerning democracy, and the status of the Constitution relative to it, that everything ultimately proved to turn. But in 1911, as Lodge was speaking, his opponents were still divided in their answers. Most took the less grave view, namely, that the Constitution was originally satisfactorily democratic, had then been perverted, but that certain democratizing constitutional reforms would quite readily restore it to its original condition of excellence. Cast in such terms, this was still a debate among friends. Lodge and his opponents both agreed that the United States should have a democratic form of government and that the Constitution had established a good version of one. However, while Lodge was content that all was still satisfactorily democratic, his opponents were convinced otherwise. They proposed to graft some democratizing reforms on to the otherwise acceptable Constitution; he warned that these reforms were not really compatible with the rest of the Constitution, and chided them for their too simple faith in popular wisdom as directly and immediately applied to policy and legal questions. The issue between them came down to a question about the nature of democracy and how best to arrange or constitute it in America.

Now, this is a serious question but it is also a limited one, and it is an example of the archetypal American political question. That is to say, in contrast with the situation in many other countries, where the very nature of the regime is typically called into question, in the dispute between Lodge and his opponents there remained a consensus as to the fundamental type of regime the United States should have— namely, constitutional democracy—but serious, even bitter, conflict as to the particular constitutional arrangements. Each side could suspect the other of concealing more vehement aims under the common rhetoric of approval for constitutional democracy; and, if long exacerbated by concurrent social and economic discontents, the issues could of course escalate into profound conflict. But so long as both held to the agreement on the democratic character of the original Constitution, and claimed it as their standard, it remained a moderate debate within the boundaries of the American constitutional order.

### Smith and the Betrayal of the Democratic Promise

But even as Lodge was speaking, another, graver answer to the question about the democratic status of the Constitution was gathering force. Only four years earlier, in 1907, J. Allen Smith had published *The Spirit of American Government*, in which for the first time fully and passionately, a crucial turn was made in the Populist and Progressive argument. It was not true, Smith argued, that an originally democratic Constitution had been perverted to contemporary plutocratic purposes. Rather, democracy had never really gotten off the ground in America; the hopeful democratic promise of the Revolution had been deliberately betrayed from the very beginning by selfish "aristocratic" forces which had calculatedly framed the Constitution so as to prevent democratic majority rule and thus perpetuate privilege. Because democratic ideas had taken strong hold "among the masses," Smith said, the Founders were obliged to frame a government which conferred "at least the form of political power upon the people." But it was a sham conferral; they devised a "system of government which was just popular enough not to excite general opposition and which at the same time gave to the people as little as possible of the substance of political answer."

This was to deepen and darken the debate. The issue was no longer an intra-democratic dispute over the meaning and tendency of the Constitution, but a struggle between democracy and its foes, between democrats yearning to revive the old Revolutionary spirit and reactionaries entrenched behind the barriers of a Constitution, the spirit of which had always been anti-democratic. In principle, Smith's analysis invited those whom he succeeded in persuading to a far greater rejection of the entire constitutional system than anything contemplated by his predecessors. If the Constitution had indeed been the handiwork of a reactionary oligarchy, then all of its mechanisms and processes, its entire "spirit," must be understood as tending against the people and in favor of oligarchy. This was to create, in those who followed Smith's account of the founding, a frame of mind which was receptive to claims for radical political reconstruction.

And Smith's account—varied, elaborated, restated—became in time the dominant teaching regarding the founding among that part of American public opinion shaped by the intellectual and academic community. With that part of public opinion, the Constitution came to stand as if permanently on trial before a skeptical or hostile jury—and the more educated the jurors, the more skeptical or hostile they were likely to be. Nowadays we hear much of political alienation, of distrust in our fundamental institutions; while other factors are undoubtedly involved, this alienation is surely not unconnected with an account of the founding that nurtures a frame of mind prepared, to paraphrase Burke, to sniff radical constitutional defects "on every tainted breeze."

### From Revolution to Reaction?

Preeminent among those who taught a version of Smith's account of the founding are, of course, Charles A. Beard and Vernon L. Parrington. In his *An Economic Interpretation of the Constitution of the United States,* published in 1913, Beard developed an original version of the Smith view, emphasizing especially economic determinism, but in general manipulating data and conclusions in the manner that became characteristic of contemporary political science. Beard's influence was immense and—despite cogent rejoinders by many, especially E. S. Corwin—his argument came to be treated as having settled the fundamental question; for decades, government and history textbooks simply followed the Beard account. On another front, Vernon L. Parrington, whose *Main Currents in American Thought* (the first volume of which was published in 1927) was dedicated to J. Allen Smith, gave a general account of American literature which had its inspiration in Smith's account of the founding. Parrington built upon this base a general view of American life as the conflict between a crabbed old-world liberalism and a generous democratic outlook that derived from French romantic thought, with Hamilton and Jefferson starring as the rival champions. By the 1930's, in the worlds of both social science and literary criticism, Smith, Beard, and Parrington had achieved an amazing hegemony. Few who grew up in those years will have forgotten the sense of enlightenment, of emancipation, and of avant-garde intellectualism that came as one discovered these authors or their views.

Those views were encountered in the leading political science, history, and literary texts used in colleges and universities, in widely-read journals, and in scholarly and popular works generally. Among political science texts, examples are too numerous to need mentioning. One example among historians is the influential text of Samuel Eliot Morison and Henry Steele Commager, *The Growth of the American Republic.* The authors in their own way so fully accepted the dominant view that they presented a section of their chapter on the founding under the heading, "The Thermidorean Reaction." Thermidor! As if America under the Articles had had any resemblance to Robespierrean democracy, and as if the Constitution had anything like the anti-revolutionary character of French government after Thermidor. Under the impact, apparently, of the postwar revisionist attacks on Beard, this heading was silently dropped from later editions—but without, as I recall it, much change in the thrust of the argument. The chapter on the founding generation in Richard Hofstadter's *The American Political Tradition,* perhaps the most influential text among college students, also takes basically the same view. Hofstadter joins with an economic interpretation of the Framers a criticism of their outmoded Calvin-*cum*-Hobbes psychology, but the teaching is the same: democracy feared, democracy rejected; the Constitution as the expression of an outmoded undemocratic outlook still functioning as the barrier against which the forces of modern democracy must contend. A standard literary text—*Literary History of the United States,* by Spiller, Thorp, Johnson, Canby—deals with the founding political questions, understandably, somewhat more perfunctorily; but any lack of boldness in detail is amply made up for by the title of the chapter on the founding. It is "Revolution and Reaction," a favorite formulation of all those who take the Smith-Beard-Parrington position.

The overall character of this teaching constitutes a kind of drama in three acts, with a fourth act always trying to get itself written. As already indicated, Act I is the Revolution, with its brave Declaration of democratic equality and the hopeful democratic beginnings in the new states under the Articles of Confederation. Act II is the Constitution, reactionary and retrograde with respect to democracy, stifling the promising beginnings in the interest of economic privilege or in the name of a constricted, timorous, too jealous love of liberty. Act III is American history to date, in which frustrated democracy struggles against and gradually overcomes the confining Constitution; that is, by such means as constitutional amendment, legislation, and judicial interpretation, and through informal social and political developments, the country is thought to have become somewhat more democratic. However, since on this view the constricting Constitution is still there, and the struggle for democracy is not yet won, there is an Act IV always waiting to be written. The dramatic action here would consist in the final triumph of democracy. Democracy would no longer have to work its cramped way within the constraints of a Constitution always inimical to it, but would at last fully actualize itself and, by means of a new constitutional ordering, become the open, comprehensive, and fundamental law of the land.

So thoroughly has Lodge's "discordant outcry" become the conventional academic wisdom, that now it is the Constitution which seems to be the discordant element—an outmoded formal structure, either irrelevant to contemporary democratic needs or in conflict with them. No wonder there is a sense of faltering and uncertainty as we confront our Bicentennial. Abstracting from all other causes of concern, this understanding of the founding would be enough to darken the mood of the Bicentennial and of the reflections to which it gives rise.

### Two Views of the Founding

The spirit in which we celebrate the Bicentennial will thus in considerable degree depend upon our understanding of the founding. If we continue to view it as fundamentally flawed—that is, as characterized by an improperly resolved question regarding the relationship of democracy and liberty—then we should unhesitatingly seize upon the Bicentennial as the occasion for new beginnings, as an opportunity to rally the nation toward a proper reconstituting of democracy. But if that view of the founding is false, in both history and political philosophy, then we ought, equally unhesitatingly, to make the Bicentennial the occasion for renewed appreciation of our fundamental institutions and rededication to their perpetuation.

But which view of the founding is the right one? The now dominant view or the traditional one it supplanted? The question may be conveniently discussed in terms of our two fundamental documents, the Declaration and the Constitution, and the relationship between liberty and democracy as expressed in them. These are the two great charters of our national existence, representing the beginning of our founding and its consummation; in them are incarnated the two principles—liberty and democracy—upon the basis of which our political order was established, and upon the understanding of which in each generation our political life in some important way depends. Inevitably, then, the dispute about the founding has in a sense always revolved about the understanding of the Declaration and the Constitution and how they stand toward each other.

Now, all parties to the dispute agree that one of these documents stands somehow fundamentally for liberty, and the other one for democracy. But which is which? Interestingly and conveniently, in the two conflicting views of the founding the status of the two documents is exactly reversed. In the now dominant view, the Declaration is understood as a democratic manifesto, or at least as positing principles that logically point to the democratic form of government; and the Constitution is understood as having turned against the democracy of the Declaration in the name of liberty, but in actuality of privilege masquerading as liberty. But in the older view, the one held by the leading men who wrote the two documents—and the correct view, as I shall argue—the matter was understood just the other way round. The Declaration is understood as holding forth only the self-evident truths regarding liberty and, thus, as doing no more than declaring liberty the only legitimate end of all government, whatever its form; and it is the Constitution which is viewed as having opted for democracy, as embodying the bold and unprecedented decision to achieve, in so large a country as this, a free society under the democratic form of government.

Now there is something startling to contemporary Americans, something unpersuasive on its face, in this old-fashioned view of the relation between the Declaration and the Constitution, of liberty and democracy. How can it really be, one might ask, that the glowing, resounding, revolutionary Declaration was limited to the principle of liberty while the sober—one might say, phlegmatic—Constitution represented the bold establishment of democratic government? But the old-fashioned view is startling only to those who have made democracy, understood as the achievement of human equality in every respect, *the* comprehensive political good, superior to liberty or comfortably comprehending it. Eighteenth-century Americans had not yet become so complacent about democracy. Indeed, the founding generation would have balked at the language used above in speaking of the Declaration as *limited* to liberty, as *only* making liberty the end of government. They could not have accepted the implication that democracy was something higher than liberty and beyond it in worth and dignity. On the contrary, *for the founding generation it was liberty that was the comprehensive good, the end against which political things had to be measured; and democracy was only a form of government which, like any other form of government, had to prove itself adequately instrumental to the securing of liberty.*

### The Horizon of Liberty

To understand the founding, then, we must understand anew the horizon or perspective of liberty within which the Declaration and the Constitution were conceived, and the status of democracy within that horizon. A statement of Hamilton from *The Federalist,* which it should be remembered Jefferson unreservedly regarded as the authoritative commentary on the Constitution, will help to renew our understanding. In *The Federalist* Number 9, Hamilton is defending the idea of popular republican government (by which, he says elsewhere, he meant "representative democracy") from its critics. He acknowledges, first, the force of their argument; "it is not to be denied," he says, that the history of all earlier popular republics is so wretched, so disfigured by disorders, as to make plausible the critics' contempt of popular government. Indeed, if there were not some new, improved way to devise a popular republic, then "the enlightened friends to liberty would have been obliged to abandon the cause of that species of government as indefensible." Hamilton of course proceeds to argue that the Constitution will establish just such a novel and defensible system. But the crucial point for us here is the priority of liberty as the end of government, the merely instrumental status of all forms of government, and the peculiarly questionable status of the popular form—democracy—up to the time of the American founding. I cannot conceive of a single author of the Declaration or a leading Framer of the Constitution who would have disagreed with Hamilton's formulation. They all saw the relationship of the Declaration and the Constitution in exactly the same light.

Now this liberty, the preciousness and precariousness of which are now obscured by a complacent contemporary egalitarianism, seemed then a very grand and novel idea to those who drafted our two national documents. They regarded liberty as a modern idea, as the extraordinary achievement of 17th- and 18th-century political thought. With that achievement in mind, George Washington, for example, said that Americans lived in "an Epocha when the rights of mankind were better understood and more clearly defined, than at any former period." This understanding and clarity were all part of the new "science of politics" to which Hamilton referred. It rested, as Leo Strauss has persuasively explained, upon a crucial turn in political thought made by the great philosophic predecessors of the Americans—a turn toward practicable liberty rather than utopian virtue as the end at which governments ought to aim. For thinkers like Locke and Montesquieu it thus became the task of government to provide the framework for a safe and free society in which all equally could enjoy their "unalienable rights . . . [to] life, liberty, and the pursuit of happiness." Such prescriptions for political liberty, the American Founders thought, gave hope at last for the "relief of man's estate," and it was with such prescriptions in mind that they drafted the Declaration and the Constitution.

### Equality as Equal Political Liberty

Once this is understood, one can turn directly to the text of the Declaration and hope to read it as it was intended. Here is the crucial passage:

> We hold these Truths to be self-evident, that all Men are created equal, that they are endowed by their Creator with certain unalienable Rights, that among these are Life, Liberty and the Pursuit of Happiness—That to secure these Rights, Governments are instituted among Men, deriving their just Powers from the Consent of the Governed, that whenever any Form of Government becomes destructive of these Ends, it is the Right of the People to alter or to abolish it, and to institute new Government, laying its Foundations on such principles, and organizing its Powers in such Form, as to them shall seem most likely to effect their Safety and Happiness.

Two of the key phrases— "created equal" and "consent of the governed"—have been particularly misunderstood because they have been wrenched out of context. Written within the horizon of liberty of the founding generation, they have been understood instead within the horizon of egalitarian democracy to which later generations have tended. The Declaration does not mean by "equal" anything at all like the general human equality which so many now make their political standard. Jefferson's original draft of the Declaration is especially illuminating in this respect. All men, Jefferson first wrote, "are created equal and independent" and from that "equal creation they derive rights inherent and inalienable." The word "independent" is especially instructive; it refers to the condition of men in the state of nature. In fact, this famous passage of the Declaration, in both its original and final formulations, must be understood as dealing entirely with the question of the state of nature and with the movement from it into political society.

*The social contract theory upon which the Declaration is based teaches not equality as such but equal political liberty.* The reasoning of the Declaration is as follows. Each man is equally born into the state of nature in a condition of absolute *independence* of every other man. That equal independence of each from all, as John Locke put it, forms a "Title to perfect Freedom" for every man. It is this equal perfect freedom, which men leave behind them when they quit the state of nature, from which they derive their equal "unalienable rights" in civil society. The equality of the Declaration, then, consists entirely in the equal entitlement of all to the rights which comprise political liberty, and nothing more. Thus Lincoln wisely interpreted the Declaration: "The authors of that notable instrument . . . did not intend to declare all men equal in all respects. They did not mean to say all were equal in color, size, intellect, moral developments, or social capacity. They defined with tolerable distinctness, in what respects they did consider all men created equal—equal in 'certain inalienable rights, among which are life, liberty, and the pursuit of happiness.' "

Now "to secure these rights," men quit the insecure state of nature and "Governments are instituted among men, deriving their just powers from the consent of the governed." Here we have the unambiguous meaning of the other phrase in the Declaration that is now so typically misunderstood. It has been transformed to mean rule by the consent of majorities, that is, consent according to the procedures of the democratic form of government. *But the Declaration does not say that consent is the means by which the government is to operate; it says that consent is necessary only to institute or establish the government.* It does not prescribe that the people establish a democratic form of government which *operates* by means of their consent. Indeed, the Declaration says that they may organize government on "such principles" as they choose, and that they may choose "any form of government" they deem appropriate to secure their rights. (In this, the Declaration was again simply following Locke, who taught that when men consent "to joyn into and make one Society," they "might set up what form of Government they thought fit.") And by "any form of government," the Declaration emphatically includes—as any literate 18th-century reader would have understood—not only the democratic form of government, but also a mixed form, and the aristocratic and monarchic forms as well. That is why, for example, the Declaration has to submit facts to a "candid world" to prove the British king guilty of a "long train of abuses." Tom Paine, by way of contrast, could dispose of King George more simply. Paine deemed George III unfit to rule simply because he was a *king* and kingly rule was illegitimate as such. The fact that George was a "Royal Brute" was only frosting on the cake; for Paine his being royal was sufficient warrant for deposing him. But the Declaration, on the contrary, is obliged to prove that George was indeed a brute. That is, the Declaration holds George III "unfit to be the ruler of a free people" not because he was a king, but because he was a *tyrannical* king. Had the British monarchy continued to secure to the colonists their rights, as it had prior to the long train of abuses, the colonists would not have been entitled to rebel. It was only the fact, according to the Declaration, that George had become a tyrannical king that supplied the warrant for revolution. Indeed, most of the signers of the Declaration probably would have cheerfully agreed that the English "mixed monarchy" had been, and perhaps still was for the English themselves, the best and freest government in the history of mankind.

Thus the Declaration, accurately speaking, is neutral on the question of forms of government; any form is legitimate, provided it secures equal freedom and is instituted by popular consent. But as to how to secure that freedom the Declaration, in its famous passage on the principles of government, is silent.

### The "Inconveniences of Democracy"

The Framers of the Constitution were not lacking in guidance from that same new science of politics which had taught them to make liberty the end of government. Especially in Montesquieu's *The Spirit of the Laws,* there was guidance for the construction of, and statesmanship within, the various forms of government. Montesquieu understood that every form of government has its own peculiar excellences, and also its own peculiar tendency to corruption or degeneration. In this, Montesquieu was simply in agreement with the great tradition of political thought. For example, in Aristotle's fundamental typology of regimes, there are six basic forms—three that are "true" forms, namely, monarchy, aristocracy, and "polity," and their three perversions, that is, the forms into which each tends to degenerate, namely, tyranny, oligarchy, and "democracy." On the basis of this typology, Aristotle teaches how to arrange or constitute the regime, whatever type it is, so as to help it be its distinctive best self in its circumstances, and so as to guard against its distinctive degenerative tendency. Montesquieu likewise has a typology of regimes (or forms of government, more precisely), and an analysis of their peculiar excellences and degenerative tendencies. In this regard, then, despite the vast differences between them, Aristotle and Montesquieu are at one.

Their common reasoning is as follows. Every regime or form of government has to have a "ruling element," some part of the whole—whether it be the monarch, the few, or the many—which has to have the final political power. But that power is always susceptible to perversion or abuse. In each political order, the slide to perversion or abuse follows the path of weakness peculiar to that order, and prudent founders and statesmen take pains to guard against the slide.[1]

If we understand that the American Founders, like all sensible men before them, regarded *every* form of government as problematic, in the sense of having a peculiar liability to corruption, and accepted the necessity to cope with the problematics peculiar to their *own* form of government, we will be able to emancipate ourselves from a particularly misleading and persuasive error made by those who follow the now dominant account of the founding. In this account, much is made argumentatively and rhetorically of the fact that the Framers frequently delivered themselves of very sharp criticism of the defects and dangers of democracy. Perhaps the favorite exemplary quotation is that of Edmund Randolph who, at the Federal Convention, traced the evils of the day to their origin in the "turbulence and follies of democracy." Generations of students have shared with their instructors the titillating satisfaction of shocked disdain for the crudely anti-democratic bias of the Founders, as revealed in that remark and similar utterances. The inference drawn from such criticisms of the peculiar defects of democracy has been that the Founders naturally rejected what they regarded as defective. But we may now understand the matter in a different light. *Of course,* the Founders criticized the defects and dangers of democracy and did not waste much breath on the defects and dangers of the other forms of government. For a very good reason. They were not founding any other kind of government; they were establishing a democratic form, and it was the dangers peculiar to it against which all their efforts had to be bent.

An especially clear example, as always, is James Madison's discussion of the separation of powers as it was structured in the proposed Constitution. The separation of powers, he explains in *The Federalist* Number 48, should be differently arranged in many vital details, according to the form of government with which one is dealing. Where there is an hereditary monarch, for example, or in a small direct democracy, the danger of corruption and abuse is different from what it will be in the "representative republic" that is being established by the Constitution. And in accordance with the difference in the danger, the allocations and arrangements of the separated powers likewise ought to be different. Madison spends very little time, however, in discussing the provisions that should be made against dangers elsewhere. rather, he devotes himself to the problems of the form of government at hand—namely, the democratic republic to be established under the Constitution. Sufficient unto a Founder are the evils of the form he is founding.

Properly understood, then, the extent and intensity of the founding generation's concern for the defects and dangers of the democratic form, far from indicating their rejection of democracy, is proof of their acceptance of it and of their determination—copiously expressed, if only one will listen to them—to cope with it. Thus Madison coolly analyzed the "inconveniences of democracy," but only in order to deal with them in a manner "consistent with the democratic form of Government." Similarly, in *The Federalist* Number 9, Hamilton claims that the Founders are employing the newly discovered and improved means "by which the excellencies of republican government may be retained and its imperfections lessened or avoided." And above all, there is Madison, whose Number 10 of *The Federalist* is rightly regarded as the most important original political writing by an American. In it Madison presents his solution to the old problem of majority faction (the tyranny of the majority, as we call it) which had earned for popular governments the just "opprobrium" under which they had hitherto always labored. Madison proudly claims that under the Constitution that form of government will be rescued and can at last "be recommended to the esteem and adoption of mankind."

How utterly the intention and achievement of the Founders are hidden from us by an account of the founding which denies them their democratic *bona fides!* That intention consisted above all in trying to establish a system faithful to the "spirit and form of popular government" in which individual liberty would be made secure. It was the "honorable determination," Madison wrote in *The Federalist* Number 39, of every American "votary of freedom to rest all our political experiments on the capacity of mankind for self-government." Here we have the very heart of the matter: As votaries of freedom, *individual liberty was to the Founders the comprehensive, unproblematic good; and they were determined to secure that good by an experiment in democracy.*

### The Political Science of Liberty

Now wherein lay the difficulty and the danger? We may turn to Montesquieu for guidance to the Founders' understanding of their task. Accepting Locke's perspective on liberty, Montesquieu was the great teacher of the political science of liberty, of the means by which it could be made secure in various forms of government, or, failing that, then at least means by which constraints upon liberty could be moderated. In Book XI of *The Spirit of the Laws* Montesquieu states the problem. No form of government is free "by its nature"; that is, none has liberty built securely into its very form. This is because, as observed above, every form of government consists in giving power to some ruler or body of rulers. And "eternal experience" teaches that, if this power is unrestrained, it will inevitably come to be abused. But how to restrain that necessary power? It is in the very "disposition of things" that power can only be restrained by another power. This restraint, this prevention of unrestrained political power, is for Montesquieu the very definition of political liberty. "The political liberty of the citizen is a tranquility of mind arising from the opinion each has of his safety." When will the citizen be warranted in holding such an opinion? The answer is: when, within the bounds of the possible, his government has been so constituted that no other citizen or body of citizens is unrestrainedly able to employ the powers of government to oppress him.

It is at precisely this point that we can see the modernity of Montesquieu. Montesquieu does not seek to restrain rulers (except, interestingly, in despotisms) by means of the teachings of religion, or by such instruction in virtue as will moderate them or make them friends to liberty. Nor does he rely primarily on the traditional prescription of the "mixed regime," that means of arranging government so that both Lords and Commons, both patricians and plebians, both oligarchs and demos, have to concur in the public measures. Montesquieu turns instead toward a purely institutional means for securing liberty—above all, the separation of powers. His political science is a political science of institutions (and also, it can only be mentioned here, of such a "constitutional" arrangement of the interests and passions as will be conducive of the same mild results sought through institutional means).

In the 19th century, there were many who mocked Montesquieu for his fear of political power and for his cautious institutional strategies. Such men had a confidence in power on the basis of "a conception of human nature," as Parrington described it in another context, "as potentially excellent and capable of indefinite development." But let those now mock who read the 20th century as warranting credence in such a conception of human nature, as entitling men to adventures in unrestrained power. The American Founders, at any rate, preferred to follow men like Montesquieu and the teachings of modern liberty, and chose to find democratic means under the Constitution to secure that liberty. Their great merit consisted in taking the political science of liberty, as that is expressed in the Declaration, and elaborating it into its first full application to the democratic form of government under the Constitution. That was their intention. This has been shown. That it was also their achievement would require an argument beyond the scope of the present essay. But this can be said: It is an intention and achievement which anyone raised under the present scholarly dispensation is incapable of understanding and appreciating.

## The American Posture Toward Democracy

From the relationship of the Declaration and the Constitution, as it was understood by the founding generation, there emerges what can be called the American posture toward democracy. Henry Cabot Lodge, with whose post-Centennial reflections this essay began, understood that posture well because he understood the founding in the traditional way which I have attempted to restore: "The makers of the Constitution . . . knew that what they were establishing was a democracy." But "the vital question was how should this be done." With the history of democracy's past failures in mind, they were determined to "so arrange the government that it should be safe as well as strong. . . . They did not try to set any barrier in the way of the popular will, but they sought to put effective obstacles in the path to sudden action which was impelled by popular passion, or popular whim. . . ." This was the issue as it confronted Lodge: Should the American posture toward democracy remain that of self-doubt and self-restraint, of reliance on representative institutions, on the separation of powers, and all the other self-imposed moderating devices of the Constitution? Or should the political thrust of society be in the direction of government by a more immediate and direct popular will?

For us the issue has become very much graver. With us now, it is not just a question of imprudent democratizing reforms, but a vast inflation of the idea of equality, a conversion of the idea of equal political liberty into an ideology of equality. The underlying complaint against the American political order is no longer a matter of mere reforms, or even of wholesale constitutional revision, although there is always a kind of itch in that direction, but rather a critique of the entire regime in the name of a demand for equality in every aspect of human life. It is a demand which consists in a kind of absolutization of a single principle, the principle of equality, and at the same time an absolutization of the democratic form of government understood as the vehicle for that complete equality. This is a different posture toward democracy indeed than that embodied in the American founding.

The deepest political question Americans can ponder during their Bicentennial celebration is precisely this rivalry of democratic postures or outlooks, the original one of the founding and the newer one based on egalitarianism. The pondering of this question involves considerations far beyond the scope of this essay. But this much can be said: It is a rivalry that will not be fairly contested, a question that will not be wisely pondered, so long as the American political order is understood in the light of the account of the founding that I have been criticizing. That account prejudges the question; it denies democratic credentials to the traditional American posture toward democracy and thereby tilts the scales in favor of egalitarian claims against the present constitutional order. The Bicentennial is a good occasion for the restoration of those credentials.

### Notes

1. To emphasize their common reasoning in this matter is not, however, to minimize the vast difference between Aristotle, the great exponent of ancient political science, and Montesquieu, of the modern. Aristotle has in mind the enhancement in each regime, to the extent possible, of a high conception of virtue and justice; Montesquieu has in mind the security of individual liberty. In accordance with this difference, Aristotle and Montesquieu categorize the various kinds of regimes differently, diagnose differently what their degenerative tendencies are, and prescribe differently because of the different things each is trying to achieve or protect in the various regimes. This difference between the ancient and modern views is illuminated in an observation of Leo Strauss. From the point of view of modern thought, he says, "what you need is not so much formation of character and moral appeal [which ancient thought required] as the right kind of institutions, institutions with teeth in them." The American Founders followed Montesquieu in their reliance on institutions, and not the ancients regarding the necessity of character formation.

---

# The Origin and Scope of the American Doctrine of Constitutional Law.[1]

James B. Thayer

## I.

How did our American doctrine, which allows to the judiciary the power to declare legislative Acts unconstitutional, and to treat them as null, come about, and what is the true scope of it?

It is a singular fact that the State constitutions did not give this power to the judges in express terms; it was inferential. In the earliest of these instruments no language was used from which it was clearly to be made out. Only after the date of the Federal constitution was any such language to be found; as in Article XII. of the Kentucky constitution of 1792. The existence of the power was at first denied or doubted in some quarters; and so late as the year 1825, in a strong dissenting opinion, Mr. Justice Gibson, of Pennsylvania, one of the ablest of American judges, and afterwards the chief justice of that State, wholly denied it under any constitution which did not expressly give it. He denied it, therefore, under the State constitutions generally, while admitting that in that of the United States the power was given; namely, in the second clause of Article VI., when providing that the constitution, and the laws and treaties made in pursuance thereof, "shall be the supreme law of the land; and the judges in every State shall be bound thereby, anything in the constitution or laws of any State to the contrary notwithstanding."[2]

So far as the grounds for this remarkable power are found in the mere fact of a constitution being in writing, or in judges being sworn to support it, they are quite inadequate. Neither the written form nor the oath of the judges necessarily involves the right of reversing, displacing, or disregarding any action of the legislature or the executive which these departments are constitutionally authorized to take, or the determination of those departments that they are so authorized. It is enough, in confirmation of this, to refer to the fact that other countries, as France, Germany, and Switzerland, have written constitutions, and that such a power is not recognized there. "The restrictions," says Dicey, in his admirable Law of the Constitution, "placed on the action of the legislature under the French constitution are not in reality laws, since they are not rules which in the last resort will be enforced by the courts. Their true character is that of maxims of political morality, which derive whatever strength they possess from being formally inscribed in the constitution, and from the resulting support of public opinion."[3]

How came we then to adopt this remarkable practice? Mainly as a natural result of our political experience before the War of Independence,—as being colonists, governed under written charters of government proceeding from the English Crown. The terms and limitations of these charters, so many written constitutions, were enforced by various means,—by forfeiture of the charters, by Act of Parliament, by the direct annulling of legislation by the Crown, by judicial proceedings and an ultimate appeal to the Privy Council. Our practice was a natural result of this; but it was by no means a necessary one. All this colonial restraint was only the usual and normal exercise of power. An external authority had imposed the terms of the charters, the authority of a paramount government, fully organized and equipped for every exigency of disobedience, with a king and legislature and courts of its own. The superior right and authority of this government were fundamental here, and fully recognized; and it was only a usual, orderly, necessary procedure when our own courts enforced the same rights that were enforced here by the appellate courts in England. These charters were in the strict sense written *law*: as their restraints upon the colonial legislatures were enforced by the English courts of last resort, so might they be enforced through the colonial courts, by disregarding as null what went counter to them.[4]

The Revolution came, and what happened then? Simply this: we cut the cord that tied us to Great Britain, and there was no longer an external sovereign. Our conception now was that "the people" took his place; that is to say, our own home population in the several States were now their own sovereign. So far as existing institutions were left untouched, they were construed by translating the name and style of the English sovereign into that of our new ruler,—ourselves, the People. After this the charters, and still more obviously the new constitutions, were not so many orders from without, backed by an organized outside government, which simply performed an ordinary function in enforcing them; they were precepts from the people themselves who were to be governed, addressed to each of their own number, and especially to those who were charged with the duty of conducting the government. No higher power existed to support these orders by compulsion of the ordinary sort. The sovereign himself, having written these expressions of his will, had retired into the clouds; in any regular course of events he had no organ to enforce his will, except those to whom his orders were addressed in these documents. How then should his written constitution be enforced if these agencies did not obey him, if they failed, or worked amiss?

Here was really a different problem from that which had been presented under the old state of things. And yet it happened that no new provisions were made to meet it. The old methods and the old conceptions were followed. In Connecticut, in 1776, by a mere legislative Act, the charter of 1662 was declared to continue "the civil

Constitution of the State, under the sole authority of the People thereof, independent of any King or Prince whatsoever;" and then two or three familiar fundamental rules of liberty and good government were added as a part of it. Under this the people of Connecticut lived till 1818. In Rhode Island the charter, unaltered, served their turn until 1842; and, as is well known, it was upon this that one of the early cases of judicial action arose for enforcing constitutional provisions under the new order of things, as against a legislative Act; namely, the case of Trevett *v.* Weeden, in the Rhode Island Supreme Court in 1786.[5]

But it is instructive to see that this new application of judicial power was not universally assented to. It was denied by several members of the Federal convention, and was referred to as unsettled by various judges in the last two decades of the last century. The surprise of the Rhode Island legislature at the action of the court in Trevett *v.* Weeden seems to indicate an impression in their minds that the change from colonial dependence to independence had made the legislature the substitute for Parliament, with a like omnipotence.[6] In Vermont it seems to have been the established doctrine of the period that the judiciary could not disregard a legislative Act; and the same view was held in Connecticut, as expressed in 1795 by Swift, afterwards chief justice of that State. In the preface to 1 D. Chipman's (Vermont) Reports, *22 ct seq.,* the learned reporter, writing (in 1824) of the period of the Vermont Constitution of 1777, says that "No idea was entertained that the judiciary had any power to inquire into the constitutionality of Acts of the legislature, or to pronounce them void for any cause, or even to question their validity." And at page 25, speaking of the year 1785, he adds: "Long after the period to which we have alluded, the doctrine that the constitution is the supreme law of the land, and that the judiciary have authority to set aside . . . Acts repugnant thereto, was considered anti-republican." In 1814,[7] for the first time, I believe, we find this court announcing an Act of the State legislature to be "void as against the constitution of the State and the United States, and even the laws of nature." It may be remarked here that the doctrine of declaring legislative Acts void as being contrary to the constitution, was probably helped into existence by a theory which found some favor among our ancestors at the time of the Revolution, that courts might disregard such acts if they were contrary to the fundamental maxims of morality, or, as it was phrased, to the laws of nature. Such a doctrine was thought to have been asserted by English writers, and even by judges at times, but was never acted on. It has been repeated here, as matter of speculation, by our earlier judges, and occasionally by later ones; but in no case within my knowledge has it ever been enforced where it was the single and necessary ground of the decision, nor can it be, unless as a revolutionary measure.[8]

In Swift's "System of the Laws of Connecticut," published in 1795,[9] the author argues strongly and elaborately against the power of the judiciary to disregard a legislative enactment, while mentioning that the contrary opinion "is very popular and prevalent." "It will be agreed," he says, "it is as probable that the judiciary will declare laws unconstitutional which are not so, as it is that the legislature will exceed their constitutional authority." But he makes the very noticeable admission that there may be cases so monstrous,—*e.g.,* an Act authorizing conviction for crime without evidence, or securing to the legislature their own seats for life,—"so manifestly unconstitutional that it would seem wrong to require the judges to regard it in their decisions." As late as 1807 and 1808, judges were impeached by the legislature of Ohio for holding Acts of that body to be void.[10]

## II.

When at last this power of the judiciary was everywhere established, and added to the other bulwarks of our written constitutions, how was the power to be conceived of? Strictly as a judicial one. The State constitutions had been scrupulous to part off the powers of government into three; and in giving one of them to each department, had sometimes, with curious explicitness, forbidden it to exercise either of the others. The legislative department, said the Massachusetts constitution in 1780,[11]—

> "Shall never exercise the executive and judicial powers, or either of them; the executive shall never exercise the legislative and judicial powers or either of them; the judicial shall never exercise the legislative and executive powers or either of them; to the end, it may be a government of laws, and not of men."

With like emphasis, in 1792, the constitution of Kentucky[12] said:—

> "Each of them to be confided to a separate body of magistracy; to wit, those which are legislative to one, those which are executive to another, and those which are judiciary to another. No person or collection of persons, being of one of these departments, shall exercise any power properly belonging to either of the others, except in the instances hereinafter expressly permitted."

Therefore, since the power now in question was a purely judicial one, in the first place, there were many cases where it had no operation. In the case of purely political acts and of the exercise of mere discretion, it mattered not that other departments were violating the constitution, the judiciary could not interfere; on the contrary, they must accept and enforce their acts. Judge Cooley has lately said:[13]—

> "The common impression undoubtedly is that in the case of any legislation where the bounds of constitutional authority are disregarded, . . . the judiciary is perfectly competent to afford the adequate remedy; that the Act indeed must be void, and that any citizen, as well as the judiciary itself, may treat it as void, and refuse obedience. This, however, is far from being the fact."

Again, where the power of the judiciary did have place, its whole scope was this; namely, to determine, for the mere purpose of deciding a litigated question properly submitted to the court, whether a particular disputed exercise of power was forbidden by the constitution. In doing this the court was so to discharge its office as not to deprive another department of any of its proper power, or to limit it in the proper range of its discretion. Not merely, then, do these questions, when presenting themselves in the courts for judicial action, call for a peculiarly large method in the treatment of them, but especially they require an allowance to be made by the judges for the vast and not definable range of legislative power and choice, for that wide margin of considerations which address themselves only to the practical judgment of a legislative body. Within that margin, as among all these legislative considerations, the constitutional law-makers must be allowed a free foot. In so far as legislative choice, ranging here unfettered, may select one form of action or another, the judges must not interfere, since *their* question is a naked judicial one.

Moreover, such is the nature of this particular judicial question that the preliminary determination by the legislature is a fact of very great importance, since the constitutions expressly intrust to the legislature this determination; they cannot act without making it. Furthermore, the constitutions not merely intrust to the legislatures a preliminary determination of the question, but they contemplate that this determination may be the final one; for they secure no revision of it. It is only as litigation may spring up, and as the course of it may happen to raise the point of constitutionality, that any question for the courts can regularly emerge. It may be, then, that the mere legislative decision will accomplish results throughout the country of the profoundest importance before any judicial question can arise or be decided,—as in the case of the first and second charters of the United States Bank, and of the legal tender laws of thirty years ago and later. The constitutionality of a bank charter divided the cabinet of Washington, as it divided political parties for more than a generation. Yet when the first charter was given, in 1791, to last for twenty years, it ran through its whole life unchallenged in the courts, and was renewed in 1816. Only after three years from that did the question of its constitutionality come to decision in the Supreme Court of the United States. It is peculiarly important to observe that such a result is not an exceptional or unforeseen one; it is a result anticipated and clearly foreseen. Now, it is the legislature to whom this power is given,—this power, not merely of enacting laws, but of putting an interpretation on the constitution which shall deeply affect the whole country, enter into, vitally change, even revolutionize the most serious affairs, except as some individual may find it for his private interest to carry the matter into court. So of the legal tender legislation of 1863 and later. More important action, more intimately and more seriously touching the interests of every member of our population, it would be hard to think of. The constitutionality of it, although now upheld, was at first denied by the Supreme Court of the United States. The local courts were divided on it, and professional opinion has always been divided. Yet it was the legislature that determined this question, not merely primarily, but once for all, except as some individual, among the innumerable chances of his private affairs, found it for his interest to raise a judicial question about it.

It is plain that where a power so momentous as this primary authority to interpret is given, the actual determinations of the body to whom it is intrusted are entitled to a corresponding respect; and this not on mere grounds of courtesy or conventional respect, but on very solid and significant grounds of policy and law. The judiciary may well reflect that if they had been regarded by the people as the chief protection against legislative violation of the constitution, they would not have been allowed merely this incidental and postponed control. They would have been let in, as it was sometimes endeavored in the conventions to let them in, to a revision of the laws before they began to operate.[14] As the opportunity of the judges to check and correct unconstitutional Acts is so limited, it may help us to understand why the extent of their control, when they do have the opportunity, should also be narrow.

It was, then, all along true, and it was foreseen, that much which is harmful and unconstitutional may take effect without any capacity in the courts to prevent it, since their whole power is a judicial one. Their interference was but one of many safeguards, and its scope was narrow.

The rigor of this limitation upon judicial action is sometimes freely recognized, yet in a perverted way which really operates to extend the judicial function beyond its just bounds. The court's duty, we are told, is the mere and simple office of construing two writings and comparing one with another, as two contracts or two statutes are construed and compared when they are said to conflict; of declaring the true meaning of each, and, if they are opposed to each other, of carrying into effect the constitution as being of superior obligation,—an ordinary and humble judicial duty, as the courts sometimes describe it. This way of putting it easily results in the wrong kind of disregard of legislative considerations; not merely in refusing to let them directly operate as grounds of judgment, but in refusing to consider them at all. Instead of taking them into account and allowing for them as furnishing possible grounds of legislative action, there takes place a pedantic and academic treatment of the texts of the constitution and the laws. And so we miss that combination of a lawyer's rigor with a statesman's breadth of view which should be found in dealing with this class of questions in constitutional law. Of this petty method we have many specimens; they are found only too easily to-day in the volumes of our current reports.

In order, however, to avoid falling into these narrow and literal methods, in order to prevent the courts from forgetting, as Marshall said, that "it is a constitution we are expounding," these literal precepts about the nature of the judicial task have been accompanied by a rule of administration which has tended, in competent hands, to give matters a very different complexion.

### III.

Let us observe the course which the courts, in point of fact, have taken, in administering this interesting jurisdiction.

They began by resting it upon the very simple ground that the legislature had only a delegated and limited authority under the constitutions; that these restraints, in order to be operative, must be regarded as so much law; and, as being law, that they must be interpreted and applied by the court. This was put as a mere matter of course. The reasoning was simple and narrow. Such was Hamilton's method in the Federalist, in 1788,[15] while discussing the Federal constitution, but on grounds applicable, as he conceived, to all others. So, in 1787, the Supreme Court of North Carolina had argued that no Act of the legislature could alter the constitution;[16] that the judges were as much bound by the constitution as by any other law, and any Act inconsistent with it must be regarded by them as abrogated. Wilson, in his Lectures at Philadelphia in 1790–1791,[17] said that the constitution was a supreme law, and it was for the judges to declare and apply it; what was subordinate must give way; because one branch of the government infringed the constitution, it was no reason why another should abet it. In Virginia, in 1793, the judges put it that courts were simply to look at all the law, including the constitution: they were only to expound the law, and to give effect to that part of it which is fundamental.[18] Patterson, one of the justices of the Supreme Court of the United States, in 1795, on the Pennsylvania circuit,[19] said that the constitution is the commission of the legislature; if their Acts are not conformable to it, they are without authority. In 1796, in South Carolina,[20] the matter was argued by the court as a bald and mere question of conformity to paramount law. And such, in 1802, was the reasoning of the General Court of Maryland.[21] Finally, in 1803 came Marbury v. Madison,[22] with the same severe line of argument. The people, it was said, have established written limitations upon the legislature; these control all repugnant legislative Acts; such Acts are not law; this theory is essentially attached to a written constitution; it is for the judiciary to say what the law is, and if two rules conflict, to say which governs; the judiciary are to declare a legislative Act void which conflicts with the constitution, or else that instrument is reduced to nothing. And then, it was added, in the Federal instrument this power is expressly given.

Nothing could be more rigorous than all this. As the matter was put, the conclusions were necessary. Much of this reasoning, however, took no notice of the remarkable peculiarities of the situation; it went forward as smoothly as if the constitution were a private letter of attorney, and the court's duty under it were precisely like any of its most ordinary operations.

But these simple precepts were supplemented by a very significant rule of administration,—one which corrected their operation, and brought into play large considerations not adverted to in the reasoning so far mentioned. In 1811,[23] Chief Justice Tilghman, of Pennsylvania, while asserting the power of the court to hold laws unconstitutional, but declining to exercise it in a particular case, stated this rule as follows:—

> "For weighty reasons, it has been assumed as a principle in constitutional construction by the Supreme Court of the United States, by this court, and every other court of reputation in the United States, that an Act of the legislature is not to be declared void unless the violation of the constitution is so manifest as to leave no room for reasonable doubt."

When did this rule of administration begin? Very early. We observe that it is referred to as thoroughly established in 1811. In the earliest judicial consideration of the power of the judiciary over this subject, of which any report is preserved,—an *obiter* discussion in Virginia in 1782,[24]—while the general power of the court is declared by other judges with histrionic emphasis, Pendleton, the president of the court, in declining to pass upon it, foreshadowed the reasons of this rule, in remarking,—

> "How far this court, in whom the judiciary powers may in some sort be said to be concentrated, shall have power to declare the nullity of a law passed in its forms by the legislative power, without exercising the power of that branch, contrary to the plain terms of that constitution, is indeed a deep, important, and, I will add, a tremendous question, the decision of which would involve consequences to which gentlemen may not . . . have extended their ideas."

There is no occasion, he added, to consider it here. In 1793, when the General Court of Virginia held a law unconstitutional, Tyler, Justice, remarked,[25]—

> "But the violation must be plain and clear, or there might be danger of the judiciary preventing the operation of laws which might produce much public good."

In the Federal convention of 1787, while the power of declaring laws unconstitutional was recognized, the limits of the power were also admitted. In trying to make the judges revise all legislative acts before they took effect, Wilson pointed out that laws might be dangerous and destructive, and yet not so "unconstitutional as to justify the judges in refusing to give them effect."[26] In 1796 Mr. Justice Chase, in the Supreme Court of the United States,[27] said, that without then determining whether the court could declare an Act of Congress void, "I am free to declare that I will never exercise it but in a very clear case." And in 1800, in the same court,[28] as regards a statute of

Georgia, Mr. Justice Patterson, who had already, in 1795, on the circuit, held a legislative Act of Pennsylvania invalid, said that in order to justify the court in declaring any law void, there must be "a clear and unequivocal breach of the Constitution, not a doubtful and argumentative implication."

In 1808 in Georgia[29] it was strongly put, in a passage which has been cited by other courts with approval. In holding an Act constitutional, Mr. Justice Charlton, for the court, asserted this power, as being inseparable from the organization of the judicial department. But, he continued, in what manner should it be exercised?

> "No nice doubts, no critical exposition of words, no abstract rules of interpretation, suitable in a contest between individuals, ought to be resorted to in deciding on the constitutional operation of a statute. This violation of a constitutional right ought to be as obvious to the comprehension of every one as an axiomatic truth, as that the parts are equal to the whole. I shall endeavor to illustrate this: the first section of the second article of the constitution declares that the executive function shall be vested in the governor. Now, if the legislature were to vest the executive power in a standing committee of the House of Representatives, every mind would at once perceive the unconstitutionality of the statute. The judiciary would be authorized without hesitation to declare the Act unconstitutional. But when it remains doubtful whether the legislature have or have not trespassed on the constitution, a conflict ought to be avoided, because there is a possibility in such a case of the constitution being with the legislature."

In South Carolina, in 1812,[30] Chancellor Waties, always distinguished for his clear assertion of the power in the judiciary to disregard unconstitutional enactments, repeats and strongly reaffirms it:—

> "I feel so strong a sense of this duty that if a violation of the constitution were manifest, I should not only declare the Act void, but I should think I rendered a more important service to my country than in discharging the ordinary duties of my office for many years. . . . But while I assert this power and insist on its great value to the country, I am not insensible of the high deference due to legislative authority. It is supreme in all cases where it is not restrained by the constitution; and as it is the duty of legislators as well as judges to consult this and conform their acts to it, so it should be presumed that all their acts do conform to it unless the contrary is manifest. This confidence is necessary to insure due obedience to its authority. If this be frequently questioned, it must tend to diminish the reverence for the laws which is essential to the public safety and happiness. I am not, therefore, disposed to examine with scrupulous exactness the validity of a law. It would be unwise on another account. The interference of the judiciary with legislative Acts, if frequent or on dubious grounds, might occasion so great a jealousy of this power and so general a prejudice against it as to lead to measures ending in the total overthrow of the independence of the judges, and so of the best preservative of the constitution. The validity of the law ought not then to be questioned unless it is so obviously repugnant to the constitution that when pointed out by the judges, all men of sense and reflection in the community may perceive the repugnancy. By such a cautious exercise of this judicial check, no jealousy of it will be excited, the public confidence in it will be promoted, and its salutary effects be justly and fully appreciated."[31]

## IV.

I have accumulated these citations and run them back to the beginning, in order that it may be clear that the rule in question is something more than a mere form of language, a mere expression of courtesy and deference. It means far more than that. The courts have perceived with more or less distinctness that this exercise of the judicial function does in truth go far beyond the simple business which judges sometimes describe. If their duty were in truth merely and nakedly to ascertain the meaning of the text of the constitution and of the impeached Act of the legislature, and to determine, as an academic question, whether in the court's judgment the two were in conflict, it would, to be sure, be an elevated and important office, one dealing with great matters, involving large public considerations, but yet a function far simpler than it really is. Having ascertained all this, yet there remains a question—the really momentous question—whether, after all, the court can disregard the Act. It cannot do this as a mere matter of course,—merely because it is concluded that upon a just and true construction the law is unconstitutional. That is precisely the significance of the rule of administration that the courts lay down. It can only disregard the Act when those who have the right to make laws have not merely made a mistake, but have made a very clear one,—so clear that it is not open to rational question. That is the standard of duty to which the courts bring legislative Acts; that is the test which they apply,—not merely their own judgment as to constitutionality, but their conclusion as to what judgment is permissible to another department which the constitution has charged with the duty of making it. This rule recognizes that, having regard to the great, complex, ever-unfolding exigencies of government, much which will seem unconstitutional to one man, or body of men, may reasonably not seem so to another; that the constitution often admits of different interpretations; that there is often a range of choice and judgment; that in such cases the constitution does not impose upon the legislature any one specific opinion, but leaves open this range of choice; and that whatever choice is rational is constitutional. This is the principle which the rule that I have been illustrating affirms and supports. The meaning and effect of it are shortly and very strikingly intimated by a remark of Judge Cooley,[32] to the effect that one who is a member of a legislature may vote against a measure as being, in his judgment, unconstitutional; and, being subsequently placed on the bench, when this measure, having been passed by the legislature in spite of his opposition, comes before him judicially, may there find it his duty, although he has in no degree changed his opinion, to declare it constitutional.

Will any one say, You are over-emphasizing this matter, and making too much turn upon the form of a phrase? No, I think not. I am aware of the danger of doing that. But whatever may be said of particular instances of unguarded or indecisive judicial language, it does not appear to me possible to explain the early, constant, and emphatic statements upon this subject on any slight ground. The form of it is in language too familiar to courts, having too definite a meaning, adopted with too general an agreement, and insisted upon quite too emphatically, to allow us to think it a mere courteous and smoothly transmitted platitude. It has had to maintain itself against denial and dispute. Incidentally, Mr. Justice Gibson disputed it in 1825, while denying the whole power to declare laws unconstitutional.[33] If there be any such power, he insisted (page 352), the party's rights "would depend, not on the greatness of the supposed discrepancy with the constitution, but on the existence of any discrepancy at all." But the majority of the court reaffirmed their power, and the qualifications of it, with equal emphasis. This rule was also denied in 1817 by Jeremiah Mason, one of the leaders of the New England bar, in his argument of the Dartmouth College case, at its earlier stage, in New Hampshire.[34] He said substantially this: "An erroneous opinion still prevails to a considerable extent, that the courts . . . ought to act . . . with more than ordinary deliberation, . . . that they ought not to declare Acts of the legislature unconstitutional unless they come to their conclusion with absolute certainty, . . . and where the reasons are so manifest that none can doubt." He conceded that the courts should treat the legislature "with great decorum, . . . but . . . the final decision, as in other cases, must be according to the unbiassed dictate of the understanding." Legislative Acts, he said, require for their passage at least a majority of the legislature, and the reasons against the validity of the Act cannot ordinarily be so plain as to leave no manner of doubt. The rule, then, really requires the court to surrender its jurisdiction. "Experience shows that legislatures are in the constant habit of exerting their power to its utmost extent." If the courts retire, whenever a plausible ground of doubt can be suggested, the legislature will absorb all power. Such was his argument. But notwithstanding this, the Supreme Court of New Hampshire declared that they could not act without "a clear and strong conviction;" and on error, in 1819, Marshall, in his celebrated opinion at Washington, declared, for the court, "that in no doubtful case would it pronounce a legislative Act to be contrary to the Constitution."

Again, when the great Charles River Bridge Case[35] was before the Massachusetts courts, in 1829, Daniel Webster, arguing, together with Lemuel Shaw, for the plaintiff, denied the existence or propriety of this rule. All such cases, he said (p. 442,) involve some doubt; it is not to be supposed that the legislature will pass an Act palpably unconstitutional. The correct ground is that the court will interfere when a case appearing to be doubtful is made out to be clear. Besides, he added, "members of the legislature sometimes vote for a law, of the constitutionality of which they doubt, on the consideration that the question may be determined by the judges." This Act passed in the House of Representatives by a majority of five or six.

> "We could show, if it were proper, that more than six members voted for it because the unconstitutionality of it *was* doubtful; leaving it to this court to determine the question. If the legislature is to pass a law because its unconstitutionality is doubtful, and the judge is to hold it valid because its unconstitutionality is doubtful, in what a predicament is the citizen placed! The legislature pass it *de bene esse;* if the question is not met and decided here on principle, responsibility rests nowhere. . . . It is the privilege of an American judge to decide on constitutional questions. . . . Judicial tribunals are the only ones suitable for the investigation of difficult questions of private right."

But the court did not yield to this ingenious attempt to turn them into a board for answering legislative conundrums. Instead of deviating from the line of their duty for the purpose of correcting errors of the legislature, they held that body to its own duty and its own responsibility. "Such a declaration," said Mr. Justice Wilde in giving his opinion, "should never be made but when the case is clear and manifest to all intelligent minds. We must assume that the legislature have done their duty, and we must respect their constitutional rights and powers." Five years later, Lemuel Shaw, who was

Webster's associate counsel in the case last mentioned, being now Chief Justice of Massachusetts, in a case[36] where Jeremiah Mason was one of the counsel, repeated with much emphasis "what has been so often suggested by courts of justice, that . . . courts will . . . never declare a statute void unless the nullity and invalidity are placed beyond reasonable doubt."

A rule thus powerfully attacked and thus explicitly maintained, must be treated as having been deliberately meant, both as regards its substance and its form. As to the form of it, it is the more calculated to strike the attention because it marks a familiar and important discrimination, of daily application in our courts, in situations where the rights, the actions, and the authority of different departments, different officials, and different individuals have to be harmonized. It is a distinction and a test, it may be added, that come into more and more prominence as our jurisprudence grows more intricate and refined. In one application of it, as we all know, it is constantly resorted to in the criminal law in questions of self-defence, and in the civil law of tort in questions of negligence,—in answering the question what might an individual who has a right and perhaps a duty of acting under given circumstances, reasonably have supposed at that time to be true? It is the discrimination laid down for settling that difficult question of a soldier's responsibility to the ordinary law of the land when he has acted under the orders of his military superior. "He may," says Dicey, in his "Law of the Constitution,"[37] as it has been well said, be liable to be shot by a court-martial if he disobeys an order, and to be hanged by a judge and jury if he obeys it. . . . Probably," he goes on, quoting with approval one of the books of Mr. Justice Stephen, ". . . it would be found that the order of a military superior would justify his inferiors in executing any orders for giving which they might fairly suppose their superior office to have good reasons. . . . The only line that presents itself to my mind is that a soldier should be protected by orders for which he might reasonably believe his officer to have good grounds."[38] This is the distinction adverted to by Lord Blackburn in a leading modern case in the law of libel.[39] "When the court," he said, "come to decide whether a particular set of words . . . are or are not libellous, they have to decide a very different question from that which they have to decide when determining whether another tribunal . . . might not unreasonably hold such words to be libellous." It is the same discrimination upon which the verdicts of juries are revised every day in the courts, as in a famous case where Lord Esher applied it a few years ago, when refusing to set aside a verdict.[40] It must appear, he said, "that reasonable men could not fairly find as the jury have done. . . . It has been said, indeed, that the difference between [this] rule and the question whether the judges would have decided the same way as the jury, is evanescent, and the solution of both depends on the opinion of the judges. The last part of the observation is true, but the mode in which the subject is approached makes the greatest difference. To ask 'Should we have found the same verdict,' is surely not the same thing as to ask whether there is room for a reasonable difference of opinion." In like manner, as regards legislative action, there is often that ultimate question, which was vindicated for the judges in a recent highly important case in the Supreme Court of the United States,[41] viz., that of the reasonableness of a legislature's exercise of its most undoubted powers; of the permissible limit of those powers. If a legislature undertakes to exert the taxing power, that of eminent domain, or any part of that vast, unclassified residue of legislative authority which is called, not always intelligently, the police power, this action must not degenerate into an irrational excess, so as to become, in reality, something different and forbidden,—*e.g.,* the depriving people of their property without due process of law; and whether it does so or not, must be determined by the judges.[42] But in such cases it is always to be remembered that the judicial question is a secondary one. The legislature in determining what shall be done, what it is reasonable to do, does not divide its duty with the judges, nor must it conform to their conception of what is prudent or reasonable legislation. The judicial function is merely that of fixing the outside border of reasonable legislative action, the boundary beyond which the taxing power, the power of eminent domain, police power, and legislative power in general, cannot go without violating the prohibitions of the constitution or crossing the line of its grants.[43]

It must indeed be studiously remembered, in judically applying such a test as this of what a legislature may reasonably think, that virtue, sense, and competent knowledge are always to be attributed to that body. The conduct of public affairs must always go forward upon conventions and assumptions of that sort. "It is a *postulate,*" said Mr. Justice Gibson, "in the theory of our government . . . that the people are wise, virtuous, and competent to manage their own affairs."[44] "It would be indecent in the extreme," said Marshall, C. J.,[45] "upon a private contract between two individuals to enter into an inquiry respecting the corruption of the sovereign power of a State." And so in a court's revision of legislative acts, as in its revision of a jury's acts, it will always assume a duly instructed body; and the question is not merely what persons may rationally do who are such as we often see, in point of fact, in our legislative bodies, persons untaught it may be, indocile, thoughtless, reckless, incompetent,—but what those other persons, competent, well-instructed, sagacious, attentive, intent only on public ends, fit to represent a self-governing people, such as our theory of government assumes to be carrying on our public affairs,—what such persons may reasonably think or do, what is the permissible view for them. If, for example, what is presented to the court be a question as to the constitutionality of an Act alleged to be *ex post facto,* there can be no assumption of ignorance, however probable, as to anything involved in a learned or competent discussion of that subject. And so of the provisions about double jeopardy, or giving evidence against one's self, or attainder, or jury trial. The reasonable doubt, then, of which our judges speak is that reasonable doubt which lingers in the mind of a competent and duly instructed person who has carefully applied his faculties to the question. The rationally permissible opinion of which we have been talking is the opinion reasonably allowable to such a person as this.

The ground on which courts lay down this test of a reasonable doubt for juries in criminal cases, is the great gravity of affecting a man with crime. The reason that they lay it down for themselves in reviewing the civil verdict of a jury is a different one, namely, because they are revising the work of another department charged with a duty of its own,—having themselves no right to undertake *that* duty, no right at all in the matter except to hold the other department within the limit of a reasonable interpretation and exercise of its powers. The court must not, even negatively, undertake to pass upon the facts in jury cases. The reason that the same rule is laid down in regard to revising legislative acts is neither the one of these nor the other alone, but it is both. The courts are revising the work of a co-ordinate department, and must not, even negatively, undertake to legislate. And, again, they must not act unless the case is so very clear, because the consequences of setting aside legislation may be so serious.

If it be said that the case of declaring legislation invalid is different from the others because the ultimate question here is one of the construction of a writing; that this sort of question is always a court's question, and that it cannot well be admitted that there should be two legal constructions of the same instrument; that there is a right way and a wrong way of construing it, and only one right way; and that it is ultimately for the court to say what the right way is,—this suggestion appears, at first sight, to have much force. But really it begs the question. Lord Blackburn's opinion in the libel case[46] related to the construction of a writing. The doctrine which we are now considering is this, that in dealing with the legislative action of a co-ordinate department, a court cannot always, and for the purpose of all sorts of questions, say that there is but one right and permissible way of construing the constitution. When a court is interpreting a writing merely to ascertain or apply its true meaning, then, indeed, there is but one meaning allowable; namely, what the court adjudges to be its true meaning. But when the ultimate question is not that, but whether certain acts of another department, officer, or individual are legal or permissible, then this is not true. In the class of cases which we have been considering, *the ultimate question is not what is the true meaning of the constitution, but whether legislation is sustainable or not.*

It may be suggested that this is not the way in which the judges in fact put the matter; *e.g.,* that Marshall, in McCulloch *v.* Maryland[47] seeks to establish the court's own opinion of the constitutionality of the legislation establishing the United States Bank. But in recognizing that this is very often true, we must remember that where the court is sustaining an Act, and finds it to be constitutional in its own opinion, it is fit that this should be said, and that such a declaration is all that the case calls for; it disposes of the matter. But it is not always true; there are many cases where the judges sustain an Act because they are in doubt about it; where they are not giving their own opinion that it is constitutional, but are merely leaving untouched a determination of the legislature; as in the case where a Massachusetts judge concurred in the opinion of his brethren that a legislative Act was "competent for the legislature to pass, and was not unconstitutional," "upon the single ground that the Act is not so clearly unconstitutional, its invalidity so free from reasonable doubt, as to make it the duty of the judicial department, in view of the vast interests involved in the result, to declare it void."[48] The constant declaration of the judges that the question for them is not one of the mere and simple preponderance of reasons for or against, but of what is very plain and clear, clear beyond a reasonable doubt,—this declaration is really a steady announcement that their decisions in support of the constitutionality of legislation do not, as of course, import their own opinion of the true construction of the constitution, and that the strict meaning of their words, when they hold an Act constitutional, is merely this,—not unconstitutional beyond a reasonable doubt. It may be added that a sufficient explanation is found here of some of the decisions which have alarmed many people in recent years,—as if the courts were turning out but a broken reed.[49] Many more such opinions are to be expected, for, while legislatures are often faithless to their trust, judges sometimes have to confess the limits of their own power.

It all comes back, I think, to this. The rule under discussion has in it an implied recognition that the judicial duty now in question touches the region of political administration, and is qualified by the necessities and proprieties of administration. If our doctrine of constitutional law—which finds itself, as we have seen, in the shape of a narrowly stated substantive principle, with a rule of administration enlarging the otherwise too restricted substantive rule—admits now of a juster and simpler conception, that is a very familiar situation in the development of law. What really took place in adopting our theory of constitutional law was this: we introduced for the first time into the conduct of government through its great departments a judicial sanction, as among these departments,—not full and complete, but partial. The judges were allowed, indirectly and in a degree, the power to revise the action of other departments and to pronounce it null. In simple truth, while this is a mere judicial function, it involves, owing to the subject-matter with which it deals, taking a part, a secondary part, in the political conduct of government. If that be so, then the judges must apply methods and principles that befit their task. In such a work there can be no permanent or fitting *modus vivendi* between the different departments unless each is sure of the full co-operation of the others, so long as its own action conforms to any reasonable and fairly permissible view of its constitutional power. The ultimate arbiter of what is rational and permissible is indeed always the courts, so far as litigated cases bring the question before them. This leaves to our courts a great and stately jurisdiction. It will only imperil the whole of it if it is sought to give them more. They must not step into the shoes of the law-maker, or be unmindful of the hint that is found in the sagacious remark of an English bishop nearly two centuries ago, quoted lately from Mr. Justice Holmes:[50]—

> "Whoever hath an absolute authority to interpret any written or spoken laws, it is he who is truly the lawgiver, to all intents and purposes, and not the person who first wrote or spoke them."[51]

## V.

Finally, let me briefly mention one or two discriminations which are often overlooked, and which are important in order to a clear understanding of the matter. Judges sometimes have occasion to express an opinion upon the constitutionality of a statute, when the rule which we have been considering has no application, or a different application from the common one. There are at least three situations which should be distinguished: (1) where judges pass upon the validity of the acts of a co-ordinate department; (2) where they act as advisers of the other departments; (3) where as representing a government of paramount authority, they deal with acts of a department which is not co-ordinate.

(1) The case of a court passing upon the validity of the act of a co-ordinate department is the normal situation, to which the previous observations mainly apply. I need say no more about that.

(2) As regards the second case, the giving of advisory opinions, this, in reality, is not the exercise of the judicial function at all, and the opinions thus given have not the quality of judicial authority.[52] A single exceptional and unsupported opinion upon this subject, in the State of Maine, made at a time of great political excitement,[53] and a doctrine in the State of Colorado, founded upon considerations peculiar to the constitution of that State.[54] do not call for any qualification of the general remark, that such opinions, given by our judges,—like that well-known class of opinions given by the judges in England when advising the House of Lords, which suggested our own

practice,—are merely advisory, and in no sense authoritative judgments.[55] Under our constitutions such opinions are not generally given. In the six or seven States where the constitutions provide for them, it is the practice to report these opinions among the regular decisions, much as the responses of the judges in Queen Caroline's Case, and in MacNaghten's Case, in England, are reported, and sometimes cited, as if they held equal rank with true adjudications. As regards such opinions, the scruples, cautions, and warnings of which I have been speaking, and the rule about a reasonable doubt, which we have seen emphasized by the courts as regards judicial decisions upon the constitutionality of laws, have no application. What is asked for is the judge's own opinion.

(3) Under the third head come the questions arising out of the existence of our double system, with two written constitutions, and two governments, one of which, within its sphere, is of higher authority than the other. The relation to the States of the paramount government as a whole, and its duty in all questions involving the powers of the general government to maintain that power as against the States in its fulness, seem to fix also the duty of each of its departments; namely, that of maintaining this paramount authority in its true and just proportions, to be determined by itself. If a State legislature passes a law which is impeached in the due course of litigation before the national courts, as being in conflict with the supreme law of the land, those courts may have to ask themselves a question different from that which would be applicable if the enactments were those of a co-ordinate department. When the question relates to what is admitted not to belong to the national power, then whoever construes a State constitution, whether the State or national judiciary, must allow to that legislature the full range of rational construction. But when the question is whether State action be or be not conformable to the paramount constitution, the supreme law of the land, we have a different matter in hand. Fundamentally, it involves the allotment of power between the two governments,—where the line is to be drawn. True, the judiciary is still debating whether a legislature has transgressed its limit; but the departments are not co-ordinate, and the limit is at a different point. The judiciary now speaks as representing a paramount constitution and government, whose duty it is, in all its departments, to allow to that constitution nothing less than its just and true interpretation; and having fixed this, to guard it against any inroads from without.

I have been speaking of the national judiciary. As to how the State judiciary should treat a question of the conformity of an Act of their own legislature to the paramount constitution, it has been plausibly said that they should be governed by the same rule that the Federal courts would apply. Since an appeal lies to the Federal courts, these two tribunals, it has been said, should proceed on the same rule, as being parts of one system. But under the Judiciary Act an appeal does not lie from every decision; it only lies when the State law is *sustained* below. It would perhaps be sound on general principles, even if an appeal were allowed in all cases, here also to adhere to the general rule that judges should follow any permissible view which the co-ordinate legislature has adopted. At any rate, under existing legislation it seems proper in the State court to do this, for the practical reason that this is necessary in order to preserve the right of appeal.[56]

The view which has thus been presented seems to me highly important. I am not stating a new doctrine, but attempting to restate more exactly and truly an admitted one. If what I have said be sound, it is greatly to be desired that it should be more emphasized by our courts, in its full significance. It has been often remarked that private rights are more respected by the legislatures of some countries which have no written constitution, than by ours. No doubt our doctrine of constitutional law has had a tendency to drive out questions of justice and right, and to fill the mind of legislators with thoughts of mere legality, of what the constitution allows. And moreover, even in the matter of legality, they have felt little responsibility; if we are wrong, they say, the courts will correct it.[57] If what I have been saying is true, the safe and permanent road towards reform is that of impressing upon our people a far stronger sense than they have of the great range of possible harm and evil that our system leaves open, and must leave open, to the legislatures, and of the clear limits of judicial power; so that responsibility may be brought sharply home where it belongs. The checking and cutting down of legislative power, by numerous detailed prohibitions in the constitution, cannot be accomplished without making the government petty and incompetent. This process has already been carried much too far in some of our States. Under no system can the power of courts go far to save a people from ruin; our chief protection lies elsewhere. If this be true, it is of the greatest public importance to put the matter in its true light.[58]

### Notes

1. Read at Chicago, August 9, 1893, before the Congress on Jurisprudence and Law Reform.
2. This opinion has fallen strangely out of sight. It has much the ablest discussion of the question which I have ever seen, not excepting the judgment of Marshall in *Marbury v. Madison,* which, as I venture to think, has been overpraised. Gibson afterwards accepted the generally received doctrine. "I have changed that opinion," said the Chief Justice to counsel, in *Norris v. Clymer,* 2 Pa. St., p. 281 (1845), "for two reasons. The late convention [apparently the one preceding the Pennsylvania constitution of 1838] by their silence sanctioned the pretensions of the courts to deal freely with the Acts of the legislature; and from experience of the necessity of the case."
3. Ch. ii. p. 127, 3d ed. President Rogers, in the preface to a valuable collection of papers on the "Constitutional History of the United States, as seen in the Development of American Law," p. 11, remarks that "there is not in Europe to this day a court with authority to pass on the constitutionality of national laws. But in Germany and Switzerland, while the Federal courts cannot annul a Federal law, they may, in either country, declare a cantonal or State law invalid when it conflicts with the Federal law." Compare Dicey, *ubi supra,* and Bryce, Am. Com., i. 430, note (1st ed.), as to possible qualifications of this statement.
4. For the famous cases of *Lechmere v. Winthrop* (1727–28), *Phillips v. Savage* (1734), and *Clark v. Tousey* (1745), see the Talcott Papers, Conn. Hist. Soc. Coll., iv. 94, note. For the reference to this volume I am indebted to the Hon. Mellen Chamberlain, of Boston. The decree of the Privy Council, in *Lechmere v. Winthrop,* declaring "null and void" a provincial Act of nearly thirty years' standing, is found in Mass. Hist. Soc. Coll., sixth series, v. 496.
5. Varnum's Report of the case (Providence, 1787); s. c. 2 Chandler's Crim. Trials, 269.
6. And so of the excitement aroused by the alleged setting aside of a legislative Act in New York in 1784, in the case of *Rutgers v. Waddington.* Dawson's edition of this case, "With an Historical Introduction" (Morrisania, 1866), pp. xxiv *et seq.* In an "Address to the People of the State," issued by the committee of a public meeting of "the violent Whigs," it was declared (pp. xxxiii) "That there should be a power vested in Courts of Judicature, whereby

they might control the Supreme Legislative power, we think is absurd in itself. Such powers in courts would be destructive of liberty, and remove all security of property." For the reference to this case, and a number of others, I am indebted to a learned article on "The Relation of the Judiciary to the Constitution" (19 Am. Law Rev. 175) by William M. Meigs, Esq., of the Philadelphia bar. It gives all the earliest cases. As Mr. Meigs remarks, the New York case does not appear to be really one of holding a law *unconstitutional.*

7. *Dupuy v. Wickwire,* 1 D. Chipman, 237.
8. This subject is well considered in a learned note to Paxton's Case (1761), Quincy's Rep 51, relating to Writs of Assistance, understood to have been prepared by Horace Gray, Esq., now Mr. Justice Gray, of the Supreme Court of the United States. See the note at pp. 520–530. James Otis had urged in his argument that "an Act of Parliament against the Constitution is void" (Quincy, 56, n., 474). The American cases sometimes referred to as deciding that a legislative Act was void, as being contrary to the first principles of morals or of government,—*e.g.,* in Quincy, 529, citing *Bowman v. Middleton,* 1 Bay, 252, and in 1 Bryce, Am. Com., 431, n., 1st ed., citing *Gardner v. Newburgh,* Johns. Ch. Rep. 162,—will be found, on a careful examination, to require no such explanation.
9. Vol. i. pp. 50 *et seq.*
10. Cooley, Const. Lim., 6th ed., 193, n.; 1 Chase's Statutes of Ohio, preface, 38–40. For the last reference I am indebted to my colleague, Professor Wambaugh.
11. Part I. Art. 30.
12. Art I.
13. Journal of the Michigan Pol. Sc. Association, vol. i. p. 47.
14. The constitution of Colombia, of 1886, art. 84, provides that the judges of the Supreme Court may take part in the legislative debates over "bills relating to civil matters and judicial procedure." And in the case of legislative bills which are objected to by "the government" as unconstitutional, if the legislature insist on the bill, as against a veto by the government, it shall be submitted to the Supreme Court, which is to decide upon this question finally. Arts. 90 and 150. See a translation of this constitution by Professor Moses, of the University of California, in the supplement to the Annals of the American Academy of Political and Social Science, for January, 1893.

We are much too apt to think of the judicial power of revising the acts of the other departments as our only protection against oppression and ruin. But it is remarkable how small a part this played in any of the debates. The chief protections were a wide suffrage, short terms of office, a double legislative chamber, and the so-called executive veto. There was, in general, the greatest unwillingness to give the judiciary any share in the law-making power. In New York, however, the constitution of 1777 provided a Council of Revision, of which several of the judges were members, to whom all legislative Acts should be submitted before they took effect, and by whom they must be approved. That existed for more than forty years, giving way in the constitution of 1821 to the common expedient of merely requiring the approval of the executive, or in the alternative, if he refused it, the repassing of the Act, perhaps by an increased vote, by both branches of the legislature. In Pennsylvania (Const. of 1776, § 47) and Vermont (Const. of 1777, § 44) a Council of Censors was provided for, to be chosen every seven years, who were to investigate the conduct of affairs, and point out, among other things, all violations of the constitution by any of the departments. In Pennsylvania this arrangement lasted only from 1776 to 1790; in Vermont from 1777 to 1870. In framing the constitution of the United States, several of these expedients, and others, were urged, and at times adopted; *e.g.,* that of New York. It was proposed at various times that the general government should have a negative on all the legislation of the States; that the governors of the States should be appointed by the United States, and should have a negative on State legislation; that a Privy Council to the President should be appointed, composed in part of the judges; and that the President and the two houses of Congress might obtain opinions from the Supreme Court. But at last the convention, rejecting all these, settled down upon the common expedients of two legislative houses, to be a check upon each other, and of an executive revision and veto, qualified by the legislative power of reconsideration and enactment by a majority of two-thirds;—upon these expedients, and upon the declaration that the constitution, and constitutional laws and treaties, shall be the supreme law of the land, and shall bind the judges of the several States. This provision, as the phrasing of it indicates, was inserted with an eye to secure the authority of the general government as against the States, *i.e.*, as an essential feature of any efficient Federal system, and not with direct reference to the other departments of the government of the United States itself. The first form of it was that "legislative Acts of the United States, and treaties, are the supreme law of the respective States, and bind the judges there as against their own laws."

15. No. 78, first published on May 28, 1788. See Lodge's edition, pp. xxxvi and xliv.
16. *Den d. Bayard v. Singleton,* 1 Martin, 42.
17. Vol i. p. 460.
18. *Kemper v. Hawkins,* Va. Cas. 20.
19. *Vanhorne's Lessee v. Dorrance,* 2 Dall. 304.
20. *Lindsay v. Com'rs,* 2 Bay, 38.
21. *Whittington v. Polk,* 1 II. and J. 236.
22. 1 Cranch, 137.
23. *Com. v. Smith,* 4 Bin. 117.
24. *Com. v. Call,* 4 Call, 5.
25. *Kemper v. Hawkins,* Va. Cases, p. 60.
26. 5 Ell. Deb. 344.
27. *Ware v. Hylton,* 3 Dall. 171.
28. *Cooper v. Telfair,* 4 Dall. 14.
29. *Grimball v. Ross,* Charlton, 175.
30. *Adm'rs of Byrne v. Adm'rs of Stewart,* 3 Des. 466.
31. This well-known rule is laid down by Cooley (Const. Lim., 6th ed., 216), and supported by emphatic judicial declarations and by a long list of citations from all parts of the country. In *Ogden v. Saunders,* 12 Wheat. 213 (1827), Mr. Justice Washington, after remarking that the question was a doubtful one, said: "If I could rest my opinion in favor of the constitutionality of the law . . . on no other ground than this doubt, so felt and acknowledged, that alone would, in my estimation, be a satisfactory vindication of it. It is but a decent respect due to the . . . legislative body by which any law is passed, to presume in favor of its validity, until its violation of the constitution is proved beyond all reasonable doubt. This has always been the language of this court when that subject has called for its decision; and I know it expresses the honest sentiments of each and every member of this bench." In the Sinking Fund Cases, 99 U.S. 700 (1878), Chief Justice Waite, for the court, said: "This declaration [that an Act of Congress is unconstitutional] should never be made except in a clear case. Every possible presumption is in favor of the validity of a statute, and this continues until the contrary is shown beyond a rational doubt. One branch of the government cannot encroach on the domain of another without danger. The safety of our institutions depends in no small degree on a strict observance of this salutary rule." In Wellington *et al.,* Petitioners, 16 Pick. 87 (1834), Chief Justice Shaw, for the court, remarked that it was proper "to repeat what has been so often suggested by courts of justice, that when called upon to pronounce the invalidity of an Act of legislation [they will] never declare a statute void unless the nullity and invalidity of the Act are placed, in their judgment, beyond reasonable doubt." In *Com. v. Five Cents Sav. Bk.,* 5 Allen, 428 (1862), Chief Justice Bigelow, for the court, said: "It may be well to repeat the rule of exposition which has been often enunciated by this court, that where a statute has been passed with all the forms and solemnities required to give it the force of law, the presumption is in favor of its validity, and that the court will not declare it to be . . . void unless its invalidity is established beyond reasonable doubt." And he goes on to state a corollary of this "well-established rule." In *Ex parte* M'Collum, 1 Cow. p. 564 (1823), Cowen, J. (for the court), said: "Before the court will deem it their duty to declare an Act of the legislature unconstitutional, a case must be presented in which there can be no rational doubt." In the *People v. The Supervisors of Orange,* 17 N.Y. 235 (1858), Harris, J. (for the court), said: "A legislative Act is not to be declared void upon a mere conflict of interpretation between the legislative and the judicial power. Before proceeding to annul, by judicial sentence, what has been enacted by the law-making power, it should clearly appear that the Act cannot be supported by any reasonable intendment or allowable presumption." In *Perry v. Keene,* 56 N. H. 514, 534 (1876), Ladd, J. (with the concurrence of the rest of

the court), said: "Certainly it is not for the court to shrink from the discharge of a constitutional duty; but, at the same time, it is not for this branch of the government to set an example of encroachment upon the province of the others. It is only the enunciation of a rule that is now elementary in the American States, to say that before we can declare this law unconstitutional, we must be fully satisfied—satisfied beyond a reasonable doubt—that the purpose for which the tax is authorized is private, and not public." In The Cincinnati, etc., Railroad Company, 1 Oh. St. 77 (1852), Ranney, J. (for the court), said: "While the right and duty of interference in a proper case are thus undeniably clear, the principles by which a court should be guided in such an inquiry are equally clear, both upon principle and authority. . . . It is only when manifest assumption of authority and clear incompatibility between the constitution and the law appear, that the judicial power can refuse to execute it. Such interference can never be permitted in a doubtful case. And this results from the very nature of the question involved in the inquiry. . . . The adjudged cases speak a uniform language on this subject. . . . An unbroken chain of decisions to the same effect is to be found in the State courts." In Syndics of *Brooks v. Weyman,* 3 Martin (La.), 9, 12 (1813), it was said by the court: "We reserve to ourselves the authority to declare null any legislative Act which shall be repugnant to the constitution; but it must be manifestly so, not susceptible of doubt." (Cited with approval in *Johnson v. Duncan,* Ib. 539) In *Cotton v. The County Commissioners,* 6 Fla. 610 (1856), Dupont, J. (for the court), said: "It is a most grave and important power, not to be exercised lightly or rashly, nor in any case where it cannot be made plainly to appear that the legislature has exceeded its powers. If there exist upon the mind of the court a reasonable doubt, that doubt must be given in favor of the law. . . . In further support of this position may be cited any number of decisions by the State courts. . . . If there be one to be found which constitutes an exception to the general doctrine, it has escaped our search."

32. Const. Lim., 6th ed., 68; cited with approval by Bryce, Am. Com., 1st ed., i. 431.
33. *Eakin v. Raub,* 12 S. and R. 330.
34. Farrar's Rep. Dart. Coll. Case, 36.
35. 7 Pick. 344.
36. Wellington, Petr., 16 Pick. 87.
37. 3d ed., 279–281.
38. It was so held in *Riggs v. State,* 3 Cold. 85 (Tenn., 1866), and *United States v. Clark,* 31 Fed. Rep. 710 (U.S. Circ. Ct., E. Dist. Michigan, 1887, Brown, J.). I am indebted for these cases to Professor Beale's valuable collection of Cases on Criminal Law (Cambridge, 1893). The same doctrine is laid down by Judge Hare in 2 Hare, Am. Const. Law, 920.
39. *Cap. and Counties Bank v. Henty,* 7 App. Cas, p. 776.
40. *Belt v. Lawes,* Thayer's Cas. Ev. 177, n.
41. *Chic.&c. Ry. Co. v. Minnesota,* 134 U.S. 418. The question was whether a statute providing for a commission to regulate railroad charges, which excluded the parties from access to the courts for an ultimate judicial revision of the action of the commission, was constitutional.
42. Compare Law and Fact in Jury Trials, 4 Harv. Law Rev. 167, 168.
43. There is often a lack of discrimination in judicial utterances on this subject,—as if it were supposed that the legislature had to conform to the judge's opinion of reasonableness in some other sense than that indicated above. The true view is indicated by Judge Cooley in his Principles of Const. Law, 2d ed., 57, when he says of a particular question: "Primarily the determination of what is a public purpose belongs to the legislature, and its action is subject to no review or restraint so long as it is not manifestly colorable. All cases of doubt must be solved in favor of the validity of legislative action, for the obvious reason that the question is legislative, and only becomes judicial when there is a plain excess of legislative authority. A court can only arrest the proceedings and declare a levy void when the absence of public interest in the purpose for which the funds are to be raised is so clear and palpable as to be perceptible to any mind at first blush." And again, on another question, by the Supreme Court of the United States, Waite, C. J., in *Terry v. Anderson,* 95 U.S. p. 633: "In all such cases the question is one of reasonableness, and we have therefore only to consider whether the time allowed in this Statute [of Limitations] is, under all the circumstances, reasonable.

Of that the legislature is primarily the judge; and we cannot overrule the decision of that department of the government, unless a palpable error has been committed." See *Pickering Phipps v. Ry. Co.,* 66 Law Times Rep. 721 (1892), and a valuable opinion by Ladd, J., in *Perry v. Keene,* 56 N. H. 514 (1876).

44. *Eakin v. Raub,* 12 S. and R., p. 355.

45. *Fletcher v. Peck,* 6 Cr., p. 131.

46. *Cap. and Count. Bank v. Henty,* 7 App Cas. 741.

47. Wheat. 316.

48. *Per* Thomas, J., the Opinion of Justices, 8 Gray, p. 21.

49. "It matters little," says a depressed, but interesting and incisive writer, in commenting, in 1885, upon the Legal Tender decisions of the Supreme Court of the United States, "for the court has fallen, and it is not probable it can ever again act as an effective check upon the popular will, or should it attempt to do so, that it can prevail." The "Consolidation of the Colonies," by Brooks Adams, 55 Atlantic Monthly, 307.

50. By Professor Gray in 6 Harv. Law Rev. 33, n., where he justly refers to the remark as showing "that gentlemen of the short robe have sometimes grasped fundamental legal principles better than many lawyers."

51. Bishop Hoadly's Sermon preached before the King, March 31, 1717, on "The Nature of the Kingdom or Church of Christ." London: James Knapton, 1717. It should be remarked that Bishop Hoadly is speaking of a situation where the supposed legislator, after once issuing his enactment, never interposes. That is not strictly the case in hand; yet we may recall what Dicey says of amending the constitution of the United States: "The sovereign of the United States has been roused to serious action but once during the course of ninety years. It needed the thunder of the Civil War to break his repose, and it may be doubted whether anything short of impending revolution will ever again arouse him to activity. But a monarch who slumbers for years is like a monarch who does not exist. A federal constitution is capable of change, but, for all that, a federal constitution is apt to be unchangeable."

52. *Com. v. Green,* 12 Allen, p. 163; *Taylor v. Place,* 4 R. I, p. 362. See Thayer's Memorandum on Advisory Opinions (Boston, 1885), Jameson, Const. Conv., 4th. ed., Appendix, note   , p. 667, and a valuable article by H. A. Dubuque, in 24 Am. Law Rev. 369, on "The Duty of Judges as Constitutional Advisers."

53. Opinion of Justices, 70 Me., p. 583 (1880). *Contra,* Kent, J., in 58 Me., p. 573 (1870): "It is true, unquestionably, that the opinions given under a requisition like this have no judicial force, and cannot bind or control the action of any officer of any department. They have never been regarded as binding on the body asking for them." And so Tapley, J., ibid, p. 615: "Never regarding the opinions thus formed as conclusive, but open to review upon every proper occasion;" and Libby, J., in 72 Me., p. 562–3 (1881): "Inasmuch as any opinion now given can have no effect if the matter should be judicially brought before the court by the proper process, and lest, in declining to answer, I may omit the performance of a constitutional duty, I will very briefly express my opinion upon the question submitted." Walton, J., concurred; the other judges said nothing on this point.

54. *In re* Senate Bill, 12 Colo. 466,—an opinion which seems to me, in some respects ill considered.

55. Macqueen's Pract. Ho. of Lords. pp. 49, 50.

56. Gibson, J., in *Eakin v. Raub,* 12 S. and R., p. 357. Compare Ib., p. 352. The same result is reached by the court, on general principles, in the Tonnage Tax Cases, 62 Pa. St. 286: "A case of simple doubt should be resolved favorably to the State law, leaving the correction of the error, if it be one, to the Federal judiciary. The presumption in favor of a co-ordinate branch of the State government, the relation of her courts to the State, and, above all, the necessity of preserving a financial system so vital to her welfare, demand this at our hands" (Agnew, J., for the court).

57. A singular result of the importance of constitutional interpretation in the American government . . . is this, that the United States legislature has been very largely occupied in purely
legal discussions. . . . Legal issues are apt to dwarf and obscure the more substantially
important issue of principle and policy, distracting from these latter the attention of the
nation as well as the skill of congressional debates."—1 Bryce, Am. Com., 1st ed., 377. On
page 378 he cites one of the best-known writers on constitutional law, Judge Hare, as saying
that "In the refined and subtle discussion which ensues, right is too often lost sight of, or
treated as if it were synonymous with might. It is taken for granted that what the constitution
permits it also approves, and that measures which are legal cannot be contrary to morals."
See also Ib., 410.

58. La volonté populaire: tel est, dans les pays libres de l'ancien et du Nouveau Monde, la source
et la fin de tout pouvoir. Tant qu'elle est saine, les nations prospèrent malgré les imperfections
et les lacunes de leurs institutions; si le bon sens fait défaut, si les passions l'emportent, les
constitutions les plus parfaites, les lois les plus sages, sont impuissantes. La maxime d'un
ancien: *quid leges sine moribus?* est, en somme, le dernier mot de la science politique.—*Le
Système Judiciaire de la Grande Bretagne,* by le Comte de Franqueville, i. 25 (Paris: J.
Rothschild, 1893).

---

# The Notion of a Living Constitution†

William H. Rehnquist

At least one of the more than half-dozen persons nominated during the past
decade to be an Associate Justice of the Supreme Court of the United States has been
asked by the Senate Judiciary Committee at his confirmation hearings whether he
believed in a living Constitution.[1] It is not an easy question to answer; the phrase
"living Constitution" has about it a teasing imprecision that makes it a coat of many
colors.

One's first reaction tends to be along lines of public relations or ideological sex
appeal, I suppose. At first blush it seems certain that a *living* Constitution is better
than what must be its counterpart, a *dead* Constitution. It would seem that only a
necrophile could disagree. If we could get one of the major public opinion research
firms in the country to sample public opinion concerning whether the United States
Constitution should be *living* or *dead,* the overwhelming majority of the responses
doubtless would favor a *living* Constitution.

If the question is worth asking a Supreme Court nominee during his confirmation
hearings, however, it surely deserves to be analyzed in more than just the public
relations context. While it is undoubtedly true, as Mr. Justice Holmes said, that

† This observation is the revised text of the ninth annual Will E. Orgain Lecture, delivered at
The University of Texas School of Law on March 12, 1976.

"general propositions do not decide concrete cases,"[2] general phrases such as this have a way of subtly coloring the way we think about concrete cases.

Professor McBain of the Columbia University Law School published a book in 1927 entitled *The Living Constitution.*[3] Professor Reich of the Yale Law School entitled his contribution to a book-length symposium on Mr. Justice Black *The Living Constitution and the Court's Role.*[4] I think I do no injustice to either of these scholars when I say that neither of their works attempts any comprehensive definition of the phrase "living Constitution." The phrase is really a shorthand expression that is susceptible of at least two quite different meanings.

The first meaning was expressed over a half-century ago by Mr. Justice Holmes in *Missouri v. Holland*[5] with his customary felicity when he said:

> . . . When we are dealing with words that also are a constituent act, like the Constitution of the United States, we must realize that they have called into life a being the development of which could not have been foreseen completely by the most gifted of its begetters. It was enough for them to realize or to hope that they had created an organism; it has taken a century and has cost their successors much sweat and blood to prove that they created a nation.[6]

I shall refer to this interpretation of the phrase "living Constitution," with which scarcely anyone would disagree, as the Holmes version.

The framers of the Constitution wisely spoke in general language and left to succeeding generations the task of applying that language to the unceasingly changing environment in which they would live. Those who framed, adopted, and ratified the Civil War amendments[7] to the Constitution likewise used what have been aptly described as "majestic generalities"[8] in composing the fourteenth amendment. Merely because a particular activity may not have existed when the Constitution was adopted, or because the framers could not have conceived of a particular method of transacting affairs, cannot mean that general language in the Constitution may not be applied to such a course of conduct. Where the framers of the Constitution have used general language, they have given latitude to those who would later interpret the instrument to make that language applicable to cases that the framers might not have foreseen.

In my reading and travels I have sensed a second connotation of the phrase "living Constitution," however, one quite different from what I have described as the Holmes version, but which certainly has gained acceptance among some parts of the legal profession. Embodied in its most naked form, it recently came to my attention in some language from a brief that had been filed in a United States District Court on behalf of state prisoners asserting that the conditions of their confinement offended the United States Constitution. The brief urged:

> We are asking a great deal of the Court because other branches of government have abdicated their responsibility. . . . Prisoners are like other 'discrete and insular' minorities for whom the Court must spread its protective umbrella because no other branch of government will do so. . . . This Court, as the voice and conscience of contemporary society, as the measure of the modern conception of human dignity, must declare that the [named prison] and all it represents offends the Constitution of the United States and will not be tolerated.

Here we have a living Constitution with a vengeance. Although the substitution of some other set of values for those which may be derived from the language and intent of the framers is not urged in so many words, that is surely the thrust of the message. Under this brief writer's version of the living Constitution, nonelected members of the federal judiciary may address themselves to a social problem simply because other branches of government have failed or refused to do so. These same judges, responsible to no constituency whatever, are nonetheless acclaimed as "the voice and conscience of contemporary society."

If we were merely talking about a slogan that was being used to elect some candidate to office or to persuade the voters to ratify a constitutional amendment, elaborate dissection of a phrase such as "living Constitution" would probably not be warranted. What we are talking about, however, is a suggested philosophical approach to be used by the federal judiciary, and perhaps state judiciaries, in exercising the very delicate responsibility of judicial review. Under the familiar principle of judicial review, the courts in construing the Constitution are, of course, authorized to invalidate laws that have been enacted by Congress or by a state legislature but that those courts find to violate some provision of the Constitution. Nevertheless, those who have pondered the matter have always recognized that the ideal of judicial review has basically antidemocratic and antimajoritarian facets that require some justification in this Nation, which prides itself on being a self-governing representative democracy.

All who have studied law, and many who have not, are familiar with John Marshall's classic defense of judicial review in his opinion for the Court in *Marbury v. Madison*.[9] I will summarize very briefly the thrust of that answer, with which I fully agree, because while it supports the Holmes version of the phrase "living Constitution," it also suggests some outer limits for the brief writer's version.

The ultimate source of authority in this Nation, Marshall said, is not Congress, not the states, not for that matter the Supreme Court of the United States. The people are the ultimate source of authority, they have parceled out the authority that originally resided entirely with them by adopting the original Constitution and by later amending it. They have granted some authority to the federal government and have reserved authority not granted it to the states or to the people individually. As between the branches of the federal government, the people have given certain authority to the President, certain authority to Congress, and certain authority to the federal judiciary. In the Bill of Rights they have erected protections for specified individual rights against the actions of the federal government. From today's perspective we might add that they have placed restrictions on the authority of the state governments in the thirteenth, fourteenth, and fifteenth amendments.

In addition, Marshall said that if the popular branches of government—state legislatures, the Congress, and the Presidency—are operating within the authority granted to them by the Constitution, their judgment and not that of the Court must obviously prevail. When these branches overstep the authority given them by the Constitution, in the case of the President and the Congress, or invade protected individual rights, and a constitutional challenge to their action is raised in a lawsuit brought in federal court, the Court must prefer the Constitution to the government acts.

John Marshall's justification for judicial review makes the provision for an independent federal judiciary not only understandable but also thoroughly desirable. Since the judges will be merely interpreting an instrument framed by the people, they should be detached and objective. A mere change in public opinion since the adoption of the Constitution, unaccompanied by a constitutional amendment, should not change the meaning of the Constitution. A merely temporary majoritarian groundswell should not abrogate some individual liberty truly protected by the Constitution.

Clearly Marshall's explanation contains certain elements of either ingenuousness or ingeniousness, which tend to grow larger as our constitutional history extends over a longer period of time. The Constitution is in many of its parts obviously not a specifically worded document but one couched in general phraseology. There is obviously wide room for honest difference of opinion over the meaning of general phrases in the Constitution; any particular Justice's decision when a question arises under one of these general phrases will depend to some extent on his own philosophy of constitutional law. One may nevertheless concede all of these problems that inhere in Marshall's justification of judicial review, yet feel that his justification for nonelected judges exercising the power of judicial review is the only one consistent with democratic philosophy of representative government.

Marshall was writing at a time when the governing generation remembered well not only the deliberations of the framers of the Constitution at Philadelphia in the summer of 1787 but also the debates over the ratification of the Constitution in the thirteen colonies. The often heated discussions that took place from 1787, when Delaware became the first state to ratify the Constitution,[10] until 1790, when recalcitrant Rhode Island finally joined the union,[11] were themselves far more representative of the give-and-take of public decisionmaking by a constituent assembly than is the ordinary enactment of a law by Congress or by a state legislature. Patrick Henry had done all he could to block ratification in Virginia,[12] and the opposition of the Clinton faction in New York had provoked Jay, Hamilton, and Madison to their brilliant effort in defense of the Constitution, the *Federalist Papers*.[13] For Marshall, writing the *Marbury v. Madison* opinion in 1803, the memory of the debates in which the people of the thirteen colonies had participated only a few years before could well have fortified his conviction that the Constitution was, not merely in theory but in fact as well, a fundamental charter that had emanated from the people.

One senses no similar connection with a popularly adopted constituent act in what I have referred to as the brief writer's version of the living Constitution. The brief writer's version seems instead to be based upon the proposition that federal judges, perhaps judges as a whole, have a role of their own, quite independent of popular will, to play in solving society's problems. Once we have abandoned the idea that the authority of the courts to declare laws unconstitutional is somehow tied to the language of the Constitution that the people adopted, a judiciary exercising the power of judicial review appears in a quite different light. Judges then are no longer the keepers of the covenant; instead they are a small group of fortunately situated people with a roving commission to second-guess Congress, state legislatures, and state and federal administrative officers concerning what is best for the country. Surely there is no justification for a third legislative branch in the federal government, and there is even less justification for a federal legislative branch's reviewing on a policy basis the laws enacted by the legislatures of the fifty states. Even if one were to disagree with me on this point, the members of a third branch of the federal legislature at least ought to be elected by and responsible to constituencies, just as in the case of the other two branches of Congress. If there is going to be a council of revision, it ought to have at least some connection with popular feeling. Its members either ought to stand for reelection on occasion, or their terms should expire and they should be allowed to continue serving only if reappointed by a popularly elected Chief Executive and confirmed by a popularly elected Senate.

The brief writer's version of the living Constitution is seldom presented in its most naked form, but is instead usually dressed in more attractive garb. The argument in favor of this approach generally begins with a sophisticated wink—why pretend that there is any ascertainable content to the general phrases of the Constitution as they are written since, after all, judges constantly disagree about their meaning? We are all familiar with Chief Justice Hughes' famous aphorism that "We are under a Constitution, but the Constitution is what the judges say it is."[14] We all know the basis of Marshall's justification for judicial review, the argument runs, but it is necessary only to keep the window dressing in place. Any sophisticated student of the subject knows that judges need not limit themselves to the intent of the framers, which is very difficult to determine in any event. Because of the general language used in the Constitution, judges should not hesitate to use their authority to make the Constitution relevant and useful in solving the problems of modern society. The brief writer's version of the living Constitution envisions all of the above conclusions.

At least three serious difficulties flaw the brief writer's version of the living Constitution. First, it misconceives the nature of the Constitution, which was designed to enable the popularly elected branches of government, not the judicial branch, to keep the country abreast of the times. Second, the brief writer's version ignores the Supreme Court's disastrous experiences when in the past it embraced contemporary, fashionable notions of what a living Constitution should contain. Third, however socially desirable the goals sought to be advanced by the brief writer's version, advancing them through a freewheeling, nonelected judiciary is quite unacceptable in a democratic society.

It seems to me that it is almost impossible, after reading the record of the Founding Fathers' debates in Philadelphia, to conclude that they intended the Constitution itself to suggest answers to the manifold problems that they knew would confront succeeding generations. The Constitution that they drafted was indeed intended to endure indefinitely, but the reason for this very well-founded hope was the general language by which national authority was granted to Congress and the Presidency. These two branches were to furnish the motive power within the federal system, which was in turn to coexist with the state governments; the elements of government having a popular constituency were looked to for the solution of the numerous and varied problems that the future would bring. Limitations were indeed placed upon both federal and state governments in the form of both a division of powers and express protection for individual rights. These limitations, however, were not themselves designed to solve the problems of the future, but were instead designed to make certain that the constituent branches, when *they* attempted to solve those problems, should not transgress these fundamental limitations.

Although the Civil War Amendments[15] were designed more as broad limitations on the authority of state governments, they too were enacted in response to practices that the lately seceded states engaged in to discriminate against and mistreat the newly emancipated freed men. To the extent that the language of these amendments is general, the courts are of course warranted in giving them an application coextensive with their language. Nevertheless, I greatly doubt that even men like Thad Stevens and John Bingham, leaders of the radical Republicans in Congress, would have thought any portion of the Civil War Amendments, except section five of the fourteenth amendment,[16] was designed to solve problems that society might confront a century later. I think they would have said that those amendments were designed to prevent from ever recurring abuses in which the states had engaged prior to that time.

The brief writer's version of the living Constitution, however, suggests that if the states' legislatures and governors, or Congress and the President, have not solved a particular social problem, then the federal court may act. I do not believe that this argument will withstand rational analysis. Even in the face of a conceded social evil, a reasonably competent and reasonably representative legislature may decide to do nothing. It may decide that the evil is not of sufficient magnitude to warrant any governmental intervention. It may decide that the financial cost of eliminating the evil is not worth the benefit which would result from its elimination. It may decide that the evils which might ensue from the proposed solution are worse than the evils which the solution would eliminate.

Surely the Constitution does not put either the legislative branch or the executive branch in the position of a television quiz show contestant so that when a given period of time has elapsed and a problem remains unsolved by them, the federal judiciary may press a buzzer and take its turn at fashioning a solution.

The second difficulty with the brief writer's version of the living Constitution lies in its inattention to or rejection of the Supreme Court's historical experience gleaned from similar forays into problem solving.

Although the phrase "living Constitution" may not have been used during the nineteenth century and the first half of this century, the idea represented by the brief writer's version was very much in evidence during both periods. The apogee of the living Constitution doctrine during the nineteenth century was the Supreme Court's decision in *Dred Scott v. Sanford*.[17] In that case the question at issue was the status of a Negro who had been carried by his master from a slave state into a territory made free by the Missouri Compromise. Although thereafter taken back to a slave state, Dred Scott claimed that upon previously reaching free soil he had been forever emancipated. The Court, speaking through Chief Justice Taney, held that Congress was without power to legislate upon the issue of slavery even in a territory governed by it, and that therefore Dred Scott had never become free.[18] Congress, the Court held, was virtually powerless to check or limit the spread of the institution of slavery.

The history of this country for some thirty years before the *Dred Scott* decision demonstrates the bitter frustration which that decision brought to large elements of the population who opposed any expansion of slavery. In 1820 when Maine was seeking admission as a free state and Missouri as a slave state, a fight over the expansion of slavery engulfed the national legislative halls and resulted in the Missouri Compromise,[19] which forever banned slavery from those territories lying north of a line drawn through the southern boundary of Missouri.[20] This was a victory for the antislavery forces in the North, but the Southerners were prepared to live with it. At the time of the Mexican War in 1846, Representative David Wilmot of Pennsylvania introduced a bill, later known as the Wilmot Proviso,[21] that would have precluded the opening to slavery of any territory acquired as a result of the Mexican War.[22] This proposed amendment to the Missouri Compromise was hotly debated for years both in and out of Congress.[23] Finally in 1854 Senator Stephen A. Douglas shepherded through Congress the Kansas-Nebraska Act,[24] which in effect repealed the Missouri Compromise and enacted into law the principle of "squatter sovereignty": the people in each of the new territories would decide whether or not to permit slavery.[25] The enactment of this bill was, of course, a victory for the proslavery forces in Congress and a defeat for those opposed to the expansion of slavery. The great majority of the antislavery groups, as strongly as they felt about the matter, were still willing to live with the decision of Congress.[26] They were not willing, however, to live with the *Dred Scott* decision.

The Court in *Dred Scott* decided that all of the agitation and debate in Congress over the Missouri Compromise in 1820, over the Wilmot Proviso a generation later, and over the Kansas-Nebraska Act in 1854 had amounted to absolutely nothing. It was, in the words of Macbeth, "A tale told by an idiot, full of sound and fury, signifying nothing."[27] According to the Court, the decision had never been one that Congress was entitled to make; it was one that the Court alone, in construing the Constitution, was empowered to make.

The frustration of the citizenry, who had thought themselves charged with the responsibility for making such decisions, is well expressed in Abraham Lincoln's First Inaugural Address:

> [T]he candid citizen must confess that if the policy of the government, upon vital questions affecting the whole people, is to be irrevocably fixed by decisions of the Supreme Court, the instant they are made, in ordinary litigation between parties in personal actions, the people will have ceased to be their own rulers, having to that extent practically resigned their government into the hands of that eminent tribunal.[28]

The *Dred Scott* decision, of course, was repealed in fact as a result of the Civil War and in law by the Civil War amendments. The injury to the reputation of the Supreme Court that resulted from the *Dred Scott* decision, however, took more than a generation to heal. Indeed, newspaper accounts long after the *Dred Scott* decision bristled with attacks on the Court, and particularly on Chief Justice Taney, unequalled in their bitterness even to this day.

The brief writer's version of the living Constitution made its next appearance, almost as dramatically as its first, shortly after the turn of the century in *Lochner v. New York*.[29] The name of the case is a household word to those who have studied constitutional law, and it is one of the handful of cases in which a dissenting opinion has been overwhelmingly vindicated by the passage of time. In *Lochner* a New York law that limited to ten the maximum number of hours per day that could be worked by bakery employees was assailed on the ground that it deprived the bakery employer of liberty without due process of law. A majority of the Court held the New York maximum hour law unconstitutional, saying, "Statutes of the nature of that under review, limiting the hours in which grown and intelligent men may labor to earn their living, are mere meddlesome interferences with the rights of the individual. . . ."[30]

The fourteenth amendment, of course, said nothing about any freedom to make contracts upon terms that one thought best, but there was a very substantial body of opinion outside the Constitution at the time of *Lochner* that subscribed to the general philosophy of social Darwinism as embodied in the writing of Herbert Spencer in England and William Graham Sumner in this country. It may have occurred to some of the Justices who made up a majority in *Lochner,* hopefully subconsciously rather than consciously, that since this philosophy appeared eminently sound and since the language in the due process clause was sufficiently general not to rule out its inclusion, why not strike a blow for the cause? The answer, which has been vindicated by time, came in the dissent of Mr. Justice Holmes:

> [A] constitution is not intended to embody a particular economic theory, whether of paternalism and the organic relation of the citizen to the state or of *laissez faire*. It is made for people of fundamentally differing views, and the accident of our finding certain opinions natural and familiar or novel and even shocking ought not to conclude our judgment upon the question whether statutes embodying them conflict with the Constitution of the United States.[31]

One reads the history of these episodes in the Supreme Court to little purpose if he does not conclude that prior experimentation with the brief writer's expansive notion of a living Constitution has done the Court little credit. There remain today those, such as wrote the brief from which I quoted, who appear to cleave nevertheless to the view that the experiments of the Taney Court before the Civil War, and of the Fuller and Taft Courts in the first part of this century, ended in failure not because they sought to bring into the Constitution a principle that the great majority of objective scholars would have to conclude was not there but because they sought to bring into the Constitution the *wrong* extraconstitutional principle. This school of thought appears to feel that while added protection for slave owners was clearly unacceptable and safeguards for businessmen threatened with ever-expanding state regulation were not desirable, expansion of the protection accorded to individual liberties against the state or to the interest of "discrete and insular" minorities,[32] such as prisoners, must stand on a quite different, more favored footing. To the extent, of course, that such a distinction may legitimately be derived from the Constitution itself, these latter principles do indeed stand on an entirely different footing. To the extent that one must, however, go beyond even a generously fair reading of the language and intent of that document in order to subsume these principles, it seems to me that they are not really distinguishable from those espoused in *Dred Scott* and *Lochner*.

The third difficulty with the brief writer's notion of the living Constitution is that it seems to ignore totally the nature of political value judgments in a democratic society. If such a society adopts a constitution and incorporates in that constitution safeguards for individual liberty, these safeguards indeed do take on a generalized moral rightness or goodness. They assume a general social acceptance neither because of any intrinsic worth nor because of any unique origins in someone's idea of natural justice but instead simply because they have been incorporated in a constitution by the people. Within the limits of our Constitution, the representatives of the people in the executive branches of the state and national governments enact laws. The laws that emerge after a typical political struggle in which various individual value judgments are debated likewise take on a form of moral goodness because they have been enacted into positive law. It is the fact of their enactment that gives them whatever moral claim they have upon us as a society, however, and not any independent virtue they may have in any particular citizen's own scale of values.

Beyond the Constitution and the laws in our society, there simply is no basis other than the individual conscience of the citizen that may serve as a platform for the launching of moral judgments. There is no conceivable way in which I can logically demonstrate to you that the judgments of my conscience are superior to the judgments of your conscience, and vice versa. Many of us necessarily feel strongly and deeply about our own moral judgments, but they remain only personal moral judgments until in some way given the sanction of law.

As Mr. Justice Holmes said in his famous essay on natural law:

> Certitude is not the test of certainty. We have been cocksure of many things that were not so. . . . One cannot be wrenched from the rocky crevices into which one is thrown for many years without feeling that one is attacked in one's life. What we most love and revere generally is determined by early associations. I love granite rocks and barberry bushes, no doubt because with them were my earliest joys that reach back through the past eternity of my life. But while one's experience thus makes certain preferences dogmatic for oneself, recognition of how they came to be so leaves one able to see that others, poor souls, may be equally dogmatic about something else. And this again means skepticism.[33]

This is not to say that individual moral judgments ought not to afford a springboard for action in society, for indeed they are without doubt the most common and most powerful wellsprings for action when one believes that questions of right and wrong are involved. Representative government is predicated upon the idea that one who feels deeply upon a question as a matter of conscience will seek out others of like view or will attempt to persuade others who do not initially share that view. When adherents to the belief become sufficiently numerous, he will have the necessary armaments required in a democratic society to press his views upon the elected representatives of the people, and to have them embodied into positive law.

Should a person fail to persuade the legislature, or should he feel that a legislative victory would be insufficient because of its potential for future reversal, he may seek to run the more difficult gauntlet of amending the Constitution to embody the view that he espouses. Success in amending the Constitution would, of course, preclude succeeding transient majorities in the legislature from tampering with the principle formerly added to the Constitution.

I know of no other method compatible with political theory basic to democratic society by which one's own conscientious belief may be translated into positive law and thereby obtain the only general moral imprimatur permissible in a pluralistic, democratic society. It is always time consuming, frequently difficult, and not infrequently impossible to run successfully the legislative gauntlet and have enacted some facet of one's own deeply felt value judgments. It is even more difficult for either a single individual or indeed for a large group of individuals to succeed in having such a value judgment embodied in the Constitution. All of these burdens and difficulties are entirely consistent with the notion of a democratic society. It should not be easy for any one individual or group of individuals to impose by law their value judgments upon fellow citizens who may disagree with those judgments. Indeed, it should not be easier just because the individual in question is a judge. We all have a propensity to want to do it, but there are very good reasons for making it difficult to do. The great English political philosopher John Stuart Mill observed:

> The disposition of mankind, whether as rulers or as fellow-citizens, to impose their own opinions and inclinations as a rule of conduct on others, is so energetically supported by some of the best and by some of the worst feeling incident to human nature, that it is hardly ever kept under restraint by anything but want of power. . . .[34]

The brief writer's version of the living Constitution, in the last analysis, is a formula for an end run around popular government. To the extent that it makes possible an individual's persuading one or more appointed federal judges to impose on other individuals a rule of conduct that the popularly elected branches of government would not have enacted and the voters have not and would not have embodied in the Constitution, the brief writer's version of the living Constitution is genuinely corrosive of the fundamental values of our democratic society.

### Notes

1. *See Hearings on Nominations of William H. Rehnquist and Lewis F. Powell, Jr., Before the Senate Comm. on the Judiciary*, 92d Cong., 1st Sess. 87 (1971).
2. *Lochner* v. *New York*, 198 U.S. 45, 76 (1905) (Holmes, J., dissenting).
3. H. McBain, The Living Constitution (1927).
4. Reich, *The Living Constitution and the Court's Role*, in Hugo Black and the Supreme Court 133 (S. Strickland ed. 1967).
5. 252 U.S. 416 (1920).
6. *Id.* at 433.
7. U.S. Const. amends. XIII, XIV, XV.
8. *Fay* v. *New York*, 332 U.S. 261, 282 (1947) (Jackson, J.).
9. 5 U.S. (1 Cranch) 137 (1803).
10. 2 F. Thorpe, The Constitutional History of the United States 18 (1901).
11. *Id.* at 191.
12. *Id.* at 81, 87, 91–95.
13. *Id.* at 134–39.
14. C. Hughes, Addresses 139 (1908).

15. U.S. Const. amends. XIII, XIV, XV.
16. "The Congress shall have power to enforce, by appropriate legislation, the provisions of this article." U.S. Const. amend. XIV, § 5.
17. 60 U.S. (19 How.) 393 (1857).
18. *Id.* at 452.
19. Act of March 6, 1820, ch. 22, 3 Stat. 545.
20. *See* 2 F. Thorpe, *supra* note 10, at 366–71, 433.
21. Act of June 19, 1862, ch. 111, 12 Stat. 432.
22. 2 F. Thorpe, *supra* note 10, at 430.
23. *Id.* at 430–32.
24. Act of May 30, 1854, ch. 59, 10 Stat. 277.
25. *See* 2 F. Thorpe, *supra* note 10, at 518–21.
26. *See id.* at 524–36.
27. Shakespeare, *Macbeth,* V.v. 19.
28. First Inaugural Address by Abraham Lincoln, March 4, 1861, in A. Lincoln, Speeches and Letters 171–72 (M. Roe ed. 1894).
29. 198 U.S. 45 (1905).
30. *Id.* at 61.
31. *Id.* at 75–76 (Holmes, J., dissenting).
32. *United States* v. *Carolene Prods.* Co., 304 U.S. 144, 152 n.4 (1938).
33. O. W. Holmes, *Natural Law,* in Collected Legal Papers 310, 311 (1920).
34. J. S. Mill, On Liberty, in 43 Great Books of the Western World 273 (R. Hutchins ed. 1952).

# The Constitution and the Courts

The great tides and currents which engulf the rest of men do not turn
aside in their course and pass the judges by.

*Benjamin N. Cardozo*

The federal judges therefore must not only be good citizens and men of
education and integrity, qualities necessary for all magistrates, but must
also be statesmen; they must know how to understand the spirit of the
age, to confront those obstacles that can be overcome, and to steer out of
the current when the tide threatens to carry them away, and with them
the sovereignty of the union and obedience to its laws.

*Alexis de Tocqueville*

---

## The Constitution and the Courts

Alexis de Tocqueville

Their judicial institutions exercise a great influence on the condition of the
Anglo-Americans, and they occupy a very important place among political institutions,
properly so called: in this respect they are peculiarly deserving of our attention. But
I am at a loss how to explain the political action of the American tribunals without
entering into some technical details respecting their constitution and their forms of
proceeding; and I cannot descend to these minutiae without wearying the reader by
the natural dryness of the subject. Yet how can I be clear and at the same time brief?
I can scarcely hope to escape these different evils. Ordinary readers will complain that
I am tedious, lawyers that I am too concise. But these are the natural disadvantages
of my subject, and especially of the point that I am now to discuss.

The great difficulty was, not to know how to constitute the Federal government,
but to find out a method of enforcing its laws. Governments have generally but two
means of overcoming the opposition of the governed: namely, the physical force that
is at their disposal, and the moral force that they derive from the decisions of the
courts of justice.

A government which should have no other means of exacting obedience than
open war must be very near its ruin, for one of two things would then probably happen
to it. If it was weak and temperate, it would resort to violence only at the last extremity
and would connive at many partial acts of insubordination; then the state would

gradually fall into anarchy. If it was enterprising and powerful, it would every day have recourse to physical strength, and thus would soon fall into a military despotism. Thus its activity and its inertness would be equally prejudicial to the community.

The great end of justice is to substitute the notion of right for that of violence and to place a legal barrier between the government and the use of physical force. It is a strange thing, the authority that is accorded to the intervention of a court of justice by the general opinion of mankind! It clings even to the mere formalities of justice, and gives a bodily influence to the mere shadow of the law. The moral force which courts of justice possess renders the use of physical force very rare and is frequently substituted for it; but if force proves to be indispensable, its power is doubled by the association of the idea of law.

A federal government stands in greater need than any other of the support of judicial institutions, because it is naturally weak and exposed to formidable opposition. If it were always obliged to resort to violence in the first instance, it could not fulfill its task. The Union, therefore, stood in special need of a judiciary to make its citizens obey the laws and to repel the attacks that might be directed against them. But what tribunals were to exercise these privileges? Were they to be entrusted to the courts of justice which were already organized in every state? Or was it necessary to create Federal courts? It may easily be proved that the Union could not adapt to its wants the judicial power of the states. The separation of the judiciary from the other powers of the state is necessary for the security of each and the liberty of all. But it is no less important to the existence of the nation that the several powers of the state should have the same origin, follow the same principles, and act in the same sphere; in a word, that they should be correlative and homogeneous. No one, I presume, ever thought of causing offenses committed in France to be tried by a foreign court of justice in order to ensure the impartiality of the judges. The Americans form but one people in relation to their Federal government; but in the bosom of this people diverse political bodies have been allowed to exist, which are dependent on the national government in a few points and independent in all the rest, which have all a distinct origin, maxims peculiar to themselves, and special means of carrying on their affairs. To entrust the execution of the laws of the Union to tribunals instituted by these political bodies would be to allow foreign judges to preside over the nation. Nay, more; not only is each state foreign to the Union at large, but it is a perpetual adversary, since whatever authority the Union loses turns to the advantage of the states. Thus, to enforce the laws of the Union by means of the state tribunals would be to allow not only foreign, but partial judges to preside over the nation.

But the number, still more than the mere character, of the state tribunals made them unfit for the service of the nation. When the Federal Constitution was formed, there were already thirteen courts of justice in the United States which decided causes without appeal. That number has now increased to twenty-four. To suppose that a state can exist when its fundamental laws are subjected to four-and-twenty different interpretations at the same time is to advance a proposition contrary alike to reason and to experience.

The American legislators therefore agreed to create a Federal judicial power to apply the laws of the Union and to determine certain questions affecting general interests, which were carefully defined beforehand. The entire judicial power of the Union was centered in one tribunal, called the Supreme Court of the United States.

But to facilitate the expedition of business, inferior courts were added to it, which were empowered to decide causes of small importance without appeal, and, with appeal, causes of more magnitude. The members of the Supreme Court are appointed neither by the people nor by the legislature, but by the President of the United States, acting with the advice of the Senate. In order to render them independent of other authorities, their office was made inalienable; and it was determined that their salary, when once fixed, should not be diminished by the legislature. It was easy to proclaim the principle of a Federal judiciary, but difficulties multiplied when the extent of its jurisdiction was to be determined.

As the Constitution of the United States recognized two distinct sovereignties, in presence of each other, represented in a judicial point of view by two distinct classes of courts of justice, the utmost care taken in defining their separate jurisdictions would have been insufficient to prevent frequent collisions between those tribunals. The question then arose to whom the right of deciding the competency of each court was to be referred.

In nations that constitute a single body politic, when a question of jurisdiction is debated between two courts, a third tribunal is generally within reach to decide the difference; and this is effected without difficulty because in these nations questions of judicial competence have no connection with questions of national sovereignty. But it was impossible to create an arbiter between a superior court of the Union and the superior court of a separate state, which would not belong to one of these two classes. It was therefore necessary to allow one of these courts to judge its own cause and to take or retain cognizance of the point that was contested. To grant this privilege to the different courts of the states would have been to destroy the sovereignty of the Union *de facto,* after having established it *de jure;* for the interpretation of the Constitution would soon have restored to the states that portion of independence of which the terms of the Constitution deprived them. The object of creating a Federal tribunal was to prevent the state courts from deciding, each after its own fashion, questions affecting the national interests, and so to form a uniform body of jurisprudence for the interpretation of the laws of the Union. This end would not have been attained if the courts of the several states, even while they abstained from deciding cases avowedly Federal in their nature, had been able to decide them by pretending that they were not Federal. The Supreme Court of the United States was therefore invested with the right of determining all questions of jurisdiction.

This was a severe blow to the sovereignty of the states, which was thus restricted not only by the laws, but by the interpretation of them, by one limit which was known and by another which was unknown, by a rule which was certain and one which was arbitrary. It is true, the Constitution had laid down the precise limits of the Federal supremacy; but whenever this supremacy is contested by one of the states, a Federal tribunal decides the question. Nevertheless, the dangers with which the independence of the states is threatened by this mode of proceeding are less serious than they appear to be. We shall see hereafter that in America the real power is vested in the states far more than in the Federal government. The Federal judges are conscious of the relative weakness of the power in whose name they act; and they are more inclined to abandon the right of jurisdiction in cases where the law gives it to them than to assert a privilege to which they have no legal claim.

After establishing the competence of the Federal courts the legislators of the Union defined the cases that should come within their jurisdiction. It was determined, on the one hand, that certain parties must always be brought before the Federal courts, without regard to the special nature of the suit; and, on the other that certain causes must always be brought before the same courts, no matter who were the parties to them. The party and the cause were therefore admitted to be the two bases of Federal jurisdiction.

Ambassadors represent nations in amity with the Union, and whatever concerns these personages concerns in some degree the whole Union. When an ambassador, therefore, is a party in a suit, its issue affects the welfare of the nation, and a Federal tribunal is naturally called upon to decide it.

The Union itself may be involved in legal proceedings, and in this case it would be contrary to reason and to the customs of all nations to appeal to a tribunal representing any other sovereignty than its own; the Federal courts alone, therefore, take cognizance of these affairs.

When two parties belonging to two different states are engaged in a suit, the case cannot with propriety be brought before a court of either state. The surest expedient is to select a tribunal which can excite the suspicions of neither party, and this is naturally a Federal court.

When the two parties are not private individuals, but states, an important political motive is added to the same consideration of equity. The quality of the parties, in this case, gives a national importance to all their disputes; and the most trifling litigation between two states may be said to involve the peace of the whole Union.

The nature of the cause frequently prescribes the rule of competency. Thus, all questions which concern maritime affairs evidently fall under the cognizance of the Federal tribunals. Almost all these questions depend on the interpretation of the law of nations, and in this respect they essentially interest the Union in relation to foreign powers. Moreover, as the sea is not included within the limits of any one state jurisdiction rather than another, only the national courts can hear causes which originate in maritime affairs.

The Constitution comprises under one head almost all the cases which by their very nature come before the Federal courts. The rule that it lays down is simple, but pregnant with an entire system of ideas and with a multitude of facts. It declares that the judicial power of the Supreme Court shall extend to all cases in law and equity *arising under the laws of the United States.*

Two examples will put the intention of the legislator in the clearest light.

The Constitution prohibits the states from making laws on the value and circulation of money. If, notwithstanding this prohibition, a state passes a law of this kind, with which the interested parties refuse to comply because it is contrary to the Constitution, the case must come before a Federal court, because it arises under the laws of the United States. Again, if difficulties arise in the levying of import duties that have been voted by Congress, the Federal court must decide the case, because it arises under the interpretation of a law of the United States.

This rule is in perfect accordance with the fundamental principles of the Federal Constitution. The Union, as it was established in 1789, possesses, it is true, a limited sovereignty; but it was intended that within its limits it should form one and the same people. Within those limits the Union is sovereign. When this point is established and admitted, the inference is easy; for if it is acknowledged that the United States, within the bounds prescribed by their Constitution, constitute but one people, it is impossible to refuse them the rights which belong to other nations. But it has been allowed, from the origin of society, that every nation has the right of deciding by its own courts those questions which concern the execution of its own laws. To this it is answered that the Union is in such a singular position that in relation to some matters it constitutes but one people, and in relation to all the rest it is a nonentity. But the inference to be drawn is that in the laws relating to these matters the Union possesses all the rights of absolute sovereignty. The difficulty is to know what these matters are; and when once it is settled (and in speaking of the means of determining the jurisdiction of the Federal courts I have shown how it was settled), no further doubt can arise; for as soon as it is established that a suit is Federal—that is to say, that it belongs to the share of sovereignty reserved by the Constitution to the Union—the natural consequence is that it should come within the jurisdiction of a Federal court.

Whenever the laws of the United States are attacked, or whenever they are resorted to in self-defense, the Federal courts must be appealed to. Thus the jurisdiction of the tribunals of the Union extends and narrows its limits exactly in the same ratio as the sovereignty of the Union augments or decreases. I have shown that the principal aim of the legislators of 1789 was to divide the sovereign authority into two parts. In the one they placed the control of all the general interests of the Union, in the other the control of the special interests of its component states. Their chief concern was to arm the Federal government with sufficient power to enable it to resist, within its sphere, the encroachments of the several states. As for these communities, the general principle of independence within certain limits of their own was adopted on their behalf; there the central government cannot control, nor even inspect, their conduct. In speaking of the division of authority, I observed that this latter principle had not always been respected, since the states are prevented from passing certain laws which apparently belong to their own particular sphere of interest. When a state of the Union passes law of this kind, the citizens who are injured by its execution can appeal to the Federal courts.

Thus the jurisdiction of the Federal courts extends, not only to all the cases which arise under the laws of the Union, but also to those which arise under laws made by the several states in opposition to the Constitution. The states are prohibited from making *ex post facto* laws in criminal cases; and any person condemned by virtue of a law of this kind can appeal to the judicial power of the Union. The states are likewise prohibited from making laws that may impair the obligation of contracts. If a citizen thinks that an obligation of this kind is impaired by a law passed in his state, he may refuse to obey it and may appeal to the Federal courts.

This provision appears to me to be the most serious attack upon the independence of the states. The rights accorded to the Federal government for purposes obviously national are definite and easily understood; but those with which this clause invests it are neither clearly appreciable nor accurately defined. For there are many political laws that affect the existence of contracts, which might thus furnish a pretext for the encroachments of the central authority.

I have shown what the rights of the Federal courts are, and it is no less important to show how they are exercised. The irresistible authority of justice in countries in which the sovereignty is undivided is derived from the fact that the tribunals of those countries represent the entire nation at issue with the individual against whom their decree is directed; and the idea of power is thus introduced to corroborate the idea of right. But it is not always so in countries in which the sovereignty is divided; in them the judicial power is more frequently opposed to a fraction of the nation than to an isolated individual, and its moral authority and physical strength are consequently diminished. In Federal states the power of the judge is naturally decreased and that of the justiciable parties is augmented. The aim of the legislator in confederate states ought therefore to be to render the position of the courts of justice analogous to that which they occupy in countries where the sovereignty is undivided; in other words, his efforts ought constantly to tend to maintain the judicial power of the confederation as the representative of the nation, and the justiciable party as the representative of an individual interest.

Every government, whatever may be its constitution, requires the means of constraining its subjects to discharge their obligations and of protecting its privileges from their assaults. As far as the direct action of the government on the community is concerned, the Constitution of the United States contrived, by a master stroke of policy, that the Federal courts, acting in the name of the laws, should take cognizance only of parties in an individual capacity. For, as it had been declared that the Union consisted of one and the same people within the limits laid down by the Constitution, the inference was that the government created by this Constitution, and acting within these limits, was invested with all the privileges of a national government, of which one of the principal is the right of transmitting its injunctions directly to the private citizen. When, for instance, the Union votes an impost, it does not apply to the states for the levying of it, but to every American citizen, in proportion to his assessment. The Supreme Court, which is empowered to enforce the execution of this law of the Union, exerts its influence not upon a refractory state, but upon the private taxpayer; and, like the judicial power of other nations, it acts only upon the person of an individual. It is to be observed that the Union chose its own antagonist; and as that antagonist is feeble, he is naturally worsted.

But the difficulty increases when the proceedings are not brought forward *by,* but *against* the Union. The Constitution recognizes the legislative power of the states; and a law enacted by that power may violate the rights of the Union. In this case a collision is unavoidable between that body and the state which has passed the law, and it only remains to select the least dangerous remedy. The general principles that I have before established show what this remedy is.

It may be conceived that in the case under consideration the Union might have sued the state before a Federal court, which would have annulled the act; this would have been the most natural proceeding. But the judicial power would thus have been placed in direct opposition to the state, and it was desirable to avoid this predicament as much as possible. The Americans hold that it is nearly impossible that a new law should not injure some private interests by its provisions. These private interests are assumed by the American legislators as the means of assailing such measures as may be prejudicial to the Union, and it is to these interests that the protection of the Supreme Court is extended.

Suppose a state sells a portion of its public lands to a company, and that a year afterwards it passes a law by which the lands are otherwise disposed of and that clause of the Constitution which prohibits laws impairing the obligation of contracts is thereby violated. When the purchaser under the second act appears to take possession, the possessor under the first act brings his action before the tribunals of the Union and causes the title of the claimant to be pronounced null and void. Thus, in point of fact, the judicial power of the Union is contesting the claims of the sovereignty of a state; but it acts only indirectly and upon an application of detail. It attacks the law in its consequences, not in its principle, and rather weakens than destroys it.

The last case to be provided for was that each state formed a corporation enjoying a separate existence and distinct civil rights, and that it could therefore sue or be sued before a tribunal. Thus a state could bring an action against another state. In this instance the Union was not called upon to contest a state law, but to try a suit in which a state was a party. This suit was perfectly similar to any other cause except that the quality of the parties was different; and here the danger pointed out at the beginning of this chapter still exists, with less chance of being avoided. It is inherent in the very essence of Federal constitutions that they should create parties in the bosom of the nation which present powerful obstacles to the free course of justice.

When we have examined in detail the organization of the Supreme Court and the entire prerogatives which it exercises, we shall readily admit that a more imposing judicial power was never constituted by any people. The Supreme Court is placed higher than any other known tribunal, both by the nature of its rights and the class of justiciable parties which it controls.

In all the civilized countries of Europe the government has always shown the greatest reluctance to allow the cases in which it was itself interested to be decided by the ordinary course of justice. This repugnance is naturally greater as the government is more absolute; and, on the other hand, the privileges of the courts of justice are extended with the increasing liberties of the people; but no European nation has yet held that all judicial controversies, without regard to their origin, can be left to the judges of common law.

In America this theory has been actually put in practice; and the Supreme Court of the United States is the sole tribunal of the nation. Its power extends to all cases arising under laws and treaties made by the national authorities, to all cases of admiralty and maritime jurisdiction, and, in general, to all points that affect the law of nations. It may even be affirmed that, although its constitution is essentially judicial, its prerogatives are almost entirely political. Its sole object is to enforce the execution of the laws of the Union; and the Union regulates only the relations of the government with the citizens, and of the nation with foreign powers; the relations of citizens among themselves are almost all regulated by the sovereignty of the states.

A second and still greater cause of the preponderance of this court may be adduced. In the nations of Europe the courts of justice are called upon to try only the controversies of private individuals; but the Supreme Court of the United States summons sovereign powers to its bar. When the clerk of the court advances on the steps of the tribunal and simply says: "The State of New York *versus* The State of Ohio," it is impossible not to feel that the court which he addresses is no ordinary body; and when it is recollected that one of these parties represents one million, and the other two millions of men, one is struck by the responsibility of the seven judges, whose decision is about to satisfy or to disappoint so large a number of their fellow citizens.

The peace, the prosperity, and the very existence of the Union are vested in the hands of the seven Federal judges. Without them the Constitution would be a dead letter: the executive appeals to them for assistance against the encroachments of the legislative power; the legislature demands their protection against the assaults of the executive; they defend the Union from the disobedience of the states, the states from the exaggerated claims of the Union, the public interest against private interests, and the conservative spirit of stability against the fickleness of the democracy. Their power is enormous, but it is the power of public opinion. They are all-powerful as long as the people respect the law; but they would be impotent against popular neglect or contempt of the law. The force of public opinion is the most intractable of agents, because its exact limits cannot be defined; and it is not less dangerous to exceed than to remain below the boundary prescribed.

Not only must the Federal judges be good citizens, and men of that information and integrity which are indispensable to all magistrates, but they must be statesmen, wise to discern the signs of the times, not afraid to brave the obstacles that can be subdued, nor slow to turn away from the current when it threatens to sweep them off, and the supremacy of the Union and the obedience due to the laws along with them.

The President, who exercises a limited power, may err without causing great mischief in the state. Congress may decide amiss without destroying the Union, because the electoral body in which the Congress originates may cause it to retract its decision by changing its members. But if the Supreme Court is ever composed of imprudent or bad men, the Union may be plunged into anarchy or civil war.

The original cause of this danger, however, does not lie in the constitution of the tribunal, but in the very nature of federal governments. We have seen that in confederate states it is especially necessary to strengthen the judicial power, because in no other nations do those independent persons who are able to contend with the social body exist in greater power, or in a better condition to resist the physical strength of the government. But the more a power requires to be strengthened, the more extensive and independent it must be made; and the dangers which its abuse may create are heightened by its independence and its strength. The source of the evil is not, therefore, in the constitution of the power, but in the constitution of the state which renders the existence of such a power necessary.

## "Line Drawing" between Judicial Restraint and Judicial Activism: The Supreme Court of the United States in the Political Process

Henry J. Abraham

I

In order to comprehend the ebb and flow of the political struggle in the United States, it is necessary to keep in mind that the American democracy is based, at least institutionally, upon the concept of the separation of powers, duly modified by that of the attendant checks and balances. At times, the former, and to a much lesser extent the latter, may be considerably more of a theoretical than a practical phenomenon; but it represents an omnipresent, and not infrequently an omnipotent, aspect of the governmental process in the United States. It is one of the two or three cardinal characteristics of what to many an observer, domestic as well as foreign, have been the mysteries of American politics . . . mysteries that have prompted some to quote an Arthur Guiterman ditty:

> Providence, that watches over children,
>    drunks and fools,
> With silent miracles and other esoterica,
> Continue to suspend the ordinary rules,
> And take care of the United States of America.

That, appealing and attractively facile though it may be, is hardly a satisfactory explanation of the problem. The presence of the separation of powers, discounted by its checks and balances, however, *is* of its very essence.

The chief weapon at the disposal of the Supreme Court in the separation of power *cum* checks and balances struggle or game has been its overriding power of *judicial review,* a power possessed in theory by the judiciaries of sixty-five other countries—normally those with a federal structure of democratic government—yet effectively by only a few, among them Australia, Canada, and India. It is a power utterly absent, however, in such unitary democratic states as Britain—where the courts do, of course, have power to interpret and to adjudicate, but not to exercise a judicial veto over legislative or executive action; where Walter Bagehot's nineteenth century comment, that there is nothing Parliament cannot do except change a man into a woman and a woman into a man, still applies. At the risk of being obvious, judicial review, properly defined in its fullest majesty, signifies the following, and only the following: the power of *any* court of record, no matter how high or low, *to hold unconstitutional,* and hence unenforceable, any law, any official action actually or allegedly based upon it, and any illegal action by a public official, no matter in which branch of the government he or she may function, that the court of record deems—upon careful, normally painstaking, reflection, and in line with the canons of the taught

Reprinted with permission of the author, Henry J. Abraham.

tradition of the law as well as judicial self-restraint—to be in conflict with the written Constitution. Of course, in a very real sense, judicial review also denotes the positive judicial power *to uphold,* to validate, governmental actions—but the negative is by far the more dramatic and traumatic application. In other words, by invoking the power of judicial review, a court applies the *superior* of two laws, which at the level of the federal judiciary of the United States signifies the written Constitution, as amended and interpreted, instead of a legislative statute or some action by a public official allegedly or actually based upon either.

It is well to remember that the United States Supreme Court itself has rarely invoked this, its *ultimate,* power. It much prefers to resort to its penultimate power, that of statutory construction—as it did with its highly contentious decision in the Weber case[1] in June of 1979—which permits it to have its proverbial cake and yet eat it—a tactic not exactly viewed inevitably with particular favor by legislators! Of some 90,000 federal public and private laws passed to date (early 1980) by the United States Congress, the Supreme Court has struck down as unconstitutional only 122 or 123 provisions in whole or in part. (If parts of a law are savable, the Court will always strive to do so.) More than 1,000 state and local laws and provisions of *state* constitutions, on the other hand, have run wholly or partly afoul of that judicial checkmate since 1789 (but we are here primarily concerned with the problem on the national level). It should be noted that after the famous decision in *Marbury* v. *Madison*[2]—in which John Marshall, our fourth, and generally regarded as our greatest, chief justice—he was certainly our most influential—established or divined the doctrine of judicial review, no other federal legislation was declared unconstitutional by his Court (and only thirty-six *state* statutes fell) during the remaining thirty-two of his long tenure of thirty-four and one-half years (the third longest on the high bench, exceeded only by Mr. Justice Douglas's incredible almost thirty-seven years and Mr. Justice Stephen J. Field's thirty-four and three-fourths years.[3] Yet merely one year later Marshall made certain that judicial authority was to be understood as being equally applicable to the executive branch by ruling in *The Flying Fish* case[4] that President Adams had exceeded his powers in ordering the Navy to seize vessels bound to *or* from a French port because Congress had specifically authorized seizure of ships only going *to* French ports. Of course, regardless of its utilization of judicial review, the Marshall Court wielded immense power—coming on the heels of a very inauspicious beginning under three ambivalent and/or disinterested leaders of a then lowly-regarded and rather inactive Court—and, guided by the dominant figure of the assertive chief justice of the United States, did more than either of the two other branches to make the young United States a strong, a vigorous, a powerful nation and its Constitution a living effective elastic basic law. Not until Mr. Chief Justice Taney's contentious decision in *Dred Scott* v. *Sandford*[5] in 1857—a holding that was intended to stem the tides of the oncoming Civil War, and had precisely the opposite effect, and which featured nine opinions, six on the majority side, one concurring, and two dissenting—not until then was another federal statute struck down by the Supreme Court (here the "Missouri Compromise"). Of course, the greatest crisis evoked by the exercise of power by the Court did not arrive until, dominated by the four key doctrinaires among the so-called "Nine Old Men" of the Hughes Court—Associate Justices Sutherland, Van Devanter, Butler, and McReynolds—it declared unconstitutional no less than thirteen crucial

New Deal laws between 1934–36, many of these by 5:4 votes—laws heavily and overwhelmingly endorsed by both the executive and the legislative branches. Since that time, however, only fifty provisions of Congressional statutes have fallen—all of these, in fact, since 1943. And we ought to observe at once that all except three of these fifty did so because they were regarded by the Court as unacceptably infringing *personal rights and/or liberties* safeguarded under the Constitution.

## II

It should thus be clear that the always live argument as to the proper role of the judiciary is not really concerned with the rare exercise of its ultimate power of judicial review *per se,* but with the applications of its interpretative powers, generally embracing those delineating legislative and/or executive authority, especially the former, on both the federal and state governmental levels. It is here that the central line-drawing question between "judicial restraint" and "judicial activism" arises; it is here that both professionals and laymen, sooner or later, inexorably ask the central question of whether the judiciary, whether its justices, merely "judge" each case on its intrinsic merit, or whether they also "legislate?" Do they, to put it into somewhat different but analogous terms, "find" or "make" law? Do they, in effect, engage in what has often been styled as "social engineering?" In theory, all the members of any judicial tribunal do is to judge the controversies over which they have jurisdiction and arrive at a decision in accordance with the legal aspects of the particular situation at issue. Yet especially the nine justices of the United States Supreme Court are frequently charged with "legislating" rather than "judging" in handing down their decisions. This charge usually admits, and indeed grants, that the Court must of course possess the power to *interpret* legislation, and, if "absolutely justified" by the particular issue at hand, even strike down legislation that is unconstitutional beyond "rational question." The charge against the Court insists, however, that a line must be drawn between the imposition of judicial *judgment* and the exercise of judicial *will.* The latter is described as legislating, presumably the function of the legislature, and hence reserved to it. But, no matter how desirable one may be in the eyes of a good many observers, *is* it possible to draw such a line?

It is, of course, *im*possible. As with every "line," questions arise at once as to *how, where, when* and by *whom* it shall be drawn. Nor do the justices claim to have a ready-made answer to the problem, although Mr. Justice Owen Roberts, for one, attempted in the famed 1936 case of *United States* v. *Butler*[6] to draw that line once and for all by way of an often-quoted passage from his opinion for a majority of six (which here declared the New Deal's Agricultural Act of 1933 unconstitutional):

> When an act of Congress is appropriately challenged in the Courts as not conforming to the constitutional mandate the judicial branch of Government has only one duty—*to lay the articles of the Constitution next to the act and to decide whether the latter squares with the former.*[7]

In theory, this is a praiseworthy formula; in practice, it is hardly a realistic assessment, for it is invoked by judges who must decide the meaning of the all-important verb *to square.* The responses to the *Butler* decision—culled from contemporary press commentary—is illustrative of the enigma: "Bravo," applauded the *opponents* of the New

Deal, "great judicial statesmanship, proper and precise interpretation of the written Constitution!" Countered the *proponents* of the New Deal, "An unwarranted, outrageous assumption of legislative authority, an arrogant disregard of constitutional limitations on judicial power." And soon thereafter President Roosevelt moved to "pack" the Court with members who would read the Constitution *his* way.

The reaction to the *Butler* case is but one example of the ever recurring problem. Another famous illustration of a set of diametrically opposite-in-reaction postures is that of the decisions in *Dred Scott* v. *Sandford* (in 1877)[8] and *Brown* v. *Board of Education* (in 1954)[9], where friend and foe of racial equality may be found first on one, then on the opposite side of the scale of plaudits, depending upon the course of the decision and the commitment of the commentator! It would seem that, to a large extent, official as well as private reaction is more or less a matter of whose ox is being gored, to use Al Smith's happy phrase.


### III

It is not, however, quite so simple—although unquestionably reactions to Supreme Court decisions are normally highly subjective. Nor is the key to the problem—in what Professor Alpheus T. Mason well styled as "an unrealistic dictum"[10]—the well-known, on-its-face logical, statement by Mr. Chief Justice Stone, who was among the three dissenters in the aforementioned *Butler* decision, when he thus admonished the six adherents to Mr. Justice Roberts' majority opinion:

> . . . while unconstitutional exercise of power by the executive and legislative branches is subject to judicial restraint, the only check on our own exercise of power is our sense of self-restraint.[11]

To be sure, as the *Butler* decision-era Court amply demonstrated, the assertion does have a meritorious ring. Yet it far too sweepingly glosses over the facts of political life, facts that have amply demonstrated the long-run clout of the other two branches, especially that of the legislature. Moreover, it is but a short step from the Stone statement to a contentious pronouncement by Charles Evans Hughes, publicly voiced in 1907 while serving as governor of New York—and one he later grew to regret—that "We are under a Constitution, but the Constitution is what the judges say it is." While a priori appealing, the Hughes assertion goes considerably beyond that by Mr. Justice Stone; moreover, being a campaign statement—although that of future associate justice and later chief justice of the United States—it failed to point to the complexities inherent in such a facile pronouncement, complexities that do include, but are certainly not confined to, the very real sense of selfrestraint[12] that, to a greater or lesser degree, is almost always present on the bench.

It is obvious, however, that the judges do "legislate." They do make law. One of the most consistent advocates of judicial selfrestraint, Mr. Justice Oliver Wendell Homes, Jr., recognized "without hesitation" that judges do and must "legislate." (More than once he would quip: "Why, I made some law myself—last Monday.") But, he added significantly, the judges "can do so only interstitially; they are confined from molar to molecular motions."[13] Judges are human, as indeed all of us are human—but they also are judges, which most of us are not. Being human, they have human reactions. "Judges are men, not disembodied spirits; as men they respond to human situations," in Mr. Justice Frankfurter's words. Mr. Justice McReynolds insisted that a judge neither can be, nor should he be, "an amorphous dummy, unspotted by human emotions"—and he assuredly was amply "spotted!" And Mr. Justice Cardozo spoke elegantly of the cardiac promptings of the moment, musing that "[T]he great tides and currents which engulf the rest of men do not turn aside in their course and pass the judges by."[14]

Yet, as indicated, being human does not stand alone in the judicial decision-making process. A jurist is also presumably a qualified and conscientious member of the tribunal; he or she is in no sense of the term a free agent—free to render a decision willynilly. There is a deplorable tendency on the part of many observers to over-simplify the judicial decision-making process. To a very real degree, jurists are "rigidly bound within walls that are unseen" by the average layman. These walls are built of the heritage of the Anglo-Saxon law; the spirit of that law; the impact of the cases as these have come down through the years; the regard for *stare decisis* (although there may well conveniently be several precedents from which to choose), for a genuine sense of historical continuity with the past, as Holmes put it, "is not a duty, it is only a necessity,"[15] because to him, "a page of history is worth more than a pound of logic;" and there is, further, the already discussed and so crucial practice of judicial self-restraint[16]—in brief sum, *the taught tradition of the law.*

Moreover, the judges are very well aware of at least two other cardinal facts of judicial life: the first is that they have no power for such enforcement—witness the Little Rock (Arkansas) and the Tuscaloosa (Alabama) and Oxford (Mississippi) troop dispatches by Presidents Eisenhower and Kennedy, respectively, in order to support and implement federal court orders to desegregate public schools and universities. The second is that judicial decisions may be reversed by statutory legislative action, albeit with varying degrees of effectiveness and indubitably with very considerable toil and trouble, of which a telling illustration is the enactment of the Crime Bill of 1968, with its three-pronged attack on the Court, subsequent to the *Miranda* decision.[17] Or they may be reversed by constitutional amendment, of which the Twenty-Sixth Amendment, providing for the eighteen-year-old vote at the state level, is a recent example. The Supreme Court's only power is essentially a moral one, namely, its power to persuade. For purse and sword are in other hands, as Alexander Hamilton put it so well two centuries ago now, those of the legislative and the executive, respectively. Yet not only do we often expect too much from the Court, we let it—or wish it to—settle policy matters that ought to be, yet for a variety of reasons are not, tackled by the other two branches of government. This is demonstrated by such contentious issues as desegregation-integration; reapportionment-redistricting; criminal justice; privacy; separation of Church and State—and we then assault the judicial holding! As Anthony Lewis has observed so perceptively in addressing the vexatious issue of the proper judicial role, "judicial interventions on fundamental issues are most clearly justified [only] when there is no other remedy for a situation that threatens the national fabric—when the path of political change is blocked,"[18] always, however, assuming constitutional warrant. This was indeed true of the areas of endemic racial segregation and persistent legislative mal-, mis- and nonapportionment—assuredly so in terms of the initial grabbing of the proverbial constitutional bull by the horns a few decades ago. But it has become a fair question whether the judiciary, especially at the level of the trial courts in their expansive perceptions of equity powers, has begun to overreach itself of late in these two realms, particularly in the former—note, for example, the controversial use of those judicial equity powers in governmental structure, forced school busing, racial pairing, racial quotas, and the live issue of affirmative action—"reverse discrimination," generally.

Be that as it may, the demonstrably expansive judicial intervention in such contentious criminal justice rulings as *Miranda* v. *Arizona,*[19] for one, was arguably of dubious justification, at least in part. For there, by reading a particular, multifaceted code of police procedure into the general language of the Constitution, the Court very likely overreached itself. Nor, or so it would seem, was that intervention readily justifiable in the Court's recent highly questionable involvement with a host of marginally judicial and questionably judicious aspects of the vexatious realm of abortion[20] (regardless of whether or not one agrees with the results it reached), where, in effect, the Court has legislated a detailed Federal Abortion Code. Nor, to point to another realm, is it clearly justifiable in the Court's increasing involvement—some have styled it "meddling"—with matters of discipline in the public schools,[21] or, for that matter, in school administration concerns of a local nature generally. Nor, rather obviously, it would appear, is it the judiciary's proper role to decree, as a U.S. district court judge recently did in Alabama, that—in addition to a host of other highly specific requirements—"dieticians and recreational officers in state penal institutions possess college degrees."[22] Nor did the law (here the Civil Rights Act of 1964) permit what a five-member Supreme Court ruling in effect held it permitted in the *Weber* case[23]—as the five-member majority opinion's author, Mr. Justice Brennan, quite frankly acknowledged. But he justified the racial quotas in private employment there at issue by what he identified as "the *spirit"* of the law, rather than its letter.[24] This judicial *coup de main* was accomplished notwithstanding the *crystal clear* prohibitory language of the Act's Title VII, Section 703 (a), (c), (d), especially (j),[25] as well as the equally incontestibly clear legislative *history* of the statute.[26] In *Weber* the controlling opinion majority thus did not merely go *beyond* Title VII's legislative *language and legislative history,* it went *against* it.

Our courts should not be regarded as wastebaskets of social problems, and their judges should not be viewed as social engineers—which does not mean, of course, that law does not play an efficacious role in social reform. It does, however, point to the inescapable fact that the other branches *must* do their jobs—and, alas, they often do not—for it is such a temptation to pass the buck! In sum, it must be resolutely understood that our constitutional constellation does not conceive of the courts as society's primary lawmakers; it does not provide for government by the judiciary. The Constitution *does* provide for a republican form of government, based upon popular sovereignty. If we disapprove of the performance of our elected officials we can effect a change.

Of course, the Supreme Court of the United States is engaged in the political process. But, in Mr. Justice Felix Frankfurter's admonitory prose, it is "the Nation's ultimate judicial tribunal, not a super-legal-aid bureau."[27] Neither is the Court, in the second Mr. Justice John Marshall Harlan's words, "a panacea for every blot upon the public welfare, nor," he warned, "should this Court, ordained as a judicial body, be thought of as a general haven for reform movements."[28] Of course, the justices—who have quite succinctly been styled "inevitably teachers in a vital national seminar"[29]—consult their own policy preferences. But they are expected to do so in an institutional setting that forces responsibility upon them. They must meet and maintain high standards of integrity, intelligence, logic, reflectiveness, and consistency. They must demonstrate a sense of history, coupled with the realities and vagaries of public affairs, a task that has been aptly called "the hunch of intuition about the inner life of American democracy!"[30] They have the exciting, yet delicate, task of heeding the "felt necessities of the time,"[31] in Mr. Justice Holmes' inspired if hardly noncontentious phrase—for is it not the *legislature's* task to do that feeling?—while committed to holding aloft the banner of constitutional fundamentals.

No institution of government can be devised by human beings that will be satisfactory to all people at all times. The Court is much better at saying what the government may *not* do than in prescribing what the government *must* do and *how* it must go about doing it—the latter is essentially the task of the political branches. Indeed, the Court should resolutely shun prescriptive policy making—but the temptations seem to be sporadically irresistible. It has quite enough to do in constitutional and statutory application and interpretation. Thus it may well be questioned, on grounds of both wisdom and justification, whether the Court should become involved, as it has become increasingly of late, in such realms as *economic* equality as distinct from *political and legal* equality—by now often going beyond the basic constitutional guarantee of equality of *opportunity* to that of equality as a prima facie requirement of *condition or result*. Or, to turn to a different area of societal concern, one might well query whether the Court should deal with *private* morality as distinct from *public* morality, as it has done, for example, in the obscenity syndrome. Paraphrasing Harvard's famed Constitutional Law expert Paul Freund, the question is not whether the Court can do everything, but whether it can do something—and do that in its appropriate sphere. Naturally, these lines are often as brittle and elusive as they are vexatious—and the Court can escape neither controversy nor criticism. In Mr. Justice Holmes' oft-quoted words: "We are very quiet up there, but it is the quiet of a storm center, as we all know." As an institution at once legal, political, and human, it possesses both the assets and liabilities that attend these descriptive characteristics.

## IV

Yet when all is said and done, the Court, at the head of the United States judiciary, is not only the most fascinating, the most influential, and the most powerful judicial body in the world—it is also the "living voice of [the] Constitution," as Lord Bryce once phrased it. As such, it is both arbiter and educator, and, in essence, represents the sole solution short of anarchy under the American system of government as we know it—witness its seminal message in *United States* vs. *Nixon,*[32] with the entire nation's and most of the world's eye turned upon it. It must act, in the words of one commentator, "as the instrument of national moral values that have not been able to find other governmental expression"[33]—again, however, always assuming that it functions within its authorized sphere of constitutional adjudication, within the parameters of the judicial role—a *caveat* that some members of the judiciary are apt to ignore or forget at times. In its appropriate role, however, the Court operates admirably as the "collective conscience of a sovereign people."[34] Also in that role it functions as the natural forum for the individual and the small group. It *is* the ultimate guardian of our basic civil rights and liberties.

And even if a transfer of the judicial guardianship to other institutions of government were theoretically desirable, which few thoughtful citizens believe, it would be politically impossible. "Do we desire constitutional questions," asked Charles Evans Hughes, then not on the bench, in his fine book on the Court, "to be determined by political assemblies and partisan divisions?"[35] The response must be a ringing "NO!" In the 1955 Godkin lectures, which he was to deliver at Harvard University when death intervened, Mr. Justice Robert H. Jackson had expressed his conviction eloquently and ably: "The people have seemed to feel that the Supreme Court, whatever its defects, is still the most detached, dispassionate, and trustworthy custodian that our system affords for the translation of abstract into constitutional commands."[36] And we may well agree with Thomas Reed Powell that the logic of constitutional law is the common sense of the Supreme Court of the United States—even if that is not indubitably always in evidence. George Reedy, L.B.J.'s press secretary, gauged the matter rather perceptively recently when he said that he "liked what the Court was doing, but could not avoid the apprehension that it was taking an awful lot of money out of the bank and would do well to put a little of it back from time to time."[37] The Court might well ponder the shrewd insight of that message.

Still, in the long run—if not inevitably in the short—common constitutional sense has usually served the Court well in its ceaseless striving as a voice of reason, to maintain the blend of continuity and change that constitutes the *sine qua non* for desirable stability in the basic governmental processes of this representative democracy under its remarkable elastic, but written, Constitution. In that role, and notwithstanding the voyeurism to which its activities were subjected in the insensitive tome, *The Brethren*,[38] the Court will—for it must—live in history.

### Notes

1. *Steelworkers* v. *Weber*, 98 S. Ct. 2721 (1979).
2. Cranch 137 (1803).
3. In fourth place stands Mr. Justice Black, who served thirty-four years and a bit more than a month, at his retirement in September of 1971, falling just five months short of the all-time longevity record. Fifth is Mr. Justice John Marshall Harlan, the Elder, who served exactly thirty-four years.
4. 2 Cranch 170 (1804).
5. 19 Howard 393 (1957).
6. 297 U.S. 1 (1936).
7. *Ibid.,* at 62.
8. 19 Howard 393.
9. 347 U.S. 783.
10. "The Case for Judicial Activism," LVI *The Yale Review* 2 (Winter, 1967), pp. 197–211.
11. 297 U.S. 1 (1936), at 78. (Italics added.)

12. Professor Philip Kurland—an expert on the subject—makes six basic assumptions for the doctrine of self-restraint:

"One is history and the obligation that constitutionalism imposes to adhere to the essential meaning put in the document by its framers. A second is the intrinsically undemocratic nature of the Supreme Court. A third is a corollary to the second, an abiding respect for the judgments of those branches of the government that are elected representatives of their constituents. A fourth is the recognition that judicial error at this level is more difficult of correction than other forms of judicial action. A fifth is respect for the judgments of earlier courts. But (sixth), the essential feature of judicial restraint that has gained most attention and aroused the greatest doubts probably because few men are themselves big enough to abide by its command—is the notion of rejection of personal preference." (*Mr. Justice Frankfurter and the Supreme Court* (Chicago: University of Chicago Press, 1971), p. 5).

13. *Southern Pacific Co.* v. *Jensen*, 224 U.S. 205 (1916), at 221.

14. Benjamin N. Cardozo, *The Nature of the Judicial Process* (New Haven: Yale University Press, 1921), p. 169.

15. As quoted by Alpheus T. Mason and William M. Beaney in *American Constitutional Law*, 6th ed. (Englewood Cliffs, N.J.: Prentice-Hall, Inc., 1978), p. XXVI.

16. For a list of sixteen "maxims" of this self-restraint, see my *The Judicial Process: An Introductory Analysis of the Courts of the United States, England, and France*, 4th ed. (New York: Oxford University Press, 1980), ch. IX.

17. *Miranda* v. *Arizona*, 384 U.S. 433 (1966).

18. *The New York Times*, November 15, 1971, p. 41 (Italics added.)

19. 384 U.S. 433 (1966).

20. *Roe* v. *Wade*, 410 U.S. 113 and *Doe* v. *Bolton*, 410 U.S. 179 (1973), followed by decisions in 1976, 1977, 1978 and 1979.

21. *Goss* v. *Lopez*, 419 U.S. 565 (1975); *Baker* v. *Owen*, 423 U.S. 907 (1975).

22. *Pugh* v. *Locke*, 406 F. Supp. 318 (1976), at 334. (M.D., Ala., 1976: Judge Frank M. Johnson.) *Pugh* required "in working order one toilet per 15 inmates, one urinal or one foot of urinal trough per 15 inmates, one shower per 20 inmates, and one lavatory per 10 inmates," at 334; "Each inmate who requires a special diet for reasons of health or religion shall be provided a diet to meet his or her individual need," at 334; "Visitors shall not be subjected to any unreasonable searches," at 334; a minimum number of custodial staff at each institution, at 335.

23. *Steelworkers* v. *Weber*, 99 S. Ct. 2721 (1979).

24. *Ibid.*, at 2731.

25. The section states: "Nothing contained in this subchapter shall be interpreted to require any employer, employment agency, labor organization, or joint labor-management committee subject to this sub-chapter to grant preferential treatment to the race, color, religion, sex, national origin of such individual or group *on account of an imbalance which may exist with respect to the total number or percentage of persons of any race, color, religion, sex, or national origin employed by any employer, referred or classified for employment by any employment agency or labor organization*, admitted to membership or classified by any labor organization, or admitted to, or employed in any apprenticeship or other training program *in comparison with the total number or percentage of persons of such race, color, religion, sex, or national origin in any community, state, section or other area, or in any available work force in any community, state, section, or other area."* (Italics added.)

26. E.g., 111 Cong. Dec. 1518 (1964); *Ibid.*, pp. 1540, 2557, 2558, 4764, 5423, 6509, 6566, 7213, 7218, 7418–20, 8921, 9943, 11768, 12617, 12691, 13080, 14328, 14484, *et seq.*

27. *Uveges* v. *Pennsylvania*, 335 U.S. 437 (1948), at 437.

28. *Reynolds* v. *Sims*, 377 U.S. 533 (1964), at 624, dissenting opinion.

29. Eugene V. Rostow, "The Democratic Character of Judicial Review," 66 *Harvard Law Review*, 195 (1952).

30. Judge Joseph C. Hutcheson, Jr., of Texas, as quoted by Eugene V. Rostow in his *The Sovereign Prerogative: The Supreme Court and the Quest for Law* (New Haven: Yale University Press, 1963), p. 110.

31. *The Common Law* (Boston: Little, Brown and Co., 1881), p. 1.
32. 418 U.S. 683 (1974).
33. Anthony Lewis, *The New York Times Magazine,* June 17, 1962, p. 38.
34. U.S. Court of Appeals' Judge J. Skelly Wright, "The Role of the Courts: Conscience of a Sovereign People," 29 *The Reporter* 5 (September 26, 1963).
35. *The Supreme Court of the United States* (New York: Columbia University Press, 1928), p. 236.
36. Robert H. Jackson, *The Supreme Court in the American System of Government* (Cambridge: Harvard University Press, 1955), p. 23.
37. As quoted in 426 *The Annals* 217 (July 1976).
38. Bob Woodward and Scott Armstrong, *The Brethren: Inside the Supreme Court* (New York: Simon and Schuster, 1979).

---

# Are the Courts Going Too Far?

Donald L. Horowitz

The last two decades have been a period of considerable expansion of judicial responsibility in the United States. Although the kinds of cases that judges have long handled still occupy most of their time, the cope of judicial business has broadened. The result has been involvement of courts in decisions that would earlier have been thought unfit for adjudication. Judicial activity has extended to welfare administration, prison administration, and mental hospital administration, to education policy and employment policy, to road building and bridge building, to automotive safety standards, and to natural resource management.

In just the past few years, courts have struck down laws requiring a period of instate residence as a condition of eligibility for welfare. They have invalidated presumptions of child support arising from the presence in the home of a "substitute father." Federal district courts have laid down elaborate standards for food handling, hospital operations, recreation facilities, inmate employment and education, sanitation, laundry, painting, lighting, plumbing, and renovation in some prisons; they have ordered other prisons closed. Courts have established equally comprehensive programs of care and treatment for the mentally ill confined in hospitals. They have ordered the equalization of school expenditures on teachers' salaries, established hearing procedures for public school discipline cases, decided that bilingual education must be provided for Mexican-American children, and suspended the use by school boards of the National Teacher Examination and of comparable tests for school supervisors. They have eliminated a high school diploma as a requirement for a fireman's job. They have enjoined the construction of roads and bridges on environmental grounds and suspended performance requirements for automobile tires and air bags. They have told the Farmers' Home Administration to restore a disaster loan program, the Forest Service to stop the clear-cutting of timber, and the Corps of Engineers to maintain the nation's nonnavigable waterways. They have been, to put it mildly, very busy, laboring in unfamiliar territory.

What the judges have been doing is new in a special sense. Although no single feature of most of this litigation constitutes an abrupt departure, the aggregate of features distinguishes it sharply from the traditional exercise of the judicial function.

First of all, many wholly new areas of adjudication have been opened up. There was, for all practical purposes, no previous judge-made law of housing or welfare rights, for example. To some extent, the new areas of activity respond to invitations from Congress or, to a much lesser extent, from state legislatures. Sometimes these take the form of judicial review provisions, written into new legislation. Sometimes they take the form of new legislation so broad, so vague, so indeterminate, as to pass the problem to the courts. They then have to deal with the inevitable litigation to determine the "intent of Congress," which, in such statutes, is of course nonexistent.

If some such developments result from legislative or even bureaucratic activity (interpretation of regulations, for example), then it is natural to see the expansion of judicial activity as a mere concomitant of the growth of the welfare state. As governmental activity in general expands, so will judicial activity.

But that is not all that is involved. Much judicial activity has occurred quite independently of Congress and the bureaucracy and sometimes quite contrary to their announced policies. The very idea is sometimes to handle a problem unsatisfactorily resolved by another branch of government. In areas far from traditional development by case law—indeed in areas often covered densely by statutes and regulations—the courts have now seized the initiative in lawmaking. In such areas, the conventional formulation of the judicial role has it that courts are to "legislate" only interstitially. With the important exception of judicial decisions holding legislative or executive action unconstitutional, this conventional formulation of what used to be the judicial role is probably not far from what judges did in fact do. It is no longer an adequate formulation.

What the courts demand in such cases, by way of remedy, also tends to be different. Even building programs have been ordered by courts, and the character of some judicial decrees has made them, *de facto,* exercises of the appropriation power. A district court order rendered in Alabama had the effect of raising the state's annual expenditure on mental institutions from $14 millions before suit was filed in 1971 to $58 millions in 1973, a year after the decree was rendered. Decisions expanding welfare eligibility or ordering special education for disturbed, retarded, or hyperactive pupils have had similar budgetary effects. "For example, it is estimated that federal court decisions striking down various state restrictions on welfare payments, like residency requirements, made an additional 100,000 people eligible for assistance."[1] It is no longer even approximately accurate to say that courts exercise only a veto. What is asked and what is awarded is often the doing of something, not just the stopping of something.

To be sure, courts have always had some say in the way public funds were spent. How else could they award damages against the government? But even in the aggregate, decisions ordering a municipality to pay for an injury sustained by someone who trips over a loose manhole cover are not generally important enough to influence the setting of public priorities. The recent decisions that require spending to achieve compliance with a newly articulated policy are something else again.

It is also true that both affirmative and negative relief (orders to do something and orders to stop doing something) have a long history in English equity jurisprudence. The hoary remedies of mandamus and specific performance both require affirmative action—but action of a very circumscribed, precise sort, the limits of which are known in advance of the decree. Mandamus traditionally compels performance of an official duty of a clear and usually trivial sort; generally, compliance is measured by performance of one or two simple acts. Specific performance compels compliance with certain kinds of contractual obligation, the exact nature of the obligation spelled out in the contract. But specific performance is not traditionally awarded to compel performance of a contract for personal services, one significant reason being that the courts would then find themselves deep in the management of a continuing relationship, perhaps a whole business enterprise.

Again, therefore, compelling the performance of certain affirmative acts is nothing new in principle, but it is new in degree. The decree of a federal district judge ordering mental hospitals to adhere to some eighty-four minimum standards of care and treatment represents an extreme in specificity, but it is representative of the trend toward demanding performance that cannot be measured in one or two simple acts but in a whole course of conduct, performance will be owned. Remedies like these are reminiscent of the kinds of programs adopted by legislatures and executives. If they are to be translated into action, remedies of this kind often require the same kinds of supervision as other government programs do.

This leads to still another difference in degree between adjudication as it once was and as it now is. Litigation is now more explicitly problem solving than grievance answering. The individual litigant, though still necessary, has tended to fade a bit into the background. Courts sometimes take off from the individual cases before them to the more general problem that the cases call up, and indeed they may assume—dubiously—that the litigants before them typify the problem.

Once again, of course, it is all too easy to fabricate an idealized judicial past that consigned judges merely to resolving individual disputes. It has not been that way. In articulating the law of negligence from one case to the next, judges have tried to lay down a standard of care calculated to reduce the incidence of personal injury and property damage without unduly raising the expense of doing so. Many other common-law rules could be described in similar terms, as much efforts to frame behavioral standards as to apply them. Some of the most formidable difficulties faced by common-law judges have arisen in cases that present the judges with an inescapable choice between doing justice in the individual case and doing justice in general.

For all that, however, the individual and his case remained indispensable. Courts paid particular attention to the interplay between the facts of the individual case and the facts of the class of cases they projected from it. Without the particular case, the task of framing standards was devoid of meaning. It is inconceivable, for example, that even a great, innovative common-law court like the New York Court of Appeals early in this century would have countenanced deciding a case that had become moot. That some issues might forever escape judicial scrutiny because of the doctrine that a moot case is not a case at all would have struck even bold judges of a few decades ago as entirely natural.

Today it is repellent to many judges. For the view has gained ground that the judicial power is, by and large, coterminous with the governmental power. One test of this is the withering of the mootness doctrine in the federal courts. The old prohibition on the decision of moot cases is now so riddled with exceptions that it is almost a matter of discretion whether to hear a moot case. The argument for deciding a case that has become moot is often the distinctly recent one that there is a public interest in the judicial resolution of important issues. In contrast, the earlier view was that there was a public interest in avoiding litigation. By the same token, dismissal for mootness has become a practice reserved for invocation when it is unimportant, inconvenient, or impolitic to decide the issues a case raised.

What this shift signifies is the increasing subordination of the individual case in judicial policymaking, as well as the expansion of judicial responsibility more nearly to overlap the responsibilities of other governmental institutions. The individual case and its peculiar facts have on occasion become mere vehicles for an exposition of more general policy problems. Consequently, somewhat less care can be devoted, by lawyers and judges alike, to the appropriateness of particular plaintiffs and to the details of their grievances.

At the same time, the courts have tended to move from the byways onto the highways of policy making. Alexander M. Bickel has captured, albeit with hyperbole, the thrust of the new judicial ventures into social policy. "All too many federal judges," he has written, "have been induced to view themselves as holding roving commissions as problem solvers, and as charged with a duty to act when majoritarian institutions do not." The hyperbole is itself significant: many federal judges regard themselves as holding no such commission, yet even they have embarked on "problem-solving" ventures. This is the surest sign that the tendency is not idosyncratic but systemic: it transcends, in some measure, individual judicial preference and calls for systematic explanation.

The remote sources of the broad sweep of judicial power in America lie deep in English and American political history. The immediate origins of recent shifts in judicial emphasis are another matter. These are several, and they have tended to build on each other.

Most obvious has been the influence of the school desegregation cases. These decisions created a magnetic field around the courts, attracting litigation in areas where judicial intervention had earlier seemed implausible. The more general judicial activism of the Warren Court signaled its willingness to test the conventional boundaries of judicial action. As this happened, significant social groups thwarted in achieving their goals in other forums turned to adjudication as a more promising course. Some organizations saw the opportunity to use litigation as a weapon in political struggles carried on elsewhere. The National Welfare Rights Organization, for example, is said to have turned to lawsuits to help create a state and local welfare crisis that might bring about a federal guaranteed income. The image of courts willing to "take the heat" was attractive, too, to legislators who were not. Such social programs as the poverty program had legal assistance components, which Congress obligingly provided, perhaps partly because they placed the onus for resolving social problems on the courts. Soon there were also privately funded lawyers functioning in the environmental, mental health, welfare rights, civil rights, and similar fields. They tended to prefer the judicial road to reform over the legislative. They raised issues never before tested in litigation, and the courts frequently responded by expanding the boundaries of judicial activity.

Major doctrinal developments both followed and contributed to the increase in number and the change in character of the issues being litigated. The loosening of requirements of jurisdiction, standing, and ripeness (to name just three) helped spread out judge-made law, moving it from the tangential questions to the great principles. If these doctrinal decisions mean anything, it is that the adjudicative format is less and less an inhibition on judicial action and that the lawsuit can increasingly be thought of as an option more or less interchangeable with options in other forums, except that it has advantages the other forums lack. Hence the time-honored tradition that those who lose in the legislature or the bureaucracy may turn to the courts has lost none of its appeal. Only the identity of those who turn from one forum to another has undergone some change. Deprived social groups have joined the advantaged in the march to the courthouse. But where the wealthy invariably want the courts to strike down action that the other branches have taken, the disadvantaged often ask the courts to take action that the other branches have decided not to take. The character of the demand for action is therefore different.

Some major obstacles of a practical sort have also been cleared away. It still takes years to conclude most litigation, but some courts have shown a willingness to expedite hearing schedules to speed up the disposition of injunction cases. It still costs large sums of money to bring suit, and reductions in foundation funding of public interest law firms are contracting their efforts. But decisions awarding attorneys' fees may have eased the hardship and proliferated the cases. In one decision, an attorney's fee was awarded even though the plaintiff's lawyer had agreed to represent him without charge. The court said the award would encourage lawyers to represent public interest clients without fees in the hope that a fee would be awarded—and no doubt it would have that effect. In 1975, the Supreme Court restricted the award of attorneys' fees in federal cases unless authorized by Congress. But many statutes do allow attorneys' fees, and proposed legislation in some areas may be more generous in allowing expert witness fees as well.

It is still true, too, that legislative remedies—when they are forthcoming—may be more systematic and inclusive than judicial remedies. Yet more often than not, the judicial remedy has a directness, a concreteness, and a lack of equivocation notably absent in schemes that emerge from the political process. More and more, the courts have turned to decrees that afford comprehensive relief, often of a far-reaching sort. Support in the Anglo-American equity tradition for a decree as broad as the occasion warrants is unmistakable. The problem of school desegregation has tested this tradition, and the judges have sometimes proved as resourceful as the English chancellors from whom their equitable powers spring. In the process, the willingness to entertain remedies as inclusive as those a legislature might provide has grown, even to the point where the judicially ordered consolidation of school districts or equalization of tax burdens across districts—wholly beyond imagination not long ago—have become debatable measures, indeed litigated issues.

All of this has taken place—perhaps could only take place—in a society given to an incomparable degree of legalism. In the United States, as Tocqueville observed long ago, "all parties are obliged to borrow, in their daily controversies, the ideas, and even the language, peculiar to judicial proceedings. . . . The language of the law thus becomes in some measure a vulgar tongue; the spirit of the law, which is produced in the schools and courts of justice, gradually penetrates beyond their walls into the bosom of society, where it descends to the lowest classes, so that at last the whole people contract the habits and the taste of the judicial magistrate." The American proclivity to think of social problems in legal terms and to judicialize everything from wage claims to community conflicts and the allocation of airline routes makes it only natural to accord judges a major share in the making of social policy. No doubt, this underlying premise in American thought was a necessary, though insufficient, condition for the expansion of judicial responsibility that has taken place over the last twenty years.

The tendency to commit the resolution of social policy issues to the courts is not likely to be arrested in the near future. The nature of the forces undergirding the tendency makes them not readily reversible. Doctrinal erosion in particular is not easily stopped. Ironically, perhaps, the traditional judicial conception of precedent makes it more difficult for courts to change course dramatically than for the other branches of government to do so. The generally greater stability of judicial personnel, appointed for life in the federal courts, appointed or elected to long terms in the states, also makes for continuity. The statutes already enacted and continuing to be enacted, lodging authority for policy making in the courts by explicit provision or by default, are enough to propel judicial activity for some time to come. And the attractiveness of passing problems to the judges is unabated. The new responsibilities of the courts are not just the product of individual states of mind.

Even to the limited extent that judges can contract their recently expanded commitments, some curious twists are possible. Supreme Court justices, appointed because a president thinks they will construe the Bill of Rights more narrowly than their predecessors, have a way of becoming entangled in institutional tradition. No contraction is likely to take place on all fronts.

Beyond that, expansive exercises in statutory construction may be untouched by a contraction in constitutional adjudication. As a matter of fact, judges who recoil at innovation in constitutional lawmaking may not see the same dangers at all in the interpretation of statutes. It is customary to think that judicial self-limitation in constitutional interpretation is important because constitutional law is a permanent inhibition on policy: a legislature cannot override an interpretation of the Constitution. In statutory law, judges may reason, basic policy choices have been made by other branches, and judicial construction may later be overridden by them. For these reasons, judges with a strong sense of institutional limitation are less likely to let it stand in the way of innovation short of constitutional interpretation.

The soundness of this conventional distinction between the scope of constitutional and nonconstitutional adjudication need not detain us here. Whether or not decisions that rest on constitutional foundations are really more permanent than those that do not is beside the point—which is simply that traditional counsels of restraint that apply to the former do not apply to the latter. Judges concerned to avoid the excesses that are believed to have characterized the Supreme Court of the 1930s and 1960s may still embark on ambitious ventures of judicial reform in the name of statutory construction.

Let me give two examples. Both, as it happens, are from the civil rights field, and both are decisions of the Supreme Court, but they might just as easily have come from some other court acting in some other field.

The first is *Griggs* v. *Duke Power Co.,* in which the Court unanimously read Title VII of the Civil Rights Act of 1964 to require the elimination of tests and diplomas as job requirements if they disqualify prospective black employees at a higher rate than whites, unless the employer can show that the test or diploma bears a "demonstrable relationship" to successful job performance. Employment practices that have no discriminatory intent, the Court said, are to be measured by "business necessity." Tests that prevent minority applicants from obtaining jobs in proportion to their numbers must be shown to "measure the person for the job and not the person in the abstract." So the Court, in an opinion by Chief Justice Burger, interpreted the Civil Rights Act.

The act had forbidden job discrimination on grounds of "race, color, religion, sex, or national origin." An amendment, added on the floor of the Senate in order to clarify and reaffirm the rights of employers to use "ability tests" to screen potential employees, had insulated such tests from scrutiny, provided the tests were "not designed, intended, or used to discriminate" on racial or other forbidden grounds. That, at least, is what the senators thought.

In the event, the Supreme Court read the word *used* to mean used intentionally or unintentionally, and so to forbid tests like the aptitude test used in *Griggs* unless the employer could prove it measured job performance in the narrow sense.

There is convincing legislative history to show that Congress intended the opposite of the result reached in Griggs. This was a provision on which Congress was at pains to make itself clear. The sponsors of the testing amendment explicitly wished to insure that no court would prohibit a testing procedure to evaluate applicants because some categories of applicants might do better on the test than others. The Senators plainly believed that general intelligence and aptitude tests were job-related and meant to exempt them from the act for that reason. It is not surprising, therefore, that the Court's handling of the legislative history is halting and embarrassed.

*Griggs* has already been interpreted very broadly by lower federal courts to require a number of significant changes in public and private employment practices. There have been suggestions that *Griggs'* requirement of expensive validation of employment tests may cause firms to abandon testing and move to more subjective (and potentially more biased) methods of screening applicants—or, on the other hand, to proportional hiring on a racial basis in order to avoid charges of discrimination. Either way, the result contravenes the twofold legislative intention, which was to forbid preferential hiring on a racial basis and "to allow an employer's bona fide use of professionally developed tests despite their disparate impact on culturally disadvantaged minorities."

In its skepticism about aptitude tests and formal credentials, *Griggs* accords with some recent research questioning the predictive value of such requirements for job performance. But *Griggs* cannot be understood as a traditional exercise in statutory exegesis.[2]

The second example is *Lau* v. *Nichols*. *Lau* arose under Title VI of the Civil Rights Act of 1964, which forbids discrimination on grounds of "race, color, or national origin" in "any program or activity receiving federal financial assistance." As a condition of federal aid, the Department of Health, Education, and Welfare had required school districts to "take affirmative steps to rectify the language deficiency" of "national-origin minority group children" unable to speak and understand English. So enlarged by the regulations, the act was read by the Supreme Court, 9–0, to require the San Francisco school system to take some action to rectify the language deficiencies of some 1,800 Chinese-American pupils (most of them born in the United States) who do not speak English.

The decision has already had important consequences across the nation. Indeed, it is one of the ironies of *Lau* that, though it was rendered in the case of Chinese-origin pupils, it will affect primarily the rights of Spanish-speaking children all over the United States. The decision has been widely interpreted—erroneously—as *requiring* "bilingual-bicultural" education, rather than remedial instruction in English. Stimulated by *Lau*, the Texas legislature has recently enacted a law making bilingual education mandatory in schools with twenty or more children whose ability in English is limited, and there are movements for bilingual education in several other states. The decision will no doubt affect instructional programs and language choice across the nation.

*Lau* may be interpreted as a judicial experiment. The Court did not hold that any particular action was required of the school system—only that inaction was forbidden. The case was remanded to the district court for the fashioning of relief, and the Court may have thought there would be time enough for a second look after a decree was entered.

This may explain the offhanded way in which the case was disposed of, for the majority and concurring opinions contain no serious discussion of the central issues of the litigation: whether it constitutes discrimination to teach all pupils in English regardless of their fluency at the time they enter school and whether, in any event, linguistic discrimination constitutes discrimination on the basis of "race, color, or national origin." Discrimination is generally thought of as differential treatment. What was complained of in *Lau* was the failure to differentiate in the instruction given pupils fluent in Chinese and not fluent in English. Similarly, linguistic loyalty and national origin are related but are not the same thing. No claim was made in *Lau* that Chinese-origin pupils were affected adversely by the policies of the school system—only that monolingual, Chinese-speaking pupils (most of whom had their "national origin" in the United States) were so affected. There is little in the language of Title VI to suggest that it contemplates affirmative action to remedy linguistic deficiencies, and there is nothing in the legislative history that hints at such a purpose.

These two seminal decisions of the Burger Court—neither of which drew a single dissent—should suffice to show that judicial participation in the making of social policy is no ephemeral development. It is part of a chain of developments that can survive the vicissitudes of constitutional "activism" and "restraint." No one could mistake these decisions for "interstitial" statutory interpretation, since they are departures from the language and legislative history of the statutes they construe. Nor does it need to be stressed that these decisions were not solely the work of judges who "view themselves as holding roving commissions as problem solvers." That they do not so regard themselves attests to the structural and enduring character of the phenomena I have been describing.

The appropriate scope of judicial power in the American system of government has periodically been debated, often intensely. For the most part, what has been challenged has been the power to declare legislative and executive action unconstitutional. Accordingly, the debate has been cast in terms of legitimacy. A polity accustomed to questioning unchecked power views with unease judicial authority to strike down laws enacted by democratically elected legislatures. Where, after all, is the accountability of life-tenured judges? This question of democratic theory has been raised insistently, especially in times of constitutional crisis, notably in the 1930s and again in the 1950s.

The last word has not been heard in these debates, and it will not soon be heard. The structure of American government guarantees the issue a long life. But, for the moment, the debate seems to have waned with the growing recognition that these are elements of overstatement in the case against judicial review. The courts are more democratically accountable, through a variety of formal and informal mechanisms, than they have been accused of being. Equally important, the other branches are in many ways less democratically accountable than they in turn were said to be by those who emphasized the special disabilities under which judges labor. Hence the many academic discussions of the need for "representative bureaucracy," for a less insular presidency, and for reform of the procedures and devices that make Congress undemocratic internally and unrepresentative externally. (That students of any single institution often tend to see that institution as the flawed one is a useful indication of the limited perspective that comes from single-minded attention to any one institution. It should properly make us chary of drawing inferences about the courts without an institutionally comparative frame of reference.)

As the debate over the democratic character of judicial review wanes, there is another set of issues in the offing. It relates not to legitimacy but to capacity, not to whether the courts *should* perform certain tasks but to whether they *can* perform them competently.

Of course, legitimacy and capacity are related. A court wholly without capacity may forfeit its claim to legitimacy. A court wholly without legitimacy will soon suffer from diminished capacity. The cases for and against judicial review have always rested in part on assessments of judicial capacity: on the one hand, the presumably superior ability of the courts "to build up a body of coherent and intelligible constitutional principle"; on the other, the presumably inferior ability to courts to make the political judgments on which exercises of the power of judicial review so often turn. If the separation of powers reflects a division of labor according to expertise, then relative institutional capacity becomes relevant to defining spheres of power and particular exercises of power.

The recent developments that I have described necessarily raise the previously subsidiary issue of capacity to a more prominent place. Although the assumption of new responsibilities can, as I have observed, be traced to exercises of the traditional power to declare laws unconstitutional, they now transcend that power. Traditional judicial review meant forbidding action, saying "no" to the other branches. Now the judicial function often means requiring action, and there is a difference between foreclosing an alternative and choosing one, between constraining and commanding. Among other things, it is this difference, and the problematic character of judicial resources to manage the task of commanding, that make the question of capacity so important.

Yet judicial intervention in matters of social policy has greatly increased and will not soon decrease. This expansion of judicial responsibility means, first, a broadening of the sphere of judge-made law into areas that might once have been called "social welfare" and were not considered "legal" at all. It also means an expansion of the scope for judicial initiative within these areas. Courts are no longer as confined to the interstices of legislation as they once were—now the statute is often a mere point of departure—and they are no longer as inhibited as they once were from delving into supervisory or administrative responsibilities in connection with the remedies they award. They are more often found requiring detailed, affirmative, and specific action than previously. They are less constrained, too, by the limitations of the cases and the litigants before them. More openly, self-consciously, and broadly than before, the courts are engaged in efforts to shape or control the behavior of identifiable social groups, groups not necessarily before the court: welfare administrators, employers, school officials, policemen.

What this means is that there is somewhat less institutional differentiation today than two decades ago. There is now more overlap between the courts and Congress in formulating policy and between the courts and the executive in both formulating and carrying out programs. That is, the types of decisions being made by the various institutions—their scope and level of generality—seem to be converging somewhat, though the processes by which the decisions are made and the outcomes of those processes may be quite different—as different as the groups who maneuver to place an issue before one set of decision makers rather than another, or who, defeated in one forum, turn hopefully to the next, believe them to be. Thus, to say that there is convergence in the business of courts and other institutions is not tantamount to saying that it makes no difference who decides a question. On the contrary, it matters a good deal, for the institutions are differently composed and organized. The real possibility of overlapping responsibilities but opposite outcomes makes the policy process a more complex and drawn-out affair than it once was.

The recency, the incompleteness, and the incremental history of these developments should not obscure their portentousness. It is just possible that these modifications in the scope of judicial power will one day amount to a major structural change. We regard as quaintly and unduly restrictive the medieval conception of legislation as mere restatement of customary law. Future generations may likewise view our distinctive association of adjudication with the grievances of individual litigants as an equally curious affectation.

It may be, of course, that something much less significant than this is in the offing. For the purposes of this discussion, it makes little difference. The changes of degree that are already visible are quite enough to raise important questions about the consequences of using the judicial process for the resolution of social policy issues.

Many of the most serious questions relate to the way in which courts get their information. Consider the position of the judge. His formal function is to decide a dispute between two parties, a role for which his training and experience generally equip him well. The legal rules and machinery through which the judge works are also geared to the controversy between the parties. Virtually all of the conventions of litigation leave the initiative to the parties. What they elicit, the judge hears. What they neglect, he neglects. The rules of evidence are also designed with the litigants' case, and that alone, in mind. Evidence about their relationship, their characteristics, their transactions, is generally relevant and admissible. Evidence about more general conditions is often inadmissible and, when admissible, is treated far more circumspectly, both by the law and by the judges who apply it.

Most of the time these rules and conventions are well adapted to the business of the courts. Focusing on litigants and their controversy is perfectly appropriate when their own controversy is all that is at stake. But when questions of social policy arise in the guise of a lawsuit, that is another matter. Then the controversy between the litigants is really secondary to the larger questions that their lawsuit raises. The judge can learn all there is to learn about the parties and their dispute without being very much wiser about the general problem their case is said to reflect.

As a matter of fact, the judge may be seriously misled if he pays close attention to the facts of the case before him, for that case is almost surely unrepresentative of the general class of cases it is supposed to represent. Enough is known about when and why people bring suit to know that the average plaintiff is not just like everybody else with a similar problem. No lawyer who seeks a favorable decision in welfare rights or prison reform or any other field will, if given a choice, be content to bring just a run-of-the-mill case to court. Instead, he will choose the worst case, the most extreme case, that comes his way.

So the cases that come to court are by no means typical, and a judge who masters the facts of the case before him has at best a very rough—and sometimes stereotyped—idea of the dimensions of his policy problem. How the courts are to inform themselves of the diverse social conditions that are increasingly relevant to decision is a question that insistently demands an answer.

The judge's difficulties, however, only begin there. After he is convinced that some unlawfulness has been identified, a remedy has to be devised. At this point, the judge, like all other policy makers, has gone into the prediction business. He has to sense what is required to get the results he aims at, and he must forecast the consequences of various alternative decrees that might be formulated.

Yet the same rules, conventions, and procedure that focus the judge's attention on the litigants and the history of their controversy also focus the judge on the past more than the future. Since court decisions declare rights and duties arising out of previous transactions, the framing of the decree usually gets far less meticulous attention than does proof of the "wrongs" which give rise to the decree. Litigation tends to be backward looking, and orienting it toward forecasting is no simple matter.

Questions also remain about the way in which court orders are carried out. Accustomed to thinking in terms of "compliance" or "noncompliance," judges do not necessarily sense the scope that exists for effectuating a judicial decree in one way rather than another. Yet what happens to a decree after it leaves the courthouse is every bit as important as what has gone before.

In fact, the accessibility and rationality of the judicial process may lead the participants to think that the problem of implementation is more straightforward than it is. One reason the policy issue is in court at all may be that action on it has been thwarted in the other branches of government by the myriad influences and interests that are represented there. In court, fewer interests are represented, and fewer still are in a position to thwart action. Hence the attractiveness of the judicial forum for groups that find it hard to get their way in the other branches.

The judicial process thus reduces the number of participants and makes it possible to cut through to an apparent solution. But the courts cannot make the complex pattern of interests disappear altogether. If all the parties who have some stake in a policy decision one way or the other are not fully represented in court, they may nonetheless reappear and make their influence felt at the implementation stage. And so the judge who decrees this or orders that may later find that he has in fact produced something rather different from what he had in mind. The simplification of social and political complexity that occurs in the courtroom is only temporary.

After a number of such experiences, sensitive judges may well wonder whether the institution over which they preside, admirably suited as it is to processing individual cases, is really the right setting in which to thrash out the perplexing social policy questions that increasingly come to court. Some judges may begin to think of ways to augment their capacity; others may prefer to emphasize the venerable canons of judicial restraint. And some may ultimately come to embrace Jeremy Bentham's blunt assertation that "amendment from the judgment seat is confusion."

### Notes

1. Stuart Scheingold, *The Politics of Rights: Lawyers, Public Policy, and Political Change.* Yale University Press, 1974, p. 126.
2. It is interesting to note that the Court has recently declined to extend the rigorous *Griggs* standards for employment tests to cases arising under the Constitution rather than under Title VII. This may suggest that the majority is unhappy with what the lower courts have done with *Griggs* and wishes to confine the impact of the decision. But it is also consistent with the thesis that some justices are willing to be bolder in statutory interpretation than in constitutional interpretation.

# Social Science and the Courts

Daniel Patrick Moynihan

From the time, at the beginning of the century, that American legal scholars and jurists began to speak of the "science of law" it was rather to be assumed that the courts would in time find themselves involved with the social sciences. This was perhaps more a matter of probability than of certainty, for it was at least possible that the "legal realists," or "progressive realists," as they are variously denominated, would have found the social science of that and subsequent periods insufficiently rigorous for their standards—a case at least some social scientists, then as now, would have volunteered to make for them. But Pound and Cardozo and Holmes were indeed realists, and seemingly were prepared to make do with what was at hand, especially when there was such a correspondence with the spirit and structure of their own enterprise.

In 1908, Pound in a seminal article, "Mechanical Jurisprudence," in the *Columbia Law Review* declared: "We have . . . the same task in jurisprudence that has been achieved in philosophy, in the natural sciences, and in politics. We have to . . . attain a pragmatic, a sociological legal science."

This passage suggests, of course, an alternative explanation for the easy acceptance of the social sciences by the lawyers: to wit, that Pound and his associates were not themselves intolerably rigorous. For what else are we to think of the suggestion, even in 1908, that philosophy and politics had been advancing arm and arm with the natural sciences toward some presumed methodological maturity!

Equally we may wonder at the legal realists' seeming perception of "natural law" as pre-scientific. It may have been for them, but it was nothing of the sort to the framers of the Constitution, for whom "natural law," as we think of it, and scientific law were parts of an integrated understanding of the behavior of both physical objects and human beings. As the late Martin Diamond has reminded us, the framers' respect for human rights, which constituted liberty as they understood it, was not an idiosyncratic "value" of a remote culture. Rather, liberty was seen as *the* primary political good, of whose goodness any intelligent man would convince himself if he knew enough history, philosophy, and science. Indeed, it was because our constitutional principles seemed so self-evident, so much at harmony with the results of enquiry in other fields, that the Founders felt such confidence in them.

But this is perhaps to cavil. The point is that as between the legal scholars and jurists of two and three generations ago, who were seeking to establish a "science of law," and those seeking to establish scientific principles and methods in, say, sociology, there was indeed that symmetry of technique and purpose which Paul Horgan has observed in the arts and sciences of most eras.

There was a corresponding bustle of organization and the discovery of like-mindedness among persons who may have thought themselvs quite alone in their new and sometimes radical purposes. At the same time that a new judicial philosophy was

Reprinted with permission from *The Public Interest,* No. 54 (Winter 1979) pp. 12–31. Copyright 1979 by National Affairs, Inc.

making its appearance, the social sciences were organizing themselves. The Anthropological Association was founded in 1902; the American Political Science Association in 1903; the American Sociological Association in 1905. The innovators in the legal and academic realms were, in the popular saying of the period, made for each other.

### Progressive Realism

Even so, the process whereby social science argument became more prominent in the proceedings and decisions of American courts was gradual, and followed the equally gradual rise to ascendency of the "progressive realists," to use Alexander M. Bickel's term, from whom, as he wrote, "the Warren Court traced its lineage."

In its most famous decision, *Brown v. Board of Education* (1954), the Warren Court drew upon a spectrum of social science—ranging from discrete psychological experiments to broad-ranging economic and social enquiry—in reversing the Court's earlier ruling in *Plessy v. Ferguson* (1896), which had established the separate-but-equal standard in racial matters. Taking their lead from the Supreme Court, subordinate Federal courts began to resort to social-science findings to guide all manner of decisions, especially in the still troubled field of schooling, but extending to questions of tax policies, of institutional confinement and care, of crime and punishment, and a hitherto forbidding range of ethical issues.

Social science had become familiar to the courts in the course of hearing advocacy before them. From the time that Louis D. Brandeis began to argue facts and figures before various courts—arguing, however, for judicial restraint in the face of legislation establishing minimum labor standards—judges had had to contend with social-science arguments presented *to* them. Brandeis's data consisted in the main of social statistics, the early measurement devices on which most subsequent social research has been based. But it should be emphasized that the "Brandeis brief" did not assert that its view of the facts was totally accurate; its purpose was merely to demonstrate that the legislature, in acting as it did, had a reasonable basis, that the facts *might* be accurate in holding, for example, that minimum standards were necessary to protect workers' health.

The Supreme Court itself soon became accustomed to and comfortable with this kind of brief. The Court's capacity to cope with social-science arguments was much on display, for example, in *Witherspoon v. Illinois* (1968). At issue was the constitutionality of an Illinois statute providing for the exclusion of jurors having scruples against the death penalty. Mr. Justice Stewart, for the Court, took note of the social-science arguments presented by those contending that the statute was illegal:

> To support this view, the petitioner refers to what he describes as 'competent scientific evidence that death-qualified jurors are partial to the prosecution on the issue of guilt or innocence.'

The Justice, in a footnote, took further note of the academic papers—nicely and accurately describing them as "surveys"—which the petitioners had presented. He went on, however, to declare:

> The data adduced by the petitioner . . . are too tentative and fragmentary to establish that jurors not opposed to the death penalty tend to favor the prosecution in the determination of guilt.

In a footnote to this passage, the Justice commented on these studies in language that will be familiar to graduate student and thesis committee alike:

> We can only speculate . . . as to the precise meaning of the terms used in those studies, the accuracy of the techniques employed, and the validity of the generalizations made.

Having thus acquitted itself in the matter of methodological rigor, and having in effect rejected the social-science data presented by the petitioners, the Court went on to rule *for* them, and to rest its decision on *other* social-science data! Specifically, Justice Stewart found that ours is a nation "less than half of whose people believe in the death penalty." To establish this he cited opinion polls for the year 1966, as compiled in the *International Review on Public Opinion,* and judged that an Illinois jury culled of "all who harbor doubts about the wisdom of capital punishment" would thus speak only "for a distinct and dwindling minority." Accordingly, the statute was deemed to fail under the Sixth Amendment.[1]

### Law, Social Science, and the Future

In these changed—or perhaps it were better to say these now developed—circumstances it would seem useful to suggest, from the point of view of the social sciences, something of the limitations of this kind of information in the judicial process. If it is quite clear that the courts employ social science with considerable deftness on some occasions, then it must be allowed that on other occasions the courts have got themselves into difficult situations by being too casual, even trusting, about the "truths" presented to them by way of research on individual and group behavior. Here it is not necessary to get into the question of where the courts might have erred. If there are those who wish to challenge particular decisions, they are free to do so under the arrangements so ably, indeed wonderfully, presided over by the American judiciary itself. It is enough to state that the social science involved in a great many judicial decisions—including, for that matter, *Brown* itself—has been sharply criticized by social scientists with differing or competing views.

Hence there are two points which a social scientist would ask jurists to consider before deciding how much further to proceed, and in what direction:

*The first point is that social science is basically concerned to predict future events, whereas the purpose of the law is to order them.* In this respect both are unavoidably entangled with politics which, as Maurice Cranston has put it, is an argument about the future. But where social science seeks to establish a fixity of *relationships* such that the consequences of behavior can be known in advance—or, rather, narrowed to a manageable range of possibilities—law seeks to dictate future performance on the basis of past *agreements*. It is the business of the law, as it were, to order alimony payments; it is the business of social science to try to estimate the likelihood of their being paid, or their effect on work behavior and remarriage in male and female parties, or similar probabilities.

In the end social science *must* be a quantitative discipline dealing with statistical probabilities. Law, by contrast, enters the realm of the merely probable at some risk. For the law, even when dealing with the most political of issues, must assert that there are the firmest, established grounds in past settlements on which to order future settlements. The primary social function of the courts is to preserve the social peace embodied in such past settlements, and to do this by establishing a competent, disinterested forum to which parties in dispute can come, ask, and be told *what it was we agreed to.* Hence Marshall's dictum in *Marbury v. Madison:* "It is emphatically the province and duty of the judicial department to say what the law *is.*"

To restate, for emphasis: The courts are very much involved with the future; indeed to declare the future is what they do, and not infrequently they do so in the largest conceivable terms. (Bickel writes that the Warren Court "like Marshall's, may for a time have been an institution seized of a great vision, that it may have glimpsed the future, and gained it.") But the basis for ordering the future is that which the judges conclude were the standards and agreements reached in the past for the purpose of such future ordering.

Hence, also, the concern of the courts to be seen to be above politics. If they are to keep the King's peace they had best not be seen to be involved in planning the King's wars. And so long as the courts confine their references to established *past* agreements—constitutions, customs, statutes, contracts—they are protected by the all-important circumstance that among the things we have agreed to is that for these purposes *the past is what the courts say it is.* It is a living past, and clearly enough it changes, but only the courts can make these changes. It is all very well for others to have opinions about what the Sixth Amendment intends with respect to the composition of juries, but it is what Justice Stewart says, in the company of a sufficient number of his colleagues, that decides, *and there is no way to disprove him.* In this sense, what the court decrees to be the past thereupon has the consequence of *being* the past. On the other hand, when the courts get into the business of predicting the *future* by the use of various social-science techniques for doing this, then others, who need not be lawyers even, much less judges, can readily dispute them, and events will tell who is right and who is wrong.

In this circumstance, perhaps the first thing a jurist will wish to know about the social sciences is: How good are they? How well do they predict? Have they attained to any of the stability that Pound observed in the natural sciences in the early years of the century? The answer must be that the social sciences are labile in the extreme. What is thought to be settled in one decade is as often as not unsettled in the very next; and even that "decent interval" is not always observed. Consider, for example, the cycles of professional opinion concerning the desirability of putting persons with various behavior disorders in institutions, as against maintaining them in their communities. True, there are some areas of stability. With a sample of 500 or so persons, a "psephologist" can predict the popular vote in a Presidential election within a few percentage points. But who will foretell the fate of the administration that follows?

It is fair to state that the unsettled condition of the social sciences represents something of a disappointment, even a surprise. It was thought, especially in economics, that matters were much further advanced than they now appear to be. With respect to the slow progress, or nonprogress, of the social sciences a range of explanations is put forward. It is said that the subject matter is more complex than that of the physical sciences. Experimental modes are usually unattainable. The disciplines are relatively new. They probably have not attracted their share of the best talent. Other reasons come readily enough to mind. But the fact of slow progress is clear enough. The judiciary is entitled to know this, for it needs to acquire the habit of caution, the more perhaps when the work presented to it declares itself to be the most rigorous and "scientific."

Consider the venerable, yet always troubled and constantly shifting "advice" which social science has to offer in the matter of crime and punishment, a subject of the greatest relevance to the judiciary. For the longest while, 20th-century criminology, such as it was, tended to hold that capital punishment did not deter capital crimes. This tendency persisted until the 1960's, when a number of empirical analyses appeared which seemed to establish a "negative association between the level of punishment and the crime rate." Concepts borrowed from economics were employed, often with great elegance, and once again (!) it was discovered that as price goes up demand goes down. We began to talk of the "elasticity of the crime rate to changes in the probability of imprisonment." Next, studies appeared which seemed to establish that capital punishment *saved lives,* as it were, by preventing subsequent capital crimes. This was important and responsible research, and bid fair to make a considerable impression on public and even judicial policy, coming as it did at a time when the courts were banning capital punishment and elements in the public began to demand its return.

In 1976, however, the National Academy of Sciences established a panel to study the relation between crime rates and the severity of punishments. Two years later, the panel concluded that "the available studies provide no useful evidence on the deterrent effect of capital punishment." Thus, research lends support to the decision of the Supreme Court in *Gregg v. Georgia* (1976), in which Justice Stewart, for the Court, declared:

> Statistical attempts to evaluate the worth of the death penalty as a deterrent to crimes by potential offenders have occasioned a great deal of debate. The results simply have been inconclusive.

It could perhaps be argued that Justice Stewart was judging just a little ahead of the evidence, *Gregg* having preceded the NAS panel report by two years. But if it is accepted that the Courts ought to be hesitant to the point of reluctance before accepting any social-science finding as final, Justice Stewart's 1976 cautionary decision seems warranted indeed.

For it is a melancholy fact that, recurrently, even the most rigorous efforts in social science come up with devastatingly imprecise stuff. Thus, a few lines after the *Summary* of the National Academy of Sciences study informed us in plain enough language that execution may or may not deter murder, another murkier passage sums up the evidence on the effect of imprisonment on other kinds of crime:

> Since the high-crime jurisdictions that are most likely to be looking to incapacitation to relieve their crime problems also tend to have relatively lower rates of time served per crime, they can expect to have the largest percentage increases in prison populations to achieve a given percentage of reduction in crime.

As English composition, the sentence itself calls for punishment of some sort. To say that high-crime jurisdictions can expect to "have" the largest percentage increases in prison populations, rather than to "require" them or some equivalent term, is to leave the reader with a sense of surpassing fuziness that all manner of mathematical notation does not overcome. Or conceal. Thus, further in the same study, we are told that the lower bound on the probability of arrest for an "index" offense is given by the formula

$$q\wedge > \quad \frac{\lambda q \wedge T\left(\dfrac{V}{A}\right)}{\dfrac{C}{A} - \dfrac{V_1}{A}}$$

and we are also told that if prison use is expanded there is a potential for "two to fivefold decreases in crime." Now one need not be much of a mathematician to know that a twofold decrease in anything will likely lead to antimatter, and that a fivefold decrease might well produce a black hole.

The profession, in a word, has a way to go.

### Social Science and Politics

*The second point is that social science is rarely dispassionate, and social scientists are frequently caught up in the politics which their work necessarily involves.* The social sciences are, and have always been, much involved with problem-solving and, while there is often much effort to disguise this, the assertion that a "problem" exists is usually a political statement that implies a proposition as to who should do what for (or to) whom. (This essay, for example, which suggests that there are limits to the value which social science can have for the courts, will almost certainly be searched for clues as to whether its implications are politically liberal, or conservative, or whatever.) Social scientists are never more revealing of themselves than when challenging the objectivity of one another's work. In some fields almost *any* study is assumed to have a more-or-less-discoverable political purpose.

Moreover, there is a distinct social and political bias among social scientists. In all fairness, it should be said that this is a matter which social scientists are quick to acknowledge, and have studied to some purpose. It all has to do, one suspects, with the orientation of the discipline toward the future: It attracts persons whose interests are in shaping the future rather than preserving the past. In any event, the pronounced "liberal" orientation of sociology, psychology, political science, and similar fields is well established.

This observation, however, leads us to one of the ironies of the present state of the social sciences. The explanatory power of the various disciplines is limited. Few serious permanencies are ever established. In a period of civilization in which the physical sciences are immensely advanced, when the methodology of proof is well established, and when discoveries rush one upon the other, there are not many things social science has to say. To the degree that it strives for the rigor of the physical sciences, its characteristic product is the null hypothesis, i.e., the discovery that two social phenomena are *not* causally related. In some circumstances this can be rather liberating for social policy. There are, for example, few recent works in social science that have had the immediate impact of James Q. Wilson's *Thinking About Crime.* After examining the research concerning the effect of rehabilitation programs on criminals in this country and abroad, Wilson concluded that no consistent effects could be shown one way or the other. Seemingly, all that could be established for certain about the future behavior of criminals is that when they are in jail they do not commit street crimes. Two centuries of hopes collapsed in that proposition, and not a few illusions. But out of the wreckage came the idea that fixed and predictable prison terms are a sensible social policy, and in short order this was being advocated across the spectrum of political opinion. Indeed, if anything, while social scientists tend to be liberal, the tendencies of social-science *findings* must be judged conservative, in that they rarely point to the possibilities of much more than incremental change. In 1959 the Yale political scientist Charles Lindblom set this forth as a necessity, the one *law* of social change, in a celebrated article entitled "The Science of Muddling Through."

The political orientation of the social sciences has been particularly evident (and is, I believe, least objectionable) in the shifting fashions in research topics. One will find a score of books, mostly of the period 1910–1950, about trade unions and strikes for every serious study of a middle-class organization such as the American Bar Association. But it is also to be noted that these preferences change with some regularity. Trade unions, having been judged "conservative," are not much written about any longer. Of late, community organizations, such as those funded by government anti-poverty efforts, have been in vogue. Tomorrow, doubtless, it will be something else again.

This is not to be understood to suggest any deliberate attempt to distort. One has little more than impressions to offer here, but it seems mostly to be a matter of a somewhat-too-ardent searching for evidence that will help sustain a hoped-for conclusion. Sometimes the search succeeds; just as often it does not. Where there is deliberate fudging in the research, success is brief and retaliation can be truly termed draconian. The social sciences are serious professions, seeking to become ever more professional. They are also highly competitive, at times perhaps damagingly so. Edward C. Banfield has described this as the Fastest-Gun-in-the-West-Effect—which is to say, the melancholy knowledge of anyone briefly on top of any particular subject matter that the graduate schools are abrim with young scholars who dream of making their own reputations by bringing him down in a brief, violent encounter. Such efforts may or may not succeed. But *anyone* who brings questionable data or methodology into the various fields can expect to be devastated. And even the most impeccable work will be challenged simply because "it is there."

The prudent jurist will be aware of this, and take it into account. That this can be done was splendidly demonstrated by the Supreme Court in its decision in *San Antonio School District v. Rodriguez* (1973). Here a class action on behalf of certain Texas schoolchildren was instituted against school authorities challenging the constitutionality, under the equal protection clause of the 14th Amendment, of the state's system of financing public education. The system was characterized by a heavy reliance on local property taxes, which is associated with substantial differences in per-pupil expenditure. Now it happens that just a very few years before this issue came to the

Court, a series of research findings appeared which were quite devastating to the previous assumption that achievement in education was more or less a direct function of spending. Best understood, this new research seemed to show that, after a point, this just wasn't so.[2]

The *Rodriguez* case was the culmination of an effort, primarily the work of academics, to disestablish the general American pattern of local-school-district financing in favor of statewide, or even nation-wide systems, with uniform per-pupil expenditures. (In passing, it may be noted that moving an issue *upwards* in the federal system has been well documented by political scientists to be a technique of effecting social reform.) In briefest summary, these scholars did not anticipate that their research establishing differentials in school expenditure would be vitiated, at least in part, by the enquiries that were simultaneously taking place which cast grave doubt on just what significance was to be attributed to such differences.

In any event, the matter did not escape the attention of Justice Powell, who, writing for the majority, observed:

> On even the most basic questions in this area the scholars and educational experts are divided. Indeed, one of the major sources of controversy concerns the extent to which there is a demonstrable correlation between educational expenditures and the quality of education—an assumed correlation underlying virtually every legal conclusion drawn by the District Courts in this case.

Further on, Justice Powell declared, "We are unwilling to assume for ourselves a level of wisdom superior to that of legislators, scholars, and educational authorities in 50 states," and found that the Texas system of school financing met the constitutional standard of the equal protection clause. It is not necessary to side either with the majority or the dissenting justices in this latter judgment to state with some confidence that, if the District Courts depended over-much in their decisions on the existence of a "demonstrable correlation between educational expenditures and the quality of education"—which Justice Powell says they did, and no dissenting Justice said they did not—then the District Courts either did not know their social science or, perhaps, did not know their social scientists.

### The Impact of Social Science

The attentive reader might well be given pause by the somewhat remonstrative suggestion that "the District Courts . . . did not know their social science." Since when, it might well be asked, has this been required of judges? Is it not sufficiently demanding to expect that they will know the law?

No, alas, it is not. Herewith we encounter what is arguably the major impact of social science on law.

The social sciences may be at an early state of development, but this has not in the least inhibited their assertiveness. It may well have served to abet it. For the moment their ambitions are truly imperial. There is little by way of human behavior which the social sciences do no *in theory* undertake to explain, to account for.

As a result, there are fewer and fewer areas of social behavior for which traditional or "common-sense" explanations will any longer suffice in serious argument. A cursory reading of the District Court decisions which preceded *Rodriguez* suggests that the judges' views on the relation of educational expenditure to educational achievement were based on nothing more than common-sense everyday opinion. And this is the point. Common-sense everyday opinion no longer persuades. Everybody asks: who *knows?* If it is theoretically possible to know something—and there are few relationships about which it is not theoretically possible to know *something*—then until the research is done, no one is in a very good position to speak!

If we may adopt for a moment the lawyers' term "material," then we may say that the range of what is material in lawsuits is now greatly expanded—or will be as the courts submit to the logic, or perhaps it may be better to speak of the spirit, of the social sciences. Some years ago Kenneth Boulding spoke of the advent of the social sciences as an historical event comparable for society to the beginnings of consciousness in human beings. That we are only at the beginning of this era does not at all limit what we expect of it; it may be, and probably is, the case that we greatly exaggerate. But that changes nothing as yet. The Supreme Court in *Rodriguez* found there was *no evidence* to support the charges. Accordingly, the Texas school-financing system was found Not Guilty. (Or was it a Scottish verdict: Not Proven?)

Thus does social science rend the "web of subjectivity," the phrase which Bickel used to describe aspects of the Warren Court. His references were primarily to the Court's reading of the past. On more than a few occasions, he wrote, "the Warren Court has purported to discover in the history of the Fourteenth Amendment, and of the Thirteenth, and of other constitutional provisions, the crutch that wasn't there." Now this can be seen to be a traditional enough critique. Here the Court interprets the past, and it is altogether to be expected that legal scholars should occasionally criticize the Court (however gently, in Bickel's case) for its interpretation of the past. But where the Court essays to predict the *future,* which is the realm of social science, the idiosyncratic and the subjective are even more conspicuous, and more subject to criticism.

As litigation concerning educational matters has illustrated some earlier propositions, it may do so also with respect to this last, most important one. Commencing at least with the *Brown* decision, the Supreme Court has held that "education is perhaps the most important function of state and local governments." But a decade prior to *Brown,* the Court ruled in *Everson v. Board of Education* (1947) that the First Amendment requires that government assistance to schools that are not in the public sector, strictly defined as not operated by government, must be severely restrained, and as near as possible nonexistent.

Here was a common enough situation for the courts. They were asked to determine what it is the Constitution decrees with respect to matters that clearly were remote from the thoughts of those who drafted the document, including its various amendments. Anyone who will trouble to read the debates concerning this part of the First Amendment—and this will not entail a great deal of trouble, for the question was debated for the equivalent of about a day in the House and a day in the Senate and the entire record in the *Annals of Congress* takes up only 119 lines—will find no mention of aid to education. Hence judges have had to interpret as best they could.

Now in the judgment of some, they have quite misinterpreted this history. In the manner that Bickel chides the Warren Court for discovering things in the history of the 13th and 14th Amendments that simply are not there, scholars such as Walter Berns, Michael Malbin, Antonin Scalia, and Philip Kurland find that, with respect to aid to nonpublic schools, the Court's interpretation of the establishment clause is non-historical. In his 1962 study, *Religion and the Law,* Philip Kurland writes: "Anyone suggesting that the answer, as a matter of constitutional law, is clear one way or the other is either deluding or deluded."

In the interest, once more, of full disclosure, I must state that I quite agree with the critics of the Court in this matter. In my view, the only *truly* comparable situation is that long period when the Supreme Court repeatedly claimed to find in the 14th Amendment a whole series of restrictions on the power of legislatures to enact labor legislation. Thus in *Lochner v. New York* (1905), the Court—striking down a 60-hour-work-week law—said that it was not at all "a question of substituting the judgment of the Court for that of the legislature," but simply that there was "no reasonable ground for interfering with the liberty of person or the right of free contract." Now there was no real difficulty in 1905 in discovering the purposes for which the 14th Amendment had been adopted, and establishing that it was in no wise enacted to prevent the New York State legislature from regulating the hours of bakers. But such nonsense had been solemnly invoked by the Supreme Court in *Allgeyer v. Louisiana* (1897) in the closing years of the 19th century and was only overruled in the fourth decade of the 20th century. It is all forgotten now, save by historians, but it was once a burning issue of American politics—as it should have been.

In just this manner, the establishment clause has been held to prevent legislatures from providing various forms of assistance to church-related schools, albeit that the establishment clause has the plain and unambiguous meaning—reflecting the Founders' intention—that Congress will not establish a national religion.

There are those who are not happy with this state of affairs, but few, one would venture, who are actively angry. We go through these things every so often, and have done so for generations. One day a Justice will come along who will make the equivalent point that Holmes made in *Lochner* when he declared, "The 14th Amendment does not enact Mr. Herbert Spencer's *Social Statics.*" It will come to be seen that the Court's rulings on aid to private schools merely reflected a particular religious point of view—i.e., that there is no public interest in the promotion of religion—which reached its peak of intellectual respectability in the 1920's and 1930's, the period in which most of the judges who made the decisions were educated.

Having stressed the shaky reliability of social science, a certain kind of fairness suggests that the infallibility of judges might usefully be questioned also. The establishment-clause decisions are an intellectual scandal. Without intending to do so, the courts in the school-aid cases have been imposing on the country their *own* religious views. This point was well understood in 1841 by John C. Spencer, Tocqueville's first American translator and New York's Secretary of State and Superintendent of Public Schools. To those who feared use of public funds for sectarian purposes, Spencer in an official report replied that all instruction is in some ways sectarian:

> No books can be found, no reading lessons can be selected, which do not contain more or less of some principles of religious faith, either directly avowed, or indirectly assumed.
>
> Even the moderate degree of religious instruction which the Public School Society imparts, must therefore be sectarian; that is, it must favor one set of opinions in opposition to another, or others; and it is believed that this always will be the result, in any course of education that the wit of man can devise.
>
> On the contrary, it would be in itself sectarian; because it would be consonant to the views of a peculiar class, and opposed to the opinions of other classes.

All this will be borne with sufficient good will and even good humor. The greater problem is for the courts, and it is a problem much complicated by social science. For social science affects what the court *can* say. Thus the case of *Tilton v. Richardson* (1971), which is the controlling decision regarding Federal aid to church-related schools. The Higher Education Facilities Act of 1963 provided Federal construction grants for college and university facilities. Tilton *et al.* sued, contending that grants to four church-related colleges and universities in Connecticut had the effect of promoting religion. The Court held that this was not so, even though it would never tolerate a Federal statute that provided construction grants to church-related high schools or suchlike institutions. Colleges and universities, the Court said, are different from elementary and secondary schools where religious matters are concerned, and college students are different from high school students.

### An Unassailable Argument

Before grappling with the decision of the majority, it will help to touch upon the dissent of Mr. Justice Douglas, who thought such aid to church-related colleges to be unconstitutional. It was an impassioned dissent: in his own words, a despairing dissent. The respect, he said, "which through history has been accorded the First Amendment is this day lost." Before coming to this sad conclusion, he presented an argument which some may view as wrong, but which is also logically quite—or almost—unassailable. By contrast, the less idiosyncratic decision of the majority is nonetheless indefensible, and it is a weakness which the advent of social science has brought about.

There is *one* unimpeachable sentence in Justice Douglas's opinion. "The First Amendment," he writes, "bars establishment of a religion." Just so. There was to be no established religion such as the Church of England or the Church of Ireland of that period. The meaning and intent of the amendment was most clear in the version considered by the House of Representatives on August 15, 1789, which read "no national religion shall be established by law." Elbridge Gerry objected, as the word "national" was a matter of contention between Federalists and Anti-Federalists, and the final version emerged, accessible in meaning to anyone who can read English. No established religion. Surely this has nothing to do with construction grants made available to religious institutions of *all* denominations. Hence a judge who is going to contend that it does, had best give considerable thought to what kinds of available evidence will tend to prove or disprove his contention. On this score Douglas was unassailable. He advanced arguments that some will find curious, but which none can refute.

To begin with, he would brook no distinction between levels of "parochial schools." They all looked alike to him. There is, he stated, a "dominant religious character" to all such schools. He then introduced in evidence the work of Loraine Boettner. A passage from Boettner's book, *Roman Catholicism,* is reproduced in a footnote. It should be clear, Boettner writes, "that a Roman Catholic parochial school is an integral part of that church." The title of ownership is vested in the bishop as an individual, a person "who is appointed by, who is under the direct control of, and who reports to the pope in Rome."

Now this "pope in Rome" is a person much on Mr. Boettner's mind. His book was published in Philadelphia in 1962, by the Presbyterian and Reformed Publishing Company, but it could as well have appeared in Edinburgh four centuries earlier. To him, very simply, the pope is an Antichrist; his church is an heretical church; its teachings utterly subversive of true religion. As for the followers of the pope, they are, in Boettner's view, to a greater or lesser degree, agents of papal subversion. On one page of his book, for example, he states that Roman Catholics ought not to be allowed to teach in *public* schools.

Boettner's full view of the matter, with respect to schools, is seen in another passage from this book which Douglas reproduces word for word in his concurring opinion in *Lemon v. Kurtzman* (1971):

> In the parochial schools Roman Catholic indoctrination is included in every subject. History, literature, geography, civics, and science are given a Roman Catholic slant. The whole education of the child is filled with propaganda. That, of course, is the very purpose of such schools, the very reason for going to all of the work and expense of maintaining a dual school system. Their purpose is not so much to educate, but to indoctrinate and train, not to teach scripture truths and Americanism, but to make loyal Roman Catholics. The children are regimented, and are told what to wear, what to do, and what to think.

Now here we are at the crux of the matter: Catholic schools do not "teach scripture truths." In Boettner's view Roman Catholic schools are heretical. In Douglas's view they are unconstitutional, i.e., they are not *Presbyterian*.

Now this is a venerable view, entertained over the years by many more Scotsmen than the Justice. Equally interesting is the passage that Douglas quotes in his dissent in *Tilton* from an article by Dr. Eugene Carson Blake which appeared in *Christianity Today* in 1959, the year after Blake completed his distinguished eight-year tenure as Stated Clerk of the General Assembly of the Presbyterian Church of the United States of America. (Douglas, to be quite fair, identifies him as "Dr. Eugene C. Blake of the Presbyterian Church.") Blake, who had studied in Edinburgh as a youth, had a lively imagination of the sort associated with that city. He had also, more rare, the gift of prophecy. It was his judgment that owing to the tax-exempt state of church properties "it is not unreasonable to prophesy that with reasonably prudent management, the churches ought to be able to control the whole economy of the nation within the predictable future." This alarmed him:

> That the growing wealth and property of the churches was partially responsible for revolutionary expropriations of church property in England in the 16th century, in France in the 18th century, in Italy in the 19th century, and in Mexico, Russia, Czechoslovakia, and Hungary (to name a few examples) in the 20th century, seems self-evident.

Now this is a range of historical reference which Gibbon would have admired, and in our time perhaps only Toynbee might have essayed. It is also of course gibberish, much as Boettner is . . . well, if not harmless, surely not serious. But these arguments are all but irrefutable. Boettner thinks the pope is an Antichrist. Douglas cites Boettner. *Who is to disprove them?* Blake thinks rich monasteries cause peasant revolts. Douglas cites Blake. *Who is to disprove them?* Douglas chose his ground well. He asserted a range of particular values and ultimate truths which he claimed to find in the Constitution; and that was that.

By contrast, the majority of the Court chose the most exposed arguments on which to rest its decision. The Chief Justice, for the majority, stated that "there are generally significant differences between the religious aspects of church-related institutions of higher learning and parochial schools." Two particular differences are cited. First, that religiously-affiliated colleges and universities do not attempt to indoctrinate their students while religiously-affiliated elementary and secondary schools do. Second, that college students are different, that "college students are less impressionable and less susceptible to religious indoctrination," that the "skepticism of the college student is not an inconsiderable barrier to any attempt to subvert the Congressional objectives and limitations."

Enter social science. For these are *researchable* subjects. The facts are *discoverable,* if not easily. It is no longer possible to make such statements and expect to be taken seriously unless one has proof.

The Court in a sense acknowledges this. Proofs are provided. One is tempted to observe that, as in the evocation of the Dreyfus case in *Penguin Island,* this was fatal. For what the Justices offer with respect to the assertion that "there are generally significant differences between the religious aspects of church-related institutions of higher learning and parochial elementary and secondary schools" is a *Harvard Law Review* article by Paul A. Freund. And what does Professor Freund report? He reports that "institutions of higher learning present quite a different question, mainly because church support is less likely to involve indoctrination and conformity at that level of instruction." The argument grows tautological. What is Freund's evidence? What studies? What survey data? *None.* No evidence of any kind. Freund is among the most distinguished legal scholars of the age. But it is not for anyone to describe the pedagogical practices of a group of colleges and universities without having inquired into the matter, preferably in accordance with reasonably well-established methodological rules. "Less likely," will not do. A modern bench requires harder data than that. Social science establishes new standards for what it is that can be taken as "self-evident," what, to use the words of the Court, "common observation would seem to support." This of course is a special problem for the Supreme Court. One cannot imagine that the bloopers of *Tilton* would have survived review—but with the Supreme Court there is no review.

Consider the second assertion, that "there is substance to the contention that college students are less impressionable and less susceptible to religious indoctrination." The Court again offers in evidence a *Harvard Law Review* article, this by Professor Donald A. Giannella. Again the tautology: Church-related colleges, Giannella writes, do not "attempt to form the religious character of the student by maintaining a highly controlled regime . . . to attempt such control of the college students is highly inappropriate, and would probably prove self-defeating." Again, no evidence, no data.

This kind of assertion by the Court is bound to be challenged. Anyone with any experience of a liberal-arts faculty would immediately suspect that psychologists would not have any reliable findings on a subject so vast as "impressionability to religious indoctrination." This almost surely would come under the heading of things researchable but not researched. The methodological problems, especially of definition, are clearly formidable.

And, indeed, in response to an enquiry which I sent, the 1978 President of the American Psychological Association, Professor M. Brewster Smith of the University of California, replied:

> There is no comparable comprehensive treatment of religious change over the high school years that I know of, and while surely a close search might turn up scattered studies, I think it is fair to say, in answer to your question, that solid evidence regarding the high school vs. college comparison in which you are interested *does not exist* (his italics).

Inasmuch as I have called the *Tilton* case into question in the course of Senate debate, allow me to be particularly explicit as to what I judge the Court to have done in this case. The Court's confidence in what some might call its "secularist" position on the establishment clause has declined steadily since it first pronounced on the matter in *Everson* in 1947. In *Tilton* it was trying to find grounds for allowing a clear intent of Congress to be carried out, and did so by distinguishing between higher-education facilities, which are the only ones affected by the law, and other facilities. But the point I would wish to make, for purposes of this essay, is that the Court, in an effort to base its decision on contemporary modes of argument, was rigorous but not rigorous enough. On examination, there is no evidence with which to support its finding. Justice Douglas, arguing in a prescientific mode, made no such mistake.

### A Great Wisdom

Is this distressing? Not, I think, unless one is distressed by the modern age. Primitive man, presumedly, had an explanation for everything. There is a sense, of course, in which science has made ignoramuses of us all. So much is *not* known. But modern man still does know more than his ancestors, even immediate ones, and we would do well to recall the saying of 19th-century Americans that "it's not ignorance that hurts, it's knowin' all those things that ain't so." Courts will learn to adapt to the changed conditions of evidence which social science imposes on contemporary argument. One would not be surprised, for example, to see the emergence of a group of lawyers trained in both disciplines, much as there are now specialists trained both as lawyers and as medical doctors. Indeed, lawyers with no more than a good undergraduate grounding in social-science methodology could have quite an impact in this area simply by establishing standards of cross-examination which are infrequently attained today.

This would be no small thing. To take yet another, and now concluding example from the field of education: Consider the controversy which broke out in the late 1970's over reinterpretations of the Equal Educational Opportunity Report, commonly known as the Coleman Report after its principal author, Professor James S. Coleman. In the late 1960's Coleman's data on pupil achievement were the basis for a number of major court decisions calling for school busing. Subsequently—in the familiar pattern—his initial interpretations were challenged. Much confusion and some bitterness followed. It is at least arguable that much of this might have been avoided had it been made clear to the courts, in the first place, either through exposition by plaintiffs or cross-examination by defendants, that Coleman had not found any race effect as such in his analysis of student-body characteristics and educational achievement. He had found a social-class effect.

Judges in the future should be able to look for such cross-examination. This will help them protect the special space that we give to the courts, for if there is one thing they don't need, it is another group of critics, claiming to know their tasks better than they.

One hopes it does not transgress any boundaries to suggest that these developments might also encourage in the courts a somewhat more easeful acceptance that, in the end, law is after all only long-established preference, codified opinion. When Pound and Cardozo and Holmes began talking of the "science of law," perhaps they, too, were mostly trying to impose a different set of opinions from those then prevailing. But at least they were doing so in an effort to get the bench back to the business of interpreting opinion as *embodied in legislation,* rather than as embodied in the education and social-class preferences of a particular body of judges. This was great wisdom, and this is precisely the import of Chief Justice Burger's decision in *Tennessee Valley Authority v. Hill* (1978) in which it was held that, inasmuch as the Tellico Dam would endanger the snail darter, it was prohibited by the Endangered Species Act. In civil but firm tones the Congress was informed that it must expect that, when called upon, the Court will enforce such laws as Congress enacts regardless of any individual appraisal of the wisdom or unwisdom of a particular course. Whether that was to be considered a warning or not will depend on one's judgment as to the balance of wisdom against unwisdom in recent Congressional enactments. But that it is the policy of the present Court, none need doubt. We may all take pleasure in the nice touch of the Chief Justice who closed his opinion not with a citation of social science, nor yet of any "science of law," but rather lines ascribed to Sir Thomas More by the contemporary playwright Robert Bolt: "The law, Roper, the law. I know what's legal, not what's right. And I'll stick to what's legal . . . I'm *not* God."

**Notes**

1. It may be that few persons will think of public-opinion polls as social science, but they represent one of our largest achievements in the field of direct measurement, having been developed largely by Lazarsfeld and his colleagues at Columbia University in the 1930's and 1940's.
2. In the interest, as lawyers say, of full disclosure, I should state that this is the intrepretation that Frederick Mosteller and I presented in a reanalysis of the Coleman data, in *On Equality of Educational Opportunity* (1972). Mr. Justice Powell cites our work, along with that of others, in a passage in his decision in *Rodriguez.*

# The Supreme Court as Republican Schoolmaster: Freedom of Speech, Political Equality, and the Teaching of Political Responsibility

Ralph A. Rossum

In the felicitous phrase of Professor Ralph Lerner, the Supreme Court is a "republican schoolmaster." It was intended by the Framers of the American Constitution to be "an educator, molder, and guardian of the manners, morals, and beliefs that sustain republican government."[1] Unfortunately, the Court has not always realized this noble intention. On occasion, what it has taught the citizenry has served more to jeopardize than to sustain republican principles. This paper explores the Court's teaching on one especially important principle: political responsibility. This principle has been selected because, as Professor Stephen Ross has observed:

> [How men] meet their responsibilities defines who and what they are. What men take themselves to be circumscribes the responsibilities they bear and how they meet them. What a man accepts as his responsibilities both represents what he takes himself to be and gives its character to what he will become in the future.[2]

This observation applies with no less force to the judiciary: What the Court takes men to be circumscribes the responsibilities they bear and how they meet them. What the Court accepts as a man's responsibilities both represents what it (and ultimately the man himself) takes that man to be and gives its character to what he will become in the future. The Supreme Court is, it must be emphasized, the leader of a "vital national seminar." Through its opinions, it teaches the citizenry its understanding of the basic principles of the American regime, including political responsibility. If the Court teaches that in the decisive respects men are fundamentally irresponsible, e.g., if it teaches that in many instances men are not to be held accountable or responsible for either their words or deeds, it should come as no surprise if this lesson is learned by the citizenry only too well. Moreover, neither should it be strange if this

Reprinted with permission of the author, Ralph A. Rossum.

teaching is followed by a substantial increase in judicial activism and, ultimately, by the emergence of what Nathan Glazer has called an "imperial judiciary." After all, why should a Supreme Court, guided by a "guardian ethic," have qualms about frustrating the wishes of a public that it knows to be decidedly irresponsible—a fact that it consistently confirms in its other opinions?[3]

This paper provisionally explores the Court's teaching on political responsibility as it is found in two distinct areas of civil liberties: freedom of speech and press and political equality.[4] These areas have been selected because they illustrate a consistency in the Court's approach to political responsibility, even on these widely divergent topics. Once they have been explored, the impact that this teaching has on the emergence of an imperial judiciary should be apparent.

### Freedom of Speech and Press

The guarantee of freedom of speech and press has been the object of a considerable amount of Court deliberation, but, as Justice Harlan pointed out in *Curtis Publishing Co.* v. *Butts,* the history of this guarantee has largely "been one of a search for the outer limits of that right." Little systematic consideration has been given by the Court to "the real problem of defining or delimiting the right itself."[5] Put simply, little attention has been focused on the purpose to be served or the end to be advanced by freedom of speech and press. Of course, statements by members of the Court can be found indicating that these First Amendment freedoms are to be understood as means to the end of self-government, i.e., that they have as their purpose to serve the political needs of a representative democracy that depends on free discussion of public affairs.[6] Justice Jackson is illustrative: The founding generation protected freedom of speech and press "because they knew no other way by which free men could conduct representative democracy."[7] With these words, he simply restated what Justice Sutherland and Thomas McIntyre Cooley had said before him: the first Amendment was designed to prevent "any action of the government by which it might prevent such free and general discussion of public matters as seems absolutely essential to prepare the people for an intelligent exercise of their rights as citizens."[8]

Increasingly, however, freedom of speech and press is no longer seen as a means "through which, in a free society, the process of popular rule may effectively function."[9] Rather, an analysis of contemporary Supreme Court opinions suggests that it has come to be viewed as a means to any end and even as an end in itself. Consideration of the "commercial speech" cases of *Bigelow* v. *Virginia,*[10] *Virginia State Board of Pharmacy* v. *Virginia Citizens Consumer Council,*[11] and *Bates* v. *State Bar of Arizona*[12] is instructive in this regard. Together, they have effectively overturned the Supreme Court's unanimous opinion in *Valentine* v. *Chrestensen*[13] that "the Constitution imposes no . . . restraint on government as respects purely commercial advertising"[14] and have bestowed the full protection of the First Amendment upon communications that may be simply characterized as "I will sell the X prescription drug at the Y price."[15]

*Bigelow* began the trend toward the protection of commercial speech. A seven member majority reversed a newspaper editor's conviction for violating a Virginia statute that made it a misdemeanor to circulate any publication that encouraged or promoted the processing of an abortion in Virginia. The defendant had published an advertisement in his newspaper that, in addition to announcing that abortions were legal in New York, offered the services of a referral agency in that state. The Court rejected the contention that the publication was unprotected because it was commercial. It called into question the continuing validity of *Chrestensen* and concluded that "the Virginia courts erred in their assumptions that advertising, as such, was entitled to no First Amendment protection."[16] As Justice Blackmun observed, "The relationship of speech to the marketplace of products or of services does not make it valueless in the marketplace of ideas."[17] Nonetheless, it did ultimately distinguish *Chrestensen*. It noted that "the advertisement published in appellant's newspaper did more than simply propose a commercial transaction. It contained factual material of clear 'public interest.'" According to the Court, "viewed in its entirety, the advertisement conveyed information of potential interest and value to a diverse audience—not only to readers possibly in need of the services offered, but also to those with a general curiosity about, or general interest in, the subject matter or the law of another State and its development, and to readers seeking reform in Virginia."[18] This emphasis on the subject matter of the advertising, however, left the status of commercial speech in considerable doubt, for, as Justice Rehnquist noted in his dissent, if the First Amendment protects "advertising, as such," "the subject of the advertisement ought to make no difference."[19]

Any confusion concerning a First Amendment exception for advertising was removed in *Virginia State Board of Pharmacy* v. *Virginia Citizens Consumer Council*. In that case, the Court considered a First Amendment challenge to a Virginia statute declaring that a pharmacist was guilty of "unprofessional conduct" if he advertised prescription drug prices. By subjecting guilty pharmacists to monetary penalties or suspension or revocation of licenses, the statute effectively prevented the advertising of prescription drug price information. The Court conceded that pharmacists who desired to advertise did not wish to report any particularly newsworthy fact or to comment on any cultural, philosophical, or political subject. Nonetheless, it held that commercial speech of that kind was entitled to the protection of the First Amendment and that the statute in question was void. Speaking for a seven member majority,[20] Justice Blackmun argued that a "particular customer's interest in the free flow of commercial information . . . may be as keen, if not keener by far, than his interest in the day's most urgent political debate."[21] It followed, for him, that commercial advertising was thereby protected by the First Amendment. Moreover, he argued, no line could be drawn "between publicly 'interesting' or 'important' commercial advertising and the opposite kind." After all,

> Advertising, however tasteless and excessive it sometimes may seem, is nonetheless dissemination of information as to who is producing and selling what product, for what reason, and at what price. So long as we preserve a predominantly free enterprise economy, the allocation of our resources in large measure will be made through numerous private economic decisions. It is a matter of public interest that those decisions, in the aggregate, be intelligent and well informed. To this end, the free flow of commercial information is indispensible.[22]

The consequences of Justice Blackmun's opinion are readily apparent. The ends served by the means of freedom of speech and press were increased to include the right of a merchant to go "door to door selling pots"[23] and "freedom for the ideas of the marketplace" has come to enjoy a parity of esteem with "freedom of the marketplace of ideas."[24]

Justice Rehnquist filed a lone dissent. As in *Bigelow,* he denied that the First Amendment offers the same protection to "the exchange of services" as to "the exchange of ideas."[25] In his estimation, the First Amendment is a means to the end of "enlightened public decision-making in a democracy." Thus, it is related to decisions "as to political, social, and other public issues, rather than the decision of a particular individual as to whether to purchase one or another kind of shampoo."[26] Responding directly to Justice Blackmun's majority opinion, Rehnquist acknowledged that "it is undoubtedly arguable that many people in the country regard the choice of shampoo as just as important as who may be elected to local, state, or national political office." But, he insisted, "that does not automatically bring information about competing shampoos within the protection of the First Amendment."[27] For Justice Rehnquist, "the importance in a 'predominantly free enterprise economy' of intelligent and well-informed decisions as to allocation of resources" is an insufficient basis for a First Amendment claim. While admitting that "there is much to be said for the Court's observation as a matter of desirable public policy," he insisted that "there is certainly nothing in the United States Constitution which requires the Virginia Legislature to hew to the teaching of Adam Smith in its legislative decisions regulating the pharmacy profession."[28]

Justice Rehnquist's fears that the Court's ruling in *Virginia State Board of Pharmacy* could not be confined to pharmacists but it would "likewise extend to lawyers, doctors, and all other professions"[29] were realized in *Bates,* in which the Court held that the disciplinary rule of the Arizona Supreme Court that prohibited attorneys from advertising in newspapers and other media was violative of the First Amendment. Justice Blackmun again spoke for the Court majority.[30] Reiterating the arguments he had made in *Virginia State Board of Pharmacy,* he stressed once more that "the consumer's concern for the free flow of commercial speech may often be far keener than his concern for urgent political dialogue" and that "commercial speech serves to inform the public of the availability, nature, and prices of products and services, and thus performs an indispensible role in the allocation of resources in a free enterprise system."[31] His assumptions remained the same; since freedom of speech and press is conceded to be a constitutionally protected means to the end of self-government, and since it is no less crucial a means to the end of the free enterprise system (considered by many people to be more important than self-government), freedom of speech and press ought therefore to be a constitutionally protected means to the end of free enterprise. In his dissent, Justice Rehnquist repeated his contention that the amount of protection that freedom of speech and press should receive is determined by the kinds of ends it serves. He concluded: "I would hold quite simply that the appellant's advertisement . . . is not the sort of expression that the Amendment was adopted to protect."[32]

As the ends that the Supreme Court has come to regard the First Amendment as serving have increased, so also have the means to these ends. As we have already noted, commercial speech is now a constitutionally protected means, even though it may be devoid of any cultural, philosophical, or political significance. Other examples also exist. To focus on just one of these, the Court has now come to consider profanity as likewise safeguarded by the First Amendment. In such cases as *Cohen* v. *California*,[33] *Rosenfeld* v. *New Jersey*,[34] and *Papish* v. *Board of Curators of the University of Missouri*[35] the Court has held that laws designed to preserve the tone of public discourse or to protect at even elemental levels the moral, aesthetic, and patriotic sensibilities of the community must fall.[36] The basic rationale for this conclusion is found in Justice *Harlan's* majority opinion in *Cohen.*

> Much linguistic expression serves a dual communicative function: It conveys not only ideas capable of relatively precise, detached explication, but otherwise inexpressible emotions as well. In fact, words are often chosen as much for their emotive as their cognitive force. We cannot sanction the view that the Constitution, while solicitous of the cognitive content of individual speech, has little or no regard for that emotive function which, practically speaking, may often be the more important element of the overall message sought to be communicated.[37]

Justice Harlan stressed that the emotive content of language can be fully as important as its intellectual content and that both are protected. It is significant to note, however, that what he described as being protected was "expression," not speech. Speech, after all, is connected with rationality, and it is man's rationality that makes him capable of governing himself and, ultimately, of participating collectively in self-government. Expression, on the other hand, is a much broader term and comes closer to describing the kinds of utterances the Court has brought within the range of First Amendment protection. Thus, although perhaps inadvertently, Justice Harlan paid honor to, while simultaneously repudiating, the sentiments of Wentworth Dillon, "Immodest words admit of no defense,/For want of decency is want of sense."[38]

Central to Justice Harlan's argument in *Cohen* is the Court's belief that any means, rational or otherwise, contributes to the "democratic dialogue" and is thereby protected.[39] This is the case because, as he concedes, "governmental officials cannot make principled distinctions in this area."[40] There is, the Court would have us believe, an "equality of status in the field of ideas."[41] In Justice Harlan's memorable language, "One man's vulgarism is another's lyric."[42] These, however, are curious sentiments for a body that was intended to serve as a "republican schoolmaster" and, by so doing, to educate, mold, and guard the "manners, morals, and beliefs" that sustain republican government.[43] If, as the Court argues, all political doctrines are to be tolerated because all are equal and none is erroneous, this in large part deprives the citizenry of the ability to evaluate regimes and serves to undermine their attachment to republican government.[44] Few cases illustrate this more forcefully than the Illinois State Supreme Court's opinion in *Village of Skokie* v. *National Socialist Party of America*.[45] The city fathers of Skokie, Illinois, a suburb of Chicago, sought to enjoin members of the American Nazi Party from marching in their village to commemorate the birthday of Adolf Hitler. The population of Skokie is overwhelmingly Jewish: Jews number over

40,000 of its 69,000 residents. Moreover, many of them survived, or lost relatives in, the Holocaust. Most of the Jewish refugees from Europe who came to the Chicago area between 1930 and 1960 settled there, and of the 12,000 members of Survivors of the Holocaust in metropolitan Chicago, 7,000 live in Skokie. The purpose of the Nazi march was readily apparent. It was not to recruit new members or to discuss abstract political ideas. Rather it was to subject these Jewish survivors and victims to still further torment. Nevertheless, the Illinois State Supreme Court refused to grant the injunction and held that the march must be permitted. It relied heavily on *Cohen* and quoted approvingly Justice Harlan's claim that "One man's vulgarism is another's lyric."[46] However, in light of the monstrous inhumanity that the march was intended to celebrate, the use of this language is astonishing. It suggests that to the Illinois Court, the Holocaust was a vulgarism at worst or a lyric at best. This moral obtuseness illustrates once again the truth of Thomas Reed Powell's words that "If you can think about something that is attached to something else, without thinking about what it is attached to, then you have what is called a legal mind."[47]

Important as this problem is, it points to a still larger one: the Court's willingness to expand the ends served by freedom of speech and press and even to increase the kinds of utterances that receive First Amendment protection has inevitably led to the view that freedom of speech and press is an end in itself.[48] This is especially true for those justices who have come to embrace either an absolutist or "clear and present danger" interpretation of the First Amendment. For them, freedom of speech and press is no longer seen as a means to the end of self government. Rather, it is an end in itself and must be preserved, even if it destroys republican government in the process. Justice Black's words in *Communist Party* v. *S.A.C. Board* are representative of this position: the remedy for the danger posed by advocating the violent overthrow of the government "must be the same remedy that is applied to the danger that comes from any other erroneous talk—education and contrary argument."[49] Moreover, "if that remedy is not sufficient, the only meaning of free speech must be that the revolutionary ideas will be allowed to prevail."[50]

The implications for political responsibility of this understanding of free speech and press are profound. As long as these First Amendment freedoms are understood to be specific means to the end of self-government, then they must somehow be related to that end, for, as Francis Canavan observes, "end or purpose is a limiting principle, regulating and restricting the uses of means to those which in some way contribute to that end. If a freedom is guaranteed for the sake of a certain end, those uses of the freedom which make no contribution to that end, or are positive hindrances to its achievement are abuses of the freedom and [may] cease to enjoy the protection of the guarantees."[51] However, once freedom of speech and press becomes a means to any end or an end in itself, it no longer needs to be exercised in the same responsible and sober fashion. *Cohen* V. *California* is again instructive. Thanks to its holding, individuals are now free to utter in all public settings the most vile, threatening, and scurrilous of epithets free from all responsibility for their speech.[52] The Court has relieved them of any need to honor the rules of propriety and good taste or the conventions of decency.[53] Consequences, however, flow from this dramatic policy. Having concluded that the people are (and should be allowed to be) fundamentally irresponsible on the important questions of freedom of speech and press, it seems unlikely, indeed, that it will now feel obligated to respect their judgments on other matters of social policy.

At this point, it might be objected that the Supreme Court is very much concerned about political responsibility and that it is striving to promote it. Justice Harlan's observations in *Cohen* could be introduced as evidence of this concern: the First Amendment put "the decision as to what views shall be voiced largely into the hands of each of us, in the hope that use of such freedom will ultimately produce a more capable citisenry and more perfect polity and in the belief that no other approach would comport with the premise of individual dignity and choice upon which our political system rests."[54]

Two immediate responses are in order. First, this same concern for producing "capable citizens" is also conspicuously absent in the Court's decisions in other areas of the law, including political equality. Second and more importantly, accepting *arguendo* that the Court is eager to promote political responsibility, the means it has chosen to employ are questionable at best. They are rather akin to teaching someone to swim by the simple expedient of throwing him in deep water and, without instruction or support, letting him fend for himself. Although this procedure may prove successful for some, for the vast majority it is likely to end in disaster. Most citizens need to be taught both the importance and the means of responsibility.[55] Traditionally in the United States, the law has been an important source of this instruction. However, at least in its opinions on freedom of speech and press, the Court is teaching neither. In fact, by conceding that it is impossible to make a principled distinction between a vulgarism and a lyric, it concedes as well that it cannot distinguish between responsibility and irresponsibility and teaches that it can give no principled account of why citizens should act in a responsible manner. The end result of this instruction is not encouraging, and it is appropriate to question whether the citizenry that is so taught by the Court is capable of producing "a more perfect polity."[56]

### Political Equality

An examination of the Court's decisions on political equality reveals an equally restricted teaching of the importance of political responsibility. The term *political equality* may be employed in conjunction with three analytically distinct principles: (1) each vote is to count equally, e.g., *Reynolds* v. *Sims*[57] and the one person, one vote principle; (2) the franchise is to be broadly available; and (3) its exercise is to be meaningful, e.g., *Williams* v. *Rhodes*[58] and its provision of greater ballot access for minority parties. The present discussion, however, will be limited simply to the second principle. In a series of recent cases, the Supreme Court has voided poll taxes,[59] military status,[60] property ownership,[61] durational residency,[62] and prior party affiliation[63] as conditions to exercise of the franchise. In so doing, it has repudiated the view that voting is not only a right but a duty and is to be engaged in only upon some demonstration of political responsibility—whether of interest in public affairs by paying a nominal poll tax, of a stake in political life stemming from ownership of property, or of a familiarity with and commitment to state politics resulting from living within the state's boundaries a respectable period of time.

This repudiation began in *Harper* v. *Virginia Board of Elections*. In this case, the Court overruled *Breedlove* v. *Suttles*[64] and invalidated Virginia's poll tax. Justice Douglas spoke for a six member majority when he declared that "voter qualifications have no relation to wealth nor to paying or not paying this or any other tax."[65] He waxed eloquently that "wealth like race, creed, or color, is not germane to one's ability to participate intelligently in the electoral process."[66] However, when it is recalled that the tax in question was the nominal sum of $1.50 a year (an amount so trivial that any claim of discrimination through such a requirement would seem appropriately dismissed as frivolous), it is difficult to accept Justice Douglas's claim that the Virginia poll tax was unconstitutional because it discriminated on the basis of wealth. Rather, it appears that Justice Douglas's action was motivated in large part by his fundamental opposition to the way in which the poll tax held the voters responsible for paying this token amount and disenfranchised those who failed to meet this responsibility.[67] Interestingly enough, Virginia defended its imposition of the poll tax on exactly these grounds. It noted that the convention that had drafted Virginia's Constitution had declared that "the voter has to pay a poll tax, prepare his own application, and case his own ballot. The plan virtually eliminates the incompetent from politics."[68] Elaborating upon this theme, it stressed in its brief in *Harper* that "the tax . . . only requires an annual payment of $1.50 by December 4 in every year and this serves as a 'simple and objective test of certain minimal capacity for ordering one's own affairs and thus of qualification to participate in the ordering of the affairs of state.' "[69]

For many, however, this attempt by Virginia to promote political responsibility through the use of the poll tax represented an undue burden on those who would otherwise wish to exercise the franchise, and they sought relief from the Court. The Brief for Appellant complained that "many persons through inadvertence or lack of diligence let the deadline go by without paying their poll taxes, but when the election draws near and candidates and issues are known, find that they cannot vote because they did not pay their poll taxes on time."[70] Joining in the chorus, the amicus curiae brief of the United States also objected that in order to qualify to vote, the voter must pay the tax well "in advance of the election—at a time, that is, when political activity is relatively quiescent and the actual election campaign has not begun."[71] To expect the public to remain concerned and aware of the problems and questions of self-government throughout the entire year and not just at election time represented an "unreasonable burden," Solicitor General Thurgood Marshall assured the Court. The Supreme Court agreed and, by invalidating the poll tax, spared the public, at least in this context, the consequences of its irresponsibility.[72]

The Court's willingness to sever the nexus between voting and political responsibility is also apparent in *Kramer* v. *Union Free School District, Phoenix* v. *Kolodziejski,* and *Hill* v. *Stone.* As a result of these cases, the Supreme Court has held that a state cannot deny the franchise to nonproperty owners in municipal elections to approve the issuance of general obligation bonds, even when the general bonded indebtedness of the municipality effectively operates as a lien on all taxable property within its borders.[73] The states defended such property qualification requirements on the grounds that they promoted responsible voting. First, they argued, these requirements encouraged more knowledgeable and interested voters. As the Brief of Appellees stressed in *Kramer:* "It is apodictic that those persons whose properties in the school district are assessed for payment through the local property tax of the cost of rendering services to the pupils and the parents of the district will have enough of an interest, through the burden on their pocketbooks, to acquire such information as they may need in order to try to evaluate the operation of the public school system and the reasonableness of expenditures."[74] Second, these qualifications served to protect those who would have a lien placed on their property for the payment of a tax from being told they would have that lien by others who would not.[75] In the words of the Texas Supreme Court, "One who is willing to vote for and impose a tax on the property of another should be willing to assume his distributive share of the burden."[76]

The Court rejected these justifications, however, and voided these requirements, contending that they erected a classification that impermissibly discriminated on the basis of wealth and disenfranchised persons otherwise qualified to vote.[77] In the context of the Court's most recent and comprehensive consideration of this matter, however, this reasoning is difficult to sustain. *Hill* v. *Stone* considered that provision of the Texas Constitution that restricted the vote in general obligation bond elections to those who had rendered taxable property with local taxing officials. All property owned by any citizen of that state—be it real, personal, or mixed—was taxable property under state law, and all citizens of the state were required by law to render all such taxable property with local taxing officials on a yearly basis in order that it could be added to local tax rolls. The rendering requirement for voting was satisfied by the listing of any single item of property, even though of purely nominal worth, and the completion of an affidavit provided at polling places with a description of any single item of property that the voter had rendered. Rendering of property immediately before the election was possible, and the voter was qualified even if he had not actually paid the tax. Viewed objectively, Texas' property ownership qualification was so easily met that it constituted no impediment to any voter who truly desired to vote in a bond election. As Justice Rehnquist noted in his dissent, "The Texas elector who renders a pair of shoes or a bicycle on election day casts a vote no different from that of a rendering cattle baron."[78] The Court, however, invalidated this qualification, asserting that it was an unconstitutional restriction of the franchise.

Contrary to its assertions, it would appear that the Court's fundamental quarrel with Texas's rendering qualification, no less than with Virginia's poll tax, is the responsibilities it imposes on those who are otherwise unwilling to assume them. Justice Rehnquist's dissent pierces to the heart of the matter: "The rendering qualification under challenge in the instant case is designed in part to prevent citizens who violate their legal obligations resulting from a bond election, however small that share may be, from influencing the process which results in the imposition of such obligations."[79] This emphasis on citizen responsibility, however, was more than the Court was willing to tolerate.

The same disregard for the importance of political responsibility is also apparent in the Court's consideration of durational residency requirements in *Dunn* v. *Blumstein*. In a 6–1 decision, it invalidated a Tennessee requirement of one year residence in the state and three months in the county as a condition of voting.[80] In so doing, the Court rejected the idea that a state may have a legitimate interest in using such requirements either to secure knowledgeable voters with a genuine interest in the governance of the community or to educate the citizenry on the importance of casting informed, considered, and responsible votes. All the knowledge and experience a voter needs to exercise the franchise could be gained in the thirty-day period before an election, the amicus curiae brief for Common Cause argued. "Advertising and news coverage reach and sustain a fever pitch only during the month before an election. Because this is so, a new resident can acquire all the knowledge he wants or needs during that period."[81] Justice Thurgood Marshall agreed, "Given modern communications, and given the clear indication that campaign spending and voter education occur largely during the month before the election, the state cannot seriously maintain that it is 'necessary' to reside for a year in the state and three months in the county in order to be knowledgeable about congressional, state, or even purely local elections."[82] The teaching from all of this is also clear, though inadvertent: efforts to foster in the public a reflective and ongoing concern for the principles, problems, and prospects of republican government and to encourage thoughtful voters to appreciate the importance of a responsible exercise of the franchise are impermissible. For the Court, responsibility is not even required in voting. However, if the citizenry may cast an irresponsible vote, what assurance is there that their policy preferences will not be equally irresponsible? And, if their policy preferences are irresponsible, what onus will attach to the Court if it simply disregards these whims or urges and imposes instead its own solutions on the problems of the day?[83]

In both of the areas this paper has explored—freedom of speech and press and political equality—the Court has shown little concern for the impact that its decisions have on the problem of political responsibility. It has shown even less apprehension for the effects that they have on judicial activism and on the rise of an imperial judiciary. This is unfortunate, for whether or not the Court acknowledges the fact, it is a "republican schoolmaster." Through its opinions in these and other areas, it provides "authoritative definitions" of what is or is not permissible in the name of liberty. In so doing, it has, as Professor Walter Berns points out, a profound effect on the opinions, habits, and tastes of the citizenry and, therefore, on the future of the American regime.[84] As a consequence, it is imperative for the Court that it consider the broader social, political, and philosophic issues latent in what may often appear to be narrow legal questions.

If the Court were to appreciate these concerns and consistently to take a stand accordingly, the growth of the "imperial" judiciary would doubtless be checked. The Court's ardor for the "guardian ethic" would soon cool as it would come to appreciate that a responsible citizenry has little need for the tutelage and guidance of a "guardian democracy." It would become increasingly aware that what the Court accepts as the citizens' responsibilities both represents what it and ultimately the citizens themselves perceive the citizenry to be and gives its character to what they will become in the future. At that juncture, the Court would again be equal to its role as educator and guardian of those principles and values upon which republican government fundamentally depends.

### Notes

1. Ralph Lerner, "The Supreme Court as Republican Schoolmaster," in *Supreme Court Review*, Philip B. Kurland, ed. (Chicago: University of Chicago Press, 1967), pp. 127–128. Theodore J. Lowi goes even further. He considers the Supreme Court to be "a primary, perhaps the primary, source of political theory in the United States. The rulings and opinions of leading decisions of the Court constitute our most important source of standards about what is good and what is bad for the public, [and] what is good or bad government." *American Government: Incomplete Conquest* (Hinsdale, Illinois: The Dryden Press, 1976), p. 556.
2. Stephen David Ross, *The Nature of Moral Responsibility* (Detroit: Wayne State University Press, 1973), p. 7.
3. See Nathan Glazer, "Toward an Imperial Judiciary?" *The Public Interest*, No. 41 (Fall, 1975), 104–123. See also Ward E. Y. Elliott, *The Rise of Guardian Democracy* (Cambridge, Mass.: Harvard University Press, 1974), p. 2.
4. A third area, the entrapment defense in criminal procedure, has already been considered elsewhere. See Ralph A. Rossum, "The Entrapment Defense and the Teaching of Political Responsibility: The Supreme Court as Republican Schoolmaster," *American Journal of Criminal Law*, Vol. 6, No. 3 (November 1978).
5. 388 U.S. 130, 148 (1967).
6. Francis Canavan, "Freedom of Speech and Press: For What Purpose?" *American Journal of Jurisprudence*, Vol. 16 (1971), 125–126. See also Alexander Meiklejohn, *Political Freedom: The Constitutional Powers of the People* (New York: Oxford University Press, 1965), pp. 28, 57, 75.
7. *Thomas* v. *Collins*, 323 U.S. 516, 545 (1945). Mr. Justice Jackson concurring.
8. *Grosjean* v. *American Press Co.*, 297 U.S. 233, 249–250 (1936). Speaking for the Court, Justice Sutherland quoted approvingly from 2 Cooley's *Constitutional Limitations*, 8th ed., p. 886. For other statements that also show that the chief function of the First Amendment guarantees of free speech and press is to serve the political needs of an open and democratic society, see *Pickering* v. *Board of Education*, 391 U.S. 563, 573 (1968); *Time* v. *Hill*, 385 U.S. 374, 389 (1967); *Mills* v. *Alabama*, 384 U.S. 214, 218 (1966); *Associated Press* v. *United States*, 326 U.S. 1, 20 (1945); *Bridges* v. *California*, 314 U.S. 252, 293 (1941), Mr. Justice Frankfurter dissenting; *Cantwell* v. *Connecticut*, 310 U.S. 296, 310 (1940); and *Thornhill* v. *Alabama*, 310 U.S. 88, 95, 101–102 (1940).
9. *Minersville School District* v. *Gobitis*, 310 U.S. 586, 599 (1940).
10. 121 U.S. 809 (1975).
11. 425 U.S. 748 (1976).
12. 433 U.S. 350 (1977).
13. 316 U.S. 52 (1942).
14. Ibid, at 54. See also *Schneider* v. *State*, 308 U.S. 147 (1939), and *Breard* v. *Alexandria*, 341 U.S. 622 (1951).
15. See *Virginia State Board of Pharmacy* v. *Virginia Citizens Consumer Council*, 425 U.S. 748, 761 (1976), and *Bates* v. *State Bar of Arizona*, 433 U.S. 350, 363 (1977).
16. 421 U.S. at 825.
17. Ibid, at 826.
18. Ibid, at 822. Compare Justice Rehnquist's comments in dissent: "Whatever slight factual content the advertisement may contain and whatever expression of opinion may be laboriously drawn from it does not alter its predominantly commercial content. 'If that evasion were successful, every merchant who desires to broadcast . . . need only append a civic appeal, or a moral platitude, to achieve immunity from the law's command.' *Valentine* v. *Chrestensen* 316 U.S. 52, 55 (1942)." *Bigelow* v. *Virginia*, 421 U.S. 809, 832 (1975).
19. 421 U.S. at 831.
20. Justice Rehnquist dissented, and Justice Stevens did not participate.

21. 425 U.S. at 763. Justice Douglas had made much the same argument in his dissent from denial of certiorari in *Dunn and Bradstreet* v. *Grove*, 404 U.S. 898, 905 (1971): "The language of the First Amendment does not except speech directed at private economic decision-making. Certainly such speech could not be regarded as less important than political expression." See also Brief of Osco Drug, Inc., as Amicus Curiae at 4, 9, *Virginia State Board of Pharmacy* v. *Virginia Citizens Consumer Council*, 425 U.S. 748 (1976): "Commercial advertising serves essential social purposes in affording to consumers information required to make prudent choices among competing products. Such information may be more important to the majority of people than the political and philosophical opinions which traditionally have been more fully protected under the First Amendment."
22. 425 U.S. at 765.
23. *Breard* v. *City of Alexandria*, 341 U.S. 622, 650 (1951). Mr. Justice Black dissenting.
24. Brief of the Association of National Advertisers, Inc., as Amicus Curiae, at 10, *Virginia State Board of Pharmacy* v. *Virginia Citizens Consumer Council*, 425 U.S. 748 (1976).
25. *Bigelow* v. *Virginia*, 421 U.S. 809, 831 (1975), and *Virginia State Board of Pharmacy* v. *Virginia Citizens Consumer Council*, 425 U.S. 748, 781 (1976).
26. *Virginia State Board of Pharmacy* v. *Virginia Citizens Consumer Council*, 425 U.S. 748, 787 (1976).
27. Ibid.
28. Ibid, at 784.
29. Ibid, at 783.
30. The Court, however, was badly split; only Justices Brennan, White, Marshall, and Stevens joined in Justice Blackmun's opinion.
31. 433 U.S. at 364.
32. Ibid, at 404. Mr. Justice Rehnquist dissenting. See also Brief of the Maryland State Bar Association, et al., as Amici Curiae at 18–22, 25, *Bates* v. *State Bar of Arizona*, 433 U.S. 350 (1977).
33. 403 U.S. 15 (1971).
34. 408 U.S. 901 (1972).
35. 410 U.S. 667 (1973).
36. See Cox, *The Role of the Supreme Court in American Government* (New York: Oxford University Press, 1976), pp. 45–46.
37. 403 U.S. at 26. In so doing, Justice Harlan repudiated Justice Murphy's claim in *Chaplinsky* v. *New Hampshire*, 315 U.S. 568, 572 (1942), that "Such utterances are no essential part of any exposition of ideas and are of such slight social value as a step to truth that any benefit that may be derived from them is clearly outweighed by the social interest in order and morality."
38. *Essay on Translated Verse* (1684), line 113.
39. See Brief for Appellant at 33–35, *Cohen* v. *California*, 403 U.S. 15 (1971).
40. *Cohen* v. *California*, 403 U.S. at 25.
41. *Police Department of the City of Chicago* v. *Mosley*, 408 U.S. 92, 96 (1972). Mr. Justice Thurgood Marshall for the majority.
42. *Cohen* v. *California*, 403 U.S. at 25.
43. Lerner, "The Supreme Court as Republican Schoolmaster," p. 128.
44. Walter F. Berns, *The First Amendment and the Future of American Democracy* (New York: Basic Books, 1976), p. 173.
45. 373 N.E. 2d 21 (1978).
46. Ibid, at 24.
47. Quoted by Thurman Arnold, "Criminal Attempts—The Rise and Fall of an Abstraction," *Yale Law Journal*, Vol. 40 (1930), p. 58.
48. See Justice Brandeis's comments in *Whitney* v. *California*, 274 U.S. 357, 375 (1927). See also Brief for Appellant at 43, *Cohen* v. *California* 403 U.S. 15 (1971): "Free speech is important not only as a means in the democratic process but also as an end in itself. The nature of man is such that he can realize self-fulfillment only if he is free to express himself."
49. 367 U.S. 1, 147 (1961). See also *Whitney* v. *California*, 274 U.S. at 377.

50. *Communist Party* v. *S.A.C. Board,* 367 U.S. at 147. Mr. Justice Black dissenting. Justice Black was, of course, echoing what Justice Holmes uttered in dissent in *Gitlow* v. *New York,* 268 U.S. 652, 673 (1925): "If in the long run the beliefs expressed in proletarian dictatorships are destined to be accepted by the dominant forces of the community, the only meaning of free speech is that they should be given their chance and have their way."

51. Canavan, "Freedom of Speech and Press: For What Purpose?" p. 102.

52. See the dissent of Chief Justice Burger in *Rosenfeld* v. *New Jersey* 408 U.S. at 902.

53. To the extent that any responsibility remains, it has been shifted to the shoulders of others. Once again, Justice Harlan's comments in *Cohen* have substantially influenced subsequent rulings. There, he observed that members of the public could "effectively avoid further bombardment of their sensibilities simply by averting their eyes." 403 U.S. at 21. The Illinois Supreme Court relied on this language in *Village of Skokie* v. *National Socialist Party of America,* 373 N.E. 2d at 26, to conclude that "the burden normally falls upon the viewer to 'avoid further bombardment of [his] sensibilities simply by averting his eyes," and that *"Cohen and Erznoznik* [v. *City of Jacksonville,* 422 U.S. 205 (1975)] direct the citizens of Skokie that it is their burden to avoid the offensive symbol if they can do so without unreasonable inconvenience."

54. *Cohen* v. *California,* 405 U.S. 15, 24 (1971). See also Justice Blackmun's comments in *Virginia State Board of Pharmacy* v. *Virginia Citizens Consumer Council,* 425 U.S. 748, 770 (1976).

55. This view of mankind may not be especially complimentary, but as Publius has observed, "It may be a reflection on human nature, that such devices should be necessary . . . but, what is government itself but the greatest of all reflections on human nature. If men were angels, no government would be necessary." *The Federalist,* No. 51, p. 349. See also No. 15, p. 96.

56. A related matter should also be noted: the Supreme Court has all but abandoned the traditional Blackstonian understanding of freedom of speech and press as no prior restraint, and profound consequences for the question of political responsibility result from this as well. Freedom of speech and press once meant that while one could not be restrained in advance from speaking or publishing, one could well be punished after the fact for one's libelous, seditious, or obscene utterances. See William Blackstone's statement on the common law: "Every free man has an undoubted right to lay what sentiments he pleases before the public: To forbid this, is to destroy the freedom of the press: But if he publishes what is improper, mischievous, or illegal, he must take the consequences of his own temerity." *Commentaries on the Laws of England,* Vol. 4, p. 152. See also James Wilson's comments in the Pennsylvania ratifying convention regarding freedom of the press in the United States: "What is meant by the liberty of the press is, that there should be no antecedent restraint upon it; but that every author is responsible when he attacks the security or welfare of the government, or the safety, character and property of the individual." John Back McMaster and Frederick D. Stone (eds.), *Pennsylvania and the Federal Constitution, 1787–1788* (Lancaster, Pennsylvania: The Historical Society of Pennsylvania, 1888), p. 308. That view has been largely replaced with the notion that the First Amendment not only prohibits all prior censorship but renders one wholly irresponsible for the content or consequences of one's expression as well.

57. 377 U.S. 533 (1964).

58. 393 U.S. 23 (1968).

59. *Harper* v. *Virginia Board of Elections,* 383 U.S. 663 (1966).

60. *Carrington* v. *Rash,* 380 U.S. 89 (1965).

61. *Kramer* v. *Union Free School District,* 395 U.S. 621 (1969), *Cipriano* v. *City of Houma,* 395 U.S. 701 (1969), *Phoenix* v. *Kolodziejski,* 399 U.S. 204 (1970), and *Hill* v. *Stone,* 421 U.S. 289 (1975).

62. *Dunn* v. *Blumstein,* 405 U.S. 330 (1972).

63. *Kusper* v. *Pontikes,* 414 U.S. 51 (1973).

64. 302 U.S. 277 (1937).

65. *Harper* v. *Virginia Board of Elections,* 383 U.S. 663, 666 (1966).

66. Ibid, at 668.

67. See 383 U.S. at 664, n. 1.

68. Quoted in Brief for Appellees at 43, *Harper* v. *Virginia Board of Elections,* 383 U.S. 663 (1966).
69. Ibid.
70. Brief for the Appellants at 26, *Harper* v. *Virginia Board of Elections,* 383 U.S. 663 (1966).
71. Brief for the United States as Amicus Curiae at 30, *Harper* v. *Virginia Board of Elections,* 383 U.S. 663 (1966).
72. See the dissents of Justices Black and Harlan, however, where the poll tax's service to "civic responsibility" was acknowledged. *Harper* v. *Virginia Board of Elections,* 383 U.S. 663, 674, 685 (1966). It should be stressed that it was conceded by all parties that Virginia's poll tax had not been used for racially discriminatory purposes. See 383 U.S. at 672.
73. In particular, in *Kramer* v. *Union Free School District,* 395 U.S. 621 (1969), the Court held that a state could not restrict the vote in school district elections to owners and lessees of real property and parents of school children because the exclusion of otherwise qualified voters was not shown to be necessary to promote a compelling state interest. In *Phoenix* v. *Kolodziejski,* 399 U.S. 204 (1970), it held invalid an Arizona statute restricting the franchise in a general obligation bond election to real property owners. And, in *Hill* v. *Stone,* 421 U.S. 289 (1975), the Court declared that Texas's requirement limiting the right to vote in city bond issue elections to persons who had "rendered" or listed real, mixed, or personal property for taxation in the election district in the year of the election was in violation of the Equal Protection Clause of the Fourteenth Amendment, for this restriction on the suffrage did not serve any compelling state interest.
74. Brief of Appellees at 4, *Kramer* v. *Union Free School District,* 395 U.S. 621 (1969). See also Justice Stewart's dissent in *Kramer,* 395 U.S. at 636–637.
75. See Brief for Poudre School District R. 1 of Larimer, Colorado, as Amicus Curiae at 15, *Phoenix* v. *Kolodziejski,* 399 U.S. 204 (1970).
76. *Montgomery Independent School District* v. *Martin,* 464 S.W. 2d 638, 642 (Tex. 1971).
77. See *Kramer* v. *Union Free School District,* 395 U.S. 621, 633 (1969), *Phoenix* v. *Kolodziejski,* 399 U.S. 204, 209 (1970), and *Hill* v. *Stone* 421 U.S. 289, 300 (1975).
78. *Hill* v. *Stone,* 421 U.S. at 303.
79. Ibid, at 307.
80. Compare Justice Douglas's language in *Lassiter* v. *Northampton County Board of Elections,* 360 U.S. 45, 51 (1959). "Residence requirements, age, previous criminal record are *obvious examples* indicating factors which a state may take into consideration in determining the qualifications of voters. The ability to read and write likewise has some relation to standards designed to promote intelligent use of the ballot." (Emphasis added.)
81. Brief for Common Cause as Amicus Curiae at 19, *Dunn* v. *Blumstein,* 405 U.S. 330 (1972).
82. *Dunn* v. *Blumstein,* 405 U.S. 330, 358 (1972).
83. In this connection, see *Bolden* v. *City of Mobile, Alabama,* 423 F. Supp. 384 (S.D. Ala. 1976). In this case, the federal court for the southern district of Alabama invalidated Mobile's sixty-five year old, three-member commission form of government. The citizens of Mobile seemed pleased with their system, having rejected in both 1963 and 1973 the opportunity to change to a mayor-council form of government, the last time by a 2–1 majority. In the mind of Judge Virgil Pittman, however, the system did not provide sufficient representation for Mobile's black minority. As a consequence, he struck it down. However, not trusting the citizens of Mobile to act responsibly and devise their own new charter, he went further and declared that his reading of the Equal Protection Clause of the Fourteenth Amendment indicated that a government must be established composed of a major and nine council members elected from single member districts. 423 F. Supp. at 404.
84. Berns, *The First Amendment and the Future of American Democracy,* ix.

# Judicial Activism:
# Toward a Constitutional Solution

Gary L. McDowell

Judicial activism tends to be like Charles Dudley Warner's weather: there is a great deal of talk, but very little action. One might think that there is nothing to be done, that judicial excesses are simply a way of life. That need not be the case. Judicial activism is a constitutional problem of the most fundamental sort, and there exists an equally fundamental constitutional solution. The problem is that we no longer look upon the Constitution in the way we should. We tend to take the Constitution not very seriously. It is the purpose of this study to point toward a constitutional solution to the problem of government by judiciary.

I

Since the time of its creation—or at least since John Marshall became chief justice in 1801—the Supreme Court has never been immune to politics. Whether from the Jeffersonian Republicans, the Jacksonians, the Abolitionists, the Radical Republicans, the Progressives, or the New Dealers, each Court throughout our history has enjoyed the praise and suffered the blame of being "political" or "activist." Whatever the time and whatever the issue, the Supreme Court has always found itself in the thick of the political debates that have animated the American political order. The current controversy over the "Egalitarian Society," with all its equitable overtones, is no different. This is due in no slight measure to the Constitution itself; for nearly every issue in American politics comes ultimately to be measured by the standard of the Constitution. Constitutionality is the fundamental source of our political legitimacy. Hence the Supreme Court—an institution "peculiarly essential in a limited constitution"[1]—eventually is dragged into the fray and asked to exercise its judgment as the final arbiter of conflicting claims of constitutionality. Such power of judgment wielded by the Court is awesome, so awesome in fact that the Founders saw fit to give it this power alone and to deny it the necessary tools of implementation. The Founders agreed with Montesquieu: "there is no liberty, if the power of judging be not separated from the legislative and executive powers."[2] Force and will, the executive and legislative powers respectively, were not intended to be components of judicial review.

Judicial review, though not explictly provided for by the Constitution, was anticipated by the Founders and assumed to be inherent in the judicial power. The power of judicial review was understood as an essentially negative power. As Alexander Hamilton succinctly put it, judicial review is "the right of the courts to pronounce legislative acts void, because contrary to the Constitution."[3] The judiciary was designed as an "intermediate body between the people and the legislature in order, among other things, to keep the latter within the limits assigned to their authority." Hamilton went on:

> The interpretation of the laws is the proper and peculiar province of the courts. A constitution is in fact, and must be, regarded by the judges as fundamental law. It therefore belongs to them to ascertain its meaning as well as the meaning of any particular act proceeding from the legislative body. If there should happen to be an irreconcilable variance between the two, that which has the superior obligation and validity ought of course to be preferred; or in other words, the constitution ought to be preferred to the statute, the intention of the people to the intention of their agents.[4]

The courts, according to Hamilton, were intended to be the "bulwarks of a limited constitution" with an institutional force sufficient to resist "legislative encroachments." Should the courts ever be "disposed to exercise *will* instead of *judgment,* the consequence would equally be the substitution of their pleasure to that of the legislative body."[5] That is, they would be substituting their will for the will of the people; they would in essence be creating a will independent of society itself.[6] Such a judicial presumption was considered by the Founders as intolerable, and provisions to check such judicial behavior are provided by the Constitution. As Hamilton observed:

> Particular misconstructions and contraventions of the will of the legislature may now and then happen; but they can never be so extensive as to amount to an inconvenience, or in any sensible degree to affect the order of the political system. This may be inferred with certainty from the general nature of the judicial power; from the objects to which it relates; from the manner in which it is exercised; from its comparative weakness, and from its total incapacity to support its usurpations by force. And the inference is greatly fortified by the consideration of the important constitutional check, which the power of instituting impeachments, in one part of the legislative body, and of determining upon them in the other, would give to that body upon the members of the judicial department.[7]

Beyond the most drastic constitutional check of impeachment, the legislature controlled the appellate jurisdiction of the Supreme Court as well as the creation and implementation of all inferior tribunals. Therefore the judiciary could be safely entrusted to exercise the power of constitutional judgment because on the basis of its power as defined by the Constitution it would be unable to take any "active resolution whatever."[8] And should it be overwhelmed by its own sense of self-righteousness and attempt to express its will rather than its judgment, it could be safely brought back to the republican fold by Congress.

Although its critics may insist that judicial vetoes of legislative enactments (e.g., the pre-1937 New Deal Court) are, in a very real sense, expressions of a judicial will, such judicial behavior still seems to fit comfortably with the original understanding of the judicial function. Certainly *proscriptive* rather than *prescriptive* judicial decrees were what was intended by those who drafted and ratified the Constitution. Until the *Brown* decisions in 1954–1955, most judicial opinions took the form of prohibiting actions it deemed unconstitutional rather than commanding actions it thought necessary to attain the good life under the Constitution. The *prescriptive* decrees of *Brown* (II),[9] *Green,*[10] *Carter,*[11] *Swann,*[12] *Hills,*[13] and *Milliken* (II)[14] are clear examples of a new judicial view of the judicial function. They are, to be sure, the results of a new sociological understanding of the inherently positive "historic equitable remedial powers" (in contradistinction to the inherently negative power of judicial review) possessed by the federal judiciary. But this new notion of equity—"sociological" equity—has been made possible only by a new and widely accepted judicial view of the Constitution itself.

## II

The object of the Constitutional Convention in 1787, it was frequently asserted, was to draft a constitution "for future generations, and not merely for the peculiar circumstances of the moment;"[15] the Founders hoped they had devised a Constitution that would "last forever" or at the very least one that would "last for ages."[16]

The Constitution was intended to be "paramount," "fundamental," and lasting, in order to achieve a steady and just administration of the laws.[17] By being held above the law, the Constitution would contribute to the necessary political stability by drawing unto itself that "veneration which time bestows on everything."[18] Certainly the Founders entertained no utopian notions that they had written the last word in republican constitutions; they knew the necessity of allowing for future amendments. But they also understood that the process of changing the fundamental and paramount law must rest not only with the people but also be cumbersome so it would not be used for "light and transient causes." It would have been dangerous to have rendered the Constitution "too mutable."[19] The Constitution was left to posterity to "improve and perpetuate,"[20] not merely to improve. And the alteration of the Constitution where necessary to meet the unforeseen exigencies of the future was left to the people, not to their deputies alone.

This older view of the Constitution as paramount to the ordinary law and to the branches of the government has become undermined to a great degree by a new judicial view of the Constitution. The latter is made up of two distinct but related lines of judicial logic: the first is that the opinions of the Supreme Court—constitutional law—have the status of "supreme Law of the Land"; the second, that the Constitution is not bound to any particular political theory and, instead of being permanent and fixed, the Constitution is free to move with amoebalike precision through history. Although this new view perhaps did not originate with the Warren Court, it received its clearest articulation by that Court.

In *Cooper* v. *Aaron*—a case involving the implementation of *Brown*—the Supreme Court elevated its opinions to the status of "supreme Law of the Land."[21] In a line of judicial reasoning that may be described as tenuous, the Court insisted that it was only recalling "some basic constitutional propositions which are settled doctrine." First, the Court pointed out that "Article VI of the Constitution makes the Constitution 'the supreme Law of the Land.' " Then, citing John Marshall's opinion in *Marbury* v. *Madison,* the Court put forth its novel doctrine:

> This decision (*Marbury*) declared the basic principle that the federal judiciary is supreme in the exposition of the law of the Constitution, and that principle has ever since been respected by this Court and the Country as a permanent and indispensable feature of our constitutional system. It follows that the interpretation of the Fourteenth Amendment enunciated in this Court in the *Brown* case is the supreme law of the land. . . .[22]

The Court in *Cooper* v. *Aaron* endeavored to obliterate the distinction between the Constitution and constitutional law; the two had never been explicitly considered as being synonymous. The Constitution, on the one hand, was considered the supreme law in that it represented the public will. It was mutable, to be sure, but only by the intricate and lengthy process of formal amendment. Constitutional law, on the other hand, was not considered the supreme law insofar as it was only the interpretation of the supreme will of the people by agents of the people and susceptible of error. The justices of the Supreme Court were no more expected to be that "philosophical race of kings wished for by Plato"[23] than any other deputy of the people—representative, senator, or president.

The Constitution is more fundamental than constitutional law in the same sense that it is more fundamental than legislative enactments.[24] Constitutional law and legislative enactments are, and must be, more mutable than the Constitution. To assume that constitutional law is by its nature somehow part of the "supreme Law of the Land" is to conjure up frightening conclusions about not only the "derelicts of constitutional law"[25] (e.g., *Dred Scott* v. *Sandford*)[26] but, more deeply, about the necessity of maintaining certainty in the administration of a republican form of government. The Court, in *Cooper* v. *Aaron,* it seems, took too seriously Charles Evans Hughes' nonjudicial *dictum* that the "Constitution is what the judges say it is."[27]

This notion of the supremacy of judicial opinions was rendered even more problematical by the related line of the new constitutional logic. In *Harper* v. *Virginia Board of Elections*[28] Mr. Justice Douglas, writing for the majority of a bitterly divided Court, insisted that:

> The Equal Protection Clause is not shackled to the political theory of a particular era. In determining what lines are unconstitutionally discriminatory, we have never been confined to historic notions of equality any more than we have restricted due process to a fixed catalogue of what was at a given time deemed to be the limits of fundamental rights.[29]

"Notions of what constitutes equal treatment for purposes of the Equal Protection Clause," Douglas emphasized, "*do* change."[30]

Between these two lines of judicial logic—the alleged supremacy of Supreme Court opinions and the notion that the meaning of the Constitution changes from one era to another—lies the fundamentally new judicial view of the Constitution, the idea of a "living Constitution." As Felix Frankfurter pointed out as early as 1937, the "people have been taught to believe that when the Supreme Court speaks it is not they who speak but the Constitution, whereas, of course, in so many vital cases, it is *they* who speak and *not* the Constitution." "And verily I believe," Frankfurter concluded, "that this is what the country needs most to understand."[31] The idea of a "living Constitution" is, in the words of Justice Black, "an attack not only on the great value of our Constitution itself, but also on the concept of a written constitution which is to survive through the years as originally written unless changed through the amending process which the Framers wisely provided."[32]

To try to instill an appreciation for the distinction between the Constitution and what the judges say it is in their opinions is no mean task. Although one may argue against the view that many of its commands are "written in Delphic language,"[33] the Constitution is certainly not free of "indeterminate language."[34] Nor is the application of the language of the Constitution a merely "mechanical process." But however indeterminate its language may be, and however much judgment may be necessary to apply its provisions, "there are large areas of clarity in constitutional language which could limit the operations of government by providing limits to the discretion of those who apply constitutional rules."[35] It is necessary, in order to "restore somewhat the distinction between the Constitution and its judicial gloss," to point out that a "coherent account of events in judicial history requires principles which transcend the cases themselves." As Sotirios Barber has argued: "The meaning of the Constitution itself is one source of those principles; as are such other sources as the deeper intentions of the Framers and the needs of current generations."[36]

In order to evaluate fully the constitutional implications of the Court's new doctrine of "sociological" equity, it is important to recall the original intention of the Constitution and to reconsider the precedents and principles of equity jurisprudence. However, it is also necessary to consider that the best interests of aggrieved social classes may be better served by the preservation of the institutional equilibrium of an emphatically limited Constitution dedicated to the rule of law rather than the transient opinions of judges, however noble their consciences or senses of "moral duty" may appear at a given moment.

### III

The indeterminacy of some provisions of the Constitution is the inevitable concomitant of a limited constitution. The task before the Philadelphia Convention in 1787 was, as Madison saw it, not to produce a "digest of laws," but rather a constitution.[37] In part owing to the limited purposes of the Constitution, its language often lacks the precise definitions that could be expected more plausibly in statutory construction. The wording of the Constitution is often terse; and its terseness has been its source both of strength and weakness. Whereas it has allowed the Constitution to endure for nearly two centuries, it has also permitted a great deal of leeway in the interpretations of its provisions. But that leeway, although permitted, is not always demanded. Only rarely is it impossible to discern what the Framers intended to convey by the language they chose. There are several sources from whence one can attempt to learn the intentions of the Framers: the record of the Philadelphia debates as kept by James Madison; the polemical writings of the ratification period, especially *The Federalist;* and the records of the state conventions that were convened to vote on the new Constitution. In addition, the debates of the First Congress shed some light on the original meaning of the Constitution. And, as James Madison would have it, recourse to the original intentions is generally the safest point of departure for constitutional interpretations.

On the basis of the Constitution, the equity power is not well-defined; indeed, it is not defined at all. But the lack of constitutional definition in no way obscures what the Framers meant by "all cases in law and equity." For the Framers, as for us, the word was backed by several centuries of jurisprudence.

The substantive concept of juridical equity—from its first formulation by Aristotle, through the Roman tradition of Cicero and Justinian, through the efforts of such English and Scottish students of jurisprudence as Ranulph de Glanville, Henrici de Bracton, Christopher St. Germain, Sir Edward Coke, Sir Francis Bacon, Thomas Hobbes, Lord Kames, and Sir William Blackstone, and up to the Founders of the American republic—remained virtually unchanged. From one century to the next the idea was transmitted with nearly every writer paying tribute to Aristotle's first pronouncement. Aristotle had pointed out:

> For that which is equitable seems to be just, and equity is justice that goes beyond the written law. These omissions (in the written law) are sometimes involuntary, sometimes voluntary, on the part of legislatures; involuntary when it may have escaped their notice, voluntary when, being unable to define for all cases, they are obliged to make a universal statement, which is not applicable to all, but only to most cases . . . for life would not be long enough to reckon all the possibilities. If then no exact definition is possible, but legislation is necessary, one must have recourse to general terms.[38]

Law, general by its nature, is limited and suffers the possibility of promoting injustice as well as justice in particular instances. It is necessary that there be a continuing opportunity for human reason to reassert itself into the realm of positive law. Equity is the power to dispense with the harsh rigor of general laws in particular cases. But equity is always to be understood as the exception rather than the rule. Equity, from the beginning, was viewed as part of the law, not as some power superior to it. Throughout the vast tradition of equity jurisprudence one maxim was held as indispensable in the administration of equity: *Aequitas sequitur legem.*

The major innovations in equity jurisprudence following Aristotle were in the procedural rather than the substantive realm. In Rome there first appeared a special office for the administration of equity. This was brought to its most complete institutional expression in England with the creation of the office of the Chancellor, or "Keeper of the King's Conscience." If there is one thing that the entire history of procedural innovations in equitable adjudication teaches, it is that equity is a potentially dangerous source of arbitrary discretion. And as kings came to be replaced by constitutions, the procedural arrangements for the dispensation of equity had to be reconsidered.

In America the debate was largely between those who followed the opinion of Sir Francis Bacon and those who followed that of Lord Kames. Bacon, on the one side, advocated a rigid separation between courts of law and courts of equity. Kames, on the other side, believed that the separation of law from equity was a chimerical idea, and that justice, if it were to be served, demanded that each court enjoy a mixed jurisdiction reaching to both law and equity. The Constitution allowed only for the judicial power to extend to "all cases in law and equity" but, like the rest of the judicial branch, left the procedural niceties to Congress.

In the Judiciary Act of 1789, Congress effected something of a balance between those who advocated a hard separation of law from equity and those who wished for equity as an unfettered judicial tool in each federal court. On the one hand, the Act extended equity jurisdiction to all federal courts, but on the other it established a firm rule as to when causes in equity could and could not be sustained. In the Process Act of 1792, Congress allowed that equity procedures in the federal courts would be "according to the principles, rules and usages which belong to a court of equity as contradistinguished from a court of common law." The Act as passed gave the Supreme Court the discretion to make such regulations as it would think proper to prescribe equity procedure in the lower courts. In that year, the Court under Chief Justice John Jay announced that in making such regulations it would "consider the practices of the Courts of Kings Bench and Chancery in England as affording outlines."

The safety provided in the Judiciary Act of 1789 and the subsequent Process Acts was to rigidly separate the procedure of equity pleadings from the procedure of pleadings at law, although leaving each court with the jurisdiction to entertain both. The draftsmen of these bills saw this procedural distinction as necessary if equity was to be kept from becoming a dangerous source of unfettered judicial discretion. This logic would be lost in the ensuing years.

In the early nineteenth century, a movement began to codify the remnants of the common law in order to reduce judicial discretion and achieve a greater degree of certainty and objectivity in the administration of the law. Although this movement was slowed (and perhaps even weakened) by the treatise writers of the 1820s and 1830s—especially by the prolific Joseph Story—it continued to gain adherents and make inroads on the structure of law in the United States. At first, the Supreme Court resisted this new spirit of innovation; but finally it too succumbed to the demands for simplification and, in the New Rules of Civil Procedure of 1938, provided for the collapse of the procedural distinction between actions at law and actions in equity. Still as late as 1949, the Court would insist that the lack of "technical niceties" in the procedural realm in no way affected the substance of equity. But without that rigid separation of pleadings it was only a matter of time until equity would no longer be held as a necessary substantive body of law and would come to be viewed as merely another set of procedural remedies available to the Court. In *Porter* v. *Warner* (1946)[39] it seemed that the Court was on the verge of giving equity a radical expansion. But it was not until 1955 that it became clear just how fluid equity had become. The Court in *Brown* (II) fashioned a new understanding of the "historic equitable remedial powers" that no longer was concerned with the individual; in place of the individual litigant the Court now put an aggrieved social class. Its remedies would no longer be decreed for the individual who had been injured by the generality of the law, but rather for whole classes of people on the basis of a deprivation of rights. The court went beyond merely enjoining discriminatory laws and attempted to fashion broad social remedies. The effect has been for the Court to enter the "political thicket" and attempt to formulate social policy.

An older political science assumed that the formulation of policies that were to reach the lives of the people were more safely written by the duly *elected* representatives of the people. Through a rather intricate system of representation, it was believed that all the conflicting opinions, passions, and interests of the populace could be filtered up into the legislature and, by a process of coalescing and politics be fashioned into public policy that resembled, at least somewhat, the public interest.[40] It was never assumed that the judiciary was competent to such a task. As Nathaniel Gorham pointed out to the delegates at the Philadelphia Convention, "Judges . . . are not to be presumed to possess any peculiar knowledge of the mere policy of public measures."[41] Madison made the same point in *The Federalist,* No. 49, when he argued that the judiciary "by the mode of their appointment, as well as by the nature and permanency of it, are too far removed from the people to share much in their prepossession."[42]

The formulation of public policy is an expression of a political will. To be legitimate, such public policies must reflect the will of the people, not the independent will of their deputies. The Judiciary has no means available to it to ascertain the public will in any meaningful sense. It is not, strictly speaking, a representative body. It must be assumed that when the court moves to make such decisions as immediate integration, busing, low-income housing development, and remedial education programs it is exercising more than mere judgment: it is making policy choices; it is exercising its own will. It is exercising a power that the Constitution specifically denies to it. The Court, under the guise of the "historic equitable remedial powers" has been endeavoring to formulate public policies for which it lacks not only the institutional capacity but, more importantly, the constitutional legitimacy.

## IV

The basic intention of the Framers, taking into account the permanent attributes of human nature—both its strengths and its weaknesses—was to create a government that could be safely administered by men over men. The end sought was a safe balance between governmental power and individual liberty or, as Madison explained in *The Federalist,* to combine "the requisite stability and energy in government with the inviolable attention due to liberty and the Republican form."[43] The Constitution was the magnificent product; it was understood to create an institutional arrangement whereby the political principles of the Declaration of Independence could be achieved and the most hallowed of the Framers' objects, political liberty, would be secured.[44] One of the most enduring threats to political liberty in a popular regime of which the Constitution took account was the problem of majority factions.[45] These were the "mortal diseases under which popular governments (had) everywhere perished."[46] Majority faction was seen as the problem of popular government, because the form of the government itself could enable an "overbearing" majority to "sacrifice to its ruling passion or interest both the public good and the rights of other citizens."[47] To prevent such popular tyranny—or at least hedge against it—the Framers sought to construct a political system laden with internal checks such as separation of powers, representation, bicameralism, federalism, and "courts of judges holding their offices during good behavior."[48] An independent and vital judiciary was deemed a peculiarly essential "auxiliary precaution" under the limited constitution being drafted.[49] As Alexander Hamilton said in *The Federalist*, No. 78:

> It is not with a view to infractions of the Constitution only that the independence of the judges may be an essential safeguard against the effects of occasional ill humors in the society. These sometimes extend no farther than to the injury of private rights of particular classes of citizens by unjust and partial laws. Here also the firmness of the judicial magistracy is of vast importance in mitigating the severity and confining the operation of such laws.[50]

The judicial power was created by the Constitution to "extend to all cases in law and equity" as a means of maintaining a constitutional equilibrium that would render governmental power safe for political liberty. Equity would be—in particular instances—an appropriate judicial power to restrain the operation and enforcement of any "unjust and partial laws." *De jure* racial discrimination is an example (to use Madison's telling description) of public policy being decided not "according to the rules of justice and the rights of the minor party, but by the superior force of an interested and overbearing majority."[51]

In the *Brown* v. *Board of Education of Topeka, Kansas* cases, the Court would have been on firmer ground—both constitutionally and jurisprudentially—had it approached the "separate but equal" doctrine as an infringement of liberty rather than as a denial of equality. Without constructing the dubious doctrine of psychological equality—a "feeling of inferiority"—the Court could have reached the merits of the case by arguing that the Equal Protection Clause was intended to secure political liberty for the Negroes and that the essence of political liberty was freedom to live one's life without the pressures of legally imposed burdens based solely on race. Such a view would have had considerably more support in the legislative history of the Fourteenth Amendment than the idea that the Amendment either intended or was simply conveniently silent on the idea of social equality for Negroes. Since it seems apparent that the Warren Court's predecessor, the Vinson Court, had been moving toward an abandonment of the "separate but equal" doctrine for some time, the Warren Court, in *Brown*, could have reversed the majority opinion in *Plessy* v. *Ferguson*[52] without ever having to enter the uncertain realm of psychology and sociology. Following the dissent of the elder John Marshall Harlan in *Plessy*, the Court, in *Brown*, could have invalidated the "separate but equal" doctrine as an unconstitutional infringement of liberty insofar as it allowed the states to deny to a portion of their citizens on the basis of "partial laws," the freedom to choose how to live their lives.

By reaching what it believed to be the psychological merits of the case in *Brown*, the Court lost sight of the problem of maintaining liberty for the individual. A "feeling of inferiority" became a problem not of the individual but of the entire race. Hence, the Supreme Court moved toward a new understanding of equal protection of the laws dedicated to generating a feeling of social equality among all citizens rather than toward insuring the political liberty of the individual citizen.[53] The "historic equitable remedial powers" of the federal judiciary were then put into service of this new understanding of equality and used in the judicial attempt to achieve a feeling of equality among the citizens. For the first time, equity was to be used explicitly for furthering a particular political goal rather than as a judicial means of confining unjust and partial laws in order better to serve liberty and justice. The result has been the new "sociological" understanding of equitable relief. From what was thought at the Founding to offer relief to individuals from "hard bargains" has come the asserted judicial power to draw the line between governmental powers and the rights of "discrete and insular minorities" and to create remedies for past encroachments against whole classes of people.

The new fusion of sociological equity with psychological equality has distorted the Court's interpretations of the Constitution. It has led the Court to attempt to fashion broad equitable remedies for the society from the particular cases and controversies brought before it. Such broad decrees of relief "fashioned and effectuated" on the basis of "equitable principles" are in essence judicially created social policies. This new wave of judicial activism is quite different from earlier activist periods.

## V

The Constitution does not leave republican safety and the security of political liberty to good intentions. It created a detailed scheme of separation of powers where there remained enough "partial agency" of each branch with the others to insure a safe separation. It sought to supply "by opposite and rival interests, the defect of better motives." As Madison explained it in *The Federalist,* No. 51:

> But the great security against a gradual concentration of the several powers in the same department, consists in giving to those who administer each department, the necessary constitutional means, and personal motives, to resist encroachments of the others. The provision for defense must in this, as in all other cases, be made commensurate to the danger of attack. Ambition must be made to counteract ambition. The interest of the man must be connected with the constitutional rights of the place.[54]

Although it was the legislative power the Founders feared most, they were not blind to the possibility that each department might be inclined to extend its authority beyond the limits safely assigned to it. The judiciary was intended "from the nature of its functions" to be the branch "least dangerous to the political rights of the Constitution." The liberty of the people would be safe from judicial power only "so long as the judiciary remains truly distinct from both the legislative and executive."[55] The formulation of policy is a distinctly legislative function; a judiciary that undertakes to make such choices infringes upon the legislative power. To violate the separation of powers an institutional collusion is not required—the violation occurs when any of the branches of the government proceeds to exercise the *power* that was assigned by the Constitution to one of the coordinate branches.

Recognizing that such judicial usurpations could take place, the Framers made provisions to check it. Most obviously, the executive could refuse to enforce the decisions of the court, or the legislature could initiate impeachment proceedings. But on a more practical level, the Constitution provides for a more appropriate pressure on a recalcitrant Court.[56] On the basis of the Constitution, Congress possesses the power to regulate the appellate jurisdiction of the Supreme Court as well as the power to constitute and regulate all inferior tribunals. In all the areas that the Court has reached under the new "sociological" equity, the equity power can be regulated by Congress in the form of rules of civil procedure.

There seems to be sufficient evidence to support a call for a return to the older mode of civil procedure whereby law and equity were procedurally distinct. Such a course would recover the older understanding of the problematical nature of equity jurisprudence and preclude, in the telling language of the "Federal Farmer," the judges from switching from their shoes of law to their shoes of equity whenever they find that the law restrains them. The most apparent objection to such a recovery of the old method of procedure would be that which led to its demise in the first place. The rigid procedural distintion between law and equity is cumbersome and slow. To borrow out of context the language of Chief Justice Burger, such a separated system of pleadings "may be administratively awkward, inconvenient, and even bizarre in some situations and may impose burdens on some." But "such awkwardness and inconvenience" cannot be sufficient to deny an enforcement of the Constitution's provisions for a separation of the powers of government.

Republican safety and political liberty are of a more elevated status under the Constitution than a concern for efficiency in the administration of the government. To counter the resistance of those who would deny the necessity of recovering the past to the extent of separating equity from law, we could find no better authority, nor one more appropriate, than the greatest American student of equity jurisprudence, Joseph Story:

> If there be any truth, which a large survey of human experience justifies us in asserting, it is, that, in proportion as a government is free, it must be complicated.[57]

### Notes

1. Jacob Cooke, ed., *The Federalist,* (Middletown: Wesleyan University Press, 1961) No. 78, p. 524. All references are to this edition.
2. Ibid., p. 524.
3. Ibid., p. 524.
4. Ibid., pp. 525–526.
5. Ibid., p. 526.
6. *The Federalist,* No. 51, p. 351.
7. *The Federalist,* No. 81, p. 546.
8. *The Federalist,* No. 78, p. 523.
9. 349 U.S. 294 (1955).
10. 391 U.S. 430 (1968).
11. 396 U.S. 290 (1968).
12. 402 U.S. 1 (1971).

13. 425 U.S. 284 (1976).
14. 433 U.S. 267 (1977).
15. James Wilson, speech in the Philadelphia Convention, in Max Farrand, ed., *Records of the Federal Convention,* 4 vols. (New Haven: Yale University Press, 1937), II, p. 125. Herein after cited as Farrand.
16. James Madison, speeches in the Philadelphia Convention, I Farrand 422; 462. Consider other remarks of a similar nature by Madison and Gouvernor Morris at II Farrand 126; 361.
17. *The Federalist,* Nos. 14, 37, 53, 63, 78.
18. *The Federalist,* No. 49, p. 340.
19. *The Federalist,* No. 43, p. 296.
20. *The Federalist,* No. 14, p. 89.
21. 358, U.S. 1 (1958).
22. 358 U.S. 1, 18–19.
23. *The Federalist,* No. 49, p. 340.
24. *The Federalist,* No. 78.
25. Philip B. Kurland, *Politics, the Constitution, and the Warren Court* (Chicago: University of Chicago Press, 1971), p. 86.
26. 19 Howard 393 (1857). See Don E. Fehrenbacher, *The Dred Scott Case: Its Significance in American Law and Politics,* (New York: Oxford University Press, 1978), for the most recent, and apparently definitive treatment of this landmark case.
27. As quoted in Henry J. Abraham, *The Judicial Process,* (3rd ed: New York: Oxford University Press, 1975 p. 324.
28. 383 U.S. 663 (1966).
29. 383 U.S. 663, 669.
30. Ibid.
31. Max Friedman, *Roosevelt and Frankfurter: Their Correspondence, 1928–1945* (Boston: Little, Brown and Co., 1968), p. 383.
32. Dissenting opinion in *Harper* v. *Virginia Board of Elections,* 383 U.S. 663, 678.
33. Kurland, *Politics, the Constitution, and the Warren Court,* p. xiv.
34. Sotirios A. Barber, *The Constitution and the Delegation of Congressional Power* (Chicago: University of Chicago Press, 1974).
35. Ibid.
36. Ibid., p. 9.
37. *The Papers of James Madison,* Rutland and Hobson, eds., volume X, p. 196.
38. Aristotle, *Rhetoric,* I.xiii.13–14.
39. 328 U.S. 395 (1946).
40. See especially James Madison's speech of 31 May 1787, in the Philadelphia Convention, I Farrand 49–50; and his later observations in *The Federalist,* Nos. 10 and 51.
41. II Farrand 73.
42. *The Federalist,* No. 49, p. 341.
43. *The Federalist,* No. 37, p. 233.
44. See Bernard Bailyn, *The Ideological Origins of the American Revolution;* and Martin Diamond, "The Declaration and the Constitution: Liberty, Democracy, and the Founders," in Glazer and Kristol, eds., *The American Commonwealth: 1976.*
45. *The Federalist,* Nos. 10 and 51. See Martin Diamond, "Democracy and *The Federalist:* A Reconsideration of the Framers' Intents," 53 *American Political Science Review* 52 (1959).
46. *The Federalist,* No. 10, p. 57.
47. Ibid., pp. 60–61.
48. *The Federalist,* No. 9, p. 51.
49. *The Federalist,* No. 78, p. 524.
50. Ibid., p. 528.
51. *The Federalist,* No. 10, p. 57.

52. 163 U.S. 537 (1896). On the movement of the Court toward abandoning the "separate but equal" doctrine see Robert J. Harris, *The Quest for Equality,* Henry J. Abraham, *Freedom and the Court,* and Raoul Berger, *Government by Judiciary.* Consider the opinions of the Court in *Missouri ex rel. Gaines* v. *Canada,* 305 U.S. 337 (1938); *Sipuel* v. *Oklahoma,* 332 U.S. 631 (1948); *Sweatt* v. *Painter,* 339 U.S. 629 (1950); and *McLaurin* v. *Oklahoma State Regents,* 339 U.S. 637 (1950). On the debates over the Fourteenth Amendment see Alfred Avins, ed., *The Reconstruction Amendments' Debates,* (Richmond: Virginia Commission on Constitutional Government, 1967).
53. The Constitution was viewed by its creators as a means of securing personal political liberty, not as a means of forcing an artificial equality of condition. Such men as Elbridge Gerry early in the Philadelphia Convention warned of the "danger of the levilling (sic) spirit" and the "evils" that often "flow from the excess of democracy." Such a leveling spirit was generally considered to be the antithesis of political liberty and private rights. And even though history and recent experience supported Charles Pinckney when he observed that among the peoples of the United States "there are fewer distinctions of fortunes and less of rank, than among the inhabitants of any other nation," it was clear to some that Amercia was still not "one homogeneous mass, in which everything that affects a part will affect in the same manner the whole." As James Madison explained:

> In all civilized Countries the people fall into different classes havg. a real or supposed difference of interests. There will be creditors and debtors, farmers, merchts. and manufacturers. There will be particularly the distinction of rich and poor. It was true as had been observed (by Mr. Pinckney) we had not among us those hereditary distinction which were a great source of the contests in the ancient Govts. as well as the modern States of Europe, nor those extremes of wealth and poverty which characterize the latter. . . . In framing a system which we intend to last for ages, we shd. not lose sight of the changes which ages will produce. An increase of population will of necessity increase the proportion of those who will labor under all the hardships of life and secretly sigh for a more equal distribution of its blessings.

> The solution for this hard political fact was not to attempt to reduce mankind to a homogeneous mass, but rather to encourage such a diversity and multiplicity of interests that a majority faction would be rendered highly improbable. See I Farrand 48; 398; 422; and *The Federalist,* Nos. 10 and 51.
54. *The Federalist,* No. 51, p. 349.
55. *The Federalist,* No. 78.
56. *The Federalist,* No. 81.
57. Joseph Story, "The Science of Government," in *Miscellaneous Writings,* p. 619.

# The Constitution and Federalism

> Conceiving that an individual independence of the States is utterly irre-
> concileable with their aggregate sovereignty; and that a consolidation of
> the whole into one simple republic would be as inexpedient as it is unat-
> tainable, I have sought for some middle ground, which may at once sup-
> port a due supremacy of the national authority, and not exclude the local
> authorities wherever they can be subordinately useful.
>
> *James Madison*

---

## *The Federalist* on Federalism: "Neither a National nor a Federal Constitution, but a Composition of Both"

Martin Diamond

Something surprising confronts the contemporary reader who turns to *The Federalist* to see what it has to say about federalism. Expecting to find the original source
of his view of American federalism, he finds instead a very different understanding
from ours of the nature of federalism and of the federal character of American government. We think that the invention of federal government was the most important
contribution made by the American founders to the art of government and we thus
regard the system they devised as the very paradigm of what we call "federal government." Indeed, as we shall see, most contemporary definitions of federalism are little
more than generalized descriptions of the way we Americans divide governing power
between the states and the central government. It is surprising, therefore, to discover
that *The Federalist* does not likewise characterize the American constitutional system
as a "federal government." Instead, it tells us that the "proposed Constitution . . . is
in strictness neither a national nor a federal constitution; but a composition of both."[1]

This formulation is typical of the way the entire founding generation saw the
matter. For example, the proceedings of the Federal Convention—especially in the
famous compromise regarding the House and Senate—show that the delegates likewise
understood the terms federal and national in a way that required characterizing the
Constitution as a compound or composition of both elements. But what Madison and
the founding generation carefully distinguished as partly federal and partly national,
we have for a long time blended or blurred under the single term federal. Alexis de
Tocqueville saw this happening: "Clearly here we have not a federal government but
an incomplete national government. Hence a form of government has been found which
is neither precisely national nor federal; but things have halted there, and the new
word to express this new thing does not yet exist."[2] Although it may well have been

politically salutary that things "halted" at the old word federal, much may thereby have been lost in precision. And that is the concern of this review of what *The Federalist* teaches about federalism, namely, to suggest that it would be analytically useful to restore *The Federalist's* "strict" distinction between the federal and the national elements in our compound political system, and therewith to restore also *The Federalist's* understanding of federalism in general.

*The Federalist* was operating with the typology, so to speak, composed of two fundamental modes of political organization, the federal and the national. The founders thought that they had combined these two fundamental modes or "elements" into a "compound" system. We disagree and think, instead, that they invented a third fundamental mode or element, which we call federal government. In so thinking, we are operating with a typology composed of three elemental forms: confederation, federal government, and national or unitary government. The difference between our thinking and that of the founders evidently turns on the distinction that we make, and they did not, between confederalism and federalism. That familiar distinction will be found in almost all contemporary writing on federalism. But *The Federalist* and the whole founding generation saw no more difference between confederalism and federalism than we see, say, between the words inflammable and flammable; nothing more was involved than the accidental presence or absence of a nonsignifying prefix. For the founders, then, there were only two basic modes to choose from: confederal/federal as opposed to national/unitary; confederal/federal being that mode which preserves the primacy and autonomy of the states, and the national/unitary being that mode which gives unimpeded primacy to the government of the whole society. Given their bipartite typology or framework, the founders had to view the Constitution as being a "composition" of the two elemental modes and, given our tripartite one, we have to see the Constitution as elementally federal. The question is who is right, we or they? Which is the more useful mode of analysis?

It is instructive, and perhaps disconcerting, to learn that our modern distinction between confederalism and federalism derives from John Calhoun. His *Discourse on the Constitution and Government of the United States* begins with a severe and systematic attack on *The Federalist's* view of federalism. In particular, Calhoun argues that its view of American government as compoundly federal and national is a "deep and radical error."[3] Now Calhoun had some very practical reasons for rejecting the "compound" view. He could not admit that there was anything national at all about the central government because that would open the door to an effective national jurisdiction over South Carolina's slave interests. Yet, because the central government under the Constitution was so palpably stronger than under the Articles of Confederation, Calhoun could not characterize it as confederal/federal, which was the only category left to him according to the bipartite typology then still universally accepted. Moreover, Calhoun did not really want to return to the old Articles; he was not averse to having a government as powerful as that under the Constitution, provided it could be rendered safe for southern interests. Calhoun solved all of his problems by inventing a new category of "federal government" which he contradistinguished from both a confederacy and a national government.

Not surprisingly, Calhoun saw "federal government" as differing rather more from the national form, which posed the threat to southern interests, than from the confederal form. Indeed, Calhoun's new "federal government" turns out to be nothing but a confederacy in all respects save one; unlike a confederacy, which has at its center "a mere congress of delegates,"[4] it has a real central government to carry its powers into execution. This becomes clear if we examine his famous and shrewdly labeled theory of the "concurrent majority." The concurrent *majority* is in fact a system of *unanimous* concurrence; according to Calhoun's scheme, the central government can act only when its measures have the unanimous concurrence of majorities in every sovereign sub-unit of the system. This requirement of unanimity (an exaggeratedly confederal requirement) guaranteed that nothing could be done without the voluntary concurrence of South Carolina. Whatever South Caroline concurred in, however, would then be executed, not with confederal weakness, but directly upon individuals throughout the country with the full force of a national government. Is it not clear, then, that far from being contradistinguished from confederation and national government, Calhoun's "federal government" is in fact nothing but a compound of these two fundamental forms? He combined an exaggeratedly confederal/federal means of arriving at central decisions with a wholly national means of execution, and then arbitrarily assigned to his peculiar compound the new label of federal government.

This appears to have been an important source of our contemporary understanding of federalism. While we have largely rejected his theory of the concurrent majority, we have nonetheless taken over Calhoun's tripartite framework and the elemental status it assigns to federal government. Many scholars have, of course, been perfectly aware that the founding generation conceived their handiwork differently than Calhoun did and we do. But the difference has not been taken seriously. Either there has been a patronizing assumption that our understanding has scientifically superseded theirs, or the difference has been shrugged off as a mere matter of their having their terminology and we ours.[5] But this is surely too serious a matter to be so quickly dismissed; if *The Federalist* is analytically right in its compound view, then we have lost ground in our understanding of federalism. After all, is it not as obscurantist in political things, as it would be in, say, physics or chemistry, to confuse as a new element what in fact is only a compound? In both bases, it would be rendered difficult if not impossible to see how the essential parts of the compound worked and, thereby, to know how to achieve, preserve, or improve it.

To resolve our dispute with *The Federalist*, as to whether our political system is compoundly federal and national or integrally federal, we need a satisfactory definition of federalism. Unfortunately, the current conventional definition will not do. Consider the following from the standard contemporary work on federalism by Professor K. C. Wheare. Like Calhoun, Wheare disagrees with *The Federalist's* compound theory and also sees federal government as a distinctive form differing from both the confederal and the national forms. He defines this distinctive federal principle as "the method of dividing powers so that the general and regional governments are each, within a sphere, co-ordinate and independent."[6] Nearly all contemporary definitions concur in the single point of this one, namely, the reduction of federalism solely to the idea of the division of the governing power.[7] Indeed, the "division of power" definition of federalism is so familiar that it is hard to force ourselves to examine it closely. But its shortcomings will become evident if we ask precisely what is federal about such a division of power. Clearly there is nothing federal at all about the "general" government; it is just a national government like every other one, save that its jurisdiction is not complete. The only thing federal, then, is the retention by the "regional governments" of some portion of the governing power. But this is manifestly nothing more than to define arbitrarily as uniquely federal what is merely the combination of an incomplete national government with the retention in the member units of a confederal/federal autonomy in some respects. In short, the modern theory turns out to be an arbitrarily unacknowledged and hence obscuring version of *The Federalist's* compound theory. *The Federalist* openly alerts us to the national and federal elements in the compound, enabling us to see when it is becoming more simply national or more simply federal, and thereby enabling us to take appropriate action. By lumping together under the term federal government what *The Federalist* keeps separately visible, the modern definition makes it harder for us to see and evaluate such changes in the compound system.

But more importantly, the modern definition is a badly truncated version of *The Federalist's* compound theory. It blinds us to a whole range of federal phenomena that *The Federalist's* understanding of federalism properly comprehends. A moment's reflection reminds us what is left out. Consider the Senate; every school child knows (or at least used to be taught) that the Senate is a peculiarly federal part of American government. *The Federalist*, as we shall see, can readily explain what is federal about the Senate. And so can we all, unless we take seriously the modern definition of federalism, which makes the federalness of the Senate quite inexplicable. After all, the Senate has nothing to do with the reserved powers of the states, which is the sole federal desideratum according to the modern definition. The Senate is a part of the general government of the whole society. But it is a *federal* part of that government. And that is what the truncated modern definition cannot reach—the federal elements in the structure and procedures of the central government itself. By limiting federalism to the reserved jurisdiction of the states, the modern definition obliges us, insofar as we take it seriously, to conceive the central government as purely national. It thus contradicts what our commonsense tells us about the federal character of the Senate and, as we shall see, it tends to blind us to other federal elements in the design of our central government.

*The Federalist's* compound theory offers a clearer and fuller account of federalism, albeit not in the handy form of a definition. We must glean that definition from the various ways *The Federalist* replies to the main charge made by the opponents of the proposed Constitution, namely, that it had departed from the federal form in favor of the "consolidated" national form. In *Federalist 39*, where the charge is most systematically dealt with, Madison examines five ways to "ascertain the real character of the government" relative to the federal-national question.[8] By examining them closely, we will be able to piece together *The Federalist's* understanding of federalism.

First, the mode by which the Constitution is to be ratified, Madison argues, is federal and not national, because only the voluntary assent of each state, taken as a distinct and independent body politic, joins it to the Union. Second, Madison examines the sources of the legislative and executive branches of the central government. The House of Representatives is national because it derives from the whole people treated as a single body politic; the people will be represented in it, Madison says, exactly as they would be in any unitary state. Contrarily, the Senate is a federal element in the central government because it derives from, and represents equally, the states treated as "political and coequal societies." The Presidency has a "very compound source" because the electoral votes allotted to the states "are in a compound ratio, which considers them partly as distinct and coequal societies, partly as unequal members of the same society." The presidential aspect of the central government thus "appears to be of a mixed character presenting at least as many *federal* as *national* features."[9] Third, the government's mode of operation, in exercising its enumerated powers, is national because it reaches directly to individual citizens like any other national government (like any *government*, one might say). Fourth, as to the extent of its powers, Madison cautiously says that the government "cannot be deemed a national one," because it has a limited, enumerated jurisdiction. Madison means that the new system is national as to the extent of powers entrusted, but is federal insofar as a substantial portion of the governing powers autonomously remains with the states as distinct political societies. (Notice that Madison is here treating as but one aspect of federalism what the modern definition treats as the whole of it. In his first three considerations, Madison had been inquiring into what was federal in the formation, structure, and operation of the central government, that is, into crucial aspects of federalism which the modern defintion excludes from its purview.)

Fifth, and finally, Madison judges the amending process to be neither wholly federal nor wholly national. His argument on this brings to the fore the logic and language of his theory of federalism.

> [Were the amending process] wholly national, the supreme and ultimate authority would reside in the *majority* of the people of the Union; and this authority would be competent at all times, like that of a majority of every national society, to alter or abolish its established Government. Were it wholly federal on the other hand, the concurrence of each State in the Union would be essential to every alteration that would be binding on all. . . . In requiring more than a majority, and particularly in computing the proportion by *States*, not by *citizens*, it departs from the *national*, and advances toward the *federal* character: In rendering the concurrence of less than the whole number of States sufficient it, loses again the *federal*, and partakes of the *national* character.[10]

This is the way the federal principle was understood in 1787 and, for that matter, in all earlier political writings. We are now in a position to summarize it. Having the nature of a "league or contract,"[11] federalism is a relation of independent, equal bodies politic that join together for limited purposes and carry those out, as the Latin root (*foedus, fides*) of the word reminds us, only by the obligation of good faith, rather than by governmental, which is to say coercive, authority. Insofar as any governmental structure, process, power, or practice conforms to the primacy of the separate bodies politic, to their equal status within the federal association, to the limited nature of that association, and to its operational dependence upon faithful compliance rather than political coercion, the structure, process, power, or practice is federal; insofar as it departs toward the principle of a complete, coercive government of a single body politic, it is national. Indeed, one may even contrast federalism, not only with national government, but with government as such. This is in fact what Alexander Hamilton argues in *Federalist 15*. The Constitution differs from the Articles of Confederation, he argues, because it incorporates "those ingredients which may be considered as forming the characteristic difference between a league and a government."[12]

Because they thus understood federalism, the leading Framers of the Constitution were convinced that no "merely federal" system would suffice for the purposes of union.[13] For those purposes, the federal principle of voluntary association was inadequate; a true government of the whole was required. "Mr. Govr. Morris explained the distinction between a *federal* and *national, supreme*, Govt.; the former being a mere compact resting on the good faith of the parties; the latter having a compleat and *compulsive* operation."[14] Accordingly, in the Virginia Plan, the leading Framers proposed "a *national* Government . . . consisting of a *supreme* Legislative, Executive & Judiciary."[15] Happily, as we may now say, they did not wholly succeed in their plan to institute "one supreme power, and one only";[16] federal elements were worked back into their national design. Had the nationalists wholly succeeded, the Preamble of the Constitution would have had to read "in order to form a perfect Union," not just a "*more* perfect" one. Had the opponents of the Constitution succeeded, the country would have remained under the radically imperfect Union provided by the Articles of Confederation. The phrase "a more perfect Union" is no grammatical solecism, but an accurate description of the compromised, compoundly federal and national system that resulted from the Convention and that Madison had the theoretical apparatus to analyze so precisely.

*The Federalist's* theory of federalism is not only analytically superior to our contemporary approach in explaining the American political system as originally devised, but it also illuminates the federal-national balance of the system as it has developed historically. The Senate is again a good case in point. It has developed in some respects into a more nationally oriented body than the House, where localist tendencies are very strong. Yet why should this be so if the Senate, because of the equal suffrage of the states, is the formally federal branch of the legislature? Should that not have made the Senate primarily parochial rather than national in outlook? It could be suggested that its not having become so is but one more example of the way formal, institutional factors propose, while underlying historical and behavioral forces informally dispose in unanticipated ways. We need not have recourse to the mysterious working of such forces in order to explain why the Senate developed both federal and national characteristics. Using *The Federalist's* compound theory, we can see that the Senate was formally constituted in a more compound manner than is usually appreciated. Now the leading Framers had always intended some sort of senate to balance and moderate the more immediately democratic House of Representatives; as the democratic analogue of the traditional upper or aristocratic house, it was intended to be the branch that took the longer and more systematic, as it were, the more national view. But the Connecticut Compromise (national House, federal Senate) threatened to balk that intention. The leading Framers feared that the Senators, as had been so many delegates to the Confederal Congress, would be too closely bound by state interests and views to function, as desired, on behalf of long-run national considerations. They succeeded in mitigating the federal character of the Senate by means of four subtle formal departures from the practice under the Articles of Confederation. One was the provision for per capita voting ( "each Senator shall have one Vote"). The Articles had required each state's delegates to cast a single ballot as a delegation; this forced them to form, as it were, an ambassadorial judgment on behalf of the state. The constitutional per capita provision invites and enables Senators to form individual legislative judgments just as do members of the national House of Representatives.

The other departures were three closely linked provisions, all of which likewise tended to lessen the federal control of the states over the Senators. One disallowed the states the power they had under the Articles to recall their delegates at any time. Another provided for the six-year senatorial term; and the third permitted indefinite and uninterrupted eligibility for re-election. The Articles had provided that no person could serve more than three years during any six-year period, the aim being to keep the delegates on a short leash with frequent rustication, so to speak, back to the states.

It is easy to summarize the significance of all these departures. The *federal* aim of the Articles was to reduce the delegates as much as possible to the status of agents of their states. The *national* aim of the Constitution was to make the Senators, despite the federally equal suffrage of the states, more nearly into representatives in the Burkean sense, free to serve long-run national interests as the deliberative process suggested. To appreciate the effectiveness of these provisions in permitting the Senate to develop a national outlook despite its partly federal basis, think how very much more federal (like Congress under the Articles) it would have been had the state delegations been obliged to vote as a unit and had the Senators been obliged to function under the threat of state recall. By contrast, imagine that the states had not been made the electoral districts for the Senate and, as was strongly urged at the Convention, that districts had been based upon the same national population principle as the House of Representatives. How very much *less* federal—how very much less committed to the primacy of state interests and views—the Senate and all of American politics would then have become. The peculiarly mixed character of the Senate as it actually developed becomes more visible and intelligible when we understand it in the light of *The Federalist's* theory of a compoundly federal and national constitutional basis.

Indeed, that theory of federalism can make more visible and intelligible the compound complexity of the whole American political system. It is thus especially valuable to those who treasure the federal elements in the compound and who fear that those elements are weakening, because it enables them to see more clearly what and where the sources of federal vitality are throughout the whole political system. As we have seen, these are of two fundamental kinds: everything connected with the division of governing power, and everything connected with the federal elements in the central government. The importance of the first source, the balance between state power and the enumerated powers of the central government, is understandable enough under the modern theory of federalism; indeed, that is all it comprehends. It also is that source or aspect of federalism most familiar and intelligible to students of constitutional law. Ever since *McCulloch v. Maryland*, the question of the extent of the enumerated powers has been, to use Marshall's phrase, "perpetually arising."[17] In any event, it happens to be a question that is perpetually gratifying to lawyers and the courts because it is so amenable to legal disputation and judicial determination. But

*The Federalist*, as this review has argued, directs our attention to what may be called the political rather than the legal side of federalism. It emphasizes that other and neglected source of federalism, namely, the federal elements in the design of the central government itself and in its politics. Both sources of federalism, not just the one emphasized in the modern theory and in constitutional law, sustain the federal vitality of American government and political life, a vitality achieved by keeping interest, affection, power, and energy alive and well at the state level of politics in an otherwise homogenizing and centralizing age. Neither source should be neglected.

The status of the first of these two has been rendered increasingly problematic since the time of the New Deal. For decades the limiting doctrine of delegated and enumerated powers has been eroded, and the scope of national government has been vastly expanded. True, the strength of the states in the system has not been weakened to a corresponding degree. This is because the states have likewise vastly increased the scope of their activities. Although perhaps not an unmixed blessing, it means that the state is still that government which most affects citizens in their daily lives. Heedless of many learned pronouncements on their obsolescence, the states have thus stubbornly retained more of their federal vigor than might have been expected. Nonetheless, those who are concerned to preserve the federalism in the American compound remain concerned to limit the growth of national government relative to the states, as one indispensable support for that federalism. To this end, it is especially necessary to restore the moral and intellectual *bona fides* of the constitutional doctrine of enumerated powers as a crucial resource for limiting that growth.

But those concerned to preserve federalism must also devote their energies to that other support of American federalism to which *The Federalist* alerts them, namely, the federal elements in the central government. One such element now under heavy attack is the Electoral College. But the federal aspect to the Electoral College controversy has received relatively little attention: indeed, it is regarded as irrelevant to it. The argument has been that because the President is the representative of "all the people," he should be elected by them in a wholly national way, unimpeded by the interposition of the states through the Electoral College. Given the prevailing understanding of federalism, the "general" government is supposed to be purely national; from this perspective, the participation of the states in presidential selection does indeed seem to be an unjustifiable intrusion, and the potential "mischiefs" resulting from that intrusion seem insupportable. But from the perspective of *The Federalist's* compound theory of American government, there is no reason why the President, admittedly the representative of "all the people," cannot represent them and, hence, be elected by them in a way corresponding to the American government's compoundly federal and national character.

The Presidency, especially the modern Presidency, is no doubt the most nationalizing single element in the American political system, and quite rightly so. Yet the method by which the President is elected has also operated for years in a countervailing federalizing fashion, and just as rightly so. Every Presidential election—the nominating campaigns as well as the electoral campaign itself—is a dramatic reaffirmation that the states are the basis of American political life. Nothing is more vigorously federal than this informal manifestation of federalism in political practice. But it all depends upon the formal structure of the Electoral College as originally conceived and as subsequently statutorily modified by the states. The informal federalizing effect of the Electoral College derives in the first instance from the "compound ratio" by which the states figure in the original constitutional design. Still more federalizing is the general ticket or unit-rule system (the state's entire electoral vote goes to the popular vote winner in the state) which, for nearly a century and a half, almost all the states have employed. Any removal of these federalizing elements, any change toward a purely national mode of Presidential election, would have a corresponding nationalizing effect on the spirit and practice of American politics. The nominating process—primaries and national party conventions—now is radically decentralized by force of the Electoral College's use of the states as states; the nominating process naturally takes its cues from the electing process. If the President were elected in a single national election, the same "cuing" process would continue, but in reverse.

However unproblematic such a centralizing effect might have seemed to partisans of electoral reform some years ago, it seems very problematic indeed now when circumstances are so changed. The thrust of much recent social and political criticism has been against the homogenizing and centralizing tendencies of mass society and its tendency to diminish political participation. *The Federalist* alerts us to the federal implications of the Electoral College and its potential for countervailing those tendencies. To nationalize the Presidential election, especially in this age of electronic media, is to reduce Presidential politics to a single arena with room for little participation. By preserving the federal importance of the states in the process, the Electoral College scatters the Presidential contest into fifty-one arenas (the states and the District of Columbia), with correspondingly enlarged opportunity for the vastly greater number of political participants.

The modern theory of federalism tends to blind us to such peripheral possibilities of federalism in the Presidential election process and throughout our political system. *The Federalist's* theory is superior in clarity and comprehensiveness. The reason this can be so, despite nearly two centuries of eventful history since *The Federalist* was written, is that its political understanding was not limited to the historical period within which it was produced. Rather, it speaks to perennial political issues and, especially, to those peculiar to the genius of American politics. Publius (the pen name Hamilton, Madison, and Jay used in writing the essays) remains our most instructive political thinker. Making accessible to contemporary use his subtle understanding of federalism and of the compoundly federal and national American republic has been the intention of this review.

### Notes

1. *The Federalist* No. 39, at 257 (J. Cooke ed. 1961) [hereinafter to this edition without reference to editor]. Professor Cooke's edition is the definitive modern edition of *The Federalist*.
2. A. de Tocqueville, *Democracy in America* 143 (J. Mayer and M. Lerner eds. 1966).
3. J. Calhoun, *A Disquisition on Government and a Discourse on the Constitution or Government of the United States 156* (R. Cralle ed. 1851).
4. *Id.* at 163.
5. A recent example of the latter is Gunther, *Toward "A More Perfect Union": Framing and Implementing the Distinctive Nation-Building Elements of the Constitution*, 2 Stan. Law., Fall 1976, at 5. In this otherwise very thoughtful essay, Professor Gunther takes note of *The Federalist's* compound theory, but then treats it only as belonging to "the terminology of that day." *Id.*

6. K. Wheare, *Federal Government II* (3d ed. 1953).
7. An example in a recent American textbook can be found in M. Cummings and D. Wise, *Democracy under Pressure* (3d ed. 1977): "[T]he United States has a *federal* system of government, in which power is constitutionally shared by a *national* government and fifty state governments." Id. at 63 (emphasis added). See also W. Bennett, *American Theories of Federalism* 10 (1961) (The "essence of federalism" is evidenced by any "political system in which there is a constitutional distribution of powers between provincial governments and a common central authority."); R. Rikir, *Federalism* 5 (1964) ( "The essential institutions of federalism are, of course, a government of the federation and a set of governments of the member units. . . .")
8. The quotations in the analysis that follows are taken from *The Federalist* No. 39, at 250–57. The concept of federalism is discussed throughout *The Federalist*; other papers that are especially relevant are numbers 15–17, 23, 27, 45, and 46.
9. *The Federalist* No. 39, at 255 (emphasis in original).
10. *Id.* at 257 (emphasis in original).
11. Samuel Johnson's dictionary defined "confederacy" as: "A league; a contract by which several persons or bodies of men engage to support each other; union; engagement; federal compact." The definition of "federal" said: "Relating to a league or contract." The entry for "federate" said: "Leagued; joined in confederacy." I. S. Johnson, *A Dictionary of the English Language* (Philadelphia 1818) (1st Amer. ed. from 11th London ed.).
12. *The Federalist* No. 15, at 95.
13. I. M. Farrand, *The Records of the Federal Convention of 1787,* at 33 (rev. ed. 1937).
14. *Id.* at 31 (emphasis in original).
15. *Id.* at 33 (emphasis in original).
16. *Id.* at 31 (remark of Gouverneur Morris).
17. 17 U.S. (4 Wheat.) 316, 405 (1819).

---

# The Meaning of the Tenth Amendment

Walter Berns

The powers not delegated to the United States by the Constitution, nor prohibited by it to the States, are reserved to the States respectively, or to the people.

## I

No aspect of the United States Constitution has been so vigorously and so persistently disputed as its division of powers between the national government and the governments of the several states. Whatever may be said of the intent of the men who controlled the 1787 convention and, thereby, may be said to have authored the constitutional document, there can be scarcely any doubt of the intent of the men who provided the principal opposition to its ratification. They spoke in opposition out of a concern for the integrity and authority of the states. They formulated, in the several state ratifying conventions, the original drafts of the first ten amendments to the

From *A Nation of States: Essays on the American Federal System* (second edition), edited by Robert A. Goldwin. Copyright © 1974 by the Public Affairs Conference Center, Kenyon College, Gambier, Ohio. Reprinted by permission.

Constitution which were debated and formally proposed by the First Congress, and they, and their heirs, have resisted the exercise of national authority down to the present day. Fear of national power is a theme running the entire course of our history.

This fear cannot be dismissed as unreasonable. The authors of *The Federalist* might seek to discount it by arguing that the mere likely danger was state usurpation of national authority, but their arguments, whatever their effect on the issue then at stake—the ratification of the new Constitution—are not convincing to us who read them with the advantage of a knowledge of subsequent events. "Several important considerations have been touched in the course of these papers," wrote Madison in *Federalist* 45, "which discountenance the supposition that the operation of the federal government will by degrees prove fatal to the state governments. The more I revolve the subject, the more fully I am persuaded that the balance is much more likely to be disturbed by the preponderancy of the last than of the first scale."[1] Yet within a decade he was to join Jefferson in denouncing federal power in the name of state sovereignty. Hamilton, too, argued that it "will always be far more easy for the state governments to encroach upon the national authorities than for the national government to encroach upon the state authorities [because, just as] a man is more attached to his family than to his neighborhood, to his neighborhood than to the community at large, the people of each state would be apt to feel a stronger bias towards their local governments than towards the government of the Union," unless, he warned, "the force of that principle should be destroyed by a much better administration of the latter"[2]—which he promptly set out to provide.

In 1788, Madison and Hamilton might wonder, or at least pretend to wonder, why the proposed Constitution should engender such alarm among the friends of state authority. "If the new Constitution be examined with accuracy and candor," Madison asserted disarmingly, "it will be found that the change which it proposes consists much less in the addition of NEW POWERS to the Union than in the invigoration of its ORIGINAL POWERS [i.e., under the Articles of Confederation]. The regulation of commerce, it is true, is a new power; but that seems to be an addition which few oppose and from which no apprehensions are entertained."[3] And why should there be apprehensions when, according to Hamilton, "the supervision of agriculture and of other concerns of a similar nature, all those things, in short, which are proper to be provided for by local legislation, can never be desirable cares of a general jurisdiction."[4] Yet in 1942 the Supreme Court was to uphold as a valid exercise of the commerce power an Act of Congress making it an offense for a farmer to grow wheat—including wheat to be fed to his own livestock or to be ground into flour and made into bread for his own family—in excess of a quota established by a federal government agency; and in 1969 the Court held that a snack bar in a remote recreational facility on a small Arkansas lake, miles from any interstate highway or even major state road and reachable only on country roads, was nevertheless engaged in interstate commerce insofar as it affected this commerce within the meaning of the Civil Rights Act of 1964.[5] There can be little doubt that if, as the advocates of the cause of the states have argued at least since Jefferson's 1791 opinion on the constitutionality of the bank, and as Madison and Hamilton seem to concede in certain passages of *The Federalist*, the Framers of the Constitution intended the powers of the federal government to be "few and defined" and to be "exercised principally on external objects [such] as war, peace, negotiation, and foreign commerce,"[6] then surely our history demonstrates that the fears of 1788 were not unfounded and that the charges of federal usurpation, leveled by Jefferson and by Madison himself, in 1798, and by others down into the present day, are not without merit. Whether they have this merit depends on the intended meaning of the Constitution as a whole. While in one sense the meaning of the Tenth Amendment, the subject of this paper, is obvious and beyond dispute, in another sense whatever meaning it has depends altogether on the meaning of the Constitution as a whole, and it will be necessary to address this larger question. Those who invoke the Tenth Amendment in order to resist federal power belong to the states-sovereignty school of the Constitution (although, as we shall see, their reliance on the Amendment can only mean their abandonment of the essential element in the states-sovereignty theory).

## II

The enactment of the infamous Alien and Sedition Laws provoked Jefferson and Madison's charges of federal usurpation in their Kentucky and Virginia Resolutions of 1798. The so-called Tariff of Abominations of 1828 and the somewhat less "abominable" tariff of 1832 were followed by South Carolina's Ordinance of Nullification; and the 1954 Supreme Court decision in *Brown v. Board of Education*, the school segregation case, was followed by various southern protests, including James Jackson Kilpatrick's *The Sovereign States: Notes of a Citizen of Virginia.* [7] In each case, as well as in others, the exercise of federal power brought forth not only a protest but a statement, or restatement, of the states-sovereignty theory of the Constitution.

This theory rests on a series of related propositions, the first of which being that it was the individual and separate states, not "one people," that declared independence of Great Britain, from which it follows that the states preceded the United States in time. Thus, or so it is alleged, the states, and not "we the people," created the United States, and more specifically, the United States is a compact entered into by the sovereign states with each other. The states and the United States stand in the legal relation of principal and agent, and the Constitution is the agreement stating the terms of the relationship. Whenever the agent, the United States, exceeds the terms of the agreement, it is the right of each of the principals, that is, each sovereign state, so to declare. This declaration may assume the form of an "interposition," a "nullification," or, in the extreme case, an abrogation (with notice) of the agreement itself, otherwise known as secession.

The advocates of states sovereignty, as well as their opponents, have always known that clashes of authority are inevitable—indeed, it would be disingenuous for anyone addressing himself to the question of a federal union to deny the possibility, in fact, the inevitability, of disputes concerning the legitimate extent of federal and state authority; they have always known, therefore, that the decisive question is who is to arbitrate these disputes. The essence of states sovereignty consists in the proposition that it is the right of the states to perform the role of arbiter or judge. Jefferson declared in the first of the Kentucky Resolutions,

. . . that the Government created by this compact was not made the exclusive or final *judge* of the extent of the powers delegated to itself; since that would have made its discretion, and not the Constitution, the measure of its powers; but that as in all other cases of compact among parties having no common Judge, each party has an equal right to judge for itself, as well of infractions as of the mode and measure of redress.

Madison, in the Virginia Resolutions, made the same point: ". . . in case of a deliberate, palpable, and dangerous exercise of other powers not granted by the said compact, the States, who are parties thereto, have the right and are in duty bound to interpose for arresting the progress of the evil. . . ." The decisive role of the states is claimed more emphatically in his 1799 Report on the Resolutions: "The states then, being the parties to the constitutional compact, and in their sovereign capacity, it follows of necessity that there can be no tribunal above their authority to decide, in the last resort, whether the compact made by them be violated. . . ."[8] The function performed historically by the Supreme Court of the United States belongs by right, according to the doctrine of states sovereignty, to the individual states.

### III

It will be necessary to return briefly to the subject of states sovereignty in the concluding section of this paper, but here it must be pointed out that the meaning of the Tenth Amendment assumes importance, as we said above, only after the essence of the states-sovereignty doctrine has been abandoned. The reason for this is almost obvious: if the states themselves were intended to be the judges of the legitimate extent of their own and of federal power (if, for example, the Constitution contained a provision authorizing the state legislatures to exercise a kind of review of federal legislation), they would not require a tenth amendment to remind them that they intended, when they established the Constitution, to set limits to their agent's (that is, the federal government's) power. Under this condition, there would be no need of a tenth amendment. Thus, by taking a stand on the ground of the Amendment, the states— rights advocates have retreated to a second line of defense: they have conceded, whether they realize it or not, the right of the federal government, and in practice the Supreme Court, to arbitrate federal-state relations. The Tenth Amendment would make no sense as an admonition addressed to the states. It can be understood only as an admonition to the Supreme Court that the federal government may not legitimately exercise all the powers of government.

According to Chief Justice Stone in his opinion for the Court in *United States v. Darby*, the

> amendment states but a truism that all is retained which has not been surrendered. There is nothing in the history of its adoption to suggest that it was more than declaratory of the relationship between the national and state governments as it had been established by the Constitution before the amendment or that its purpose was other than to allay fears that the new national government might seek to exercise powers not granted, and that the states might not be able to exercise fully their reserved powers.[9]

The evidence supports this view of the Amendment.

If, for example, we consult what are widely (but not universally) considered the most authoritative commentaries on the Constitution, we find Joseph Story declaring as follows:

> This amendment is a mere affirmation of what, upon any just reasoning, is a necessary rule of interpreting the constitution. Being an instrument of limited and enumerated powers, it follows irresistibly, that what is not conferred, is withheld, and belongs to the state authorities, if invested by their constitutions of government respectively in them; and if not so invested, it is retained BY THE PEOPLE, as a part of their residuary sovereignty.[10]

Story's first statement deserves comment: he says the Amendment is a mere affirmation of a necessary rule of *interpreting* the Constitution. It is not a rule of the law of the Constitution, which is to say that no court can base its holding in any case on the Amendment because the Amendment does not contain terms that can provide a rule of law. In this respect it differs from the commerce clause, for example, which empowers Congress to regulate not all commerce but only some commerce: "The Congress shall have Power . . . To regulate Commerce with foreign Nations, and among the several States, and with the Indian Tribes." Unlike the Tenth Amendment, which merely declares that what is not granted is reserved, the commerce clause specifies what commercial powers are granted and, implicitly, what commercial powers are reserved, and thereby provides the terms in which the constitutionality of congressional legislation can be determined. That is to say, a litigant can challenge an Act of Congress that purports to be a regulation of commerce with the argument that the activity being regulated is not commercial in nature, or if commercial, is not commerce with foreign nations or among the several states or with the Indian tribes, but is rather part of that commerce regulation of which is, by the commerce clause itself, reserved to the states.

The Tenth Amendment, on the other hand, contains no terms that the courts can use to settle any legal case or controversy. Litigants have referred to it in the course of resisting the exercise of federal power, but, since every Act of Congress is alleged to rest on some specific power-granting clause, courts have been required to look to those other clauses to determine whether the power being exercised is authorized; that is, to look to other clauses, such as the commerce clause, for the rules by which cases can be decided. Thus, it is not by chance that in the annotated Constitution, 147 pages are devoted to commerce clause cases decided by the Supreme Court, and only eight to cases in which the Tenth Amendment is referred to, and in the latter cases the references occur in the context of interpreting other parts of the Constitution.[11] In Thomas Reed Powell's words, the Tenth Amendment is a "canon of political policy [that] may carry a counsel of caution in deciding whether some proposed measure is really within or without the scope of national authority."[12] It is an accessory to interpretation of the Constitution: it is not and cannot provide a rule of law of the Constitution.

After alluding to the debate of the First Congress on the Amendment, to which we shall refer below. Story concludes his commentary on this part of the Constitution in these words:

> It is plain . . . that it could not have been the intention of the framers of this amendment to give it effect, as an abridgment of any of the powers granted under the constitution, whether they are express or implied, direct or incidental. Its sole design is to exclude any interpretation, by which other powers should be assumed beyond those, which are granted. All that are granted in the original instrument, whether express or implied, whether direct or incidental, are left in their original state. . . . The attempts, then, which have been made from time to time, to force upon this language an abridging, or restrictive influence, are utterly unfounded in any just rule of interpreting the words, or the sense of the instrument. Stripped of the ingenious disguises in which they are clothed, they are neither more nor less than attempts to foist into the text the word "expressly": to qualify what is general, and obscure what is clear and defined.[13]

The attempts to which Story refers have succeeded more than once in our constitutional history, and it is largely from them that the Amendment has become a matter of controversy.

In the early case of *Calder v. Bull*, the Supreme Court had to decide whether a Connecticut legislative enactment setting aside a decree of a probate court constituted an ex post facto law and was therefore void under Article I, Section 9, of the Constitution. In the course of deciding in favor of the state legislature, Justice Samuel Chase, in a wholly unnecessary dictum (for the decision turned on the meaning of ex post facto), declared that "all the powers delegated by the people of the United States to the federal government are defined, and no *constructive* powers can be exercised by it,"[14] which means that the federal government is limited to the exercise of those powers *expressly* delegated to it by the Constitution. But it is emphatically not true that all the powers of the federal government are "defined" in the Constitution—unless the word "defined" is used so loosely as to deprive it of all meaning. Rather, it is emphatically true that the full scope of federal power can be determined only by "construction"—reasonable construction, but construction nevertheless. The reference here is, of course, to the last clause of Article I, Section 8, wherein Congress is given the power to "make all Laws which shall be necessary and proper for carrying into Execution the foregoing Powers, and all other Powers vested by this Constitution in the Government of the United States, or in any Department or Officer thereof."[15] Powers that are "necessary and proper for carrying into Execution other powers that are expressly granted cannot be said to be "defined," at least not in themselves; if they are defined at all, it is only by reference to something else, and the referring terms, "necessary and proper," are not lacking in ambiguity. What is necessary and proper, furthermore, is a matter requiring "construction."

What Chase did implicitly in *Calder v. Bull*, namely, to "foist" the word "expressly" into the text of the Tenth Amendment, was done explicitly by later Supreme Court justices. The 1868 case of *Lane County v. Oregon* involved the issuance of $150 million in federal notes, which, according to the Act of Congress, were to be "receivable in payment of all taxes . . . to the United States," with one exception, and were to be regarded as "lawful money and legal tender in payment of all debts, public and private, within the United States," with another exception not relevant to the case. Oregon subsequently passed a law requiring sheriffs to pay over to the county treasurers "the full amount of the state and school taxes, in gold and silver coin"; and the county treasurers to pay over to the state treasurer "the State tax in gold and silver coin." Lane County tendered the amount due to the state in United States notes, and the state sued to recover the full amount in gold and silver coin, as required by state law. The state court awarded judgment to the state, and Lane County appealed to the federal Supreme Court on the grounds that its tender of United States notes was warranted by the Act of Congress and that the state law, if construed to require payment only in coin, was repugnant to the Act of Congress. The Supreme Court affirmed the judgment below by denying that Congress in the legal-tender statute had intended to include taxes imposed by state authority, which meant that there was no conflict between the congressional statute and the state law. In his opinion for a unanimous Court, Chief Justice Salmon P. Chase (not the Chase of *Calder v. Bull*), found it expedient to make so general and, under the circumstances, unnecessary references to the Constitution. "But in many articles of the Constitution," he wrote, "the necessary existence of the States, and, within their proper sphere, the independent authority of the States, is distinctly recognized. To them nearly the whole charge of interior regulation is committed or left; to them and to the people all powers not *expressly* delegated to the national government are reserved."[16]

Once again the decision did not turn on the meaning of the Tenth Amendment but, in this case, on the meaning of a statute. Yet it is worth noting that the Chief Justice, in giving the Act of Congress the narrowest of interpretations so as to uphold the right of the state to require its taxes to be paid in coin, saw fit to "foist into the text the word 'expressly,' " which, as we shall see, the framers of the Amendment were very careful to keep out of the text.

The third and most famous (or infamous) case in this line of Tenth Amendment decisions is *Hammer v. Dagenhart*. The statute attacked in this case was an Act of Congress prohibiting, not the production of goods by child labor, but merely the shipment of such goods into another state (or, more precisely, the offering for such shipment of such goods). The Supreme Court, in an opinion by Justice Day that has been subjected to more devastating criticism than perhaps any opinion ever written by a Supreme Court Justice with the possible exception of Taney's opinion for the Court in *Dred Scott v. Sandford*, denied that the power to regulate commerce among the states included the power to prohibit commerce—in spite of the fact that the Court had recently upheld the prohibition of interstate commerce in lottery tickets, to name only one item, which Day distinguished with a wholly specious argument, and in spite of the fact that Jefferson's administration had prohibited *all* foreign commerce, on the basis of the authority given Congress by the same clause that Congress relied on here. Justice Day saw the law to be an attempt on the part of Congress to force the states to abolish child labor (although, strictly speaking, its effect was merely to deny to a manufacturer the benefits of commerce outside his state if he employed children), and declared that the "grant of authority over a purely federal matter was not intended to destroy the local power always existing and carefully reserved to the States in the Tenth Amendment to the Constitution."[17] One page later he wrote as follows:

> In interpreting the Constitution it must never be forgotten that the Nation is made up of States to which are entrusted the powers of local government. And to them and to the people the powers not *expressly* delegated to the National Government are reserved. *Lane County v. Oregon,* 7 Wall. 71, 76. The power of the States to regulate their purely internal affairs by such laws as seem wise to the local authority is inherent and has never been surrendered to the general government.[18]

As Holmes pointed out in his powerful dissent (concurred in by three other members of the Court), the matter being regulated here was not an internal affair; the statute became operative only when a local manufacturer sought to "foist" his products onto the out-of-state market. And once again it should be noted that the citing of the Tenth Amendment was accompanied by a distortion of its text, by, that is, the foisting "into the text the word 'expressly.' " Once again it is proper to point out that the decision turned on the interpretation of another clause in the Constitution—here the commerce clause; and it should be plain from Day's language quoted above that the Tenth Amendment does not provide a rule of law out, instead, a rule of interpretation. And, once again, the application of this rule was accompanied by the distortion of the text of the Amendment. Reference to the Amendment in the context of denying federal power does not require such distortion; that is, it is surely possible in the course of determining the extent of federal power to be guided by the "counsel of caution" that the federal government is one of limited powers, without having to distort the text.[19] Just as surely, the United States is left with fewer powers if the states (and the people) are said to have reserved all powers not *expressly* delegated to it. In fact, the application of this judicially-amended rule of interpretation seems to lead, as it did in *Hammer v. Dagenhart,* to a denial of a power that is expressly delegated. Mr. Kilpatrick is absolutely correct when he says that the "Supreme Court . . . has no authority to repeal any provision of the Constitution. . . . [And] so long as the Tenth Amendment remains a part of the Constitution, it is elementary that it must be given full meaning. . . ."[20] But neither does the Supreme Court have the authority to amend the Constitution by adding words to it and then giving a full meaning to the amended Amendment—especially when the framers of the Amendment were unusually careful to omit the very word added by the Court in these three cases.

In his famous opinion for the full Court in *McCulloch v. Maryland,* Chief Justice Marshall, in the course of determining the scope of Congress's power under the "necessary and proper" clause, stressed the fact that, unlike the similar clause in the Articles of Confederation, the Tenth Amendment does not include the word "expressly." "The men who drew and adopted this amendment," Marshall declared, "had experienced the embarrassments resulting from the insertion of this word in the Articles of Confederation, and probably omitted it to avoid those embarrassments."[21] But the states-rights advocates are never willing to accept Marshall's credentials as constitutional expositor. "To be sure," Mr. Kilpatrick writes of his fellow Virginian's opinion,

"John Marshall, not long after the Union was formed, was to seize upon the fact that the restriction went only to the 'powers not delegated,' and not to the 'powers not *expressly* delegated,' as if this made some large difference."[22] But it made a difference to James Madison (whose credentials *are* accepted by Mr. Kilpatrick) and to a majority of the House of Representatives who, in 1789, in the First Congress, formally proposed the Tenth Amendment. Responding to the motion of South Carolina's Tucker to amend the proposed amendment by adding the word "expressly," Madison said he objected to the addition "because it was impossible to confine a Government to the exercise of express powers; [and because] there must necessarily be admitted powers by implication, unless the constitution descended to recount every minutia." The debate that ensued was very short, not one rising to support Tucker, and the motion was lost without a taking of the yeas and nays.[23] On the basis of this evidence one would be entitled to argue that Madison and his fellow members of the First Congress made a serious mistake, but it is not legitimate to argue that they made it unwittingly and without being aware of the significant difference between the Amendment as it appears in the Constitution and the Amendment as it appears in Tucker's version, in at least three Supreme Court decisions, and in the constitution propounded by Mr. Kilpatrick and his fellow advocates of states sovereignty.

By this time it should be obvious that there can be no legitimate dispute concerning the meaning of the Tenth Amendment: it is merely declaratory of the division of powers between nation and states made in the original, unamended Constitution. This much was conceded by counsel for the state of Maryland in its great dispute with the Bank of the United States in *McCulloch v. Maryland*: "We admit, that the Tenth Amendment to the Constitution is merely declaratory; that it was adopted *ex abundanti cautela* [out of an abundance of caution]; and that with it nothing more is reserved than would have been reserved without it."[24] The only legitimate dispute, and the focus of that case, is the division of powers made in the unamended Constitution, and specifically, the effect of the "necessary and proper" clause on that division. What is not delegated to the United States is, without question—for the Tenth Amendment so declares—reserved to the states or to the people; but among the powers delegated is the power to make all laws that are "necessary and proper for carrying into Execution" all the other powers expressly granted. As to the meaning of the Tenth Amendment, then, there can be no doubt; but what are necessary and proper laws is a question on which honest and intelligent men can differ and have differed throughout our constitutional history. And nowhere in this history has this question been so fully argued and so uncompromisingly answered as in the case of *McCulloch v. Maryland*. This question, fraught with such divergent tendencies, makes the decision in this case one of the most important decisions, if not *the* most important decision, ever handed down by the Court.

*McCulloch v. Maryland* involved the constitutionality of a Maryland tax levied on all notes issued by banks other than those chartered by the state, unless such banks paid annually the sum of $15,000 to the state. McCulloch was the cashier of the Baltimore branch of the Bank of the United States who refused to pay the tax, and the state sued to recover the statutory penalties. Judgment was rendered against him in the state court and, after affirmance by the Maryland Court of Appeals, he sued out a writ of error to the Supreme Court of the United States. The first question, and the only one directly relevant to this discussion, was whether Congress has the power to incorporate a bank. The question was not new in 1819, for it had been asked of Hamilton, Jefferson, and Randolph by President Washington in 1791 after Congress had passed a bill establishing the first Bank of the United States; and the significance of the Court's decision in 1819 is best grasped by reading the answers of Hamilton and Jefferson to Washington's question, because in those answers is to be found the essence of the national-state dispute: disagreement on the kind of country intended by the Framers of the Constitution. In Hamilton's view, the principles by which Jefferson construed the various provisions of the Constitution "would be fatal to the just and indispensable authority of the United States."[25] And so they would—to his United States. In Jefferson's view, a principle of constitutional construction that would permit Congress to incorporate a bank "would reduce the whole instrument to a single phrase, that of instituting a Congress with power to do whatever would be for the good of the United States,"[26] and that Congress should have such powers implied a nation that, according to his principles, was incompatible with republican government.

This disagreement on the constitutionality of the Bank is usually described in terms of liberal or loose as opposed to strict construction of the Constitution, and it was this, certainly. Hamilton, starting from the proposition that the powers of the national government are sovereign as to those objects "intrusted to its management," and that these sovereign powers include the means requisite to the ends of the powers, unless specifically denied in the Constitution, or immoral, or "contrary to the *essential ends* of political society," concludes that the power "to erect a corporation" is a sovereign power. This does not mean that Congress may erect a corporation "for superintending the police of the city of Philadelphia," because Congress is "not authorized to *regulate* the *police* of that city." But Congress, because it is expressly authorized to "lay and collect taxes," may certainly establish a bank to facilitate the exercise of this power. A bank is not "absolutely or indispensably" necessary to collect axes, but the true construction of the word "necessary" in the "necessary and proper" clause, in the grammatical as well as the popular sense of the word, is "*needful, requisite, incidental, useful*, or *conducive* to." The degree to which "a measure is necessary can never be a *test* of the legal right to adopt it; that must be a matter of opinion, and can only be a *test* of expediency."

To Jefferson, the power to incorporate a bank was not among the enumerated powers, and the carrying "into execution" of the "enumerated powers" does not require a bank. A bank may be convenient in that its bills "would have a currency all over the States," but by the same argument it would be "still more convenient" to have a bank, "whose bills should have a currency all over the world," and it certainly "does not follow from this superior conveniency, that there exists anywhere a power to establish such a bank. . . ." The Constitution restricts Congress "to the *necessary* means, that is to say, to those means without which the grant of power would be nugatory."[27]

Thus, their dispute narrows down to, and the effect of the Tenth Amendment depends on, the meaning of the word *necessary*, whether it should be construed loosely or strictly. This cannot be answered by an application of the principles of grammar or even of philology; on the contrary, the answer must be obtained by the rules applicable to the interpretation of legal documents, which Jefferson then started in a wholly unobjectionable form: "It is," he said, "an established rule of construction, where a phrase will bear either of two meanings, to give it that which will allow some meaning to the other parts of the instrument, and not that which would render all the others useless." But what is the meaning of the Constitution? That is, what is the purpose of the Constitution? The fundamental dispute underlying the grammatical disagreement concerns the purpose of the Constitution or, in short, the kind of country the United States was intended to be. It was because John Marshall and his associates on the Supreme Court agreed with Hamilton's view of the nature of the United States that they adopted his interpretation of the "necessary and proper" clause in their decision on the Bank in *McCulloch v. Maryland*, and held the incorporating of a bank to be among the powers of Congress and the Maryland tax to be illegal. It was because they shared his view of the nature, or character, of the United States that they never added the word "expressly" to the Tenth Amendment: and, because so much of Marshall's opinion for the Court is taken bodily from Hamilton's opinion on the constitutionality of the Bank, it is inconceivable that they were not cognizant of the alternatives between which they had to choose, for these alternatives are readily seen by comparing Hamilton's opinion with Jefferson's.

Hamilton's United States enacts laws whose objects are "to give encouragement to the enterprise of our own merchants, and to advance our navigation and manufactures." Commerce is to be the way of the nation and "money is the very hinge on which commerce turns." It is banks that provide the money, not only in the form of loans, but also in the form of notes circulating as a credit upon the coin and other property deposited with them. Banks facilitate commerce, they provide the credit needed for commerce; indeed, Congress' power to regulate commerce authorizes it to erect a corporation whose purpose is, by collecting the capital of a number of individuals, to permit the development of a "new and unexplored branch of trade . . . with some foreign county." This United States is necessarily to be heavily involved in foreign affairs, which makes war a likely possibility, and banks are a convenient source of the loans needed to fight wars. (And when the United States conquers in these wars, it will not be doubted that it possesses "sovereign jurisdiction over the conquered territory," a jurisdiction "competent to any species of legislation.") This is an aggressive country, busily and extensively engaged in many affairs, of growing authority in the world of business and the world of nations. It requires an active government with sufficient powers to provide direction and to promote its interests. "The means by which *national* exigencies are to be provided for, *national* inconveniences obviated, *national* prosperity promoted, are of such infinite variety, extent, and complexity, that there must of necessity be a great latitude of discretion in the selection and application of those means."[28] The powers attached, of necessity in Hamilton's view, to the office of the presidency of such a country are broad enough to promote the national interest, broad enough, in fact, to permit scope for statesmanship as this was traditionally understood. "If the *end* be clearly comprehended within any of the specified powers, and if the measure have an obvious relation to that *end*, and is not forbidden by any particular provision of the Constitution, it may safely be deemed to come within the compass of the national authority." Marshall's version of this in his opinion upholding the constitutionality of the Second Bank, reads as follows: "Let the end be legitimate, let it be within the scope of the constitution, and all means which are appropriate, which are plainly adapted to that end, which are not prohibited, but consist with the letter and spirit of the constitution, are constitutional."[29]

Counsel for the state of Maryland knew what was at stake in the case, what hinged on its outcome. "To derive such a tremendous authority from implication," he pleaded, "would be . . . to change the whole scheme and theory of the government."[30] But by 1819, the nation had probably been irreversibly set in the Hamiltonian direction, despite the rhetoric of the Jacksonians, and the question before the Court was more likely whether an attempt should be made to turn it around. There is no question but that Jefferson's United States lay in the opposite direction. This is to be seen in his insistence that the powers of the national government be restricted to those enumerated plus those absolutely and indispensably needed to carry into execution those that were enumerated; in his theory of the presidency with the authority only to execute the laws; and mostly in his insistence, stemming from Rousseau, that republican government was possibly only in a simply society marked by an equality of conditions. Such a society would be based on agriculture. Thus, it was altogether consistent for him to resist the Bank and the theory of the Constitution that authorized its incorporation, on the ground that the Bank bill toppled the "pillars of our whole system of jurisprudence," the "most ancient and fundamental laws of the several States; such as those against Mortmain, the laws of Alienage, the rules of descent, the acts of distribution, the laws of escheat and forfeiture, the laws of monopoly."

The Bank bill, in short, and in Jefferson's opinion, broke down the basic laws of an agricultural society, one of them at least deriving from feudal times, and, with the exception of the laws of distribution and the laws preventing monopoly, all of them dealing with real property. Banks promoted other kinds of property and another kind of United States. A bill to incorporate a national bank was contrary to the spirit of the Constitution, because it fostered a way of life contrary to the one intended by the Framers as he understood it. More particularly, the Bank bill was in conflict with the "most ancient and fundamental laws of the several States," and was therefore unconstitutional. He advised President Washington accordingly.

Washington, however, signed the bill into law and the Marshall court upheld the constitutionality of the Second Bank, because, in part, Marshall and his colleagues agreed with the theory of constitutional construction advanced by Madison in Congress during the debate on the Bank bill in 1791: "Interference with the power of the States was no constitutional criterion of the power of Congress." If the power was not given, Madison continued, "Congress could not exercise it; if given, they might exercise it, although it should interfere with the laws, or even the Constitution of the States."[31] And Marshall and his colleagues agreed with this theory of constitutional construction because they agreed with Hamilton's view of the United States:

> Throughout this vast republic, from the St. Croix to the Gulph of Mexico, from the Atlantic to the Pacific, revenue is to be collected and expended, armies are to be marched and supported. The exigencies of the nation may require, that the treasure raised in the north should be transported to the south, that raised in the east conveyed to the west, or that this order should be reversed. Is that construction of the constitution to be preferred which would render these op-

erations difficult, hazardous, and expensive? Can we adopt that construction (unless the words imperiously require it) which would impute to the framers of that instrument, when granting these powers for the public good, the intention of impeding their exercise by withholding a choice of means.[32]

## IV

We have argued in this paper that the meaning of the Tenth Amendment is beyond legitimate dispute, that it is merely declaratory of the distribution of powers made in the original Constitution, that the attempts to rely on it for a rule of constitutional law rather than of construction require a distortion of the text, and that the decisive argument concerns the meaning of the "necessary and proper" clause. We have argued further that the meaning of this clause hinges on the intent of the Framers. Did they intend to establish a simple society based on an equality of conditions (and not a society whose government has as its "first object . . . the protection of different and unequal faculties of acquiring property"),[33] a simple society made possible and maintained by a life devoted to agriculture and a passive government, or, on the contrary, a busy commercial society, based on trade and manufacturing, and requiring an active, aggressive, powerful government? Assuming that the Constitution itself would lend itself to either of these diverse and incompatible ways of life, and assuming that the issue had not yet been decided in 1791 at the time of the debate on the constitutionality of the Bank, indeed, that it had still to be decided with finality in 1819 at the time of *McCulloch v. Maryland*, can there be any doubt that today the decision has long since been made? Is it not inconceivable today, and has it not been so for a long time, that the national interest of the United States can be promoted (and who does not want to promote it?) by a government restricted to the exercise of those powers "absolutely and indispensably" necessary?

This is an argument from necessity and not an argument based on the intrinsic merits of such a government. It is an argument that does not palliate the discontent of the advocates of states rights who continue to insist not only that it might have been otherwise, but that it was intended to be otherwise: Mr. Kilpatrick, in 1957, long after the decisive battle had been fought, entitled his book *The Sovereign States: Notes of a Citizen of Virginia*. In it he insists not only that the Tenth Amendment was intended to place stringent limitations on the national government, not only that the word *necessary* was intended to mean absolutely necessary, but that the states were intended to arbitrate disputes between national and state governments: he contends for the states-sovereignty doctrine in its entirety by arguing that *Martin v. Hunter's Lessee* was decided incorrectly. This assertion deserves a brief response.

One of the lengthy debates in the First Congress came on the bill to establish a federal judiciary, although the only extended discussion was devoted to the part that was to become Section 3 of the Judiciary Act of 1789, the section providing for the establishment of the federal district courts. There were vigorous arguments against such establishment and in favor of reliance on the existing state court systems, yet the motion in the House to strike the provision from the bill was defeated 11–31.[34] On the all-important Section 25, which authorizes the Supreme Court to review and reverse the judgments of the state courts,[35] no debate took place; or if it took place, it was not recorded. But is not the deed, even without the words, significant, perhaps even conclusive, since so many members of Congress had been delegates to the Constitutional Convention, and can be presumed to have known what they were doing? And what they did was to establish the Supreme Court as arbiter of the conflicts between state and national laws, between state laws and the federal Constitution and treaties made under the authority of the United States. The states-sovereignty doctrine cannot exist with this law of the First Congress, so that when Virginia found itself involved in the struggle over the ownership of the Fairfax lands, and its highest court refused to obey the mandate of the Supreme Court of the United States, it did so by denying the constitutionality of this section of the Judiciary Act. This judgment was reversed by a unanimous Supreme Court in the famous case of *Martin v. Hunter's Lessee* in 1816, in an opinion written by Madison's appointee to the Court, Joseph Story.[36]

This settled the matter, so far as the law of the Constitution is concerned; it did not settle the matter so far as Mr. Kilpatrick is concerned. He is one of "many Americans . . . who pray earnestly that one day the fight may be resumed."[37] But of him and those who would fight this battle with him, we would ask whether any other decision, in 1816 or at any other time, past or future, would be compatible with the second clause of Article VI—not of the Articles of Confederation but of the Constitution of the United States—which provides that "this Constitution, and the Laws of the United States which shall be made in Pursuance thereof; and all Treaties made, or which shall be made, under the Authority of the United States, shall be the supreme law of the Land; and the Judges in every State shall be bound thereby, any Thing in the Constitution or Laws of any State to the Contrary notwithstanding."

And we would also direct their attention to one of the major ironies of American history: Jefferson, by purchasing Louisiana, did more than anyone to bring about a country extending from "sea to shining sea" and unable to avoid a place among the major powers of the world, thereby rendering impossible his dream of a simple, Rousseauian republic whose life was to be based on the land and whose government was to be restricted to a few enumerated powers. The purchase made a shambles of his constitutional theories, and he knew it; he said the purchase was unconstitutional, but he made it and had to suffer in silence the indignity of listening to his party friends defending his action as an exercise of an authority derived from the "necessary and proper" clause.[38] "Even in 1804," wrote Henry Adams, "the political consequences of the act were already too striking to be overlooked."

> Within three years of his inauguration Jefferson bought a foreign colony without its consent and against its will, annexed it to the United States by an act which he said made blank paper of the Constitution; and then he who had found his predecessors too monarchical, and the Constitution too liberal in powers—made himself monarch of the new territory, and wielded over it, against its protests, the powers of its old kings."[39]

And when Gallatin, his Secretary of the Treasury, took steps to establish a branch bank of the United States at New Orleans, he protested that "this institution is one of the most deadly hostility existing against the principles and form of our Constitution"[40]—but he acquiesced in its establishment. Henry Adam's comment on the entire episode is singularly appropriate today, and should be weighed by all those who, like Mr. Kilpatrick, are drawn to the old cause of their intellectual mentor:

> Such an experience was final; no century of slow and half-understood experience could be needed to prove that the hopes of humanity lay thenceforward, not in attempting to restrain the government from doing whatever the majority should think necessary, but in raising the people themselves till they should think nothing necessary but what was good.[41]

### Notes

1. *The Federalist Papers*, ed. Clinton Rossiter (New York: New American Library, 1961).
2. *The Federalist* 17. Madison made much the same argument in number 46.
3. *The Federalist* 45.
4. *The Federalist* 17.
5. *Wickard* v. *Filburn*, 317 U.S. III (1942); Daniel v. Paul, 395 U.S. 298 (1969).
6. *The Federalist* 45.
7. James Jackson Kilpatrick, *The Sovereign States: Notes of a Citizen of Virginia* (Chicago: Henry Regnery Comparny, 1957).
8. For an example of the application of this theory, see South Carolina's "Ordinance to Nullify certain acts of the Congress of the United States, purporting to be laws laying duties and imposts on the importation of foreign commodities," enacted November 24, 1832, and printed in Commager, *Documents of American History* (New York: F. S. Crofts & Company, 1934), Vol. I, pp. 261–62.
9. 312 U.S. 100. 124 (1941).
10. Story, *Commentaries on the Constitution of the United States* (1833), Sec. 1900.
11. *The Constitution of the United States of America: Analysis and Interpretation* (Washington: Government Printing Office, 1964).
12. Child Labor, Congress and the Constitution," 3 *Selected Essays on Constitutional Law* 527–28.
13. Story, *op. cit.*, Sec. 1901. Story is referring to the fact that the Articles of Confederation contained, in a clause otherwise similar to the Tenth Amendment, the word "expressly." This matter is discussed below.
14. 3 Dall. 386, 387 (1798).
15. It was part of the politics of states rights to ignore this clause when defining federal power. Mr. Kilpatrick quotes—with approval—the statement of Judge William Cabell in the Virginia court in the Fairfax lands case to the effect that to "the Federal government are confided certain powers, specially enumerated. . . ." Kilpatrick, *op. cit.*, p. 122.
16. 7 Wall. 71, 76 (1858). Italics supplied.
17. 247 U.S. 251, 274 (1918).
18. 247 U.S. 251, 275. Italics supplied.
19. See, for instance, *Civil Rights Cases*, 109 U.S. 3 (1883), and *Schechter Poultry Corp. v. United States*, 295 U.S. 495 (1935). In another case, one that can be said to come closer than any other to relying on the Tenth Amendment for its rule of decision, *Collector v. Day* 11 Wall. 113 (1871), Justice Nelson correctly quotes the Amendment (p. 124), but on the next page he quotes, with obvious approval, Chase's misquotation in *Lane County v. Oregon*. He then goes on to hold that Congress has no power to impose an income tax on the salary of a state judge—an absurd decision that was overruled in *Graves v. O'Keefe*, 306 U.S. 466 (1939).

20. Kilpatrick, *op. cit.*, p. 47.
21. 4 Wheat. 316, 406–7 (1819). Article II of the Articles of Confederation reads as follows: "Each state retains its sovereignty, freedom and independence, and every Power, Jurisdiction and right, which is not by this Confederation expressly delegated to the United States, in Congress assembled."
22. Kilpatrick, *op. cit.*, p. 47.
23. *Annals of Congress*, Vol. I, p. 790.
24. 4 Wheat. 316, 363 (1819).
25. "Opinion as to the Constitutionality of the Bank of the United States," in *Works of Alexander Hamilton*, Lodge ed. (1885), Vol. III, p. 180.
26. "Opinion on the Constitutionality of a National Bank," in *The Writings of Thomas Jefferson*, Ford ed., Vol. V, p. 286.
27. Cf. Madison's statement in the debate on the Tenth Amendment, p. 151 above.
28. Italics supplied.
29. 4 Wheat. 316, 421 (1819).
30. *Ibid.*, p. 365.
31. *Writings*, Hunt, ed., Vol. VI, p. 28. But Madison opposed the Bank bill because, he said, the power to incorporate it was not given. Whether this was consistent with his argument against the attempt to add the word "expressly" to the Tenth Amendment, we need not consider, for Madison was anything but consistent. True, his opposition to a bank of the United States did not change, but in a letter to Spencer Roane of September 2, 1819, he said, in the course of denouncing the Court's decision in *McCulloch v. Maryland*, that the "very existence of [the states] is a control on the pleas for a constructive amplification of the powers of the General Government"—that is, the mere existence of the states is a limitation on the powers of the national government. This is a direct contradiction of his statement during the 1791 debate on the Bank bill.
32. *McCulloch v. Maryland*, 4 Wheat. 316, 408 (1819).
33. *The Federalist* 10.
34. *Annals of Congress*, Vol. I, p. 866.
35. "Sec. 25: *And be it further enacted*, That a final judgment or decree in any suit, in the highest court of law or equity of a State in which a decision in the suit could be had, where is drawn in question the validity of a treaty or statue of, or an authority exercised under the United States, and the decision is against their validity; or where is drawn in question the validity of a statute of, or an authority exercised under any State, on the ground of their being repugnant to the constitution, treaties or laws of the United States, and the decision is in favour of such their validity . . . may be re-examined and reversed or affirmed in the Supreme Court of the United States upon a writ of error. . . ."
36. 1 Wheat. 304 (1816).
37. Kilpatrick, *op. cit.*, p. 125.
38. Henry Adams, *History of the United States of America* (New York, 1890), Vol. II, p. 103.
39. *Ibid.*, p. 130.
40. *Ibid.*, p. 131.
41. *Ibid.*, p. 130.

## States' Rights and Vested Interests

Robert J. Harris

"Constitutional law," wrote Edward S. Corwin in 1941, "has always a central interest to guard."[1] During much of the history of the American Republic this central interest has been private property. Political theory, always an important ingredient of constitutional law, also has some central interest to protect, and in the United States two of the more important constitutional or political theories that have been utilized to protect the vested rights of property, corporate as well as private, have been the theory of natural law, with its Anglo-Saxon emphasis on natural rights, and the dogma of states' rights, particularly since the day of John C. Calhoun. In some ways these doctrines have supplemented each other; at times they have been mutually inconsistent; and each, as is true of many political ideas, has been used as a double-edged sword which can cut in opposite directions.

One of the most notable examples of the versatility of a political idea is to be found in the various purposes to which the principle of the law of nature or natural rights was bent, once as a revolutionary device to topple the altars of religion and the thrones of kings, and later as an instrument for the protection of the vested interests of property rights. In this regard natural law and the natural rights doctrines served well the corporate masters of the American economy, not only in the opinions of Supreme Court judges which emphasized the natural rights of artificial persons at the expense of those of natural persons,[2] but also served the purposes of the Liberty League in the 1930's and Senator Taft later in proclaiming liberty to all the land in a manner that was somewhat different from that used by the Minute Men or by those who stormed the Bastille. The doctrine of States' Rights, though less important than theories of natural law and natural rights, has nevertheless made significant contributions to American politics and law and endures with a persistent if perverse vitality.

Earlier states' rights doctrine as propounded by Thomas Jefferson, John Taylor of Caroline, and John C. Calhoun were only a portion of a broader political theory which was systematic to the extent that it assumed certain principles concerning the nature of the state and society, the nature of man, and the ends of government. As a portion of a general political theory, states' rights were a means for the attainment of primary ends and hardly an absolute even as a means. Thus what may be called the classical theory of states' rights as enunciated by Jefferson and John Taylor was liberally compounded with theories of agrarianism, natural rights, an advocacy of the dispersal of all power whether political or economic, and attacks on the granting of special privileges to banking, commerce, and industry. Though not systematically organized, Taylor's writings on the subject are among the most extended and consistent. Taylor assumed, as states' righters have assumed with only differences of detail since, that the thirteen colonies became sovereign independent states when they achieved independence; that the constitution was a compact which did not create a central state

Reprinted with permission from the Southern Political Science Association, © 1953.

or nation; that the general government could not be the judge of its own powers through the Supreme Court or any other organ; that conflicts between state and federal authority were to be judged and resolved by the states, if necessary by amendment; and that federal powers should not be extended by interpretation or implication. However, as Mr. Mudge has pointed out, Taylor made all these assumptions in defense "of the radical philosophy of the Revolution," and attacked "nationalism, geographical majorities, legal privilege that allows the few to plunder the many, and the growing power of an urban industrial group symbolized in the protective tariff with the resultant impoverishment of the yeomanry."[3] Taylor's writings abound in denunciations of "a few maritime capitalists," "the garbage of aristocracy," the depredations of pecuniary capitalists, the tariff, the tyrannical stock-jobbing system, and the general government as "the associate and ally of patronage, funding, armies and many other interests" subsisting upon agriculture. With Jefferson, Taylor was convinced that agriculture is morally superior to any other form of economic activity. He regarded the factory system as a device not only for the monopolization of capital and labor but also for the regimentation of individuals which was degrading to human nature.[4]

Calhoun's theories were more systematic, less concerned with specific attacks on a central bank, corporate charters, and the like, but were designed to combat the tariff as an enemy of the southern agrarian economy and to protect the "peculiar institution" of slavery. He extended, refined, and perfected Taylor's doctrines in ways that need only passing notice. Calhoun reserved liberty exclusively to the ruling class, rejected the egalitarian doctrines of the Declaration of Independence, denied generally the doctrine of natural rights in its traditional context, and converted the principle of states' rights into an instrumentality primarily for the protection of property rights, with the protection of slavery foremost in his consideration. In so doing he extracted from states' rights principles most of the vestiges of revolutionary and natural rights philosophy and liberal agrarian humanitarianism. In the writings of both Calhoun and Taylor, however, states' rights are a weapon against the vested interests of finance and industrial capital in the basic conflict with agrarianism.

The political and legal doctrines of states' rights received juristic recognition to a limited extent during much of the period when Chief Justice Taney presided over the Supreme Court. The opinions of the Taney Court are replete with references to state sovereignty[5] with the usual overtones to the effect that there are mutually exclusive areas of governmental power.[6] In emphasizing state sovereignty, however, the Taney Court unlike its latter day exponents emphatically enunciated the idea of active state governments effectively regulating banks, corporations, and economic activities generally in the interest of the common welfare. In pursuance of these ideas the Taney Court considerably contracted the latitudinarian limitations of the contracts clause to enable the states to regulate corporations,[7] enlarged state powers over the economy by the holding in the *Cooley* case which established the long standing rule that the commerce clause in the absence of Congressional action does not prevent state regulation of interstate commerce in areas not requiring uniform action,[8] and by relaxing the prohibition against the states' making anything but gold or silver legal tender in payment of debts to enable the states to charter banks and empower them to issue notes as legal tender.[9]

These extensions of state power rest upon the assumption expressed in the *Charles River Bridge*[10] case to the effect that "while the rights of property are sacredly guarded, we must not forget that the Community also have rights, and that the happiness and well-being of every citizen depends on their faithful preservation."[11] Similarly, in *West River Bridge Co. v. Dix* we find Justice Daniel declaring that the power and duty of eminent domain "are to be exerted not only in the highest acts of sovereignty, and in the external relations of governments; they reach and comprehend likewise the interior polity and relations of social life, which should be regulated with reference to the advantage of the whole society." Continuing, he asserted that

> Under every established government, the tenure of property is derived mediately or immediately from the sovereign power of the political body, organized in such mode or exerted in such way as the community or state may have thought proper to ordain. It can rest on no other guarantee. . . . Upon any other hypothesis, the law of property would be simply the law of force.[12]

To the Taney Court, therefore, states' rights were synonymous with the power and the duty of the states to regulate the vested interests of property, private or corporate, in the interest of the welfare of the whole people of the state.

Lee's surrender at Appomattox did not signal the end of states' rights doctrines, but rather the triumph of finance and industrial capitalism whose onward march was fostered by a perversion of the doctrine of states' rights, which had the effect not only of extracting whatever remained of its liberal and humanitarian elements but also of converting it into a symbol that was apolitical in that it became a vehicle of inaction not merely a federal power but state power as well. The mercantile and agrarian capitalism of the eras of Marshall and Taney required relatively little regulation. Much of this could be provided at the state and local levels through the medium of the common law as supplemented by state legislation. However, the triumph of industrial capitalism operating through the medium of a corporate collectivism centralized and extended economic power and created clusters of private government which first neutralized state powers and then overcame them, to challenge the political power of the nation. The rise of the railroads, the centralization of industry in the trusts, and the growing dependence of agricultural producers and wage earning consumers upon remote but powerful transportation, grain elevator, and manufacturing companies inevitably produced irresistible demands for more effective state regulation and for federal action in areas formerly occupied by the states or unoccupied at all.

These demands were ultimately translated into the Granger legislation of the 1870's and subsequent protective labor legislation at the state level. Congress responded with the Interstate Commerce Act, and Anti-Trust and Pure Foods and Drugs legislation. Beaten in the halls of Congress and the state legislatures, the defeated capitalists sought refuge in the courts, and ultimately in the Supreme Court. State regulatory legislation was assailed as unconstitutional on the ground that it either violated the due process clause of the Fourteenth Amendment or interfered with the power of Congress to regulate interstate commerce. Federal legislation of a similar character was assailed as invasion of the reserved rights of the states. Such assaults met with limited success, and the net result was seriously to limit the Taney conception of state sovereignty by the due process clause as an all encompassing protection of vested property and contract rights, and the Marshall and later conceptions of national power by what Justice Holmes once called "some invisible radiation" from the general terms of the Tenth Amendment.[13] In many of these cases too, even when governmental power was sustained, articulate dissenters mustered substantial minorities to herald other results once they should become a majority, and insubstantial majorities qualified ruling opinions by paying homage to states' rights. Hence, it is not surprising, as Justice Frankfurter has described the judicial process in another connection, how hints became suggestions which were to be translated into dicta and then progressively distorted into rules of decision.[14] Ultimately, therefore, the seed of juristic states' rights planted by Chief Justice Taney and his Court flourished under the tender care of Justices Field and Brewer and Chief Justice Fuller, and provided a rich harvest for Chief Justice White, and Justices Day, Vandevanter, McReynolds, Sutherland, and Butler.

The doctrine that the Tenth Amendment limits the exercise of expressly delegated federal power was fully accepted by the Court in *Hammer v. Dagenhart*[15] where the Court invalidated the first child labor act of Congress as an invasion of the reserved rights of the states in the guise of regulating interstate commerce. In the opinion of the Court, Justice Day in effect amended the Tenth Amendment by declaring that "the powers not expressly delegated to the National Government" are reserved to the states or to the people. Similar reasoning was employed to reach the same result in the *Child Labor Tax* case. Dual federalism as a device to protect vested interests against national legislation reached its full fruition in the *Schechter,*[16] *Carter Coal*[17] and *Butler* cases,[18] which voided respectively the National Industrial Recovery Act, the first Bituminous Coal Act, and the first Agricultural Adjustment Act on the ground among others that they invaded the reserved rights of the states.

In the *Schechter* case Congress was held to have no power to regulate the trade practices and working conditions in the wholesale live poultry industry because at most they produced only indirect effects upon interstate commerce. The argument of the government that low wages and long hours of work in the live poultry industry constituted a burden upon commerce was regarded by Chief Justice Hughes as an implication

> that the Federal authority under the commerce clause should be deemed to extend to the establishment of rules to govern wages and hours in intrastate trade and industry generally throughout the country, thus overriding the authority of the States to deal with domestic problems arising from labor conditions in their internal commerce.
>
> It is not the province of the Court, to consider the economic advantage or disadvantages of such a centralized system. It is sufficient to say that the Federal Constitution does not provide for it. Our growth and development have called for wide use of the commerce power of the Federal Government in its control over the expanded activities of interstate commerce and in protecting that commerce from burdens, interferences, and conspiracies to restrain and monopolize it. But the authority of the Federal Government may not be pushed to such an extreme as to destroy the distinction, which the commerce clause itself establishes, between commerce "among the several States" and the internal concerns of a State.[19]

Of a similar import is the declaration of Justice Sutherland in the *Carter* case that:

> The employment of men, the fixing of their wages, hours of labor and working conditions, the bargaining in respect of these things . . . each and all constitute intercourse for the purposes of production, not of trade. . . . Extraction of coal from the mine is the aim and the completed result of local activities. Commerce in the coal mined is not brought into being by force of these activities, but by negotiations, agreements, and circumstances entirely apart from production. Mining brings the subject matter of commerce into existence. Commerce disposes of it.[20]

In this manner the Court held federal regulation of the soft coal industry invalid in a made case between the president of a coal company and the company itself on the ground that it invaded the reserved rights of the states, in spite of the official protests of the Attorneys General of the coal producing states that the rights of their states were not being invaded and the legislation was necessary.

At the same time the commerce clause was being defined in terms of the Tenth Amendment, the Court was also delimiting the federal taxing power along similar lines. In *United States v. Butler*[21] the Tenth Amendment attained its fullest development as a limit upon the power of the federal government to tax. Here the processing taxes of the first Agricultural Adjustment Act which were earmarked for the payment of benefits to farmers to curtail production were declared unconstitutional over the dissent of three justices. Justice Roberts, for the majority, concluded that Congress had no power to regulate agricultural production and that the tax was a mere incident of such regulation designed to coerce farmers into compliance to the subversion of the power reserved to the states. The *Butler* case, like all the other invalidating federal legislation as a violation of the Tenth Amendment, subordinated federal power to the existence of state power and subverted the supremacy clause of the Constitution.

The physical and legal inability of the states to regulate business enterprises operating on a national scale, and the use of the Tenth Amendment as a bar to federal action, combined to produce a large area in which no government could function and in which corporate clusters of economic power erected so to speak their own private governments which affected the daily lives of more people than did civil or official government. Judicial power in such a scheme lost its character either as an organ to extend national power under Marshall's conception or as a so-called impartial umpire between the nation and the states as competing sovereignties in the Taney view. It became instead a partisan promoter of private business collectively organized and managed to be free from governmental regulation.

The theory of juristic states' rights deserves brief notice in another of its aspects. Under the mysteries of judicial review a state as such has no standing in the federal courts to challenge the validity of federal action allegedly encroaching upon its rights unless it can show an injury to its interests in a proprietary capacity. Thus Georgia and Mississippi were unable to challenge the validity of the Reconstruction Acts.[22] Private persons or corporations suffering an injury, usually economic, do have such a standing, and have it almost exclusively. This phase of juristic federalism is well illustrated by the case of *Carter v. Carter Coal Co.* Mr. Robert L. Stern has given an interesting account of the litigation in this case.[23] According to him, on the same day that the first Bituminous Coal Act became law, the directors of the Carter Coal Company met in New York. The board consisted of James Carter, who was president, his father, vice-president, and C. A. Hall, an employee of the company. James Carter presented a letter in which he asserted that the coal act was unconstitutional and recommended that the company refuse to adhere to the coal code. His father agreed that act was unconstitutional, but thought the company should not run the risk of paying the tax on coal required of non-members in the event the act should be sustained. The third director agreed with the elder Carter, and the board adopted a resolution rejecting James Carter's proposals. This action was subsequently approved by a majority of the voting stock held by James Carter's father and mother who outvoted him and his wife.

James Carter then brought a suit to enjoin the company of which he was president from adhering to the coal code and complying with it. Although to find adversity of parties and interests in such circumstances is to find it almost anywhere, the federal courts took jurisdiction of the suit as an actual case or controversy within the meaning of Article III. The Act was challenged as unconstitutional on the allegation, among others, that it invaded the reserved rights of the states. When the case went to the Supreme Court seven states presented briefs as *amici curiae* to sustain the validity of the Act on the ground that it did not invade their rights. On these briefs the states of Illinois, Indiana, New Mexico, Pennsylvania, and Washington were represented by their Attorneys General; Kentucky was represented by an Assistant Attorney General; and Ohio was represented by a lawyer in the Attorney General's office. In sustaining the contentions of Carter, the Court in effect declared that a private citizen or a corporation is prepared to know better when states' rights are being invaded than the states themselves, even when acting through their chosen legal counsel. This phase of juristic states' rights clearly demonstrates that the distensions and distortions of the Tenth Amendment prior to 1937 had little or nothing to do with the rights of states as states, but almost everything with economic interests whose spokesmen profess a solicitude for states' rights.

Juristic states' rights or dual federalism went into a decline in the *National Labor Relations Act* cases[24] and was effectively laid to rest in *United States v. Darby Lumber Co.*[25] However, the slogan of states' rights remains as a political symbol. The spectre of a centralized federal bureaucracy invading the reserved rights of the states has been repeatedly invoked by the electric light and power companies to combat federal power policies; by the American Medical Association in its successful attempt to defeat a national health insurance program; by southern politicians and others in their effort to preserve the power of a white majority to oppress and exploit a black minority; by employers to combat ameliorative federal labor legislation, although these same employers favor and have favored federal regulation to curb unions; by oil companies and others to defeat national title to the oil in the submerged lands in the Tidelands oil controversy. That these same groups would be equally opposed to effective state action in these areas of governmental activity is amply illustrated by lobbying activities in state legislatures and by the filed briefs and oral arguments of corporation counsel in the federal courts challenging the validity of state legislation regulating public utilities, providing for protection of labor, and establishing mild social reforms on the ground that at the state level such legislation deprived vested interests of liberty or property. Moreover, the public utilities and employers manifested little concern for the right of the states to regulate utility services and rates and to formulate policies in the area of labor legislation so long as they had recourse to injunctions in the federal courts to restrain the enforcement of rate orders of state public utility commissions or to break strikes in labor disputes, although judicial intervention in both areas struck at the basic power of the states to govern men and things within their dominion.

Vested interests seeking economic gain, and candidates motivated by desire for public office, have cooperated to impress upon the public mind the picture of the federal government as an aggressive enemy. This is well illustrated by the controversy over Tidelands oil. Although the *California, Louisiana,* and *Texas* decisions affected adversely only the claims of three states and indirectly, at least, fostered the interests of the other forty-five, they provoked wails of anger and anguish not merely from the oil interests and the three affected states, but in addition from national organizations of state and local officials, private interests other than oil companies masquerading under the banner of states' rights, and not surprisingly from the oligarchy of the American Bar Association in its customary and self-appointed rôle as the custodian and defender of vested interests against "socialism," "statism, " and "bureaucracy" in Washington. The efforts of the Truman Administration ro prosecute the claims of the national government contributed to some extent to the rise of the States' Rights or Dixiecrat party in 1948, a novel third party in that it looked exclusively to the past, not without hopes, to be sure, of controlling the future.

In committee hearings and Congressional debates representatives of oil companies, officials of state governments, and members of Congress removed traditional states' rights doctrines from their venerable shrouds and restated them with an articulation that would have won the applause of John Taylor and John C. Calhoun, albeit for opposite purposes. Admittedly the doctrine of states' rights does coincide in this controversy with the governmental interests of the three coastal states involved, but it has been the well financed lobby of the oil interests which successfully used states' rights propaganda to induce a majority of Senators and Representatives from other states to vote not merely against what the Supreme Court has called the paramount rights of the national government, but against the interests of their own states.

The solicitude of the oil companies for states' rights is hardly based on convictions derived from political theory but rather on fears that federal ownership may result in the cancellation or modification of state leases favorable to their interests, their knowledge that they can successfully cope with state oil regulatory agencies, and uncertainty concerning their ability to control a federal agency. The position of the oil companies is reflected in the public press and other propaganda media of Louisiana and Texas which have persistently distorted the decisions of the Supreme Court affecting the submerged lands, depicted the actions of the federal government as the "Tidelands grab" by an oppressive central government from sovereign states, and in general misrepresented the basic facts of the controversy. It is no exaggeration to state that the oil companies and their adherents in this controversy corroborate the thesis of Brooks Adams to the effect that business, of all elements in the national community, stands most in need of law and order, and yet at the same time is the most lawless.[26]

Whatever political validity the doctrine of states' rights may have had in the formative period of the union has been lost in the transition of the American economy from a simple and decentralized agrarian and commercial order, in which the individual or family was the economic unit, into a highly centralized and unified industrial order in which the corporation is the economic unit. By 1938, according to the final report of the Temporary National Economic Committee, there were thirty corporations with assets of more than one billion dollars each; by contrast only ten states had within their borders property and wealth valued at more than the assets of the Metropolitan Life Insurance Company and the American Telephone and Telegraph Company, and eighteen states had a smaller assessed valuation of property than the smallest of these industrial or financial giants. Even after we take into account the assessment of property at less than its value and the failure of assessors to list much personal property at all, the contrast between the governmental power of the states and the economic power of large financial and industrial combinations is startling, and has become more so in the years that have intervened since 1938.[27]

Parallel to giantism in industry is the economic concentration of power into the hands of a relatively few corporations, In 1935, for example, 4.6 per cent of all the corporations engaged in transportation and public utilities controlled 93 per cent of all such assets; 2.6 per cent of all financial corporations controlled 78 per cent of the corporate assets in this area; and 1.5 per cent of all manufacturing companies controlled 66 per cent of all manufacturing assets. Viewed from another angle one company produced all the virgin aluminum, a production it now shares with a few small companies; three companies produced 86 per cent of all the automobiles; three produced 61 per cent of the steel; and four 58 per cent of the whiskey.[28] Added to these may be mentioned concentration in the manufacture of farm machinery, the production of copper, the refining of oil, and the processing of foods.

Although the data cited above were collected by the Temporary National Economic Committee in the 1930's, a number of factors contributed to concentration in industry during and following the second World War. The larger industries were generally more favored in the awarding of war and defense contracts and the allocation of priorities on raw materials; during much of the war period the prosecution of anti—trust actions by the Department of Justice was largely suspended except for actions against cartel arrangements limiting the production of essential war materials; and the profits by big business were used for plant expansions and the acquisition of smaller firms. In isolated instances, to be sure, new companies have arisen, as in the aluminum industry, but the Aluminum Company of American still dominates its field. The trend in all economic activity is therefore toward concentration of wealth and the centralization of economic power.[29] To suppose that a decentralized political order operating under the traditional separation of powers and checks and balances can effectively control a centralized economic order, or even act as a counter-check, is to ignore the facts of economic and political life. In one form or another centralization of economic power is accompanied by political and administrative centralization.

These vast concentrations not only exercise enormous powers over workers, consumers, and stockholders, but they possess in addition a great influence over government. They have used government as a lever to pry advantages from various groups by exploiting the law as a means of outlawing the methods whereby competitors operate business, denying freedom of choice to the consumer, and fixing prices from which retailers cannot deviate under the euphemism of fair trade, consumer protecttion, or self-government in industry. Through trade associations, price leadership, and other devices the strongest of these concentrations, usually organized on a unitary rather than a federal basis, exert great powers over smaller competitors. To talk of states' rights in such a context is not only to ignore political realities, but to pervert John Taylor's principle to the aid of the very thing he detested most—a stock-jobbing paper aristocracy.

The doctrine of states' rights, in addition to ignoring the facts of economic and political life, has always been an inconsistency within itself. Each political party has made it a battle cry when out of power, only to alarm its opponents by its centralizing tendencies when in power. Individual politicians have shown a notable ambivalence on the subject as illustrated by the public careers and views of Webster and Calhoun; the former beginning as a particularist and ending as a nationalist, the latter beginning as a nationalist voting for tariffs, internal improvements, and a central bank, and ending as a nullificationist. Each in his own way corroborated Harrington's dictum that empire follows property, and each also followed property. Even John Taylor, the most consistent advocate of state sovereignty, made exceptions for his cherished agrarians by advocating a soil conservation program and the establishment of a national tool office at public expense for experimenting with foreign tools suitable for use in America, as of greater value than a patent office in listing inventions for industrial use.[30]

Today state sovereignty is even more of an anomaly in view of extensive federal grants of money to the states. Senators, Representatives, and governors of southern states who most ardently repeat the ritual of state sovereignty go to the federal treasury with outstretched and eager hands. During the summer and autumn of 1952 the governors of Texas and Louisiana, while angrily denouncing federal encroachments on states' rights, like the Emperor Henry in proceeding to Canossa, appealed to Washington as humble mendicants seeking indulgences in the form of drought relief for their states. In the fiscal year 1950–51 the states of Alabama, Arkansas, Florida, Georgia, Louisiana, Mississippi, North Carolina, South Carolina, Tennessee, Texas, and Virginia contributed a total of $6,267,108,000 to the federal treasury and received back in federal grants-in-aid, exclusive or direct federal spending, a total of $653,125,000, or slightly better than 10 per cent of their total contributions. These eleven states paid into the federal treasury 12.52 per cent of all internal revenue collections and received in return between 27 and 28 per cent of federal grants-in-aid, while having a population amounting to 25¼ per cent of the national total. Some states have fared better than others. Thus Arkansas and Mississippi received in return more than a third of what they paid in, and South Carolina approximately 16 per cent. Louisiana's federal grants of $79,933,000 make its loss of tidelands oil revenues look less significant, and render the action of its legislature in petitioning Congress for a constitutional convention to propose an amendment to the Constitution limiting income taxes to a maximum of 25 per cent on any income incongruous with reality.

These data demonstrate that a significant number of the southern states are financially dependent upon the federal government, and this fact in turn suggests that dependence is inconsistent with either rights or responsibilities. Moreover, such data stand in direct repudiation of the picture of the federal government as an enemy of the states and the people as painted by newspaper editors, politicians in and out of office, and other leaders of "thought" and "opinion." They point rather, as do other data, to a co-operative federalism which stresses programs and results rather than barren elocution about rights, state sovereignty, or national supremacy.

It should be emphasized that the foregoing observations do not point to the conclusion that the states do not have a vital importance to the American scheme of government or that federalism should be replaced by a unitary government. On the contrary, the states display and should display a marked vigor in all kinds of activities. It is important therefore that our conceptions of federalism in a technological and industrial order characterized by a considerable amount of unity, and endowed with a wide range of political and economic powers, should not be determined or influenced by outworn shibboleths which were popular in some quarters a century ago. Likewise, when the dogma of states' rights is used to perpetuate public wrongs, it is time for one to make a choice. In making that choice it is appropriate to recall Justice Black's statement in *Testa v. Katt*[31] that "the States of the Union constitute a nation." Finally, to emphasize the connection between states' rights and vested interests is not to overlook at various periods in our history the connection between nationalism and vested interests—but that is a separate problem.

### Notes

1. Edward S. Corwin, *The Constitution and What It Means Today* (7th Ed.; Princeton: Princeton University Press, 1941), p. viii. See also the preface to the 10th edition, p. vi. In 1941 Professor Corwin declared that "Today it appears to be that of organized labor."
2. See Charles A. Beard, "Corporations and Natural Rights," 12 *The Virginia Quarterly Review* 337 ff. (1936).
3. Eugene Tenbroeck Mudge, *The Social Philosophy of John Taylor of Caroline* (New York: Columbia University Press, 1939), p. 5. See also John Taylor, *An Inquiry into the Principles and Policy of the Government of the United States* (Fredericksburg, Va.: Green and Cady, 1814); *Construction Construed, and Constitutions Vindicated* (Richmond: Shepherd and Pollard, 1820); *Tyranny Unmasked* (Washington: Davis and Force, 1822); *New Views of the Constititution of the United States* (Washington: Way and Gideon, 1823); and *Arator* (Georgetown: J. M. and J. B. Carter, 1813).
4. Mudge, *op. cit.*, pp. 1–9, 27–88.
5. Carl B. Swisher, *Roger B. Taney* (New York: The Macmillan Company, 1935), pp. 409–410.
6. *Kentucky v. Dennison*, 24 Howard 66 (1861). See also *Ableman v. Booth*, 21 Howard 506 (1859).
7. *Charles River Bridge v. Warren Bridge*, 11 Peters 420 (1837); *West River Bridge Co. v. Dix*, 6 Howard 507 (1848).
8. *Cooley v. Board of Port Wardens*, 12 Howard 199 (1851).
9. *Briscoe v. Bank of the Commonwealth of Kentucky*, 11 Peters 257 (1837).
10. *Charles River Bridge v. Warren Bridge*, 11 Peters 420 (1837).
11. *Charles River Bridge v. Warren Bridge*, 11 Peters 420, 548 (1837).
12. *West River Bridge Co. v. Dix*, 6 Howard 507, 532 (1848).
13. *Missouri v. Holland*, 252 U.S. 416, 434 (1920).
14. See *United States v. Rabinowitz*, 339 U.S. 56, 75 (1950) (dissenting opinion).
15. *Hammer v. Dagenhart*, 247 U.S. 251, 275 (1918).
16. *A. L. A. Schechter Poultry Corporation v. United States*, 295, U.S. 495 (1935).
17. *Carter v. Carter Coal Co.*, 298 U.S. 238 (1936).
18. *United States v. Butler*, 297 U.S. 1 (1936).

19. *A. L. A. Schechter Poultry Corporation v. United States*, 295 U.S. 495, 549 (1935).
20. *Carter v. Carter Coal Co.*, 298 U.S. 238, 303–304 (1936).
21. *United States v. Butler*, 297 U.S. 1 (1936).
22. *Mississippi v. Johnson*, 4 Wallace 475 (1867); *Georgia v. Stanton*, 6 Wallace 318 (1868).
23. Robert L. Stern, "The Commerce Clause and the National Economy, 1933–1946," 59 *Harvard Law Review* 645, 667–668 (1946).
24. *National Labor Relations Board v. Jones and Laughlin Steel Corporation*, 301 U.S. 1 (1937); *National Labor Relations Board v. Fruehauf Trailer Co.*, 301 U.S. 49 (1937); *National Labor Relations Board v. Friedman-Marks Clothing Co.*, 301 U.S. 58 (1937); *Associated Press v. National Labor Relations Board*, 301 U.S. 103 (1937); *Washington, Virginia and Maryland Coach Co. v. National Labor Relations Board*, 301 U.S. 142 (1937).
25. *United States v. Darby*, 312 U.S. 100 (1941).
26. Brooks Adams, *The Theory of Social Revolutions* (New York: The Macmillan Company, 1913), pp. 212–213.
27. Temporary National Economic Committee, *Final Report and Recommendations*, pp. 676–677.
28. Temporary National Economic Committee, *Hearings*, Pt. 1, pp. 115, 137.
29. For concentration trends since 1940 see, House of Representatives, *Hearings*, Committee on the Judiciary, Subcommittee on the Study of Monopoly Power, 81st and 82d Congresses; and *House Report No. 255*, March 13, 1951. See also, Federal Trade Commission *Report on the Concentration of Productive Facilities* (Washington, D.C.: United States Government Printing Office, 1947); United States Senate Select Committee on Small Business, Subcommittee on Monopoly, *Report* of March 31, 1952; Federal Trade Commission, *The Merger Movement* (Washington, D.C.: United States Government Printing Office, 1948); and *Economic Concentration and World War II*, Report of the Smaller War Plants Corporation, 79th Congress, 2d Session, Senate Print No. 6, 1946.
30. Mudge, *op. cit.*, p. 164.
31. *Testa v. Katt*, 330 U.S. 386, 389 (1947).

---

# Advantages of the Federal System in General, and Its Special Utility in America

Alexis de Tocqueville

In small states, the watchfulness of society penetrates everywhere, and a desire for improvement pervades the smallest details; the ambition of the people being necessarily checked by its weakness, all the efforts and resources of the citizens are turned to the internal well-being of the community and are not likely to be wasted upon an empty pursuit of glory. The powers of every individual being generally limited, his desires are proportionally small. Mediocrity of fortune makes the various conditions of life nearly equal, and the manners of the inhabitants are orderly and simple. Thus, all things considered, and allowance being made for the various degrees of morality and enlightenment, we shall generally find more persons in easy circumstances, more contentment and tranquillity, in small nations than in large ones.

From *Democracy in America*, Volumes I and II, by Alexis de Tocqueville, translated by Henry Reeve, revised by Francis Bowen, and edited by Philips Bradley. Copyright 1945 and renewed 1973 by Alfred A. Knopf, Inc. Reprinted by permission of Alfred A. Knopf.

When tyranny is established in the bosom of a small state, it is more galling than elsewhere, because, acting in a narrower circle, everything in that circle is affected by it. It supplies the place of those great designs which it cannot entertain, by a violent or exasperating interference in a multitude of minute details; and it leaves the political world, to which it properly belongs, to meddle with arrangements of private life. Tastes as well as actions are to be regulated; and the families of the citizens, as well as the states are to be governed. This invasion of rights occurs but seldom, however, freedom being in truth the natural state of small communities. The temptations that the government offers to ambition are too weak and the resources of private individuals are too slender for the sovereign power easily to fall into the grasp of a single man; and should such an event occur, the subjects of the state can easily unite and overthrow the tyrant and the tyranny at once by a common effort.

Small nations have therefore always been the cradle of political liberty; and the fact that many of them have lost their liberty by becoming larger shows that their freedom was more a consequence of their small size than of the character of the people.

The history of the world affords no instance of a great nation retaining the form of republican government for a long series of years; and this has led to the conclusion that such a thing is impracticable. For my own part, I think it imprudent for men who are every day deceived in relation to the actual and the present, and often taken by surprise in the circumstances with which they are most familiar, to attempt to limit what is possible and to judge the future. But it may be said with confidence, that a great republic will always be exposed to more perils than a small one.

All the passions that are most fatal to republican institutions increase with an increasing territory, while the virtues that favor them do not augment in the same proportion. The ambition of private citizens increases with the power of the state; the strength of parties with the importance of the ends they have in view; but the love of country, which ought to check these destructive agencies, is not stronger in a large than in a small republic. It might, indeed, be easily proved that it is less powerful and less developed. Great wealth and extreme poverty, capital cities of large size, a lax morality, selfishness, and antagonism of interests are the dangers which almost invariably arise from the magnitude of states. Several of these evils scarcely injure a monarchy, and some of them even contribute to its strength and duration. In monarchical states the government has its peculiar strength; it may use, but it does not depend on, the community; and the more numerous the people, the stronger is the prince. But the only security that a republican government possesses against these evils lies in the support of the majority. This support is not, however, proportionably greater in a large republic than in a small one; and thus, while the means of attack perpetually increase, in both number and influence, the power of resistance remains the same; or it may rather be said to diminish, since the inclinations and interests of the people are more diversified by the increase of the population, and the difficulty of forming a compact majority is constantly augmented. It has been observed, moreover, that the intensity of human passions is heightened not only by the importance of the end which they propose to attain, but by the multitude of individuals who are animated by them at the same time. Everyone has had occasion to remark that his emotions in the midst of a sympathizing crowd are far greater than those which he would have felt in solitude. In great republics, political passions become irresistible, not only because they aim at gigantic objects, but because they are felt and shared by millions of men at the same time.

It may therefore be asserted as a general proposition that nothing is more opposed to the well-being and the freedom of men than vast empires. Nevertheless, it is important to acknowledge the peculiar advantages of great states. For the very reason that the desire for power is more intense in these communities than among ordinary men, the love of glory is also more developed in the hearts of certain citizens, who regard the applause of a great people as a reward worthy of their exertions and an elevating encouragement to man. If we would learn why great nations contribute more powerfully to the increase of knowledge and the advance of civilization than small states, we shall discover an adequate cause in the more rapid and energetic circulation of ideas and in those great cities which are the intellectual centers where all the rays of human genius are reflected and combined. To this it may be added that most important discoveries demand a use of national power which the government of a small state is unable to make: in great nations the government has more enlarged ideas, and is more completely disengaged from the routine of precedent and the selfishness of local feeling; its designs are conceived with more talent and executed with more boldness.

In time of peace the well-being of small nations is undoubtedly more general and complete; but they are apt to suffer more acutely from the calamities of war than those great empires whose distant frontiers may long avert the presence of the danger from the mass of the people, who are therefore more frequently afflicted than ruined by the contest.

But in this matter, as in many others, the decisive argument is the necessity of the case. If none but small nations existed, I do not doubt that mankind would be more happy and more free; but the existence of great nations is unavoidable.

Political strength thus becomes a conditon of national prosperity. It profits a state but little to be affluent and free if it is perpetually exposed to be pillaged or subjugated; its manufactures and commerce are of small advantage if another nation has the empire of the seas and gives the law in all the markets of the globe. Small nations are often miserable, not because they are small, but because they are weak; and great empires prosper less because they are great than because they are strong. Physical strength is therefore one of the first conditions of the happiness and even of the existence of nations. Hence it occurs that, unless very peculiar circumstances intervene, small nations are always united to large empires in the end, either by force or by their own consent. I do not know a more deplorable condition than that of a people unable to defend itself or to provide for its own wants.

The federal system was created with the intention of combining the different advantages which result from the magnitude and the littleness of nations; and a glance at the United States of America discovers the advantages which they have derived from its adoption.

In great centralized nations the legislator is obliged to give a character of uniformity to the laws, which does not always suit the diversity of customs and of districts; as he takes no cognizance of special cases, he can only proceed upon general principles; and the population are obliged to conform to the requirements of the laws, since legislation cannot adapt itself to the exigencies and the customs of the population, which is a great cause of trouble and misery. This disadvantage does not exist in confederations; Congress regulates the principal measures of the national government, and all the details of the administration are reserved to the provincial legislatures. One can hardly imagine how much this division of sovereignty contributes to the well-being of each of the states that compose the Union. In these small communities, which are never agitated by the desire of aggrandizement or the care of self-defense, all public authority and private energy are turned towards internal improvements. The central government of each state, which is in immediate relationship with the citizens, is daily apprised of the wants that arise in society; and new projects are proposed every year, which are discussed at town meetings or by the legislature, and which are transmitted by the press to stimulate the zeal and to excite the interest of the citizens. This spirit of improvement is constantly alive in the American republics, without compromising their tranquillity; the ambition of power yields to the less refined and less dangerous desire for well-being. It is generally believed in America that the existence and the permanence of the republican form of government in the New World depend upon the existence and the duration of the federal system; and it is not unusual to attribute a large share of the misfortunes that have befallen the new states of South America to the injudicious erection of great republics instead of a divided and confederate sovereignty.

It is incontestably true that the tastes and the habits of republican government in the United States were first created in the townships and the provincial assemblies. In a small state, like that of Connecticut, for instance, where cutting a canal or laying down a road is a great political question, where the state has no army to pay and no wars to carry on, and where much wealth or much honor cannot be given to the rulers, no form of government can be more natural or more appropriate than a republic. But it is this same republican spirit, it is these manners and customs of a free people, which have been created and nurtured in the different states, that must be afterwards applied to the country at large. The public spirit of the Union is, so to speak, nothing more than an aggregate or summary of the patriotic zeal of the separate provinces. Every citizen of the United States transfers, so to speak, his attachment to his little republic into the common store of American patriotism. In defending the Union he defends the increasing prosperity of his own state or country, the right of conducting its affairs, and the hope of causing measures of improvement to be adopted in it which may be favorable to his own interests; and these are motives that are wont to stir men more than the general interests of the country and the glory of the nation.

On the other hand, if the temper and the manners of the inhabitants especially fitted them to promote the welfare of a great republic, the federal system renders their task less difficult. The confederation of all the American states presents none of the ordinary inconveniences resulting from large associations of men. The Union is a great republic in extent, but the paucity of objects for which its government acts assimilates it to a small state. Its acts are important, but they are rare. As the sovereignty of the Union is limited and incomplete, its exercise is not dangerous to liberty; for it does not excite those insatiable desires for fame and power which have proved so fatal to great republics. As there is no common center to the country, great capital cities, colossal wealth, abject poverty, and sudden revolutions are alike unknown; and political passion, instead of spreading over the land like a fire on the prairies, spends its strength against the interests and the individual passions of every state.

Nevertheless, tangible objects and ideas circulate throughout the Union as freely as in a country inhabited by one people. Nothing checks the spirit of enterprise. The government invites the aid of all who have talents or knowledge to serve it. Inside of the frontiers of the Union profound peace prevails, as within the heart of some great empire; abroad it ranks with the most powerful nations of the earth; two thousand miles of coast are open to the commerce of the world; and as it holds the keys of a new world, its flag is respected in the most remote seas. The Union is happy and free as a small people, and glorious and strong as a great nation.

# The Constitution and Separation of Powers

> In framing a government which is to be administered by men over men, the great difficulty lies in this: you must first enable the government to control the governed; and in the next place oblige it to control itself.
>
> *James Madison*

## Separation of Powers and Checks and Balances: The Delicate Balance between Republican Liberty and Power

Paul Peterson

Separation of powers and checks and balances are doctrines that appropriately bring to mind the concern of the Framers with creating a regime of liberty. In this connection, separation of powers and checks and balances are appropriately thought of as key structural devices in the creation of such a regime. However, to focus on separation of powers and checks and balances as means of exclusively achieving liberty is inappropriate given the complex of commitments found in the thought of the Framers. Such an exclusive focus usually serves to make the thought of the Framers and, thereby, the nature of the constitutional system itself more obscure than it need be. For instance, one famous American government textbook concludes that Americans at the time of the founding viewed government "as something to be handcuffed, hemmed in, and rendered harmless" and that separation of powers and checks and balances were important tools utilized to achieve this end. Three pages later, the bewildered student is informed that the main reason the Framers gathered in Philadelphia "was to create a *strong* national government."[1] The failure of the authors to explain this disparity would seem to stem from their failure to perceive that the Framers were committed to both liberty and power while at the same time desiring to avoid the excesses of either.

The tendency of many constitutional commentators, scholarly and nonscholarly, conservative and liberal, to focus exclusively on the concern for liberty simplifies the thought of the Framers, but that simplicity does not aid clarification. What is needed is a means of reconciling Hamilton's assertion in *The Federalist,* No. 70 that "energy in the executive is a leading character in the definition of good government" with the concern for liberty.[2] Too energetic an executive can be destructive of liberty. Yet the Framers in their proper concern for liberty did not go so far as to render the government harmless.[3] Again, they desired both power and liberty. It is our contention that just as separation of powers and checks and balances were key devices in constructing a regime of liberty, so were they also, paradoxically, key devices in providing the new government with the desired quantity of energy.

The doctrine of separation of powers was hardly new to the Framers of the Constitution. As James Bryce notes:

> No general principle of politics laid such hold on the constitution-makers and statesmen of America as the dogma that the separation of these three functions [executive, legislative, judicial] is essential to freedom. It had already been made the groundwork of several State constitutions. It is always reappearing in their writings: it was never absent from their thoughts.[4]

While the doctrine itself was not new, the Framers of the Constitution were to devise a new use for it, a use that would allow them to blend the heretofore irreconcilable ends of republicanism and energetic or powerful government. The Framers did believe in the traditional use of separation of powers to prevent the corrupting accumulation of all powers in the same hands. A proper understanding, however, of their new, more subtle, use of separation of powers and checks and balances should help to restore the deeper and more complex political teaching of the Framers.

The problem of striking and maintaining the delicate balance between power and liberty manifests itself most clearly in the Presidency. Just as deliberation characterizes the activities of the legislative branch, so is energy the quality that should characterize the executive. In recognition of the point that the two branches of government possess different principles, Hamilton writes in *The Federalist,* No. 70:

> Those politicians and statesmen who have been the most celebrated for the soundness of their principles and for the justness of their views have declared in favor of a single executive and a numerous legislature. They have, with great propriety, considered energy as the most necessary qualification of the former, and have regarded this as most applicable to power in a single hand; while they have, with equal propriety, considered the latter as best adapted to deliberation and wisdom, and best calculated to conciliate the confidence of the people and to secure thier privileges and interests.[5]

It is the executive power that most lends itself to energy. If it is energy that is desired, then it is the executive branch that must be constituted in a manner that will produce the potentiality for the exercise of energy. Thus, we have Hamilton's famous dictum: "Energy in the *executive* is a leading character in the definition of good government." Because the legislative and judicial branches are intended to produce other qualities, one would not look for them to produce energy. To speak of energy in the legislative or judicial branches would be something akin to an oxymoron.

Hamilton seems well aware of how revolutionary is the intention to have both liberty and power in a republican scheme when he addresses himself at the outset of *The Federalist,* No. 70 to those who believe liberty and power to be mutually exclusive: "There is an idea, which is not without its advocates, that a vigorous executive is inconsistent with the genius of republican government." Here stated is the problem: vigor, action, power on the one hand, the principles of republican liberty on the other. Do we want both? Can we have both? In fact, Hamilton does not explicitly argue that a vigorous executive is compatible with the principles of republican government. Rather, he merely asserts that the enlightened well-wishers to republican government must at least hope that the two are indeed compatible. "A feeble executive implies a feeble execution of the government." A poorly executed government, whatever it is in theory, must be, in practice, a bad government. Thus, "all mean of sense will agree in the necessity of an energetic executive."[6] This theoretical problem of matching a strong or energetic executive with republican liberty was one of the greatest problems facing the Federal Convention of 1787. A proper understanding of separation of powers and checks and balances in the American framework requires careful attention to how this problem was resolved.

On the floor of the Convention, Hamilton, as in *The Federalist*, was well aware of the dilemma: "As to the Executive, it seemed to be admitted that no good one could be established on Republican principles. Was not this giving up the merits of the question; for can there be a good Govt. without a good Executive."[7] The theoretical problem was intensified by the extent of the republic. As Gouverneur Morris recognized, "it has been a maxim in political Science that Republican Government is not adapted to a large extent of Country, because the energy of the Executive Magistry can not reach the extreme parts of it."[8] The kind of energy necessary for an executive to govern successfully over such an extensive land was commonly associated with a monarchical arrangement.[9] While the Framers shied away from a monarchical arrangement, recent history had made them well aware of the inability of a constitutional scheme such as the Articles of Confederation to govern in the manner they desired. The country was an extensive one and the choice was pretty much as Morris put it. "We must either then renounce the blessings of the Union, or provide an Executive with sufficient vigor to pervade every part of it."[10] Did the Convention dare squint in the direction of monarchy in order to secure the blessings of union?

The path to the creation of the Presidency in the Federal Convention is a difficult one. The problem of the Presidency was, as Charles Thach states, "in the largest sense of the term . . . the chief and the most difficult problem to be solved."[11] So labored and confusing is the path of creation that Clinton Rossiter writes: "I have followed the tortuous progress of the incipient Presidency through Madison's *Notes* several times, and I am still not sure how the champions of the strong executive won their smashing victory."[12] The doctrines of separation of powers and checks and balances allowed the advocates of a strong executive to carry the day and allowed them to construct an energetic executive within a framework of republican liberty. Separation of powers and checks and balances prevented the Framers from being impaled on the horns of the dilemma of the necessity for a strong executive on the one hand and the apparent incompatibility of a strong executive with republican principles on the other.

The doctrines of separation of powers and checks and balances would allow for the creation of an executive with sufficient power to govern, that would be, in Edward S. Corwin's words, "capable of penetrating to the remotest parts of the Union."[13] At the same time, these doctrines would prevent the creation of an uncontrolled executive power, a power that could become too aloof from the people or the public good. Indeed, while some at the Convention expressed fear of too powerful an executive, there were others, such as Madison, who argued from the doctrine of separation of powers on behalf of an executive powerful enough to be independent of the legislature. As most commentators on the founding period of the Presidency have noted, by 1787 much of the fear against a powerful executive had subsided in American politics and, at the same time, there was growing concern over the grant of power that had been given to the legislatures in the states. In one of the most famous speeches of the Convention, Madison captured this spirit of concern.

> Experience had proved a tendency in our governments to throw all power into the Legislative vortex. The Executives of the States are in general little more than Cyphers; the legislatures omnipotent. If no effectual check be devised for restaining the instability and encroachments of the latter, a revolution of some kind or other would be inevitable. The preservation of Republican Govt. therefore required some expedient for the purpose, but required evidently at the same time that in devising it, the genuine principles of that form should be kept in view.[14]

The remedy Madison had in view was a stronger executive. Implied in his argument is the case for a singular executive, thus increasing the efficiency and energy of that branch and also serving as a check on instability. A singular executive also has the virtue of being more visible, thereby increasing his responsibility. As Hamilton noted: "[O]ne of the weightiest objections to a plurality in the executive . . . is that it tends to conceal faults and destroy responsibility."[15] Singularity in the executive, then, provides greater energy and is in keeping with the genuine principles of republicanism in that it provides for greater responsibility than would a dual or multiple executive. More explicit in Madison's argument is the case for an independent executive and for a judicious mixing of powers as opposed to a strict separation of powers. Here both of what M. J. C. Vile calls "the two central positions of modern American constitutional thought"[16] come into play. An independent executive is necessary to a sufficient remedy for the ills of too much legislative power. An executive dependent upon the legislature for his office and/or the power to act could not effectively check the excesses of legislative power. Experience had shown that. Madison made his case for executive independence on one of the two central positions—separation of powers. "If it be essential to the preservation of liberty that the Legisl: Execut: and Judiciary powers be separate, it is essential to a maintenance of the separation, that they should be independent of each other."[17]

Checks and balances—the second of these two central positions—come into play with the necessity for a check on the instability and encroachments of the legislature. A judicious mixing of powers that allows the executive to participate in the legislative process through his veto power provides the independent executive with the most notable structural check on legislative power. A month-and-a-half before his "legislative vortex" speech, Madison put forth a straightforward argument for the necessity of checks. He argued that there is a diversity of interests in every country, e.g., rich and poor, debtors and creditors, various religious sects, and that checks "which will destroy the measures of an interested majority" must be introduced. "[I]n this view a negative in the Ex: is not only necessary for its own safety, but for the safety of a minority in Danger of oppression from an unjust and interested majority."[18] Later in the Convention, Madison most clearly showed the theoretical relationship between separation of powers and checks and balances.

> If a Constitutional discrimination of the departments on paper were a sufficient security to each agst. encroachments of the others, all further provisions would indeed be superfluous. But experience had taught us a distrust of that security; and that it is necessary to introduce such a balance of powers and interests, as will guarantee the provisions on paper. Instead therefore of contenting ourselves with laying down the Theory in the Constitution that each department ought to be separate and distinct, it was proposed to add a defensive power to each which should maintain the Theory in practice. In so doing we did not blend the departments together. We erected effectual barriers for keeping them separate.[19]

Compared to the separation of powers, the doctrine of checks and balances was a recent arrival to the scene of accepted principles of American political thought, and many saw it as being contradictory to the separation of powers. That is, the powers of the branches of government must either be separate or mixed, but both conditions cannot exist together. Although there was little opposition to the principle of mixing of powers at the Convention, opposition to this principle did arise when the final draft of the Constitution was presented for ratification. In *The Federalist,* No. 47, Madison deals with this problem regarding the compatibility of a mixture of powers and the doctrine of the separation of powers. It is noted that "one of the principal objections inculcated by the more respectable adversaries to the Constitution is its supposed violation of the political maxim that the legislative, executive, and judiciary departments ought to be separate and distinct."[20]

In expressing his allegiance to the principle of the separation of powers, Madison gives an indication of the argument he will make when he states in these now famous words: "The accumulation of all powers, legislative, executive, and judiciary, in the same hands, whether of one, a few, or many, and whether hereditary, self-appointed, or elective, may justly be pronounced the very definition of tyranny." The separation of powers is not to be viewed as a distinct labeling of functions peculiar to each branch of government with no branch acting in the specified domain of the others; rather, separation of powers, from Madison's view, is primarily the argument he presented to the Convention for an independent executive. All powers are not to be in the hands of one man or group, but nothing in the doctrine of the separation of powers prevents the various branches from having shared powers. This argument is made abundantly clear when Madison presents the theoretical argument for the separation of powers. Beginning with Montesquieu, that "oracle who is always consulted and cited on this subject," Madison notes that "the British Constitution was to Montesquieu what Homer has been to the didactic writers on epic poetry." It can be seen in the British constitution "that the legislative, executive, and judicial departments are by no means totally separate and distinct from each other." Citing specific examples of a mixing of functions rather than a distinct separation of functions in the British constitution, Madison concludes:

> From these facts, by which Montesquieu was guided, it may clearly be inferred that in saying 'There can be no liberty where the legislative and executive powers are united in the same person, or body of magistrates' or, 'if the power of judging be not separated from the legislative and executive powers,' he did not mean that these departments ought to have no *partial agency* in, or no *control* over, the acts of each other.[21]

Separation of powers means only that the branches of government and their proper powers should not be in the same hands and does not preclude a mixing of the functions or powers among the branches. The doctrine of the separation of powers would not preclude executive participation in the legislative process through the use of an executive veto.[22]

Madison then moves from the theoretical argument regarding the separation of powers to the experience of the practical application of that principle in the state constitutions. Looking at the constitutions of the several states, Madison sees that, "notwithstanding the emphatical and, in some instances, the unqualified terms in which this axiom has been laid down, there is not a single instance in which the several departments of power have been kept absolutely separate and distinct." Finally, Madison concludes his observations, both theoretical and practical, writing that the charge against the proposed Constitution of violating "the sacred maxim of free government," the separation of powers, "is warranted neither by the real meaning annexed to that maxim by its author, nor by the sense in which it has hitherto been understood in America."[23]

Hamilton's treatment of the veto power in *The Federalist,* No. 73 can be seen not only as a defense of the Constitution's mixing of powers, but also as showing the relationship of separation of powers to checks and balances. Hamilton notes the propensity of the legislature to intrude upon the rights and absorb the powers of the other departments, the insufficiency of a mere parchment delineation of the boundaries of the various departments, and the inference from these observations of the necessity of furnishing each department with constitutional means for its defense. "From these clear and indubitable principles results the propriety of a negative, either absolute or qualified, in the executive upon the acts of the legislative branches."[24] As Madison had suggested at the Convention and again in *The Federalist,* No. 48, something more than parchment delineation was needed to insure what was desired by a separation of powers. In the case of the executive, this something more was the power of the veto, which would provide the executive department with a constitutional check to protect itself from any possible attempts by the legislature branch to absorb unduly any powers of the executive. Checks and balances strengthen the separation of powers rather than weaken it. Gordon Wood refers to the presidential veto as "the major bulwark against legislative encroachment and the chief means of maintaining executive independence."[25]

The doctrine of separation of powers was used to justify the independence of the president, and then the doctrine of checks and balances was used to insure that independence. As we have seen, Madison used the doctrine of separation of powers to show that in fact an absolute separation of powers, strictly speaking, had not been secured by the state constitutions. Checks and balances provided this security in the proposed Constitution of 1787. The new system would be able to provide what was desired by the doctrine of separation of powers but which had not been provided by the previous American constitutions, namely, a sufficient guard against tyranny. However, this could be gained only with a significant increase in the power of the executive branch. That increase was necessary to guard against legislative tyranny, but that power could also be used for other ends—ends anticipated and desired by the Framers. The new system of separation of powers would have a dual effect: first, the power of the legislative branch could now be more effectively checked; and second, the quantity of energy necessary to check the legislative branch is greatly increased, thereby increasing the energy or the power of the new government as a whole. That increase in energy is rendered safe in a republican government by a due dependence of both branches on the people and the fact that each branch must operate within a system of separation of powers and checks and balances. The American system of separation of powers and checks and balances has the peculiar effect of both increasing power and making the exercise of this increased power safe.

Most of the substantive arguments at the Federal Convention regarding various aspects of the Presidency have a separation-of-powers flavor to them. That is, the overall role of the executive department in the separation-of-powers arrangement seems to have been a major concern in filling out the details of the office. For instance, Madison's advocacy of the veto power was tied to the separation-of-powers argument in that it would aid in keeping the executive independent of the legislature. This is also true of the consideration of the proposed length of term, re-eligibility, impeachment, and the mode of election. Relating to the issue of the executive's length of term, Elbridge Gerry argued for a longer term because "that the Executive shd. be independent of the Legislature is a clear point. The longer the duration of his appointment the more will his dependence be diminished."[26] The problems of length of term, re-eligibility, and mode of election were all tied together in an intricate knot, with the desire to make the executive independent of the legislature being the chief obstacle to untying the knot.[27] If the executive were to be chosen by the legislature, then he should not be eligible for re-election so not be become dependent upon the legislature in seeking re-election, and, as Gerry argued, the term should be of substantial length. Yet many delegates were opposed to denying the executive his re-eligibility, believing that re-eligibility was the best inducement for good conduct in office. But if a shorter term with re-eligibility were accepted, a mode of election other than that by the legislature would have to be chosen if a realistic hope for the maintenance of executive independence were to be realized.[28] With regard to impeachment, Max Farrand has observed, "what is perhaps the clearest indication of intention to make the office an important one is that the executive [of the Virginia Plan] was rendered subject to impeachment."[29] Impeachment would have been even more important in a scheme of separated powers if the executive were to be chosen for a substantial length of time. While the independence of the executive of the Virginia Plan would have suffered by the addition of a procedure of impeachment, surely this would be an indication that the Framers did have much in mind for the executive even at this early stage of the Convention. A procedure for impeachment would serve as an effective check on an execuitve that might get out of hand by becoming disproportionately powerful for even the strong executive advocates.

The mode of election presented perhaps the most difficult problem of the Convention. As James Wilson commented, "this subject has greatly divided the House, and will also divide people out of doors. It is in truth the most difficult of all on which we have had to decide."[30] Given the state of modern political science literature on the Electoral College and the need for reform, there is a certain irony in reading Hamilton's comments on the mode of election in the *Federalist,* no. 68.

> The mode of appointment of the Chief Magistrate of the United States is almost the only part of the system, of any consequence, which has escaped without severe censure or which has received the slightest mark of approbation from its opponents. The most plausible of these, who has appeared in print, has even deigned to admit that the election of the President is pretty well guarded. I venture somewhat further, and hesitate not to affirm that if the manner of it be not perfect, it is least excellent. It unites in an eminent degree all the advantages the union of which was to be desired.[31]

Despite Hamilton's argument for the excellence of the mode of apointment, Forrest McDonald describes the electoral college system as "an awkward scheme, irrational almost to the point of absurdity, and it was so greeted by most of the delegates." To McDonald the creation of the Electoral College and its relationship to a system of checks and balances were almost an accident founded upon the Electoral College being "a system that would overcome every objection that had been raised against every other method." "The committee had devised the electoral college as a half-baked compromise with an immediate issue, and as such it worked. The convention's most vexing problem had been solved, and dissenters had been deprived of their last weapon."[32] The notion of a system of electors was with the Convention almost from from the beginning. Direct election by the people, election by the state legislatures, and a system of electors were all modes of executive appointment that came up time and time again during the course of the Convention. Whereas it is true that as late as September 6, the Convention was still dealing with an executive to be chosen by the national legislature, the sense of the Convention seems by this time aligned for a mode of appointment that would make the executive independent of the national legislature.

As early as July 25, Madison presented a cogent anlaysis of the predominant modes of appointment that had been considered to that date. Eliminating all but two of various defects, Madison concluded: "The Option before us then lay between an appointment by Electors chosen by the people—and an immediate appointment by the people."[33] Madison's constant concern throughout the Convention that an executive independent of the legislature was crucial to a maintenance of a true separation of powers; the desire of the Convention to create an executive that would be more than a mere cypher; and the powerful analysis, such as Madison's July 25 speech, that was brought to the problem by the advocates of a strong executive brought the Convention to a consensus, albeit an uneasy consensus, that simply would not allow for an executive that would be chosen by the national legislature with no mitigating influences. Although McDonald argues "and thus, almost by accident, was created the maginificent system of checks and balances of the United States Constitution,"[34] the course of the Convention would seem to indicate that, more correctly, the antithesis is the case. That is, the desire for an independnet executive and the implications of that desire for a system of both separated powers and checks and balances led to a mode of appointment that preserved that element of independence which the Framers wanted in the executive. True, the Electoral College was a compromise, but it was not simply a last-minute compromise and, thereby, an accident. It had a theoretical justification for its existence in that it provided what was wanted in a mode of election by most of the Convention delegates.

Returning to Hamilton's analyais of the completed product in *The Federalist,* No. 68, just how much the Framers believed could be obtained by the electoral college mode of appointment can be seen. Most of the desirable traits cited by Hamilton as being gained by the use of a system of electors are also cited by the advocates of a similar system in the Convention for purposes of strengthening the executive branch. Among the strengths of the electoral college system listed by Hamilton are: the operation of the sense of the people in the choice of the executive, the immediate election would be made by those most capable of analyzing the candidates, it afforded little opportunity to tumult and disorder, it provided for checks on cabal and intrigue, and it provided for the independence of the executive for a continued stay in office from all but the people themselves. *The Federalist,* No. 68 could be compared with Madison's Convention speech of July 25, in which he eliminates modes of election other than by electors or by the people directly because they endanger the independence of the executive and praises the system of electors because it handles well the problem of cabal and intrigue.

The most important advantage of the Electoral College was in securing the independence of the executive. Here a second irony arises from a modern reading of Hamilton's analysis of the mode of appointment. The Framers viewed a separation of powers as being essential to the principles of republican liberty, and it was through the separation of powers that they were able to solve the dilemma of the need for a strong executive and the apparent incompatibility of such an executive with republican principles. That the principle of separation of powers is not only essential to the Framers' understanding of liberty, but that it is also tied to democratic principle, Madison makes clear in *The Federalist,* No. 51 when he writes that if the principle of separation of powers were "rigorously adhered to, it would require that all the appointments for the supreme executive, legislative, and judiciary magistracies should be drawn from the same fountain of authority, the people, through channels having no communication whatever with one another."[35] The mode of election decided upon at the Convention did not meet this qualification of rigorous adherence and, in fact, was also a deviation from the electoral system portion of the option Madison felt was left to the Convention. Madison's option was between electors *chosen by the people* and a more immediate election by the people themselves. The Constitution calls for each state to appoint the electors "as the legislature thereof may direct." Despite this deviation from both a rigorous adherence to the principle of separation of powers and from the democratic principle, Hamilton still sees the executive as being democratic in nature.

> It was desirable that the sense of the people should operate in the choice of the person to whom so important a trust was to be confided. This end will be answered by committing the right of making it, not to any preestablished body, but to men chosen by the people for the special purpose, and at the particular conjuncture.[36]

There is considerable irony for the modern reader in this portrayal of the electoral system as being a democratic mode of election when much of the modern literature depicts the Electoral College as an archaic and undemocratic system of election that is at odds with the rest of the American political system. In characterizing the Electoral College as undemocratic or even antidemocratic, undemocratic and antidemocratic motives are often applied to the Framers. Yet it should be apparent from Hamilton's analysis that although the mode of appointment may be a deviation of some degree from pure democratic principle, that deviation does not make the Electoral College either undemocratic or antidemocratic, and it cannot be deduced from this deviation that such motives can be applied accurately to the Framers. To attribute such motives would seem questionable, particularly in light of Hamilton's own language in *The Federalist,* No. 68.

One of the more persuasive analyses of the mode of presidential appointment as being of a character other than democratic comes not from a source who seeks democratic reform, but from one who seeks to maintain the balance of a mixed regime that he sees as having been the intent of the Framers. Paul Eidelberg, in arguing that the American regime is a mixed regime wherein the Presidency represents the monarchical element, cites the constitutional grant of authority for choosing electors, which is given to the state legislature rather than to the people as evidence in support of his understanding of the regime and the role of the presidency. In analyzing Hamilton's *The Federalist,* no. 68, Eidelberg argues, "as Hamilton well knew, the Constitution does not even grant the people a right to choose Electors! . . . The manner of appointing Electors is absolutely under the control of the state legislatures, at whose discretion the people may exercise the privilege which is now accorded them."[37] Whereas the whole of Eidelberg's thesis as to the monarchial nature of the presidency does not rest upon this argument, a different view of the intent of the Framers can be gained by looking at this clause of the Constitution in light of the federal principle, rather than attempting to understand it in terms of democratic principle. Besides being a republican regime, the United States is also established on a federal principle. The clause of Article II, Section I, of the Constitution granting authority for appointing electors to the state legislatures would seem to be in accord with this federal principle. Thus Hamilton's use of democratic language with regard to the selection of the electors, which would not be a necessary result of the meaning of Article II, Section I, could be explained as anticipation on the Framers' part that the various state legislatures would turn to the people as the appropriate mode for choosing the Electors. Eidelberg considers this possibility in a note citing Lucius Wilmerding's *The Electoral College:*

"It is Wilmerding's position that the general sentiment of the Convention was to have the Electors chosen by the people. But even he admits that 'too many members of the Federal Convention expressed a contrary view.' " Although rejecting this interpretation, Eidelberg adds, "I do not wish to suggest, however, that the evidence is conclusive as to how the majority of the Convention intended to have Electors chosen."[38]

In rejecting the view that it was the general sentiment or belief of the Convention that the people should choose the electors, Eidelberg scoffs at Wilmerding for citing such Federalists as Hamilton, Morris, Rufus King, and Timothy Pickering in support of a democratic interpretation of the Presidency. "Whatever their views on the manner of choosing Electors, these men would have deplored the democratic conception of the Presidency which underlies Wilmerding's thesis."[39] Yet, there were those, even of a Federalist bent, who supported a democratic executive. As early as June 1, James Wilson was declaring, "at least that in theory he was for an election by the people."[40] By July 19, Wilson "perceived with pleasure that the idea was gaining ground, of an election mediately or immediately by the people."[41] In his July 25 speech discussed earlier, Madison, in considering the option of the two modes of election that he viewed as then being left to the Convention, concluded: "The remaining mode was an election by the people or rather by the (qualified part of them) at large. With all its imperfections he liked this best."[42] Not only was there this spirit for making the Presidency a popularly-based institution present at the Convention, but it was represented by some of those who were most influential in the framing of the Presidency, as evidenced by the remarks of Wilson and Madison. Indeed, of Wilson's role in the creation of the Presidency, Thach writes, "to James Wilson belongs the credit of crystallizing the concept and laying it before the Convention."[43] Given the understanding of the separation of powers expressed in *The Federalist*, No. 51—that the appointments for each department "should be drawn from the same fountain of authority, the people," in the most rigorous adherence to the principle of separation of powers—it can be seen that the desire to create an independent executive would then also be tied to a democratic concept of the office, if not necessarily the most democratic concept.[44]

Hamilton concludes his analysis of the Presidency in *The Federalist* by returning to the starting point of his outline of the nature of the office and to the dilemma of the Convention—the compatability of an energetic executive with republican principles. Hamilton asks: "Does it also combine the requisites to safety, in the republican sense— a due dependence on the people, a due responsibility?"[45] Just as the democratic selection of the president allows for his independence, so does the democratic selection allow for a due dependence on the people. Separation of powers, so essential in the eyes of the Framers to republican liberty, also provided the key for the Framers that made an energetic executive compatible with republican principles. By justifying an energetic executive and making it capable of exercising the desired qualities of decision, activity, secrecy, and dispatch, separation of powers and checks and balances were crucial devices in the creation of a new government that was both free and powerful. With the enhancement of the desired qualities of energy, the new government was now better able to perform competently the tasks assigned to it.

What we see with the Presidency and this new use of the separation of powers doctrine that justifies a strong president is a bit of modeling based on mixed regime theory. Energy had been thought for two thousand years to be the principle of monarchical government or a principle of mixed government. This is what had made mixed government such a powerful model both in theory and in practice: it secured energy and guarded against the abuse of power through its own system of checks and balances based upon giving each of the two major classes, the few and the many, a branch of the government. The American President, through its unity, four-year term, and independence from the legislature branch, will also secure energy. The president's energy will not be that of a monarch, but it will be significantly greater than that of the 18th century state governors. The American President, however, will also be republican in that he will be dependent on the people. While the president's term will be longer than that of any of the state governors, it will be far short of the life term of a monarch.

The Framers of the American Constitution did not make the same mistake as those men who framed the original state constitutions. The framers of the state constitutions, with their belief that energy was the principle of only monarchial or mixed government and with this belief supported by their own conflicts with a monarch and the monarch's appointed executives in the colonial governments, used monarchy as their only model of executive power and, accordingly, sought to restrict their executives. Madison notes of the framers of the state constitutions, "that they seem never for a moment to have turned their eyes from the danger, to liberty, from the overgrown and all-grasping prerogative of an hereditary magistrate, supported and fortified by an hereditary branch of the legislative authority."[46] Recognizing that their executive would be a republican executive, the Framers of the American Constitution realized that a new balance would have to be struck to compensate for the errors that occurred during the period in which the state constitutions had been written. This new balance would lead to a strengthened executive and a republican government that would now be capable of energy.

A common error among those who offer commentaries on the creation of the Presidency is to compare the president with the monarchial model found in the 18th century English system. In any such comparison, the powers of the president are considerably more restricted than would be those of the crown. Such a comparison lends credence to those who maintain that the Framers were fearful of executive power and sought to severely restrict it. Such comparison, however, ignores the eleven years of experience between 1776 and 1787. While this comparison is appropriate for and explains the weak executives of the state constitutions written in 1776 and 1777, the appropriate comparison for the Constitution of 1787 is between the weak state governors and the strong executive of the new Constitution. This comparison provides a much different, and more accurate, insight into the intentions of the Framers.

A prominent example of this error of analysis is Raoul Berger's examination of presidential-congressional relations in *Executive Privilege: A Constitutional Myth.* Berger in making the case not for separation of powers, but for congressional supremacy, writes:

> The Framers did not endow the President with more power than the King had, but with less; they removed notable powers formerly exercised under the Crown prerogative and lodged them in Congress, not the President. All this was subsumed by Madison when he wrote in *Federalist* No. 51 that 'in a republican form of government, the legislature necessarily predominates.' Congress, it cannot be unduly emphasized, was to be the senior partner, from whom, it follows, no junior could conceal the state of the Union.[47]

While Berger is correct that the Framers did not intend a system in which the President could conceal the state of the union from Congress, his reliance on Madison's statement concerning the predomination of the legislative branch is strange when that statement is seen in the overall framework of *The Federalist's* consideration of separation of powers. For Madison this is a descriptive statement, not a prescriptive one. It is this predomination that makes the exercise of legislative power particularly dangerous in republican government. This is why Madison warns that "in a representative republic . . . it is against the enterprising ambition of this department [the legislature] that the people ought to indulge all their jealousy and exhaust all their precautions."[48]

Because of the domination of the branch that places a primacy on representation, the executive must be removed from the burden of junior partnership that was placed on him in the states by the erroneous reasoning of the framers of those constitutions, made independent of the legislative authority, and strengthened. The statement concerning the predomination of the legislative branch, which Berger sees as a sign of Madison advocating Congressional supremacy, is in fact a warning from Madison about the dangers of such supremacy and a warning that republican regimes are particularly susceptible to legislative tyranny. The Constitution and the Presidency are grounded in these warnings. As we have seen, by having an executive powerful enough to guard against legislative tyranny, the government will also have the institutional means to supply the positive dimensions of energy: decision, activity, secrecy, and dispatch.

### Notes

1. James MacGregor Burns and J. W. Peltason, *Government by the People,* 8th Basic Edition (Englewood Cliffs, New Jersey: Prentice-Hall, Inc., 1972), pp. 44, 47. Emphasis added. Subsequent editions of this text, with the addition of Thomas Cronin as a joint author, have eliminated this blatant statement of the confusion, although the confusion itself still exists in a less obvious fashion.
2. Alexander Hamilton, James Madison, and John Jay, *The Federalist Papers,* edited by Clinton Rossiter (New York: Mentor Books, 1961), No. 70, p. 423.
3. See Madison's discussion of the work of the Federal Convention in *The Federalist,* No. 37 for a sensitive treatment of the problem of reconciling these conflicting demands. "Among the difficulties encountered by the convention, a very important one must have lain in combining the requisite stability and energy in government with the inviolable attention due to liberty and to the republican form" (P. 226.)

4. James Bryce, *The American Commonwealth,* revised edition, 2 volumes (New York: The Macmillan Company, 1910), I, p. 29.
5. *The Federalist,* No. 70. p. 424.
6. Ibid., p. 423. Just how revolutionary was the claim that a vigorous executive was compatible with republican government can be seen from the following remarks by John Page of Virginia addressed to Congress in 1789:

> The doctrine of energy in Government, as I said before, is the true doctrine of tyrants. . . . Energy of Government may be the destruction of liberty; it should not, therefore, be too much cherished in a free country. A spirit of independence should be cultivated. . . .
>
> The liberty and security of our fellow-citizens is our great object, and not the prompt execution of the laws. Indecision, delay, blunders, nay, villainous actions in the administration of Government, are trifles compared to legalizing the full exertion of a tyrannical despotism. (As quoted in Leonard D. White, *The Federalists*[New York: The Free Press, 1948], p. 22.)

Here Page is shown vigorously articulating this fundamental cause of the political science challenged by the Federalists after ratification of a constitution establishing a republican regime and a vigorous executive.
7. Max Farrand (ed.), *The Records of the Federal Convention of 1787.* 4 vols. (New Haven: Yale University Press, 1966). I, p. 289.
8. Ibid., II, p. 52.
9. The problem of how much monarchical sentiment there was at the Convention "really hinges," as Charles Thach says, "on the definition of monarchy." (*The Creation of the Presidency 1775–1789* [Baltimore: The John Hopkins University Press, 1923, 1969], p. 80.) If monarchy means, as Hamilton used it, an hereditary executive, then there was probably little or no monarchical sentiment present. (Farrand, *Records of the Federal Convention,* I, p. 290.) Yet, this does not do away with the fear that many of the delegates had of the creation of an executive with many of the wide-ranging powers often associated with monarchs and to which these delegates chose to attach the adjective monarchical.
10. Farrand, *Records of the Federal Convention,* II, p. 52.
11. Thach, *Creation of the Presidency,* p. 76. In a letter to Thomas Jefferson in which he relates the proceedings of the Convention, Madison describes the deliberations concerning the executive as being "peculiarly embarrassing." Farrand, *Records of the Federal Convention,* III, p. 132.)
12. Clinton Rossiter, *The American Presidency,* 2nd ed., revised (New York: The New American Library, 1962), p. 72.
13. Edward S. Corwin, *The President: Office and Powers,* 4th ed. (New York: New York University Press, 1968), p. 10.
14. Farrand, *Records of the Federal Convention,* II, p, 35. In *The Federalist,* No. 48, Madison makes a similar argument: "[E]xperience assures us that the efficacy of the provision [that is, separation of powers without checks and balances] has been greatly overrated; and that some more adequate defense is indispensably necessary for the more feeble against the more powerful members of the government. The legislative department is everywhere extending the sphere of its activity and drawing all power into its impetuous vortex." (pp. 308–309.)
15. *The Federalist.* No. 70, p. 427. See Paul Peterson, "The Meaning of Republicanism in *The Federalist*," *Publius* 9 (Spring, 1979), pp. 49–51, for a discussion of the new Federalist teaching on republican responsibility.
16. M. J. C. Vile, *Constitutionalism and the Separation of Powers* (Oxford: Clarendon Press, 1967), p. 153.
17. Farrand, *Records of the Federal Convention,* II, p. 34.
18. Ibid., I, p. 108.
19. Ibid., II, p. 77.
20. The *Federalist,* No. 47, p. 301.
21. Ibid., pp. 301–302. Emphasis in the original.

22. One cannot help but be charmed by Michael Reagan's statement that "the conventional wisdom on the separation of powers, which holds that the President has no legislative role and the legislature no executive role, has been thoroughly discredited by a generation of research." (*The New Federalism* [New York: Oxford University Press, 1972], p. 5.) Anyone with even a rudimentary knowledge of *The Federalist* has no need of a generation of research to dispel such "conventional wisdom," unless, of course, Reagan means the generation of research conducted in the 1780s.

23. *The Federalist,* No. 47, pp. 304, 308.

24. *The Federalist,* No. 73, p. 442.

25. Gordon S. Wood, *The Creation of the American Republic, 1776–1787* (Chapel Hill: University of North Carolina Press for the Institute of Early American History and Culture, Williamsburg, Virginia, 1969), p. 552.

26. Farrand, *Records on the Federal Convention,* 11, p. 102.

27. This is not to suggest that everyone at the Convention favored an independent executive. For instance, Roger Sherman "was for the appointment by the Legislature, and for making him absolutely dependent on that body, as it was the will of that which was to be executed. An independence of the Executive on the supreme Legislative, was in his opinion the very essence of tyranny if there was any such thing." (Farrand, *Records of the Federal Convention,* I, p. 68.) Sherman's statement can be seen as a representative sample of the political science that the Framers generally and, in the case of the presidency, specifically Hamilton challenged in their attempt to make compatible the apparently incompatible ends of republicanism and energy.

28. It could be argued that effective executive independence could have been maintained through a parlimentary government of cabinet responsibility, but given the concerns of the Convention, this alternative, had it been advocated, would certainly have been rejected as leaving the executive too dependent upon the legislature, primarily because the Convention did not have an historical model to which it could turn for different conclusions. Several commentators (e.g., Corwin, p. 14; Rossiter, p. 75) have noted the crucial decisions made at the Convention that mitigated against a possible evolution toward a parlimentary government. In opposition to most of these commentators who maintain that the Framers were not grounded in the theory of parliamentary government because it was but an immature structure in England at that time, Vile argues that the Framers were aware of this alternative and rejected it because of a fear of legislative dominance. Whether or not the Framers were aware of a parliamentary alternative, as Vile believes, he does read the mood of the Convention correctly, and if this alternative were known, it most surely was rejected for the reason cited by Vile. (Vile, *Constitutionalism and the Separation of Powers,* pp. 154–156.) Perhaps even more significant is that a parliamentary system would have strayed too far from federal principles to have been accepted in 1787.

29. Max Farrand, *The Framing of the Constitution of the United States* (New Haven: Yale Univesity Press, 1913), p. 279.

30. Farrand, *Records of the Federal Convention,* II, p. 501.

31. *The Federalist,* No. 68, pp. 411–412.

32. Forrest McDonald, *The Formation of the American Republic* (Baltimore: Penguin Books, Inc., 1967), pp. 185–186.

33. Farrand, *Records of the Federal Convention,* II, p. 110.

34. McDonald, Formation of the American Republic, p. 186.

35. *The Federalist,* No. 51, p. 321.

36. *The Federalist,* No. 68, p. 412.

37. Eidelberg, *Philosophy of the American Constitution,* p. 184.

38. Ibid., pp. 310–11, n. 11.

39. Ibid.

40. Farrand, *Records of the Federal Convention,* 1, p. 68.

41. Ibid., II, p. 56.

42. Ibid., p. 111.

43. Thach, *Creation of the Presidency,* p. 176.

44. By maintaining that the Presidency is a democratic office, I do not mean to suggest that it is democratic in the crudest sense, that is, that there was no thought of structuring the mode of election so as to promote a particular kind of majority. The entire constitutional system, including the Presidency, is designed to promote a qualitative majority, that is, the rule of reason rather than passion.
45. *The Federalist,* No. 77, pp. 463–464.
46. *The Federalist,* No. 48, p. 309.
47. Raoul Berger, *Executive Privilege: A Constitutional Myth* (New York: Bantam Books, 1974), pp. 14–15.
48. *The Federalist,* No. 48, p. 309.

---

# The Steel Seizure Case: A Judicial Brick without Straw

Edward S. Corwin

President Truman's seizure of the steel industry without specific statutory warrant[1] brings to a new pitch a developing reliance on the "Executive Power" which began almost at the inception of the Federal Government. True, this development has not always proceeded at the same pace; while at times it has seemed to be arrested, during the last fifty years its maturation has been virtually uninterrupted. Moreover, the forces, interests and events which have energized the development are today more potent than ever.

The opening clause of Article II of the Constitution reads: "The executive Power shall be vested in a President of the United States of America." The records of the Constitutional Convention make it clear that the purposes of this clause were simply to settle the question whether the executive branch should be plural or single and to give the executive a title.[2] Yet, in the very first Congress to assemble under the Constitution, the opening clause of Article II was invoked by James Madison and others in order to endow the President with power to remove officers whose appointments had been made with the advice and consent of the Senate. Madison's view prevailed,[3] and was finally ratified by the Supreme Court in 1926.[4] The same theory was invoked by Hamilton in support of President Washington's Proclamation of Neutrality upon the outbreak of war between France and Great Britain.[5] This time the Court's acquiescence was not long delayed. Even in the act of asserting the power of the Court to pass upon the constitutionality of acts of Congress, Chief Justice Marshall said: "By the Constitution of the United States the President is invested with certain important political powers, in the exercise of which he is to use his own discretion, and is accountable only to his country in his political character, and to his own conscience."[6] Even Thomas Jefferson, cousin and congenial enemy of Marshall, had said of the executive power in an official opinion as Secretary of State in 1790: "The Executive [branch of the government], possessing the rights of self-government from nature, cannot be controlled in the exercise of them but by a law, passed in the forms of the Constitution."[7]

Reprinted with permission from *Columbia Law Review,* © 1953.

Throughout the last half century the theory of presidential power has recruited strength from a succession of "strong" presidents, from an economic crisis, from our participation in two world wars and a "cold" war, and finally from organization of the labor movement. Moreover, the constitutional basis of the doctrine has shifted somewhat since the early nineteenth century. It no longer relies exclusively, or even chiefly, on the opening clause of Article II. To the terminology of political disputation in the Jacksonian period it is indebted for such concepts as "residual," "resultant" and "inherent" powers. Thanks to Lincoln, it is able to invoke the president's duty to "take care that the laws," *i.e.,* all the laws, "be faithfully executed," and his power as commander-in-chief of the armed forces. Of more recent origin is the quite baffling formula of an "aggregate of powers vested in the President by the Consitution and the laws."[8]

The chief constitutional value which overextension of presidential power threatens is, of course, the concept of a "government of laws and not of men"—the "Rule of Law" principle. In 1882 Justice Samuel Miller gave classical expression to this principle in the following words: "No man . . . is so high that he is above the law. . . . All officers of the government . . . are creatures of the law, and are bound to obey it."[9] Yet eight years later this same great judge queried whether the president's duty to "take care that the laws be faithfully executed is limited to the enforcement of the acts of Congress or treaties . . . [in] their *express terms,*" or whether it embraces also "the rights, duties and obligations growing out of the Constitution itself . . . and all the protection implied by the nature of the government under the Constitution?"[10] The answer assumed is evident.

In 1895 the *Debs* case,[11] a landmark in the judicial history of Article II, was decided. Here the Court held that the United States has at all times the right to enter its courts to ask for an injunction to protect "matters which by the Constitution are entrusted to the care of the nation." The "United States" here meant the President. The significance of the Court's choice of terminology is that it was not basing its holding on the duty of the president "to take care that the laws be faithfully executed," but on a broader principle—national interest.

The procession of "strong" presidents was headed by Theodore Roosevelt, who asserts in his *Autobiography* that the principle which governed him in his exercise of the presidential office was that he had not only a right but a duty "to do anything that the needs of the Nation demanded unless such action was forbidden by the Constitution or by the laws."[12] Although in his book, *Our Chief Magistrate and His Powers,* Ex-President Taft warmly protested against the notion that the president has any constitutional warrant to attempt the role of a "Universal Providence,"[13] yet, as Chief Justice, he later relied on the opening clause of Article II as a grant of power.[14] He also interpreted the *Debs* case as signifying that the national executive may seek an injunction in any case involving a widespread public interest.[15]

As for the influence of the labor movement and the resultant consolidation of labor's political strength in a few great organizations subject to a highly autocratic leadership, it is sufficient to mention that, between the anthracite strike of 1902 and the bituminous coal strike of 1946, presidents intervened in a purely personal or political capacity in no fewer than twenty-six strikes.[16] Indeed, President Truman's course of action in dealing with the bituminous coal situation in 1946 may be regarded as having both foreshadowed his conduct in the steel strike of 1952[17] and influenced judicial attitudes in some measure in the *Youngstown* (Steel Seizure) case.[18]

*The Facts of the Youngstown Case.* To avert a nation-wide strike of steel workers which he believed would jeopardize the national defense, President Truman, on April 8th, 1952, issued Executive Order 10340[19] directing the Secretary of Commerce to seize and operate most of the country's steel mills. The order cited no specific statutory authorization, but invoked generally the powers vested in the president by the Constitution and laws of the United States. Secretary Sawyer forthwith issued an order seizing the mills and directing their presidents to operate them as managers for the United States in accordance with his regulations and directions. The President promptly reported these events to Congress,[20] conceding Congress' power to supersede his order; but Congress failed to take action either then or a fortnight later, when the President again raised the problem in a special letter.[21] Of course, in the Defense Production Act of 1950,[22] the Labor Management Relations (Taft-Hartley) Act of 1947[23] and the Selective Service Act of 1948,[24] Congress had in fact provided other procedures for dealing with such situations; and in the elaboration of these statutory schemes it had repeatedly declined to authorize governmental seizures of property to settle labor disputes. The steel companies sued the Secretary in a federal district court, praying for a declaratory judgment and injunctive relief. The district judge issued a preliminary injunction, which the court of appeals stayed. On certiorari to the court of appeals, the Supreme Court affirmed the district court's order by a vote of six to three. Justice Black delivered the opinion of the Court in which Justices Frankfurter, Douglas, Jackson and Burton concurred; Justice Clark expressly limited his concurrence to the judgment of the Court. All these Justices presented what are termed "concurring" opinions. The Chief Justice, speaking for himself and Justices Reed and Minton, dissented.

*The Doctrine of the Opinion of the Court.* The chief point urged in Justice Black's opinion is that there was no statute which expressly or impliedly authorized the President to take possession of the steel mills. On the contrary, in its consideration of the Taft-Hartley Act in 1947, Congress refused to authorize governmental seizures of property as a method of preventing work stoppages and settling labor disputes. Authority to issue such an order in the circumstances of the case was not deducible from the aggregate of the executive powers under Article II of the Constitution; nor was the Order maintainable as an exercise of the president's power as commander-in-chief of the armed forces. The power sought to be exercised was the lawmaking power. Even if it were true that other presidents have taken possession of private business enterprises without congressional authority in order to settle labor disputes, Congress was not thereby divested of its exclusive constitutional authority to make the laws necessary and proper to carry out all powers vested by the Constitution "in the Government of the United States, or in any Department or Officer thereof."[25]

The pivotal proposition of the opinion is, in brief, that inasmuch as Congress could have ordered the seizure of the steel mills, there was a total absence of power in the president to do so without prior congressional authorization. To support this thesis no proof in the way of past opinion, practice or adjudication is offered. Justice Black's attitude toward this matter of authority is, in fact, decidedly cavalier. The closing paragraph of his opinion reads:

> The Founders of this Nation entrusted the lawmaking power to the Congress alone in both good and bad times. It would do no good to recall the historical events, the fears of power and the hopes for freedom that lay behind their choice. Such a review would but confirm our holding that this seizure order cannot stand.[26]

The somewhat different truth of the matter is that the framers of the Constitution were compelled to defend their handiwork against the charge that it violated "the political maxim that the legislative, executive, and judicial departments ought to be separate and distinct."[27] To meet this charge Madison sought to show in the *Federalist* that the three departments ought not to be so far separated as to have no control over each other.[28] In his opinion for the Court in *Ex parte Grossman*,[29] decided 137 years later, Chief Justice Taft adopted the same point of view: the fact that when two departments both operate upon the same subject matter the action of one may cancel that of the other *affords no criterion of the constitutional powers of either*. Rather the question is what does *the pertinent historical record* show with regard to presidential action in the field of congressional power?

*The Historical Record.* Our history contains numerous instances in which, contrary to the pattern of departmental relationship assumed in the Black opinion, presidential action has occurred within a recognized field of congressional power and has, furthermore, fully maintained its tenancy until Congress adopted superseding legislation. And Congress' right to supersede was not contested. In brief, the mere existence in Congress of power to do something has not, of itself, excluded the president from the same field of power until Congress finally acted. But once this happened, its legislation was forthwith recognized as governing the subject and as controlling presidential action in the area.

An early example of this pattern of departmental relationship is afforded by the case of the *Flying Fish*,[30] in which Chief Justice Marshall denied that the president had power to order the seizure of a vessel bound from a French port, *because* Congress had acted in the same field of power:

> It is by no means clear that the president of the United States whose high duty it is to "take care that the laws be faithfully executed," and who is commander in chief of the armies and navies of the United States, might not, without any special authority for that purpose, in the then existing state of things, have empowered the officers commanding the armed vessels of the United States, to seize and send into port for adjudication, American vessels which were forfeited by being engaged in this illicit commerce. But when it is observed that [an act of Congress] gives a special authority to seize on the high seas, and limits that authority to the seizure of vessels bound, or sailing to, a French port, the legislature seem to have prescribed that the manner in which this law shall be carried into execution, was to exclude a seizure of any vessel not bound to a French port.[31]

Another field which the President and Congress have occupied successively is extradition. In 1799 President Adams, in order to execute the extradition provisions of the Jay Treaty, issued a warrant for the arrest of one Jonathan Robbins. As Chief Justice Vinson recites in his opinion:

> This action was challenged in Congress on the ground that no specific statute prescribed the method to be used in executing the treaty. John Marshall, then a member of the House of Representatives, in the course of his successful defense of the President's action, said: "Congress, unquestionably, may prescribe the mode, and Congress may devolve on others the whole execution of the contract; but, till this be done, it seems the duty of the Executive department to execute the contract by any means it possesses."[32]

Not until 1848 did Congress enact a statute governing extradition cases and conferring on the courts, both State and Federal, the duty of handling them.[33]

The power of the president to act until Congress acts in the same field is also shown in these instances. The first Neutrality Proclamation, issued by President Washington in 1793, was also without congressional authorization.[34] The following year Congress enacted the first neutrality statute,[35] and subsequent proclamations of neutrality have been based on an act of Congress governing the matter. The president may, in the absence of legislation by Congress, control the landing of foreign cables in the United States and the passage of foreign troops through American territory, and has done so repeatedly.[36] Likewise, until Congress acts, he may govern conquered territory[37] and, "in the absence of attempts by Congress to limit his power," may set up military commissions in territory occupied by the armed forces of the United States.[38] He may determine in a manner binding on the courts whether a treaty is still in force as law of the land, although again the final power in the field rests with Congress.[39] One of the president's most ordinary powers and duties is that of ordering the prosecution of supposed offenders against the laws of the United States. Yet Congress may do the same thing under the "necessary and proper" clause.[40] On September 22, 1862, President Lincoln issued a proclamation suspending the privilege of the writ of habeas corpus throughout the Union in certain classes of cases. By an act passed March 3, 1863, Congress ratified his action and at the same time brought the whole subject of military arrests in the United States under statutory control.[41] Conversely, when President Wilson failed in March, 1917, to obtain Congress' consent to his arming American merchant vessels with defensive arms, he went ahead and did it anyway, "fortified not only by the known sentiments of the majority in Congress but also by the advice of his Secretary of State and Attorney General."[42]

To turn to the specific matter of property seizures, Justice Frankfurter's concurring opinion in the *Youngstown* case is accompanied by appendices containing a synoptic analysis of legislation authorizing seizures of industrial property and also a summary of seizures of industrial plants and facilities by presidents without definite statutory warrant. Eighteen such statutes are listed, all but the first of which were enacted between 1916 and 1951. Of presidential seizures unsupported by reference to specific statutory authorization he lists eight as occurring during World War I. One he fails to mention is the seizure of the Marconi Wireless Station at Siasconset in the late summer of 1914, as a result of the company's refusal to give assurance that it would comply with naval censorship regulation.[43] To justify these seizures it was deemed sufficient to refer to "the Constitution and laws" generally. For the World War II period he lists eleven seizures in justification of which no statutory authority was cited. The first of these was the seizure of North American Aviation, Inc. of Englewood, Claifornia. In support of this action Attorney General Jackson, as Chief Justice Vinson points out in his dissenting opinion, "vigorously proclaimed that the President had the moral duty to keep this Nation's defense effort a 'going concern.' "[44] Said the then Attorney General:

> For the faithful execution of . . . [the] laws the President has back of him not only each general law-enforcement power conferred by the various acts of Congress but the aggregate of all such laws plus that wide discretion as to method vested in him by the Constitution for the purpose of executing the laws.[45]

In the War Labor Disputes Act of June 25, 1943,[46] all such seizures were put on a statutory basis. Congress having at last acted on the subject, its expressed will thereafter governed.

In *United States v. Pewee Coal Co.,*[47] the Court had before it the claim of a coal mine operator whose property was seized by the President without statutory authorization, "to avert a nation-wide strike of miners." The company brought an action in the Court of Claims to recover under the Fifth Amendment for the total operating losses sustained during the period in which this property was operated by the United States. The court awarded judgment for $2,241.46 and the Supreme Court sustained this judgment, a result which, by implying the validity of the seizure,[48] supported the Government's position in the *Youngstown* case.[49]

The doctrine dictated by the above considerations as regards the exercise of executive power in the field of legislative power was well stated by Mr. John W. Davis, principal counsel on the present occasion for the steel companies, in a brief which he filed nearly forty years ago as Solicitor General. The brief defended the action of the president in withdrawing certain lands from public entry, although his doing so was at the time contrary to express statute. "Ours," the brief reads,

> is a self-sufficient Government within its sphere. (*Ex parte Siebold,* 100 U.S. 371, 395; *in re Debs,* 158 U.S. 56, 564, 578.) "Its means are adequate to its ends" (*McCulloch v. Maryland,* 4 Wheat, 316, 424), and it is rational to assume that its active forces will be found equal in most things to the emergencies that confront it. While perfect flexibility is not to be expected in a Government of divided powers, and while division of power is one of the principal features of the Constitution, it is the plain duty of those who are called upon to draw the dividing lines to ascertain the essential, recognize the practical, and avoid a slavish formalism which can only serve to ossify the Government and reduce its efficiency without any compensating good. The function of making laws is peculiar to Congress, and the Executive can not exercise that function to any degree. But this is not to say that all of the *subjects* concerning which laws might be made are perforce removed from the possibility of Executive influence. The Executive may act upon things and upon men in many relations which have not, though they might have, been actually regulated by Congress. In other words, just as there are fields which are peculiar to Congress and fields which are common both, in the sense that the Executive may move within them until they shall have been occupied by legislative action. These are not the fields of

legislative prerogative, but fields within which the lawmaking power may enter and dominate whenever it chooses. This situation results from the fact that the President is the active agent, not of Congress, but of the Nation. As such he performs the duties which the Constitution lays upon him immediately, and as such, also, he executes the laws and regulations adopted by Congress. He is the agent of the people of the United States, deriving all his powers from them and responsible directly to them. In no sense is he the agent of Congress. He obeys and executes the laws of Congress, not because Congress is enthroned in authority over him, but because the Constitution directs him to do so.

Therefore it follows that in ways short of making laws or disobeying them, the Executive may be , under a grave constitutional duty to act for the national protection in situations not covered by the acts of Congress, and in which, even, it may not be said that his action is the direct expression of any particular one of the independent powers which are granted to him specifically by the Constitution. Instances wherein the President has felt and fulfilled such a duty have not been rare in our history, though, being for the public benefit and approved by all, his acts have seldom been challenged in the courts.[50]

*Some Logical Considerations.* If the legislative power and executive power are not always mutually exclusive, neither, on the other hand, are the legislative and judicial powers. Replying to the contention in *Wayman v. Southard*[51] that it was unconstitutional for Congress to delegate to the courts its power to regulate their practice. Chief Justice Marshall answered that while Congress cannot delegate powers which are "strictly and exclusively legislative," the courts do have certain rule-making powers with respect, for example, to the returning of writs and processes and the filing of pleadings which Congress might have retained but which it had the right to confer on the judicial department.[52] Indeed, if the President was forbidden to seize the steel mills by virtue of the fact that Congress could have done so, the right of the Court to "invalidate" the seizure becomes highly questionable; and, as all admitted, Congress could have invalidated the seizure.

Actually the President was exercising the same *kind* of power that he would have exercised had the Taft-Hartley Act, for example, made provision for such a seizure "when necessary to avert a serious strike." The Court's opinion says, however:

> The President's order does not direct that a congressional policy be executed in a manner prescribed by Congress—it directs that a presidential policy be executed in a manner prescribed by the President. The preamble of the order itself, like that of many statutes, sets out reasons why the President believes certain policies should be adopted, proclaims these policies as rules of conduct to be followed, and again, like a statute, authorizes a government official to promulgate additional rules and regulations consistent with the policy proclaimed and needed to carry that policy into execution.[53]

So what? The same thing can be said of orders of the Interstate Commerce Commission setting "reasonable rates," something which Congress can do directly any time it chooses to by-pass or override the Commission. Besides, the chief factors of the "national emergency" described in Executive Order 10340 put into operation "cognate powers" of President and Congress which may be merged indefinitely in the former at the option of Congress.[54]

*The Concurring Opinions*. Justice Frankfurter begins the material part of his opinion with the statement:

> We must . . . put to one side consideration of what powers the President would have had if there had been no legislation whatever bearing on the authority asserted by the seizure, or if the seizure had been only for a short, explicitly temporary period, to be terminated automatically unless Congressional approval were given.[55]

He then enters upon a review of the proceedings of Congress which attended the enactment of the Taft-Hartley Act, and concludes that Congress expressed its intention to withhold the seizure power "as though it had said so in so many words."[56]

Justice Douglas' contribution consists in the argument that a necessary result of the condemnation provision of the Fifth Amendment is that the branch of government with "the power to pay compensation for a seizure is the only one able to authorize a seizure or make lawful one that the President has effected."[57] This contention overlooks such cases as *Mitchell v. Harmony*.[58] *United States v. Russell*,[59] *Portsmouth Harbor Land & Hotel Co. v. United States*[60] and *United States v. Pewee Coal Co.*,[61] in all of which a right of compensation was recognized to exist in consequence of a taking of property or damage to property which resulted from acts stemming ultimately from constitutional powers of the president. In *United States v. Pink*,[62] Justice Douglas quoted with approval the following words from the *Federalist:* "All constitutional acts of power, whether in the executive or in the judicial department, have as much . . . validity and obligation as if they proceeded from the legislature."[63] If this is so as to treaty obligations, then all the more must it be true of obligations which are based directly on the Constitution.[64]

Justice Jackson's rather desultory opinion contains little that is of direct pertinence to the constitutional issue. Important, however, is his contention, which seems to align him with Justice Frankfurter, that Congress has "not left seizure of private property an open field but has covered it by three statutory policies inconsistent with this seizure." From this he reasons that ". . . we can sustain the President only by holding that seizure of such strike-bound industries is within his domain and beyond control by Congress."[65] The opinion concludes:

> In view of the case, expedition and safety with which Congress can grant and has granted large emergency powers, certainly ample to embrace this crisis, I am quite unimpressed with the rgument that we should affirm possession of them without statute. . . . But I have no illusion that any decision by this Court can keep power in the hands of Congress if it is not wise and timely in meeting its problems. A crisis that challenges the President equally, or perhaps primarily, challenges Congress. If not good law, there was worldly wisdom in the maxim attributed to Napoleon that "The tools belong to the man who can use them." We may say that power to legislate for emergencies belongs in the hands of Congress, but only Congress itself can prevent power from slipping through its fingers.[66]

Justice Burton says that the Taft-Hartley Act, read in the light of its legislative history,[67] significantly fails to provide authority for seizures. He also agrees that "Congress authorized a procedure which the President declined to follow."[68] Justice Clark bases his position directly on *Little v. Barreme*.[69] The President must, he says, follow the procedures laid down in the Taft-Hartley, Selective Service and Defense Production

Acts.[70] At the same time he endorses the view, "taught me not only by the decision of Chief Justice Marshal in *Little v. Barreme,* but also by a score of other pronouncements of distinguished members of this bench," that "the Constitution does grant to the President extensive authority in times of grave and imperative national emergency."[71]

*Dissenting Opinion.* Chief Justice Vinson launched his dissent, for himself and Justices Reed and Minton, with a survey of the elements of the emergency which confronted the President: the Korean war, the obligations of the United States under the United Nations Charter and the Atlantic Pact, the Appropriations Acts by which Congress voted vast sums to be expended in our defense and that of our European allies, the fact that steel is a basic constituent of war matériel. He reproaches the Court for failing to give consideration to the President's finding of an emergency. According to the Court, he said, "the immediacy of the threatened disaster" is "irrelevant"; and the President, unable to use the executive power to avert the disaster, "must confine himself to sending a message to Congress." The opinion of the Chief Justice musters impressive evidence to show that the steel seizure, considering the emergency involved, fits into the picture of past presidential emergency action. And "plaintiffs admit that the emergency procedures of Taft-Hartley are not mandatory."[72]

*Résumé and Evaluation. Youngstown* will probably go down in history as an outstanding example of the *sic volo, sic jubeo* frame of mind into which the Court is occasionally maneuvered by the public context of the case before it. The doctrine of the case, as stated in Justice Black's opinion of the Court, while purporting to stem from the principle of the separation of powers, is a purely arbitrary construct created out of hand for the purpose of disposing of this particular case, and is altogether devoid of historical verification. Nor do the concurring opinions contribute anything to the decision's claim to be regarded seriously as a doctrine of constitutional law. Their importance consists in the suggestion, cogently urged by Justice Frankfurter and endorsed by Justices Jackson, Burton and Clark, that the President should have heeded the intention of the Taft-Hartley Act. Only Justice Clark, however, guided by Marshall's opinion in the early case of *Little v. Barreme,* had the courage to draw the appropriate conclusion: Congress having entered the field, its ascertainable intention supplied the law of the case. Justice Clark accordingly refused to concur in the opinion of the Court, while voting for its decision.

The Chief Justice's dissenting opinion is impressive for its delineation of the emergency and convincing in its summation of evidence regarding presidential emergency power. In view of the attitude of the concurring justices, however, his assertion as to the bearing of Taft-Hartley on the problem before the Court is deceptive. The statement that Taft-Hartley was "not mandatory" is equivocal. Granting that the Act was not intended to require the president to resort to it in preference to permitting the situation to take an uncontrolled course, yet resort to it may very well have been intended as an indispensable preliminary to a seizure. This conclusion is borne out by the fact that when the procedures provided by the act fail, the president is required to submit a report and recommendations to Congress for action. In the opinion of the writer the case was rightly decided, but for wrong reasons. The line of reasoning suggested by Justices Frankfurter, Jackson, Burton and Clark should have been pursued to its logical end, as by Justice Clark it was.[73]

The question remains whether the record of the case is of value for constitutional law and practice. It is. (1) That the president does possess "residual" or "resultant" powers over and above, or in consequence of, his specifically granted powers to take temporary alleviative action in the presence of serious emergency is a proprosition to which all but Justices Black and Douglas would probably have assented in the absence of the complicating issue that was created by the president's refusal to follow the procedures laid down in the Taft-Hartley Act. (2) Such residual powers being conceded, it would follow logically that a seizure of property made by exercise of them would give rise to a constitutional obligation on the part of the United States to render "just compensation" in accordance with the requirements of the Fifth Amendment. (3) It is also fairly evident that the Court would never venture to traverse a presidential finding of "serious" emergency which was prima facie supported by judicially cognizable facts, but would wave aside a challenge to such a finding as raising a "political question." (4) The Court would unquestionably have assented to the proposition that in all emergency situations the last word lies with Congress when it chooses to speak such last word. And the moral from all this is plain: namely, that escape must be sought from "presidential autocracy" by resort not to the judicial power, but to the legislative power—in other words, by resort to timely action by Congress and to procedures for the meeting of emergency situations so far as these can be intelligently anticipated.

And—not to give the thing too fine a point—what seems to be required at the present juncture is a new Labor Disputes Act which ordains procedures for the handling of industry-wide strikes in terms so comprehensive and explicit that the most headstrong president cannot sidestep them without manifest attaint to the law, the Constitution and his own oath of office. "Presidential autocracy," when it is justified, is an inrush of power to fill a power vacuum. Nature abhors a vacuum; so does an age of emergency. Let Congress see to it that no such vacuum occurs.

### Notes

1. *Youngstown Sheet & Tube Co.* v. *Sawyer,* 343 U.S. 579 (1952).
2. 2 Farrand, *Records of the Federal Convention* 171, 185 (rev. ed. 1937).
3. Corwin, *The President: Office and Powers* 102–14, 428 (3d ed. 1948).
4. *Myers* v. *United States,* 272 U.S. 52 (1926).
5. Corwin, *op. cit. supra* note 3, at 217 *et seq.,* 465, 474–75.
6. *Marbury* v. *Madison,* 1 Cranch 137, 166 (U.S. 1803).
7. 5 *Writings of Jefferson* 209 (Ford ed. 1895).
8. 40 Ops. Att'y Gen. 312, 319 (1944).
9. *United States* v. *Lee,* 106 U.S. 196, 220 (1882).
10. *In re* Neagle, 135 U.S. 1, 64 (1889).
11. *In re* Debs, 158 U.S. 564 (1895).
12. Roosevelt, *An Autobiography* 389 (1913).
13. Taft, *Our Chief Magistrate and His Powers* 144 (1916).
14. See *Myers* v. *United States,* 272 U.S. 52, 118 (1926).
15. See *Taft, The Presidency* 90 *et seq.* (1916).
16. Corwin, *op. cit. supra* note 3, at 453–54 (figures compiled by Professor Dishman of Dartmouth College).
17. Corwin, *Constitution of Powers in a Secular State* 76 n.20 (1951). See also *id.* 62 n.8a.
18. *Youngstown Sheet & Tube Co.* v. *Sawyer,* 343 U.S. 579 (1952)
19. 17 Fed. Reg. 3139 (1952).

20. 98 Cong. Rec. 3962 (April 9, 1952).

21. 98 Cong. Rec. 4192 (April 21, 1952).

22. 64 Stat. 798 (1950), as amended, 50 U.S.C. App. § 2071 (Supp. 1952).

23. 61 Stat. 136 (1947), as amended, 29 U.S.C. §§ 141–197 (Supp. 1952).

24. 62 Stat. 604 (1948), 50 U.S.C. App. §§ 451–462 (Supp. 1952).

25. U.S. Const. Art. I, § 8. See *Youngstown Sheet & Tube Co.* v. *Sawyer,* 343 U.S. 579, 660–61 (1952).

26. *Id.* at 589.

27. *The Federalist,* No. 47 at 245 (Everyman's ed. 1929).

28. *The Federalist,* No. 48 (Madison).

29. 267 U.S. 87 (1925). "The Federal Constitution nowhere expressly declares that the three branches of the Government shall be kept separate and independent. All legislative powers are vested in a Congress. The executive power is vested in a President. The judicial power is vested in one Supreme Court and in such inferior courts as Congress may from time to time establish. The Judges are given life tenure and a compensation that may not be diminished during their continuance in office, with the evident purpose of securing them and their courts an independence of Congress and the Executive. Complete independence and separation between the three branches, however, are not attained, or intended, as other provisions of the Constitution and the normal operation of government under it easily demonstrate." *Id* at 119–20.

30. *Little* v. *Barreme,* 2 Cranch 170 (U.S. 1804).

31. *Id.* at 177–78 *quoted in Youngstown Sheet & Tube Co.* v. *Sawyer,* 343 U.S. 579, 660–61 (1952) (Clark, J., concurring). Justice Clark added: "I know of no subsequent holding of this Court to the contrary." *Ibid.*

32. *Youngstown Sheet & Tube Co.* v. *Sawyer,* 343 U.S. 579, 684 (1952), citing 10 Annals of Congress 619 (1948).

33. Rev. State. §§ 5270–79 (1878), as amended, 18 U.S.C. §§ 651–76 (1946).

34. For the controversy thereby precipitated between Hamilton (Pacificus) and Madison (Helvidius), see Corwin, *The President's Control of Foreign Relations* c. 1 (1917).

35. 1 Stat. 381 (1794). The act was the direct outcome of suggestions made by Washington in his message of December 3, 1793. See 1 Richardson, *Messages and Papers of the Presidents* 139 (1896).

36. 22 Ops. Att'y Gen. 13 (1898); see *Tucker* v. *Alexandroff,* 183 U.S. 424, 434–35 (1902). An act was passed May 27, 1921, 42 Stat. 8 (1921), 47 U.S.C. § 34 (1946) which requires presidential license for the landing and operation of cables connecting the United States with foreign countries. See Wright, *The Control of American Foreign Relations* 302 n.75 (1922).

37. *Santiago* v. *Nagueras,* 214 U.S. 260 (1909).

38. *Madsen* v. *Kinsella,* 343 U.S. 341 (1952).

39. *Charlton* v. *Kelly,* 229 U.S. 447 (1913). See also Botiller v. Dominquez, 130 U.S. 238 (1889).

40. See *Sinclair* v. *United States,* 279 U.S. 263, 289, 297 (1929).

41. 12 Stat. 755 (1863).

42. Berdahl, *War Powers of the Executive in the United States* 69 (1921).

43. Attorney General Gregory's justification of this action, 30 Ops. Att'y Gen. 291 (1914), more or less set the style for similar future opinions.

44. *Youngstown Sheet & Tube Co.* v. *Sawyer,* 343 U.S. 579, 695 (1952)

45. 89 Cong. Rec. 3992 (1943).

46. 57 Stat. 163 (1943).

47. 341 U.S. 114 (1951).

48. Such suits are based on the Tucker Act, 24 Stat. 505 (1887), as amended, 28 U.S.C. §§ 41 (20), 250 (1) (2), 287 (1946), and are founded upon the Constitution of the United States. "The constitutional prohibition against taking private property for public use without just compensation is directed against the Government, and not against individual or public officers proceeding without the authority of legislative enactment." *Hooe* v. *United States*, 218 U.S. 322, 335–36 (1910). See *United States* v. *North American Co.*, 253 U.S. 330, 333 (1920). While the above quoted language is doubtless correct as an interpretation of the Tucker Act, it ignores the constitutional obligation of the United States to compensate for acts of "taking" which stem from the president's power, especially his power as commander-in-chief. See *United States* v. *Causby*, 328 U.S. 256, 267 (1946); notes 58–61 *infra*.

49. "The relatively new technique of temporary taking by eminent domain is a most useful administrative device: many properties, such as laundries, or coal mines, or railroads, many be subjected to public operation for a short time to meet war or emergency needs, and can then be returned to their owners." *United States* v. *Pewee Coal Co.*, 341 U.S. 114, 119 (1951) (Reed, J., concurring).

50. Brief for Appellant, pp. 75–77, *United States* v. *Midwest Oil Co.*, 236 U.S. 459 (1915). Assistant Att'y Gen. Knaebel's name was also on the brief.

51. 10 Wheat, 1 (U.S. 1825).

52. *See id.* at 42–43.

53. *Youngstown Sheet & Tube Co., v. Sawyer,* 343 U.S. 579, 588 (1952).

54. *United States* v. *Curtiss-Wright Corp.,* 299 U.S. 304, 319–29 (1936).

55. *Youngstown Sheet & Tube Co.* v. *Sawyer,* 343 U.S. 579, 597 (1952).

56. *Id.* at 602.

57. *Id.* at 631–32.

58. 13 How. 115 (U.S. 1852).

59. 13 Wall, 623 (U.S. 1871).

60. 260 U.S. 327 (1922).

61. 341 U.S. 114 (1951).

62. 315 U.S. 203, 230 (1942).

63. *The Federalist,* No. 64, at 330 (Everyman's ed. 1929).

64. See 40 *Ops. Att'y Gen.* 250, 253 (1942).

65. *Youngstown Sheet & Tube Co.* v. *Sawyer,* 343 U.S. 579, 639–40 (1952).

66. *Id.* at 653–54.

67. *93 Cong. Rec* 3835–36 (1947).

68. *Youngstown Sheet & Tube Co.* v. *Sawyer,* 343 U.S. 579, 659 (1952).

69. 2 Cranch 170 (U.S. 1804).

70. *Youngstown Sheet & Tube Co.* v. *Sawyer,* 343 U.S. 579, 663–65 (1952).

71. *Id.* at 662.

72. *Id.* at 705.

73. The case for the President is not improved by Congress' adoption of the following provision as a part of the Defense Production Act Amendments of 1952, Pub. L. No. 429, 82d Cong., 2d Sess. § 115 (June 30, 1952): "Section 503 of the Defense Production Act of 1950, as amended, is hereby amended by adding at the end thereof the following: 'It is the sense of the Congress that, by reason of the work stoppage now existing in the steel industry, the national safety is imperiled, and the Congress therefore requests the President to invoke immediately the national emergency provisions (sections 206 to 210, inclusive) of the Labor-Management Relations Act, 1947, for the purpose of terminating such work stoppage.' "

## Separation of Powers and Presidential Prerogative: The Case of *Myers v. United States* Reconsidered

L. Peter Schultz

I

Almost from the beginning of our political existence under the Constitution of 1787, the question has been debated as to whether and by whom executive officers may be removed from office. The Constitution itself is silent on this question, if one distinguishes between the removal of an executive officer and an impeachment and conviction of such as an officer. The question of removal was vigorously debated by the first Congress, and at least until 1820, the President could remove all executive officers at his pleasure. However, after 1820, Congress began to limit the president's removal power, these limitations culminating in the Tenure of Office Act passed by Congress on 2 March 1867, which provided that all officers appointed by and with the consent of the Senate could not be removed without the consent of the Senate.[1] It was this act with which President Andrew Johnson refused to comply, his refusal leading to his impeachment by the House of Representatives and his trial by the Senate. Although President Johnson was acquitted by the Senate, this did not settle the removal question, and it arose again in the case of *Myers* v. *the United States*,[2] decided by the Supreme Court in 1926. The facts of the case were as follows.

Myers was appointed postmaster of the first class at Portland, Oregon, for a term of four years, under an Act of Congress of 12 July 1876.[3] According to that act:

> Postmasters of the first, second, and third classes shall be appointed and may be removed by the President by and with the advice and consent of the Senate and shall hold their offices for four years unless sooner removed or suspended according to law.[4]

On 2 February 1920, Myers was removed from office by order of the Postmaster General, acting under the direction of President Wilson. The Senate was never notified of Myers' removal, nor a successor nominated, and therefore a hearing before a Senate committee was not held. Because the president acted without the consent of the Senate, Myers protested his removal, took no other employment and brought suit in the Court of Claims for his salary from the date of his removal. Myers lost his suit in that Court, because it was deemed that he had lost his right to his salary due to unnecessary delay in suing. The Supreme Court, however, because it held that Myers had not been tardy in bringing his suit, found it necessary to confront the issue of the constitutionality of the law's removal provision.[5] The Court held, in a six to three decision, that "the President's power of removal of executive officers appointed by him with the advice and consent of the Senate is full and complete without the consent of the Senate."[6] Thus, the removal provision of the statute in question was unconstitutional and Myers was not entitled to his salary.

Reprinted with permission of the author, L. Peter Schultz.

**II**

Chief Justice Taft's opinion in the *Myers* case has customarily been considered with regard to its historical accuracy and with regard to its constitutional underpinnings. On both counts, Taft's opinion has been found wanting, and this even by those who are sympathetic to the decision itself.[7]

The historical accuracy of Taft's opinion is crucial because of the great weight he gave in his opinion to "the decision of 1789." According to Taft, in 1789 the first Congress made what was in effect "a legislative declaration that the power to remove officers appointed by the President and the Senate is vested in the President alone."[8] That is, Taft argued that the first Congress decided that the Senate was constitutionally excluded from the removal of executive officers appointed by and with the advice and consent of the Senate, and that Congress could not vest the Senate with any part of this power. Moreover, Taft asserted that this was the practice of the government for seventy-four years.[9]

Both the dissenters in the *Myers* case and other commentators have concluded that Taft's account of the decision of 1789 was grossly inaccurate. On the key point of Senate participation in removals, most have agreed with Brandeis' statement in dissent that the action of the first Congress:

> Did not involve a decision of the question whether Congress could confer upon the Senate the right, and impose upon it the duty, to participate in removals. It involved merely the decision that the Senate does not, in the absence of a legislative grant thereof, have the right to share in the removal of an officer appointed with its consent.[10]

Similarly, Edward S. Corwin concluded that "a mere fraction of a fraction, a minority of a minority of the House, can be shown to have attributed the removal power to the President on grounds of executive prerogative."[11] According to Corwin, most members of the House took the constitutionally correct position, and "attributed the broadest discretion to Congress" to regulate removals.[12]

According to the dissenters and to other commentators, Taft misconstrued the decision of 1789, if it can be called that. What Taft saw as a legislative declaration on a constitutional issue was nothing more than an ordinary exercise of power under the necessary and proper clause.

In order to assess the validity of this critique, it is essential to review the actions of the first Congress with regard to the removal question. On the surface, it appears that what transpired supports Taft's assessment of the decision of 1789. The removal power was discussed on two different occasions, and the final version of the bill in question supports Taft's argument.

On May 19 it was moved that Congress establish the Department of Foreign Affairs, headed by a secretary, "who shall be appointed by the President, by and with the advice and consent of the Senate; and to be removable by the president."[13] There ensued a discussion of this removal clause, but at the end of the day it was "carried by a considerable majority."[14] On June 16, however, the Department of Foreign Affairs again came up for discussion, and the focus of this discussion was the removal clause. This discussion occupied the House until June 22, when "Mr. Benson moved to amend the bill, by altering the clause so as to imply the power of removal to be in the President alone."[15] Benson moved to add the following language to the bill: "that there should be a chief clerk of the Department, who should have custody of all records, books and papers whenever the Secretary shall be removed from office by the President." Benson also said that "if he succeeded in this amendment, he should move to strike out the words, 'to be removable by the President,' which appeared somewhat like a grant [of power by the legislature]."[16] Two votes were then taken in the House on June 22, the first in which the House agreed to the additional language, and the second in which the House agreed to strike the original language. As Madison explained it, the purpose of these actions was to expunge "everything like an ambiguity" of a legislative grant of power, and to declare the "the sense of the House explicitly . . . that the Constitution vests the power [of removal] in the President."[17]

It appears then that the action of the House supports Taft's argument that the first Congress declared that the removal power was constitutionally vested in the president. And to some extent, the dissenters agree with Taft. Brandeis did not deny that the language of the act supported Taft's interpretation. Indeed, Brandeis admitted that the clause in question "involved a denial of the claim that the Senate had a constitutional right to participate in removals." But Brandeis did deny that the first Congress meant to declare that the Senate was *constitutionally* excluded from removals. According to Brandeis, this could not have been the intention of the first Congress, because the language in question "was adopted . . . by aid of votes [of those] who believed it expedient for Congress to confer the power of removal on the President."[18] Further, Brandeis suggested that those who thought the Constitution vested the removal power in the president alone were a distinct minority.[19] Similarly, Justice McReynolds, who also dissented, calculated that only nine of twenty-four members who spoke supported this interpretation.[20] Thus, the dissenters argued that Taft's opinion oversimplified what actually happened in the House in 1789, and that this led Taft to the erroneous conclusion that the House had decided the Senate was constitutionally excluded from the removal power.

Is it true? Did Taft oversimplify the events of the first Congress and draw an erroneous conclusion about the meaning of the legislation? The answer is both "yes" and "no." This is, yes, Taft did oversimplify the actions of the first Congress; but no, he did not draw an erroneous conclusion about the legislation in question. To explain.

An analysis of the two votes taken on Benson's two motions reveals the presence of three relatively equal "parties." First, there were those who voted in favor of Benson's two motions, who may be labeled, following Corwin, the "Presidential party."[21] These members probably agreed with Madison that the removal power was vested in the president alone. Second, there were those members who voted against Benson's first motion and in favor of the second to delete the original language from the bill. Again, Corwin correctly labels this party the "Senatorial party," because its members thought that the Senate was constitutionally entitled to participate in removals.[22] However, this party came to argue that it would be improper for the House to make any decision on the removal question, that this was for the courts to decide. Therefore, they voted to delete all references to removal from the bill.

Several things should be emphasized at this point. First, these two parties were equal in number, there being fifteen in each. Secondly, at least a majority of the House thought that the removal question was decided, one way or another, by the Constitution. That is, contrary to the analysis and interpretation offered by Brandeis and Corwin, most members of the House did not think that Congress had the power to vest the removal power where it pleased.

However, there was a third party, totaling sixteen, who voted in favor of Benson's first motion, but against his second. Corwin labels this party the "Congressional party," arguing that they thought Congress had the utmost latitude in dealing with the removal power.[23] This assessment is wrong, for this party, or at least some of its members, agreed with Madison that the Senate was constitutionally excluded from removals.

Consider, for example, Mr. Boudinot. Although Boudinot indicated that he would vote against Benson's second motion, he argued that the removal power was constitutionally vested in the president alone. According to Boudinot, because the Constitution vested all executive power "in the President . . . *ex officio,* he would remove, *without limitation.*"[24] However, he favored retaining the original language to avoid the appearance of "fickleness," and because "debate had arisen, . . . he was clear for having a *legislative declaration* in order to avoid future inconvenience."[25] Similarly, Mr. Sylvester and Mr. Sedgwick, identified by Corwin as spokesmen for the "Congressional party," also thought that the removal power inhered in the President by virtue of the Constitution.[26]

In fact, only two of the seven members of the House who spoke and voted in favor of Benson's first motion and against the second seemed to have held the view that "the Legislature had the power to establish offices on what terms they pleased," viz., Lawrence and Hartley.[27] The other two members of the "Congressional party" who expressed their sentiments, Lee and Thatcher, shared the view of Boudinot, Sylvester and Sedgwick.[28]

All members of the "Congressional party" did not, therefore, think that Congress could vest the removal power where it pleased. Also, it should be emphasized that were this so, the more rational alternative would have been to vote against Benson's motions. This would have preserved the original language, thereby preserving the implication of a congressional grant of the removal power to the president. And, in fact, two members of the House did so vote, and both argued that "the Legislature have a right to vest it [the removal power] where they pleased."[29]

It is fair to conclude, then, that although Taft did not present a complete picture of the first Congress, his assessment of the decision of 1789 was more correct than that offered by Corwin or Brandeis. It may be said with certainty that at least twenty members of the House thought that the removal power was constitutionally vested in the President alone. This is a good deal more than "a mere fraction of a fraction, a minority of a minority."[30] Moreover, only four members of the House thought that Congress had complete discretion with regard to removals, the position taken by both Brandeis and Corwin.

## III

History then seems to be on Taft's side. But what of the Constitution? That is, does it support Taft's position and opinion in the *Myers'* case and, by implication, the position of the first Congress?

With regard to Taft, we must first be clear about the extent of his opinion and the Court's decision in *Myers*. Did Taft believe, as Corwin argued, that "the logic of the case renders all executive or administrative officers . . . removable by the President at will?"[31] Or did Taft believe that Congress could, within limits, regulate the removal of some executive officials "without doing violence to the logic of [the] decision in *Myers*?"[32] The latter view is, we think, correct.

According to Taft, Congress "may prescribe incidental regulations controlling and restraining . . . the exercise of the power of removal,"[33] at least with regard to "inferior officers" and certainly with regard to any officer not appointed by the president, by and with the advice and consent of the Senate. As one commentator has noticed:

> It is specifically declared in Chief Justice Taft's opinion that when Congress exercises its power of vesting the appointment of "inferior officers" in the heads of departments or in the courts of law it may control or limit by statute the removal of such officers; but that if [Congress] does not do so the President may remove them in the exercise of his general executive authority.[34]

Both Brandeis and Corwin are wrong then when they argue that Taft's opinion renders unconstitutional any legislation regulating the removal of any executive officers, however appointed. As his lectures at Columbia University in 1913 illustrate, Taft was fully aware of the inconveniences of the spoils system. Taft deemed any concern by the president with inferior officers a waste of the president's time and energy. Such concerns diverted the president's attention from those high political duties that comprise the most important part of the president's constitutional responsibilities. In Taft's opinion, "the President should not be required to exercise his judgment to make appointments except to . . . the most important offices;" the President should not have to waste his time considering "who shall be postmistress at the town of Devil's Lake in North Dakota."[35]

Taft did not argue, then, that the president's power to remove extends to all executive officers. For Taft, the proper arrangement is suggested by the Constitution's "excepting clause," which authorizes Congress to "vest the Appointment of such inferior officers, as they think proper, in the President alone, in the Courts of Law, or in Heads of Departments."[36] Congress could, indeed should, vest the appointment of all inferior officers in someone other than the president, a "simple expedient" Taft argued, that would allow Congress to prevent the "evil of political executive removals,"[37] such as that of Myers. Having taken this simple expedient, Congress may then enact "incidental regulations controlling and restraining the [department heads] in the exercise of the power of removal."[38] And, as Taft indicated that a provision prohibiting the removal of military officers except by court martial is constitutional, at least in time of peace, congressional power over removals is quite broad, extending even to the prohibition of arbitrary removals in some cases.[39]

Why then was the provision of the law in question unconstitutional? Taft gave two reasons. First, it was unconstitutional because it regulated the removal of an executive officer, who was appointed by the president, by and with the advice and consent of the Senate. Had Myers been appointed by the Postmaster General, Congress could legitimately regulate his removal.

Second, the provision of the law in question was unconstitutional, because it authorized the Senate to participate in the removal process. According to Taft, whereas Congress may enact "incidental regulations controlling and restricting the exercise of the power of removal," it cannot draw to itself the power of removing executive officers, as this would "infringe the constitutional principle of the separation of powers."[40] The removal clause at issue in *Myers* violated the separation of powers, because it associated "the Senate with the President in the exercise of a purely Executive function."[41]

We may then summarize Taft's opinion in *Myers* as follows. As the Constitution distinguishes between superior and inferior officers, the latter need not, indeed should not, serve at the pleasure of the president. These inferior officers should be appointed by department heads and protected from arbitrary removals. According to Taft's decision in *Myers,* the Constitution need not be construed as demanding a spoils system controlled by the president. It is for Congress, however, to avoid such a system by adopting the "simple expedient" of vesting the appointment of all inferior officers in the department heads and by regulating their removals. Contrary to Brandeis' assertion, Taft did not argue that the president possessed an absolute and uncontrollable right to remove all executive officers and that any legislation relating thereto is unconstitutional. Rather, the more moderate position emerges that with regard to superior officers, or those appointed by the president, by and with the advice and consent of the Senate, the removal power is vested completely in the president. With regard to inferior officers, Congress may regulate their removal through "incidental" regulations. In no case, however, may Congress exercise the removal power itself or participate therein, as this would violate the separation of powers by taking "from the President a part of his constitutional power and dividing it with the Senate."[42]

Now, the dissenters rejected Taft's interpretation for two reasons. First, because it conflicts with their understanding of the separation of powers, and second, because it seems to lead to "uncontrollable" executive powers, i.e., powers beyond the reach of legal limitation. Each of these objections is plausible and, therefore, needs to be discussed.

The dissenters in *Myers* take the very common view that the separation of powers is more fiction than fact. At most, the Constitution created "separated institutions sharing powers."[43] Accordingly, Brandeis argued that "the separation of powers did not make each branch completely autonomous,"[44] while McReynolds argued that we "have no such thing as three totally distinct and independent departments. . . ."[45] Strictly speaking, of course, these statements are correct, and Taft agreed. But both Brandeis and McReynolds meant that the Framers rejected the separation of powers, not merely qualified them. Separated power means independent power, and the dissenters understood the Framers to be fearful of all unchecked power, and especially unchecked executive power. As Brandeis expressed this,

> The doctrine of the separation of powers was adopted . . . not to promote efficiency but to preclude the exercise of arbitrary power. The purpose was, not to avoid friction, but, by means of the inevitable friction incident to the distribution of governmental powers among three departments, to save the people from autocracy.[46]

Although this is a very common understanding of the Constitution, it does not, we think, square with the Constitution itself or with early interpretations of it by its leading Framers. For example, it is possible to distinguish between "shared" powers and "checked" powers. Strictly speaking, a "shared" power is one possessed jointly by different departments, whereas a "checked" power is possessed by one department, whose action is subject to ratification by another department. Where power is "shared," either department may exercise it, with the approval of the other. But in this sense, there are no shared powers under the Constitution.

Consider, for example, the appointment power, which the Senate does not share with the president. The Senate does not, or should not, exercise this power in any way. And it is for this reason that the practice of "Senatorial courtesy" may be questioned under the Constitution. As Taft said with regard to the president's veto, that it was intended as "a brake rather than a steam chest,"[47] so too with regard to the Senate's participation in appointments. This qualification of the separation of powers theory allows the Senate to check presidential action, but does not allow the Senate to control appointments. Thus, it is fair to say that the Senate does not share the appointment power with the president.

If one distinguishes between "checked" and "shared" powers, there is something to be said for Taft's argument that the Constitution does not grant the legislature a share of the executive power. In brief, the Constitution intended to establish an independent executive, and therefore the qualifications of the separation principle found in Article II ought to be "strictly construed."[48]

Even more interesting, however, is that Madison's argument in *The Federalist*, No. 51 leads to a similar conclusion.

There, after stating that in order to remedy the "inconvenience" of legislative predominance in representative republics, it is necessary to divide the legislature, Madison claimed that it was necessary to take "still further precautions."[49]

As the weight of the legislative authority requires that it should be divided, the weakness of the executive may require . . . that it should be fortified. An absolute negative on the legislature appears, at first view, to be the natural defense with which the executive magistrate should be armed. But perhaps it would neither be altogether safe nor alone sufficient. On ordinary occasions it might not be exerted with the requisite firmness, and on extraordinary occasions it might be perfidiously abused. May not this defect of an absolute negative be supplied by some qualified connection between this weaker department and the weaker branch of the stronger department, by which the latter may be led to support *the constitutional rights* of the former, without being too much detached from the rights of its own department?[50]

According to Madison, therefore, the Constitution qualifies the appointment power and the treaty power in order to *strengthen* the executive. This arrangement lends legitimacy to executive actions that might appear illegitimate if undertaken by the president alone. Apparently Madison was aware that while certain powers ought to be vested in the president alone, such an arrangement would in fact undermine the independence of the executive. This is especially true in a representative republic, where the authority of the legislature, if not its power, always predominates. Thus, what is theoretically an "unchaste connexion"[51] of the legislature and executive, is redeemed by its offspring, separation of powers in practice, meaning executive independence. And Taft's rule of constitutional interpretation, that "the branches should be kept separate in all cases in which they are not expressly blended, and [that] the Constitution should be expounded to blend them no more than it affirmatively requires,"[52] seems well-adapted to a constitution that establishes a government of separated powers.

But what of the charge that Taft's interpretation leads to "uncontrollable" executive power? Is this true? And if so, does this not mean that Taft's interpretation of the Constitution is fundamentally flawed?

There can be little doubt that Taft's interpretation does lead to uncontrollable executive power of some sort. Under Taft's interpretation, all executive officers appointed by the president, by and with the advice and consent of the Senate, serve at the president's pleasure. Obviously, the president's removal power is constitutionally complete and may not be limited by law.

However, it is important to see that this doctrine of uncontrollable executive power is difficult to avoid in a government of separated powers, or even one of separated institutions. For example, Brandeis does not completely avoid this doctrine in his dissent. According to Brandeis, a removal power is inherent in any government, "being an essential of effective government."[53] Moreover, Brandeis claimed that "the power of removal is . . . an executive act,"[54] and that the "Power to remove, as well as to suspend, a high political officer, might conceivably be deemed indispensable to democratic government and, hence, inherent in the President."[55]

Whatever else might be said of Brandeis' argument, it serves to illustrate the difficulty of denying some kind of presidential prerogative in a government of separated powers. For if Brandeis were consistently to follow his argument that the removal of high political officers is "inherent in the President,"[56] he would create exactly what he maintains is "not to be learned in American governments," viz., the doctrine of "an uncontrollable power of removal in the Chief Executive."[57] And this doctrine would apply to the most significant political officers of the government, other than the president.

This difficulty of denying and avoiding some kind of presidential prerogative may also be illustrated by considering three rulings of the Supreme Court, dealing with the removal power, that were made prior to *Myers*. The three cases are *Parsons v. the United States*,[58] *Shurtleff v. the United States*,[59] and *Wallace v. the United States*.[60]

In *Parsons*, the Court had before it a suit for salary brought by a former United States district attorney, who had been removed by the president under a statute that established a four-year term of office but that was silent as the president's power of removal. The Court held that Parsons' removal was legitimate, arguing that "a provision for removal from office . . . was not necessary . . . because of the fact that [the president] was then regarded as being clothed with such a power in any event."[61] According to the Court, this decision was consistent with the decision of 1789 and with "the constant and uniform practice of the Government" since then.[62]

Although in *Myers*, McReynolds suggested that the Court had erred in *Parsons*, he agreed with that if Congress created an office without specifying a term and without providing for removal, the president may remove at his pleasure. This practice was, McReynolds argued, "entirely consistent with implied legislative consent; the power to remove being commonly incident to the right to appoint when not forbidden by law."[63] However, McReynolds argued in *Myers* not that the removal power is incident to appointment, but that it comes to the president from Congress. McReynolds was not entirely consistent by agreeing with the "silence doctrine," in that it implies that the removal power is constitutionally vested in the president.

This implication was made explicit by the Court in the *Shurtleff* case, a decision that McReynolds did not criticize. In this case, the Court had before a claim for pay by a former executive officer, whose office carried a fixed term, but who also could be removed by the president for inefficiency, neglect of duty, or malfeasance in office. Shurtleff brought suit, claiming that because he was not given a hearing and because the president had made no charges against him, he had been improperly removed. In effect, he argued that the statute in question, by specifying causes for removal, prohibited the President from removing him for other reasons.[64]

Addressing this contention, the Court disagreed, arguing

> The right of removal would exist if the statute had not contained a word on the subject. *It does not exist by virtue of the grant* [in the law], but it inheres in the right to appoint, unless limited by the Constitution or statute. It requires plain language to take it away.[65]

While McReynolds did not disagree with the *Shurtleff* decision, clearly that decision conflicted with the argument of the dissenters in *Myers* that the removal power comes from Congress. The *Shurtleff* decision also conflicts with McReynolds' assessment of *Parsons*. For according to McReynolds, if Congress established a fixed term of office *without* providing explicitly for removal, the Court should assume that Congress did not intend to grant it.[66] It would seem to follow, therefore, that if Congress had established a term of office *and* specified causes for removal, the Court should hold removals made for other causes illegitimate.

Thus, both *Parsons* and *Shurtleff* conflict with the dissenters doctrine that the removal power is granted by Congress, not the Constitution. In *Parsons,* the Court ruled that in the absence of a legislative grant of the removal power, the President possesses that power completely. And in *Shurtleff,* the Court ruled that the President's power to remove was broader than that conferred upon him by act of Congress.

Furthermore, there is another principle followed by the Court, which also conflicts with the dissenters' understanding of the removal power, *viz.*, the rule that if the Senate "consents" to a presidential removal, the president's action is deemed legitimate, even though it conflicts with a statute regulating removal. This rule was followed by the Court in *Wallace* v. *the United States,* which was decided by the same justices that decided the *Myers* case.

In *Wallace,* the Court had before it a claim by a former army officer that his removal had been improper because the president had ignored a part of the statute regulating his removal. Upon learning that he was to be removed from the army, Wallace had requested a court martial, to which he was entitled by law. The president, however, denied his request. Taft, in his opinion for a unanimous court, held that the removal was valid, even though the president had violated the law, because the Senate "consented" to the removal by approving the nomination of Wallace's successor. According to Taft, "*none* of the limitations in the statutes affect [the President] when exercised by and with the consent of the Senate."[67]

When viewed in light of the dissenters' argument in *Myers* that the President's duty to execute the laws "does not go beyond the laws,"[68] the removal of Wallace was clearly invalid. As McReynolds said in *Myers*, "A certain repugnance must attend the suggestion that the President may ignore any provision of an Act of Congress under which he has proceeded."[69] And as McReynolds stressed, this repugnance should be particularly keen in "a government of laws not of men." But why should the consent of the Senate clothe with legitimacy presidential disobedience to a duly enacted law limiting the president's removal power? Obviously, such consent cannot do so if presidential power extends no further than that conferred by law. And this would be true even though one grants that "the Constitution by direct grant vests the President with all executive power."[70] For as McReynolds emphasized in *Myers:*

> it does not follow [from this] that [the President] can proceed in defiance of congressional action. Congress, by clear language is empowered to make all laws necessary and proper for carrying into execution the power in [the President]. [If] he [or she] were authorized only to appoint an officer of a certain kind, for a certain period, removable only in a certain way, [and] he [or she] undertook to proceed under the law so far as agreeable, but repudiated the remainder, I submit that *no warrant can be found for such conduct.*[71]

As this language makes perfectly clear, the implication of the *Wallace* decision is incompatible with the logic of the dissenters' arguments in *Myers*. At the very least, the *Wallace* decision implies that the president possesses the removal power by virtue of the Constitution, and therefore that he may proceed in defiance of congressional action."

## IV

By way of conclusion, it is fair to say that Taft's opinion for the Court in *Myers* is entitled to more respect than it has hitherto received. Despite some deficiencies, Taft's historiography is more accurate than that of the dissenters and even that of Corwin. As we have seen, a substantial part of the first House, even a majority, "attributed the removal power to the president on grounds of executive prerogative."[72]

But more importantly, we have seen that it is difficult to avoid the doctrine of "uncontrollable" executive power, despite Brandeis' contention that such a doctrine is inconsistent with the Constitution. In fact, Brandeis himself spoke in favor of this doctrine in *Myers*, even though he did not do so on constitutional grounds. Moreover, the Supreme Court's decisions in *Parsons* and *Shurtleff* recognize executive prerogative, defined by Blackstone as "the discretionary power of acting for the public good when the positive laws are silent."[73] Indeed, in *Wallace*, the Court even went beyond this definition, upholding a presidential removal that was in violation of the law.

Thus, it would appear that the Constitution, in establishing a government of separated powers, makes prerogative men of virtually everyone who interprets it. To be sure, some may be more high-flying prerogatives than others, but most important is the distance one has to go to avoid recognizing some kind of presidential prerogative under the Constitution of 1787.

## Notes

1. U.S., *Statutes at Large,* vol. 14 (December 1865 to March 1867), "An act regulating the tenure of certain civil officers," March 2, 1867.
2. *Myers v. the United States,* 272 U.S. 52 (1926), hereafter cited as Myers.
3. U.S., *Statutes at Large,* vol. 19 (December, 1875 to March, 1877), "An act regulating the appointment and removal of certain postmasters," July 12, 1876.
4. Ibid.
5. Myers, p. 107.
6. Ibid.
7. Edward S. Corwin, "Tenure of Office and The Removal Power Under the Constitution," *Columbia Law Review* 27:353–399. Robert E. Cushman, "Constitutional Law in 1926–1927." *American Political Science Review* 22:70–107.
8. Myers, p. 114.
9. Ibid.
10. Ibid, p. 284.
11. Corwin, "Tenure of Office," p. 362.
12. Ibid., p. 369.
13. *History of Congress,* column 371. Hereafter cited as *History.*
14. Ibid., p. 383.
15. Ibid., p. 578.
16. Ibid.
17. Ibid.
18. Myers, p. 284–285.
19. Ibid., p. 284.
20. Ibid., p. 194.
21. Corwin, "Tenure of Office," p. 360.
22. Ibid., p. 361.
23. Ibid., 362.
24. *History,* col., 583, emphasis added.
25. Ibid, emphasis added.
26. Ibid., col., 561–562 and 461.
27. Ibid., col., 538, 578.
28. Ibid., col., 525–6, 376.
29. Mr. Cadwalader and Mr. Tucker.
30. Corwin, "Tenure of Office," p. 362.
31. Ibid., p. 358.
32. Cushman, "Constitutional Law," p. 76.
33. Myers., p. 161.
34. Cushman, "Constitutional Law," ibid.
35. Taft, *Our Chief Magistrate and His Powers,* p. 67, 70.
36. U.S., *Constitution,* art. II, sec. 2, c. 2.
37. Myers, p. 162.
38. Ibid., p. 161.
39. Ibid., pp. 161–162.
40. Ibid., p. 161.
41. Ibid., p. 70, *amicus curiae* brief of Senator Pepper.
42. Ibid., p. 69.
43. Richard Neustadt, *Presidential Power* (New York: John Wiley, 1960), p. 23.
44. Myers, p. 291.
45. Ibid., p. 183.
46. Ibid., p. 293.
47. Taft, *Our Chief Magistrate,* p. 16.
48. Myers, p. 118.
49. *The Federalist Papers* (Mentor Edition), p. 322.
50. Ibid., pp. 322–323.

51. *History*, p. 557.
52. Myers, p. 116.
53. Ibid., p. 245.
54. Ibid.
55. Ibid., p. 247.
56. Ibid., p. 247.
57. Ibid., p. 292.
58. 167 U.S. 324 (1897)
59. 189 U.S. 311 (1902)
60. 257 U.S. 541 (1922)
61. *Parsons*, 339.
62. Ibid.
63. Myers., p. 187.
64. *Shurtleff*, 312.
65. Shurtleff, 313, emphasis added.
66. Myers, 187.
67. Wallace, 545, emphasis added.
68. Myers, 177, Holmes dissenting.
69. Ibid., 183.
70. Ibid., 231.
71. Ibid., 231–32, emphasis added.
72. Corwin, "Tenure of Office," p. 362.
73. Ibid., 234, cited by McReynolds.

---

# The Supreme Court and Congress's Responsibilities in Foreign Affairs

Sotirios A. Barber

Shortly before World War II Edward S. Corwin considered the Constitution's allocation of powers over foreign affairs and called it "an invitation [to Congress and the president] to struggle for the privilege of directing American foreign policy."[1] For much of our history, however, Congress has declined this invitation. Despite periods of congressional assertiveness in foreign affairs (often, though not always, after major wars), the presidency has proved to be the pre-eminent power over the long haul, and especially from the beginning of World War II to the political conflicts in the late 1960s over Vietnam. Presidential primacy in foreign affairs cannot be explained by comparing the executive and legislative powers enumerated in the Constitution. A united and determined Congress could easily have used its power to declare war, its vast lawmaking powers over foreign commerce and the military, and its control of governmental appropriations to subordinate the president's powers as commander-in-chief and chief executive. At the beginning of the republic, one may well have taken as emblematic of the president's future in foreign affairs the power of a minority of the Senate to defeat the president's treaty proposals, a power that could have reduced to ceremonial proportions the president's power to receive foreign ambassadors (thereby

Reprinted with permission of the author, Sotirios A. Barber.

extending formal diplomatic recognition to their governments).[2] The enumerated powers, therefore, cannot explain presidential primacy; but the different organizational characteristics of the two institutions can. A body, such as Congress, that cannot act until it has overcome the fragmentation of many different interests is no match for the presidency in a policy area demanding what the Framers called the strength or "energy" and the "[d]ecision, activity, secrecy, and dispatch" that "will more generally characterize the proceedings of one man, in a much more eminent degree, than the proceedings of any greater number."[3] Congress has appreciated its limitations in foreign policy for most of our history, and it has supported executive preeminence through acts of *deference* (as in its acquiescence to executive agreements in lieu of treaties) and through acts of *delegation*. By an act of delegation is meant a law of Congress that authorizes the president to make decisions of a kind that Congress itself is authorized to make by the Constitution, decisions such as America's basic import-export policies, basic policies governing the sale of American arms and nuclear fuel to foreign nations, and, ultimately, the decision to go to war.

This study is concerned with the general constitutional principles that ought to govern congressional delegations of power in foreign affairs. It is written at a time when the pendulum of foreign affairs shows signs of swinging back toward the presidency after an unparalleled decade of congressional assertiveness, a decade of reaction to the presidential "imperialism" associated with Vietnam and Watergate. This decade of assertiveness probably began with the National Commitments Resolution of the Senate in 1969, which insisted that Congress be consulted before the United States made any future commitments to foreign nations. During this decade Congress used its appropriations power to bring an end to American involvement in Vietnam. Congress passed the War Powers Resolution of 1973 over President Nixon's veto, an act requiring congressional approval for the use of American armed forces abroad. Congress limited the president's power to control the flow of appropriations by the Budget and Impoundment Act of 1974. Opposition in Congress successfully prevented President Carter from withdrawing American troops from Korea. The Panama Canal Treaties of 1978 saw an unprecedented degree of Senate involvement in negotiating treaty terms. And the Soviet invasion of Afghanistan gave sufficient strength to Senate conservatives to shelve the SALT II Treaty.

Some observers have criticized these and other acts of congressional activism in foreign affairs on the theory that Congress has contributed to the inconsistencies, fluctuations, and disunity that marked our foreign policy during the Carter presidency.[4] But it is hard to see how a unified and stable foreign policy can be achieved without the kind of congressional support that does not evaporate when the going gets rough. Consider Vietnam. Within a week after President Johnson requested it in August 1964, Congress passed the Tonkin Resolution, a virtual blank check to the President to decide whether and how far to wage war in Southeast Asia. Some members of Congress had their doubts about the unrestrictive language of the resolution, but they were drowned out by congressional leaders who demanded that Congress stand solidly with the president in a show of "unity."[5] Far from real unity, which, for us, is born of thoughtful conviction that our course is feasible and right, the Tonkin Resolution was a mere expression of faith in the president. The outcome of the war should have proved to us that faith is no substitute for deliberation. A contemporary observer wisely says: "History . . . provides abundant evidence that there is no monopoly on wisdom—or for that matter on bad judgment—on either end of Pennsylvania Avenue. Nor is there any guarantee that the President or Congress will not be mistaken at the same time. It is only the modest theory of the Constitution that they are less likely to be."[6] If independent deliberation on Congress's part leads to struggle with the president, what Professor Corwin called an invitation to struggle might also be seen as a constitutional *duty* to struggle.

But, as stated earlier, the pendulum may be swinging back toward the more usual situation of congressional abdication in foreign policy. The 1980 election suggests that many Americans want a revival of strong presidential leadership in foreign affairs coupled with a tougher attitude toward our enemies and a stronger military. Of course, a tougher foreign policy may mean new risks abroad, and ever-prudent politicians in Congress may react to risky situations by letting the president take these new risks on alone—that is, by evading their responsibility to deliberate the big questions of foreign policy and actively to stand with the president or against him, as duty dictates. Avoiding hot potatoes has been regarded as rational behavior for politicians who value political survival above all else and who feel that the voters are more likely to punish them for being wrong than reward them for courage and foresight.[7] But congressional abdication is not a rational response to the need for better leadership, because leadership is something that is recognizable only against a background of actual or potential resistance to what would-be leaders want to do. Leadership involves turning people around, showing a better way to those with minds of their own. Leadership generates a commitment to stand together, in sacrifice if need be, and this kind of dedication is not found in those whose political insecurities move them to play it safe and pass the buck. Congressional activism is thus a condition of presidential leadership, and it is a mistake to believe that the former defeats the latter, even though the former can prevent the superficial *appearance* of the latter.

We saw discouraging signs of a return to congressional passivity in the last year of the Carter presidency. After the Soviets invaded Afghanistan the President announced the so-called Carter Doctrine that America would fight to defend the Persian Gulf from "outside" intervention. Later the president announced that he would not permit the war between Iran and Iraq to close the Strait of Hormuz to oil shipments; he even moved the Navy into position to execute this policy. These were serious moves. They could have committed the nation to war, and they could have done so without congressional concurrence, despite the fact that there was ample time for advance consultation with Congress. These moves violated the letter and certainly the spirit of the National Commitments Resolution and the War Powers Resolution. Many observers have wondered whether these resolutions would meet the test of events. They have not. They have been ignored not only by the president but also by Congress. And one cannot help noting that they were ignored in an election year.

## Congressional Buckpassing and the Supreme Court

Congress evades its responsibilities either by deferring to executive initiatives in silence, as it did when President Truman went to war in Korea, or by enacting a law that transfers policy-making authority, as it did in the Tonkin Resolution. The Supreme Court can do little about the first kind of evasion because it will not order Congress to take an affirmative action like passing a bill. The only way the Court could oppose what I am calling a case of congressional deference to the executive would be to declare subsequent executive actions unconstitutional because they are not authorized by Congress. The Vietnam and Korean Wars could have been held unconstitutional because they were not fought pursuant to a congressional declaration of war. But the justices of the Supreme Court have ways of avoiding questions they do not want to decide, and, at this point in our history, they are likely to call unauthorized executive acts in foreign affairs "political questions," that is, constitutional questions that, in the opinion of the justices, the Constitution leaves to the political branches. Just how or why the Constitution should be read to require that most of its provisions should be applied by courts while some should be applied by the political branches is a controversial matter in constitutional law.[8] I shall not discuss it here. It is enough for our purposes to note that the Court can be expected to invoke the "political questions" doctrine in cases where the president has made a foreign policy decision without any prior act of Congress supporting or opposing what the president has done. Thus, some evasions of congressional responsibility are beyond what we currently understand to be the power of the judiciary.

But the courts can reach the second kind of evasion, the kind that takes place through formal delegations of congressional power. A rule of constitutional law says that Congress cannot delegate its powers to others—that, in other words, Congress cannot pass a law authorizing the president or other agency to decide questions of policy that the Constitution gives Congress the responsibility for deciding. This rule, usually called the "rule of nondelegation," or the "delegation doctrine," is not an expressed rule of the Constitution, and its precise historical origins are disputed.[9] A few scholars have tried to deny that it is a genuine rule of constitutional law, and no one has ever treated it as an absolute ban on any and all congressional delegations of power. There is virtual unanimity, however, that *some* limits on congressional delegations are implicit in the provision of Article I that vests "All legislative Powers herein granted . . . in a Congress of the United States." And the Supreme Court has at least given lipservice to the nondelegation doctrine over the years, permitting delegations only when it believes—or when it says it believes—that Congress has made the big decisions and is delegating power over mere subordinate matters. Sometimes the courts will take language in the law as evidence that Congress has made the big decision in a particular case, as it did when it approved a delegation of power to the president to vary tariff rates on certain foreign goods in order to "equalize . . . differences in costs of production" between those goods and the American goods with which they were competing in American markets.[10] When statutory language insufficiently indicates the general policy goal that Congress has in mind, the courts sometimes construe the statute as aiming at a certain goal, as it did when it read a statute delegating power to establish minimum quality tests for imported tea as evincing a desire on Congress's part to exclude the lowest grades of tea.[11] The Court has also permitted Congress to make the effectiveness of its policy choices contingent on facts to be ascertained by others, as when it permitted an embargo against a foreign nation to be made effective on a presidential finding of fact that the foreign nation refused to cease harassing American shipping.[12] By specifying factual findings to be made or by giving some indication (in the language of the statute or in its history) of the policy goals whose details are to be filled in by the recipients of delegated power, Congress supplies what are sometimes referred to as adequate *standards* for guiding the exercise of delegated power. The delegation doctrine, therefore, has resulted in, and is also known as, the *standards requirement,* a requirement that Congress delegate only when it gives some indication that the delegation is a means to the achievement of an end that Congress has selected among competing ends.[13] Thus, Congress itself must make the big decisions when it delegates power to others, or so the Court would have us believe when it upholds an act of Congress against the charge that it violates the rule of nondelegation or the standards requirement. By applying the standards requirement, the judiciary can do its part in reminding Congress that it has a constitutional duty to meaningfully deliberate and decide what the nation should do to solve most of its biggest problems at home and abroad. And because the courts agree that the standards requirement is itself a rule of constitutional law, the judiciary does its duty when it uses the standards requirement to remind Congress of its duties.

But a glance at Supreme Court history reveals that the justices have rarely used the delegation doctrine to declare an act of Congress unconstitutional. The problem is that the standards requirement is too loose and flexible to amount to much more than a warning to Congress not to go too far. But how far is too far? There is simply no formula for answering this question. There is no mathematical line between the big questions and many questions of "facts to be found" or "details to be filled in." Since 1813 the Supreme Court has permitted many controversial transfers of power from Congress to other agencies covering virtually every phase of government. And while the Court usually upholds these delegations as satisfying the constitutional requirement of standards, the standards expressed in the language of the statute or discovered by the Court in the legislative background are often too broad to indicate what Congress wants, even in a general way. In 1910, for example, the Court approved a transfer of power to the Interstate Commerce Commission to fix railroad rates that would be "just and reasonable," and in 1933 the Court upheld a delegation to the Federal Communications Commission to issue radio station licenses as required by the "public convenience, interest, and necessity."[14] These are hardly the kind of "standards" that would provide policy direction to those administering the statutes. As government became more complex, broad delegations became commonplace, and the Court responded by using the standards requirement more as a way of rationalizing broad delegations than as a rule for setting the limits to delegations. Professor C. Herman Pritchett reports that as a result of such decisions, by the mid-1930s "there was a widespread assumption" that the standards requirement "was one of the dead letters of American constitutional law."[15]

This pattern of decision continues to the present day. But it was interrupted in 1935 when the Supreme Court considered two cases involving sections of the National Industrial Recovery Act, a key but ill-fated part of President Roosevelt's program for extricating the country from the Great Depression. In *Panama Refining Co.* v. *Ryan*[16] the Court considered a provision that empowered the president to decide whether to prohibit interstate shipments of oil produced in excess of state regulations that were aimed at holding oil production down. At that time overproduction of oil was responsible for prices so low (as low as twenty-five cents per barrel!) that small oil producers were being driven out of business. By letting the president influence the availability of this "hot oil," Congress, in effect, delegated power to influence the amount of competition to be permitted in one of our major industries. In *Schechter Poultry Corp* v. *United States*[17] the Court considered another provision of the Recovery Act concerned with the level of industrial competition. In this section, perhaps the most extreme delegation in our history, Congress empowered the president to set the rules of "fair competition" for all of the nation's industries. Congress had gone too far in both cases, said the Court, for it had failed to provide adequate standards for guiding the president's discretion. As Chief Justice Hughes put it for the majority in *Panama*, "The Constitution has never been regarded as denying the Congress the necessary resources of flexibility and practicality, which will enable it to perform its functions in laying down policies and establishing standards, while leaving to selected instrumentalities the making of subordinate rules within prescribed limits and the determination of facts to which the policy declared by the legislature is to apply." But, the chief justice continued, "this cannot be allowed to obscure the limitations of the authority to delegate, if our constitutional system is to be maintained."[18] Thus, after a century of permissiveness toward congressional delegations, the Court finally brought itself to draw the line. To be sure, *Panama* and *Schechter* prescribe no formulas for limiting delegations. But they do prove that mere verbalisms like the old standards requirement can suddenly become effective rules of decision—that lines can be drawn even after generations of acquiescence. They prove that as long as judges give lipservice to the standards requirement, there are limits on how much power Congress can delegate.

The spirit of *Panama* and *Schechter* were not to survive the war and postwar eras. Although it is arguable that no delegation has been as extreme as that invalidated in *Schechter*, by the middle of World War II delegations were as broad as they ever were before the Recovery Act, and the Court had returned to its old ways of using the delegation doctrine more for rationalizing delegations than for limiting them. Today's Court still gives only lipservice to the standards requirement. Nevertheless lipservice has to be counted as better than nothing at all, it can keep an idea alive enough to spring back, as *Panama* and *Schechter* attest.

### The Delegation Doctrine of the Curtiss-Wright Case

In light of how the Court has stretched the traditional requirement of legislative standards, few could ask for a more permissive approach to the problem of preventing congressional buckpassing. Surely one could wonder what purpose a more permissive doctrine would serve. And it is certain that a more permissive doctrine could not be squared with the idea that Congress has duties in lawmaking that it cannot evade.

Nevertheless, a more permissive test of constitutional delegations is available, and, incredibly, there is some indication that some members of the Burger Court favor it over the more traditional approach employed in *Panama and Schechter*. The more permissive doctrine is that set forth by Justice George Sutherland in *United States* v. *Curtiss-Wright Export Corp.*,[19] decided in 1936, the year after the decisions in *Panama* and *Schechter*. A brief look at Justice Sutherland's theory will show why its revival would bear unhappy consequences for constitutional law and why the old standards requirement is much to be preferred despite its current ineffectiveness.

Justice Sutherland's opinion for a nearly unanimous Court in *Curtiss-Wright* is unique, and in a rather curious way. On the one hand, it is the Supreme Court's most famous pronouncement on the nature, constitutional status, and distribution of the foreign affairs powers among the branches of our government. It is widely cited in the scholarly literature of constitutional law, and it would have a place on any list of landmark cases in Supreme Court history. On the other hand, its meaning has always been a subject of controversy, and, most remarkably, its precise rule of decision has yet to be followed by the Court in another case involving a delegation in foreign affairs. *Curtiss-Wright* was invoked by Assistant Attorney General William H. Rehnquist in the days when he was defending President Nixon's actions in Vietnam and Cambodia before Congress.[20] And Justice Rehnquist did manage to slip a reaffirmation of *Curtiss-Wright* into a 1975 decision involving a minor delegation of rule-making power to the tribal council of an Indian tribe over liquor sales on a reservation, a decision to be discussed below.[21] But, at best, this was the Court's first reaffirmation of *Curtiss-Wright*. Despite repeated opportunities before 1975, the Court carefully avoided reaffirming *Curtiss-Wright* for almost forty years. Probably no other Supreme Court decision has been subjected to this paradoxical treatment of being respected as a landmark while carefully avoided as a precedent for so long. A review of the facts and the doctrine of *Curtiss-Wright* may explain why.

In May, 1934, Congress responded to the public's revulsion over the nasty war in the Chaco territory between Bolivia and Paraguay by giving President Roosevelt authority in the Chaco Resolution to prohibit arms sales to these governments if he should find that an embargo of American arms would contribute to peace. Satisfied that sufficient arms would not be available from other suppliers, the president concluded that an embargo of American arms would help, and he put the embargo into effect, as he was authorized to do by the Chaco Resolution.[22] The Curtiss-Wright Co. was prosecuted for selling machine guns to Bolivia in violation of the embargo, but a federal district court dismissed the case on grounds that the Chaco Resolution was an unconstitutional delegation of power. The reader will recall that this was only several months after the decisions in *Panama* and *Schechter,* a time when the lower courts could have expected that the Supreme Court was tightening up the standards requirement. The government appealed, and the Supreme Court disagreed with the district court on the constitutionality of the Chaco Resolution.

Up to this point in its history the Court had not treated delegations in foreign affairs differently from delegations in domestic affairs. All delegations were treated the same under one general theory: that Congress could not delegate without providing some guidance for the exercise of delegated power. If one had ignored the historical context and the legislative history of the Chaco Resolution—and there was no justification for doing that—one might have said the language of the resolution did not indicate whether Congress really wanted an arms embargo. One might have said, in other words, that Congress was passing the buck on the big question of whether peace between our neighbors was more important to us than some other value, like profits from the sale of arms. I emphasize that it was not necessary to read the resolution as an act of congressional indecision about what to do, for the legislative history would have supported a construction of the resolution that required an embargo for as long as an embargo would contribute to peace. Congress clearly expected an embargo, and it got one the day after the Chaco Resolution was passed. No violence would have been done to congressional intent, therefore, by construing the resolution as mandating an embargo on the factual contingency that it would work. Nor would the Court have departed from its own practices by engaging in this kind of statutory construction, for the Court had looked beyond statutory language for legislative purposes in delegation cases at least since 1825.[23] Nevertheless, Justice Sutherland veered from traditional practice in delegation cases and chose not to read a requisite level of legislative purpose into the resolution. This left him with three remaining options: (1) uphold the delegation under the rule of *Panama* and *Schechter* in spite of the alleged absence of standards in the act or the history of the act, or (2) invalidate the resolution, or (3) formulate a new theory to cover delegations of this kind. Option (1) would have weakened *Panama* and *Schechter* (as later decisions were to do); option (2) would have been unfair to Congress. This left option (3), and a new theory was born—a theory that exempts delegations in foreign affairs from the level of guidance required for delegations over domestic matters. I emphasize again that this choice was not necessary. Justice Sutherland could have saved the resolution without weakening *Panama* and *Schechter* simply by construing the delegation to mandate an embargo that would serve the cause of peace. This course would have been faithful to the fact of legislative history and to traditional judicial practice in delegation cases.

The new theory began with the proposition that there was a constitutional difference between powers over foreign affairs and powers over domestic affairs. The several states had originally possessed the domestic powers that the national government now possessed; the states granted these powers to the national government when the Constitution was ratified. But, said Justice Sutherland, power over foreign affairs had not been granted by the Constitution because the States had never possessed these powers; the foreign affairs powers had passed directly from Great Britain to the Continental Congress at the time of the Revolution. Thus, the Continental Congress handled the foreign affairs of the united colonies before the states formed a constitutional union for domestic purposes.[24] Justice Sutherland needed this theory because he looked on the nondelegation doctrine of *Panama* and *Schechter* as originating in a maxim of the common law that prohibited an agent who possessed delegated power from redelegating that power to someone else.[25] Sutherland believed that the reason Congress could not delegate domestic powers was because these powers had originally been delegated to Congress by other entities, the states. Congress could not delegate domestic powers because there was a sense in which they did not fully belong to Congress: they were *vested* in Congress by the states as a *trust* to be exercised in behalf of the people. But a similar rule of nondelegation did not govern the transfer of the foreign affairs powers because Congress did not come by these powers through an original act of delegation, according to Justice Sutherland.

A second part of Justice Sutherland's theory held that Congress may delegate more freely to the president in foreign affairs because the United States could not achieve equal status among nations without the kind of executive leadership demanded by the nature of foreign affairs. He spoke of the "very delicate, plenary, and exclusive power of the President as the sole organ of the federal government in the field of international relations—a power which does not require as a basis for its exercise an act of Congress, but which, of course, like any other governmental power, must be exercised in subordination to the applicable provisions of the Constitution."[26] This argument shows that Justice Sutherland looked upon the nondelegation doctrine of *Panama* and *Schechter* as something more than a restriction on Congress's power to delegate—he looked on it as a restriction on governmental power as a whole. The suggestion is that when Congress indicates a policy goal to be achieved in foreign policy and delegates subordinate power to the President, Congress is limiting the president and therewith the government as a whole. Apparently Justice Sutherland believed that when it came to the big questions of foreign policy, the nation would be stronger if the president were relatively free of congressional interference.

Historians have criticized Justice Sutherland's theory as inconsistent with the views of the Framers. A recent study by Professor Charles A. Lofgren shows that there was a difference of opinion in the founding period on whether the foreign affairs powers (and other powers) were originally in the possession of the several states or the people of the whole union—the *people* of the union as opposed to the *government* of the union. In either case, the Framers would have believed that Congress possessed foreign affairs powers as the result of an act of delegation (by the people of the union, if not the states), and that premise would have limited Congress's power to delegate.[27] Professor Lofgren also shows that there is little historical support for Justice Sutherland's view that the president should have indefinite discretion in making foreign policy. Justice Sutherland cited a famous statement made by John Marshall when he was a member of Congress that the president "is the sole organ of the nation in its external relations, and its sole representative with foreign nations." But Professor Lofgren shows that Marshall's statement pertained to the *execution* or *conduct* of foreign policy, not the *making* of decisions as to what general goals the nation would pursue in international affairs.[28]

If Justice Sutherland's theory is defective on historical grounds, it also offends logic and common sense. If Congress can abdicate to the president because of the way the foreign affairs powers came to be possessed by Congress, and if the president has foreign affairs powers that can be exercised without a delegation from Congress, then the president got those powers through the same process that Congress got its powers. The president, therefore, could freely delegate these powers just as Congress can freely delegate its powers. Congress and the president could even decide to delegate the foreign affairs powers of the government as a whole, say, to another government. These results follow *if* the way one gets one's powers determines the freedom with which one can delegate them, as Justice Sutherland presupposed. Of course, these results would be completely inconsistent with the idea that government holds *all* its powers in trust. For if it does, it has a duty to exercise those powers in the people's behalf. The idea that the government holds its powers in trust for the people's benefit excludes the right of the government as a whole to abdicate those powers. And if the president and Congress hold their powers in trust, they cannot abdicate their several powers either.

Remarkably, Justice Sutherland once agreed that the foreign affairs powers of Congress were held in trust and that they could not be abdicated. He published this view in a book on the foreign affairs powers four years before he was appointed to the Court. In his book he insisted that even when emergencies force the nation to place great reliance on the executive, Congress still cannot lawfully evade its responsibilities. Several parts of the book are incompatible with the theory of *Curtiss-Wright,* as the following passage illustrates:

> The war powers, with the exception of those pertaining to the office of Commander-in-Chief, are vested in Congress, and that body must exercise its own judgment with respect to the extent and character of their use. The advice and counsel of the President should be given great weight, but the acceptance of the President's recommendations must be the result of intelligent approval and not of blind obedience. Any other course involves a double betrayal of official trust—usurpation of power by the president and abdication of duty on the part of Congress.[29]

The second part of Justice Sutherland's argument is that Congress should be permitted to delegate freely in foreign affairs because the president is more capable of handling the problems of foreign affairs. This argument has deceptive appeal because the president is obviously more competent when it comes to *executing* or *conducting* foreign policy. It is also obvious that the president can use these powers to influence the *making* of foreign policy (as President Carter did when he decided to receive the Chinese ambassador) and that the line between *making* and *conducting* foreign policy is often arbitrary (as is typically the case when presidents communicate with other governments about the terms of treaties). However, none of this supports the conclusion that Congress should deliberately evade its admitted responsibilities, as it did in authorizing President Johnson to decide whether to fight in Vietnam. That the president has important, even crucial, duties in foreign affairs is beyond question, but to argue that the president can perform Congress's duties better than Congress can is to argue that the Framers erred in vesting those responsibilities in Congress in the first place. Whether the Framers erred is a question thoughtful persons should be willing to consider, not only with respect to Congress's powers but also with respect to such other obstacles to executive power as the Supreme Court's protection of individual rights. We might remember that the Court itself burdened President Nixon's foreign policy by permitting the publication of the Pentagon Papers. It is no paradox to say that even the presidency can get in the way of executive power, for the presidency is an office constituted largely of rules and traditions that seriously limit the flexibility of those persons who occupy the office. We might ask, for example, whether it is a good idea to have presidential elections every four years regardless of what is going on in the world. A serious exploration of Justice Sutherland's argument would soon find us discussing issues at the heart of constitutional government, including the viability of constitutionalism itself in a world many feel is too unstable for the kind of deliberation that should go on in legislatures and too dangerous for the protection of individual rights that should go on in courts.

I am not arguing that we should remain committed to our traditional notions of constitutional government at all costs. I am arguing that *Curtiss-Wright* offends those notions and that those who take our traditions seriously should see great risks in Justice Sutherland's theory. As we reflect on those risks we might wonder whether Justice Sutherland's theory offers any compensating gains. It does not. It might have been a moderate and reasonable theory at a time when really strict standards were required for domestic delegations, for then it merely would have called for a relaxation of standards, not their virtual elimination. But the standards requirement has always been a liberal one, even at the time of *Panama* and *Schechter,* and certainly today. If Justice Sutherland's theory ever served a practical need (consistent with the Constitution), it ceased doing so within a few years after the Chaco Resolution, as we see in the fact that the Supreme Court has used the test of *Panama* and *Schechter* to uphold very permissive delegations in foreign and domestic affairs alike since the beginning of World War II. Invoking *Curtiss-Wright* today can serve no purpose consistent with the proposition that somewhere there is a line to be drawn between congressional delegations and congressional abdications of power.

### The Reappearance of Curtiss-Wright

I have pointed out that the Supreme Court avoided reaffirming *Curtiss-Wright* until Justice Rehnquist used it to decide a delegation question in 1975. The case was *United States* v. *Mazurie.*[30] Here the Court considered a delegation without expressed standards to the tribal council of an Indian tribe to regulate liquor sales on a reservation. The Court could have upheld this delegation by reading general legislative standards into the act, as it had done so many times in the past. For example, the Court could have said that it was Congress's purpose to authorize tribal licensing of alcoholic beverages in accordance with the needs of 'good order and tribal custom.'[31] But Justice Rehnquist elected a different course. He upheld the delegation by arguing that the tribal council enjoyed "a certain degree of independent authority over . . . tribal life," and that the recognized limits on Congress's power to delegate are "less stringent in cases where the entity exercising the delegated authority itself possesses independent authority over the subject matter."[32] The sole precedent cited in behalf of this last proposition was *Curtiss-Wright,* and no one dissented or sought to uphold the delegation by the traditional tests.

*Mazurie* presents a number of problems which cannot be fully explored here. But a brief mention of them will be sufficient for the reader to appreciate the potential of the case. We note, to begin with, that despite Justice Sutherland's careful distinction between domestic delegations and delegations in foreign affairs, *Mazurie* applies *Curtiss-Wright* to a delegation over domestic affairs. We note also that Justice Rehnquist does not discuss what he means by an entity with "independent authority." In light of the fact that the Court has long regarded the Indian tribes as "wards of the nation," and "dependent communities" over which Congress has plenary authority,[33] the president and the states have far stronger claims to "independent authority" than the Indian tribes. The executive agencies and the independent regulatory agencies might even claim a relatively greater "independent authority" on separation of powers grounds. We note, finally, that Justice Rehnquist reaffirms *Curtiss-Wright* at a time when "limitations . . . less stringent" than those required for ordinary delegations can only mean no limitations at all, for it is hard to see how anything short of formal abdication could be less stringent than the delegations the Court upholds today. As one reflects on these problems, it appears well within the language of *Mazurie* to rationalize virtually unlimited transfers of congressional power in domestic and foreign affairs alike, and to the president, the states, and even other agencies who could successfully claim "a certain degree of independent authority."

We can only speculate why the Court gave these possibilities a foothold in constitutional law. Justice Rehnquist may have seen *Mazurie* as an opportunity to vindicate his constitutional defense of some of President Nixon's actions in foreign affairs. As an assistant attorney general, he once cited *Curtiss-Wright* in support of President Nixon's authority to bomb Cambodia;[34] he even suggested *Curtiss-Wright* supported presidential impoundments of foreign affairs appropriations.[35] *Mazurie* presented an opportunity to read *Curtiss-Wright* as an acknowledgement of great executive independence in foreign policy. As for the other justices, a few may simply have overlooked the final wording in what must have appeared to be a case involving a relatively minor delegation. One can hope this explains the vote of most of the justices, for if it does, they are not likely to take *Mazurie* as a precedent for delegations with a greater national impact. The remaining justices may have considered it pointless to insist on an approach different from that of the justice assigned to write the Court's opinion. They may have felt that no matter what one's theory, the practical results would be the same, for the distinction between more stringent and less stringent delegations was meaningless in light of the degree to which the modern Court has stretched the nondelegation doctrine of *Panama* and *Schechter*.[36] Indeed, some might even have applauded Justice Rehnquist's approach as a step closer to the realities of contemporary judicial decision, since little tribute is left for the old standards requirement beyond what Professor Pritchett calls "tortuous explanations and legal fiction that what is [unguided] delegation in fact is not [unguided] delegation in law."[37]

### A Concluding Thought on Law and Lipservice

However we explain the vote in *Mazurie,* the opinion was a mistake. If we take it seriously as constitutional doctrine we all but destroy the idea that Congress has responsibilities it cannot evade. The doctrine of *Panama* and *Schechter* is much to be preferred simply because it keeps the idea of constitutional duty alive. Regrettably, the Court has reduced the nondelegation doctrine of *Panama* and *Schechter* to an empty verbalism. But lipservice is a service of sorts, for lipservice can remind Congress of its constitutional duty. And when the Court goes through the motions of rationalizing acts of congressional buckpassing, it too is reminded of its constitutional duty. That is not to say the Court is *doing* its duty, for if it were, it would take the nondelegation doctrine seriously and apply it honestly. But when the Court *pretends* to be doing its duty it acknowledges that duty by honoring it at least in appearance.

Let me concede that *Mazurie* is closer to the realities of modern decision in delegation cases and that applying this modernized doctrine of *Curtiss-Wright* would be more honest than pretending that Congress always does its best to delegate only after it has decided the big questions of public policy. Some might prefer an approach like *Mazurie's* because it brings legal doctrine closer to the actual facts of judicial and congressional behavior—because it reduces the tension between what we actually do and what we believe we ought to be doing. One can agree, of course, that it is wrong to have too much of a gap between word and deed. But that does not mean that any and every closing of that gap is right. Doing the right thing means bringing conduct up to the level of what we think is right, not dropping what we think is right down to the level of our actual behavior. As long as constitutional law is really law it will provide the government with rules and principles to which its conduct should conform. It will cease to be law when it is made to conform to whatever the conduct of government may be. A tension between law and fact is therefore not unequivocally regrettable, for the tension can move us to look for ways of reconciling law and fact in favor of law. An approach to congressional duty like the one employed in *Mazurie* may reduce the tension between law and fact, but it does so at the expense of law. That is why, despite all the hypocrisy, the rule of *Panama* and *Schechter* is better law than the rule of *Curtiss-Wright* and *Mazurie.*

It has been almost fifty years since the Court invalidated a congressional delegation of power. But that in itself is no proof that the old nondelegation doctrine is dead. We should remember that well over a hundred years had passed before the Court first struck down a congressional delegation. This lengthy span of time did not prevent the Court from asserting limits on the freedom to delegate because the Court had continued to give lipservice to the idea that limits did exist, somewhere. There is no reason to believe that the Court will not want to reassert those limits in the future as it did in the past—especially now that Congress is showing signs of ignoring responsibilities of the kind it acknowledged in the War Powers Resolution of 1973. Because all can imagine (if not expect) future situations in which the Court should draw the line, the Court should not weaken tools for doing so. This is what will happen if *Mazurie* and *Curtiss-Wright* are permitted to close the gap between law and fact at the expense of law. Should the spirit move, the Justices can find a legal way to raise the level of congressional decision and resolve as long as the law is given by *Panama* and *Schechter.* In the meantime, the justices will continue to exercise their power to review the constitutionality of legislative delegations and other governmental acts. The official justification for this power of judicial review has always included the belief that government has an obligation to bring its behavior into conformity with the law of the Constitution. Judges who take their own claims to power seriously should look for ways to keep the idea of constitutional duty alive.

### Notes

1. Edward S. Corwin (ed.), *The President: Office and Powers,* 4th rev. ed., (New York: New York University Press, 1957), p. 171.
2. Charles Black, *Perspectives in Constitutional Law* (Englewood Cliffs, N.J.: Prentice Hall, 1963), pp. 56–59.
3. Jacob E. Cooke (ed.), *The Federalist* (Middletown, Conn.: Wesleyan University Press, 1961), p. 472.
4. See Cecil V. Crabb, Jr. and Pat M. Holt, *Invitation to Struggle: Congress, the President, and Foreign Policy* (Washington, D.C.: Congressional Quarterly Press, 1980), pp. 204–06.
5. Sotirios A. Barber, *The Constitution and the Delegation of Congressional Power* (Chicago: The University of Chicago Press, 1975), pp. 98–100.
6. Crabb and Holt, *Invitation to Struggle,* p. 135.

7. Barber, *Delegation of Congressional Power,* p. 4.
8. See C. Herman Pritchett, *The American Constitution* 2nd ed., (New York: McGraw-Hill, 1968), pp. 176–77.
9. Barber, *Delegation of Congressional Power,* ch.2.
10. *J. W. Hampton, Jr., & Co.* v. *United States,* 276 U.S. 394 (1928).
11. *Butterfield* v. *Stranahan,* 192 U.S. 470 (1903).
12. *The Brig Aurora* v. *United States,* 7 Cranch. 383 (1813).
13. Barber, *Delegation of Congressional Power,* pp. 36–51.
14. *Interstate Commerce Commission* v. *Illinois Central R.R.,* 215 U.S. 452 (1910); *Federal Radio Commission* v. *Nelson Brothers,* 289 U.S. 266 (1933).
15. Pritchett, *The American Constitution,* p. 200.
16. 293 U.S. 388 (1935).
17. 295 U.S. 495 (1935).
18. 293 U.S. 488, at 421.
19. 299 U.S. 304 (1936).
20. See nn. 34, 35 below.
21. *United States* v. *Mazurie,* 419 U.S. 544.
22. For the history of the Chaco Resolution see John A. Garraty (ed.), *Quarrels That Have Shaped the Constitution* (New York: Harper & Row, 1962), ch. XIV.
23. Barber, *Delegation of Congressional Power,* pp. 63–72.
24. 299 U.S. 304, at 315–16.
25. See Patrick W. Duff and Horace E. Whiteside, "Delegata Potestas Non Potest Delegari: A Maxim of American Constitutional Law," 14 *Cornell Law Quarterly* p. 195 (1929).
26. 299 U.S. 304, at 219–22.
27. Charles A. Lofgren, "*United States* v. *Curtiss-Wright Export Corp.:* An Historical Reassessment," 83 *Yale Law Journal* 1, pp. 12–20.
28. Ibid., pp. 24–25.
29. George Sutherland, *Constitutional Power and World Affairs,* (New York: Columbia University Press, 1919), pp. 110–11.
30. 419 U.S. 544.
31. Cf. *United States* v. *Sharpnack,* 355 U.S. 286 (1958).
32. 419 U.S. 544, at 556–57
33. *United States* v. *Kagama,* 118 U.S. 357, at 383–84 (1886). *Kagama* is cited in *Mazurie* at 557.
34. See Senate Committee on Foreign Relations, 91st Cong., 2nd Sess., *Documents Relating to the War Powers of Congress, The President's Authority as Commander in Chief and the War in Indochina* 175, p. 181 (1970).
35. See Joint Hearings before the Senate Ad Hoc Subcomm. on Impoundment of Funds of the Comm. on Government Operations and the Subcomm. on Separation of Powers of the Comm. on the Judiciary on S. 373, 93d Cong., 1st Sess. pp. 368–69 (1973).
36. See Marshall, J., concurring in *National Cable Television Association* v. *United States,* 415 U.S. 336, at 378 (1974).
37. Pritchett, *The American Constitution,* p. 198.

# The Dred Scott Decision

Abraham Lincoln

Fellow Citizens:—I am here to-night, partly by the invitation of some of you, and partly by my own inclination. Two weeks ago Judge Douglas spoke here on . . . the Dred Scott decision, . . . I listened to the speech at the time, and have read the report of it since. It was intended to controvert opinions which I think just, and to assail (politically, not personally,) those men who, in common with me entertain those opinions. For this reason I wished then, and still wish, to make some answer to it, which I now take the opportunity of doing.

. . . The Dred Scott decision . . . declares two propositions—first, that a negro cannot sue in the U.S. Courts; and secondly, that Congress cannot prohibit slavery in the Territories. It was made by a divided court—dividing differently on the different points. Judge Douglas does not discuss the merits of the decision; and, in that respect, I shall follow his example, believing I could no more improve on McLean and Curtis, than he could on Taney.

He denounces all who question the correctness of that decision, as offering violent resistance to it. But who resists it? Who has, in spite of the decision, declared Dred Scott free, and resisted the authority of his master over him?

Judicial decisions have two uses—first, to absolutely determine the case decided, and secondly, to indicate to the public how other similar cases will be decided when they arise. For the latter use, they are called "precedents" and "authorities."

We believe, as much as Judge Douglas, (perhaps more) in obedience to, and respect for the judicial department of government. We think its decisions on Constitutional questions, when fully settled, should control, not only the particular cases decided, but the general policy of the country, subject to be disturbed only by amendments of the Constitution as provided in that instrument itself. More than this would be revolution. But we think the Dred Scott decision is erroneous. We know the court that made it, has often over-ruled its own decisions, and we shall do what we can to have it to over-rule this. We offer no *resistance* to it.

Judicial decisions are of greater or less authority as precedents, according to circumstances. That this should be so, accords both with common sense, and the customary understanding of the legal profession.

If this important decision had been made by the unanimous concurrence of the judges, and without any apparent partisan bias, and in accordance with legal public expectation, and with the steady practice of the departments throughout our history, and had been in no part, based on assumed historical facts which are not really true; or, if wanting in some of these, it had been before the court more than once, and had there been affirmed and re-affirmed through a course of years, it then might be, perhaps would be, factious, nay, even revolutionary, to not acquiesce in it as a precedent.

Speech delivered at Springfield, Illinois, June 26, 1857.

But when, as it is true we find it wanting in all these claims to the public confidence, it is not resistance, it is not factious, it is not even disrespectful, to treat it as not having yet quite established a settled doctrine for the country—But Judge Douglas considers this view awful. Hear him:

"The courts are the tribunals prescribed by the Constitution and created by the authority of the people to determine, expound and enforce the law. Hence, whoever resists the final decision of the highest judicial tribunal, aims a deadly blow to our whole Republican system of government—a blow, which if successful would place all our rights and liberties at the mercy of passion, anarchy and violence. I repeat, therefore, that if resistance to the decisions of the Supreme Court of the United States, in a matter like the points decided in the Dred Scott case, clearly within their jurisdiction as defined by the Constitution, shall be forced upon the country as a political issue, it will become a distinct and naked issue between the friends and the enemies of the Constitution—the friends and enemies of the supremacy of the laws."

Why this same Supreme court once decided a national bank to be constitutional; but Gen. Jackson, as President of the United States, disregarded the decision, and vetoed a bill for a recharter, partly on constitutional ground, declaring that each public functionary must support the Constitution, *"as he understands it."* But hear the General's own words. Here they are, taken from his veto message:

"It is maintained by the advocates of the bank that its constitutionality in all its features, ought to be considered as settled by precedent, and by the decision of the Supreme Court. To this conclusion I cannot assent. Mere precedent is a dangerous source of authority, and should not be regarded as deciding questions of constitutional power, except where the acquiescence of the people and the States can be considered as well settled. So far from this being the case on this subject, an argument against the bank might be based on precedent. One Congress in 1791, decided in favor of a bank; another in 1811 decided against it. One Congress in 1815 decided against a bank; another in 1816 decided in its favor. Prior to the present Congress, therefore, the precedents drawn from that source were equal. If we resort to the States, the expressions of legislative, judicial and executive opinions against the bank have been probably to those in its favor as four to one. There is nothing in precedent, therefore, which if its authority were admitted, ought to weigh in favor of the act before me."

I drop the quotations merely to remark that all there ever was, in the way of precedent up to the Dred Scott decision, on the points therein decided had been against that decision. But hear Gen. Jackson further—

"If the opinion of the Supreme Court covered the whole ground of this act, it ought not to control the co-ordinate authorities of this Government. The Congress, the executive and the court, must each for itself be guided by its own opinion of the Constitution. Each public officer, who takes an oath to support the Constitution, swears that he will support it as he understands it, and not as it is understood by others."

Again and again have I heard Judge Douglas denounce that bank decision, and applaud Gen. Jackson for disregarding it. It would be interesting for him to look over his recent speech, and see how exactly his fierce philippics against us for resisting Supreme Court decisions, fall upon his own head. It will call to his mind a long and fierce political war in this country, upon an issue which, in his own language, and, of course, in his own changeless estimation, was "a distinct and naked issue between the friends and the enemies of the Constitution," and in which war he fought in the ranks of the enemies of the Constitution.

I have said, in substance, that the Dred Scott decision was, in part, based on assumed historical facts which were not really true; and I ought not to leave the subject without giving some reasons for saying this; I therefore give an instance or two, which I think fully sustain me. Chief Justice Taney, in delivering the opinion of the majority of the Court, insists at great length that negroes were no part of the people who made, or for whom was made, the Declaration of Independence, or the Constitution of the United States.

On the contrary, Judge Curtis, in his dissenting opinion, shows that in five of the then thirteen states, to wit, New Hampshire, Massachusetts, New York, New Jersey and North Carolina, free negroes were voters, and, in proportion to their numbers, had the same part in making the Constitution that the white people had. He shows this with so much particularity as to leave no doubt of its truth; and, as a sort of conclusion on that point, holds the following language:

"The Constitution was ordained and established by the people of the United States, through the action, in each State, of those persons who were qualified by its laws to act thereon in behalf of themselves and all other citizens of the State. In some of the States, as we have seen, colored persons were among those qualified by law to act on the subject. These colored persons were not only included in the body of 'the people of the United States,' by whom the Constitution was ordained and established; but in at least five of the States they had the power to act, and, doubtless, did act, by their suffrages, upon the question of its adoption."

Again, Chief Justice Taney says: "It is difficult, at this day to realize the state of public opinion in relation to that unfortunate race, which prevailed in the civilized and enlightened portions of the world at the time of the Declaration of Independence, and when the Constitution of the United States was framed and adopted." And again, after quoting from the Declaration, he says: "The general words above quoted would seem to include the whole human family, and if they were used in a similar instrument at this day, would be so understood."

In these the Chief Justice does not directly assert, but plainly assumes, as a fact, that the public estimate of the black man is more favorable *now* than it was in the days of the Revolution. This assumption is a mistake. In some trifling particulars, the condition of that race has been ameliorated; but, as a whole, in this country, the change between then and now is decidedly the other way; and their ultimate destiny has never appeared so hopeless as in the last three or four years. In two of the five States—New Jersey and North Carolina—that then gave the free negro the right of voting, the right has since been taken away; and in a third—New York—it has been greatly abridged; while it has not been extended, so far as I know, to a single additional State, though the number of the States has more than doubled. In those days, as I understand, masters could, at their own pleasure, emancipate their slaves; but since then, such legal restraints have been made upon emancipation, as to amount almost to prohibition. In those days, Legislatures held the unquestioned power to abolish slavery in their respective States; but now it is becoming quite fashionable for State Constitutions to withhold that power from the Legislatures. In those days, by common consent, the spread of the black man's bondage to new countries was prohibited; but now, Congress decides that it *will not* continue the prohibition, and the Supreme Court decides that it *could not* if it would. In those days, our Declaration of Independence was held sacred by all, and thought to include all; but now, to aid in making the bondage of the negro universal and eternal, it is assailed, and sneered at, and construed, and hawked at, and torn, till, if its framers could rise from their graves, they could not at all recognize it. All the powers of earth seem rapidly combining against him. Mammon is after him; ambition follows, and philosophy follows, and the Theology of the day is fast joining the cry. They have him in his prison house; they have searched his person, and left no prying instrument with him. One after another they have closed the heavy iron doors upon him, and now they have him, as it were, bolted in with a lock of a hundred keys, which can never be unlocked without the concurrence of every key; the keys in the hands of a hundred different men, and they scattered to a hundred different and distant places; and they stand musing as to what invention, in all the dominions of mind and matter, can be produced to make the impossibility of his escape more complete than it is.

It is grossly incorrect to say or assume, that the public estimate of the negro is more favorable now than it was at the origin of the government.

Three years and a half ago, Judge Douglas brought forward his famous Nebraska bill. The country was at once in a blaze. He scorned all opposition, and carried it through Congress. Since then he has seen himself superseded in a Presidential nomination, by one indorsing the general doctrine of his measure, but at the same time standing clear of the odium of its untimely agitation, and its gross breach of national faith; and he has seen that successful rival Constitutionally elected, not by the strength of friends, but by the division of adversaries, being in a popular minority of nearly four hundred thousand votes. He has seen his chief aids in his own State, Shields and Richardson, politically speaking, successively tried, convicted, and executed, for an offense not their own, but his. And now he sees his own case, standing next on the docket for trial.

There is a natural disgust in the minds of nearly all white people, to the idea of an indiscriminate amalgamation of the white and black races; and Judge Douglas evidently is basing his chief hope, upon the chances of being able to appropriate the benefit of this disgust to himself. If he can, by much drumming and repeating, fasten the odium of that idea upon his adversaries, he thinks he can struggle through the storm. He therefore clings to this hope, as a drowning man to the last plank. He makes an occasion for lugging it in from the opposition to the Dred Scott decision. He finds the Republicans insisting that the Declaration of Independence includes ALL men, black as well as white; and forthwith he boldly denies that it includes negroes at all, and proceeds to argue gravely that all who contend it does, do so only because they want to vote, and eat, and sleep, and marry with negroes! He will have it that they cannot be consistent else. Now I protest against that counterfeit logic which concludes that, because I do not want a black woman for a *slave* I must necessarily want her for a *wife*. I need not have her for either, I can just leave her alone. In some respects she certainly is not my equal; but in her natural right to eat the bread she earns with her own hands without asking leave of any one else, she is my equal, and the equal of all others.

Chief Justice Taney, in his opinion in the Dred Scott case, admits that the language of the Declaration is broad enough to include the whole human family, but he and Judge Douglas argue that the authors of that instrument did not intend to include negroes, by the fact that they did not at once, actually place them on an equality with whites. Now this grave argument comes to just nothing at all, by the other fact, that they did not at once, *or ever afterwards,* actually place all white people on an equality with one or another. And this is the staple argument of both the Chief Justice and the Senator, for doing this obvious violence to the plain unmistakable language of the Declaration. I think the authors of that notable instrument intended to include *all* men, but they did not intend to declare all men equal *in all respects.* They did not mean to say all were equal in color, size, intellect, moral developments, or social capacity. They defined with tolerable distinctness, in what respects they did consider all men created equal—equal in "certain inalienable rights, among which are life, liberty, and the pursuit of happiness." This they said, and this meant. They did not mean to assert the obvious untruth, that all were then actually enjoying that equality, nor yet, that they were about to confer it immediately upon them. In fact they had no power to confer such a boon. They meant simply to declare the *right,* so that the *enforcement* of it might follow as fast as circumstances should permit. They meant to set up a standard maxim for free society, which should be familiar to all, and revered by all; constantly looked to, constantly labored for, and even though never perfectly attained, constantly approximated, and thereby constantly spreading and deepening its influence and augmenting the happiness and value of life to all people of all colors everywhere. The assertion that "all men are created equal" was of no practical use in effecting our separation from Great Britain; and it was placed in the Declaration, not for that, but for future use. Its authors meant it to be, thank God, it is now proving itself, a stumbling block to those who in after times might seek to turn a free people back into the hateful paths of despotism. They knew the proneness of prosperity to breed tyrants, and they meant when such should re-appear in this fair land and commence their vocation they should find left for them at least one hard nut to crack.

I have now briefly expressed my view of the *meaning* and *objects* of that part of the Declaration of Independence which declares that "all men are created equal."

Now let me hear Judge Douglas' view of the same subject, as I find it in the printed report of his late speech. Here it is:

"No man can vindicate the character, motives and conduct of the signers of the Declaration of Independence except upon the hypothesis that they referred to the white race alone and not to the African, when they declared all men to have been created equal—that they were speaking of British subjects on this continent being equal to British subjects born and residing in Great Britain—that they were entitled to the same inalienable rights, and among them were enumerated life, liberty and the pursuit of happiness. The Declaration was adopted for the purpose of justifying the colonists in the eyes of the civilized world in withdrawing their allegiance from the British crown, and dissolving their connection with the mother country."

My good friends, read that carefully over some leisure hour, and ponder well upon it—see what a mere wreck—mangled ruin—it makes of our once glorious Declaration.

"They were speaking of British subjects on the continent being equal to British subjects born and residing in Great Britain!" Why, according to this, not only negroes but white people outside of Great Britain and America are not spoken of in that instrument. The English, Irish and Scotch, along with white Americans, were included to be sure, but the French, Germans and other white people of the world are all gone to pot along with the Judge's inferior races.

I had thought the Declaration promised something better than the condition of British subjects; but no, it only meant that we should be *equal* to them in their own oppressed and *unequal* condition. According to that, it gave no promise that having kicked off the King and Lords of Great Britain, we should not at once be saddled with a King and Lords of our own.

I had thought the Declaration contemplated the progressive improvement in the condition of all men everywhere; but no, it merely "was adopted for the purpose of justifying the colonists in the eyes of the civilized world in withdrawing their allegiance from the British crown, and dissolving their connection with the mother country." Why, that object having been effected some eighty years ago, the Declaration is of no practical use now—mere rubbish—old wadding left to rot on the battle-field after the victory is won.

I understand you are preparing to celebrate the "Fourth," tomorrow week. What for? The doings of that day had no reference to the present; and quite half of you are not even descendants of those who were referred to at that day. But I suppose you will celebrate; and will even go so far as to read the Declaration. Suppose after you read it once in the old fashioned way, you read it once more with Judge Douglas' version. It will then run thus: "We hold these truths to be self-evident that all British subjects who were on this continent eighty-one years ago, were created equal to all British subjects born and *then* residing in Great Britain."

And now I appeal to all—to Democrats as well as others,—are you really willing that the Declaration shall be thus frittered away?—thus left no more at most, than an interesting memorial of the dead past? thus shorn of its vitality, and practical value; and left without the *germ* or even the suggestion of the individual rights of man in it?

But Judge Douglas is especially horrified at the thought of the mixing blood by the white and black races: agreed for once—a thousand times agreed. There are white men enough to marry all the white women, and black men enough to marry all the black women; and so let them be married. On this point we fully agree with the Judge; and when he shall show that his policy is better adapted to prevent amalgamation than ours we shall drop ours, and adopt his. Let us see. In 1850 there were in the United States 405,751 mulattoes. Very few of these are the offspring of whites and *free* blacks; nearly all have sprung from black slaves and white masters. A separation of the races is the only perfect preventive of amalgamation but as an immediate separation is impossible the next best thing is to *keep* them apart *where* they are not already together. If white and black people never get together in Kansas, they will never mix blood in Kansas. That is at least one self-evident truth. A few free colored persons may get into the free States, in any event; but their number is too insignificant to amount to much in the way of mixing blood. In 1850 there were in the free states, 56,649 mulattoes; but for the most part they were not born there—they came from the slave States, ready made up. In the same year the slave States had 348,874 mulattoes all of home production. The proportion of free mulattoes to free blacks—the only colored classes in the free states—is much greater in the slave than in the free states. It is worthy of note too, that among the free states those which make the colored man the nearest to equal the white, have, proportionably the fewest mulattoes the least of amalgamation. In New Hampshire, the State which goes farthest towards equality between the races, there are just 184 Mulattoes while there are in Virginia—how many do you think? 79,775, being 23,126 more than in all the free States together.

These statistics show that slavery is the greatest source of amalgamation; and next to it, not the elevation, but the degeneration of the free blacks. Yet Judge Douglas dreds the slightest restraints on the spread of slavery, and the slightest human recognition of the negro as tending horribly to amalgamation.

This very Dred Scott case affords a strong test as to which party most favors amalgamation, the Republicans or the dear Union-saving Democracy. Dred Scott, his wife and two daughters were all involved in the suit. We desired the court to have held that they were citizens so far at least as to entitle them to a hearing as to whether they were free or not; and the, also, that they were in fact and in law really free. Could we have had our way, the chances of these black girls, ever mixing their blood with that of white people would have been diminished at least to the extent that it could not have been without their consent. But Judge Douglas is delighted to have them decided to be slaves, and not human enought to have a hearing, even if they were free, and thus left subject to the forced concubinage of their masters, and liable to become the mothers of mulattoes in spite of themselves—the very state of case that produces nine tenths of all the mulattoes—all the mixing of blood in the nation.

Of course, I state this case as an illustration only, not meaning to say or intimate that the master of Dred Scott and his family, or any more than a percentage of masters generally, are inclined to exercise this particular power which they hold over their female slaves.

I have said that the separation of the races is the only perfect preventive of amalgamation. I have no right to say all the members of the Republican party are in favor of this, nor to say that as a party they are in favor of it. There is nothing in their platform directly on the subject. But I can say a very large proportion of its members are for it, and that the chief plank in their platform—opposition to the spread of slavery—is most favorable to that separation.

Such separation, if ever effected at all, must be effected by colonization; and no political party, as such, is now doing anything directly for colonization. Party operations at present only favor or retard colonization incidentally. The enterprise is a difficult one; but "when there is a will there is a way;" and what colonization needs most is a hearty will. Will springs from the two elements of moral sense and self-interest. Let us be brought to believe it is morally right, and, at the same time, favorable to, or, at least, not against our interest, to transfer the African to his native clime, and we shall find a way to do it, however great the task may be. The children of Israel, to such numbers as to include four hundred thousand fighting men, went out of Egyptian bondage in a body.

How differently the respective courses of the Democratic and Republican parties incidentally bear on the question of forming a will—a public sentiment—for colonization, is easy to see. The Republicans inculcate, with whatever of ability they can, that the negro is a man; that his bondage is cruelly wrong, and that the field of his oppression ought not to be enlarged. The Democrats deny his manhood; deny, or dwarf to insignificance, the wrong of his bondage; so far as possible, crush all sympathy for him, and cultivate and excite hatred and disgust against him; compliment themselves as Union-savers for doing so; and call the indefinite outspreading of his bondage "a sacred right of self-government."

The plainest print cannot be read through a gold eagle; and it will be ever hard to find many men who will send a slave to Liberia, and pay his passage while they can send him to a new country, Kansas for instance, and sell him for fifteen hundred dollars, and the rise.

# The Constitution and Civil Liberty

> The Bill of Rights provides a fitting close to the parenthesis around the Constitution that the preamble opens. But the substance is a design of government with powers to act and a structure to make it act wisely and responsibly. It is in that design, not in its preamble or its epilogue, that the security of American civil and political liberty lies.
>
> *Herbert J. Storing*

---

## The Bill of Rights

Hugo L. Black

I am honored to be the first speaker in your new annual series of James Madison lectures. The title of the series suggested the title of my talk: The Bill of Rights. Madison lived in the stirring times between 1750 and 1836, during which the Colonies declared, fought for, and won their independence from England. They then set up a new national government dedicated to Liberty and Justice. Madison's role in creating that government was such a major one that he has since been generally referred to as the Father of our Constitution. He was a most influential member of the Philadelphia Convention that submitted the Constitution to the people of the states; he alone kept a comprehensive report of the daily proceedings of the Convention; he was an active member of the Virginia Convention that adopted the Constitution after a bitter fight; finally, as a member of the First Congress, he offered and sponsored through that body proposals that became the first ten amendments, generally thought of as our Bill of Rights. For these and many other reasons, Madison's words are an authentic source to help us understand the Constitution and its Bill of Rights. In the course of my discussion I shall have occasion to refer to some of the many things Madison said about the meaning of the Constitution and the first ten amendments. In doing so, I shall refer to statements made by him during the Bill of Rights debates as reported in the *Annals of Congress*. There has been doubt cast upon the accuracy of the reports of Congressional debates and transactions in the *Annals*. I am assured by Mr. Irving Brant, the eminent biographer of Madison, that Madison's discussions of the Bill of Rights as reported in the *Annals* are shown to be correct by Madison's own manuscripts on file in the Library of Congress.[1]

Reprinted with permission from *New York University Law Review,* 865, (1960), Black, The Bill of Rights.

This article was delivered as the first James Madison Lecture at the New York University School of Law on February 17, 1960.

What is a bill of rights? In the popular sense it is any document setting forth the liberties of the people. I prefer to think of our Bill of Rights as including all provisions of the original Constitution and Amendments that protect individual liberty by barring government from acting in a particular area or from acting except under certain prescribed procedures. I have in mind such clauses in the body of the Constitution itself as those which safeguard the right of habeas corpus, forbid bills of attainder and ex post facto laws, guarantee trial by jury, and strictly define treason and limit the way it can be tried and punished. I would certainly add to this list the last constitutional prohibition in Article Six that "no religious Test shall ever be required as a Qualification to any Office or public Trust under the United States."

I shall speak to you about the Bill of Rights only as it bears on powers of the Federal Government. Originally, the first ten amendments were not intended to apply to the states but, as the Supreme Court held in 1833 in *Barron v. Baltimore*,[2] were adopted to quiet fears extensively entertained that the powers of the big new national government "might be exercised in a manner dangerous to liberty." I believe that by virtue of the Fourteenth Amendment, the first ten amendments are now applicable to the states, a view I stated in *Adamson v. California*.[3] I adhere to that view. In this talk, however, I want to discuss only the extent to which the Bill of Rights limits the Federal Government.

In applying the Bill of Rights to the Federal Government there is today a sharp difference of views as to how far its provisions should be held to limit the lawmaking power of Congress. How this difference is finally resolved will, in my judgment, have far-reaching consequences upon our liberties. I shall first summarize what those different views are.

Some people regard the prohibitions of the Constitution, even its most unequivocal commands, as mere admonitions which Congress need not always observe. This viewpoint finds many different verbal expressions. For example, it is sometimes said that Congress may abridge a constitutional right if there is a clear and present danger that the free exercise of the right will bring about a substantive evil that Congress has authority to prevent. Or it is said that a right may be abridged where its exercise would cause so much injury to the public that this injury would outweigh the injury to the individual who is deprived of the right. Again, it is sometimes said that the Bill of Rights' guarantees must "compete for survival against general powers expressly granted to Congress and that the individual's right must, if outweighed by the public interest, be subordinated to the Government's competing interest in denying the right. All of these formulations, and more with which you are doubtless familiar, rest, at least in part, on the premise that there are no "absolute" prohibitions in the Constitution, and that all constitutional problems are questions of reasonableness, proximity, and degree. This view comes close to the English doctrine of legislative omnipotence, qualified only by the possibility of a judicial veto if the Supreme Court finds that a congressional choice between "competing" policies has no reasonable basis.

I cannot accept this approach to the Bill of Rights. It is my belief that there *are* "absolutes" in our Bill of Rights, and that they were put there on purpose by men who knew what words meant, and meant their prohibitions to be "absolutes." The whole history and background of the Constitution and Bill of Rights, as I understand it, belies the assumption or conclusion that our ultimate constitutional freedoms are no more than our English ancestors had when they came to this new land to get new freedoms. The historical and practical purposes of a Bill of Rights, the very use of a written constitution, indigenous to America, the language the Framers used, the kind of three-department government they took pains to set up, all point to the creation of a government which was denied all power to do some things under any and all circumstances, and all power to do other things except precisely in the manner prescribed. In this talk I will state some of the reasons why I hold this view. In doing so, however, I shall not attempt to discuss the wholly different and complex problem of the marginal scope of each individual amendment as applied to the particular facts of particular cases. For example, there is a question as to whether the First Amendment was intended to protect speech that courts find "obscene." I shall not stress this or similar differences of construction, nor shall I add anything to the views I expressed in the recent case of *Smith v. California*.[4] I am primarily discussing here whether liberties *admittedly* covered by the Bill of Rights can nevertheless be abridged on the ground that a superior public interest justifies the abridgment. I think the Bill of Rights made its safeguards superior.

Today most Americans seem to have forgotten the ancient evils which forced their ancestors to flee to this new country and to form a government stripped of old powers used to oppress them. But the Americans who supported the Revolution and the adoption of our Constitution knew firsthand the dangers of tyrannical governments. They were familiar with the long existing practice of English persecutions of people wholly because of their religious or political beliefs. They knew that many accused of such offenses had stood, helpless to defend themselves, before biased legislators and judges.

John Lilburne, a Puritan dissenter, is a conspicuous example.[5] He found out the hard way that a citizen of England could not get a court and jury trial under English law if Parliament wanted to try and punish him in some kind of summary and unfair method of its own. Time and time again, when his religious or political activities resulted in criminal charges against him, he had demanded jury trials under the "law of the land" but had been refused. Due to "trials" either by Parliament, its legislative committees, or courts subservient to the King or to Parliament, against all of which he vigorously protested as contrary to "due process" or "the law of the land," Lilburne had been whipped, put in the pillory, sent to prison, heavily fined and banished from England, all its islands and dominions, under penalty of death should he return. This last sentence was imposed by a simple Act of Parliament without any semblance of a trial. Upon his defiant return he was arrested and subjected to an unfair trial for his life. His chief defense was that the Parliamentary conviction was a nullity, as a denial of "due process of law," which he claimed was guaranteed under Magna Charta, the 1628 Petition of Right, and statutes passed to carry them out. He also challenged the power of Parliament to enact bills of attainder on the same grounds—due process of law. Lilburne repeatedly and vehemently contended that he was entitled to notice, an indictment, and court trial by jury under the known laws of England; that he had a right to be represented by counsel; that he had a right to have witnesses summoned in his behalf and be confronted by the witnesses against him; that he could not be compelled to testify against himself. When Lilburne finally secured a jury, it courageously acquitted him, after which the jury itself was severely punished by the court.

Prompted largely by the desire to save Englishmen from such legislative mockeries of fair trials, Lilburne and others strongly advocated adoption of an "Agreement of the People" which contained most of the provisions of our present Bill of Rights. That Agreement would have done away with Parliamentary omnipotence. Lilburne pointed out that the basic defect of Magna Charta and statutes complementing it was that they were not binding on Parliament since "that which is done by one Parliament, as a Parliament, may be undone by the next Parliament: but an "Agreement of the People" begun and ended amongst the People can never come justly within the Parliament's cognizance to destroy."[6] The proposed "Agreement of the People," Lilburne argued, could be changed only by the people and would bind Parliament as the supreme "law of the land." This same idea was picked up before the adoption of our Federal Constitution by Massachusetts and New Hampshire, which adopted their constitutions only after popular referendums. Our Federal Constitution is largely attributable to the same current of thinking.

Unfortunately, our own colonial history also provided ample reasons for people to be afraid to vest too much power in the national government. There had been bills of attainder here; women had been convicted and sentenced to death as "witches"; Quakers, Baptists, and various Protestant sects had been persecuted from time to time. Roger Williams left Massachusetts to breathe the free air of new Rhode Island. Catholics were barred from holding office in many places. Test oaths were required in some of the colonies to bar any but Christians from holding office. In New England Quakers suffered death for their faith. Baptists were sent to jail in Virginia for preaching, which caused Madison, while a very young man, to deplore what he called that "diabolical hell-conceived principle of persecution."[7]

In the light of history, therefore, it is not surprising that when our Constitution was adopted without specific provisions to safeguard cherished individual rights from invasion by the legislative, as well as the executive and judicial departments of the National Government, a loud and irresistible clamor went up throughout the country. These protests were so strong that the Constitution was ratified by the very narrowest of votes in some of the states. It has been said, and I think correctly, that had there been no general agreement that a supplementary Bill of Rights would be adopted as soon as possible after Congress met, the Constitution would not have been ratified. It seems clear that this widespread demand for a Bill of Rights was due to a common fear of political and religious persecution should the national legislative power be left unrestrained as it was in England.

The form of government which was ordained and established in 1789 contains certain unique features which reflected the Framers' fear of arbitrary government and which clearly indicate an intention absolutely to limit what Congress could do. The first of these features is that our Constitution is written in a single document. Such constitutions are familiar today and it is not always remembered that our country was the first to have one. Certainly one purpose of a written constitution is to define and therefore more specifically limit government powers. An all-powerful government that can act as it pleases wants no such constitution—unless to fool the people. England had no written constitution and this once proved a source of tyranny, as our ancestors well knew. Jefferson said about this departure from the English type of government: "Our peculiar security is in the possession of a written Constitution. Let us not make it a blank paper by construction."[8]

A second unique feature of our Government is a Constitution supreme over the legislature. In England, statutes, Magna Charta and later declarations of rights had for centuries limited the power of the King, but they did not limit the power of Parliament. Although commonly referred to as a constitution, they were never the "supreme law of the land" in the way in which our Constitution is, much to the regret of statemen like Pitt the elder. Parliament could change this English "Constitution"; Congress cannot change ours. Ours can only be changed by amendments ratified by three-fourths of the states. It was one of the great achievements of our Constitution that it ended legislative omnipotence here and placed all departments and agencies of government under one supreme law.

A third feature of our Government expressly designed to limit its powers was the division of authority into three coordinate branches none of which was to have supremacy over the others. This separation of powers with the checks and balances which each branch was given over the others was designed to prevent any branch, including the legislative, from infringing individual liberties safeguarded by the Constitution.

Finally, our Constitution was the first to provide a really independent judiciary. Moreover, as the Supreme Court held in *Marbury v. Madison,*[9] correctly I believe, this judiciary has the power to hold legislative enactments void that are repugnant to the Constitution and the Bill of Rights. In this country the judiciary was made independent because it has, I believe, the primary responsibility and duty of giving force and effect to constitutional liberties and limitations upon the executive and legislative branches. Judges in England were not always independent and they could not hold Parliamentary acts void. Consequently, English courts could not be counted on to protect the liberties of the people against invasion by the Parliament, as many unfortunate Englishmen found out, such as Sir Walter Raleigh, who was executed as the result of an unfair trial, and a lawyer named William Prynne, whose ears were first cut off by court order and who subsequently, by another court order, had his remaining ear stumps gouged out while he was on a pillory. Prynne's offenses were writing books and pamphlets.

All of the unique features of our Constitution show an underlying purpose to create a new kind of limited government. Central to all of the Framers of the Bill of Rights was the idea that since government, particularly the national government newly created, is a powerful institution, its officials—all of them—must be compelled to exercise their powers within strictly defined boundaries. As Madison told Congress, the Bill of Rights' limitations point "sometimes against the abuse of the Executive power, sometimes against the Legislative, and in some cases against the community itself; or, in other words, against the majority in favor of the minority."[10] Madison also explained that his proposed amendments were intended "to limit and qualify the powers of Government, by excepting out of the grant of power those cases in which the Government ought not to act, or to act only in a particular mode."[11] In the light of this purpose let us now turn to the language of the first ten amendments to consider whether their provisions were written as mere admonitions to Congress or as absolute commands, proceeding for convenience from the last to the first.

The last two Amendments, the Ninth and Tenth, are general in character, but both emphasize the limited nature of the Federal Government. Number Ten restricts federal power to what the Constitution delegates to the central government, reserving all other powers to the states or to the people. Number Nine attempts to make certain that enumeration of some rights must "not be construed to deny or disparage others retained by the people." The use of the words, "the people," in both these Amendments strongly emphasizes the desire of the Framers to protect individual liberty.

The Seventh Amendment states that "In Suits at common law, where the value in controversy shall exceed twenty dollars, the right of trial by jury shall be preserved . . . ." This language clearly requires that jury trials must be afforded in the type of cases the Amendment describes. The Amendment goes on in equally unequivocal words to command that "no fact tried by a jury, shall be otherwise re-examined in any Court of the United States, than according to the rules of the common law."

Amendments Five, Six, and Eight relate chiefly to the procedures that government must follow when bringing its powers to bear against any person with a view to depriving him of his life, liberty, or property.

The Eighth Amendment forbids "excessive bail," "excessive fines," or the infliction of "cruel or unusual punishments." This is one of the less precise provisions. The courts are required to determine the meaning of such general terms as "excessive" and "unusual." But surely that does not mean that admittedly "excessive bail," "excessive fines," or "cruel punishments" could be justified on the ground of a "competing" public interest in carrying out some generally granted power like that given Congress to regulate commerce.

Amendment Six provides that in a criminal prosecution an accused shall have a "speedy and public trial, by an impartial jury of the State and district wherein the crime shall have been committed, which district shall have been previously ascertained by law, and to be informed of the nature and cause of the accusation; to be confronted with the witnesses against him; to have compulsory process for obtaining witnesses in his favor, and have the Assistance of Counsel for his defence." All of these requirements are cast in terms both definite and absolute. Trial by jury was also guaranteed in the original Constitution. The additions here, doubtless prompted by English trials of Americans away from their homes, are that a trial must be "speedy and public," "by an impartial jury," and in a district which "shall have been previously ascertained by law." If there is any one thing that is certain it is that the Framers intended both in the original Constitution and in the Sixth Amendment that persons charged with crime by the Federal Government have a right to be tried by jury. Suppose juries began acquitting people Congress thought should be convicted. Could Congress then provide some other form of trial, say by an administrative agency, or the military, where convictions could be more readily and certainly obtained, if it thought the safety of the nation so required? How about secret trials? By *partial* juries? Can it be that these are not absolute prohibitions?

The Sixth Amendment requires notice of the cause of an accusation, confrontation by witnesses, compulsory process and assistance of counsel. The experience of centuries has demonstrated the value of these procedures to one on trial for crime. And this Amendment purports to guarantee them by clear language. But if there are no absolutes in the Bill of Rights, these guarantees too can be taken away by Congress on findings that a competing public interest requires that defendants be tried without notice, without witnesses, without confrontation, and without counsel.

The Fifth Amendment provides:

> No person shall be held to answer for a capital, or otherwise infamous crime, unless on a presentment or indictment of a Grand Jury, except in cases arising in the land or naval forces, or in the Militia, when in actual service in time of War or public danger; nor shall any person be subject for the same offence to be twice put in jeopardy of life or limb; nor shall be compelled in any criminal case to be a witness against himself, nor be deprived of life, liberty, or property, without due process of law; nor shall private property be taken for public use, without just compensation.

Most of these Fifth Amendment prohibitions are both definite and unequivocal. There has been much controversy about the meaning of "due process of law." Whatever its meaning, however, there can be no doubt that it must be granted. Moreover, few doubt that it has an historical meaning which denies Government the right to take away life, liberty, or property without trials properly conducted according to the Constitution and laws validly made in accordance with it. This, at least, was the meaning of "due process of law" when used in Magna Charta and other old English Statutes where it was referred to as "the law of the land."

The Fourth Amendment provides:

> The right of the people to be secure in their persons, houses, papers, and effects, against unreasonable searches and seizures, shall not be violated, and no Warrants shall issue, but upon probable cause, supported by Oath or affirmation, and particularly describing the place to be searched, and the persons or things to be seized.

The use of the word "unreasonable" in this Amendment means, of course, that not *all* searches and seizures are prohibited. Only those which are *unreasonable* are unlawful. There may be much difference of opinion about whether a particular search or seizure is unreasonable and therefore forbidden by this Amendment. But if it *is* unreasonable, it is absolutely prohibited.

Likewise, the provision which forbids warrants for arrest, search or seizure without "probable cause" is itself an absolute prohibition.

The Third Amendment provides that:

> No Soldier shall, in time of peace be quartered in any house, without the consent of the Owner, nor in time of war, but in a manner to be prescribed by law.

Americans had recently suffered from the quartering of British troops in their homes, and so this Amendment is written in language that apparently no one has ever thought could be violated on the basis of an overweighing public interest.

Amendment Two provides that:

> A well regulated Militia, being necessary to the security of a free State, the right of the people to keep and bear Arms, shall not be infringed.

Although the Supreme Court has held this Amendment to include only arms necessary to a well-regulated militia, as so construed, its prohibition is absolute.

This brings us to the First Amendment. It reads:

> Congress shall make no law respecting an establishment of religion, or prohibiting the free exercise thereof; or abridging the freedom of speech, or of the press; or the right of the people peaceably to assemble, and to petition the Government for a redress of grievances.

The phrase "Congress shall make no law" is composed of plain words, easily understood. The Framers knew this. The language used by Madison in his proposal was different, but no less emphatic and unequivocal. That proposal is worth reading:

> The civil rights of none shall be abridged on account of religious belief or worship, nor shall any national religion be established, nor shall the full and equal rights of conscience be in any manner, or on any pretext, infringed.

> The people shall not be deprived or abridged of their right to speak, to write, or to publish their sentiments; and the freedom of the press, as one of the great bulwarks of liberty, shall be inviolable.

> The people shall not be restrained from peaceably assembling and consulting for their common good; nor from applying to the Legislature by petitions, or remonstrances, for redress of their grievances.[12]

Neither as offered nor as adopted is the language of this Amendment anything less than absolute. Madison was emphatic about this. He told the Congress that under it "The right of freedom of speech is secured; the liberty of the press is expressly declared to be *beyond the reach of this Government* . . . ."[13] (Emphasis added in all quotations.) Some years later Madison wrote that "it would seem scarcely possible to doubt that *no power whatever* over the press was supposed to be delegated by the Constitution, as it originally stood, and that the amendment was intended as a *positive and absolute reservation of it.*"[14] With reference to the positive nature of the First Amendment's command against infringement of religious liberty, Madison later said that "there is not a shadow of right in the general government to intermeddle with religion,"[15] and that "this subject is, for the honor of America, perfectly free and unshackled. The *government has no jurisdiction over it.*"[16]

To my way of thinking, at least, the history and language of the Constitution and the Bill of Rights, which I have discussed with you, make it plain that one of the primary purposes of the Constitution with its amendments was to withdraw from the Government all power to act in certain areas—whatever the scope of those areas may be. If I am right in this then there is, at least in those areas, no justification whatever for "balancing" a particular right against some expressly granted power of Congress. If the Constitution withdraws from Government all power over subject matter in an area, such as religion, speech, press, assembly, and petition, there is nothing over which authority may be exerted.

The Framers were well aware that the individual rights they sought to protect might be easily nullified if subordinated to the general powers granted to Congress. One of the reasons for adoption of the Bill of Rights was to prevent just that. Specifically the people feared that the "necessary and proper" clause could be used to project the generally granted Congressional powers into the protected areas of individual rights. One need only read the debates in the various states to find out that this is true. But if these debates leave any doubt, Mr. Madison's words to Congress should remove it. In speaking of the "necessary and proper" clause and its possible effect on freedom of religion he said, as reported in the *Annals of Congress:*

> Whether the words are necessary or not, he did not mean to say, but they had been required by some of the State Conventions, who seemed to entertain an opinion that under the clause of the Constitution, which gave power to Congress to make all laws *necessary and proper* to carry into execution the Constitution, and the laws made under it, enabled them to make laws of such a nature as might infringe the rights of conscience, and establish a national religion; to prevent these effects he presumed the amendment was intended, and he thought it as well expressed as the nature of the language would admit.[17]

It seems obvious to me that Congress, in exercising its general powers, is expressly forbidden to use means prohibited by the Bill of Rights. Whatever else the phrase "necessary and proper" may mean, it must be that Congress may only adopt such means to carry out its powers as are "proper," that is, not specifically prohibited.

It has also been argued that since freedom of speech, press, and religion in England were narrow freedoms at best, and since there were many English laws infringing those freedoms, our First Amendment should not be thought to bar similar infringements by Congress. Again one needs only to look to the debates in Congress over the First Amendment to find that the First Amendment cannot be treated as a mere codification of English law. Mr. Madison made a clear explanation to Congress that it was the purpose of the First Amendment to grant greater protection than England afforded its citizens. He said:

> In the declaration of rights which that country has established, the truth is, they have gone no farther than to raise a barrier against the power of the Crown; the power of the Legislature is left altogether indefinite. Although I know whenever the great rights, the trial by jury, freedom of the press, or liberty of conscience, come in question in that body, the invasion of them is resisted by able advocates, yet their Magna Charta does not contain any one provision for the security of those rights, respecting which the people of America are most alarmed. The freedom of the press and rights of conscience, those choicest privileges of the people, are unguarded in the British Constitution.
>
> But although the case may be widely different, and it may not be thought necessary to provide limits for the legislative power in that country, yet a different opinion prevails in the United. States.[18]

It was the desire to give the people of America greater protection against the powerful Federal Government than the English had had against their government that caused the Framers to put these freedoms of expression, again in the words of Madison, "beyond the reach of this Government."

When closely analyzed the idea that there can be no "absolute" constitutional guarantees in the Bill of Rights is frightening to contemplate even as to individual safeguards in the original Constitution. Take, for instance, the last clause in Article Six that "no religious Test shall ever be required" for a person to hold office in the United States. Suppose Congress should find that some religious sect was dangerous because of its foreign affiliations. Such was the belief on which English test oaths rested for a long time and some of the states had test oaths on that assumption at the time, and after, our Constitution was adopted in 1789. Could Congress, or the Supreme Court, or both, put this precious privilege to be free from test oaths on scales, find it outweighed by some other public interest, and therefore make United States officials and employees swear they did not and never had belonged to or associated with a particular religious group suspected of disloyalty? Can Congress, in the name of overbalancing necessity, suspend habeas corpus in peacetime? Are there circumstances under which Congress could, after nothing more than a legislative bill of attainder, take away a man's life, liberty, or property? Hostility of the Framers toward bills of attainder was so great that they took the unusual step of barring such legislative punishments by the States as well as the Federal Government. They wanted to remove any possibility of such proceedings anywhere in this country. This is not strange in view of the fact that they were much closer than we are to the great Act of Attainder by the Irish Parliament, in 1688, which condemend between two and three thousand men, women, and children to exile or death without anything that even resembled a trial.[19]

Perhaps I can show you the consequences of the balancing approach to the Bill of Rights liberties by a practical demonstration of how it might work. The last clause of the Fifth Amendment is: "nor shall private property be taken for public use, without just compensation." On its face this command looks absolute, but if one believes that it should be weighed against the powers granted to Congress, there might be some circumstances in which this right would have to give way, just as there are some circumstances in which it is said the right of freedom of religion, speech, press, assembly and petition can be balanced away. Let us see how the balancing concept would apply to the just compensation provision of the Bill of Rights in the following wholly imaginary judicial opinion of Judge X:

"This case presents an important question of constitutional law. The United States is engaged in a stupendous national defense undertaking which requires the acquisition of much valuable land throughout the country. The plaintiff here owns 500 acres of land. The location of the land gives it a peculiarly strategic value for carrying out the defense program. Due to the great national emergency that exists, Congress concluded that the United States could not afford at this time to pay compensation for the lands which it needed to acquire. For this reason an act was passed authorizing seizure without compensation of all the lands required for the defense establishment.

"In reaching a judgment on this case, I cannot shut my eyes to the fact that the United States is in a desperate condition at this time. Nor can I, under established canons of constitutional construction, invalidate a Congressional enactment if there are any rational grounds upon which Congress could have passed it. I think there are such grounds here. Highly important among the powers granted Congress by the Constitution are the powers to declare war, maintain a navy, and raise and support armies. This, of course, means the power to conduct war successfully. To make sure that Congress is not unduly restricted in the exercise of these constitutional powers, the Constitution also gives Congress power to make all laws 'necessary and proper to carry into execution the foregoing powers . . . .' This 'necessary and proper' clause applies to the powers to make war and support armies as it does to all the other granted powers.

"Plaintiff contends, however, that the Fifth Amendment's provision about compensation is so absolute a command that Congress is wholly without authority to violate it, however great this nation's emergency and peril may be. I must reject this contention. We must never forget that it is a constitution we are expounding. And a constitution, unlike ordinary statutes, must endure for ages; it must be adapted to changing conditions and the needs of changing communities. Without such capacity for change, our Constitution would soon be outmoded and become a dead letter. Therefore its words must never be read as rigid absolutes. The Bill of Rights' commands, no more than any others, can stay the hands of Congress from doing that which the general welfare imperatively demands. When two great constitutional provisions like these conflict—as here the power to make war conflicts with the requirements for just compensation—it becomes the duty of courts to weigh the constitutional right of an individual to compensation against the power of Congress to wage a successful war.

"While the question is not without doubt, I have no hesitation in finding the challenged Congressional act valid. Driven by the absolute necessity to protect the nation from foreign aggression, the national debt has risen to billions of dollars. The Government's credit is such that interest rates have soared. Under these circumstances, Congress was rationally entitled to find that if it paid for all the lands it needs it might bankrupt the nation and render it helpless in its hour of greatest need. Weighing as I must the loss the individual will suffer because he has to surrender his land to the nation without compensation against the great public interest in conducting war, I hold the act valid. A decree will be entered accordingly."

Of course, I would not decide this case this way nor do I think any other judge would so decide it today. My reason for refusing this approach would be that I think the Fifth Amendment's command is absolute and not to be overcome without constitutional amendment even in times of grave emergency. But I think this wholly fictitious opinion fairly illustrates the possibilities of the balancing approach, not only as to the just compensation clause, but as to other provisions of the Bill of Rights as well. The great danger of the judiciary balancing process is that in times of emergency and stress it gives Government the power to do what it thinks necessary to protect itself, regardless of the rights of individuals. If the need is great, the right of Government can always be said to outweigh the rights of the individual. If "balancing" is accepted as the test, it would be hard for any conscientious judge to hold otherwise in times of dire need. And laws adopted in times of dire need are often very hasty and oppressive laws, especially when, as often happens, they are carried over and accepted as normal. Furthermore, the balancing approach to basic individual liberties assumes to legislators and judges more power than either the Framers or I myself believe should be entrusted, without limitation, to any man or any group of men.

It seems to me that the "balancing" approach also disregards all of the unique features of our Constitution which I described earlier. In reality this approach returns us to the state of legislative supremacy which existed in England and which the Framers were so determined to change once and for all. On the one hand, it denies the judiciary its constitutional power to measure acts of Congress by the standards set down in the Bill of Rights. On the other hand, though apparently reducing judicial powers by saying that acts of Congress may be held unconstitutional only when they are found to have no rational legislative basis, this approach really gives the Court, along with Congress, a greater power, that of overriding the plain commands of the Bill of Rights on a finding of weighty public interest. In effect, it changes the direction of our form of government from a government of limited powers to a government in which Congress may do anything that Courts believe to be "reasonable."

Of course the decision to provide a constitutional safeguard for a particular right, such as the fair trial requirements of the Fifth and Sixth Amendments and the right of free speech protection of the First, involves a balancing of conflicting interests. Strict procedures may release guilty men; protecting speech and press may involve dangers to a particular government. I believe, however, that the Framers themselves did this balancing when they wrote the Constitution and the Bill of Rights. They appreciated the risks involved and they decided that certain rights should be guaranteed regardless of these risks. Courts have neither the right nor the power to review this original decision of the Framers and to attempt to make a different evaluation of the importance of the rights granted in the Constitution. Where conflicting values exist in the field of individual liberties protected by the Constitution, that document settles the conflict, and its policy should not be changed without constitutional amendments by the people in the manner provided by the people.

Misuse of government power, particularly in times of stress, has brought suffering to humanity in all ages about which we have authentic history. Some of the world's noblest and finest men have suffered ignominy and death for no crime—unless unorthodoxy is a crime. Even enlightened Athens had its victims such as Socrates. Because of the same kind of bigotry, Jesus, the great Dissenter, was put to death on a wooden cross. The flames of inquisitions all over the world have warned that men endowed with unlimited government power, even earnest men, consecrated to a cause, are dangerous.

For my own part, I believe that our Constitution, with its absolute guarantees of individual rights, is the best hope for the aspirations of freedom which men share everywhere. I cannot agree with those who think of the Bill of Rights as an 18th Century straitjacket, unsuited for this age. It is old but not all old things are bad. The evils it guards against are not only old, they are with us now, they exist today. Almost any morning you open your daily paper you can see where some person somewhere in the world is on trial or has just been convicted of supposed disloyalty to a new group controlling the government which has set out to purge its suspected enemies and all those who had dared to be against its successful march to power. Nearly always you see that these political heretics are being tried by military tribunals or some other summary and sure method for disposition of the accused. Now and then we even see the convicted victims as they march to their execution.

Experience all over the world has demonstrated, I fear, that the distance between stable, orderly government and one that has been taken over by force is not so great as we have assumed. Our own free system to live and progress has to have intelligent citizens, citizens who cannot only think and speak and write to influence people, but citizens who are free to do that without fear of governmental censorship or reprisal.

The provisions of the Bill of Rights that safeguard fair legal procedures came about largely to protect the weak and the oppressed from punishment by the strong and the powerful who wanted to stifle the voices of discontent raised in protest against opression and injustice in public affairs. Nothing that I have read in the Congressional debates on the Bill of Rights indicates that there was any belief that the First Amendment contained any qualifications. The only arguments that tended to look in this direction at all were those that said "that all paper barriers against the power of the community are too weak to be worthy of attention."[20] Suggestions were also made in and out of Congress that a Bill of Rights would be a futile gesture since there would be no way to enforce the safeguards for freedom it provided. Mr. Madison answered this argument in these words:

> If they[the Bill of Rights amendments] are incorporated into the Constitution, independent tribunals of justice will consider themselves in a peculiar manner the guardians of those rights; they will be an impenetrable bulwark against any assumption of power in the Legislative or Executive; they will be naturally led to resist every encroachment upon rights expressly stipulated for in the Constitution by the declaration of rights.[21]

I fail to see how courts can escape this sacred trust.

Since the earliest days philosophers have dreamed of a country where the mind and spirit of man would be free; where there would be no limits to inquiry; where men would be free to explore the unknown and to challenge the most deeply rooted beliefs and principles. Our First Amendment was a bold effort to adopt this principle—to establish a country with no legal restrictions of any kind upon the subjects people could investigate, discuss and deny. The Framers knew, better perhaps than we do today, the risks they were taking. They knew that free speech might be the friend of change and revolution. But they also knew that it is always the deadliest enemy of tyranny. With this knowledge they still believed that the ultimate happiness and security of a nation lies in its ability to explore, to change, to grow and ceaselessly to adapt itself to new knowledge born of inquiry free from any kind of governmental control over the mind and spirit of man. Loyalty comes from love of good government, not fear of a bad one.

The First Amendment is truly the heart of the Bill of Rights. The Framers balanced its freedoms of religion, speech, press, assembly and petition against the needs of a powerful central government, and decided that in those freedoms lies this nation's only true security. They were not afraid for men to be free. We should not be. We should be as confident as Jefferson was when he said in his First Inaugural Address:

> If there be any among us who would wish to dissolve this Union or to change its republican form, let them stand undisturbed as monuments of the safety with which error of opinion may be tolerated where reason is left free to combat it.[22]

### Notes

1. See also Brant, The Madison Heritage, 35 N.Y.U.L. Rev. 882 (1960).
2. 32 U.S. (7 Pet.) 242, 249 (1833).
3. 332 U.S. 46, 71–72 (1947) (dissenting opinion).
4. 361 U.S. 147, 155 (1959) (concurring opinion).
5. See The Trial of John Lilburn and John Wharton (Star Chamber 1637) in 3 How. St. Tr. 1315 (1816).
6. Leveller Manifestoes of the Puritan Revolution 423 (Wolfe ed. 1944).
7. 1 Rives, History of the Life and Times of James Madison 44 (1859).
8. 4 Jefferson, Writings 506 (Washington ed. 1859).
9. U.S. (1 Cranch) 137 (1803).
10. 1 Annals of Cong. 437 (1789).
11. Ibid.
12. 1 Annals of Cong. 434 (1789).
13. 1 Annals of Cong. 738 (1789).
14. 6 Madison, Writings 391 (Hunt ed. 1906).
15. 5 Madison, Writings 176 (Hunt ed. 1904).
16. Id. at 132.
17. 1 Annals of Cong. 730 (1789). (Emphasis added.)
18. 1 Annals of Cong. 436 (1789).
19. See *Joint Anti-Fascist Refugee Comm.* v. *McGrath,* 341 U.S. 123, 146–49 (1951) (appendix to concurring opinion of Black, J.).
20. 1 Annals of Cong. 437 (1789).
21. 1 Annals of Cong. 439 (1789).
22. 8 Jefferson, Writings 2–3 (Washington ed. 1859).

---

# The Constitution and the Bill of Rights

Herbert J. Storing

The foundation of the American constitutional system was not completed, it is widely agreed, until the adoption of the first ten admendments in 1791. The absence of a bill of rights from the original Constitution had, of course, been a major item in the Antifederalist position. "No sooner had the Continental Congress laid the proposed Constitution before the people for ratification," Irving Brant writes, "than a great cry went up: it contained no Bill of Rights."[1] According to Robert Rutland, whose book *The Birth of the Bill of Rights, 1776–1791* is the major history of these events, "The Federalists, failing to realize the importance of a bill of rights, miscalculated public opinion and found themselves on the defensive almost from the outset of the ratification struggle."[2] Another scholar, Bernard Schwartz, says: "Here, the Antifederalists had the stronger case and their opponents were on the defensive from the beginning. It was, indeed, not until the Federalists yielded in their rigid opposition on Bill of Rights Amendments that ratification of the Constitution was assured. On the Bill of Rights issue, it is the Antifederalist writings which are the more interesting and even the more influential."[3]

Reprinted with permission from Kennikat Press Corporation, © 1978.

So, as the story is generally told, the Federalists gave us the Constitution, but the Antifederalists gave us the Bill of Rights. Moreover, it seems quite plausible today, when so much of constitutional law is connected with the Bill of Rights, to conclude that the Antifederalists, the apparent losers in the debate over the Constitution, were ultimately the winners. Their contribution to the scheme of American constitutional liberty seems to be a more fundamental one. Rutland puts this point well: "The facts show that the Federal Bill of Rights and the antecedent state declarations of rights represented, more than anything else, the sum total of American experience and experimentation with civil liberty up to their adoption."[4]

We all have a tendency to look at the past through the glass of our present concerns and presuppositions. That is altogether understandable; it can be given a plausible justification; it is sometimes said to be the only thing we can do. The result, however, is that we tend to speak to the past rather than to let the past try to speak to us. I want to try to reconstruct some of the debate over the Bill of Rights in a way that will enable it to speak to us. I think the result will be to show that the common view that the heart of American liberty is to be found in the Bill of Rights is wrong. That view rests, I think, on a misreading of the events of the American founding and reflects and fosters a misunderstanding of the true basis of American constitutional liberty.

To begin, we need to remind ourselves of some of the central facts about the way the Constitution was ratified. On 17 September 1787 the convention sitting in Philadelphia finished its business and sent its proposed constitution to Congress for transmittal to the states, there to be considered in conventions specially elected for that purpose. The Federalists in several states moved quickly to secure ratification. The Pennsylvania legislature began discussing the calling of a convention, even before the Constitution had been acted upon by Congress, and provided for a convention to meet on 21 November. Delaware was, however, the first to ratify, on 7 December, followed by Pennsylvania on 12 December. The Pennsylvania ratification was accompanied by charges of steamrolling and unfair tactics; the opposition remained unreconciled and demanded a second national convention. There followed ratification in rapid succession by New Jersey, Georgia, and Connecticut. By the middle of January 1788, however, no major state had ratified except Pennsylvania, where the opposition was still strong.

The Massachusetts convention met on 14 January, and the evidence suggests that there was probably a majority against the Constitution or at least that the Antifederalists were very strong. The Massachusetts convention saw intensive debate, accompanied by equally intensive parliamentary and political maneuvering. Finally, for reasons that will always be debated, John Hancock, the hitherto absent president of the convention, made an appearance and proposed that along with ratification the convention recommend a series of amendments to "remove the fears and quiet the apprehensions of many of the good people of the commonwealth, and more effectually guard against an undue administration of the federal government. . . ."[5] This proposal, supported by Samuel Adams, secured ratification in Massachusetts on 6 February by the still close vote of 187 to 168. Indeed, it is scarcely too much to say that this formula secured the ratification of the Constitution; for some version of it was used in every state that ratified after Massachusetts, with the exception of Maryland but including the crucial and doubtful states of Virginia and New York. The Constitution was ratified, then, on the understanding that an early item on the national agenda would be the consideration of widely desired amendments.

The story is completed in the First Congress. When the new government began functioning in 1789, James Madison introduced in the House of Representatives a series of amendments which, after consideration there and in the Senate, were framed as twelve proposed amendments and sent to the states for ratification. Two of these amendments (of minor importance) were not ratified by the states.[6] The others were ratified in 1791 and became the first ten amendments to the Constitution—our Bill of Rights.

The reader of the debates of the First Congress can hardly avoid being struck by the persistence with which Madison pressed his proposals and the coolness with which they were initially received. The House of Representatives was hard at work getting the government organized and underway. It was engaged in establishing the executive departments and providing for a national revenue system; the Senate was working on a bill to establish the federal judiciary (where several of the main questions raised in proposals for amendment would have to be faced). It seemed sensible to most of Madison's colleagues to concentrate on getting the government well launched, to acquire some experience in it, and to avoid a premature reopening of the divisive debate over ratification. It is true that Madison had explicitly committed himself to the position that the First Congress should propose amendments to be submitted to the states; "amendments, if pursued with a proper moderation and in a proper mode, will be not only safe, but may serve the double purpose of satisfying the minds of well meaning opponents, and of providing additional guards in favour of liberty."[7] Nevertheless, Madison could have explained, altogether plausibly, to his Virginia constituents that he had introduced amendments as promised, but that they had been postponed until the House could finish the obviously more pressing business of launching the new government. Yet in the face of resistance from political friends as well as foes, Madison pressed forward. Why?

Madison's insistent sponsorship of amendments has to be seen, I think, as the final step in the strikingly successful Federalist strategy to secure an effective national government. I do not claim that this strategy was conceived at the beginning of the ratification debate—it developed as events emerged—or that all Federalists were parties to it; if they had been, Madison would not have had the opposition he did at the outset of the debate on amendments. But I think it is fairly clear that Madison knew what he was doing: he meant to complete the Federalist ratification victory, and in fact he did so.

Madison's proposals were designed primarily to prevent two things from happening. The first aim was to thwart the move for a general convention to consider amendments under the authority of Article V of the Constitution. A second convention was a favorite plan of the Antifederalists; the Federalists feared that such a convention might be—was indeed, intended to be—a time bomb that would destroy the essentials of the Constitution. The second and related aim was to snuff out the attempt to revise the basic structure and powers of the new federal government, which was the main thrust of Antifederal opposition. All the state ratifying conventions that proposed amendments included suggestions to strengthen the states and limit the powers of Congress relating to such crucial matters as federal elections, taxes, military affairs, and commercial regulation. Madison made clear that he had no intention of proposing, or accepting, any amendments along these lines. "I should be unwilling to see a door opened for a reconsideration of the whole structure of Government—for a reconsideration of the principles and the substance of the powers given; because I doubt, if such a door were opened, we should be very likely to stop at that point which would be safe to the Government itself."[8] Madison's strategy was to seize the initiative for amendments, to use the Federalist majority in the First Congress to finish the unavoidable business of amendments in such a way as to remove from the national agenda the major Antifederalist objections—and incidentally to secure some limited but significant improvements in the Constitution, especially in securing individual rights.

Thus, on 6 June Madison offered his proposals, mustering all his remarkable influence to urge on the friends of the Constitution the prudence of showing their good faith and tranquilizing the public mind by putting forward amendments "of such a nature as will not injure the Constitution" and yet could "give satisfaction to the doubting part of our fellow-citizens." He urged also that "it is possible the abuse of the powers of the General Government may be guarded against in a more secure manner than is now done, while no one advantage arising from the exercise of that power shall be damaged or endangered by it." "We have," he said, "in this way something to gain, and, if we proceed with caution, nothing to lose."[9]

Secure in the knowledge of a large majority back of him (once he could get it to move), Madison proposed amendments designed to correct minor imperfections in the structure of government, which I pass over here,[10] to secure traditional individual rights, and to reserve to the states powers not granted to the federal government. These proposals were recast by the House, but little of substance was added or taken away. A comparison of Madison's original proposals and the first ten amendments of the Constitution shows both the value of a serious and thoughtful deliberative process in improving the original language and the dominance of Madison's impulse. The crucial fact is that none of the amendments regarded by the opponents to the Constitution as fundamental was included.

Indeed, in one of his proposals Madison tried to turn the table on the Antifederalists by using the Bill of Rights momentum to make what he regarded as a substantial improvement in the constitutional design. He proposed that "no state shall violate the equal right of conscience, or the freedom of the press or the trial by jury in criminal cases." Admitting that many state constitutions already had such provisions, Madison saw no reason against double security. And he shrewdly observed that

> nothing can give a more sincere proof of the attachment of those who opposed this Constitution to these great and important rights, than to see them join in obtaining the security I have now proposed; because it must be admitted, on all hands, that the State Governments are as liable to attack these individual privileges as the General Government is, and therefore ought to be as cautiously guarded against.[11]

This amendment, which Madison thought "the most valuable amendment in the whole list,"[12] was eventually rejected by the Senate, as perhaps he expected it would be. It reflected, nonetheless, Madison's long-standing view that the chief danger to American liberty lay in the incapacity, instability, and injustice of state governments.

Madison's proposals were first referred to the committee of the whole house; later, after a good deal of controversy about how to proceed, they were referred to a select committee of eleven, on which Madison sat. To this select committee were also referred, pro forma, all the amendments proposed by the state ratifying conventions. But the committee reported out Madison's amendments only. The majority had now committed itself to action, and Madison's proposals were briskly moved through the House, over some objections of unseemly haste, echoing similar briskness and similar complaints in the early stages of the ratification of the Constitution itself. Attempts by Antifederalists such as Aedanus Burke and Elbridge Gerry to secure consideration of the more fundamental amendments proposed by the state ratifying conventions were courteously but firmly and quickly turned aside.

The objective of amendments, Madison had said, was to "give satisfaction to the doubting part of our fellow-citizens." But they did not give satisfaction. Burke spoke for most of his fellow Antifederalists when he contended that Madison's amendments were "very far from giving satisfaction to our constituents; they are not those solid and substantial amendments which the people expect. They are little better than whip-syllabub, frothy and full of wind, formed only to please the palate; or they are like a tub thrown out to a whale to secure the freight of the ship and its peaceable voyage." Samuel Livermore thought Madison's amendments were "no more than a pinch of snuff; they went to secure rights never in danger."[13] And when later the amendments went to the states the main opposition to their ratification came not from the friends but from the former enemies of the Constitution, whose opinion the amendments were supposed to placate. Their view, generally speaking, was that expressed by Samuel Chase to John Lamb of New York. "A declaration of rights alone will be of no essential service. Some of the powers must be abridged, or public liberty will be endangered and, in time, destroyed."[14] Of course, Madison knew that his amendments would not satisfy the hard-core Antifederalists. His strategy was rather to isolate them from the large group of common people whose opposition did rest, not on fundamental hostility to the basic design of the Constitution but on a broad fear that individual liberties were not sufficiently protected. By conciliatory amendments, he told Jefferson, he hoped "to extinguish opposition to the system, or at least break the force of it, by detaching the deluded opponents from the designing leaders."[15] However little the Antifederalist leaders ultimately relied on the absence of a bill of rights, too many reams of paper and hours of speaking had been devoted to it to make it now very plausible for them to dismiss a Federalist-sponsored bill of rights as mere froth. Bristling (pleasurably, one supposes) at accusations from the Antifederalists of lack of candor, Madison could ask "whether the amendments now proposed are not those most strenuously required by the opponents of the Constitution?" Have not the people been "taught to believe" that the Constitution endangered their liberties and should not be adopted without a bill of rights?[16] And by whom had they been taught? That liberty had never been in serious danger under the Constitution is what the Federalists had claimed; but under Madison's prodding they were now moderately yielding to their opponents' sensibilities. Those opponents could not expect to make much headway by admitting that the Federalists had been right on the bill of rights issue all along. "It is a fortunate thing," Madison solemnly declared in the house, "that the objection to the Government has been made on the ground I stated; because it will be practicable, on that ground, to obviate the objection, so far as to satisfy the public mind that their liberties will be perpetual, and this without endangering any part of the Constitution, which is considered as essential to the existence of the Government by those who promoted its adoption."[17] The Antifederalist leaders objected to what Madison had *not* included in his amendment, but they had been neatly boxed in.

In September 1789 Edmund Pendleton wrote to Madison:

> . . . I congratulate you upon having got through the Amendments to the Constitution, as I was very anxious that it should be done before your adjournment, since it will have a good effect in quieting the minds of many well meaning Citizens, tho' I am of opinion that nothing was further from the wish of some, who covered their Opposition to the Government under the masque of uncommon zeal for amendments and to whom a rejection or a delay as a new ground of clamour would have been more agreeable. I own also that I feel some degree of pleasure, in discovering obviously from the whole progress, that the public are indebted for the measure to the friends of Government, whose Elections were opposed under pretense of their being averse to amendments.[18]

My argument thus far is that the primary significance of the Bill of Rights is seen most clearly in what it does not include. Madison's successful strategy was to finish the debate over ratification by pushing forward a set of amendments that almost everyone could accept and that excluded all the Antifederalists' fundamental proposals. There is also a more positive and substantial significance. To consider this we need to understand first why there was no bill of rights in or attached to the Constitution as originally drafted. The most obvious answer is that it was only after the convention in Philadelphia had spent three months constructing a government that it occurred to anyone to attach a bill of rights to it. By the time Mason and Gerry did propose a bill of rights on 12 September, it was clear to almost everyone that the convention needed to finish its business and put its proposal to the country. It seemed likely, moreover, despite Mason's contention to the contrary, that the drafting of a bill of rights would turn out to be a long and difficult business.

But why was a bill of rights not considered earlier? And why, even admitting that it might be difficult to draw up, could it be dispensed with? There is a bewildering diversity of arguments made by defenders of the Constitution to explain why a bill of rights was undesirable or unnecessary. These are not always consistent or very plausible; but at bottom there are a couple of powerful and, I think, deeply compelling arguments.[19] The most widely discussed argument against a federal bill of rights was made by James Wilson in his influential "State House" speech on 6 October 1787. Wilson pointed to the fact that the general government would possess only specifically enumerated powers, unlike the state governments, which possessed broad, general grants of authority. Thus, in the case of the states, "everything which is not reserved is given," but in the case of the general government "everything which is not given is reserved." Once this distinction is understood, the pointlessness of a federal bill of rights emerges:

> for it would have been superfluous and absurd to have stipulated with a federal body of our own creation, that we should enjoy those privileges of which we are not divested, either by the intention or the act that has brought the body into existence. For instance, the liberty of the press, which has been a copious source of declamation and opposition—what control can proceed from the Federal government to shackle or destroy that sacred palladium of national freedom?[20]

Wilson articulated here a fundamental principle of the American Constitution, that the general government possesses only enumerated powers. It is, however, open to the objection that enumerated powers must imply other powers (an implication strengthened by the necessary and proper clause) and that a train of implied powers may lead to encroachments on state prerogatives. Madison made a kind of concession to this argument by proposing in one of his amendments that "the powers not delegated by this Constitution, nor prohibited by it to he States, are reserved to the States respectively." Attempts to insert "expressly" before "delegated," thus restoring the language of the Articles of Confederation and more tightly restraining federal authority, failed (though the ubiquitous "expressly" proved extremely difficult to eliminate from American political debate). Indeed, the House accepted Charles Carroll's motion to add "or to the people," which was presumably meant to narrow the states' claim to reserved powers.[21] Thus emerged what is now the Tenth Amendment. But this amendment was quite rightly seen by the Antifederalists as no substantial concession at all. It merely stated the obvious in a coldly neutral way: that what was not granted was reserved.

Losing the battle of "expressly delegated" was merely the sign of the Antifederalists' loss of the battle over the basic character of the Constitution. They threw up, however, a second, less than best, defense against the possibility of unjust enlargement of federal powers, and that was the campaign to give specific protection to especially important or exposed individual rights. This was part of the serious argument for a bill of rights; and Madison's response here was more substantial, as we have seen. The result is the prudent and successful scheme of limited government that we now enjoy in the United States, with both its Constitution and its Bill of Rights. Security is provided at both ends: limited grants of power; protection of individual rights. This scheme is well known enough to require from me little in the way of either explanation or praise. Perhaps a view from the founding might caution us, however, not to exaggerate its benefits. Justice Black to the contrary notwithstanding, it is impossible in any interesting case to define the rights protected in the amendments with sufficient exactness to permit their automatic application. A bill of rights cannot eliminate the need for political judgment, and therewith the risk of abuse. James Iredell, in his reply to George Mason's "Objections" to the Constitution, displayed the ambiguity, for example, of "cruel and unusual punishments" and at the same time the impossibility of exhaustive particularization.[22] Alexander Hamilton defied anyone to give a definition to "liberty of the press" "which should not leave the utmost latitude for evasion." "I hold it to be impracticable; and from this, I infer that its security, whatever fine declarations may be inserted in any constitution respecting it, must altogether depend on public opinion, and on the general spirit of the people and of the government. And here, after all . . . must we seek for the only solid basis of all our rights."[23]

It is interesting to consider what our constitutional law would be like today if there had been no Bill of Rights. Its focus would presumably be to a far greater extent than it is today on the powers of the government. We might expect a more searching examination by the Supreme Court of whether federal legislation that seems to conflict with cherished individual liberties is indeed "necessary and proper" to the exercise of granted powers. We might expect a fuller articulation than we usually receive of whether, in Marshall's terms, "the end" aimed at by given legislation "is legitimate." Might this not foster a healthy concern with the problems of *governing,* a healthy sense of responsible self-government?

Doubtless a jurisprudence without a Bill of Rights would also have to find ways of scrutinizing the impact of legislation on the individual. How could that be done? Could the individual "take advantage of a natural right founded in reason," one Antifederalist asked; "could he plead it and produce Locke, Sydney, or Montesquieu as authority?"[24] Perhaps he could. One Federalist said that while there was no way to predict in advance what laws may be "necessary and proper," "this we may say—that, in exercising those powers, the Congress cannot legally violate the natural rights of an individual."[25] Another insisted that "no power was given to Congress to infringe on any one of the natural rights of the people by this Constitution; and, should they attempt it without constitutional authority, the act would be a nullity, and could not be enforced."[26] Such views have found expression in the Supreme Court by men who would rest their findings of governmental usurpation squarely on the inherent purposes and limitations of all legitimate, free government. "I do not hesitate to declare," Justice Johnson said in Fletcher v. Peck, "that a state does not possess the power of revoking its own grants. But I do it on a general principle, on the reason and nature of things: a principle which will impose laws even on the Deity."[27] And Justice Chase, in *Calder v. Bull,* insisted that

> There are certain vital principles in our free Republican governments, which will determine and overrule an apparent and flagrant abuse of legislative power; as to authorize manifest injustice by positive law; or to take away that security for personal liberty, or private property, for the protection whereof the government was established. An act of the Legislature (for I cannot call it law) contrary to the great first principles of the social compact, cannot be considered a rightful exercise of legislative authority.[28]

Of course, government *does* "violate" the natural rights of the individual, at least in the sense that it legitimately prevents him from enjoying the fullness of his rights. The question that always has to be asked is whether individual rights have been unnecessarily or unreasonably abridged. Such questions are not easy to answer, with or without a bill of rights. Any formulation of the standard of natural rights is problematical and obscure. But is it much more cloudy or contingent than "cruel and unusual punishment," "excessive bail," or "freedom of the press?" Would the nationalization of civil rights which Professor Fellman has discussed in this series have been less well guided by something like Cardozo's standard of "implicit in the concept of ordered liberty."[29] than it has been by the tortuous reasoning induced by preoccupation with the issue of "incorporation?" Without a bill of rights our courts would probably have developed a kind of common law of individual rights to help to test and limit governmental power. Might the courts thus have been compelled to confront the basic questions that "substantive due process," "substantive equal protection," "clear and present danger," etc., have permitted them to conceal, even from themselves? Is it possible that without a bill of rights we might suffer less of that ignoble battering between absolutistic positivism and flaccid historicism that characterizes our constitutional law today?

I stray from my principal concern, though not, I think, from the spirit of the argument I am examining. The basis of the Federalist argument was that the whole notion of a bill of rights as generally understood is alien to American government. It was derived from Britain where there was no written constitution and where individual liberties were secured by marking out limits on royal prerogative. Here the Constitution itself is a bill of rights, the Federalists often argued, meaning that it was derived from the people themselves, that it provided for a sound system of representation, and that it granted limited powers to a balanced government. Quoting from the opening of the preamble, *Publius* said, "Here is a better recognition of popular rights than volumes of aphorisms which make the principal figure in several of our State bills of rights and which would sound much better in a treatise of ethics than in a constitution of government."[30] This argument shows the redundancy of any declaration of the right of people to establish their own government, but it does not reach the chief problem of popular government, which is majority tyranny. Protecting individuals and minorities against unjust action by the majority, or the government reflecting the wishes of the majority, is a major benefit of a bill of rights in the Antifederalist view. Like most Federalists, Madison never denied this, but he did not think it very reliable. The solution has to be found at a deeper level, in the functioning of a large, differentiated commercial society. And so far as the possible dangers from government are concerned, protection must be found in the very constitution of that government. Thus, Thomas McKean told his Pennsylvania colleagues that although a bill of rights "can do no harm, I believe, yet it is an unnecessary instrument, for in fact the whole plan of government is nothing more than a bill of rights—a declaration of the people in what manner they choose to be governed."[31] In the words of another Federalist:

> Where the powers to be exercised, under a certain system, are in themselves consistent with the people's liberties, are legally defined, guarded and ascertained, and ample provision made for bringing condign punishment to all such as shall overstep the limitations of the law—it is hard to conceive of a greater security for the rights of the people.[32]

But admitting that a bill of rights was not necessary, what harm could it do? "A bill of rights may be summed up in a few words," Patrick Henry told his fellow Virginians. "What do they tell us?—That our rights are reserved. Why not say so? Is it because it will consume too much paper?"[33] By 1789 Madison conceded this; he told Congress that we have nothing to lose and something to gain by amendments to secure individual rights. Why not concede the point earlier? Madison admitted that "some policy had been made use of, perhaps, by gentlemen on both sides of the question."[34] On the Federalist side, an unyielding resistance to a bill of rights is to be explained by a fear that it would divert the campaign for ratification of the Constitution into what surely would have been a long and circuitous route to amendments, a route along which the essentials of the Constitution would have been extremely difficult to protect. As long as the Constitution remained unratified, Madison wrote to George Eve in 1783, "I opposed all previous alterations as calculated to throw the States into dangerous contentions, and to furnish the secret enemies of the Union with an opportunity of promoting its dissolution."[35]

There was also, I think, a deeper and more positive reason for what appears to many scholars a rigid and defensive opposition to a bill of rights. The Federalists were determined that Americans not be diverted, in a more fundamental sense, from the main task of providing themselves with effective government. Jefferson, writing from France, admitted to Madison that bills of rights have an occasional tendency to cramp government in its useful exertions; but he thought that such inconvenience was short-lived, moderate, and reparable.[36] The friends of the Constitution, on the other hand, feared that an undue concern with rights might be fatal to American liberty. "Liberty may be endangred by the abuses of liberty," *Publius* warned, "as well as by the abuses of power, and the former rather than the latter is apparently most to be apprehended by the United States."[37] James Iredell saw in the old state bills of rights evidence that "the minds of men then [were] so warmed with their exertions in the cause of liberty as to lean too much perhaps toward a jealousy of power to repose a proper confidence in their own government."[38] The Federalists feared that Americans were all too wont to fall into easy and excessive criticism of all proposals for effective government. They saw in the arguments against the Constitution a tendency to drift into the shallow view that Americans could somehow get along without government—without the tough decisions, the compulsion, the risk that government must always involve. The main political business of the American people, they thought, was and would continue to be not to protect themselves against political power but to accept the responsibility of governing themselves. The Federalists did not deny that government, once established, may need protecting against, but they tried to make sure that that would always be seen for the secondary consideration it is. The lesson that the furor over a bill of rights threatened to obscure was, in Edmund Pendleton's words, that "there is no quarrel between government and liberty. The war is between government and licentiousness, faction, turbulence, and other violations of the rules of society, to preserve liberty."[39]

It was altogether appropriate, from this Federalist point of view, that the Bill of Rights should have emerged from a separate set of deliberations, occurring after the Constitution had been framed and accepted and its government set in motion. Even at this point, however, the Federalist concession was less than might at first appear. We have seen that by taking the initiative for amendments Madison confined discussion to a bill of rights (plus a few, noncontroversial changes) and excluded that whole set of major Antifederalist proposals that would limit the powers of the general government or otherwise change the basic design of the Constitution. We must now see that Madison also took a narrow view of the meaning of a bill of rights as such, with the aim of preserving not only the constitutional scheme but also the vigor and capacity of government.

In their extraordinary exchange of views between 1787 and 1789, Thomas Jefferson pressed on Madison his opinion in favor of a bill of rights.[40] But the significant fact is not that Madison came to favor a bill of rights—he said truthfully that he had always favored it under the right circumstances. What is significant is the time he chose to move for a bill of rights, the kinds of rights protected, and the form the Bill of Rights took.

> I will own that I never considered this provision [of a bill of rights] so essential to the Federal Constitution as to make it improper to ratify it, until such an amendment was added; at the same time, I always conceived, that in a certain form, and to a certain extent, such a provision was neither improper nor altogether useless.[41]

Jefferson repeatedly described the kinds of protection he wanted in terms like the following: "a bill of rights providing clearly and without the aid of sophisms for freedom of religion, freedom of press, protection against standing armies, restriction against monopolies, the eternal and unremitting force of the habeas corpus laws, and trials by jury in all matters of fact triable by the law of the land and not by the law of Nations."[42] Three of these amounted to substantial restrictions on the power of government to act—the restrictions on monopolies, standing armies, and the suspension of habeas corpus; Jefferson clearly thought that they were vital barriers against governmental tyranny. It is equally clear that Madison consistently opposed all such amendments as obstacles to effective government. He did not include them in his original proposals (though there had been such proposals from the state ratifying conventions), and he and the Federalist majority beat down all attempts to secure such amendments.

There is, moreover, a deeper stratum in Madison's concern to prevent bills of rights from inhibiting government. The Antifederalists' advocacy of a bill of rights was concerned with more than specific protections; their overriding concern here was to make sure that government was rooted firmly in natural rights and justice. One of the confusions to the modern ear in the debate over the Bill of Rights and in the language of the old state bills of rights is the jumbling together of natural rights, civil rights, basic principles of justice, maxims of government, and specific legal protections. The state bills of rights were full of "oughts" and general principles. The Virginia Declaration of Rights of 1776 provides, for example: "That all men are by nature equally free and independent, and have certain inherent rights, of which, when they enter into a state of society, they cannot, by any compact deprive or divest their posterity; namely, the enjoyment of life and liberty, with the means of acquiring and possessing property, and pursuing and obtaining happiness and safety." Again, "Government is, or ought to be, instituted for the common benefit, protection, and security of the people, nation or community." The legislative and executive powers "should be separate and distinct from the judiciary"; "elections . . . ought to be free"; jury trial in civil cases "is preferable to any other, and ought to be held sacred."

Bills of rights were often described by their advocates as having as their purpose "to secure to every member of society those unalienable rights which ought not to be given up to any government."[43] Yet bills of rights, as we know them today, do not protect natural rights. And there seems to be something empty in the declarations of natural rights in a Constitution. That was the Federalist view. Thus, the acerbic Dr. Rush praised the framers for not disgracing the Constitution with a bill of rights: "As we enjoy all our natural rights from a pre-occupancy, antecedent to the social state," it would be "absurd to frame a formal declaration that our natural rights are acquired from ourselves."[44] The Antifederalists insisted, on the contrary, that the main purpose of a bill of rights is to provide an explicit set of standards in terms of which a government can be judged and, when necessary, resisted. A good bill of rights is a book in which a people can read the fundamental principles of their political being. "Those rights characterize the man, essentially the true republican, the citizen of this continent; their enumeration, in head of the new constitution, can inspire and conserve the affection for the native country, they will be the first lesson of the young citizens becoming men, to sustain the dignity of their being. . . . "[45] This is what explains the affirmation of natural rights, the "oughts," the unenforceable generality of the state bills of rights and of many of the Antifederalists' proposals. In Patrick Henry's words:

> There are certain maxims by which every wise and enlightened people will regulate their conduct. There are certain political maxims which no free people ought ever to abandon—maxims of which the observance is essential to the security of happiness. . . . We have one, sir, *that all men are by nature free and independent, and have certain inherent rights, of which, when they enter into society, they cannot by any compact deprive or divest their posterity.* We have a set of maxims of the same spirit, which must be beloved by every friend to liberty, to virtue, to mankind: our bill of rights contains those admirable maxims.[46]

This was the reason that the state bills of rights preceded their constitutions and could be described as the foundation of government. Edmund Randolph put it as well as anyone in his comment on the Virginia bill of rights:

> In the formation of this bill of rights two objectives were contemplated: one, that the legislature should not in their acts violate any of those cannons [sic]; the other, that in all the revolutions of time, of human opinion, and of government, a perpetual standard should be erected around which the people might rally, and by a notorious record be forever admonished to be watchful, firm and virtuous. The corner stone being thus laid, a constitution, delegating portions of power to different organs under certain modifications, was of course to be raised upon it.[47]

The problem with a bill of rights as a "perpetual standard" or a set of maxims to which people might rally is that it may tend to undermine stable and effective government. The Virginia Declaration of Rights asserted that free government depends on "a frequent recurrence to fundamental principles." The Federalists doubted that. Recurrence to first principles does not substitute for well-constituted and effective government. In some cases, it may interfere. Does a constant emphasis on unalienable natural rights foster good citizenship or a sense of community? Does a constant emphasis on popular sovereignty foster responsible government? Does a constant emphasis on a right to abolish government foster the kind of popular support that any government needs? The Federalists did not doubt that these first principles are true, that they may be resorted to, that they provide the ultimate source and justification of government. The problem is that these principles, while true, can also endanger government. Even rational and well-constituted governments need and deserve a presumption of legitimacy and permanence.[48] A bill of rights that presses these first principles to the fore tends to deprive government of that presumption.

For this reason, I think, Madison drastically limited the kind of standard-setting, maxim-describing, teaching function of bills of rights that the Antifederalists thought so important. In the hands of Madison and the majority of the First Congress, the Bill of Rights became what it is today: not the broad principles establishing the ends and limits of government, not "maxims" to be learned and looked up to by generations of Americans, not statements of those first principles to which a healthy people should, according to the Virginia Declaration of Rights, frequently resort; but specific protections of traditional civil rights.

With two exceptions, all the "oughts," all the statements of general principle, were excluded from Madison's original proposals—and these two were themselves eliminated before the House of Representatives finished its work. One of Madison's amendments would have declared that the powers delegated by the Constitution "are appropriated to the departments to which they are respectively distributed" so that no department shall exercise powers vested in another.[49] This was rather weakly defended by Madison in the House, where it was accepted; but it was rejected by the Senate, and no one seems to have regretted its loss. The second and most important residue of the old maxims was Madison's first proposal, which was a statement that all power derives from the people, that government ought to be instituted for the benefit of the people, and that the people have a right to change the government when they find it adverse or inadequate to its purposes.[50] This proposal was later reduced by a committee (on which Madison sat) to a brief and ill-fitting preface to the preamble ( "Government being intended for the benefit of the people, and the rightful establishment thereof being derived from their authority alone. We the People of the United States. . . ."). It was finally dropped altogether as a result of the acceptance of Sherman's proposal to have the amendments added at the end of the Constitution. The separation of powers amendment was to be given a separate article of its own, a clear breach of the economy of the Constitution; yet there was no other place for it. Even more striking is the awkward placing of Madison's first proposal prior to the preamble and the intolerable grammatical cumbersomeness of the Committee of Eleven version. Both these drafting inelegancies derived from Madison's determination to fit all of the amendments into the existing text of the Constitution.

Virtually, all the advocates of a bill of rights assumed that it should come at the head of the Constitution; Madison wanted it in the body; it came finally at the tail.[51] Madison's argument was that "there is a neatness and propriety in incorporating the amendments into the Constitution itself; in that case the system will remain uniform and entire. . . . " He wanted to avoid a form that would emphasize the *distinction*, common in the states, between the Constitution and the Bill of Rights. On the other hand, Roger Sherman, who was far from keen on having amendments at all, argued that to try to interweave the amendments with the Constitution was to mix brass, iron, and clay; "The Constitution is the act of the people and ought to remain entire." George Clymer supported Sherman; the amendments should be kept separate so that the Constitution "would remain a monument to justify those who made it; by a comparison the world would discover the perfection of the original and the superfluity of the amendments." Madison sought to secure his amendments against the possibility of their being held merely redundant and ineffective; he wanted them to "stand upon as good a foundation as the original work." When he said that a separate set of amendments would "create unfavourable comparisons," he was concerned to avoid a denigration of the amendments. But neither did he wish to elevate them to a distinct, primary position. His proposed form was designed to secure protection for the most widely agreed rights that would be both authoritative and inconspicuous. Sherman had his way, for reasons that do not fully emerge from the report of the debate. Ironically, the result seems to have been exactly the opposite of what Sherman intended, and yet to have gone beyond what Madison wanted. Separate listing of the first ten amendments has elevated rather than weakened their status. The over-all result is a Bill of Rights that is much less than the broad, preambular statement of basic principles that the enthusiastic proponents of bills of rights had in mind. At the same time it is—or has in this century become—rather more significant (not less, as Sherman and his friends wanted) than scattered protections of individual rights inserted into the Constitution would have been.

What can we say in conclusion in answer to our original questions? What is the significance of the absence of a bill of rights from the original Constitution and of its subsequent addition?

First, the basic justification for the absence of a bill of rights was that the main business of a free people is to establish and conduct good government; that is where the security of freedom must be sought. For the Americans in the 1870s, still warm with the ultimate truths of natural rights and revolution, the rhetoric of bills of rights might serve as a delusive substitute for the hard tasks of self-government.

Yet, second, bills of rights are an appropriate second step. Governments do tend to abuse their powers; and while the main protections are to be found in representation and social and political checks, a bill of rights can provide useful supplemental security.

Third, the initiative seized by Madison in the First Congress enabled the Federalists to complete their ratification victory by using amendments to better secure individual rights as the vehicle for decisively (if not finally) laying to rest the major Antifederal objections to the powers of the general government.

Fourth, the traditional notion of a bill of rights was drastically narrowed by largely eliminating the usual declarations of first principles, frequent resort to which Madison thought caused serious harm to government by disturbing that healthy crust of prejudice needed to support even the most rational government.

At the same time, however, and finally, the civil rights that were secured by the new Bill of Rights were limited and defined enough to be capable of effective (though not unproblematical) enforcement. The oft-described transformation of the moralistic "ought nots" of the old bills of rights into the legal "shall nots" of the United States Bill of Rights *is* a true and important part of the story. But I hope it is now clear that that transformation was possible only as a result of a drastic narrowing and lowering deliberately intended to secure the central place for the establishment and conduct of free government as the main business of a free people.

Yet there is still in our Bill of Rights an echo of the earlier declarations of natural rights and maxims of well-constituted free governments. This is especially true of the First Amendment, which might be described as a statement in matter-of-fact legal form of the great end of free government, to secure the private sphere, and the great means for preserving such a government, to foster an alert and enlightened citizenry. In the form of a protection of civil liberties, then, the First Amendment echoes the great principles of natural liberty and free government that played so large a role in the state bills of rights.[52] The preamble contains a similar echo of the basic principle of human equality and popular sovereignty. The Bill of Rights provides a fitting close to the parenthesis around the Constitution that the preamble opens. But the substance is a design of government with powers to act and a structure arranged to make it act wisely and responsibly. It is in that design, not in its preamble or its epilogue, that the security of American civil and political liberty lies.

### Notes

1. *The Bill of Rights: Its Origin and Meaning* (Indianapolis: The Bobbs Merrill Co., 1965), p. 46.
2. (Chapel Hill: University of North Carolina Press, 1955), p. 125.
3. Bernard Schwartz, *The Bill of Rights: A Documentary History* (New York: Chelsea House Publishers, 1971), p. 527.
4. *The Birth of the Bill of Rights*, p. v.
5. Jonathan Elliot, ed., *Debates in the Several State Conventions on the Adoption of the Federal Constitution*, II, 122–23, 177.
6. See below, note 10.
7. Letter to George Eve, 2 January 1789, Gaillard Hunt, ed., *The Writings of James Madison* (New York: G. P. Putnam's Sons, 1904), V, 320.
8. *The Debates and Proceedings of the Congress of the United States* (Washington, 1834), I, 433.
9. Ibid., p. 432.
10. Amendments were proposed (1) to insure at least one representative for each thirty thousand people until the size of the House should reach a certain limit, when the proportion would be reduced; and (2) to make increases in the salaries of congressmen apply only after the next election of representatives. Versions of these two amendments were included in the twelve amendments proposed by the Congress, but failed to be ratified by a sufficient number of states.
11. Ibid., p. 441.
12. Ibid., p. 755.
13. Ibid., pp. 745, 775.
14. 13 January 1788, Isaac Leake, *Memoir of the Life and Times of General John Lamb* (Albany: J. Munsell, 1850), p. 310.
15. Letter to Thomas Jefferson, 29 March 1789, Hunt, ed., V, 335, see *Debates of the Congress of the United States*, I, 432–33.
16. Ibid., p. 746.
17. Ibid., p. 433.
18. 2 September 1789, *The Letters and Papers of Edmund Pendleton, 1734–1803*, ed. David John Mays (Charlottesville: University Press of Virginia, 1967), II, 558.
19. One of the arguments made by the Federalists was that specific restrictions might imply powers not intended to be granted and that a listing of powers might endanger rights not listed. There was enough plausibility in this argument to lead the First Congress to add and the states to ratify what is now the Ninth Amendment.
20. John B. McMaster and Frederick Stone, *Pennsylvania and the Federal Constitution* (Lancaster: Historical Society, Penna., 1888), pp. 143–44.
21. *Debates of the Congress of the United States*, vol. I, 436, 761, 767–68.
22. Paul Leicester Ford, *Pamphlets on the Constitution* (Brooklyn, N.Y., 1888), p. 360.

23. *Federalist*, no. 84. "It would be quite as significant to declare that government ought to be free, that taxes ought not to be excessive, etc., as that the liberty of the press ought not to be restrained." The state bills of rights did in fact contain many such "ought" statements which were intended to foster that "spirit of the people" on which Hamilton depends.

24. "Essay by A Farmer," *Maryland Gazette,* 15 February 1788.

25. Essay by "Aristides," *Maryland Journal and Baltimore Advertiser,* 4 March 1788.

26. Theophilus Parsons in the Massachusetts ratifying convention, Elliot, ed., II, 162.

27. 6 Cranch 87, 143 (1810).

28. 3 Dallas 386, 387 (1798).

29. *Palko* v. *Connecticut,* 302 U.S. 319, (1937).

30. *Federalist,* no. 84.

31. McMaster and Stone, p. 252.

32. Essay by "Atticus," *Boston Independent Chronicle,* 28 November 1787.

33. Elliot, ed., III, 448.

34. *Debates of the Congress of the United States,* I, 436.

35. Letter to George Eve, 2 January 1789, Hunt, ed., V, 318.

36. Letter to James Madison, 15 March 1789, Julian Boyd, ed., *The Papers of Thomas Jefferson* (Princeton: Princeton University Press, 1958), XIV, 660.

37. *Federalist,* no. 63.

38. Ford, pp. 359–60.

39. Elliot, ed., III, 37.

40. The main letters in this exchange are Madison to Jefferson, 24 October 1787, 17 October 1788, 8 December 1788; and Jefferson to Madison, 20 December 1787, 31 July 1788, 15 March 1789. These are conveniently available in Boyd, ed., XII–XIV, and in Schwartz.

41. *Debates of the Congress of the United States,* I, 436.

42. Jefferson to Madison, 20 December 1787, Boyd, ed., XII, p. 440.

43. Elliot, ed., IV, 137.

44. McMaster and Stone, p. 295.

45. *Virginia Independent Chronicle,* 25 June 1788. See *An Additional Number of Letters from the Federal Farmer to the Republican* (New York, 1788), p. 144.

46. Elliot, ed., III, 137; see essay by "A Delegate" in *Virginia Independent Chronicle,* 18 June, 25 June 1787.

47. Schwartz, p. 249.

48. See *Federalist,* no. 49.

49. *Debates of the Congress of the United States,* I, 435–36.

50. Ibid., pp. 433–34. Already this proposal significantly modified the language of the Virginia Declaration of Rights and the proposal of the Virginia convention, from which it was drawn, in the direction of supporting government. It does not begin, as the earlier versions do, with any declarations of natural rights of individuals; Madison's beginning point is already a society. The "inherent rights of which man cannot be divested," of the Virginia Declaration of Rights, are here converted into "benefits of the people" for the sake of which government is instituted. The right "to reform, alter or abolish government" (in the Virginia Declaration of Rights) or the rejection of the "slavish doctrine of non-resistance" (in the proposals of the Virginia ratifying convention) is moderated to a right to "reform or change government."

51. This debate appears in *Debates of the Congress of the United States,* I, 707–17.

52. It is of course significant in this connection that the First Amendment is addressed to Congress (the structure of the Bill of Rights is provided by the traditional legislative, executive, judicial sequence) and that for that reason, and because of the breadth of its terms, its interpretation and enforcement are unusually problematical.

## The Private I:
## Some Reflections on Privacy and the Constitution

Philip B. Kurland

This is the third of the Nora and Edward Ryerson Lectures. The Lecture, as President Wilson has told you, honors a member of the faculty by asking him to speak to his peers and superiors about a subject with which he purports to be familiar. And I have received no greater honor. But as George Stigler might have told me, had I asked: there is no such thing as a free honor. It has to be earned and in this case, according to mandate of the lectureship, the honor is to be earned by making "a significant statement about [the lecturer's] most important work or interests."

That charge rested easily on the shoulders of my predecessors. Professors Franklin and Chandrasekhar, both Distinguished Service Professors at this University, who, between them, probably have as many honorary degrees as there are universities in this country. The historian and the astronomer and astrophysicist, between them, take all knowledge for their province. All the past belongs to Franklin, and the future, which lies in the stars, is the realm of Chandrasekhar. That leaves me only the present, and as Shakespeare once put it: "Past and to become seem best; things present worst."[1]

The audience will surely find what I am about to say neither "significant" nor "important." All that I hope to achieve here is to reveal some things that I am thinking, or think I am thinking, about a subject that is frequently the object of Supreme Court judgments. I would invoke three excuses for failing to afford you the "important" or the "significant."

The first is Mr. Justice Holmes's justification for banality, that "at this time we need education in the obvious more than investigation of the obscure."[2]

The second excuse derives from the nature of the medium. For a lecture, like an essay, at best, must be "tentative, reflective, suggestive, contradictory, and incomplete." Its vindication, if any, depends on whether it adequately reflects "the perversities and complexities" of the subject.[3] Its function is to invite thought, not to foreclose it.

And my third excuse is to be found in reminding you of Richard Steele's catechism on lawyers: "What's the first excellence in a lawyer? Tautology. What the second? Tautology. What the third? Tautology."[4]

I expect that I have put off the moment of truth about as long as I can. Let me tell you then what my subject is. The title of this paper was concocted some months ago, long before the paper was composed. I selected the title because it would allow almost anything that I could find to say to fit the rubric. My subtitle is an afterthought and not much less opaque. It is: "Some Reflections on Privacy and the Constitution." And I must emphasize that I propose to address only constitutional aspects of privacy, a subject both more arcane and less learned than the sociological, psychological, or political treatments that have been given the subject of privacy by those more erudite than I.[5]

The problem of privacy in politico-legal terms is a part of, if it does not exceed, the basic controversy that has troubled this nation from the beginning. It is concerned essentially with the competing interests of society, usually acting through government, on the one hand, and the individual acting on his own, on the other. But in this context, society is not merely its formalized organization, that is, government, but all of its components and institutions, private as well as public. The problem presented by the right to privacy is to establish the protection of the individual against intrusion on his freedom of action, freedom of choice, and freedom of thought, not only by government, but by others, particularly by others combined in association to multiply the power—physical, economic, moral—that would be available to an individual.

The task of protecting one individual's privacy against invasion by another individual or group is assigned to the government. The problem of protecting an individual's privacy against invasion by the government is also, *faute de mieux*, assigned to the government. And so the greatest, but not the exclusive, problem of privacy is the question how to contain the government which is its own regulator. Here, as elsewhere, we have turned to the courts to establish some protections by purporting to interpret the Constitution. All branches of all government, state and federal, must abide the constitutional limitations on their authority. When the states or the national executive or legislature violate the Constitution, appeal is to the courts. When the federal courts themselves violate the Constitution, the only appeal is to public opinion.

For many, the Constitution is a text that should be construed like a deed of real property or at least like a contract. Strict construction has been the rhetorical demand of such disparate practitioners of the black art of government as Mr. Justice Hugo Black, Senator Sam J. Ervin, and President Richard M. Nixon. But strict constructionists are only those who are gifted to see the true meaning of the exalted words of the Constitution, in the same way that it was given to Calvin and Luther to know that Rome was in error. It is not so much a matter of proof as it is a matter of faith or revelation.

For some, strict construction means not that the original words of the Constitution are definitive but only that the first construction given those words by the Supreme Court is definitive. Thus, precedents are to be deemed unchangeable except by the process of amendment provided in the Constitution itself. There are other strict constructionists—most of them—who would require adherence only to those precedents and judgments that conform to their personal predilections.

In whatever form, strict construction has never been anything more than a rhetorical tool. In part, this is due to the fact that many of the phrases of the Constitution do not lend themselves to simplistic readings. The document is not a series of rules—even abstract rules. It always has been read—and has to be read—in terms of the constantly changing political, social, and economic conditions that give rise to the issues that come before the Court. Constitutional limitations, like all law, are a reflection of the needs of a society. The law does not create the society, the society creates the law.

The arcane aspect of American constitutional law, then, derives from the fact that the Constitution is largely a document of the imagination but is always treated as if it were real. And over a period of time it has become the imagination of the Justices of the Supreme Court that has come to be considered definitive in the changing construction of words that have remained constant. And this is neither more nor less true of the so-called constitutional doctrine of privacy, of which I speak, than of other parts of an instrument that was framed as a fundamental and living charter of government.

Once the authority for ultimate construction of the meaning of the Constitution was conceded to the courts, as it seems to have been, the peculiarities of the common-law system of adjudication affords the only restraints on the Court's freedom of choice among competing arguments as to the appropriate reading of the basic document. And this restraint, as Chief Justice Stone long ago told us, is essentially self-restraint.[6] But the common-law process means, among other things, that the rule pronounced by a court is not an abstract rule but one composed to resolve a particular case or controversy. It may be applied in future cases that fall within its ambit, but it is not designed as a general rule of conduct for all within the national realm. Although the Justices do not acknowledge or always realize that the judicial approach necessitates the resolution of a particular dispute between particular litigants, the constitutional requirement in Article III of a case or controversy—an adversary judicial proceeding—does impose restrictions on judicial behavior that are, more or less, controlling.

Thus, if the Court has been appropriately labelled "a continuing constitutional convention," its method of doing business is different from those of an actual constitutional convention. It is not a representative body; it is not politically responsible to any constituency. If we cannot demand of the Supreme Court a "true" reading of the Constitution, or even a consistent one, we have a right to a reasoned one.

The concept of a constitutional right of privacy remains largely undefined. There are at least three facets that have been partially revealed, but their form and shape remain to be fully ascertained. The first is the right of the individual to be free in his private affairs from governmental surveillance and intrusion. The second is the right of an individual not to have his private affairs made public by the government. The third is the right of an individual to be free in action, thought, experience, and belief from governmental compulsion. Obviously, none of these rights as so stated is absolute. And the questions addressed by the law are to what degree these constitutional rights may or must be conditioned.

While the rights to be free from governmental surveillance and publicity and command are problems of constitutional law, they are also subject to protection by legislative action, by statutes which reflect the judgment of the lawmakers rather than the compulsion of the Constitution. Moreover, there may be rights to be free of surveillance and publicity and command by others than governmental actors. The legislative and common-law rights protecting against imposition by nongovernmental actions fall outside the scope of this effort, although the principles that may guide the formation of appropriate law are not irrelevant to the constitutional rights of privacy.

The origins of the constitutional doctrine of privacy are not difficult to discover. At least for a lawyer, they are to be found in two specific judicial controversies that preceded our Constitution and even the Declaration of Independence. They were encapsulated by Mr. Justice Frankfurter in 1946:

> Indeed, so unhappy was the experience with police search for papers and articles "in home or office" . . . that it was once maintained that no search and seizure is valid. To Lord Coke has been attributed the proposition that warrants could not be secured even for stolen property. . . . Under early English doctrine even

search warrants by appropriate authority could issue only for stolen goods. . . .
Certainly warrants lacking strict particularity as to location to be searched or
articles to be seized were deemed obnoxious. . . . An attempt to exceed these
narrow limits called forth the enduring judgment of Lord Camden in *Entick* v.
*Carrington* . . . in favor of freedom against police intrusions. And when appeal
to the colonial courts on behalf of these requisite safeguards for the liberty of
the people failed . . . a higher tribunal resolved the issue. The familiar comment
of John Adams on Otis' argument in *Paxton's* case can never become stale:
"American independence was then and there born; the seeds of patriots and
heroes were then and there sown, to defend the vigorous youth, the *non sine diis
animus infans*. Every man of a crowded audience appeared to go away, as I did,
ready to take arms against writs of assistance. Then and there was the first
scene of the first act of opposition to the arbitrary claims of Great Britain. Then
and there the child Independence was born. In fifteen years, namely 1776, he
grew up to manhood and declared himself free."[7]

In *Paxton's* case in the Superior Court of the Colony of Massachusetts, with
the soon to become infamous Thomas Hutchinson presiding, the judiciary held that
writs of assistance, general warrants that specified neither place to be searched nor
persons or goods to be seized, were valid against the colonial merchant smugglers'—
whom we now call "patriots"—claim for freedom. The principle which caught the
fancy of the colonial audience and particularly the merchant smugglers was not that
announced in the court, but that put forth by their counsel, James Otis, as reported
by John Adams:

> This writ is against the fundamental principles of English law. . . . Only for
> felonies may an officer break and enter—and then only by special not general
> warrant. For general warrants there is only the precedent of the Star Chamber
> under the Stuarts.
>
> An act against the Constitution is void. An act against general equity is
> void. If an act of Parliament should be passed in the very words of this petition
> for writs of assistance, it would be void.[8]

Obviously then—and perhaps even now—like beauty, constitutional principles lie in
the eyes of the beholder.

*Entick* v. *Carrington*,[9] the decision at Common Pleas in England, by a good
friend of the American colonists, Lord Camden, later reached a conclusion opposite
to that of the Massachusetts court. Following upon successful attacks on general
warrants by Wilkes, also an ally of the Americans in the Revolutionary period, Lord
Camden in *Entick* outlawed general warrants unauthorized by legislation where the
objective of the search was not smuggled goods but seditious libel. His primary reliance
was on the sacred rights of property:

> The great end, for which men entered into society, was to secure their property.
> That right is preserved sacred and incommunicable in all instances, where it has
> not been taken away or abridged by some public law for the good of the
> whole. . . .
>
> Papers are the owner's goods and chattels; they are his dearest property;
> and are so far from enduring a seizure, that they will hardly bear an inspection;
> and though the eye cannot by the laws of England be guilty of a trespass, yet
> where private papers are removed and carried away, the secret nature of those

goods will be an aggravation of the trespass, and demand more considerable damages in that respect. Where is the written law that gives any magistrate such a power? I can safely answer, there is none; and therefore it is too much for us without such authority to pronounce a practice legal, which would be subversive of all the comforts of society. . . .[10]

Both Otis's argument in *Paxton* and the argument for Wilkes resorted to appeals to "the constitution." Mr. Recorder Eyre asserted: "No legal authority [exists], in the present case, to justify the action. No precedents, no legal determinations, not an act of parliament itself, is sufficient to warrant any proceeding contrary to the spirit of the constitution."[11] Lord Camden refused to go so far. His proposition was simply that if the acts of the ministers in issuing and effecting a general warrant were valid, it would be authorized by law. "If it is law, it will be found in our books. If it is not to be found there, it is not the law."[12]

The English courts then and still are committed to legislative supremacy rather than judicial supremacy as the prime rule of their constitution. The constitutional principle then, as now, was stated in Dicey: "For liberty of the individual is nothing more than the residue of his conduct which remains unfettered by law."[13]

Events take on a different image when viewed under the lens of time. It was fifty years after *Paxton's* case that Adams recorded the observation that in Otis's arguments against the writs of assistance "the child Independence was born." If this were true in fact, it is passing strange that there was no reference in the Declaration of Independence, in the composition of which Adams had a hand, to the abuses of general warrants. The ban on general warrants did, however, show up in Madison's bill of rights and became the Fourth Amendment to the American Constitution, with this language:

The right of the people to be secure in their persons, houses, papers, and effects, against unreasonable searches and seizures, shall not be violated, and no Warrants shall issue, but upon probable cause, supported by Oath or affirmation, and particularly describing the place to be searched, and the persons or things to be seized.

In its language, the Amendment, which closely followed those already in effect in the States of the new nation, did little more than outlaw the general warrant which, after all, was the issue contested in *Paxton, Wilkes,* and *Entick.* But courts also behave in retrospect as Adams did in his romantic reading of *Paxton's* case. And toward the end of the nineteenth century, in a landmark case, *Boyd* v. *United States,*[14] the Court invalidated a federal statute calling for production of private books, invoices, and papers. Mr. Justice Bradley enlarged upon *Entick* v. *Carrington:*

The principles laid down in this opinion affect the very essence of constitutional liberty and security. They reach farther than the concrete form of the case then before the court, with its adventitious circumstances; they apply to all invasions on the part of the government and its employes of the sanctity of a man's home and the privacies of life. It is not the breaking of his doors, and the rummaging of his drawers, that constitutes the essence of the offense; but it is the invasion of his indefeasible right of personal security, personal liberty and private property, where that right has never been forfeited by his conviction of some public offense.[15]

In 1928 Mr. Justice Brandeis dissented from a judgment of the Supreme Court that wiretapping did not violate the Fourth Amendment.[16] In dissent, Bradeis offered the broadest reading of the right of the people to be free from government snooping. He wrote there that the authors of the Constitution

> recognized the significance of man's spiritual nature, of his feelings and of his intellect. They knew that only a part of the pain, pleasure, and satisfactions of life are to be found in material things. They sought to protect Americans in their beliefs, their thoughts, their emotions and their sensations.[17]

And then he went on to state his conception of the limits on governmental interference:

> [The authors of the Constitution] conferred, as against the Government, the right to be let alone—the most comprehensive of rights and the right most valued by civilized men.[18]

One of my more perspicacious students suggested that were we to translate Brandeis's "right to be let alone" into French, it might come out "laissez faire." But laissez faire had already taken on a different connotation—or at least a different clientele—from that which Brandeis intended. In *Olmstead,* Brandeis was speaking of the rights of individuals, not business entities. His first use of this phrase—"the right to be let alone"—could be found in what is always described as a seminal article he had written as a young lawyer, not on the right to be free from government inhibition, but on the right to be free from newspaper publicity, the publication by nongovernment agencies of matters of private concern. Although Brandeis's language dates from 1890, it is equally apposite today. Indeed, that is the problem. We have not advanced very much on the front of the private right of privacy any more than we have on the front of the public right of privacy. The early Brandeis paper opened this way:

> . . . the question whether our law will recognize and protect the right to privacy in this and in other respects must soon become before the courts for consideration.
>
> Of the desirability—indeed of the necessity—of some such protection, there can, it is believed, be no doubt. The press is overstepping in every direction the obvious bounds of propriety and of decency. Gossip is no longer the resource of the idle and of the vicious, but has become a trade, which is pursued with industry as well as effrontery. To satisfy a prurient taste the details of sexual relations are spread broadcast in the columns of the daily papers. To occupy the indolent, column upon column is filled with idle gossip, which can only be procured by intrusion upon the domestic circle. The intensity and complexity of life, attendant upon advancing civilization, have rendered necessary some retreat from the world, and man, under the refining influence of culture, has become more sensitive to publicity, so that solitude and privacy become more essential to the individual; but modern enterprise and invention, through invasions upon his privacy, subjected him to mental pain and distress, far greater than could be inflicted by mere bodily injury. Nor is the harm wrought by such invasions confined to the suffering of those who may be made the subjects of journalistic or other enterprise. In this, as in other branches of commerce, the supply creates the demand.

Each crop of unseemly gossip, thus harvested, becomes the seed of more, and, in direct proportion to its circulation, results in a lowering of societal standards and morality. Even gossip apparently harmless, when widely and persistently circulated, is potent for evil. It both belittles and perverts. It belittles by inverting the relative importance of things, thus dwarfing the thoughts and aspirations of a people. When personal gossip attains the dignity of print, and crowds the space available for matters of real interest to the community, what wonder that the ignorant and thoughtless mistake its relative importance. Easy of comprehension, appealing to that weak side of human nature which is never wholly cast aside by the misfortunes and frailties of our neighbors, no one can be surprised that it usurps the place of interest in brains capable of other things. Triviality destroys at once robustness of thought and delicacy of feeling. No enthusiasm can flourish, no generous impulse can survive under its blighting influence.[19]

The right of privacy from nongovernmental intrusion has never flourished, despite Brandeis's hopes and anticipation.[20] This has been due in no small part to the public commitment to voyeurism revealed not only in the news stories but in the newspaper columns giving advice to the woebegone and to the ill and in the gossip columns. (Even the mighty *New York Times* has succumbed to publishing gossip columns.) To a greater degree, however, the doctrine has failed because of judicial expansion of the concept of freedom of the press. The Court has rightly perceived that the Constitution provides for a free press but makes no demands for a responsible press. And in this case freedom and responsibility are antonyms. The press itself, which rejects privacy of others, however, is outraged at the refusal to accord it privacy in its own affairs. Its claim for constitutional protection against the necessity to reveal sources of its news stories was effectively denied—with good reasons—by the Supreme Court.[21]

But I have strayed from my subject. Brandeis's position in *Olmstead* in 1928, that wiretapping constitutes the same kind of invasion of privacy as does the physical entry, search, and seizure of the common law, became the law by Supreme Court decision in 1967:

We conclude that the underpinnings of *Olmstead* and *Goldman* have been so eroded by our subsequent decisions that the "trespass" doctrine there enunciated can no longer be regarded as controlling. The Government's activities in electronically listening to and recording the petitioner's words violated the privacy upon which he justifiably relied while using the telephone booth and thus constituted a "search and seizure" within the meaning of the Fourth Amendment. The fact that the electronic device employed to achieve that end did not happen to penetrate the wall of the booth can have no constitutional significance.[22]

It should be seen, then, that two hundred years of litigation did not really advance the privacy doctrine much beyond the limits originally afforded by the Court of Common Pleas in *Entick* v. *Carrington* in 1765, except that a "taking" by eye or ear was also forbidden by the Fourth Amendment. All that *Katz* provided was an equation between electronic invasion and physical invasion. The underlying concepts were stated by Lord Camden both in terms of trespass, as already quoted,[23] and in terms that accord more with our Fifth Amendment than our Fourth:

It is very certain, that the law obligeth no man to accuse himself; because the necessary means of compelling self-accusation, falling upon the innocent as well as the guilty, would be both cruel and unjust; and it should seem that search for evidence is disallowed upon the same principle. There too the innocent would be confounded with the guilty.[24]

The constitutional law of privacy, deriving from the Fourth and Fifth Amendments, had generally, therefore, afforded little scope for the promulgation of the Brandeisian doctrine of a right to be let alone. The fact is that the search and seizure protections have primarily served those guilty of crime as a means for evading punishment. In some measure that is because, until recently, the Fourth Amendment has not been seen as a proper predicate for private suit against wrongdoing officials who have engaged in such gross forms of invasion of privacy as would constitute illegal searches and seizures.[25] At the same time, the Court has refused relief when a plaintiff's claim is that he had been subjected to "mere surveillance" by the military.[26] But the Fourth Amendment has been utilized essentially by criminal defendants seeking to exclude from evidence those matters secured by invalid searches and seizures. The law on the subject is immense but technical. It rests on the dubious hypothesis that the police will be chastened by their inability to secure convictions where they have behaved improperly and, therefore, will abstain from such improper behavior not only against the guilty but, as Lord Camden said, against the innocent as well. Whether the "exclusionary rule" has been effective in this respect is a debated question. Most, however, will now concede that the police will be effectively chastened only by more direct means than protecting defendants against convictions. Mr. Justice Cardozo long ago stated the inadequacy of the exclusionary rule.[27] His analysis remains cogent, but ineffective. The Supreme Court has imposed the exclusionary rule on all the States.[28]

I don't mean to diminish the importance of the judicial applications of the Fourth Amendment. Anyone who has read Orwell's *1984* must be cognizant of the necessity for all possible restraints on governmental oversight of individual activity. As Mr. Justice Frankfurter stated in 1946:

> The course of decision in this Court has thus far jealously enforced the principle of a free society secured by the prohibition of unreasonable searches and seizures. Its safeguards are not to be worn away by a process of devitalizing interpretation. . . . It is not only under Nazi rule that police excesses are inimical to freedom. It is easy to make light of insistence on scrupulous regard for the safeguards of civil liberties when invoked on behalf of the unworthy. It is too easy. History bears testimony that by such disregard are the rights of liberty extinguished, heedlessly at first, then stealthily, and brazenly in the end.[29]

Judge Hand put the same proposition in these words: "Nor should we forget that what seems fair enough against a squalid huckster of bad liquor may take on a very different face, if used by a government determined to suppress political opposition under the guise of sedition."[30]

With the recent revelations about Plumbers and Watergate, and FBIs and Kings, and CIA covert activities—with vivid memories of Gestapo and Ogpu—the purpose of the Fourth Amendment is not abstract or amorphous but real and immediate. The present question is whether existent restraints are adequate. No, I would not demean the concept of the Fourth Amendment's barriers against search and seizure and wiretapping. But they rest on the slender reed of judicial refusal to authorize searches and seizures, or to condemn broad administrative and judicial subpoenas, and on the effectiveness of the exclusionary rule, at a time when almost any activity can be asserted to be criminal and justify a warrant and when the exclusionary rule is hardly a deterrent at all.

Government imposition on individuals, however, goes far beyond the improprieties covered by the judicial gloss on the Fourth Amendment. And a broader concept of privacy, such as that suggested by Brandeis, would have implications that would ward off that kind of totalitarianism for which the secret police and government surveillance are only means and not ends. If something more than trespass and self-crimination underlay the judgment in *Entick* v. *Carrington*, it was the fact that the writ was issued by a ministry that had created its own authority to do so, that the writ was returned to the ministry's own functionaries for determination of proper action against the person and materials seized. The executive—not the legislature—made its own rules and executed them. Kafka's *Trial* was hardly worse.

It should, however, be obvious that the problems of government administration have changed only in quantity and not in quality in the two centuries between English autocratic bureaucracies and American democratic bureaucracies. Once again—if not still—we are enmeshed by legislation without representation. Once again appointed government officials make the laws—by way of regulations and guidelines and executive orders, when not by simple ukase; once again the same agents determine the liability of individuals under the rules that they have created and the remedies that are to be exacted from the hapless object of their benignity. Usually, these days, the goal is accomplished with the assistance rather than the resistance of the judiciary.

A concept of privacy limited to the Fourth and Fifth Amendment privileges against search and seizure and self-crimination and preventing inappropriate publicity of information that it has commandeered offers little defense against ever-increasing government encroachment. But surely there is possibility in the Brandeisian notion of a right to be let alone. And there has been a recent flurry of opinions by the Supreme Court to suggest that the Brandeis concept might have some merit. In 1965, in a case called *Griswold* v. *Connecticut*,[31] the Supreme Court broke loose its privacy doctrine from Fourth and Fifth Amendment moorings. There was in the case no trespass on person or property, either literal or figurative; there was no issue of self-crimination; there was no real question of improper publicity. The question was about the capacity of the State of Connecticut to inhibit the conduct of its adult citizens by forbidding them the use of contraceptives. Not even the nine men in the marble palace could bring the case within the search-and-seizure canon. But, if not the Fourth Amendment, where? Ordinarily no Supreme Court Justice will openly pronounce the possibility that he is being totally creative of constitutional rights or that he is exercising judgment based on personal values. What the Justices seemed to believe, however—probably because they were all over forty and none had yet been converted by the precepts of Professor Marcuse and the Berkeley "free speech movement"—was that sexual intercourse, especially between married couples, was a private affair. And so, Mr. Justice Douglas, speaking for a majority, held that a ban on the use of contraceptives by married couples was an invasion of privacy that the Constitution could not condone. If one asked where in the Constitution such a doctrine of privacy might be found, the answer was that it would be found in the "penumbras" and "emanations" of various parts of the Bill of Rights:

> Various guarantees create zones of privacy. The right of association contained in the penumbras of the First Amendment is one, as we have seen. The Third Amendment in its prohibition against the quartering of soldiers "in any house" in time of peace without the consent of the owner is another facet of that privacy. The Fourth Amendment explicitly affirms the "right of the people to be secure in their persons, houses, papers, and effects against unreasonable searches and seizures." The Fifth Amendment in its Self-Incrimination Clause enables the citizen to create a zone of privacy which government may not force him to surrender to his detriment. The Ninth Amendment provides: "The enumeration in the Constitution of certain rights, shall not be construed to deny or disparage others retained by the people." . . . We have had many controversies over these penumbral rights of "privacy and repose." . . . These cases bear witness that the right of privacy which presses for recognition here is a legitimate one. The present case, then, concerns a relationship lying within the zone of privacy created by several fundamental constitutional guarantees. And it concerns a law which, in forbidding the use of contraceptives rather than regulating their manufacture or sale, seeks to achieve its goals by means having a maximum destructive impact upon that relationship. Such a law cannot stand in light of the familiar principle, so often applied by this Court, that a "governmental purpose to control or prevent activities constitutionally subject to state regulation may not be achieved by means which sweep unnecessarily broadly and thereby invade the area of protected freedom." . . . Would we allow the police to search the sacred precincts of marital bedrooms for telltale signs of the use of contraceptives? The very idea is repulsive to the notions of privacy surrounding the marriage relationship.
>
> We deal with a right of privacy older than the Bill of Rights—older than our political parties, older than our school system. Marriage is a coming together for better or for worse, hopefully enduring, and intimate to the degree of being sacred. The association promotes a way of life, not causes; a harmony in living, not political faiths; a bilateral loyalty, not commercial or social projects. Yet it is an association for as noble a purpose as any involved in our prior decisions.[32]

Mr. Justice Harlan's concurring opinion would have relied on the meaning implicit in the Fourteenth Amendment's—and thereby the Fifth Amendment's—prohibition against depriving any person of his life, liberty, or property without due process of law. His emphasis, too, was upon the sacred nature of the marital relationship. And like Chief Justice Warren and Justices Brennan and Goldberg, he would rule that where the government attempts to regulate such a valued right of privacy, it must justify its actions by what amounts to an almost insuperable burden of proof. And therein lies whatever hope there may be for a developing law of privacy, the transfer of the burden, as has occurred frequently in free speech and equal protection cases, from the individual to prove the irrationality of a statute to the state to prove the necessity for the statute.

An astute observer of the judicial process, Professor Paul Brest, has asked, "If the Constitution does not enact Herbert Spencer's *Social Statics,* does it enact John Stuart Mill's *On Liberty*(1859)?"[33] Brest was referring to Mill's "one very simple principle": "That the sole end to which mankind are warranted, individually or collectively, in interfering with the liberty of action of any of their number is self-protection"; that government may control the individual only "to prevent harm to others"; "His own good, either physical or moral, is not a sufficient warrant. . . . Over himself, over his own body and mind, the individual is sovereign."[34]

Brest's question was intended to be rhetorical. In the famous *Lochner* case, Holmes had told us that the Constitution did not incorporate Herbert Spencer's *Social Statics.*[35] I am arrogant enough to suggest that Holmes was wrong, that the Fourteenth Amendment, as read by the Court in the last third of the nineteenth century and for some time thereafter, did "enact Mr. Herbert Spencer's *Social Statics.*"[36] I should like to think that the Court would now incorporate Mill's *On Liberty,* but I have no hope. In part my lack of hope derives from subsequent decisions in this area, in part from the considerations I shall detail at more length very shortly.

The law in this area has not been dictated by principle or precedent. Mr. Justice Cardozo long ago described the ailment to which the Supreme Court has succumbed in the further development of the constitutional right of privacy. He wrote:

> A fertile source of perversion in constitutional theory is tyranny of labels. Out of the vague precepts of the Fourteenth Amendment a court frames a rule which is general in form, though it has been wrought under the pressue of particular situations. Forthwith another situation is placed under the rule because it is fitted to the words, though related faintly, if at all, to the reasons that brought the rule into existence.[37]

And so, despite the emphasis in *Griswold* on sacredness of marriage, the Court decided that an equally compelling situation for invoking the concept of privacy was afforded when the sexual intercourse that was inhibited by the state was that of unwed couples. The reasoning in the second case was set forth by Mr. Justice Brennan:

> It is true that in *Griswold* the right of privacy in question inhered in the marital relationship. Yet the marital couple is not an independent entity with a mind and heart of its own, but an association of two individuals each with a separate intellectual and emotional make-up. If the right of privacy means anything, it is the right of the *individual,* married or single, to be free from unwarranted governmental intrusion into matters so fundamentally affecting a person as the decision whether to bear or beget a child.[38]

The opinion thus contains a marked advance on the establishment of a doctrine, even as it marked a retreat from the rationalization that brought the doctrine into existence in the first place. Privacy is an attribute of the individual: his right "to be free from unwarranted . . . intrusion into matters [that] fundamentally affect a person." Perhaps it extends beyond the individual to the household, as our founding fathers might have thought. Indeed, it was thus that Jefferson spoke of privacy:

> Happiness, Jefferson too would insist, lies outside the public realm, "in the lap and love of my family, in the society of my neighbors and my books, in the wholesome occupation of my farms, and my affairs," in short, in the privacy of a home upon whose life the public has no claim.[39]

If the Declaration of Independence which we are so assiduously celebrating this year were a constitutional document, the basis for the doctrine of privacy might properly be found in the phrase "the pursuit of happiness."

Whether it is confined to individuals, as suggested in *Baird,* or extends to households, as originally stated in *Griswold,* it does not pertain to groups or organizations less limited than the family. There may be, as David Riesman has told us, a "lonely crowd," but it cannot be a "private" crowd.

Mr. Chief Justice Burger dissented in the *Baird* case, suggesting that the conclusion smacked of "substantive due process," that is, it was nothing more than the Justices substituting their judgment for the judgment of the legislature. And in the abortion cases, the next explication of the privacy doctrine—one more consistent with the Mill doctrines than with any other—Mr. Justice Stewart, joining the judgment of the Court, displayed an honesty of expression seldom indulged by members of the Court:

> So it was clear to me then, and it is equally clear to me now, that the *Griswold* decision can be rationally understood only as holding that the Connecticut statute substantively invaded the "liberty" that is protected by the Due Process Clause of the Fourteenth Amendment. As so understood *Griswold* stands as one in a long line of cases under the doctrine of substantive due process, and I now accept it as such.[40]

If, therefore, one looks for a home for a developing constitutional doctrine of privacy, it will most likely be found where Justices Harlan and Stewart have placed it: in the Due Process Clauses of the Fifth and Fourteenth Amendments.

Whether this particular orphan of constitutional adjudication will ever grow to maturity and find any home at all is more dubious. So far, its growth has been less than promising. Outside the realm of Fourth Amendment rights, the Court seems to have found a constitutionally protected privacy only with regard to sexual intercourse and the consequences thereof, such as abortion. And, it should be noted, in recent days the Court has refused to interfere—it has not, as the newspapers would have it, stamped its imprimatur—in a state law that makes a crime of sexual intercourse between consenting adults of the same sex.[41] Whether this portends a retreat even from the limited concessions to the Brandeis notion of the right to be let alone remains to be seen. Only one thing is certain and that is that there is no assurance that the Supreme Court will ever feel obliged to adhere to any of its precedents except those enlarging its own jurisdiction.

There is a flux in other areas of privacy adjudication. Whether a state may ever publish a list of alcoholics who should not be sold packaged liquors is unclear, but it is certain that it cannot do so without first affording a hearing to the person to be labelled a drunk.[42] On the other hand, it has been recently decided that a policeman is not precluded by civil rights laws or the Constitution from circulating a picture of a person accused but never convicted of shoplifting.[43]

The future of any constitutional privacy doctrine is in grave doubt. My own expectations are negative. For American constitutional law is, ultimately if not immediately, a consequence of the social conditions and values and needs and desires of the American people. What Holmes declared to be true of the common law in 1881 remains true of constitutional law today:

> The felt necessities of the time, the prevalent moral and political theories, intuitions of public policy, avowed or unconscious, even the prejudices which judges share with their fellow-men, have had a good deal more to do than the syllogism in determining the rules by which men should be governed.[44]

My own view is that the constitutional right of privacy, especially in Brandeis's sense of a right to be let alone, will always be a minimal and never a major force in constitutional law. ("What, *never*? Hardly ever!")*

There are two reasons for my conclusion, both of which require some explication. The first is that a constitutional concept of privacy is undefined and consequently confused with a great many other notions that are related but should not be identified with it, because such identification both distorts and demeans it. The second is that "the felt necessities of the time, the prevalent moral and political theories" are inconsistent with the Brandeis conception and are moving away from it rather than toward it.

The right of privacy is undefined, perhaps, because it is undefinable. Like the grand concepts of liberty and equality, privacy may be too large to be clearly identified. Indeed, privacy may be only another name for the freedom of the individual. Judge Learned Hand once essayed an attempt at definition of liberty. At the outset he rejected as unworthy the assurance that it means the avoidance of "license and anarchy on the one hand, and tyranny and despotism on the other."[45] He started, instead, with the proposition that "I think I am free when I can do what I want; this tiny protoplasmal center of radiant energy demands that alien impacts shall not thwart its insistences and its self-assertions."[46] He concluded:

> It is the faith that our collective fate in the end depends upon the irrepressible fertility of the individual, and the finality of what he chooses to call good. It is the faith that neither principalities, nor powers, nor things present, nor things to come, can rightfully suppress that fertility or deny that good. It is the faith in the indefectible significance of each one of us . . .[47]

Learned Hand was, however, a realist. And he recognized that the odds were heavy against "the possibility of the individual expression of life on the terms of him who has to live it."

> Liberty is so much latitude as the powerful choose to accord to the weak. So much perhaps has to be admitted for abstract statement; anything short of it appears to lead to inconsistencies. At least no other formula has been devised which will answer. If a community decides that some conduct is prejudicial to itself, and so decides by numbers sufficient to impose its will upon dissenters, I know of no principle which can stay its hand. . . .

*Gilbert and Sullivan, *H. M. S. Pinafore,* Act I.

And yet, so phrased, we should all agree, I think, that the whole substance of liberty has disappeared. It is intolerable to feel that we are each in the power of the conglomerate mass of Babbitts, whose intelligence we do not respect, and whose standards we may detest. . . . [T]here was a meaning in Jefferson's hatred of the interposition of collective pressure . . .[S]hall we not feel with him that it is monstrous to lay open the lives of each to whatever current notions of propriety may ordain.[48]

The essence of Brandeis's notion was that there were some areas of personal, individual conduct that were not subject to the kind of coercion that Hand was talking about. And the very notion of the national Constitution is that there are aspects of individual behavior that no government, federal or state, could subject to control. To the best of their not inconsiderable ability, the authors of the Constitution and the Bill of Rights detailed those areas. And among the guarantees was that contained in the Fifth Amendment, that no person shall be deprived of life, liberty, or property without due process of law.

There was an emphasis in the Massachusetts Declaration of Rights of 1780 that reinforces the notion of the right to be let alone. "It is essential to the preservation of the rights of every individual, his life, liberty, property, and character, that there be an impartial interpretation of the laws, and administration of justice."[49] The emphasis differs from the national constitution in the use of the word "individual," rather than "person," for it is to the individual that rights of privacy pertain, and "individual" might never have been translated, as the Supreme Court was to interpret "person," to include corporations.[50] And the individual and human nature of the rights were also emphasized by the addition to "life, liberty, and property" of the word "character," which might well be translated as "personality."

Sir Isaiah Berlin was also speaking about the individual, the human criterion of privacy, when he suggested that a controlling principle for the governance of society was that "there are frontiers not artifically drawn, within which men should be inviolable, these frontiers being defined in terms of rules so long and widely accepted that their observance has entered into the very conception of what is a human being."[51]And it is the idea of the uniqueness of the human quality that makes the concept of privacy so important.

The difference between being a person and being an object is, I submit, also of the essence of the concept of privacy. T. S. Eliot captured the difference and the notion of the loss of privacy in some lines in his play *The Cocktail Party*:

Yes, it's unfinished;
And nobody likes to be left with a mystery.
But there's more to it than that.
There's a loss of personality;
Or rather, you've lost touch with the person
You thought you were. You no longer feel quite human.
You're suddenly reduced to the status of an object—
A living object, but no longer a person.
It's always happening, because one is an object
As well as a person. But we forget about it
As quickly as we can. When you've dressed for a party
And are going downstairs, with everything about you

> Arranged to support you in the role you have chosen,
> Then sometimes, when you come to the bottom step
> There is one more step than your feet expected
> And you come down with a jolt. Just for a moment
> You have the experience of being an object
> At the mercy of the malevolent staircase.
> Or, take a surgical operation.
> In consultation with the doctor and the surgeon,
> In going to bed in the nursing home,
> In talking to the matron, you are still the subject,
> The centre of reality. But, stretched on the table,
> You are a piece of furniture in a repair shop
> For those who surround you, the masked actors;
> All there is of you is your body
> And the "you" is withdrawn. . . .[52]

Privacy is being a person, an individual, a human being and not an object. But in the relationship between individual and government, the individual is almost always an object to be controlled and not an individual to be set free. So all government control of human behavior is an invasion of privacy, an infringement of personality. Yet, some government is, of course, necessary. And, as Eliot said, "one is an object as well as a person." But where government control is not necessary or essential to the function of the state, it ought not to be acceptable to the constitutional limits implied in Brandeis's "right to be let alone." This will usually be true wherever the government inhibits a person's actions "for his own benefit." Or where the government grants a benefit on a condition that it could not otherwise impose. It is not a proper governmental function to buy up personal rights. Every law that compels a person to do what he would not choose to do is or should be constitutionally suspect.

Surely some such compulsion is more suspect than others. It would be difficult to argue that a distaste for paying taxes should exempt a person from doing so, even if the taxes are spent for purposes regarded by the taxpayer as odious. And compulsions relating to property may be less suspect than compulsions relating to personal action, although there is little doubt that originally the Constitution spoke in Lockean terms of property as an essential ingredient of liberty. Moreover, there will obviously be greater justification for some invasions of personal privacy than for others. The lines will be hard to draw. But the goal is worth seeking and the judiciary may yet make its contribution. For, to quote still another poet:

> . . . a man's reach should exceed his grasp.
> Or what's a heaven for.[53]

Certainly the Supreme Court's reach has always, in its brightest moments, exceeded its grasp. And, in recent times, it has more and more sought to resolve a free society's most serious difficulties. Why not this one?

If I must, then, leave to the evolution of judicial decisions the definition of constitutional privacy, I would offer some suggestions about distinctions that ought to make the task a little easier.

It is of the first importance, I should submit, that a distinction be drawn between the idea of privacy and the idea of secrecy. Edward Shils in his postmortem analysis of the problems of the McCarthy Era, in his book *The Torment of Secrecy,* pointed out that: "Privacy is the voluntary withholding of information reinforced by a willing indifference. Secrecy is the compulsory withholding of knowledge, reinforced by a prospect of sanctions for disclosure."[54] There is, for my purposes, a more important distinction to be noted, especially because Shils was speaking of only one aspect of privacy, the right against unauthorized disclosure of information. When one recognizes the potential for constitutional privacy in Brandeisian terms, then the distinction must also be found in the fact that privacy is an individual right while secrecy is a governmental, or at least a corporate, concern. Obviously the right of the individual—in his individual capacity—not to have his affairs publicized and to be let alone must rest on a different rationalization than the right or power of a government to be let alone or to conceal data from its own citizens or others. Individual liberty is not the same as, indeed it is frequently the opposite of, governmental authority.

Not only is secrecy not the same as privacy, events since World War II, if not before, make it apparent that the demand for secrecy is frequently the cause for invasion of privacy, both in the Brandeisian sense and in the more familiar terms of the Fourth Amendment concepts of search and seizure. Government spying, both in the McCarthy and Nixon eras, has been justified in terms of the necessity for maintaining government secrecy. Government secrecy has only two justifications. Neither of them is individual liberty. The first is *raison d'état,* for which the current rubric is "national security." The second is administrative convenience, including both the notion of the necessity for confidential communications and the high nuisance costs of disseminating all information that any one may demand.

Any attempt to cover both secrecy and privacy under one constitutional definition must necessarily work to the diminution of the individual protection or the expansion of the secrecy power, and possibly both. But it should be noted that if the Supreme Court can find a constitutional basis, made up of whole cloth, for executive privilege,[55] which is a secrecy proposition, it should even more readily find in the Constitution the basis for an expansive privacy doctrine. The latter—individual privacy—is consistent with the Constitution's primary function of limitation on arbitrary governmental power. The former—government secrecy—is not; indeed, it is inconsistent with it.

A second kind of confusion is frequently effected by the use of the label of privacy to cover the opposite of secrecy, the movement for "freedom of information."[56] There is a relationship between privacy and freedom of information, but again there is certainly no identity. The essence of the one is publicity, which is anathema to the other. Freedom of information imposes on the government and others the duty to produce data in their possession, but particularly data that has been collected about an individual. Certainly one of the reasons for requiring disclosure is to permit an individual whose privacy has been invaded to learn about the invasion and, presumably, to take appropriate steps to secure redress for past incursions and to prevent the future use of the data for improper purposes, that is, for breaches of one or more of the three aspects of individual privacy.

At the same time, freedom of information may itself result in invasion of privacy, as where the data to be published to the applicant authorized to secure it reveals information of a private nature about other individuals. Thus, when the Buckley Amendment compels the disclosure to a student of the contents of his school records, it may compel the disclosures of confidential data of another individual,[57] such as a professor's confidential communications about that student. This is equally true of an unedited FBI file, which may contain information about others than the subject of the file.

This problem does not exist where the compulsory disclosure—freedom of information—relates to governmental actions. Here the invasion, if any, is not of privacy but solely of secrecy. Even here, however, the line is a fine one. For every government official is also a private individual. We have become enamored of compulsory disclosure of financial and other data about government employees. When there is no connection between the information to be secured and the corruption to be prevented or corrected, it is clearly an invasion of the government employee's privacy. The more so when the data sought is not that of the individual employee but that of his relatives and associates.[58] Publicity may be a healthy preventative of, or corrective for, governmental malfeasance, but only to the degree that it actually relates to possible malfeasance and not when it simply exposes the private affairs of an individual because he happens to be a government employee. Some of the psychological tests administered to actual or putative government employees are clearly an unwarranted invasion of their privacy.

Again, we should not confuse Brandeis's right of the individual to be let alone with what was once known as "laissez faire." In the nineteenth century and well into the twentieth, the concept of individuals and individual freedom was perverted into a form of constitutional protection against the regulation of corporate and organizational economic activities. It should be clear that privacy is an individual's right and not that of a corporation, or a class, or an association. When the affairs regulated are not those of individuals but those of groups, the concern is not privacy. This is not, of course, to suggest that corporations, classes, organizations, and associations are not entitled to constitutional protections, including certainly those of due process of law and freedom of speech and press and political activities. It is simply to say that the right of privacy is essentially the right of a person, an individual, a human being.

The right of privacy cannot bear the burden of including freedom of corporations and unions from regulation. To broaden it so is to destroy it. The rejection of substantive due process in the economic regulation cases has been too strong to be overcome now. But those cases, with the possible exception of *Belle Terre*,[59] which upheld an ordinance limiting the use of private houses to one family, were all directed against interference with state regulation of economic enterprises,[60] not personal behavior. It is economic due process that has been rejected, not substantive due process, which implies a judgment that the state or federal legislature has not carried its burden of persuading the Court of the necessity for the legislation. As Mr. Justice Stewart said, *Griswold* and *Doe* are in fact substantive due process decisions,[61] but they are not economic due process cases. The same standard of judicial review, requiring the government to prove the necessity for its legislation rather than indulging a presumption of validity, has been established in the area of equal protection of the laws,[62] in the area of First Amendment rights,[63] and even in the right-to-travel cases,[64] where the constitutional authority is as undefinable as it is in the "privacy" area. Again, "laissez-faire" was a claim by corporations for freedom from economic regulation, privacy is a claim by individuals for freedom of personal behavior. The two may overlap, but should not be confused.

It is, however, neither the lack of clarity in the concept of privacy nor its confusion with equally important and related ideas that makes me doubt its future growth or even its preservation. For to me it appears—as I have said—that "constitutional privacy" is not a "felt necessity of the time." Rather it is a demand for freedom that runs against the current of most of the major social movements and changes that are receiving the Supreme Court's imprimatur as well as those of the legislature, the executive, and even most academics.

I am saying that I think the right of privacy is not now a highly valued one in our society and of decreasing rather than increasing popularity. Although of ancient vintage—it derives perhaps from the first bite of the apple of the Tree of Knowledge—it cannot be said to be pervasively regarded as a necessity or even an affordable luxury by most American citizens. It was an earlier generation that thought "The world is too much with us; late and soon." Our own demands seem to be for more rather than less.

Privacy is a factor of decency and civility which are waning—perhaps waned—elements in a society where sadism and violence constitute our primary form of entertainment; where guns are cherished and butter damned, because butter kills; where politeness is regarded as superfluous at best and male chauvinism at worst; where language is debased and becomes meaningless; where the criminal is regarded as the victim of society rather than society the victim of the criminal; where Andy Warhol is art and Pierre Bonnard is "kitsch"; where music is reduced to mathematical formulas, produced by mechanical air pumps, played by a computer; where adults are more concerned with the gossip columns and sports pages of the newspaper than any others; where learning is valueless if it is not "practical"; where reason is suspect and emotion is king. (Excuse me, my biases are showing.) The Oxford Professor of Poetry recently described our times: "An age that puts its trust in the ordering intellect will distrust and underplay the instincts. An age like ours which worships the instinctual will become anti-rational. It is no accident that our age has seen reason and lucidity sink to their lowest levels of esteem since man came down from the trees."[65] And, in such a society, the right of privacy is esteemed no greater than lucidity and reason.

In such a society, privacy is valued highly by some self-styled intellectuals and by some petit bourgeois, but mostly by those who, in the great tradition of the Fourth and Fifth Amendments, seek protection against arrest and conviction for crime. Gerald Heard once told us why the intellectual demands privacy. "We can only understand the intellectual's intellectualization of their own emotion when we realize that what they sense and dread is their individuality's destruction."[66]

Those concerned with Learned Hand's sacredness of the individual are a rapidly diminishing number. So, too, are those capable of feeling shame, or embarrassment, or guilt, or fear, which are so often the consequence of invasion of privacy. All of these old-fashioned emotions are being exorcized from our society, individually and collectively, by our modern witch doctors.

There are, too, more potent forces at work diminishing the possibility of constitutional privacy. And foremost among these is the service state, that form of government that came upon us directly after the New Deal and the Second World War. (One need only describe the chronology without assigning cause and effect.) It is since that time that so much more of our lives has increasingly become the object of governmental control.

The essence of understanding the English constitutionalists is to be found in the premise that "Liberty of the individual is nothing more than the residue of his conduct which remains unfettered by any Law."[67] This, too, it should be seen, is the definition of the third aspect of constitutional privacy, the right to be let alone, to remain ungoverned, "unfettered by any law." In a service state, such as our nation has now become, that residue is declining at a rapid rate. And Americans are no longer fettered only by laws made by elected legislatures, the fetters are far more frequently chains that are forged by individuals and bureaus, often without legislative authority and sometimes in the face of legislative policy to the contrary. (In recent days, *The New York Times* has reported the unedifying spectacle of several Senators petitioning an administrative agency to promulgate a rule of law for which these Senators are unable to secure the support of a majority of the Congress. Administrative agencies no longer go to Congress for authority to act; they are now recipients of pleas from Congressmen that the agencies make the laws.) Thus liberty is no longer limited by laws alone, but far more frequently by executive orders, by administrative regulations, by bureaucratic guidelines, by simple exercise of discretion at the lowest level of the pyramid and even by judicial actions forging major policy determinations for society without constitutional or legislative authority. Everywhere we hear—to the chagrin and cost of the individual citizen and his freedoms—of inherent constitutional powers of government not to be seen in, and most difficult to infer from, the Constitution: inherent powers of the President, inherent powers of the Congress, inherent powers of the judiciary.

Allow me a long quotation from Professor Edward Shils, who, because he knows far more on this subject than I do, should have been delivering this lecture. Writing of privacy and the service state, he said:

> The night watchman state is now only a dim trace of the past. The area of what is public has grown, and the domain of the private has retracted. . . . Governments believe that they must be responsible for the enhancement of the economic strength of their societies and the physical well-being of their peoples. Doing or trying to do so much, they think they must increase their knowledge proportionately. . . .
>
> They also wish to know more about those whom they rule. They believe that they need to know more to confer on them the benefits they desire. They believe they must know about them to protect the order from which they wish to move forward to further improvements. The acquisition of knowledge needed for these purposes increases the desire for more knowledge. The knowledge which is sought is knowledge of particular individuals and institutions and general knowledge about social and economic systems. . . .
>
> This expansion diminishes the sphere of the private. To restriction by regulation it adds intrusion by knowledge. The diminution of privacy by intrusive perception of the personal and corporate private spheres is greatly aided by the development of new professions for the acquisition of knowledge about human

beings, by the growth in the numbers of economists, sociologists, anthropologists, educationists, psychologists, political scientists, and by the techniques of research cultivated by these professions. It is also aided by the strengthening of old professions (or occupations) such as those attending to detection, intelligence, and counterintelligence.[68]

Yes, the universities, too, contribute to the barriers we continually erect against individual privacy. And, like all invaders of privacy, they share a self-righteousness that affords self-justification. But, as Mr. Justice Frankfurter once noted: "Self-righteousness gives too slender an assurance of rightness."[69]

Let me touch on just one more major social movement that surely inhibits the growth of a right of individual privacy. This time the immediate sponsor was not the legislature or the bureaucracies, although they have come round to supporting the movement, but the judiciary. I refer to the egalitarian movement that derived its original impetus from the Supreme Court's decision in *Brown* v. *Board of Education*,[70] a judgment with which I have no quarrel, indeed, which I wholeheartedly endorse. There was a time when, as Mr. Justice Holmes told us, the Equal Protection Clause was the "usual last resort of constitutional arguments."[71] It has since become the primary resort for those who would change the social structure through judicial action. But more has changed than lawyer's rhetoric.

*Brown* v. *Board of Education* and its successors mark the fundamental shift of constitutional limitations from protection of individual rights to protection of class rights. They have helped destroy the objective of a classless society which, I believe, was of the essence of a democratic dream. They moved the constitutional concept of equality from Jeffersonian political equality, which was a means, to substantive equality, which is an end. They moved the measurement from equality of opportunity to equality of condition. They spawned what Daniel Boorstin has called, in a book of that title, *The Sociology of the Absurd,* which is no longer sociology, but jurisprudence, and which is no longer absurd, but real. But most important, for my immediate purposes, was the implied rejection, by the enlargement of the Equal Protection Clause in the way the Court has done it, of the importance of the individual, the rights of the individual, the integrity of the individual.

Daniel Bell has recently written of this phenomenon:

> It is this erosion of the immediate, the personal, and the individual, and the rise of bureaucratic authority, which lead to so much irritation and disquiet. In the United States, the tension between liberty and equality, which framed the great philosophical debates in Europe, was dissolved by an individualism which encompassed both. Equality meant a personal identity, free of arbitrary class distinctions. It is the loss of that sense of individuality, promised by equality, which gives rise to a very different populist reaction today, both among the "left" and the "right," than in the past.[72]

Without individuality, there is no function for privacy. When we become fungibles to be manipulated by government, there can be no recognition of idiosyncrasies, no private realms to husband against intrusion. We are reduced to extirpating differences, not maintaining them. Distinctions, in fact, become discriminations in law and are labelled invidious and therefore unconstitutional.

With the lack of popular demand, with the bureaucracies of the service state expanding their ken, with egalitarianism the dominant juris-prudential theme,[73] it seems to me that the Private I is a phantom, not the ghost of an actuality, but the specter of a dream never to be realized.

I continue to think, however, that privacy as a constitutional concept is fundamental to a free people. It inhibits government surveillance and search and seizure, electronic and otherwise; it inhibits publicizing personal data and papers and events; it commands that men be free of unjustified governmental control, the right "to be let alone." In its pristine form, it is certainly a constitutional concept beyond realization. It is certainly beyond the puny powers of the judiciary to effect, assuming they wanted to do so, which they don't. For, from the beginning, this country has seen the contest between the ideals of Jefferson and the principles of Hamilton resolved in favor of the latter.

The question, then, is whether the mood of the country—what older historians once called "the climate of opinion"—can yet be enlisted in the cause of privacy, or individuality, or personality, or liberty, however you would label it. As I have already said, my answer is negative. The present *zeitgeist* is against the enhancement of the individual's authority over himself and in favor of the authority of Big Brother. Current political notions from left and right call for the sacrifice of individuals to the demands of society.

Judge Learned Hand, however, whose wisdom was greater than most, certainly greater than mine, spoke with more hope in an even less hopeful period of our history. It was in 1942, when the conflict between totalitarianism and freedom was being waged by force of arms, that Judge Hand memorialized Mr. Justice Brandeis and concluded in these words:

> This, the vastest conflict with which mankind has ever been faced, whose outcome still remains undecided, in the end turns upon whether the individual can survive; upon whether the ultimate value shall be this wistful, cloudy, errant You or I, or that Great Beast, Leviathan, that phantom conjured up as an *ignis fatuus* in our darkness and a scapegoat for our futility.
>
> We Americans have at last chosen sides; we believe that it may be idle to seek the Soul of Man outside Society; it is certainly idle to seek Society outside the Soul of Man. We believe this to be the transcendent stake. . . . But our faith will need again and again to be refreshed; and from the life of [Brandeis] we may gain refreshment. A great people does not go to its leaders for incantations or liturgies by which to propitiate fate or to cajole victory; it goes to them to peer into the recesses of its own soul, to lay bare its deepest desires; it goes to them as it goes to its poets and its seers. And for that reason it means little in what form this man's message may have been; only the substance of it counts. If I have read it aright, this was the substance. "You may build your Towers of Babel to the clouds; you may contrive ingeniously to circumvent Nature by devices beyond even the understanding of all but a handful; you may provide endless distractions to escape the tedium of your barren lives; you may rummage the whole planet for your ease and comfort. It shall avail you nothing; the more you struggle, the more deeply you will be enmeshed. Not until you have the courage to meet yourselves face to face; to take true account of what you find; to respect the sum of that account for itself and not for what it may

bring you; deeply to believe that each of you is a holy vessel unique and irreplaceable; only then will you have taken the first step along the path of Wisdom. Be content with nothing less; let not the heathen beguile you to their temples, or the Sirens with their songs. Lay up your Treasure in the Heaven of your hearts, where moth and rust do not corrupt and thieves cannot break through and steal."[74]

Such is my message to you about "The Private I." But I would not leave you on such a somber note. Let me close with an anecdote to which I testify as an eyewitness. Its appropriateness will be quickly apparent to you.

Some years ago a person who shall remain nameless, except to say that he was dean of a law school and later provost and president of a university, hosted a dinner party for some of his faculty members. At the end of the evening, when it came time to say good night, one of the guests apologized to the dean, saying, "I am sorry that I talked so much." The dean's reply was: "That's all right; you didn't say anything."

### Notes

1. Shakespeare, *II Henry IV*, I, c.
2. Holmes, *Collected Legal Papers* 292–293 (1920).
3. Frankfurter, *Book Review*, 77 *U. Pa. L. Rev.* 436, 437 (1929).
4. Steele, *The Funeral* 1 (1701).
5. See, for example, Shils, *Privacy and Power*, in Pool, ed., *Contemporary Political Science* 228 (1967).
6. ". . . the only check upon our own exercise of power is our own sense of self-restraint." *United States* v. *Butler*, 297 U.S. 1, 78 (1936).
7. *Davis* v. *United States*, 328 U.S. 582, 603–604 (1946).
8. Bowen, *John Adams and the American Revolution* 216 (1950).
9. 19 *How. St. Tr.* 1209 (1765).
10. *Id.* at 1065.
11. *Wilkes* v. *Wood*, 19 *How. St. Tr.* 1153, 1155 (1763).
12. 19 *How. St. Tr.* at 1066.
13. Dicey, *Law of the Constitution* lvii (9th ed. 1939).
14. 116 U.S. 616 (1886).
15. *Id.* at 630.
16. *Olmstead* v. *United States*, 277 U.S. 438 (1928).
17. *Id.* at 478.
18. *Ibid.*
19. Warren and Brandeis, *The Right to Privacy*, 4 *Harv. L. Rev.* 193 (1890).
20. See, for example, Kalven, *The Reasonable Man and the First Amendment: Hill, Butts, and Walker*, 1967 *Supreme Court Review* 267.
21. *Branzenburg* v. *Hayes*, 407 U.S. 665 (1972).
22. *Katz* v. *United States*, 389 U.S. 347, 353 (1967).
23. See text *supra*, at note 10.
24. 19 *How. St. Tr.* at 1073.
25. *Bivens* v. *Six Unknown Named Agents*, 403 U.S. 388 (1971).
26. *Laird* v. *Tatum*, 408 U.S. 1 (1972).
27. *People* v. *Defore*, 242 N.Y. 13 (1926).
28. *Mapp* v. *Ohio*, 367 U.S. 643 (1961).
29. Davis, 328 U.S. at 597.
30. *United States* v. *Kirchenblatt*, 16 F.2d 202, 203 (CA2d, 1926).
31. 381 U.S. 479 (1965).
32. *Id.* at 484–486.
33. Brest, *Processes of Constitutional Decision-Making* c. 7 (1975).

34. Quoted in Gunther, *Individual Rights in Constitutional Law* 264, n. 6 (1975).
35. *Lochner* v. *New York,* 198 U.S. 45, 75 (1905).
36. See Kurland, *Guidelines and the Constitution,* in Shultz and Aliber, eds., *Guidelines* 212 (1966).
37. *Snyder* v. *Massachusetts,* 291 U.S. 14 (1934).
38. *Eisenstadt* v. *Baird,* 405 U.S. 438, 453 (1972).
39. Arendt, *On Revolution* 125 (1963).
40. *Roe* v. *Wade,* 410 U.S. 113, 167–168 (1973).
41. *Doe* v. *Commonwealth's Attorney,* 44 *U.S.L. Week* 3543 (29 March 1976).
42. *Wisconsin* v. *Constantineau,* 400 U.S. 422 (1971).
43. *Paul* v. *Davis,* 44 *U.S.L. Week* 4337 (23 March 1976).
44. Holmes, *The Common Law* 5 (Howe ed. 1963).
45. Hand, *Liberty,* in *The Spirit of Liberty* 144 (2d ed. 1953).
46. *Id.* at 145.
47. *Id.* at 154.
48. Hand, *Sources of Tolerance, id.* at 71–73.
49. Art XXIX, in Perry and Cooper, eds., *Sources of Our Liberties* 377 (1952).
50. See the cases holding that the "liberty" provision of the Fourteenth Amendment protects natural persons rather than artificial ones. *Northwestern Life Ins. Co.* v. *Riggs,* 203 U.S. 243, 255 (1906); *Western Turf Association* v. *Greenberg,* 204 U.S. 359, 363 (1907); *Pierce* v. *Society of Sisters,* 268 U.S. 510, 535 (1925).
51. Berlin, *Two Concepts of Liberty* 51 (1958).
52. Eliot, *Complete Poems and Plays* 307 (1952).
53. Robert Browning, *Andrea del Sarto,* in Kenyon, ed. *Collected Works* 117 (1912).
54. Shils, *The Torment of Secrecy* 26 (1956).
55. *United States* v. *Nixon,* 418 U.S. 683 (1974).
56. 5 U.S.C. § 552.
57. 20 U.S.C. § 1232(g).
58. *Casper* v. *Walker,* # 75 C. 4047, U.S. Dist. Ct. N.D. 111.
59. *Village of Belle Terre* v. *Boraas,* 416 U.S. 1 (1974).
60. See McCloskey, *Economic Due Process and the Supreme Court,* 1962 *Supreme Court Review* 34.
61. Epstein, *Substantive Due Process by Any Other Name: The Abortion Cases,* 1973 *Supreme Court Review* 159.
62. See, for example, *Cleveland Bd. of Educ.* v. *LaFleur,* 414 U.S. 632 (1974).
63. See Stone, *Fora Americana: Speech in Public Places,* 1974 *Supreme Court Review* 233.
64. See Rosenheim, *Shapiro v. Thompson: "The Beggars Are Coming to Town,"* 1969 *Supreme Court Review* 303.
65. Wain, *Samuel Johnson* 157 (1974).
66. Quoted in Rosenbaum, ed., *The Bloomsbury Group* 25 (1975).
67. See note 13 supra.
68. Shils, *Privacy and Power,* in Pool, ed., *Contemporary Political Science* 232–234 (1967).
69. *Joint Anti-Fascist Refugee Committee* v. *McGrath,* 341 U.S. 123, 171 (1951).
70. 347 U.S. 483 (1954).
71. *Buck* v. *Bell,* 274 U.S. 200, 208 (1927).
72. Bell, *The End of American Exceptionalism,* in Glazer and Kristol, eds., *The American Commonwealth—1976* 209–10 (1976).
73. The academic bible that expresses the creed of egalitarianism is Professor Rawls's *A Theory of Justice* (1971). Its essential premise is that all men are equal, and to the extent this is so, the function of the state is to keep them so; to the extent the premise is false, it is the function of the state to make them equal.
74. Hand, *Mr. Justice Brandeis,* in *The Spirit of Liberty* 173–174 (2d ed. 1953).

# Freedom of Speech and Press:
# For What Purpose?

Francis Canavan

*La grandeur du génie, ne consisterait-elle pas mieux à savour dans quel cas il faut l'uniformité, et dans quel cas il faut des différences?* Montesquieu, *L' Esprit des lois*, XXIX, 18.

"The modern history of the guarantee of freedom of speech and press has been one of a search for the outer limits of that right," said Justice Harlan of the U.S. Supreme Court in 1967.[1] He went on to note that the search dates from "the fountainhead opinions of Justices Holmes and Brandeis in *Schenck, Abrams* and *Whitney*."[2] But the Court's concentration on the outer boundaries of freedom of expression, Justice Harlan felt, "has perhaps omitted from searching consideration the 'real problem' of defining or delimiting the right itself."

Justice Harlan's point was well taken. One examines the opinions of the Court since 1919 in vain for a fully thought-out and consistent philosophy of freedom of speech and press. It is not suprising that it should be so. The Court, after all, has the task of deciding cases at law and elaborates standards sufficient to the decision of the cases that come before it. It is not a philosophical academy and prudently abstains for the most part from trying to set forth the whole theory that lies behind its decisions—if indeed there is a theory consciously acknowledged and accepted by all the Justices who concur in those decisions.

The aim of this paper, then, is not to present "the" philosophy of the Court or of any of its individual members in regard to freedom of speech and press. The opinions of the Court and of individual members will be copiously quoted,[3] but in the service of an analysis and an argument which is not theirs and with which they might well disagree. In short, this paper is a brief for the author's point of view rather than an objective study of the Court's point of view.

Its thesis is that the "searching consideration" of "the 'real problem' of defining or delimiting the right" of free speech and free press, which Justice Harlan suggests is needed, must start from the purposes which the right is intended to serve, taken in relation to other purposes which the Constitution also intends to achieve. It is from these purposes that the norms and the limits of the exercise of freedom of speech and press must be derived.

In relation to its constitutional purpose, speech (taking it for the moment in a broad sense to include every kind of utterance and publication) is not always of the same kind or equally protected by the Constitution. Freedom of speech, without distinctions among kinds of speech, is no more defensible than an unqualified freedom of action, and no more desirable. A free society, after all, is as much a society in which people are free to act as one in which they are free to talk (unless one agrees with the Dublin *Opinion*'s sardonic comment that a free country is a country where you are

Reprinted with permission from the *American Journal of Jurisprudence*, © 1971.

free to complain about the restrictions). Yet freedom to act does not include freedom to perform every action, or any action in all circumstances, nor does it imply that every action is of equal value in the eyes of the law and, consequently, equally subject to or immune from restraint.

"Action," in fact, is an abstraction with little practical legal meaning until we know with what kind of action we are dealing, and the same is true of "speech." Utterances are of different qualities and unequal value in relation to the purposes for which freedom of speech is constitutionally guaranteed. A theory of freedom of speech must therefore make distinctions among kinds and grades of speech, and these distinctions will derive from the purposes which constitutionally protected speech is intended to serve.

A thorough discussion of freedom of speech would begin with the question whether this freedom should be legally protected. But let us begin where the Court begins, with the proposition that the freedom is constitutionally guaranteed[4] and is fundamental to the American political system. The Court and its members have long described freedom of speech and press as "basic to the conception of our government"[5] and as "essential to free government"[6] or to "the workings of a free society."[7] Freedom of thought and speech, as the Court said in 1937, "is the matrix, the indispensable condition, of nearly every other form of freedom."[8] Thirty years later the Court repeated the theme: "A broadly defined freedom of the press assures the maintenance of our political system and an open society."[9]

The assumption behind these assertions is that a primary purpose of the American polity is the preservation of freedom or of what the Court once called "a scheme of ordered liberty."[10] Freedom is not the only conceivable end, or necessarily the highest end, for which men might organize a political society. But the Court takes it as a fundamental American value and interprets the constitutional guarantee of freedom of speech and press in the light of that premise.

The chief function of the guarantee, in the eyes of the Court, is to serve the political needs of an open and democratic society. "The core value of the Free Speech Clause of the First Amendment," the Court has said, is "the public interest in having free and unhindered debate on matters of public importance."[11] Or, as Justices Black and Douglas said in a concurring opinion in *New York Times v. Sullivan* (1964), "Freedom to discuss public affairs and public officials is unquestionably, as the Court holds today, the kind of speech the First Amendment was primarily designed to keep within the area of free discussion."[12] The hypothesis underlying the Amendment is that "free debate of ideas will result in the wisest governmental policies."[13] Therefore, as an early authority said, the evil which the Amendment was designed to obviate was "any action of the government by means of which it might prevent such free and general discussion of public matters as seems absolutely essential to prepare the people for an intelligent exercise of their rights as citizens."[14] In the words of Justice Black, "Whatever differences may exist about interpretations of the First Amendment, there is practically universal agreement that a major purpose of that Amendment was to protect the free discussion of governmental affairs."[15]

The further purpose, according to Chief Justice Hughes, was "that government may be responsive to the will of the people and that changes may be obtained by lawful means."[16] Justice Jackson was of the opinion that "the forefathers" protected freedom of speech and press "because they knew of no other way by which free men could conduct representative democracy."[17] On another occasion he explained: "It is our philosophy that the course of government should be controlled by a consensus of the governed. This process of reaching intelligent popular decisions requires free discussion."[18]

The primary purpose of the constitutional guarantee of free speech and press, then, is political; the means by which this purpose is to be achieved has been described by the Court, in the most general terms, as "communication of information or opinion."[19] The First Amendment assumes, according to the Court, "that the widest possible dissemination of information from diverse and antagonistic sources is essential to the welfare of the public."[20] The "predominant purpose" of freedom of the press, the Court has said, "was to preserve an untrammeled press as a vital source of public information."[21] But, beyond the need for information about public affairs, the Court sees the constitutional guarantee as protecting a clash of opinions which fosters the pursuit of political truth and political good.

"Winds of doctrine should freely blow," declared Justice Frankfurter, "for the promotion of good and the correction of evil . . . [b]ecause freedom of public expression alone assures the unfolding of truth, it is indispensable to the democratic process."[22] "It was the pursuit of truth which the First Amendment was designed to protect," agreed his frequent opponents, Justices Black and Douglas.[23] The Court echoed in a more recent opinion: "It is the purpose of the First Amendment to preserve an uninhibited marketplace of ideas in which truth will ultimately prevail. . . ."[24]

The metaphor of a "free trade in ideas," with the corollary notion that "the best test of truth is the power of the thought to get itself accepted in the competition of the market,"[25] has been a favorite of the Court since the days of Justice Holmes. The theory behind the metaphor received classic expression in an opinion by Chief Judge Learned Hand of the U.S. Court of Appeals, which was quoted as follows by Justice Frankfurter:

> The interest which [the First Amendment] guards, and which gives it its importance, presupposes that there are no orthodoxies—religious, political, economic, or scientific—which are immune from debate and dispute. Back of that is the assumption—itself an orthodoxy, and the one permissible exception—that truth will be most likely to emerge if no limitations are imposed upon utterances that can with any plausibility be regarded as efforts to present grounds for accepting or rejecting propositions whose truth the utterer asserts or denies. *International Brotherhood of Electrical Workers v. Labor Board,* 181 F.2d 34, 40. In the last analysis it is on the validity of this faith that our national security is staked.[26]

The liberal orthodoxy thus expounded is, of course, no more exempt from criticism than any other orthodoxy. But let us take it as the prevailing faith of our liberal society.[27] It asserts that the aim of freedom of expression is truth but, for that very reason, no idea enters the marketplace with a legal presumption that it is true or that the expression of opposing ideas may be legally prohibited. Government serves truth, not by teaching truth or repressing error, but by protecting the market in which truth will prevail. "It cannot be the duty, because it is not the right, of the state," Justice Jackson explained, "to protect the public against false doctrine. The very purpose of the First Amendment is to foreclose public authority from assuming a guardianship of the public mind through regulating the press, speech, and religion. In this every person must be his own watchman for truth, because the forefathers did not trust any government to separate the true from the false for us."[28] It follows, as the Court was to say years later, that "the Constitution protects expression. . . without regard to . . . the truth, popularity, or social utility of the ideas and beliefs which are offered."[29]

The Constitution evenhandedly protects the expression of ideas and beliefs, but not because it is indifferent to their truth and social utility. It does so because of a faith in "the power of reason as applied through public discussion"[30] to distinguish the true from the false, the good from the evil, without interference by governmental authority. "Back of the guarantee of free speech," said Justice Frankfurter, lies "faith in the power of an appeal to reason by all the peaceful means of gaining access to the mind."[31]

The First Amendment's policy of protecting speech, according to Justice Jackson, "is rooted in faith in the force of reason."[32] The primary purpose of the Amendment's guarantee of freedom of speech and press, therefore, is to produce a government controlled by a public opinion that has been formed through free and rational debate on public issues.

The Court has also insisted, increasingly in recent years, that freedom of expression covers persuasion to action as well as exposition of ideas. The protection intended by the First Amendment, declared the Court in the heyday of the "preferred position" of First Amendment freedoms, "extends to more than abstract discussion, unrelated to action. The First Amendment is a charter for government, not for an institution of learning. 'Free trade in ideas' means free trade in the opportunity to persuade to action, not merely to describe facts."[33]

Again, in 1963, the Court said: "Abstract discussion is not the only species of communication which the Constitution protects; the First Amendment also protects vigorous advocacy, certainly of lawful ends, against governmental intrusion."[34] Thus, as the Court said in *New York Times v. Sullivan* in 1964 and has often since repeated, there is "a profound national commitment to the principle that debate on public issues should be uninhibited, robust, and wide-open, and that it may well include vehement, caustic, and sometimes unpleasantly sharp attacks on government and public officials."[35] At the same time the Court has also insisted that freedom of speech and press includes the right to receive, as well as to impart, "information and ideas."[36]

The end sought by constitutionally guaranteeing freedom of expression is not solely political, however. "The guarantees for speech and press are not the preserve of political expression or comment upon public affairs, essential as those are to healthy government."[37] For one thing, freedom of speech and press "is as much a guarantee to individuals of their personal right to make their thoughts public and put them before the community . . . as it is a social necessity required for the 'maintenance of our political system and an open society.' "[38] For another, the social goals of freedom of expression are broader than the merely political.

Thus Justice Frankfurter said: "Freedom of expression is the well-spring of our civilization. . . . For social development of trial and error, the fullest possible opportunity for the free play of the human mind is an indispensable prerequisite."[39] "The First Amendment was designed to enlarge, not to limit, freedom in literature and in the arts as well as in politics, economics, law, and other fields," said Justice Douglas. Justice Harlan agreed that the Founders "felt that a free press would advance 'truth, science, morality and arts in general' as well as responsible government."[40]

For similar reasons, the Court has extended the protection of freedom of speech and press to academic freedom. "Our Nation is deeply committed to academic freedom, which is of transcendent value to all of us and not merely to the teachers concerned. That freedom is therefore a special concern of the First Amendment. . . ."[41] The Court has even wrapped the mantle of freedom of expression around "mere entertainment," saying: "The line between the informing and the entertaining is too elusive for the protection of that basic right."[42] But in mentioning this position of the Court, we anticipate a problem that must be dealt with later, and which we will therefore pass by for the moment.

From the dicta of the Court and of individual Justices that have been quoted, one can elaborate a certain view of the purposes of the First Amendment's guarantee of freedom of speech and press. In this view, the guarantee was meant to protect and facilitate the achievement of rational ends by communication among free and ordinarily intelligent people. Chief among these ends is the successful functioning of the democratic political process. But freedom to express one's mind is an individual right as well as a means to social goals; and the social goods to be realized through free expression are much broader than the strictly political. They include the whole range of objects of the human mind, the esthetic as well as the logical and narrowly rational. It is the pursuit not only of the true and the good, but of the beautiful as well, that deserves constitutional protection. Yet what the Constitution intends to protect is always the free functioning of a mind presumed to be rational and intelligent.

Abuses of freedom of speech and press must indeed be tolerated, but not for their own sake or as if there were no differences between use and abuse. As the Court said in *Cantwell v. Connecticut,* "the people of this nation have ordained, in the light of history, that, in spite of the probability of excesses and abuses, these liberties are, in the long view, essential to enlightened opinion and right conduct on the part of the citizens of a democracy."[43] The assumption is clear that not every opinion or principle of conduct is in itself enlightened or right and worth protecting.

The problem then is how to relate the constitutional guarantee of freedom of expression to the ends it is supposed to serve. For end or purpose is a limiting principle, regulating and restricting the uses of means to those which in some way contribute to the end. If a freedom is guaranteed for the sake of a certain end, those uses of the freedom which make no contribution to that end, or are positive hindrances to its achievement, are abuses of the freedom and cease to enjoy the protection of the guarantees, *unless the effort to suppress the abuses would be an even greater hindrance to the end*.

There are many who feel that to authorize government to suppress any abuse of freedom of speech or press is necessarily and always a greater threat to the purposes for which the guarantee of freedom was established than it is to tolerate the abuses. The only acceptable solution to the problem, according to this view, is to absolutize the guarantee and to protect all utterances and publications without distinction or discrimination, so long as they remain in the realm of expression and do not pass over into the area of conduct. Among the members of the Supreme Court, the names most prominently identified with this solution of the problem are those of Justices Black and Douglas.

Their position has evolved over the years in the direction of an ever-greater absolutism. Justice Douglas, for instance, once wrote: "The validity of the obscenity laws is recognized that the mails may not be used to satisfy all tastes, no matter how perverted."[44] In later years he abandoned that view.[45] By 1966 he found sexually deviant tastes to be "values" as socially important to those who have them as the "values" of the "normal" majority, and as deserving of the protection of freedom of speech and press."[46] By 1969 he felt obliged to explain that he had consistently dissented from the view that " 'obscenity' is not protected by the Free Speech and Free Press Clauses of the First Amendment . . . but not because, as frequently charged, I relish 'obscenity.' "[47]

Similarly, in *Beauharnais v. Illinois,* Justice Douglas was apparently willing, though reluctantly, to accept the power of a State to enact a group libel law.[48] Later he was to announce: "In my view the First Amendment would bar Congress (and the States) from passing any libel law,"[49] and in this view he was joined by Justice Black.[50] Finally, although Justices Black and Douglas originally accepted the clear and present danger test as a norm for judging the limits of freedom of speech and press,[51] they now "see no place in the regime of the First Amendment for any 'clear and present danger' test, whether strict and tight as some would make it, or free-wheeling as the Court in *Dennis* rephrased it."[52]

Despite such variations, it is safe to say that the Black-Douglas position has not changed in substance but has only grown in clarity and firmness during their long tenure on the Court. By no means the earliest, but one of the more succinct statements of this position is Justice Douglas's: "The only line drawn by the Constitution is between 'speech' on the one side and conduct or overt acts on the other."[53] For a typical statement by Justice Black we may take the following: "I think the Founders of our Nation in adopting the First Amendment meant precisely that the Federal Government should pass 'no law' regulating speech and press but should confine its legislation to the regulation of conduct. So too, that policy of the First Amendment made applicable to the States by the Fourteenth, leaves the States vast power to regulate conduct, but no power at all, in my judgment, to make the expression of views a crime."[54]

The constitutional line, then, is between conduct and the expression of "ideas." The First Amendment, says Justice Black, guarantees "complete freedom for expression of all ideas."[55] "Its aim was to unlock all ideas for argument, debate, and dissemination."[56] says Justice Douglas, and it "leaves no power in government over expression of ideas."[57] They do not define, however, what constitutes an "idea." One gets the impression that for Justice Black and particularly for Justice Douglas, anything that is uttered by a human voice or comes off a printing press, whether in the form of words, photographs, or motion pictures, is an "idea" and as such is entitled to the protection of the First Amendment. Certainly, for them, obscene publications,[58] advocacy of the violent overthrow of the government,[59] and statements about the public conduct of public figures, however libelous,[60]fall into that category.

Their willingness to give free rein to the expression of all "ideas" however mindless or irrational they may be, is based on faith in the soundness of the popular mind. "I have the same confidence," said Justice Douglas, "in the ability of our people to reject noxious literature as I have in their capacity to sort out the true from the false in theology, economics, politics, or any other field."[61] Justice Black feels a similar confidence that the American people cannot be shaken in their devotion to free institutions by any amount of talk on the part of totalitarians.[62] The remedy for the danger posed by advocacy of the violent overthrow of the government, he has said, "must be the same remedy that is applied to the danger that comes from any other erroneous talk—education and contrary argument." He was willing to add: "If that remedy is not sufficient, the only meaning of free speech must be that the revolutionary ideas will be allowed to prevail."[63]

Justices Black and Douglas, therefore, insist that, to be punishable under the First Amendment, mere speech or publication must be "shown to be part of unlawful action,"[64] or, in a phrase of which Justice Douglas has become fond, it must be proved to be "brigaded with illegal action."[65] The example of punishable speech usually given, that of a person who falsely shouts fire in a crowded theatre, says Justice Douglas, is "a classic case where speech is brigaded with action. . . . They are indeed inseparable and a prosecution can be launched for the overt acts actually caused. Apart from rare instances of that kind, speech is, I think, immune from prosecution."[66]

Justice Black, as is well known, has been criticized in recent years for apostatizing from his pristine liberalism and lapsing into the conservative heresy in regard to freedom of expression. Certainly he has more than once shocked the faithful by uttering such sentiments as: "Uncontrolled and uncontrollable liberty is an enemy to domestic peace."[67] The criticism is chiefly inspired, however, by his willingness to restrict the right to engage in forms of expression that are not strictly and solely "speech," e.g., picketing and demonstrations, and by the vehemence with which he denies that aggrieved persons have the right "to use the public's streets, buildings, and property to protest whatever, wherever, whenever they want, without regard to whom such conduct may disturb."[68] But it must be emphasized that, as Justice Black sees the issue, he denies only the right to certain kinds of *conduct*; speech and publication remain immune. On the other hand, demonstrations and similar public manifestations of opinion make it clear that drawing the line between speech and conduct is not always easy.

Justice Black, supported by Justice Douglas, therefore continues to denounce what he calls the "balancing test" for deciding freedom of speech and press cases.[69] He was once willing to say that the Court must "balance the Constitutional rights of owners of property against those of the people to enjoy freedom of speech and press," provided that the Court remained "mindful of the fact that the latter occupy a preferred position."[70] But his final position, which he has consistently maintained for many years, is that no balancing of rights is permissible where freedom of speech and press is involved, because there are no "more important interests" to which the freedom may constitutionally be subordinated.[71] "The men who drafted our Bill of Rights," he says, "did all the 'balancing' that was to be done in this field."[72] The First Amendment is in itself a choice of freedom of expression over any values that can be weighted against it.[73] The question, therefore, whether in any given case the public interests to be achieved or safeguarded by suppressing expression outweigh the loss to freedom of speech or press is constitutionally illegitimate, because the First Amendment has already answered the question in the negative. In this opinion Justice Douglas concurs.[74]

For Justices Black and Douglas, it would seem, "expression" is a univocal concept. If it is not "brigaded with illegal action," expression means the same thing in relation to the First Amendment in every case, no matter what its content or mode. There can be no inquiry whether the expression has what Justice Brennan once called "saving intellectual content."[75] It is enough that something has been uttered rather than done by overt action. It follows that the Court may make no judgment on the relationship of the expression to the ends which freedom of speech and press is supposed to serve. On the contrary, according to Justices Black and Douglas, the ends of the First Amendment are always served by guaranteeing absolute freedom of expression, and no further question may constitutionally be raised.

The majority of the Court has never accepted the Black-Douglas position. Despite considerable shifts of opinion among the members of the majority, the Court has consistently maintained, in the words of Chief Justice Hughes, that "liberty of speech and press is not an absolute right and the State may punish its abuse."[76] Justice Harlan elaborated this principle in an opinion of the Court in 1961, in these terms:

> At the outset we reject the view that freedom of speech and association, . . . as protected by the First and Fourteenth Amendments, are "absolutes," not only in the undoubted sense that where the constitutional protection exists it must prevail, but also in the sense that the scope of that protection must be gathered solely from a literal reading of the First Amendment. Throughout its history this Court has consistently recognized at least two ways in which constitutionally protected freedom of speech is narrower than an unlimited license to talk. On the one hand, certain forms of speech, or speech in certain contexts, has been considered outside the scope of constitutional protection. . . . On the other hand, general regulatory statutes, not intended to control the content of speech, but incidentally limiting its unfettered exercise, have not been regarded as the type of law the First or Fourteenth Amendment forbade Congress or the States to pass, when they have been found justified by subordinating valid governmental interests, a prerequisite to constitutionality which has necessarily involved a weighing of the governmental interest involved.[77]

In the majority view, some kinds of speech or publication are not protected at all by the Constitution. In a footnote to the passage quoted above, Justice Harlan explained that the literalist view of freedom of speech and press[78]"cannot be reconciled with the law relating to libel, slander, misrepresentation, obscenity, perjury, false advertising, solicitation of crime, complicity by encouragement, conspiracy and the like."[79] The classic statement on this point, which has often since been quoted in Court opinions, was made by Justice Murphy in 1942:

> Allowing the broadest scope to the language and purpose of the Fourteenth Amendment, it is well understood that the right of free speech is not absolute at all times and under all circumstances. There are certain well-defined and narrowly limited classes of speech, the prevention and punishment of which have never been thought to raise any Constitutional problems. These include the lewd

and obscene, the profane, the libelous, and the insulting or "fighting" words—those which by their very utterance inflict injury or tend to incite an immediate breach of the peace. It has been well observed that such utterances are no essential part of any exposition of ideas, and are of such slight social value as a step to truth that any benefit that may be derived from them is clearly outweighed by the social interest in order and morality.[80]

More specific statements of the kinds of speech and publication that are not constitutionally protected, and of the reasons why they are not protected, appear in many opinions of the Court or of individual members. We shall cite a few for illustration.

"Expressions found in numerous opinions indicate that this Court has always assumed that obscenity is not protected by the freedom of speech and press," said Justice Brennan,[81] because "implicit in the history of the First Avendment is the rejection of obscenity as utterly without redeeming social importance."[82] Said Justice Roberts in *Cantwell v. Connecticut*: "No one would have the hardihood to suggest that the principle of freedom of speech sanctions incitement to riot."[83] Justice Frankfurter explained in a later case that "utterance in a context of violence can lose its significance as an appeal to reason and become part of an instrument of force. Such utterance was not meant to be sheltered by the Constitution."[84] In *Cantwell v. Connecticut* Justice Roberts also remarked: "Resort to epithets or personal abuse is not in any proper sense communication of information or opinion safeguarded by the Constitution."[85]

The Constitution does not protect libelous statements, either, said the Court[86] in an opinion in which, however, it proceeded to prohibit "a public official from recovering damages for a defamatory falsehood relating to his official conduct unless he proves that the statement was made with 'actual malice'—that is, with knowledge that it was false or with reckless disregard of whether it was false or not."[87] But even under this liberal rule, the deliberate or reckless lie is not protected. In later cases the Court explained: "Although honest utterance, even if inaccurate, may further the fruitful exercise of the rights of free speech, it does not follow that the lie, knowingly and deliberately published about a public official, should enjoy a like immunity."[88] "Calculated falsehood," therefore, is not protected by freedom of the press,[89] because "neither lies nor false communications serve the ends of the First Amendment."[90]

From the passages cited above we may draw the conclusion that the Constitution does not protect certain kinds of speech. They include, with the qualifications laid down by the Court in its opinions, libel, reckless or calculated lies, slander, misrepresentation, perjury, false advertising, obscenity and profanity, solicitation of crime and personal abuse or "fighting" words. The reason why such kinds of speech or publication are not protected is that they are of minimal or no value as an exposition of ideas, a communication of information or opinion, an appeal to reason or a step to truth and therefore do not serve the ends of the First Amendment.

Advocacy of the forcible overthrow of the government may be taken as an example of the "speech in certain contexts," which Justice Harlan said "has been considered outside the scope of constitutional protection."[91] The same would be true generally of advocacy of violation of the law. According to Chief Justice Vinson, "The important question that came to this Court immediately after the First World War was not whether, but how far, the First Amendment permits the suppression of speech which advocates conduct inimical to the public welfare." It was in answer to this question, he said, that Justices Holmes and Brandeis framed the clear and present danger test.[92]

The test was originally formulated by Justice Holmes in *Schenck v. U.S.* (1919) in these terms: "The question in every case is whether the words used are used in such circumstances and are of such a nature as to create a clear and present danger that they will bring about the substantive evils that Congress has a right to prevent."[93] It is only the present danger of immediate evil or an intent to bring it about that warrants Congress in setting a limit to the expression of opinion where private rights are not concerned," he later explained in *Abrams v. U.S.*[94] In *Dennis v. U.S.* (1951), Chief Justice Vinson reviewed the cases since *Schenck v. U.S.* and concluded: "The rule we deduce from these cases is that where an offense is specified in nonspeech or nonpress terms [i.e., where what the law forbids is an action], a conviction relying upon speech or press as evidence of violation may be sustained only when the speech or publication created a 'clear and present danger' of attempting or accomplishing the prohibited crime, e.g., interference with enlistment."[95] The results of constitutional adjudication since 1919 were again summarized by the Court in 1969 in the principle that "advocacy of the use of force or of law violation" may be forbidden or proscribed only "where such advocacy is directed to inciting or producing imminent lawless action and is likely to incite or produce such action."[96]

It is sufficient for our present purpose to remark that speech of a type that might deserve constitutional protection as, let us say, an expression of political views loses its claim to protection, even though it remains speech, when it takes on a certain relationship to illegal action. But, whereas the Court holds that "obscenity is not protected expression and may be suppressed without a showing of the circumstances which lie behind the phrase 'clear and present danger' in its application to protected speech,"[97] because obscenity is inherently valueless, a different situation is presented in a case where the clear and present danger test applies. "Many of the cases in which this Court has reversed convictions by use of this or similar tests have been based on the fact that the interest which the State was attempting to protect was itself too insubstantial to warrant restriction of speech," said Chief Justice Vinson in *Dennis v. U.S.*[98] Or, as Justice Brandeis had earlier said, "even imminent danger cannot justify resort to prohibition of these functions essential to effective democracy, unless the evil apprehended is relatively serious. Prohibition of free speech and assembly is a measure so stringent that it would be inappropriate as the means for averting a relatively trivial harm to society."[99] It follows that in order to decide whether a particular speech or publication threatens a valid social or governmental interest seriously enough to lose its constitutional immunity from punishment under the clear and present danger test, the Court must weigh the public interest involved.

In other words, the Court must engage in what Justice Black has so often denounced as "balancing" (and this doubtless explains why he and Justice Douglas eventually concluded that the clear and present danger test has no place in the interpretation of the First Amendment). The balancing process, however, is a severely limited one. On one side is speech, without differentiation among kinds of speech, and it is given great weight by the requirement that speech may not be punished unless it creates a clear and present danger of a substantive evil that government may prevent. But, on the other side, there are grades of substantive evils that fall under the power of government. Some are more serious evils than others, and only the more serious ones warrant the suppression of speech, even under the conditions of clear and present danger. Implicit in this rule is the notion of a hierarchy of public interests which, in proportion to their importance, either do or do not outweigh the value of speech.

A balancing process is also involved in cases where the law's penalties fall, not on speech or publication, but on conduct, and restriction of the exercise of freedom of speech or press is an incidental effect of the regulation of conduct. Here again an essential question is whether a public interest of sufficient weight justifies the restriction. Chief Justice Warren summarized a line of previous decisions on this point in *U.S. v. O'Brien* in 1968:

> This Court has held that when "speech" and "nonspeech" elements are combined in the same course of conduct, a sufficiently important governmental interest in regulating the nonspeech element can justify incidental limitations on First Amendment freedoms. To characterize the quality of the governmental interest which must appear, the Court has employed a variety of descriptive terms; compelling; substantial; subordinating; paramount; cogent; strong. Whatever imprecision inheres in these terms, we think it clear that a government regulation is sufficiently justified if it is within the constitutional power of the Government; if it furthers an important or substantial governmental interest; if the governmental interest is unrelated to the suppression of free expression; and if the incidental restriction on alleged First Amendment freedoms is no greater than is essential to the furtherance of that interest.[100]

"The mere fact that speech is accompanied by conduct does not mean that the speech can be suppressed under the guise of prohibiting the conduct," the Court has said.[101] On the other hand, the Court has also said that the First and Fourteenth Amendments do not "afford the same kind of freedom to those who would communicate ideas by conduct such as patrolling, marching, and picketing on streets and highways, as these amendments afford to those who communicate ideas by pure speech."[102] Borderline cases therefore arise. "We cannot accept the view that an apparently limitless variety of conduct can be labeled 'speech' whenever the person engaging in the conduct intends thereby to express an idea," said Chief Justice Warren in an opinion of the Court which rejected the claim that draft-card burning was entitled to constitutional protection as "symbolic speech."[103] But in another case the Court found that the wearing of black armbands to protest the Vietnam War by children attending a public school was "closely akin to 'pure speech' which, we have repeatedly held, is entitled to comprehensive protection under the First Amendment."[104] In other words, the more "pure" speech is, the more it escapes regulation aimed at conduct.

To refine a bit on Justice Harlan, there are at least three ways in which utterances may be found unprotected by the First Amendment. Some utterances, such as obscene or "fighting" words, are outside the ambit of the constitutional guarantee because they are of such slight social value that they do not merit the Amendment's protection. Others bear so close a relationship to illegal action that they can be punished under the clear and present danger test, "whether strict and tight as some would make it, or free-wheeling as the Court in *Dennis* rephrased it," to use Justice Douglas's words quoted above.[105] Still other expressions may be restricted, not directly, since they are in themselves protected, but incidentally to the regulation of conduct. In cases involving all three kinds of expressions the underlying problem is that of accommodating the public interest in free speech and press with other public interests which government is also charged with safeguarding or promoting. Not all members of the Court would care to admit it, but it would seem that Justice Harlan was right when he said that "a balancing of the competing interests at stake . . . is unavoidably required in this kind of constitutional adjudication, notwithstanding that it arises in the domain of liberty of speech and press."[106]

The greatest exponent of "balancing" as the appropriate process in deciding freedom of speech and press cases was Justice Frankfurter, and the heyday of the "balancing test" came during his tenure on the Court. A typical expression of his view is found in his concurring opinion in *Dennis v. U.S.*, where he rejected the argument that "clear and present danger" was the only or completely adequate norm for decision when freedom of expression was the issue. "A survey of the relevant decisions," he said, "indicates that the results which we have reached are on the whole those that would ensue from careful weighing of conflicting interests. The complex issues presented by regulation of speech in public places, by picketing and by legislation prohibiting advocacy of crime have been resolved by many factors besides the imminence and gravity of the evil threatened."[107]

"It were far better," he continued, "that the phrase [clear and present danger] be abandoned than that it be sounded once more to hide from the believers in an absolute right of free speech the plain fact that the interest in free speech, profoundly important as it is, is no more conclusive in judicial review than other attributes of democracy or than a determination of the people's representatives that a measure is necessary to assure the safety of government itself."[108]

The "balancing test" supplied the Court with the rationale for its major anti-Communist decisions in the Cold War national security cases. Thus, for example, in *American Communications Association v. Douds,* the Court upheld a Federal law that sought to discourage labor unions from choosing as their officials persons who were members or supporters of the Communist Party or of any other organization that believes in or teaches the overthrow of the United States government by illegal or unconstitutional methods. In the opinion of the Court, Chief Justice Vinson admitted that the law restricted the exercise of First Amendment freedoms by Communists and other persons subject to it, but denied that it was necessarily unconstitutional for that reason. "When particular conduct is regulated in the interest of public order," he said, "and the regulation results in an indirect, conditional partial abridgment of speech, the duty of the courts is to determine which of the two conflicting interests demands the greater protection under the particular circumstances presented." Regulation of "conduct," he granted, may be a cloak for censorship of ideas. "On the other hand, legitimate attempts to protect the public, not from the remote possible effects of noxious ideologies, but from present excesses of direct, active conduct [i.e., political strikes called by Communist union officials], are not presumptively bad because they interfere with and, in some of its manifestations, restrain the exercise of First Amendment rights."[109]

In *Dennis v. U.S.,* Chief Justice Vinson went even further in upholding the conviction of Communist leaders for conspiracy to advocate the violent overthrow of the United States government. Now the balancing test sustained the direct suppression of speech. "An analysis of the leading cases in this Court which have involved direct limitations on speech," he said, ". . . will demonstrate that this is not an unlimited, unqualified right, but that the societal value of speech must, on occasion, be subordinated to other values and considerations."[110]

Justice Frankfurter's position and the "balancing test" generally have been severely criticized. To regard the public interest in free speech as only one of several interests that have to be weighed in the balance, it is said, weakens the constitutional guarantee of freedom of expression which, if not absolute, at least enjoys a "preferred position." Furthermore, it makes the decisions of the Court in this area unpredictable, since no two cases are exactly alike, and one therfore does not know what balance the Court will strike in a future case. Finally, the criticism runs, the balancing test during the Cold War proved to be a handy device by which the Court could uphold Congressional legislation that impaired First Amendment rights, while loudly professing its devotion to those same rights in the abstract. It just happened that when the whole weight of "national security" was put on the scale against the claim of this or that "subversive" to a particular exercise of First Amendment freedoms, the government won.

One may as well admit the force that there is in this criticism. The Court has shown often enough that during the crisis of war, whether hot or cold, it will not blow the whistle on measures that the national government thinks necessary to national security, e.g., the "relocation" of Japanese-Americans during the Second World War, however much it may later deplore them in the cold, gray light of peace. It is also true "balancing," carried far enough, would result in a case-by-case jurisprudence without predictable standards of decision. And no one can deny—certainly Justice Frankfurter never did[111]—that a constitutionally guaranteed right is something more than merely one among many interests that the Court must take into account in assessing legislation.

But, when all of this has been said, it still remains that freedom of speech and press is not the only or in all circumstances the highest of constitutional values that the court must weigh. The Warren Court moved far from the Vinson Court in its application of the balancing test. But it never abandoned the principle that the "societal value of speech" may sometimes be subordinated to other values by direct or incidental limitation of freedom of expression, and that such limitation involves a weighing and balancing of the competing interests. As late as 1968, in the case of a teacher who had been dismissed for publicly criticizing the way his school board spent the taxpayers' money, the Court stated the issue in these terms: "The problem in any case is to arrive at a balance between the interests of the teacher, as a citizen, in commenting upon matters of public concern and the interest of the State, as an employer, in promoting the efficiency of the public services it performs through its employees."[112]

The Warren Court did not abolish the balancing test. What it did was to tip the balance in favor of freedom of speech and press and to become more reluctant to subordinate this freedom to other social values except in strictly defined and narrowly limited circumstances. The tipping of the balance appears most clearly in the opinions of Justice Brennan, the Warren Court's principal spokesman in freedom of speech and press cases. A typical majority in such a case, when the decision was on the liberal side, would include Justices Black and Douglas, concurring from their characteristic point of view. Added to them would be the Chief Justice, Justice Goldberg (succeeded by Justice Fortas) and Justice Brennan, who would write the opinion of the Court.

Justice Brennan's tendency is to approach the Black-Douglas position without actually joining it: speech has a "transcendent value"[113] that is nearly, but not quite, absolute. As he says, "the line between speech unconditionally guaranteed and speech which may legitimately be regulated, suppressed, or punished is finely drawn."[114] There is indeed such a line. But we must keep as much speech as possible inside the line of the unconditional guarantee and leave as little as we can outside it, because of the danger of tolerating, in the area of First Amendment freedoms, the existence of a penal statute susceptible of sweeping and improper application. . . . These freedoms are delicate and vulnerable, as well as supremely precious in our society. The threat of sanctions may deter their exercise almost as potently as the actual application of sanctions. . . . Because First Amendment freedoms need breathing space to survive, government may regulate in the area only with narrow specificity."[115]

The requirement of narrow specificity applies even to kinds of speech or publication that *per se* are outside the pale of constitutional protection. For example, in *Roth v. U.S.,* having declared that "obscenity is not protected by the freedoms of speech and press,"[116] Justice Brennan went on to say:

> The door barring federal and state intrusion into this area [freedom of speech and press] cannot be left ajar; it must be kept tightly closed and opened only the slightest crack necessary to prevent encroachment upon more important interests.[117] It is therefore vital that the standards for judging obscenity safe-guard the protection of freedom of speech and press for material which does not treat sex in a manner appealing to prurient interest.[118]

Hence, as Justice Brennan said in a later case, the Court's "insistence that regulations of obscenity scrupulously embody the most rigorous procedural safeguards" is only "a special instance of the larger principle that the freedoms of expression must be ringed about with adequate bulwarks."[119]

In like manner,

> When the State undertakes to restrain unlawful advocacy it must provide procedures which are adequate to safeguard against infringement of constitu-tionally protected rights—rights which we value most highly and which are essential to the workings of a free society. Moreover, since only considerations of the greatest urgency can justify restrictions on speech, and since the validity of a restraint on speech in each case depends on careful analysis of the particular circumstances, . . . the procedures by which the facts of the case are adjudi-cated are of special importance and the validity of the restraint may turn on the safeguards which they afford.[120]

The conclusion follows, in the words of Justice Fortas: "An order issued in the area of First Amendment rights must be couched in the narrowest terms that will accomplish the pin-pointed objective permitted by constitutional mandate and the essential needs of the public order."[121] There is still a balancing process by which competing interests are weighed against each other, but the balance, in the decisions of the Warren Court, is heavily weighted in favor of freedom of expression.[122]

Now, "balancing" assumes that there are constitutionally relevant interests that can be weighed against each other, and the Court recognizes this whenever it applies the balancing test. The Court nowhere, however, sets down the complete scales of interests which can be put into the balance. One finds statements indicating that some public interests are more important than others and hence more capable of justifying certain restrictions of freedom of speech and press. One does not find the whole hierarchy of public interests in their order of importance. More rarely one comes across suggestions that some kinds of utterance are less deserving of constitutional protection than others. But the tendency of the Court, particularly in the last decade or so, is to find "speech" either not protected at all (e.g., obscenity) or protected simply as speech, without distinction of different kinds of speech that might deserve different degrees of constitutional protection.

The Court's opinions, therefore, do not furnish a satisfactory statement of all the elements that enter into the balancing process. It is sufficient for the Court's purposes, when balancing competing interests, to decide which of them shall prevail in the case, or class of case, before it. The questions before the Court is whether, in the context of the case, this sort of restriction on utterance (or perhaps on this *kind* of utterance) is justified by the kind and the magnitude of the public interest which the restriction is intended to serve. The Court need answer no further question.

Thus, for example, in early applications of the balancing test, it was held that the public's interest in protecting the streets against littering did not outweigh the public's interest in free political discussion as served by distributing political handbills on the streets.[123] But the public's interest in protecting householders against the annoyance caused by door-to-door peddlers justified the restriction imposed on freedom of the press by an ordinance forbidding such peddling by magazine salesmen.[124] The same public interest, however, was held not to justify similar restrictions on persons distributing advertisements of a religious meeting,[125] which suggests that freedom of religious expression ranks higher than the freedom of the commercial press.

Above all such local interests rises protection of national security which is clearly the highest of the values to which the Court has been willing to see freedom of speech and press subordinated. As Chief Justice Vinson put it in *American Communications Association v. Douds,* "When compared with ordinances and regulations dealing with littering of the streets or disturbance of householders by itinerant preachers, the relative significance and complexity of the problem of political strikes [fostered by communists] and how to deal with their leaders becomes at once apparent."[126]

Out of the decision of such cases arises a body of constitutional law, in which the emphasis on freedom of expression or on government's right to restrict it shifts from decade to decade. Certainly, Chief Justice Vinson's Court struck the balance in the early 1950's differently from Chief Justice Warren's in the late 1960's. But there does not emerge a complete, coherent and fully articulated hierarchy of kinds of speech and levels of public interest in the light of which the Court makes its decisions, and it would be fruitless to try to piece one together from the dicta of the Court and its individual members over a period of more than fifty years. Yet the hierarchy is there in the Court's opinions, though seen as in a glass, darkly, and it furnishes a basis for further reflection on the several scales of values implicit in a regime of free speech and press.

For those who accept the Black-Douglas position, of course, no reflection on a hierarchy of constitutionally protected values and on the place of freedom of speech and press in that hierarchy is necessary. But it is submitted here that the Black-Douglas position is wrong. As its most severe critic, Justice Frankfurter, once wrote, "Because freedom of public expression alone assures the unfolding of truth, it is indispensable to the democratic process. But even that freedom is not absolute and is not predetermined. By a doctrinaire overstatement of its scope and by giving it an illusory absolute appearance, there is danger of thwarting the free choice and the responsibility of exercising it which are basic to a democratic society."[127]

For it is simply not true that every kind of utterance, regardless of its content or mode of expression or of the effects it may have on substantial and valid public interests is of equal intrinsic value or equally serves the ends of the First Amendment. To quote Justice Frankfurter again,

> [n]ot every type of speech occupies the same position on the scale of values. There is no substantial public interest in permitting certain kinds of utterances: "the lewd and obscene, the profane, the libelous, and the insulting or 'fighting' words. . . ." It is pertinent to the decision before us [in *Dennis v. U.S.*] to consider where on the scale of values we have in the past placed the type of speech now claiming immunity [i.e., advocacy of the forcible overthrow of the United States government]. . . . On any scale of values which we have hitherto recognized, speech of this sort ranks low.[128]

Failure or refusal to recognize that there are differences of kind and degree among utterances and modes of expression leads to the type of reasoning which Justice Frankfurter derided in his concurring opinion in *Kovacs v. Cooper:* "It is argued that the Constitution protects freedom of speech; freedom of speech means the right to communicate, whatever the physical means for so doing; sound trucks are one form of communication; ergo, that form is entitled to the same protection as any other means of communication, whether by tongue or pen. Such sterile argumentation treats society as though it consisted of bloodless categories."[129] What is perhaps more to the point, it treats the key terms, such as "speech," "press," "expression," and "communication," as though they were mere abstractions which always mean exactly the same thing and can be applied to the decision of cases in constitutional law without regard to constitutional purposes or to the concrete realities to which they refer.

The effort so to apply them leads to such profundities as Justice Douglas's remark: "I seriously doubt the wisdom of trying by law to put the fresh, evanescent, natural blossoming of sex in the category of 'sin.' "[130] If one recalls that in the case in which Justice Douglas made that remark the issue was the power of the State to forbid the sale of obscene literature to minors, one may be inclined more seriously to doubt the wisdom of trying by fiat of the Supreme Court to put the reading of pornography in the category of the fresh, evanescent, natural blossoming of sex. But what Justice Douglas really meant was that the First Amendment permits neither the State nor the Court to tell the difference. It was enough that the magazines in question came off a printing press. That fact alone put them in the category of "expression" or even of "exposition of ideas," and should therefore render their sale immune from prosecution.

Admittedly, the Black-Douglas approach to freedom of speech and press has one great advantage: simplicity. It relieves legislatures and courts of any function other than that of drawing the line between utterance and conduct. In *Beauharnais v. Illinois,* for example, the Court, speaking through Justice Frankfurter, upheld Beauharnais' conviction for distributing a leaflet that exposed Negroes as a class to contempt, derision or obloquy in violation of a State group-libel law. "Every power may be abused," Justice Frankfurter conceded, "but the possibility of abuse is a poor reason for denying Illinois the power to adopt measures against criminal libels sanctioned by centuries of Anglo-American law. 'While this Court sits,' it retains and exercises authority to nullify action which encroaches on freedom of utterance under the guise of punishing libel."[131] To which Justice Black replied: "We are told that freedom of petition and discussion are in no danger 'while this Court sits.' This case raises considerable doubt. Since those who peacefully petition for changes in the law [as Beauharnais was doing] are not to be protected 'while this Court sits,' who is? I do not agree that the Constitution leaves freedom of petition, assembly, speech, press, or worship at the mercy of a case-by-case, day-by-day majority of this court."[132]

Justice Black's sincere concern for freedom is evident. Yet he ignored the wisdom in Justice Holmes' original coinage of the phrase: "The power to tax is not the power to destroy while this Court sits."[133] It is an ancient and useful maxim in constitutional law that the power to tax is the power to destroy. But, as Holmes saw and the Court eventually came to agree, the maxim inevitably leads to ridiculous results if it is applied mechanically without consideration of the end it is meant to serve and of the circumstances in which it is used. As Holmes remarked on another occasion, "the provisions of the Constitution are not mathematical formulas having their essence in their form."[134] Some human mind or minds must apply them to the decision of cases, employing a method of reasoning appropriate to jurisprudence rather than to mathematics. In the American constitutional system, that function is assigned in the highest instance to the Supreme Court and will have to be performed by it "while this Court sits."

When deciding whether an exercise of the taxing power or any other power of government exceeds constitutional limits, the Court cannot draw a conclusion from the letter of the Constitution as though it were deriving a theorem in geometry. It must decide what the letter of the document means in the light of history, precedent and other relevant considerations; what ends it was designed to achieve or evils to avert; how they are to be reconciled and combined with other constitutional ends; and how the attainment of these ends is affected by the facts of the case.[135] Therefore, in freedom of speech and press cases, the First Amendment, to borrow a phrase from Justice Frankfurter, "is not a self-wielding sword." It is a sword that the Court has to wield in the exercise of its "duty of closer analysis and critical judgment in applying the thought behind the phrase."[136]

Such a process of analysis and judgment can issue in error, of course, and it will never result in conclusions to demonstrably true or decisions so manifestly right that they impose themselves on the mind of every honest and intelligent man. Yet it is the process in which not only the Court but its critics must engage. Constitutional rules are not self-explanatory and self-enforcing to the point of eliminating the need for judgment.

The First Amendment indeed commands Congress (and, by decision of the Supreme Court, the States, too)[137] to make no law abridging the freedom of speech or of the press. This command, however, does not relieve the Court of the obligation of deciding what freedom of speech and press is and what exercises of governmental power "abridge" it. The Court can be influenced by public opinion, checked to some extent by the other branches of the government or overruled by the exercise of the amending power. But in the performance of its function of judicial review, it is the ordinary final judge of the meaning, purpose, and limits of freedom of speech and press, as of other constitutional guarantees. If the Court is to perform its function, it must be granted a certain degree of confidence that "while this Court sits," it will exercise its authority to nullify action which encroaches on freedom of expression under the guise of punishing libel or other crimes that can be committed by words. After all, even Justices Black and Douglas must rely on the Court to nullify action which encroaches on freedom of utterance under the guise of punishing conduct, because there is normally no other body on which to rely.

These two Justices maintain, of course, that while the Court can adequately distinguish speech from conduct, to allow it to make distinctions among utterances puts freedom of expression at the capricious mercy of a majority of the Court. Justice Frankfurter argued against them throughout his career on the bench that when the Court strikes the balance between contending constitutional principles, its judgment need not and should not be based on whim, will or personal prejudice. "It must rest," he said, "on fundamental presuppositions rooted in history to which widespread acceptance may fairly be attributed."[138] Or, as he said in another context, "The Anglo-American system of law is based . . . upon the conscience of society ascertained as best it may be by a tribunal disciplined for the task and environed by the best safeguards for disinterestedness and detachment."[139] But ultimately one disagrees with the Black-Douglas position, if one does, out of a conviction that it unduly hampers rational judgment and realistic lawmaking by refusing to let legislatures and courts recognize significant differences among kinds and modes of expression.

To take a recent example from another country, in the summer of 1970 the Parliament of Northern Ireland passed a Prevention of Incitement to Hatred Act.[140] Under this Act, a person is guilty of an offense if with intent he utters words, or publishes or distributes matter, which is "threatening, abusive or insulting; being matter or words likely to stir up hatred against, or arouse fear of, any section of the public in Northern Ireland on grounds of religious belief, colour, race or ethnic or national origins." It is also an offense to spread false reports of the same tendency with intent "to provoke a breach of the peace whether immediately or at any time thereafter." Given the long and sad history of the relations between Orange and Green, Protestants and Catholics, in the North of Ireland, it is difficult to see this law as a threat to liberty rather than a defense of the peace. The kind of speech it prohibits has led to riots, to sniping from rooftops and to burning multitudes out of house and home, and will continue to do so if it is not stopped. It cannot be stopped, however, by punishing only speech "brigaded with illegal action," because the situation in Northern Ireland is much more the effect of a long-term building up of hatred than of direct incitement to immediate and overt illegal acts.

The kind of speech prohibited by this Act must be distinguished, of course, from legitimate, even if sharp, religious and political criticism. One either decides that the distinction cannot be made in practice, in which case one accepts the consequence of seeing the situation in Northern Ireland continue, or one trusts in independent courts of law, subject to review by higher courts in Great Britain, to make the distinction with reasonable accuracy. The latter course seems to be the more rational one, but it is precisely the course to which Justice Black objected in *Beauharnais v. Illinois*.

Yet distinctions must be made. Bawling invectives is not the same thing as presenting rational arguments, nor is a blaring sound truck only doing what a street-corner orator does when he sets up his soapbox. To pretend that these and a host of other types of speech are all simply and without qualification instances of "utterance" is, in the words of Justice Jackson, "to endanger the great right of free speech by making it ridiculous and obnoxious."[141]

If freedom of speech and press is to be preserved from that danger, the Court must exercise judgment on the meaning and purpose of the guarantee. The Court's judgment in this area presupposes what no one denies, that the United States is committed by the First Amendment to a regime of free speech and free press and that, as Justice Harlan said, "where the constitutional protection exists it must prevail."[142] But rational determination of where this protection prevails must include the application of several scales of values. There is a scale of kinds of utterance in relation to the ends or purposes which freedom of expression is designed to promote. Opposite it is another scale of the personal and societal values to which freedom of expression may be subordinated because they, too, merit protection by the Constitution and the laws. There is also a scale of modes or manners of expressing oneself, of very unequal value. Finally, there is a variety of communications media which, whether or not they can be arranged in a hierarchy, cannot be regarded as identical with one another for purposes either of legal regulation or of constitutional protection against such regulation.

All of these scales of value do or may enter into a judgment on freedom of speech or press. Some kinds of speech and publication enjoy no constituional protection and so stand at the bottom of the scale of the types of utterance of which the law takes cognizance. Other kinds of speech and publication, however, are above the bottom of the scale and, *per se,* merit protection. But they stand low on the scale and may be sacrificed to public interests which stand rather low on their own scale and would not justify suppressing utterances of higher value.

Thus, in 1942 the Court upheld a New York City ordinance which prohibited distribution of commercial advertising handbills on the streets, remarking: "This court has unequivocally held that the streets are proper places for the exercise of the freedom of communicating information and disseminating opinion and that, though the states and municipalities may appropriately regulate the privilege in the public interest, they may not unduly burden or proscribe its employment in these public thoroughfares. We are equally clear that the Constitution imposes no such restraint on government as respects purely commercial advertising."[143] That is to say, while advertising is not ranked with obscenity as being outside the ambit of constitutional protection, it ranks low on the scale of protected utterances. When faced with a public interest which ranks fairly low on its own scale, i.e., prevention of littering of the streets, advertising may be made to yield, whereas the expression of political opinion through the distribution of handbills would not yield. The point is that two scales of value enter into the judgment: the scale of kinds of utterance and the scale of public interests with which utterances may conflict.

As was said above, the scale of kinds of utterance is determined by their relation to the ends or purposes which the constitutional protection of speech and press was intended to promote. Freedom of speech and press figures on this scale not only as a means to other ends but as an end or value in itself. The ability to speak or publish without fear of punishment is desirable for its own sake and apart from whatever other purposes it may serve. Our law favors liberty, as Bracton said in the thirteenth century, and our Constitution today considers freedom of expression as a good in itself and protects it as such, though not absolutely.

Yet even taken as an end in itself, freedom of expression is a scaled, not a uniform, value. It would seem, at any rate, that however much people cherish the right to express themselves, they do not always attach the same importance to what they express. Casual conversation is, no doubt, a pleasure and a human good, but not of the same order as serious discussion of a serious subject. Freedom to express honest convictions, however erroneous they may be in the eyes of others or in reality, merits the status of a guaranteed right more obviously than freedom to express lightly held opinions or mere feelings. The value of freedom of expression, therefore, varies with even the subjective value of what is expressed; and of this a rational system of law may take account, even under the First Amendment.

Furthermore, freedom of expression, though valued as an end in itself, is not the highest end served by the constitutional guarantee of freedom of speech and press. The First Amendment does not protect the right to speak and to publish merely or principally because liberty-loving Americans cherish being able to talk and publish freely. The guarantee is in the Constitution chiefly as a means to ends beyond self-expression. Freedom to express oneself, therefore, while it ranks as one of the ends of the First Amendment, is not the highest of them and consequently, as Justice Harlan said, "constitutionally protected freedom of speech is narrower than an unlimited license to talk."[144]

There are higher ends which the right of free speech and press is intended to promote. The primary purpose is to serve the political needs of a representative democracy which depends on free discussion of public affairs. The guarantee also broadly serves all the social needs that can be satisfied by communication. These needs determine the relative constitutional value of the several kinds of communication.

It should be possible to arrange the kinds of utterance in a scale for purposes of constitutional interpretation. Harry M. Clor cites an example of such an effort from the case of *Roth v. U.S.,* as argued before the Supreme Court:

> The government's brief urged that the value of obscene speech be judged in the light of a comparative scale of First Amendment values based on the purpose of the amendment as interpreted in Supreme Court decisions. This scale of values was tendered as illustrative:
>
> Political speech
> Religious
> Economic
> Scientific
> General News and Information
> Social and Historical Commentary
> Literature
> Art

Entertainment
Music
Humor
Commercial Advertisements
Gossip
Comic books
Epithets
Libel
Obscenity
Profanity
Commercial Pornography

The public interest required to justify restraint would diminish as one moves down the scale and increase as one moves up. The brief then proceeds to the "weighing." Expression characterized by obscenity has extremely low value in the light of basic First Amendment purposes. Arrayed against this expression are social interests in the preservation of moral standards.[145]

As Mr. Clor points out, while the government won its case in *Roth v. U.S.*, the Court rejected its proposed rationale for the decision and refused to accept the scale of values suggested in the government's brief.[146] Rather than commit itself, even by implication, to the proposition that political, religious, economic, scientific, literary, and artistic expression are related to one another in a descending order of value, the Court simply ruled obscenity outside the pale of constitutional protection on the ground that it was "utterly without redeeming social importance."[147] Obscenity, so to speak, was declared to have no place at all on the scale of First Amendment values.

One understands the Court's reluctance to become involved, even remotely, in determining the relative merits of political and religious speech,[148] or of scientific and literary publications. There is, in fact, little reason why it should do so. For most practical purposes, these fields of expression stand constitutionally on the same plane. The Founding Fathers, as we have seen, felt that freedom of the press (and therefore of speech as well) would advance "truth, science, morality and arts in general" as well as responsible government.[149]

Not only the expression of political and religious belief, but the cultivation of all the arts and sciences is protected by the guarantee of freedom of speech and press. To allow the free operation of the human mind in all of these fields is the global end of the First Amendment, and the Court has little or no occasion to determine their relative merits and to decide whether a treatise on economics is of higher value than one on physics, or political speech ranks above a poem.

It is possible, nonetheless, that the Court might some day face the necessity of making some such determination. One might argue, for example, that while national security would in certain circumstances justify suppressing the publication of news or of scientific findings, it would not in the same circumstances justify suppressing the expression of political opinion, and this because the latter stands higher on the scale of First Amendment values. But, generally speaking, it is not necessary to determine what order of value obtains among the kinds of utterance that serve the higher ends of the Amendment.

It might well be relevant, however, for the Court to inquire whether a speech or publication is an effort to attain any of these higher ends and, if so, to what degree. Can the utterance be taken as an attempt to pursue the truth, to argue for a conception of morality, or to communicate an esthetic experience? Or is the dominant purpose of the utterance to amuse and entertain, to sell goods, to satisfy idle curiosity, to express hatred, or to furnish a vicarious experience which is subhuman and degrading? These questions imply a scale of values that puts political, religious, economic and scientific speech, the communication of general news and information and the cultivation of literature and the arts on a superior plane to mere entertainment, commercial advertising, gossip, epithets and pornography. The latter kinds of utterance serve either inferior ends of the First Amendment or no constitutional ends at all, and so may be more readily subordinated to overriding public interests or suppressed altogether.[150]

The pursuit of truth is, by universal agreement among the Justices of the Supreme Court who have spoken on the matter, a chief end of the Freedom of Speech and Press Clause. If we assume, with Chief Judge Learned Hand, that "truth will be most likely to emerge if no limitations are imposed upon utterances that can with any plausibility be regarded as efforts to present grounds for accepting or rejecting propositions whose truth the utterer asserts, or denies,"[151] then we may insist that there should at least be some plausibility. Government may not pass upon the truth of propositions in matters of belief or doctrine. But it can, and sometimes must, distinguish efforts, however mistaken, to get at truth from utterances which tend toward or reach the merely trivial or the irrational. If freedom of speech and press are meant to protect the "exposition of ideas," it is fair to require that what is exposed be an idea and not a mindless appeal to passion or to vulgar curiosity.

For example, in 1959, the Court declared unconstitutional a New York law under which a license had been denied for showing the film, *Lady Chatterley's Lover.* "What New York has done," the Court said, ". . . is to prevent the exhibition of a motion picture because it advocates an idea—that adultery under certain circumstances may be proper behavior."[152] That adultery may be engaged in with propriety is indeed an idea—if not a true one, at least a consoling one—and, like any other idea, it may be advocated through the medium of an art form. It does not follow that if a film included a clinically explicit depiction of the act of sexual intercourse as performed by partners in adultery, it would be "advocating an idea." As *Time* once remarked, voyeurism is a vice, not a point of view. Or, as Justice Harlan concluded after perusing the allegedly obscene material involved in the companion case to *Roth v. U.S.,* "I cannot say that its suppression would so interfere with the communication of 'ideas' in any proper sense of that term that it would offend the Due Process Clause."[153]

Admittedly, the Court has upon occasion denied that "saving intellectual content" is necessary for constitutional protection of publications. In *Winters v. New York* in 1948 it said:

> We do not accede to appellee's suggestion that the constitutional protection for a free press applies only to the exposition of ideas. The line between the informing and the entertaining is too elusive for the protection of that basic right. Everyone is familiar with instances of propaganda through fiction. What is one man's amusement, teaches another's doctrine. Though we can see nothing of any possible value to society in these magazines [described as exploiting "criminal deeds of bloodshed or lust"], they are as much entitled to the protection of free speech as the best of literature.[154]

The Court was careful to add to the above passage the statement that the magazines in question "are equally subject to control if they are lewd, indecent, obscene or profane." But twenty-one years later, the Court went farther and said: "Nor is it relevant that obscene materials in general, or the particular films before the Court, are arguably devoid of any ideological content. The line between the transmission of ideas and mere entertainment is much too elusive for this Court to draw, if indeed such a line can be drawn at all."[155]

This latter declaration merits even more strongly Justice Frankfurter's comment in the *Winters* case: "The essence of the Court's decision is that it gives publications which have 'nothing of any possible value to society' constitutional protection but denies to the States the power to prevent the grave evils to which, in their rational judgment, such publications give rise."[156] To maintain that publications that contain no ideas and are of no possible value to society deserve protection against the claims of a substantial public interest is tantamount to saying that speech or publication need have no rationally discernible relation to the ends of the First Amendment in order to come under its mantle.

Besides, while the line between the transmission of ideas and mere entertainment may be too elusive for a court of law to draw, it need not be assumed that this line coincides with the boundary between constitutionally protected and unprotected speech. In an obscenity case, the Court could use its own words in *Roth v. U.S.* and ask "whether to the average person, applying contemporary community standards, *the dominant theme of the material taken as a whole* appeals to prurient interest."[157] If the First Amendment was intended to foster and protect an appeal to reason, but not an appeal to prurient interest, then the clear dominance of the latter appeal over the former in a given work is enough to disqualify it for constitutional protection, even though it may contain some elements that can be called transmission of ideas. The question of proportion, in other words, is constitutionally relevant.

In cases subsequent to *Roth v. U.S.*, Justice Brennan disagreed with this proposition and rejected proportionality as a constitutional criterion in obscenity cases. For a work to be obscene in the constitutional sense, he insisted, it must be "*utterly* without redeeming social value."[158] But what is wrong with this phrase as an independent test of obscenity is precisely the word "utterly," because it makes the question of the dominant theme of the material irrelevant and renders the *Roth* definition of obscenity largely useless. By refusing to consider the question of proportion, the Court is led into a doctrinaire ignoring of the reality with which it is dealing and ends up protecting blatant pornography because it is not totally devoid of "ideas." This seems quite unnecessary for achieving the goals of the First Amendment. As Justice White said about the pornographic novel, *Fanny Hill*, "Literary style, history, teachings about sex, character description (even of a prostitute) or moral lessons need not come wrapped in such packages."[159] It should not be beyond the mental powers of a court of law to judge a package for what it is and to decide what is the dominant theme of its contents.

It is true, as the Court said in the *Winters* case, that everyone is familiar with instances of propaganda through fiction. But works of literature and of the arts aim principally at communicating an esthetic experience rather than a version of the truth. To speak of them primarily in terms of the transmission or exposition of ideas, as Justices of the Supreme Court have frequently done, and as this paper has done in the preceding paragraphs, is often to misconceive their principal function. Nevertheless, the quality of the esthetic experience which a work intends to communicate is itself an object of rational judgment which may serve as the basis for deciding whether the work is protected by the constitutional guarantee of freedom of the press.

To take a hypothetical example, let us suppose that three directors film the same battle scene in three distinct films. The first director films the battle as an adventure and wishes to communicate the experience of danger faced and overcome, of victory achieved and glory won. His film may also be intended to serve as propaganda for a "hawkish" U.S. foreign policy. The second director films the battle in order to communicate an experience of the horrors of war and to induce a revulsion against it. His film may, in addition, be intended to serve as propaganda for a "dovish" U.S. foreign policy. But, whatever one may think of either director's point of view, his filming of the battle scene communicates an acceptable vicarious experience and is a legitimate exercise of freedom of the press.

In contrast, the third director films the battle as an exercise in sadism. What he communicates is a vicarious experience of the pleasure of inflicting pain, death and degradation on human beings. To picture soldiers beating their enemies to death with their rifle butts is shocking but, properly handled, it can be a realistic portrayal of war and can serve a legitimate artistic end. But at some point the gruesomeness of such a portrayal will pass beyond any legitimate end. If the camera dwells long and lovingly on a man's face being beaten into a bloody and shapeless mass until it is no longer recognizably human, the suspicion and finally the certainty grows that what is being appealed to is nothing more than a sick appetite for violence. It is submitted that, with all due presumptions in favor of artistic freedom, reason can sometimes recognize such an appeal so clearly and unmistakably as to judge it unworthy of constitutional protection.[160] For, if freedom of expression is not an absolute end in itself, judgment must be passed on that which is expressed, and not everything that can be expressed serves the ends of the First Amendment.

It is too narrow an interpretation of freedom of speech and press to confine its protection to appeals to the mind through reasoned discourse. Appeals to the imagination and emotions through literature and the arts also deserve protection. But there is a sense in which every kind of utterance ought to be subject to reason under the First Amendment. To decide the constitutionality of limiting or suppressing an utterance requires passing rational judgment on the ends which the utterance serves and rational evaluation of those ends in the light of the purposes of the First Amendment. Literary and artistic criticism are presumably exercises of the rational human mind and so, too, is legal judgment when it bears upon works of literature and art. The refinements of literary and artistic criticism are doubtless beyond the ordinary competence of courts, for the law is far too blunt an instrument to be used as a scalpel in that kind of intellectual surgery. But rational judgment sufficient for the purposes of constitutional adjudication ought not to be beyond the abilities of the legal mind.

Justice Jackson has already been quoted as saying that the constitutional policy of protecting speech "is rooted in faith in the force of reason." He made that remark in his dissenting opinion in *Kunz v. New York*.[161] In this and in the *Terminiello* case he made a point worth citing in order to highlight the notion of rationality that underlies the various applications of freedom of speech and press.

In the *Kunz* case, the Court reversed the conviction of the Rev. Mr. Kunz, a Protestant minister, for holding a public worship service on the streets of New York City without a permit from the Police Commissioner. Kunz in previous years had had such a permit, but his application for a renewal of it had been denied. The ordinance authorizing the Commissioner to grant or deny these permits was unconstitutional, said the Court, because it vested in a public official control over the right to speak on religious subjects without appropriate legal standards to guide his action.

In his dissent, Justice Jackson chose to ignore the Court's point, which was a defect in the ordinance under which the Police Commissioner acted, and focused instead on Kunz's claim that he had a *right* to speak on religious subjects on the streets. Kunz, said Jackson, had no constitutional right to use the kind of language which he habitually used, and which was the reason why the Commissioner refused to renew his permit.

Mr. Kunz, it appears, preached his religion by attacking that of Catholics and Jews in terms that aroused their intense resentment. "A hostile reception of his subject certainly does not destroy one's right to speak," Justice Jackson admitted. "A temperate and reasoned criticism of Roman Catholicism or Judaism might, and probably would, cause some resentment and protest. But in a free society all sects and factions, as the price of their own freedom to preach their views, must suffer that freedom in others."[162]

But Kunz frequently indulged in such rhetoric as calling the Pope the Anti-Christ and the Jews Christ-killers who should have been burned in the incinerators. These, said Jackson, are not the kind of insult that can be laughed off. "They are always, and in every context, insults which do not spring from reason and can be answered by none. Their historical associations with violence are well understood, both by those who hurl and those who are struck by these missiles."[163]

"When Kunz speaks," therefore, "he poses a 'clear and present' danger to peace and order. Why, then," Justice Jackson wanted to know, "does New York have to put up with it? . . . Is the Court, when declaring Kunz has the *right* he asserts, serving the great end for which the First Amendment stands?" Jackson defined that end in these terms: "The purpose of constitutional protection of speech is to foster peaceful interchange of all manner of thoughts, information and ideas. Its policy is rooted in faith in the force of reason."[164]

He had dissented on essentially the same grounds two years earlier when the Court reversed the conviction of Fr. Terminiello, a Catholic priest, on a breach of the peace charge growing out of a speech he gave in circumstances that threatened to provoke a riot. The kind of speech Terminiello gave, Jackson said, did not deserve protection. "Unity of purpose, passion and hatred, which merges the many kinds of a crowd into the mindlessness of a mob," he remarked, "almost invariably is supplied by speeches. It is naive, or worse, to teach that oratory with this object or effect is a service to liberty. No mob has ever protected any liberty, even its own. . . ."[165]

Whatever one may think of Justice Jackson's refusal to vote with the majority of the Court in the *Kunz* and *Terminiello* cases, the point he made was a sound one. Behind the First Amendment's policy of liberating expression lies a faith in the force of reason. The Amendment assumes that what is expressed will be in some sense rational. Religious belief depends on faith rather than on rational demonstration, and the same can be said of political and other kinds of belief. But belief can be advocated and defended rationally. Even a false idea or, for that matter, an evil idea can serve the cause of truth if an effort is made to present the grounds for it (however specious) in the manner appropriate to rational argument and it is subjected to rational criticism. Literature and the arts appeal to the imagination and the emotions as much or more than to naked reason, yet they, too, are subject to rational judgment and should serve ends of which reason can approve. All of these, as well as the kind of expression that seeks to engender complete rational conviction through demonstrative argument, deserve constitutional protection. But the appeal to mere passion, uncontrolled by reason and directed to rational or antirational purposes, does not deserve protection because it does not serve "the great end for which the First Amendment stands."

There is, then, a hierarchy of kinds of speech and publication established by the ends of the First Amendment. These ends can be subsumed under "the great end," which is to liberate the human mind to pursue through thought and communication all the objects that it can propose to itself as goals of rational endeavor. These ends are not themselves all of equal rank, nor are all expressions equally related to them, hence the hierarchy. Hence, too, different degrees of protection afforded to different kinds of expression by the First Amendment against the claims of competing public interests. But ultimately, in every case, the line drawn by the Amendment is not simply between speech and conduct but between irrational and more or less rational speech.

The presumption in every case of course favors freedom of utterance. But the presumption must sometimes yield to the claims of competing public interests. In such cases the Court must take into account, not only the weight and value of the public interest alleged, but also the quality and comparative value of the kind of speech involved. This value will depend upon the rationally discernible relationship of the speech in question to one of the ends of the First Amendment. In this sense, the unifying principle of the hierarchy of kinds of speech, for purposes of constitutional adjudication, is rationality.

Over against the scale of kinds of speech and publication stands the scale of public interests to which freedom of expression may be subordinated. The interest served by a law that limits utterance should be judged, first, by its importance as a legitimate object of governmental concern. Truth is doubtless objectively a higher value than public order. But it is not a function of government under the First Amendment to protect truth—government's duty is only to keep open the channels through which presumably truth is attained—whereas preserving the elementary conditions of public order is a basic obligation of any government. But the legitimate objects of government are not all of the same importance.

Without attempting to list all such objects in their order of importance, let us mention a few for the sake of illustration. To the extent that the Court has revealed its hierarchy of public interests, national security stands at the pinnacle of it. Its disposition of some freedom of speech and association cases is illuminating on this point.

In 1958, in *N.A.A.C.P. v. Alabama*,[166] the Court unanimously found that any legitimate interest the State of Alabama might have in requiring the National Association for Advancement of Colored People to disclose its membership lists was not sufficient to outweigh the organization's interest in protecting its members against reprisals that would discourage the exercise of their constitutional right of association. In 1960 the Court handed down similar decisions in *Bates v. Little Rock*[167] and *Shelton v. Tucker*.[168]

But in 1961 the majority of the Court held that the national government did not violate the First Amendment's guarantee of freedom of speech and association by compelling the Communist Party to register and to disclose its members in compliance with the Subversive Activities Control Act of 1950. Justice Frankfurter, who wrote the opinion of the Court, answered the charge of inconsistency: "The present case differs from Thomas v. Collins and from National Assoc. for Advancement of Colored People, Bates and Shelton *in the magnitude of the public interests* which the registration and disclosure provisions are designed to protect and *in the pertinence* which registration and disclosure bear to the protection of those interests."[169]

The Court since 1961 has effectively gutted the Subversive Activities Control Act of its contents.[170] Evidently it became convinced that the threat to national security from subversion was remote and minimal and, at the same time, under Chief Justice Warren, it was putting a heavier thumb on the scale in favor of freedom of expression and association. But its earlier decision is worth mentioning because, at very nearly one and the same time, the Court denied the right of the States to compel disclosure of N.A.A.C.P. membership and affirmed the right of the national government to compel disclosure of Communist Party membership, and this because of the "magnitude" of the public interest in national security. There is little doubt that the Court would so decide again, if it thought that the situation demanded it.

The protection of the constitutional processes of democracy, of the administration of justice[171] and of public order also weigh heavily in the balance against exercises of speech and press that disrupt them. These are basic social necessities and, in fact, are essential conditions of the ordered liberty of which freedom of speech and press is a part. "The constitutional guarantee of liberty," as Justice Goldberg said, "implies the existence of an organized society maintaining public order, without which liberty itself would be lost in the excesses of anarchy."[172]

Public comfort and convenience is a lesser value, but may appropriately override some exercises of freedom of speech and press, e.g., public speeches at certain times and places. Public morality is another value that deserves protection. This writer agrees with Justice Harlan when he said: "Even assuming that pornography cannot be deemed ever to cause, in an immediate sense, criminal sexual conduct, other interests within the proper cognizance of the States may be protected by the prohibition placed on such materials. The State can reasonably draw the inference that over a long period of time the indiscriminate dissemination of materials, the essential character of which is to degrade sex, will have an eroding effect on moral standards,"[173] Justice Harlan's view hardly represents the opinion of the Court in recent years, particularly in the light of *Stanley v. Georgia,*[174] But, once it is granted that there is a public morality which government may protect, it is a reasonable view.[175]

Rights private in nature are nonetheless legitimate objects of public protection. Private reputation is a value that government may protect against certain forms of speech or publication. The Constitution does not guarantee immunity to "defamatory statements directed against the private conduct of a public official or private citizen. . . . Purely private defamation has little to do with the political ends of a self-governing society."[176]

One can also regard personal privacy as superior to some exercises of freedom of the press. Thus, when James Hill sued Time, Inc., on the ground that an article in *Life* had falsely reported that a new play, *The Desperate Hours,* portrayed an experience suffered by the Hill family, while the Supreme Court refused to decide in Hill's favor, Justice Fortas angrily dissented and said:

> I do not believe that whatever is in words, however much of an aggression it may be upon individual rights, is beyond the reach of the law, no matter how heedless of others' rights—how remote from public purpose, how reckless, irresponsible, and untrue it may be. . . . There are great and important values in our society, none of which is greater than those reflected in the First Amendment, but which are also fundamental and entitled to this Court's careful respect and protection. Among these is the right to privacy.[177]

It is not necessary to decide here whether *Life* had committed the kind of aggression on individual rights of which Justice Fortas accused it. His general principle was sound: not every utterance serves a public purpose or can stand against the claims of valid private rights. The right to personal privacy is not the highest of publicly protected values, but it is high enough in the scale to override the right to publish defamatory gossip.

There are, then, public or publicly protected private interests which are paramount to some exercises of freedom of speech and press, and this in varying degrees. The claims of public comfort and convenience are not so high as those of the impartial administration of justice. That is to say that there is an order, to use Justice Frankfurter's words, of "the magnitude of the public interests" which are served by laws that have the effect of limiting speech or publication. Rational judgment in cases contesting the constitutionality of such laws has to weigh the importance of the public interests at stake. More important interests justify more stringent limitations of freedom of expression, and this assumes that there is a scale of such interests in the order of their inherent importance.

As Justice Frankfurter indicated in the same passage, one must also consider the question of the degree of "pertinence" of a law of this kind to the public interest it is designed to safeguard. It is not enough that a public interest stand high on the scale in order to justify limiting freedom of expression. The limitation must be genuinely relevant to the interest. Here is the strength of the Warren Court's sometimes exaggerated insistence on "narrow specificity" in legislation that restricts freedom of speech and press; the sound element in this insistence is the requirement that the restriction be limited to the needs of the public interest it is said to serve.

Another element that enters into the consideration of some freedom of speech and press cases is that of urgency. As Justice Brandeis said: "If there be time to expose through discussion the falsehood and fallacies, to avert the evil by the processes of education, the remedy to be applied is more speech, not enforced silence. Only an emergency can justify repression."[178] This is another way of stating the clear and present danger test and is not, in this writer's opinion, a sufficient standard for deciding all questions concerning the limitation of speech and publication. But it generally serves well enough when the issue is the constitutionality of directly suppressing or punishing the expression of opinions thought to have consequences harmful to the public welfare.

In such a case the question is not only how important is the public interest at stake and how pertinent to that interest is the restriction of freedom of expression, but also how urgent is the necessity of applying the restriction. In cases of this kind the constitutional mandate is to avert the evil consequences that may follow from the dissemination of false and dangerous opinions by refuting them with contrary arguments. The only allowable exception to this rule is when those consequences are so imminent in the realm of action that time will not allow the process of discussion to operate.

In other words, we must ask: Is there time for rational argument to prevail? But to ask this question assumes that reason can prevail because we are dealing with the expression of views which, however wrong and harmful they may be, are nonetheless amenable to reason and can be met by rational criticism. Such, however, is not always the case.

The Prevention of Incitement to Hatred Act (Northern Ireland) mentioned above is an example of a law directed to a situation where the expression of certain religious "views" is judged not amenable to reason. It is possible that the preaching of certain racial "views" might reach the same point in this country and have to be declared not within the scope of the First Amendment.

Another example is furnished by the recent Federal legislation banning cigarette advertising from radio and television broadcasts. The constitutionality of this legislation has not been tested in the courts, but there is an obvious prima facie case against it since it restrains "expression." The case for the constitutionality of the legislation would doubtless point out that a clear public interest in health is at stake, and that the kind of expression prohibited, commercial advertising, has always been considered to rank low on the scale of constitutionally protected utterance. This argument might go on to make the point that the appeal made by cigarette commercials is directed to a mass audience, including persons of all ages and conditions, and is not made to their reason. It would be unconstitutional to ban from the airwaves a reasoned presentation of an argument that cigarettes are not really seriously harmful to health. But advertising does not depend for its effectiveness on an appeal to reason, but on the stimulation of the imagination and emotions. Therefore, if in the judgment of the national legislature, such an appeal conflicts directly with an interest of the importance of public health, it loses the constitutional protection of freedom of speech and press.

Those who find this argument unconvincing might consider the situation that would exist if we had in this country an open and widespread propaganda which extolled the joys of using heroin while carefully refraining from direct incitement to violation of the law. In such a situation, would it make sense to depend on the educational process of public discussion and wait for reason to prevail? That it would not is the substance of the argument used by Justice Stewart in his opinion concurring with the Court's decision to uphold a New York law prohibiting the sale to minors of materials judged harmful to minors, i.e., obscene literature. Justice Stewart gave this reason for his concurrence:

> The First Amendment guarantees liberty of human expression in order to preserve in our Nation what Mr. Justice Holmes called a "free trade in ideas." To that end, the Constitution protects more than just a man's freedom to say or write or publish what he wants. It secures as well the liberty of each man to

decide for himself what he will read and to what he will listen. The Constitution guarantees, in short, a society of free choice. Such a society presupposes the capacity of its members to choose. When expression occurs in a setting where the capacity to make a choice is absent, government regulation of that expression may coexist with and even implement First Amendment guarantees.[179]

This writer has considerably less faith than Justice Stewart seems to have in the notion that anyone, even an adult, buys girlie magazines as part of a "free trade in ideas." But his opinion provides confirmation of the point made above, that the conditions of a marketplace of ideas, in which reason can be expected ultimately to prevail, do not always exist.[180] Therefore, in considering whether a public interest justifies restriction of freedom of speech and press, the element of "urgency" does not always enter in. That is to say, it is not always relevant to ask whether there is time for reason to prevail, because in some situations it is unreasonable to think that reason can prevail.

To summarize, in addition to a scale of kinds of utterance that are protected in varying degrees by freedom of speech and press, there is a scale of public interests that justify, in proportion to their importance, limitations of that freedom. But the application of the latter scale must take into account the pertinence of the limitations to the interests that are alleged to justify them. It must sometimes also take into account the urgency of protecting these interests through restriction of freedom of expression rather than of waiting for the process of argument and discussion to take its course.

In addition to these two basic scales that are weighed against each other in constitutional adjudication, we may postulate another scale, that of the manners or modes of expression. Independently of the content of an utterance, the way in which it is uttered may make it more or less deserving of constitutional protection. Justice Stewart once wrote: "The Constitution protects coarse expression as well as refined, and vulgarity no less than elegance."[181] It is true that the Constitution was not written for a nation made up exclusively of ladies and gentlemen and that it protects a large range of expressions that are neither refined nor elegant. It does not follow that there are and ought to be no limits on the kind of language one is permitted to use in public, on the visual imagery that one may set before the public's eyes, or on the kind and volume of noise which one may inflict on the public's ears. The more offensive an utterance becomes in its manner of expression (as distinct from its content), the more easily it may be subordinated to public propriety and comfort, and the more nearly it approaches the point where it loses its claim to constitutional protection. As not every kind of utterance, so not every mode of utterance equally serves the ends of the First Amendment.

Finally, without entering into the subject, let us merely note that the different media of communication pose somewhat different constitutional problems. In the words of Justice Jackson: "The moving picture screen, the radio, the newspaper, the handbill, the sound truck and the street corner orator have differing natures, values, abuses and dangers. Each, in my view, is a law unto itself. . . ."[182] The Court as a whole has not been willing to consider each medium of communication a law unto itself. But, when for the first time it declared that motion pictures are protected by the guarantee of freedom of the press, the Court was careful to add: "Nor does it follow that motion pictures are necessarily subject to the precise rules governing any other particular method of expression. Each method tends to present its own peculiar problems."[183] Suffice it to say here that constitutional adjudication must take those peculiar problems into account and cannot pretend that because they are all resolved under the phrase, "freedom of speech, or of the press," they must receive uniform solutions.

It must be granted that law is of its nature not so fine or so flexible an instrument for the regulation of society's affairs as would be the perfectly nuanced judgments of a philosopher-king. But philosopher-kings, as Plato was well aware, are in notoriously short supply. On the other hand, despite its necessary rigidity and bluntness, law can and must make distinctions and recognize degrees of difference in applying its general rules to the decision of particular cases.

The distinctions will be more easily and more accurately made in regard to freedom of speech and press if we get back to asking, more insistently than we have in recent years, what are we trying to protect and why. Not everything that can be labelled "speech," or "expression," or "utterance" is worth protecting. Much of it must be granted immunity for the sake of preserving the freedom of speech and press that serves the ends of the First Amendment. But not all of it need be or should be rendered immune from legal regulation for the general good. The ends of the First Amendment, broad though they are, are not compatible with everything that it enters into the mind of man to utter, in any way in which he chooses to utter it. The quest for rationality in interpreting the Amendment's guarantees of freedom of speech and press forces us to ask, in the end, what the freedom is for.

Divorced from their original purpose, Walter Lippmann once wrote, "freedom to think and speak are not self-evident necessities. It is only from the hope and the intention of discovering truth that freedom acquires such high public significance." But, he warned,

> when the chaff of silliness, baseness, and deception is so voluminous that it submerges the kernels of truth, freedom of speech may produce such frivolity, or such mischief, that it cannot be preserved against the demand for a restoration of order or of decency. If there is a dividing line between liberty and license, it is where freedom of speech is no longer respected as a procedure of the truth and becomes the unrestricted right to exploit the ignorance, and to incite the passions, of the people. Then freedom is such a hullabaloo of sophistry, propaganda, special pleading, lobbying and salesmanship that it is difficult to remember why freedom of speech is worth the pain and trouble of defending it.[184]

Mr. Lippmann's words state the contemporary problem well. It is not to push back ever farther the outer limits of freedom of speech and press, but to remember ever more clearly why the freedom was worth defending in the first place. For when the purpose of freedom is forgotten, freedom cannot long survive.

## Notes

1. Announcing the judgment of the Court, *Curtis Publishing Co. v. Butts,* 388 U.S. 130, 148
2. *Cf.* Chief Justice Vinson's remark: "No important case involving free speech was decided by this Court prior to *Schenck v. United States,* 249 U.S. 47 (1919)." For the Court, *Dennis v. U.S.,* 341 U.S. 494, 503 (1951), *Cf.* Frankfurter, J., concurring, *Kovacs v. Cooper,*336 U.S. 77, 95 (1949).
3. A number of the statements quoted will refer to freedom of assembly as well as to freedom of speech and press, but in the mind of the Court, these freedoms are all closely related.
4. "Congress shall make no law . . . abridging the freedom of speech, or of the press." First Amendment to the Constitution of the United States. To which add: "It is no longer open to doubt that the liberty of the press, and of speech, is within the liberty safeguarded by the due process clause of the Fourteenth Amendment from invasion by State action." Hughes, C.J., for the Court, *Near v. Minnesota,*283 U.S. 697, 707 (1931).
5. Roberts, J., dissenting, *Thomas v. Collins,* 323 U.S. 516, 548 (1945).
6. Murphy, J., for the Court, *Thornhill v. Alabama,* 310 U.S. 88, 95 (1940).
7. Brennan, J., for the Court, *Speiser v. Randall,* 357 U.S. 513, 521 (1958).
8. Cardozo, J., for the Court, *Palko v. Connecticut,* 302 U.S. 319, 327 (1937).
9. Brennan, J., for the Court, *Time v. Hill,* 385 U.S. 374, 389 (1967). *Cf.* the opinions of the Court in *DeJonge v. Oregon,* 299 U.S. 353, 365 (1937), and *Roth v. U.S.,* 354 U.S. 476, 484 *Shelton v. Tucker,* 364 U.S. 479, 486 (1960); and the concurring opinion of Brandeis, J., joined by Holmes, J., in *Whitney v. California,* 274 U.S. 357, 375 (1927).
10. *Palko v. Connecticut,* 302 U.S. 319, 325 (1937).
11. *Pickering v. Board of Education,* 391 U.S. 563, 573 (1968).
12. 376 U.S. 254, 296–297. *Cf.* opinions of the Court in *Grosjean v. American Press Co.,* 297 U.S. 233, 243 (1936), and *Rosenblatt v. Baer,* 383 U.S. 75, 85 (1966).
13. Vinson, C.J., for the Court, *Dennis v. U.S.,* 341 U.S. 494, 503 (1951).
14. 2 Cooley's *Constitutional Limitations,*8th ed., p. 886, quoted with approval by Sutherland, J., for the Court, *Grosjean v. American Press Co.,* 297 U.S. 233, 249–250 (1936).
15. For the Court, *Mills v. Alabama,* 384 U.S. 214, 218 (1966).
16. For the Court, *Stromberg v. California,* 283 U.S. 359, 369 (1931). *Cf.* the opinions of the Court in *DeJonge v. Oregon,* 299 U.S. 353, 365 (1937), and *Roth v. U.S.,*354 U.S. 476, 484 (1957).
17. Concurring, *Thomas v. Collins,* 323 U.S. 516, 545 (1945).
18. Dissenting, *Terminiello v. Chicago,* 337 U.S. 1, 32 (1949).
19. Roberts, J., for the Court, *Cantwell v. Connecticut,* 310 U.S. 296, 310 (1940).
20. *Associated Press v. U.S.,* 326 U.S. 1, 20 (1945).
21. *Grosjean v. American Press Co.,* 297 U.S. 233, 250 (1936).
22. Dissenting, *Bridges v. California,* 314 U.S. 252, 291, 293 (1941).
23. Douglas, J., joined by Black, J., dissenting, *Adler v. Board of Education,* 342 U.S. 485, 511 (1952).
24. *Red Lion Broadcasting Co. v. F.C.C.,* 395 U.S. 367, 390 (1969). *Cf.* the opinion of the Court, *Thornhill v. Alabama,* 310 U.S. 88, 95 (1940).
25. Holmes, J., joined by Brandeis, J., dissenting, *Abrams v. U.S.,* 250 U.S. 616, 630 (1919).
26. Concurring in part, *Dennis v. U.S.,* 341 U.S. 494, 550 (1951). *Cf.* the opinion of the Court in *New York Times v. Sullivan,* 376 U.S. 254, 270 (1964).
27. As d'Alembert said in the *Discours préliminaire of L'Encyclopédie,* "Only the freedom to act and to think is capable of producing great works, and freedom needs only enlightenment to protect itself from excess." This is a faith which even those who are unable to suppress doubts about the unfailing efficacy of enlightenment.
28. Concurring, *Thomas v. Collins,* 323 U.S. 516, 545 (1945).
29. *N.A.A.C.P. v. Button,* 371 U.S. 415, 445 (1963).
30. Brennan, J., for the Court, *New York Times v. Sullivan,* 376 U.S. 254, 270 (1964).
31. For the Court, *Drivers Union v. Meadowmoor Co.,* 312 U.S. 287, 293 (1941). *Cf.* Justice (1941), and *Niemotko v. Maryland,* 340 U.S. 268, 282 (1951).
32. Dissenting, *Kunz v. New York,* 340 U.S. 290, 302 (1951).

33. *Thomas v. Collins,* 323 U.S. 516, 537 (1945). *Cf.* the opinion of the Court in *Terminiello v. Chicago,* 337 U.S. 1 (1949).
34. *N.A.A.C.P. v. Button,* 371 U.S. 415, 429.
35. 376 U.S. 254, 270. *Cf.* the opinions of the Court in *Bond v. Floyd,* 385 U.S. 116, 136 (1966). *Pickering v. Board of Education,* 391 U.S. 563, 573 (1968); *Red Lion Broadcasting Co. v. F.C.C.,* 395 U.S. 367, 390 (1969); *Greenbelt Cooperative Publishing Association v. Bresler,* 26 L.Ed 2d 6 (1970).
36. *Stanley v. Georgia,* 394 U.S. 557, 564 (1969). *Cf.* the opinion of the Court in *Red Lion Broadcasting Co. v. F.C.C.,* 395 U.S. 367, 390 (1969).
37. Brennan, J., for the Court *Time v. Hill,* 385 U.S. 374, 388 (1967). *Cf.* the opinion of the Court in *United Mine Workers v. Illinois Bar Association,* 389 U.S. 217, 223 (1967).
38. Harlan, J., announcing the judgment of the Court, *Curtis Publishing Co. v. Butts,* 388 U.S. 130, 149 (1967). Note that in the leading case of *Gitlow v. New York* freedom of speech and press was assumed to be "among the fundamental *personal* rights and 'liberties' protected by the due process clause of the Fourteenth Amendment," Sanford, J., for the Court, 268 U.S. 652, 666 (1925) [emphasis added]. *Cf.* Justice Jackson's dictum: "Our forefathers. . . gave the status of almost absolute individual rights to the outward means of expressing belief." Concurring and dissenting, *American Communications Association v. Douds,* 339 U.S. 382, 442 (1950).
39. Concurring in part, *Dennis v. U.S.,* 341 U.S. 494, 550 (1951).
40. Announcing the judgment of the Court, *Curtis Publishing Co. v. Butts,* 388 U.S. 130, 147 (1967). The interior quotation is from the Letter to the Inhabitants of Quebec, 1 *Journals of the Continental Congress* 108, which has often been cited by the Justices of the Court.
41. Brennan, J., for the Court, *Keyishian v. Board of Regents,* 385 U.S. 589, 603 (1967). *Cf.* the eulogies of academic freedom by Frankfurter, J., joined by Douglas, J., concurring, *Wieman v. Updegraff,* 344 U.S. 183 194–198 (1952), and Warren, C.J., announcing the judgment of the Court, *Sweezy v. New Hampshire,* 354 U.S. 234, 250 (1957).
42. *Winters v. New York,* 333 U.S. 507, 510 (1948). *Cf.* the opinion of the Court in *Stanley v. Georgia,* 394 U.S. 557, 566 (1969).
43. 310 U.S. 296, 310 (1940).
44. For the Court, *Hannegan v. Esquire, Inc.,* 327 U.S. 146, 158 (1946). *Cf.* his dissenting opinion in *Dennis v. U.S.,* 341 U.S. 494, 581 (1951).
45. See his dissenting opinion, joined by Black, J., in *Roth v. U.S.,* 354 U.S. 476, 508 (1957).
46. Dissenting, *Ginsberg vs. U.S.,* 383 U.S. 463, 489.
47. Dissenting, *Byrne v. Karalexis,* 24 L.Ed 2d 486, 487.
48. This is an inference, perhaps unjustified, from the fact that Justice Douglas joined Justice Reed in a dissenting opinion in which the latter said that he accepted "the constitutional power of a state to pass group libel laws to protect the public peace." 343 U.S. 250, 283 (1952). In his own dissenting opinion in the same case, Justice Douglas said that it would be constitutional to proscribe a conspiracy of the Nazi type "which was aimed at destroying a race by exposing it to contempt, derision, and obloquy. . . . For such a project would be more than the exercise of free speech. Like picketing, it would be free speech plus." *Ibid.,* at 284.
49. Concurring, *Rosenblatt v. Baer,* 383 U.S. 75, 90–91 (1966).
50. See his separate opinion in the same case, *ibid.,* at 95. It appears, however, that the sweeping denial of the constitutionality of libel laws means only that "the First Amendment guarantees to each person in this country the unconditional right to print what he pleases about *public* affairs." Black, J., joined by Douglas, J., dissenting, *Ginsberg v. Goldwater,* 24 I.Ed 2d 695, 696 (1970) [emphasis added]. Note that Justice Douglas once joined in a concurring opinion in which Justice Goldberg said that the Constitution does not protect "defamatory statements directed against the private conduct of a public official or private citizen." *New York Times v. Sullivan,* 376 U.S. 254, 301 (1964).
51. *E.g.,* Black J., for the Court, *Bridges v. California,* 314 U.S. 252, 263 (1941); Douglas, J., dissenting, *Dennis v. U.S.,* 341 U.S. 494, 584–585, 590 (1951); Douglas, J., dissenting, *Beauharnais v. Illinois,* 343 U.S. 250, 284–285 (1952).

52. Douglas J., concurring, *Brandenburg v. Ohio,* 395 U.S. 444, 454 (1969). Black J., concurring, *ibid.,* at 449, states his explicit agreement with this view.
53. Joined by Black, J., concurring, *Garrison v. Louisiana,* 379 U.S. 64, 82 (1964). *Cf.* the opinions of Douglas, J., joined by Black, J., in *Speiser v. Randall,* 357 U.S. 513, 535 (1958), and *DuBois Clubs v. Clark,* 389 U.S. 309, 318 (1967).
54. Dissenting, *Mishkin v. New York,* 383 U.S. 502, 518 (1966). *Cf.* his opinions, joined by Douglas, J., in *Wieman v. Updegraff,* 344 U.S. 183, 192–194 (1952), and *Yates v. U.S.,* 354 U.S. 298, 340 (1957), and his dissenting opinion in *Communist Party v. S.A.C. Board,* 367 U.S. 1, 167–168 (1961).
55. Joined by Douglas, J., concurring and dissenting, *Yates v. U.S.,* 354 U.S. 298, 343–344 (1957).
56. Joined by Warren, C.J., and Black, J., dissenting, *Times Film Corp. v. Chicago,* 365 U.S. 43, 84 (1961).
57. Concurring, *Memoirs v. Massachusetts,* 383 U.S. 413, 433 (1966). *Cf.* his dissenting opinion in *Ginsberg v. U.S.,* 383 U.S. 463, 491–492 (1966).
58. "Two members of the Court have consistently adhered to the view that a State is utterly without power to suppress, control, or punish the distribution of any writings or pictures upon the ground of their 'obscenity.' " Per curiam, *Redrup v. New York,* 386 U.S. 767, 770 (1967), where the reference is obviously to Black, J., and Douglas, J. *Cf.* e.g., their opinions in *Roth v. U.S.* 354 U.S. 476, 509 (1957), *Memoirs v. Massachusetts,* 383 U.S. 413, 426 (1966), *Ginsberg v. U.S.,* 383 U.S. 463, 491–492 (1966), *Mishkin v. New York,* 383 U.S. 502, 518 (1966), *Ginsberg v. New York,* 390 U.S. 629, 650, 655–656 (1968).
59. See, *e.g.,* their opinions in *Dennis v. U.S.,* 341 U.S. 494, 579–580, 584–585, 590 (1951), *Yates v. U.S.,* 354 U.S. 298, 343–344 (1957), *Speiser v. Randall,* 357 U.S. 513, 536 (1958), *Communist Party v. S.A.C. Board,* 367 U.S. 1, 147 (1961), *Scales v. U.S.,* 367 U.S. 203, 260, 265, 269–270 (1961), *DuBois Clubs v. Clark,* 389 U.S. 309, 314 (1967).
60. See, *e.g.,* their opinions in *New York Times v. Sullivan,* 376 U.S. 254, 293, 295 (1964), *Garrison v. Louisiana,* 379 U.S. 64, 82 (1964), *Rosenblatt v. Baer,* 383 U.S. 75, 90–91, 95 (1966),*Curtis Publishing Co. v. Butts,* 388 U.S. 130, 171–172 (1967), *Ginsberg v. Goldwater,* 24 I.Ed 2d 695, 696 (1970).
61. Joined by Black, J., dissenting, *Roth v. U.S.,* 354 U.S. 476, 514 (1957). But see his later opinions in *Ginsberg v. U.S.,* 383 U.S. 463, 491–492 (1966), and *Ginsberg v. New York,* 390 U.S. 629, 650 (1968), where it appears that the distinction between the noxious and its opposite has vanished.
62. Dissenting, *Konigsberg v. State Bar of California,* 366 U.S. 36, 78 (1961).
63. Dissenting, *Communist Party v. S.A.C. Board,*367 U.S. 1, 147 (1961). He was, of course, echoing Holmes, J., dissenting, *Gitlow v. New York,* 268 U.S. 652, 673 (1925).
64. Douglas, J., joined by Black, J., dissenting, *Roth v. U.S.,* 354 U.S. 476, 509 (1957).
65. Douglas, J., concurring, *Memoirs v. Massachusetts,* 383 U.S. 413, 426 (1966). He had earlier said: "Advocacy which is in no way brigaded with action should always be protected by the First Amendment," Concurring opinion, joined by Black, J., *Speiser v. Randall,* 357 U.S. 513, 536 (1958).
66. Concurring, *Brandenburg v. Ohio,* 395 U.S. 444, 456–457 (1969).
67. Dissenting, *Tinker v. School District,*393 U.S. 503, 524 (1969).
68. Dissenting, *Brown v. Louisiana,* 383 U.S. 131, 162 (1966). *Cf.* the opinion of the Court which he wrote in *Adderley v. Florida,* 385 U.S. 39 (1966) and his separate opinions in *Tinker v. School District,* 393 U.S. 503, 517–518 (1969) and *Gregory v. Chicago* joined by Douglas, J., 394 U.S. 111, 124 (1969).
69. See, *e.g.,* his opinions in *Konigsberg v. State Bar of California,* 366 U.S. 36, 61–62 (1961), *In re Anastaplo,* 366 U.S. 82, 110–112 (1961), *Scales v. U.S.* 367 U.S. 203, 261–262 (1961), *Time v. Hill,* 385 U.S. 374, 399–400 (1967); and the opinions of Douglas J., in *Scales v. U.S., supra,* at 270–271, and *Garrison v. Louisana,* 379 U.S. 64, 80–83 (1964).
70. For the Court, *Marsh v. Alabama,* 326 U.S. 501, 509 (1946). For a similar use of "balancing" terminology by Justice Douglas, see the opinion of the Court in *Saia v. New York,* 334 U.S. 558, 562 (1948).
71. Concurring, *Smith v. California,* 316 U.S. 147, 157–158 (1959).
72. Dissenting, *Konigsberg v. State Bar of California,* 366 U.S. 36, 61 (1961).

73. Concurring, *Time v. Hill*, 385 U.S. 374, 399–400 (1967). *Cf.* Douglas, J., joined by Black, dissenting, *Roth v. U.S.* 354 U.S. 476, 514 (1957).

74. Justices Black and Douglas also reject a "reasonableness" test for justifying limitations of speech and press which is equivalent to the "balancing" test. See, *e.g.,* their opinions in *Beauharnais v. Illinois*, 343 U.S. 250, 269–270 (1952), and *Kingsley International Pictures v. Regents*, 360 U.S. 684, 698 (1959).

75. For the Court *Ginsberg v. U.S.*, 383 U.S. 463, 470 (1966).

76. For the Court, *Near v. Minnesota*, 283 U.S. 697, 708 (1931). *Cf.* the opinions of the Court and concurring opinions in *schaefer v. U.S.*, U.S. 466, 474 (1920), *Whitney v. California*, 274 U.S. 357, 373 (1927), *Stromberg v. California*, 283 U.S. 359, 368 (1931). *Cox v. New Hampshire*, 312 U.S., 569, 574 (1941), *American Communications Association v. Douds*, 339 U.S. 382, 394 (1950), *Dennis v. U.S.*, 341 U.S. 494, 503, 508, 521, 523 (1951), *Breard v. Alexandria*, 341 U.S. 622, 642 (1961), *Roth v. U.S.*, 354 U.S. 476, 483 (1957), *Times Film Corp. v. Chicago*, 365 U.S. 43, 47 (1961).

77. *Konigsberg v. State Bar of California, 366 U.S. 36, 49–51.* See the text for references to earlier cases.

78. *Cf.* Justice Jackson's remark: "Read as literally as some would do, it [the Free Speech Clause of the First Amendment] restrains Congress in terms so absolute that no legislation would be valid if it touched free speech, no matter how obscene, treasonable, defamatory, inciting or provoking." Dissetning, *Terminiello v. Chicago*, 377 U.S. 1, 28 (1949).

79. *Supra*, at 49, note 10.

80. For the Court, *Chaplinsky v. New Hampshire*, 315 U.S. 568, 571–572. Interestingly, this opinion was joined by Justices Black and Douglas—but that was in another decade and, besides, the wench is dead.

81. For the Court, *Roth v. U.S.*, 354 U.S. 476, 481. A lengthy list of references to the earlier cases follows in the original text.

82. *Ibid.*, at 485 See *Redrup v. New York*, per curiam, 386 U.S. 767, 771 (1967) for the later use to which the phrase "utterly without redeeming importance" was put as a canon of constitutional interpretation.

83. For the Court, 310 U.S. 296, 308 (1940).

84. For the Court, *Drivers Union v. Meadowmoor Co.*, 312 U.S. 287, 293 (1941). *Cf.* the dissenting opinions of Jackson, J., in *Terminiello v. Chicago*, 337 U.S. 1, 32 (1949) and *Kunz v. New York*, 340 U.S. 290, 295, 302 (1951).

85. *Supra*, at 310, *Cf.* Murphy, J., for the Court, *Chaplinsky v. New Hampshire*, 315 U.S. 568, 571 (1942).

86. *New York Times v. Sullivan*, 376 U.S. 254. For references to earlier cases, see *ibid.*, at 268, note 6.

87. *Ibid.*, at 279.

88. *Garrison v. Louisiana*, 379 U.S. 64, 75 (1964).

89. Brennan, J., for the Court, *Time v. Hill*, 385 U.S. 374, 390 (1967).

90. White, J., for the Court, *St. Amant v. Thompson*, 390 U.S. 727, 732 (1968).

91. As he said for the Court in *Scales v. U.S.*, "It was settled in *Dennis* that the advocacy with which we are here concerned is not constitutionally protected speech." 367 U.S. 203, 228 (1961).

92. For the Court, *American Communication Association v. Douds*, 339 U.S. 382, 394 (1950).

93. For the Court, 249 U.S. 47, 52.

94. Dissenting, 250 U.S. 616, 627–628 (1919).

95. For the Court, 341 U.S. 494, 505.

96. *Brandenburg v. Ohio*, 395 U.S. 444, 447; see the text for references to the cases thus summarized. But note the earlier statement of the Court that *Dennis v. U.S.*, *supra*, and *Yates v. U.S.*, 354 U.S. 298 (1957) "have definitely laid at rest any doubt that present advocacy of *future* action for violent overthrow satisfies statutory and constitutional requirements equally with advocacy of *immediate* action to that end." *Scales v. U.S.*, 367 U.S. 203, 251 (1961). See *Yates v. U.S.*, for a precise definition of the kind of advocacy intended.

97. *Ginsberg v. New York*, 390 U.S. 629, 641 (1968).

98. For the Court, 341 U.S. 494 508 (1951). See the text for references to the cases. The Chief Justice added: "Overthrow of the Government by force and violence is certainly a substantial enough interest for the Government to limit speech."

99. Concurring, *Whitney v. California*, 274 U.S. 357, 377 (1927). *Cf.* the opinions of the Court in *Herndon v. Lowry*, 301 U.S. 242, 258 (1937), *Schneider v. State*, 308 U.S. 147, 161 (1939), *Cantwell v. Connecticut*, 310 U.S. 296, 304 (1940), *Thomas v. Collins*, 323 U.S. 516, 529–530 (1945).

100. For the Court, 391 U.S. 367, 377. See the text for references to the earlier cases.

101. *Food Employees v. Logan Valley Plaza*, 391 U.S. 308, 323 (1968).

102. *Cox v. Louisiana*, 379 U.S. 536, (1965). Justice Douglas likes to put the same idea in the phrase *"speech plus,"* e.g., "Picketing is free speech *plus*, the *plus* being physical activity that may implicate traffic and related matters." Concurring, *Food Employees v. Logan Valley Plaza, supra*, at 326.

103. *U.S. v. O'Brien*, 391 U.S. 367, 375 (1968).

104. *Tinker v. School District*, 393 U.S. 503, 505–506 (1969).

105. Note 52, *supra*.

106. Concurring and dissenting, *Smith v. California*, 361 U.S. 147, 170 (1959).

107. 341 U.S. 494, 542 (1951). See *ibid.*, at 529–539 for an extended survey of the relevant decisions.

108. *Ibid.*, at 544, *Cf.* his opinion, for the Court, in *Communist Party v. S.A.C. Board*, 367 U.S. 1, 90–91 (1961).

109. 339 U.S. 382, 399 (1950).

110. For the Court, 341 U.S. 494, 503 (1951). See the text for references to the leading cases.

111. *Cf., e.g.*, his opinions in *Bridges v. California*, 314 U.S. 252, 293 (1941) and *Kovacs v. Cooper*, 336 U.S. 77, 95 (1949).

112. *Pickering v. Board of Education*, 391 U.S. 563, 568. Mr. Pickering, to be sure, won his case against the Board, but that only means that the Court struck the balance in his favor. Nor has the Burger Court abandoned the "balancing" test. Title III of the Postal Revenue and Federal Salary Act of 1967 authorizes a householder to require that a mailer of pandering advertisements remove his name from its mailing lists and stop all future mailing to him. In upholding this statute, Burger, C. J., said for the Court: "Without doubt the public postal system is an indispensable adjunct of every civilized society and communication is imperative to a healthy social order. But the right of every person 'to be let alone' must be placed in the scales with the right of others to communicate. . . . Weighing the highly important right to communicate, but without trying to determine where it fits into constitutional imperatives, against the very basic right to be free from sights, sounds and tangible matter we do not want, it seems to us that a mailer's right to communicate must stop at the mailbox of an unreceptive addressee." *Rowan v. U.S. Post Office*, 25 I.Ed 2d 736, 742–743 (1970). Brennan, J., and Douglas, J., concurred in a separate opinion in this unanimous decision.

113. Brennan, J., for the Court, *Speiser v. Randall*, 357 U.S. 513, 526 (1958).

114. *Ibid.*, at 525. *Cf.* his opinion, for the Court, in *Bantam Books v. Sullivan, 372 U.S. 58, 66 (1963)*.

115. *Brennan, J., for the Court, N.A.A.C.P. v. Button*, 371 U.S. 415, 433 (1963). *Cf.* Stewart, J., for the Court in *Shelton v. Tucker*, 364 U.S. 479, 488 (1960), and the criticism of the policy of confining a legislature to the narrowest workable means of accomplishing its end when freedom of speech and of press are affected, expressed by Frankfurter, J., dissenting, *ibid.* at 494. See also *Dombrowski v. Pfister*, 380 U.S. 479, 487 (1965), where the need for "breathing space" issued in the doctrine that enforcement of a law might be unconstitutional because it had a "chilling effect" on the exercise of First Amendment freedoms.

116. For the Court, 354 U.S. 476, 481 (1957).

117. This is the statement denounced by Black, J., concurring, *Smith v. California*, 361 U.S. 147, 157–158 (1959), on the ground that there are no "more important interests" for the protection of which freedom of speech and press may be put in second place.

118. *Roth v. U.S., supra*, at 488.

119. For the Court, *Bantam Books v. Sullivan*, 372 U.S. 58, 66 (1963). *Cf.* his opinions for the Court in *Smith v. California*, 361 U.S. 147, 150 (1959), and *Marcus v. Search Warrant*, 367 U.S. 717, 730–731.

120. Brennan, J., for the Court, *Speiser v. Randall,* 357 U.S. 513, 521 (1958).
121. For the Court, *Carroll v. Commissioners of Princess Anne,* 393 U.S. 175, 183 (1968).
122. *Cf.,e.g.,* the opinions of the Court, per Brennan, J., in *N.A.A.C.P. v. Button,* 371 U.S. 415, 438 (1963), *Garrision v. Louisiana* 379 U.S. 64, 72–73 (1964), and *Rosenblatt v. Baer,* 383 U.S. 75, 86 (1966).
123. *Schneider v. State,* 308 U.S. 147 (1939).
124. *Breard v. Alexandra,* 341 U.S. 622 (1951).
125. *Martin v. Struthers,* 319 U.S. 141 (1943).
126. For the Court, 339 U.S. 382, 401 (1950). *Cf.* the opinion of the Court in *Communist Party v. S.A.C. Board,* 367 U.S. 1, 93 (1961).
127. Dissenting, *Bridges v. California,* 314 U.S. 252, 293 (1941).
128. Concurring opinion, 341 U.S. 494, 544–545 (1951). See the same opinion, at 549, for Frankfurter's recognition that "a public interest is not wanting in granting freedom to speak their minds even to those who advocate the overthrow of the Government by force."
129. 336 U.S. 77, 96 (1949).
130. Dissenting, *Ginsberg v. New York,* 390 U.S. 629, 650 (1968).
131. 343 U.S. 250, 263 (1952). *Cf.* the opinion of the Court in *American Communications Association v. Douds,* 339 U.S. 382, 409–410 (1950).
132. *Beauharnais v. Illinois, supra,* at 274.
133. Dissenting, *Panhandle Oil Co. v. Knox,* 277 U.S. 218, 223 (1928).
134. For the Court, *Gompers v. U.S.,* 233 U.S. 604, 610 (1914).
135. As Justice Jackson remakred, a statute must not be treated as existing in a vacuum, but must be construed in the light of all the facts of the case in which its constitutionality is contested, because "it is very easy to read a statute to permit some hypothetical violation of civil rights but difficult to draft one which will not be subject to the same infirmity." Dissenting, *Kunz v. New York,* 340 U.S. 290, 304 (1951).
136. For the Court, *Kingsley Books v. Brown,* 354 U.S. 436, 441 (1957).
137. See the remarks on this point of Jackson, J., dissenting, *Terminiello v. Chicago,* 337 U.S. 1, 28 (1949).
138. Concurring in the result, *Sweezy v. New Hampshire,* 354 U.S. 234, 267 (1957).
139. *Bartkus v. Illinois,* 359 U.S. 121, 128 (1959).
140. 1970, ch. 24 (N.I.).
141. Dissenting, *Saia v. New York,* 334 U.S. 558, 566 (1948).
142. See above, p. 107.
143. *Valentine v. Chrestenson,* 316 U.S. 52, 54 (142).
144. See above, p. 232.
145. *Obscenity and Public Morality* (Chicago and London: University of Chicago Press, 1969), p. 25.
146. *Ibid.,* pp. 27–28.
147. 354 U.S. 476, 485 (1957).
148. It can be argued, of course, that the expression of religious belief is protected by the Establishment and Free Exercise of Religion Clauses of the First Amendment, independently of the Free Speech and Press Clause.
149. See above, pp. 225–226.
150. The argument against this position comes down to the proposition that, if the Court is allowed to make any distinctions among kinds of utterance, there is no limit on the distinctions it may make. For example: "If 'obscenity' can be carved out of the First Amendment, what other like exceptions can be created? Is 'sacrilege' also beyond the pale? Are utterances or publications made with 'malice' unprotected? How about 'seditious' speech or articles? False, scandalous, and malicious writings or utterances against the Congress or the President 'with intent to defame' or to bring them 'into contempt or disrepute' or to 'excite' against them 'the hatred of the good people' or 'to stir up seditions,' or to 'excite' people to 'resist, oppose or defeat' any law were once made a crime." Douglas J., dissenting, *Byrne v. Karalexis,* 24 I.Ed 2d 486, 489 (1969). One is reminded of the words of Justice Peckham declaring a State law that limited bakers to ten hours of work a day unconstitutional: "If this statute be valid, and if, therefore, a proper case is made out in which to deny the right of an individual, sui juris, as employer or employee, to make contracts for

the labor of the latter under the protection of the provisions of the Federal Constitution, there would seem to be no length to which legislation of this nature might not go." For the Court, *Lochner v. New York,* 198 U.S. 45, 58 (1905).

151. See above, p. 223.
152. *Kingsley International Pictures v. Regents,* 360 U.S. 684, 688.
153. Concurring, *Alberts v. California,* 354 U.S. 476, 502–503 (1957). Justice Harlan, for reasons into which we need not enter here, prefers to refer to the Due Process Clause of the Fourteenth Amendment rather than to the First Amendment in cases arising under State, as distinguished from Federal laws.
154. 333 U.S. 507, 510.
155. *Stanley v. Georgia,* 394 U.S. 557, 566 (1969). The issue in this case was whether the mere private possession of obscene materials (in the particular instance, pornographic films) could constitutionally be made a criminal offense, and the Court's statement quoted here must be understood as addressed to that issue. See *U.S. v. Reidel,* 91 S.Ct. 1410 (1971), and *U.S. v. 37 Photographs,* 91 S.Ct. 1400 (1971), in which the Court rejected the argument that under *Stanley v. Georgia* individuals have a constitutional right to view pornographic material and therefore a right to obtain it on the market. Still, this writer feels that the whole tenor of the majority opinion in *Stanley* limits and weakens its declaration in *Roth v. U.S.,* 354 U.S. 476, that obscenity is not protected by the First Amendment, and he continues to think so despite the Court's ringing denial in *U.S. v. Reidel* that *Stanley* had any such intention.
156. Dissenting, 333 U.S. 507, 528 (1948).
157. 354 U.S. 476, 489 [emphasis added].
158. Announcing the judgment of the Court, *Memoirs v. Massachusetts,* 383 U.S. 413, 419, where he himself supplied the emphasis. *Cf.* his opinion in *Jacobellis v. Ohio,* 378 U.S. 184, 191 (1964) and *Redrup v. New York,* per curiam, 386 U.S. 767, 771 (1967). In no case did Justice Brennan's interpretation of "utterly without redeeming social value" as the determinative norm win the support of a majority, but his view is effectively the view of the Court because of the concurrence of Justices Black and Douglas, and others, in the judgement of the Court. For a criticism of Brennan's position on this point see Clark, J., dissenting, *Memoirs v. Massachusetts,* 383 U.S. 413, 445 (1966) and White, J., dissenting, *ibid.,* at 461.
159. *Ibid.,* at 462.
160. Obscenity, we are told, is beyond the capacity of the law adequately to define, and Justice Stewart has been laughed at for saying that, while he could not define hard-core pornography, "I know it when I see it." Concurring, *Jacobellis v. Ohio,* 378 U.S. 184, 197 (1964). But consider the following lines from *Time* for April 6, 1970. After the fall from power of Prince Sihanouk in Cambodia, the magazine reported, the "local press mocked him savagely and his half-Italian wife Princess Monique even more. Some newspapers ran composite photos of her head on anonymous nude bodies in obscene poses." The editors of *Time* evidently assumed that their readers would have no difficulty in understanding what they meant, and the people in Cambodia who made up and published the composite photographs took it for granted that their readers would know an obscene pose when they saw one. Recognizing obscenity for what it is apparently is not always so difficult as libertarians make it out to be.
161. 340 U.S. 290, 302 (1951).
162. *Ibid.,* at 301.
163. *Ibid.,* at 299.
164. *Ibid.,* at 302.
165. *Terminiello v. Chicago,* 337 U.S. 1, 32 (1949).
166. 357 U.S. 449.
167. 361 U.S. 516.
168. 364 U.S. 479.
169. *Communist Party v. S.A.C. Board,* 367 U.S. 1, 93 EMPHASIS ADDED.
170. *Albertson v. S.A.C. Board,* 382 U.S. 70 (1965) and *U.S. v. Robel,* 389 U.S. 258 (1967).
171. *Sheppard v. Maxwell,* 384 U.S. 333 (1966), however, is a curious example of an opinion in which the Court commanded trial judges to maintain the integrity of the administration of justice against the undue influence of an unrestrained press while refusing to allow any

direct restraint to be put on the press. It was an effort to preserve the competing interests of both justice and freedom of the press. But whether a realistic balance was in fact struck by the Court in this opinion is open to question.

172. For the Court, *Cox v. Louisiana,* 379 U.S. 536, 554 (1965).

173. Concurring *Alberts v. California,* 354 U.S. 476, 502 (1957). *Cf.* Warren, C. J., dissenting, *Jacobellis v. Ohio,* 378 U.S. 184, 199 (1964). The position recently taken by the majority of the President's Commission on Obscenity and Pornography is wrong, in this writer's view, because it rests on two false assumptions: (1) that "utterance" in the abstract is a value worth protecting, and (2) that limitations on it must be justified by a showing that it incites to criminal acts. On the contrary, given the minimal or nil value of obscene utterance, it is a sufficient reason for limiting or suppressing it that a legislature judges, in Justice Harlan's words, that it "will have an eroding effect on moral standards," and that it creates a fetid public atmosphere in which we all have to live.

There remains, of course, the possibility of a trade in pornography kept strictly under the counter for the benefit of "dirty old men" and no one else—but in such a situation we should still be a long way from the rottenness in the state of Denmark.

174. 394 U.S. 557 (1969).

175. A diametrically opposite view is expressed by Douglas, J., joined by Black, J., dissenting, *Roth v. U.S.* 354 U.S. 476, 509–510 (1957).

176. Goldberg, J., concurring, *New York Times v. Sullivan,* 376 U.S. 254, 301 (1964).

177. *Time v. Hill,* 385 U.S. 374, 412 (1967).

178. Concurring, *Whitney v. California,* 274 U.S. 357, 377 (1927).

179. *Ginsberg v. New York,* 390 U.S. 629, 649 (1968).

180. *Cf.* Harlan, J., dissenting in part, *Time v. Hill,* 385 U.S. 374, 407–408 (1967).

181. Dissenting, *Ginsberg v. U.S.,* 383 U.S. 463, 498 (1966).

182. Concurring, *Kovacs v. Cooper,* 336 U.S. 77, 97 (1949).

183. Clark, J., for the Court, *Burstyn v. Wilson,* 343 U.S. 495, 503 (1952).

184. *The Public Philosophy* (New York: Mentor Books, 1956), pp. 97–98.

---

# The Exclusionary Rule: A Requirement of Constitutional Principle

Lane V. Sunderland

In a government of laws, existence of the government will be imperilled if it fails to observe the law scrupulously. Our government is the potent, the omnipresent, teacher. For good or for ill, it teaches the whole people by its example. Crime is contagious. If the government becomes a law-breaker, it breeds contempt for the law; it invites every man to become a law unto himself; it invites anarchy. To declare that in the administration of the criminal law the end justifies the means—to declare that the government may commit crimes in order to secure the conviction of a private criminal—would bring terrible retribution. Against that pernicious doctrine this Court should resolutely set its face.[1]

Mr. Justice Brandeis

Reprinted with permission of the *Journal of Criminal Law and Criminology* and the author, Lane V. Sunderland.

This article was originally read as a paper at the 1976 Annual Meetings of the American Political Science Association and was later published in 69 *J. Crim. L. & C.* 141–59 (1978). I have been helped in the work of which this article is a part by Professors Peter Schotten and Richard C. Stevens. I am also indebted to Donna Palm for her research assistance.

The public has accepted—largely on faith in the judiciary—the distasteful results of the Suppression Doctrine; but the wrath of public opinion may descend alike on police and judges if we persist in the view that suppression is a solution. At best it is a necessary evil and hardly more than a manifestation of sterile judicial indignation even in the view of well motivated and well informed laymen. We can well ponder whether any community is entitled to call itself an "organized society" if it can find no way to solve this problem except by suppression of truth in the search for truth.[2]

Mr. Chief Justice Burger

The juxtaposition of these two statements leads us to the heart of the controversy between those who support and those who oppose the exclusionary rule. While some argue that exclusion of unconstitutionally seized evidence from judicial proceedings is desirable as a deterrent to unconstitutional police behavior[3] or necessary to maintain judicial integrity, others maintain that the political order cannot tolerate the freeing of individuals whose guilt would be clearly established by the introduction at trial of evidence seized unconstitutionally.[4] Do the principles of the Constitution require the exclusionary rule, or has that rule become elevated to the status of constitutional law by virtue of being an often repeated, judicially created rule of deterrence? If the forms of the Constitution do require exclusion, must the rule be applied to all police violations, no matter how minor or non-wilful the violations may be? In addressing these questions, this inquiry first examines the Supreme Court's explication of the underlying rationale of the exclusionary rule. It next presents a theory supporting the exclusionary rule as a requirement of constitutional principle, and finally attempts to determine whether or not the theory requires exclusion in all instances of police violations, or only substantial violations of rights related to search and seizure.

## I. Selected Judicial Opinions

The American origins of the exclusionary rule may be traced to 1886 when *Boyd v. United States* held unconstitutional the compulsory production of business papers under the provisions of an Act of 1874.[5] The Act authorized a court of the United States to require the defendant or claimant in revenue cases to produce in court his private books, invoices and papers, or else the allegations against the individual would be taken as confessed. Since the fifth amendment self-incrimination issue was intertwined with fourth amendment search and seizure considerations, the dispositive arguments in the case are difficult to establish. The Court simply ruled the applicable parts of the statute repugnant to the fourth *and* fifth amendments without giving a more specific explanation of its holding:

> [A] compulsory production of the private books and papers of the owner of goods sought to be forfeited in such a suit is compelling him to be a witness against himself, within the meaning of the Fifth Amendment to the Constitution; and is the equivalent of a search and seizure, and an unreasonable search and seizure, within the meaning of the Fourth Amendment.[6]

The peculiarly narrow issue resolved in *Boyd* might be interpreted in this way: does the assumption of guilt which follows from the failure to produce the private papers involved in the case amount to a compulsion to testify against oneself? Viewed from another perspective, this more inclusive issue emerges from *Boyd:* must the compelled evidence, the business papers, be excluded because the defendant had been compelled to incriminate himself by producing this evidence? It is significant that the issue of business papers may raise considerations different from evidence such as a murder weapon. Much of the Court's argument in *Boyd* would seem to apply with greater force to the former than to the latter type of evidence.

Although the Court in *Boyd* refused to compel production of the papers, the particular nature of the case rendered unnecessary a justification of the exclusionary rule or an explanation of its underlying rationale as it relates to fourth amendment issues. It should be emphasized that this was not a simple search and seizure question. Rather, the fact that the self-incrimination issue was so prevalent in the Court's reasoning, coupled with the actual wording of the fifth amendment privilege—"nor shall [any person] be compelled in any criminal case to be a witness against himself"— made it unnecessary for the Court to articulate the rationale underlying exclusion. That is, the wording of the fifth amendment privilege relates directly and explicitly to the compulsion of testimony. In *Boyd,* the Court saw the forced production of the papers as constituting compulsion to be a witness against oneself, a compulsion which was complete in nature because of the involvement of an order by the district judge which constituted a positive act by the judicial branch of government. The judicial order and the assumption of guilt following the failure to produce the papers are elements which are responsible for the characteristic fifth amendment cast of the opinion.[7] Consequently, the actual exclusion of evidence or testimony within the factual context of *Boyd* seems more deeply and apparently rooted in the fifth amendment's ban on an individual's being compelled to testify against himself than in the fourth amendment's requirements relating to searches and seizures.[8] While fourth amendment searches of a dwelling may involve an element of compulsion even when conducted under the guidelines of the Constitution, the individual is not compelled in the same sense as was true in *Boyd*.

The absence of an explicit rationale in *Boyd* was largely a result of the peculiar facts in that case.[9] Nonetheless, this lack of reasoned support for the exclusionary rule in *Boyd* offered little basis for the development of a coherent and deep-rooted explication of the doctrine in constitutional law.

Several years after *Boyd,* exclusion based on fourth amendment violations was rejected.[10] But in 1914, in the case of *Weeks v. United States,* a unanimous Court articulated an exclusionary rule based on fourth amendment considerations and rejected the common law view that evidence was admissible however that evidence was acquired.[11] The evidence on the basis of which *Weeks* was convicted was seized from his home in two warrantless searches. This evidence included private papers like those involved in *Boyd*.

*Weeks* presents a more nearly persuasive rationale for the exclusionary rule than that presented in *Boyd:*

> [T]he duty of giving to it [the fourth amendment] force and effect is obligatory upon all entrusted under our Federal system with the enforcement of the laws. The tendency of those who execute the criminal laws of the country to obtain conviction by means of unlawful seizures and enforced confessions, the latter

> often obtained after subjecting accused persons to unwarranted practices destructive of rights secured by the Federal Constitution should find no sanction in the judgments of the courts which are charged at all times with the support of the Constitution, and to which people of all conditions have a right to appeal for the maintenance of such fundamental rights.[12]

The essence of this argument is that all bodies entrusted with enforcement of the law, including the judiciary, must enforce that law as written. In the case of searches and seizures, this enforcement must be according to the commands of the fourth amendment. The second thread of the argument in *Weeks* is that the courts should not sanction any departures from the Constitution since the courts are responsible for supporting the Constitution and for maintaining fundamental constitutional rights. This argument is very similar to, although more explicit than, that made in the later cases which justify the exclusionary rule on the basis of its being necessary to maintain "judicial integrity."[13]

The emphasis on supporting particular constitutional provisions through judicial insistence on observing constitutional forms is illustrated in *Weeks*, where the Court noted:

> If letters and private documents can thus be seized and held and used in evidence against a citizen accused of an offense, the protection of the Fourth Amendment declaring his right to be secure against such searches and seizures, is of no value, and, so far as those thus placed are concerned, might as well be stricken from the Constitution. The efforts of the courts and their officials to bring the guilty to punishment, praiseworthy as they are, are not to be aided by the sacrifice of those great principles established by years of endeavor and suffering which have resulted in their embodiment in the fundamental law of the land.[14]

Both in this section of the Court's opinion and in the section quoted earlier, the reason for the exclusion is not that of deterrence. In the second excerpt, however, the rationale for exclusion shifts subtly from that of "judicial integrity" to that of preserving the great principles of the "law of the land." If the government seizes, and admits into court, evidence obtained in violation of constitutional commands, it is as if the constitutional commands or "fundamental law of the land" did not exist. While this argument may include objections to judicial involvement in violations of the "fundamental law of the land," the Court's references to sacrificing "great principles" also indicates its concern that if the judiciary does not follow the commands of the Constitution, these principles may become mere parchment declarations, meaningless to the fostering of a regime based on republican liberty. The second section of this article addresses the significance of *Weeks'* utilization of the concept "fundamental law of the land." At this point in the analysis, it is sufficient to recognize that the genesis of the exclusionary rule was not explicitly based on the rationale of deterrence as that term is understood in contemporary usage.

The course of later decisions, however, departed from the constitutional basis of the exclusionary rule. *Wolf v. Colorado,* while a fourteenth amendment decision, raised a question directly relevant to this departure:

> Does a conviction by a State court for a State offense deny the "due process of law" required by the Fourteenth Amendment, solely because evidence that was admitted at the trial was obtained under circumstances which would have rendered it inadmissible in a prosecution for violation of a federal law in a court of the United States because they deemed to be an infraction of the Fourth Amendment as applied in *Weeks v. United States. . . ?*[15]

Frankfurter's majority opinion discussed the issue of applying the exclusionary rule to the states through the fourteenth amendment in terms of enforcing the right to privacy which is at the core of the fourth amendment. He asserted without persuasive argument that the *Weeks* exclusionary rule was "not derived from the explicit requirements of the Fourth Amendment. . . . The decision was a matter of judicial implication."[16] He spoke of various means of enforcing the fourth amendment, only one of which is the exclusionary rule. Frankfurter late in the opinion stated that "though we have interpreted the Fourth Amendment to forbid the admission of such evidence, a different question would be presented if Congress under its legislative powers were to pass a statute purporting to negate the *Weeks* doctrine."[17] Frankfurter's majority opinion does not say explicitly, as does Black's concurring opinion, that the federal exclusionary rule is simply a judicially created rule of evidence.[18] Frankfurter did not see the *Weeks* opinion or the fourth amendment as clearly requiring the exclusionary rule as a matter of constitutional principle. Unfortunately, no convincing argument was offered in support of his view.

The case of *Mapp v. Ohio*[19] provides the most extended treatment of the exclusionary rule's foundations of any of the cases thus far examined. The essence of *Mapp* is that the exclusionary rule is an essential part of the fourth amendment, and the right that amendment embodies applies to the states through the due process clause of the fourteenth amendment. Or, as Francis Allen succinctly stated the case's holding: "the exclusionary rule is part of the Fourth Amendment; the Fourth Amendment is part of the Fourteenth; therefore, the exclusionary rule is part of the Fourteenth."[20] The rationale for the exclusionary rule presented in *Mapp* may roughly be divided into two different categories.[21] The Court cited several earlier cases, including *Weeks v. United States,* in what appears to be an argument supporting the exclusionary rule as a constitutional requirement, independent of its efficacy as a deterrent. In the context of this discussion, however, the Court spoke of the exclusionary rule as a "deterrent safeguard." It thereby prepared the way for a discussion of the "factual grounds" of deterrence on which *Wolf* was based, even though these grounds "are not basically relevant to a decision that the exclusionary rule is an essential ingredient of the fourth amendment as the right it embodies is vouchsafed against the States by the Due Process Clause."[22] Thus, although the Court devoted a significant portion of its opinion to a discussion of factual considerations relating to the deterrent effect of the exclusionary rule, the statements quoted seem to indicate that these considerations are not the sole or perhaps even the primary basis of its judgment in *Mapp.*

At another point in the opinion, the Court embarked on a principle defense of the exclusionary rule on grounds of constitutional principle—grounds separable from considerations of deterrence.[23] This defense is disappointingly ambiguous and insubstantial, however, and concludes, by citing *Elkins v. United States,* that the purpose of the exclusionary rule is "to deter—to compel respect for the constitutional guaranty in the only effectively available way—by removing the incentive to disregard it."[24] Thus, the foundation of this argument rests on considerations of deterrence. Only when the Court turns to considerations of "judicial integrity" does the defense of the exclusionary rule in terms of constitutional principle become substantial. The Court speaks of the potential for a government's being destroyed by its disregard of the charter of its own existence and of government as a teacher which, if it breaks the law, may breed contempt for that law. This principled rationale is of consequence in *Mapp,* but it is still not entirely clear what the Court intends as its primary rationale for the exclusionary rule.[25]

Dallin Oaks succinctly summarized a part of the difficulty with the *Mapp* opinion in stating: "The discursive prevailing opinion in *Mapp v. Ohio* quoted the *Elkins* statement and otherwise characterized the exclusionary rule as a 'deterrent safeguard,' but the decision does not clearly identify the primary basis for the rule because Justice Black's reliance on a self-incrimination theory split the majority on this question."[26] That is, Black adopted a view that evidence seized in violation of the fourth amendment must be excluded from the judicial proceeding because that evidence constitutes a compelled self-incrimination in violation of the fifth amendment. This doctrine appeared most vividly in a passage of *Boyd v. United States* quoted by Black: "[The Court declared itself] unable to perceive that the seizure of a man's private books and papers to be used in evidence against him is substantially different from compelling him to be a witness against himself"[27] Because of Black's reliance on this doctrine, identification of the primary basis for the exclusionary rule in *Mapp* becomes extremely difficult.

Absent a clear, persuasive, principled rationale in *Mapp,* it is little wonder that the rule should come under attack from those who object to the rule's practical consequences. This deficiency in *Mapp* also laid the groundwork for the later case of *Linkletter v. Walker,*[28] in which the Court held that the *Mapp* rule did not apply to state court convictions which had become final before the Court decided *Mapp. Linkletter's* seven-Justice majority rested its opinion on the deterrence rationale: "In rejecting the *Wolf* doctrine as to the exclusionary rule the purpose was to deter the lawless action of the police and to effectively enforce the Fourth Amendment. That purpose will not at this late date be served by the wholesale release of the guilty victims."[29] Further, the Court noted:

> *Mapp* had as its prime purpose the enforcement of the Fourth Amendment through the inclusion of the exclusionary rule within its rights. This, it was found, was the only effective deterrent to lawless police action. Indeed, all of the cases since *Wolf* requiring the exclusion of illegal evidence have been based on the necessity for an effective deterrent to illegal police action.[30]

With this seven-Justice majority's resting of its opinion on the policy consideration of deterrence, the way was cleared for treating the whole matter of the exclusionary rule not in terms of commands of consistent and reasoned constitutional principle, but rather in terms of the practical consideration of the efficacy of the exclusionary rule as a deterrent.[31] Other decisions dealt with retroactivity in a way similar to that of *Linkletter v. Walker*. Oaks summarized the implications of these decisions as they relate to the rationale of the exclusionary rule:

> By fixing the effective date in terms of the police conduct rather than in terms of the time at which the trial court took its action in the matter, the Court has impliedly rejected the theory of "judicial integrity" and identified the exclusionary rule's primary purpose as that of controlling police behavior. Finally, in an opinion concerning the retroactivity of its decision applying the self-incrimination privilege to the states, the Supreme Court stated that deterrence was the "single and distinct" purpose of the exclusionary rule.[32]

Given this clear emphasis on deterrence in the retroactivity cases and the uncertainty surrounding the basis of the rule in *Mapp*, it is not surprising that the rule has been criticized by members of the Court. Both *Coolidge v. New Hampshire*[33] and *Bivens v. Six Unknown Named Agents of Federal Bureau of Narcotics*[34] presented members of the Court with an opportunity to critique the rule.

It is not necessary to discuss the somewhat complex factual issues surrounding *Coolidge* or to examine the protracted opinions in the case. For our purposes, it is appropriate merely to note that four Justices expressed reservations of one type or another regarding the fourth amendment exclusionary rule as applied in the case through the fourteenth amendment. Harlan would have perpetuated the rule in federal court but would have overruled *Mapp*.[35] Justice Blackmun apparently agreed with Justice Black in the latter's rejection of the rule based on fourth amendment considerations,[36] and Chief Justice Burger wished the rule to be revised legislatively.[37]

The Chief Justice's most comprehensive and critical analysis of the exclusionary rule and his proposed alternative were explicated in *Bivens*. Decided the same day as *Coolidge, Bivens* allowed a cause of action under the fourth amendment for damages resulting from a Federal Bureau of Narcotics entry and search of petitioner's apartment and his arrest, all without a warrant.[38]

Burger began his dissent with a critique of the judicially created damage remedy, viewing it as an invasion of the legislative power. He very quickly turned to a critique of the exclusionary rule, describing the rule as having been based on a theory of deterrence.[39] His criticisms of the exclusionary rule emphasized the high price society pays for the remedy in that the criminal goes free " 'because the constable has blundered.' "[40] Burger also addressed and dismissed the argument advanced by some who justify the rule on the grounds that government must "play the game" by the rules and "cannot be allowed to profit from its own illegal acts. . . . If an effective alternative remedy is available, concern for official observance of the law does not require adherence to the exclusionary rule."[41]

Burger's argument is open to criticism, the most systematic of which will be presented in Section II. But it is necessary to recognize here that even granting the existence of alternative remedies, any individual convicted in a judicial proceeding in which the commands of the fourth amendment have not been followed is convicted outside the forms of the Constitution. Burger's argument does not adequately dispose of this objection, nor does his argument dispose of the objections raised by the case of *Weeks* to using unconstitutionally seized evidence.[42]

Burger next turned to the argument that "the relationship between the self-incrimination clause of the fifth amendment and the fourth amendment requires the suppression of evidence seized in violation of the latter."[43] Referring to the decisions of the Court holding that the fifth amendment applies only to "testimonial disclosures,"[44] Burger stated:

> [I]t seems clear that the Self-Incrimination Clause does not protect a person from the seizure of evidence that is incriminating. It protects a person only from being the conduit by which the police acquire evidence. Mr. Justice Holmes put it succinctly, "A party is privileged from producing the evidence, but not from its production."[45]

After treating these two theoretical justifications for the exclusionary rule, Burger rejected them as the relevant considerations:

> It is clear, however, that neither of these theories undergirds the decided cases in this Court. Rather the exclusionary rule has rested on the deterrent rationale—the hope that law enforcement officials would be deterred from unlawful searches and seizures if the illegally seized, albeit trustworthy, evidence was suppressed often enough and the courts persistently enough deprived them of any benefits they might have gained from their illegal conduct.[46]

After asserting that the rule rests on the rationale of deterrence, Burger turned to his critique of the exclusionary rule—a rule he regards as both "conceptually sterile" and "practically ineffective." Generally, his criticisms may be grouped into four areas. (1) "The rule does not apply any direct sanction to the individual official whose illegal conduct results in the exclusion in a criminal trial." The immediate sanction of the rule affects the prosecutor. (2) Whatever educational effect the rule might have in theory is diminished both by the fact that policemen are not likely to grasp the technicalities of appellate court opinions and by the time lag between police action and final judicial disposition. (3) The exclusionary rule has virtually no applicability and no effect in the large areas of police activity that do not result in criminal prosecutions. (4) The exclusionary rule is applied in like manner to both inadvertent errors or judgment and to deliberate and flagrant violations.[47]

In sum, Burger described the exclusionary rule as an experimental step in the tradition of the common law—a step which has turned out to be unworkable and irrational. As an alternative to the exclusionary rule, Burger set forth the outlines of a statute he recommended to Congress, the thrust of which is the abolition of the exclusionary rule and the creation of a tribunal to adjudicate claims and award damages for violations arising under the fourth amendment or relevant statutes.[48]

Prior to possible adoption of the alternative set forth above, Burger supported the narrowing of the exclusionary rule. Although he did not explicitly adopt these standards, he cited in an appendix to his opinion the tentative draft of the American Law Institute's Model Pre-Arraignment Code. The thrust of this code is the narrowing of the exclusionary rule so it applies only to substantial violations, based on considerations such as the importance of the interest involved, the magnitude and wilfulness of the violation, the extent of the invasion of privacy, and the potential in the exclusion for prevention of other violations.[49] Burger did not give a clear theoretical justification in his opinion as to why the principles of the Constitution allow or require the narrowing of the exclusionary rule, but relied on considerations of deterrence and practical matters of public policy instead.[50]

Another example of the Court's reliance on the rationale of deterrence is *United States v. Calandra*,[51] which held that a witness testifying before a grand jury may not refuse to answer questions on the ground that they are based on evidence obtained from an unlawful search and seizure. In emphasizing the deterrence rationale, the Court denied that exclusion of the evidence in the context of this case would have any substantial deterrent effect and argued that since the witness's privacy had already been invaded, it would not be further damaged by the grand jury inquiry. As the Court noted, "In sum, the rule is a judicially created remedy designed to safeguard Fourth Amendment rights generally through its deterrent effect, rather than a personal constitutional right of the party aggrieved."[52]

More recent examples of the Court's movement toward deterrence as the sole rationale for exclusion are five search and seizure decisions handed down by the Court on July 6, 1976. Although the substantive issue of fourth amendment rights involved in these cases is intrinsically interesting, the comments which follow are limited to the cases' treatment of the exclusionary rule.

*Stone v. Powell*[53] is the leading case. *Stone* and a companion case[54] held that a state prisoner who has had an opportunity in state court for full and fair litigation of fourth amendment claims is not entitled to federal habeas corpus consideration of his claim that evidence obtained in an unconstitutional search or seizure was introduced at his trial.[55] Additionally, in *United States v. Janis*,[56] the Court held that the fourth amendment exclusionary rule does not forbid the use in a federal civil proceeding of evidence seized unconstitutionally but in good faith by a state officer.

These cases reiterate the increased concentration of the Court on deterrence. In *Stone,* the Court stated:

> Although our decisions often have alluded to the "imperative of judicial integrity," . . . they demonstrate the limited role of this justification in the determination whether to apply the rule in a particular context. . . . While courts, of course, must ever be concerned with preserving the integrity of the judicial process, this concern has limited force as a justification for the exclusion of highly probative evidence.
> . . . Post-*Mapp* decisions have established that the rule is not a personal constitutional right.[57]

The Court's view of deterrence as the dispositive issue was made explicit later in the opinion when it was noted, "There is no reason to believe, however, that the overall educative effect of the exclusionary rule would be appreciably diminished if search-and-seizure claims could not be raised in federal habeas corpus review of state convictions."[58]

The Court's view of deterrence as the primary criterion justifying exclusion is stressed in *Janis* as well. The Court stated, "If, on the other hand, the exclusionary rule does not result in appreciable deterrence, then clearly, its use in the instant situation is unwarranted."[59] Moreover, the Court suggested that the concept of judicial integrity goes no further than determining the efficacy of exclusion as a deterrent in the case being adjudicated.[60]

The Court's statement in *Janis* indicates that the "judicial integrity" consideration has been collapsed into the consideration of "deterrence." This interpretation completes the transformation of the exclusionary rule from a doctrine derived, albeit inadequately, from constitutional principle, to a rule based on the judges' assessment of the rule as a deterrent.

This analysis exhibits the shift from the origins of the exclusionary rule in *Boyd*[61] and *Weeks*,[62] which stress intrinsic constitutional principles, to the retroactivity cases, *Calandra*[63] and the 1976 cases, in which public policy considerations relating to deterrence appear as the primary, if not the sole considerations.

It is this writer's opinion that the failure of the earlier cases to clearly articulate a constitutional basis for those decisions has led to this drift. In section II, I will attempt to find such a basis.

### II. A Theory of the Exclusionary Rule Based on "Due Process of Law"

In the treatment of *Boyd*, we saw no clear articulation of the rationale underlying the exclusionary rule, primarily because of the importance the Court accorded fifth amendment considerations in that case.[64] *Weeks* is more helpful in constructing a reasoned, principled defense of the exclusionary rule.[65] That case argued that all bodies, including the judiciary, entrusted with enforcement of the laws, must enforce that law as written. In the case of searches and seizures, this enforcement must be according to the commands of the fourth amendment.[66] This argument takes on added force where the judiciary is concerned, since courts are responsible for supporting the Constitution and for maintaining fundamental constitutional rights.

The part of *Weeks* on which this section of the paper is most firmly based is this:

> The efforts of the courts and their officials to bring the guilty to punishment, praiseworthy as they are, are not to be aided by the sacrifice of those great principles established by years of endeavor and suffering which have resulted in their embodiment in the *fundamental law of the land*.[67]

In other words, both courts and their officials must preserve the principles embodied in the fundamental law of the land, including the law of the Constitution.

Former Chief Justice Traynor of the California Supreme Court argued in favor of the exclusionary rule in a similar manner, stating, "[The argument against the exclusionary rule] was rejected when those [fourth amendment] provisions were adopted. In such cases had the Constitution been obeyed, the criminal could in no event be convicted."[68]

Like much of the legal argument supporting exclusion, both Traynor's insistence that the Constitution be obeyed and *Weeks'* requirement that courts be bound by the fundamental law of the land have an intuitively satisfying ring. Yet, these opinions do not present a principled and coherent argument justifying the assertion they contain, that the Constitution requires the exclusionary rule.[69] Why would an alternative remedy which obeyed the commands of the fourth amendment not be equally acceptable?[70] None of the judicial opinions relating to search and seizure adequately answers this question—a question raised most clearly by Mr. Chief Justice Burger in *Bivens*.

One answer to the question of why an alternative remedy should not simply replace the exclusionary rule is that the due process clause of the fifth amendment arguably requires the exclusionary rule, at least in certain instances of federal violations of the fourth amendment. Novelty of interpretation is not a cardinal virtue in constitutional law. However, as applied to the argument that follows, that "novelty" is diminished by three factors: (1) This interpretation has roots in the early case of *Weeks v. United States*.[71] (2) The argument supporting the Court's enforcement of the exclusionary rule, as well as much of the scholarly commentary, is based to a large degree on a kind of intuition that the Constitution requires the rule—an intuition which needs supplanting by persuasive argument. (3) Although not directly supportable through explicit historical intention or precedent, the logic of principled construction and certain cases strongly support the interpretation of the exclusionary rule set forth below.

The fourth amendment reads:

> The right of the people to be secure in their persons, houses, papers, and effects, against unreasonable searches and seizures, shall not be violated, and no Warrants shall issue, but upon probable cause, supported by Oath or affirmation, and particularly describing the place to be searched, and the persons or things to be seized.[72]

The relevant part of the fifth amendment reads, "nor [shall any person] be deprived of life, liberty or property, without due process of law."[73] It seems clear from the very words of the due process clause, that whatever technical, procedural or substantive meaning may be attached to the term, it surely means at least this: the only condition under which one may be deprived of life, liberty or property is if that deprivation be in accordance with due process of law.

Due process of law, of course, is derived from the phrase "law of the land" in section 29 of the Magna Carta: "No free man shall be taken or imprisoned or disseized or exiled or in any way destroyed, nor will we go upon him nor send upon him, except by the lawful judgment of his peers or by the law of the land."[74] The phrase, "due process of law" first appeared in 1354 in a statutory reconfirmation of this section of the Magna Carta, sometimes called the "Statute of Westminister of the Liberties of London." According to the interpretation of Rodney Mott:

> [T]he natural inference that the phrases "law of the land" and "due process of law" were intended to be synonymous is given additional weight by a direct implication in a statute issued by the same King (Henry III) nine years later. With the authority of Sir Edward Coke behind it, this interpretation has been very generally accepted, and is now the law in the United States.[75]

That is, Coke in his *Second Institutes* argued that the term "by law of the land" was equivalent to "due process of law."[76]

The equating of due process of law with law of the land has early, authoritative and continuous support from the Supreme Court of the United States as well.[77] An authoritative and often cited example of this basis in American law is the case of *Murray's Lessee v. Hoboken Land and Improvement Co.* where the Court noted, "The words due process of law, were undoubtedly intended to convey the same meaning as the words, by the law of the land."[78] It is not surprising, given his equation of due process of law with the law of the land, that Justice Curtis identified the Constitution as the first source of the content of due process of law when he stated:

> To what principles, then, are we to resort to ascertain whether this process, enacted by Congress, is due process? To this the answer must be twofold. We must examine the constitution itself, to see whether this process be in conflict with any of its provisions. If not found to be so, we must look to those settled usages and modes of proceeding existing in the common and statute law of England, before the emigration of our ancestors, and which are shown not to have been unsuited to their civil and political condition by having been acted on by them after the settlement of this country.[79]

The argument of Mr. Justice Curtis seems eminently sensible. The Constitution is the authoritative legal declaration of the American law of the land. Thus, when determining what it is that constitutes due process of law or law of the land, one looks first, as Justice Curtis emphasized, to the provisions of the Constitution.

Due process of law is, of course, a complex constitutional concept which is open to a number of interpretations, both substantive and procedural. These interpretations need not be plumbed in order to make the argument that follows. The due process clause of the fifth amendment requires that no person "be deprived of life, liberty, or property, without due process of law."[80] This requirement might be paraphrased to say that any deprivation of life, liberty or property must be in accordance with the law of the land, or, at the very least, according to the commands of the authoritative legal declaration of the American law of the land, the Constitution. According to this argument, the due process clause of the fifth amendment would allow no deprivation of life, liberty or property except insofar as the commands of the Constitution are followed throughout the proceeding. Therefore, any deprivation of life, liberty or property violating the fourth amendment search and seizure provisions would seem to violate the explicit requirements of the due process clause. That is, as a matter of constitutional principle, in any proceeding which may result in the deprivation of life, liberty or property, evidence or testimony gained through violation of the fourth amendment (or any other constitutional provision) may not be used because the due process clause of the fifth amendment prohibits such use, at least in the federal judiciary.

Contrary to recent trends, the consideration of deterrence does not assume primary importance under this interpretation. Rather, the primary consideration is that of obeying the commands of the Constitution in any proceeding depriving an individual of life, liberty or property—a requirement the due process clause makes explicit and mandatory according to the above argument. Why the exclusionary rule? Simply because the due process clause requires it, independently of the efficacy of the rule as a deterrent, or independently of the comparative efficacy of alternative remedies. Exclusion is a constitutional right emanating from the due process clause.

### III. Application of the Due Process Theory of Exclusion

Although a number of important difficulties remain to be resolved if this justification of the exclusionary rule as a mandate of the Constitution is accepted, a comprehensive analysis of each of these points is beyond the scope of the present inquiry. However, certain observations and arguments relating to the application of the theory will follow.

The fact that this theory might be interpreted to require a perfect criminal proceeding, *i.e.,* a process in which at each step every major and minor regulation of criminal procedure is scrupulously adhered to, constitutes the most evident criticism which could be made. This criticism is most appropriate in the case of a minor police violation of the fourth amendment which requires suppression of evidence essential to prove the Government's case in a criminal proceeding. Although the theory of the exclusionary rule presented in this paper differs dramatically from that of Mr. Chief Justice Burger in *Bivens,*[81] it may nonetheless satisfy certain of his legitimate reservations regarding exclusion. One of the Chief Justice's most persuasive reservations is that the exclusionary rule applies in like manner to both inadvertent errors of judgment and to deliberate and flagrant violations. Or, as Burger stated, "honest mistakes have been treated in the same way as deliberate and flagrant *Irvine*-type violations of the Fourth Amendment."[82] Burger's concern seems well placed. An important difference exists between the repeated unlawful entry of a domicile so as to conceal electronic devices, as in *Irvine,* and the merely technical, non-flagrant or otherwise insubstantial violations which may be presented by other cases.[83]

The relevant question for this inquiry is whether or not the principled argument supporting the exclusionary rule presented above allows the admission of evidence obtained under circumstances of minor, technical or non-wilful violations. The answer is arguably yes. One may, in a manner consistent with the above arguments supporting the exclusionary rule, specify certain guidelines limiting application of the rule, guidelines supported by history, reason and case law.

While it is not possible to survey either the history or contemporary adjudication of the inclusive and problematic phrase, due process of law or law of the land, certain observations regarding its origin and a common sense analysis of its application in the theoretical framework explained above are in order. The very origin of law of the land occurred in a context in which King John conceded to the barons the right to trial by their peers according to the laws of the kingdom. According to Rodney Mott, "the desire to prevent forfeitures and exactions except by a recognized legal procedure was one of the elements of Magna Carta chapter thirty-nine as it was sealed at Runnymede."[84] In another passage, Mott refers to the fact that "[t]he protest was rather against the use of brute force in a flagrant and unusual manner by the king or the violation of the law by his subordinates."[85]

William S. McKechnie described the admonition that "[n]o freeman could be punished except 'in accordance with the law of the land,' " as follows: "Their [freemen's] persons and property were protected from the King's arbitrary will by the rule that execution should be preceded by a judgment—by a judgment of peers—by a judgment according to the appropriate time-honoured 'test,' battle, compurgation, or ordeal."[86] The instructive aspect of McKechnie's commentary is his emphasis on the substitution of the King's arbitrary will for the forms which were honored by time.

George Burton Adams addressed the purpose of Magna Carta's "law of the land" provision. In his view, the baron's primary concern was John's tyrannical treatment of his vassals without regard for any process of law.[87] Bruce Lyon also emphasized the prevention of "arbitrary judgment," "tyranny," "brute force" and "royal whim" as lying at the core of this provision of Magna Carta.[88]

Mott has recorded instances in later English development of the phrase "law of the land," in which the questions at issue were those of the King's power to order arbitrary arrest and the power of judges to keep one so arrested in custody without probable cause. In examining the Petition of Right, he emphasized the revival of the idea "that due process of law granted protection from arbitrary, extraordinary, or illegal arrests."[89] These analysts of English history point to a meaning of due process which requires government to act in accordance with established legal forms and which prohibits tyrannical courses of governmental action violating these forms. It is no novel interpretation that central to the meaning of due process of law is the requirement that government be bound by established legal proceedings. What stands out in the brief excerpts from these analyses of due process of law is the degree to which terms like "flagrant," "arbitrary," "extraordinary," "royal whim" and "brute force," are associated with what were regarded as violations of law of the land in the early English history of that concept. While I am not arguing that due process of law must be frozen in its early English meaning or that there is no room for expansion of its meaning, reflection on these admittedly fragmentary comments regarding the origins of the concept is useful in making sober judgments regarding contemporary application of the doctrine.

More directly applicable to this inquiry is the meaning of and justification for due process in American constitutional history. Mr. Justice Frankfurter saw due process as embodying "a system of rights based on moral principles so deeply embedded in the traditions and feelings of our people as to be deemed fundamental to a civilized society as conceived by our whole history."[90] Another expression of the American equivalent of the law of the land is that of *Snyder v. Massachusetts*[91] that a practice or rule is invalid if it "offends some principle of justice so rooted in the traditions and conscience of our people as to be ranked as fundamental." *Twining v. New Jersey's*[92] formulation, "a fundamental principle of liberty and justice which inheres in the very idea of free government," *Palko v. Connecticut's*[93] characterization of due process as requiring those protections "implicit in the concept of ordered liberty," and *Duncan v. Louisiana's*[94] reiteration of due process as requiring those things "fundamental to the American scheme of justice" have a common basis. Each of these statements emphasizes the profound and non-trivial character of the protections associated with due process of law. Like the great English purposes associated with the origin and development of the law of the land, these American formulations lead us to a clearer understanding of the purposes of this great protection of life, liberty and property and guide us in contemporary application of due process. Such guidance indicates that it is the fundamental character of the right in question which requires it be included under the protection of due process of law.

There are certain examples of searches and seizures in American constitutional law which also emphasize "brute force," "flagrancy," the "extraordinary character" or the "fundamental" nature of the government official's misconduct. One of these cases which was decided on the basis of the due process clause of the fourteenth amendment is *Rochin v. California.*[95] This case had elements of both illegal search and seizure and self-incrimination. Mr. Justice Frankfurter, writing for the majority, disposed of the case on due process grounds. He emphasized that the judgment was based on the question of whether "the whole course of the proceedings" offended "those canons of decency and fairness which express the notions of justice of English speaking peoples."[96] Rochin was convicted after three officers, who had information he was selling drugs, entered his house and forced open his bedroom door. Rochin, who was sitting on the bed partly dressed, and whose common-law wife was in bed beside him, seized two capsules which were on a night stand and put them in his mouth. After an unsuccessful attempt to extricate the capsules, the officers took him to a hospital where a doctor pumped Rochin's stomach and produced the capsules which contained morphine. The capsules were the chief evidence on which Rochin was convicted of illegal possession of narcotics.[97]

The opinion of the Court in *Rochin* is replete with descriptions such as "unlawfully assaulting, battering, torturing and falsely imprisoning the defendant," a "shocking series of violations of constitutional rights," "lawless acts," "physical abuse," "conduct that shocks the conscience" and "brutal conduct."[98] One thread of Frankfurter's opinion for the Court is the character of the police departure from established constitutional practices. There is no question that the Court regarded the violation of constitutional rights as a violation of an important interest, a major deviation from lawful conduct and an extensive invasion of privacy. A major point of concern for the Court was that this violation was more than a mere technicality and that it constituted a side-stepping of established forms of police conduct.[99] The *nature* of the violation, not merely the fact that there was a violation of certain forms, required suppression of the evidence. In other words, the very character of due process, according to the implications of *Rochin,* requires consideration of the nature of the departure from the law of the land or the Constitution's forms in order to determine the necessity for exclusion. The flaunting or flagrant disregard of constitutional forms cannot be a part of the process by which an individual is deprived of life, liberty or property.

While Frankfurter's discussion concentrates on due process of law as requiring the imposition of "canons of decency and fairness" on the "whole course of the proceedings" and is not directed toward the theory advanced in Section II, his analysis of the police conduct as it relates to due process of law is instructive.[100] That analysis illuminates the meaning of "due process" as it developed in American constitutional law and illustrates an interpretation of and historical authority for the view that due process of law requires the exclusionary rule but not in response to *all* police violations of constitutional requirements.[101]

More directly related to the contemporary doctrine of exclusion is the application of the exclusionary rule to the states through the fourteenth amendment which was effected in the case of *Mapp v. Ohio*.[102] Although the rationale underlying the opinion was treated earlier, the specific factual context of the case deserves comment. Cleveland police officers forcibly opened a door to Mapp's residence and denied Mapp's attorney admittance to the dwelling. A paper, claimed to be a warrant, was grabbed by Mapp and placed in her bosom. Officers recovered the piece of paper in the course of a struggle, handcuffed her and manhandled her. The officers then conducted a widespread search of both the upstairs and basement of the dwelling, including drawers, personal papers and a trunk containing the obscene materials for which Mapp was ultimately convicted.[103]

Although the Court's opinion supports the exclusionary rule in its broad application to various types of police violations, the particular factual context out of which *Mapp* arose is noteworthy. The Court's recital of the facts makes clear that the police conduct involved substantial, wilful and flagrant violations of constitutional forms in which there were major deviations from lawful conduct and extensive invasions of privacy. We see phrases in the opinion such as "defiance of the law," "high-handed manner," and "[a policeman] running roughshod over appellant."[104] These characterizations together with the other actions of the police described by the Court require exclusion according to the theory and arguments advanced herein. That is, the facts of *Mapp* present an extremely strong case for exclusion when one compares the character of the police conduct there to the circumstances surrounding English development of law of the land and to the type of police actions judged to violate due process of law in *Rochin v. California*.[105] The police violations in *Mapp* were wilful, substantial and flagrant in a sense that flaunts the law of the land and in this regard go to the core of due process considerations as understood both by the doctrine of *Rochin* and by the rationale of the theory advanced herein.

It is defensible for two reasons to use the example of *Mapp's* factual context and holding to support the theory of due process and exclusion presented above, despite the fact that the Court used a different rationale to support its holding in *Mapp*. First, in spite of Professor Allen's accurate description of *Mapp's* holding,[106] the case was at bottom a fourteenth amendment due process clause case. Second, a fair reading of the Court's opinion in *Mapp* suggests the view that, apart from the consideration of deterrence, the flagrancy of the violations contributed to the way in which the Court disposed of the case.

One consequence of *Mapp* was the creation of a broad constitutional rule of exclusion applicable to flagrant police violations such as those presented in *Mapp* as well as to much less substantial violations. The exclusionary rule appears in a different and more favorable light when applied to suppress obscene materials in the context of the flagrant violations of *Mapp* than it does in the suppression of needed evidence in a murder case for a minor police violation. It is unfortunate that this case of flagrant police violations became the instrument for requiring the exclusionary rule in all cases when *Mapp* lent itself so appropriately to requiring exclusion only in cases of substantial violations of the fourteenth amendment.

In addition to the formation of a broad constitutional rule in *Mapp,* there is yet another difficulty with the decision. Its concentration on the criterion of deterrence seems to obscure treatment of considerations relating to whether or not exclusion is required as a response to all violations. By shifting the grounds of the argument to a question of due process of law or adherence to the law of the land and away from the policy question of deterrence, one is better able to adapt or limit that theory on the basis of constitutional principle.

A brief examination of certain other cases involving the exclusionary rule is extremely useful in illuminating the qualitative differences between the type of flagrant police violations described in *Mapp* and *Rochin* and certain other technical, insubstantial police violations which, nevertheless, have been held to require exclusion of evidence. The first of these cases is *United States v. Davis,*[107] the facts of which are as follows:

> FBI agents in a rural area of Alabama arrested Davis and his son pursuant to warrants charging them with the unlawful flight to avoid prosecution for the larceny of an automobile. Before the arrest procedures were completed, the defendant bolted from the house. He ran towards his house with the agents and his son in hot pursuit. He stopped at the steps, turned, and brandished a .38 calibar [sic] pistol. In the gunfire that followed, the defendant's son was wounded. When order was finally restored, the agents cared for the son until an ambulance arrived. They then took Davis to Montgomery.
>
> About three and one half hours later the agents returned to the scene to retrieve Davis' weapon. Although it was after dark, they discovered the pistol immediately upon alighting from the car because of the reflection of the porch light on the surface of the gun. The gun was recovered from the yard, and the agents left.
>
> The court held that the entry into the yard without a warrant was unreasonable.[108]

This search and seizure does not present a case of a substantial deviation from lawful conduct or a substantial invasion of privacy. Nor do the facts of *United States v. Davis* indicate that the police were guilty of a wilful violation of the law of the land. A similar criticism can be made of *United States v. Sonano,*[109] where the failure to insert an agent's name on the search warrant was fatal error although the search was otherwise sound.

> On December 23, 1971 a reliable informant advised agents of the Bureau of Narcotics and Dangerous Drugs that one Anna Betancourt . . . was expecting the delivery of a large quantity of narcotics. Previously, on December 16, 1971, the informant and Anna Betancourt had purchased a large amount of milk sugar and Christmas wrapping which were to be used to cut and wrap the narcotics. On January 4, 1972, the informant went to the Betancourt residence and was asked to leave because narcotics were on the premises. Surveilling agents then

observed a white male and female enter the house empty-handed and exit a short time later with a large paper shopping bag. They then drove to another location, deposited the shopping bag in a trash receptacle, and drove off. The bag, which was retrieved by BNDD agents, contained numerous glassine bags and Christmas wrapping paper which by chemical analysis proved to contain traces of heroin.

The agents prepared an affidavit which recited these facts. The affidavit was then presented under oath to United States Magistrate who issued the search warrant and handed it to the BNDD agent who had presented the sworn testimony. Unfortunately, the magistrate had failed to insert the name of the agent to whom it was directed.[110]

The result of this ruling was the suppression of 238 pounds of pure heroin.[111]

A final example is that of *People v. Trudeau:*[112]

During an attempted burglary of a vault at a synagogue in Southfield, Michigan, the night watchman was killed by blows to his head from a crowbar. One of the few leads was a heel print left at the scene. [A few days later] the defendant was arrested inside a United States Post Office where he had attempted to break and enter a vault.

Because of the similarity between the two jobs, the detective assigned to the murder case attended a preliminary hearing on the Post Office case in order to view the defendant's shoes. His shoes were subsequently removed by two police officers without a warrant and given to the detective.[113]

The court held that the removal of the shoes without a warrant violated the fourth amendment. The conviction was reversed and the case remanded for a new trial.[114]

The cases presented here could be dissected at great length and the admitted complexity of subtleties of search and seizure could be examined. This would not appreciably advance or illuminate the argument being presented, however. For our purposes, it is appropriate simply to compare these violations with those of *Rochin* or *Mapp* and reflect on the degree to which they are different in kind. The substantial and flagrant character of the extreme violations in *Rochin, Mapp* or *Irvine* stand in sharp contrast to the types of violations presented in *People v. Trudeau,*[115] *United States v. Davis*[116] and *United States v. Soriano.*[117]

Adoption of the view that the due process clause prohibits deprivations of life, liberty or property which are not in accordance with the law of the land—and, therefore, that the exclusionary rule is required as a matter of constitutional principle—raises the question of when exclusion is required. I suggest that limiting exclusion to instances of substantial violations of the law of the land or due process of law is consistent with the theory presented herein.

In tracing the concept of due process to its origin in the Magna Carta's law of the land provision, it was argued that the purpose of requiring adherence to the law of the land was to avoid "governmental tyranny," "the use of brute force in a flagrant manner," "arbitrary will" and "royal whim." The American judicial interpretations of due process of law have been based on the "fundamental" character of the procedure or other right in question. "Fundamental," "implicit in the concept of ordered liberty" or "a fundamental principle of liberty and justice which inheres in the very idea of free government," suggest ends similar to those the English concept of law of the land was designed to achieve.[118] That is, both the English antecedents and the American formulations emphasize a standard of governmental conduct necessary to deprive one of life, liberty or property. Whether this standard is associated with English history or with American usage, both indicate that requirements of governmental conduct are founded in the avoidance of "arbitrary," "flagrant" or "fundamental" violations of an individual's rights. The types of violations involved in *Davis, Soriano* or *Trudeau* are not "arbitrary," "flagrant" or "fundamental" in any meaningful sense of these terms. These insubstantial violations, if indeed they be clear violations of the fourth and fourteenth amendments in any objective sense, do not threaten republican liberty. Unlike the violations in *Rochin, Mapp* or *Irvine*, these insubstantial violations do not threaten the very values of political life toward which this great protection of liberty—due process of law (or law of the land)—is directed. Exclusion as a requirement of due process of law need not be extended to insubstantial violations which do not offend those great purposes which give the concept of due process its fundamental justification.

Impatience with the present law of exclusion requiring suppression in instances of both substantial and insubstantial violations of fourth and fourteenth amendment rights need not and should not lead to rejection of the doctrine in instances such as those presented by *Rochin, Mapp* or *Irvine*. Arguments such as those of Brandeis and Traynor,[119] and the opinions of the Court in cases such as *Weeks, Rochin* and *Mapp* are persuasive when viewed in the context of substantial constitutional violations; but, they lose their persuasiveness when viewed in the context of insubstantial violations illustrated by *Davis, Soriano* or *Trudeau*.

We are not without assistance in articulating standards to aid determination of what constitutes a substantial violation of constitutional requirements relating to search and seizure. The American Law Institute's Model Code of Pre-Arraignment Procedure,[120] cited by Burger in *Bivens*,[121] specifies criteria for determining substantial violations of rights relating to search and seizure. Certain of these criteria, clearly relevant to the argument advanced in this article, are (a) the extent of deviation from lawful conduct, (b) the extent to which the violation was wilful, (c) the extent to which privacy was invaded.[122] This is not the appropriate forum for extended discussion of the several criteria set forth by the American Law Institute, valuable commentary about which is contained in the Model Code of Pre-Arraignment Procedure and its tentative drafts.[123] Anyone familiar with criminal and constitutional law is aware that adequate treatment of even one of the above criteria, that of wilfulness, for example, would require lengthy analysis. I utilize these three criteria simply to indicate general directions in which the judiciary might proceed. The abbreviated remarks that follow are included to show the consistency of the criteria with the theory of exclusion presented above.

The extent of deviation from lawful conduct, point (a), is a valid criterion for determining substantiality. The factual circumstances of *Rochin* are just one example of instances in which there was an extensive deviation from lawful conduct. The facts of *Rochin*, including the forced entry, the violence employed and the forced stomach pumping, contrast sharply with the violation in the case of *People v. Trudeau*,[124] where the individual's shoes were taken during the course of a preliminary hearing, or that of *United States v. Davis*,[125] in which a gun used against FBI agents was recovered from the yard of a house.

Criterion (b) is that of wilfulness. While this element does not constitute the sole consideration in determining substantiality, it is a highly significant one. Its importance derives both from the references to English history and American case law, where purposeful disregard of established legal forms—that is, the government officer's intentionally overreaching or side-stepping the requirements of the law—illustrates the most obvious instance of an official's attempting to become a law unto himself in defiance of the established law of the land. The facts as recorded in *Rochin v. California* and *Mapp v. Ohio* seem to illustrate wilful violations of this type. Once again, they differ sharply from the cases in which evidence was suppressed as a result of non-substantial violations.[126]

The extent to which privacy is invaded, point (c), also constitutes a valid criterion by which to judge substantiality. The degree of the invasion in *Mapp,* for example, raises fundamental issues of privacy. The apparently bogus warrant, the manner in which the officers invaded the privacy of Miss Mapp's person and the widespread and non-specific nature of the search contribute to the substantial character of the violation in *Mapp.* These invasions of privacy seem even more extensive when compared with the illustrations of the minor invasions of privacy in *United States v. Davis*[127] or *People v. Trudeau.*[128]

While certain of the Institute's criteria are appropriate to the theory set forth in this paper and help clarify what constitutes a substantial violation of rights relating to search and seizure, one important difference distinguishes their proposal from the theory espoused herein. The latter theory, unlike the former proposal, does not require exclusion in all instances of governmental conduct interpreted by the judiciary to be violations of the Constitution. Examples of cases involving insubstantial violations given above exemplify possible instances in which the theory of this article would not require suppression.

The Institute's criteria do not, of course, constitute litmus paper tests of exclusion. It is evident that the three primary criteria must be balanced in light of some more nearly comprehensive standard. According to my argument, this standard consists of those ends toward which the Magna Carta'a law of the land provision was aimed and which have justified due process in its American context. Any violation of fundamental liberties, any action which threatens the principles justifying our political order, should not be sanctioned by the judiciary and should not be a part of that process which deprives an individual of life, liberty or property. By utilizing the Institute's criteria with a view toward the historical purposes of due process of law, the judiciary may achieve two important objectives. First, the principled objectives of due process will be served; second, it will be possible to avoid the present absolute view of exclusion where the violations involved are insubstantial and the result supports neither principle nor policy. Some critics may respond that this approach invites judicial uncertainty and misapplication. Such criticisms are, however, applicable to the judicial process generally and are not sufficient reason for rejecting the theory.

The argument made in Section II raises questions regarding the possible differences between applying the exclusionary rule through the fourteenth amendment as that rule involves state proceedings and the application of the doctrine at the federal level through the search and seizure provisions of the fourth amendment.[129] At the *federal* level, the theory presented in this article in support of the exclusionary rule is as follows: certain types of violations of the fourth amendment require exclusion of unconstitutionally obtained evidence because of the explicit statement in the fifth amendment that no person shall be deprived of life, liberty or property unless that deprivation be in accordance with "due process of law" or "the law of the land"; following the forms of the "law of the land" requires that any deprivation of life, liberty or property must be in accordance with the forms of the Constitution, or more specifically, in accordance with the requirements of the fourth amendment; evidence seized in substantial violation of these requirements must be suppressed. At the *state* level, the argument for exclusion here presented applies as follows: the search and seizure provisions applicable to the states through the fourteenth amendment are a part of that law of the land which binds the actions of the states; no state may deprive any person of life, liberty or property unless that deprivation be in accordance with this law of the land; evidence gained in substantial violation of these forms must be suppressed.[130]

The substantive law of search and seizure is interpreted by the Court to be identical in regard to both the state and the federal systems. Since there is no difference between what the fourth and fourteenth amendments require relating to search and seizure, my theory of exclusion would operate with equal force and be governed by the same considerations of substantiality in its application at both the state and federal levels.[131] Only substantial constitutional violations as determined by judicial interpretation would require exclusion. This theory, of course, runs counter to the proposals of the American Law Institute's Official Draft of A Model Code of Pre-Arraignment Procedure which would exclude evidence in *any* instance of constitutional violations. Examples of relatively minor violations of the Constitution's search and seizure provisions were given earlier, and grave doubts were expressed as to whether or not these cases warranted suppression under the criteria set forth to determine substantial violations.[132] These doubts would hold true in the case of both state and federal proceedings.

Another possible criticism of my theory of the exclusionary rule is that, under its operation, the criminal justice system would continue to be distracted from its primary truth-finding function by the necessity to determine whether or not police conduct within a particular factual context constitutes a *substantial* constitutional violation. There are at least two responses to this criticism. First, according to the theory presented herein, because the very principles of the Constitution require suppression under certain circumstances, the exclusionary rule cannot be viewed as merely a judicially imposed deterrent, justified by considerations of public policy. This position does not, however, preclude supplementing the exclusionary rule with other means of enforcing rights against unlawful searches and seizures such as those which might emanate from within the police department itself or from the appropriate legislative body.[133] Rather, the Constitution requires exclusion from a judicial proceeding of evidence obtained as a result of substantial violations of constitutional rights, not withstanding the existence of other possible remedies or deterrents.

A second response to the criticism that the theory espoused would distract the criminal justice system from its primary function is that articulated by Judge Henry J. Friendly:

> The beneficent aim of the exclusionary rule to deter police misconduct can be sufficiently accomplished by a practice, such as that in Scotland, outlawing evidence obtained by flagrant or deliberate violation of rights. It is no sufficient objection that such a rule would require courts to make still another determination; rather, the recognition of a penumbral zone where mistake will not call for the drastic remedy of exclusion would relieve them of exceedingly difficult decisions whether an officer overstepped the sometimes almost imperceptible line between a valid arrest or search and an invalid one. Even if there were an added burden, most judges would prefer to discharge it than have to perform the distasteful duty of allowing a dangerous criminal go free because of a slight and unintentional miscalculation by the police.[134]

While Judge Friendly's primary consideration in this passage is deterrence, the thrust of his argument is applicable to the due process argument presented herein. "Slight and unintentional miscalculation by the police" seems unrelated to the concern for preserving those great and enduring constitutional forms which are important to maintaining the rule of law and civil liberty and to avoiding tyrannical governmental conduct. While the exclusionary rule is required as a matter of principle where both the federal and state governments are concerned, the rule need not be extended to all conceivable interpretations the Court may append to the rather complex law of search and seizure. The law will undoubtedly continue to present complex and technical instances of searches and seizures which beg for legal resolution; however, it is not clear that any purpose of principle or policy is served by the exclusion of evidence in instances of insubstantial violations.[135] An argument might be made in another forum that "the law of search and seizure should be reduced to a more manageable set of rules with which law enforcement officers can live."[136] It is not necessary to the argument of this article to resolve that question, for the considerations relating to the constitutional necessity for exclusion may rest on a basis independent from the substantive law of search and seizure established through the fourth and fourteenth amendments. That basis is, of course, the due process clauses of the fifth and fourteenth amendments.

It has been argued that the exclusionary rule is a requirement of constitutional principle in instances in which constitutional rights of search and seizure are violated in a substantial manner. The present case law, resting its rationale primarily on deterrence, has neglected the development of a principled, constitutional argument. If one accepts deterrence as the sole criterion for exclusion, it follows that if exclusion does not deter, the rule should be abandoned. But, I have argued that the exclusionary rule has roots in the Constitution itself and, where substantial violations are concerned, the exclusionary rule is required, irrespective of the degree to which that rule may operate as a deterrent. While questions of deterrence may support the argument elaborated thus far, in that they may constitute a means of habituating government officers to obey the law of the land, the reasons supporting the exclusionary rule go beyond this limited justification. When the exclusionary rule is limited to substantial violations (those in which the law should be relatively clear and protective of important aspects of privacy) it is most easily defended and expresses the sense of the due process clauses that no person will be deprived of life, liberty or property unless that deprivation be in accordance with the law of the land. In this limited application, the exclusionary rule stands for the proposition that the law means what its framers said, and that in instances of substantial violations, evidence will be suppressed. Viewed from this perspective, the rule becomes more than a deterrent—it has the potential to reinforce the role of the law as a formative, civilizing influence on the police, the judicial system, the legislature and the political order as a whole.[137] These arguments apply with great force to substantial violations of fourth amendment rights. But, it is extremely difficult to see a parallel between prevention of arbitrary governmental action and preservation of fundamental rights at the root of due process and the insubstantial violations of fourth amendment rights which I would except from exclusion. The purposes of the rule of law and the requirements of the law of the land are not served in instances in which the violations are the result of the impossibility of knowing law which may not be pronounced until years after the search, are non-wilful and constitute insignificant invasions of privacy. Exclusion as a requirement of due process of law need not be extended to insubstantial violations because they do not offend those great purposes which give the concept of due process its fundamental justification.

The interpretation of due process and the exclusionary rule explicated herein is a part of the more general argument that the Constitution contains principles and that these principles impose certain requirements on governmental action, among which is the command that government be bound by the law of the land. This principled interpretation of exclusion will secure the cause of a regime based on the rule of law and a fundamental law of the land better than will a mere rule of expeditious public policy. The former is rooted in the Constitution itself—in a principle which is consistent with the requirements of criminal justice administration and the preservation of civil liberty. The latter is subject to the changing views of Justices regarding the efficacy of the exclusionary rule as a deterrent. The exclusionary rule, though long a constitutional doctrine, has not found in the case law an adequate theoretical or principled justification. The interpretation contained herein provides such justification.[138]

### Notes

1. *Olmstead* v. *United States,* 277 U.S. 438, 485 (1928) (Brandeis, J., dissenting).
2. Burger, *Who Will Watch the Watchman,* 14 AM. U.L. Rev. 1, 23 (1964).
3. *Mapp* v. *Ohio,* 367 U.S. 643, 651–59 (1961); for a summary of the most important literature advancing this argument, see generally Comment, *Trends in Legal Commentary on the Exclusionary Rule,* 65 J. Crim. L. & C. 373 (1974).
4. For a listing of periodical literature supporting this position, see *Bivens* v. *Six Unknown Named Agents of the Bureau of Narcotics,* 403 U.S. 388, 426, 27 (1971). (Burger, C. J., appendix to dissenting opinion). Burger maintained this critical stance toward exclusion in the context of right to counsel in *Brewer* v. *Williams,* 430 U.S. 387, 415–29 (1977) (Burger, C. J., dissenting).
5. 116 U.S. 606 (1886).
6. *Id.* at 634–35.
7. Allen further develops the relationship between the fourth and fifth amendments. Allen, *Federation and the Fourth Amendment: A Requiem for Wolf,* 1961 Sup. Ct. Rev. 1, 29 32.
8. 116 U.S. at 633–35.
9. *Id.* at 621–38.
10. *Adams* v. *New York,* 192 U.S. 585 (1904).

11. 232 U.S. 383 (1914).

12. *Id.* at 392.

13. *Elkins* v. *United States,* 364 U.S. 206, 222–23 (1960), *cited in Mapp* v. *Ohio,* 367 U.S. 643, 659 (1961).

14. 232 U.S. at 393.

15. 338 U.S. 25, 25–26 (1949).

16. *Id.* at 28.

17. *Id.* at 28, 33.

18. *Id.* at 39–40 (Black, J., concurring).

19. 367 U.S. 643 (1961).

20. Allen, *supra* note 7, at 26.

21. Finzen, *The Exclusionary Rule in Search and Seizure: Examination and Prognosis,* 20 Kan. L. Rev. 768, 770–71, (1972).

22. 367 U.S. at 648, 651.

23. *Id.* at 649–56.

24. 364 U.S. 206, 217, *cited in* 367 U.S. at 656. Oaks makes a thoughtful argument that the "imperative of judicial integrity" is a consideration secondary to deterrence. Oaks, *Studying the Exclusionary Rule in Search and Seizure,* 37 U. Chi. L. Rev. 665, 669–70 (1970).

25. 367 U.S. at 659–60.

26. Oaks, *supra* note 24, at 670.

27. 116 U.S. at 616, 633, *quoted in* 367 U.S. at 662 (Black, J., concurring).

28. 381 U.S. 618 (1965).

29. *Id.* at 637.

30. *Id.* at 636–37. Mr. Justice Black, in dissent, joined by Mr. Justice Douglas, explicitly dissociated himself from reliance on deterrence as the sole rationale for the exclusionary rule. Their explicit break from the majority on this point seems to underscore the majority's reliance on deterrence as the determinative basis for the decision. *Id.* at 648–50 (Black, Douglas, J. J., dissenting).

31. An early empirical study of deterrence cast grave doubts on the deterrent effect of the rule. Note, 47 NW. U.L. Rev. 493, (1952–53). A study supporting the merits of the exclusionary rule's effectiveness, and based on data of substance, was published shortly after the decision in *Mapp.* Kamisar, *Public Safety v. Individual Liberties: Some "Facts" and "Theories,"* 53 J. Crim. L.C. & P.S. 171 (1962). One widely cited and thorough study is that by Oaks which concluded, although the data neither supported nor refuted the deterrent effect of the exclusionary rule, that the rule was a failure as a deterrent. Oaks, *supra* note 24. A later empirical study concluded that the exclusionary rule did not deter police misbehavior. Spiotto, *Search and Seizure: An Empirical Study of the Exclusionary Rule and its Alternatives,* 2 J. Legal Stud. 243 (1973). A study by the Americans for Effective Law Enforcement during a 27 month period from 1970–72 indicated that appellate courts nationwide found police conduct in cases of warrantless search and seizure to be proper in six of every seven cases. Brief of Americans for Effective Law Enforcement, and the International Association of Chiefs of Police, as *amici curiae* in support of the Petitioners at 4, *California* v. *Krivda,* 409 U.S. 33 (1972) [hereinafter cited as A.E.L.E. Brief].

32. Oaks, *supra* note 24 at 670–71.

33. 403 U.S. 443 (1971).

34. 403 U.S. 388 (1971).

35. 403 U.S. at 490 (Harlan, J., concurring).

36. *Id.* at 510 (Blackmun, J., dissenting): *id.* at 496 (Black, J., concurring and dissenting).

37. *Id.* at 492–93 (Burger, C. J., dissenting).

38. 403 U.S. at 388.

39. *Id.* at 411–15.

40. *People* v. *DeFore,* 242 N.Y. 13, 21, 23–24, 150 N.E. 585, 587, 588 (1926), *cited in Bivens,* 403 U.S. at 413.

41. *Bivens,* 403 U.S. at 414 (Burger, C. J., dissenting) (citing *Olmstead* v. *United States,* 277 U.S. 438, 469, 471 (1928) and *Terry* v. *Ohio,* 392 U.S. 1, 13 (1968)).

42. See notes 6–15 *supra* and accompanying text.

43. 403 U.S. at 414.

44. *Id.*
45. *Id.* at 414–15 (citing *Johnson* v. *United States,* 228 U.S. 457, 458 (1913).
46. *Id.* at 415.
47. *Id.* at 416–18.
48. *Id.* at 422–23.
49. ALI MODEL CODE OF PRE-ARRAIGNMENT PROCEDURE 8.02(2), (3) (Tentative Draft No. 4, 1971), *cited in* 403 U.S. at 424–25. Other criteria the draft included are "whether, but for the violation, the things seized would have been discovered; and . . . the extent to which the violation prejudiced the moving party's ability to support his motion, or to defend himself in the proceeding in which the things seized are sought to be offered in evidence against him."
50. Burger cites a number of studies dealing with the concept of deterrence in an appendix to his dissenting opinion. 403 U.S. at 426–27. The Chief Justice has more recently criticized the application of the exclusionary rule outside the context of the fourth amendment. In *Brewer v. Williams,* Burger repeated his assertion that exclusion is a judicially conceived remedial device and not a personal constitutional right. In the course of arguing that the exclusionary rule is not required in all circumstances, he stated that an important factor in determining whether to require exclusion is whether the violation involved is egregious. 430 U.S. 387, 415–17 (1977) (Burger, C. J., dissenting).
51. 414 U.S. 338 (1974).
52. *Id.* at 348. For a useful discussion of the significance of *Calandra* for future decisions, see generally Barone, *Calandra—the Present Status of the Exclusionary Rule,* 4 Cap. U.L. Rev. 95 (1974).
53. 428 U.S. 465 (1976).
54. *Wolff* v. *Rice,* 428 U.S. 465 (1976).
55. *Id.* at 481–82.
56. 428 U.S. 433, 459–60 (1976).
57. 428 U.S. 465, 485–86.
58. *Id.* at 493.
59. 428 U.S. 433, 454.
60. "The primary meaning of 'judicial integrity' in the context of evidentiary rules is that the courts must not commit or encourage violations of the Constitution. In the Fourth Amendment area, however, the evidence is unquestionably accurate, and the violation is complete by the time the evidence is presented to the court. . . . The focus therefore must be on the question whether the admission of the evidence encourages violations of Fourth Amendment rights. As the Court has noted in recent cases, this inquiry is essentially the same as the inquiry into whether exclusion would serve a deterrent purpose." 428 U.S. at 458–59 n.35.
61. 116 U.S. 616 (1886).
62. 232 U.S. 383 (1914).
63. 414 U.S. 338 (1974).
64. For two useful discussions of rationales underlying the exclusionary rule see Traynor, *Mapp v. Ohio at Large in the Fifty States,* 1962, Duke, L. J. 319 (1962); Mello, *Exclusionary Rule Under Attack,* 4 Balt. L. Rev. 89 (1974).
65. 232 U.S. 383 (1914).
66. See notes 7–15 *supra* and accompanying text.
67. 232 U.S. at 393 (emphasis added).
68. *People* v. *Cahan,* 44 Cal. 2d 434, 449, 282 P.2d 905, 914 (1955).
69. This characterization seems appropriate, for much of the reasoning contained in the opinions was shown to be inadequate in terms of supporting the exclusionary rule.
70. Mr. Chief Justice Burger argues in *Bivens* that an alternative remedy would fulfill the demands of maintaining judicial integrity. 403 U.S. at 414 (Burger, C. J., dissenting).
71. 232 U.S. at 393.
72. U.S. Const. amend IV.
73. U.S. Const. amend. V.
74. Constitution of the United States of America: Analysis and Interpretation 1138 n.3 (L. Jayson ed. 1973) [herinafter cited as Constitution Annotated].

75. R. Mott, Due Process of Law, 4–5 (1973).
76. Constitution Annotated 1138, *supra* note 74, (citing H. F. Coke Institutes of the Law of England 50–51 (1641).
77. *Twining* v. *New Jersey,* 211 U.S. 78, 100 (1908). *Davidson* v. *New Orleans,* 96 U.S. 97 (1877).
78. 59 U.S. (18 How.) 272, 276 (1855).
79. *Id.* at 276–77.
80. U.S. Const. amend. V. Although developed separately, the argument contained herein in certain respects to observations contained in an extensive article by Thomas S. Schrock and Robert C. Welsh, "Up from Calandra: The Exclusionary Rule as a Constitutional Requirement," 59 *Minn. L. Rev.* 251 (1974). Serious students of the exclusionary rule should read this article for its constitutionally based defense of exclusion.
81. 403 U.S. at 411 (Burger, C. J., dissenting).
82. *Irvine* v. *California,* 347 U.S. 128 (1954), *cited in* 403 U.S. at 418.
83. 347 U.S. 128 (1953).
84. R. Mott, *supra* note 75, at 3.
85. *Id.* at 71–73.
86. W. McKechnie, Magna Carta 379 (1914).
87. G. Adams. The Origin of the English Constitution 272 (1920).
88. B. Lyon, A Constitutional and Legal History of Medieval Fngland 312–21 (1960).
89. R. Mott, *supra* note 75, at 81.
90. *Solesbee* v. *Balkcom,* 339 U.S. 9, 16 (1950). (Frankfurter, J., dissenting).
91. 291 U.S. 97, 105 (1934).
92. 211 U.S. 78. 106 (1908).
93. 302 U.S. 319–325 (1937).
94. 391 U.S. 141–149 . (1968).
95. 342 U.S. 165 (1952).
96. *Id.* at 169.
97. *Id.* at 166.
98. *Id.* at 167–72.
99. *Id.* at 172–73.
100. *Id.* at 169.
101. The *Rochin* doctrine of due process of law has, of course, been supplanted by subsequent interpretations which have simply incorporated the fourth amendment and the exclusionary rule through the fourteenth amendment. *Mapp* v. *Ohio,* 367 U.S. 643 (1961). It is useful to reflect on the factual context of *Irvine* v. *California,* 347 U.S. 128 (1954), in regard to substantial violations of constitutional rights; however, the Court did not suppress the evidence.
102. 367 U.S. 643 (1961).
103. *Id.* at 644–45.
104. *Id.*
105. 342 U.S. 165 (1952).
106. See notes 16–20 *supra* and accompanying text.
107. 423 F.2d 974 (5th Cir 1970).
108. *Id.* at 978, *quoted in* A.E.L.E. Brief, *supra* note 31, at 29–30.
109. Case No. 72–25-CR-JF. (S.D. Fla.).
110. *Id., quoted in* A.E.L.E. Brief *supra* note 31, at 343–44.
111. *Id.*
112. 385 Mich. 276, 187 N.W.2d 890 (1971).
113. A.E.L.E. Brief, *supra* note 31, at 28–29.
114. *Id.* For examples of 13 additional cases involving suppression for arguably non-substantial violations, see A.E.L.E. Brief, *supra* note 31, at 27–38.
115. 385 Mich. 276, 187 N.W. 2d 890 (1971).
116. 423 F.2d 974 (5th Cir. 1970).
117. Case No. 72–25-CR-JE (S.D. Fla.).
118. See notes 85–95 *supra* and accompanying text.

119. See notes 1, 68 *supra* and accompanying text.
120. Ali Model. Code of Pre-Arraignment Procedure (1975) [hereinafter cited Ali Code].
121. 403 U.S. at 424–25 (Burger, C. J., dissenting) (citing Ali Model Code of Pre-Arraignment Procedure §§ 8.02(2),(3) at 23–24 (Tentative Draft No. 4) (1971).
122. Ali Code, *supra* note 120, at § 290.2.
123. Other of the Institute's criteria are instructive, although not of the central importance that (a), (b), and (c) are: (d) the extent to which exclusion will tend to prevent violations of this code; (e) whether, but for the violation, the things seized would have been discovered; (f) the extent to which the violation prejudiced the moving party's ability to support his motion, or to defend himself in the proceeding in which the things seized are sought to be offered in evidence against him. ALI Code *supra* note 120, at § 290.2.

The consideration of deterrence, (d), or the extent to which exclusion will tend to prevent violations, while it may be relevant to justifying the requirement that deprivations be in accordance with the law of the land, is not according to my theory of exclusion, a determinative factor in the decision to suppress evidence. It was argued earlier that a constitutional requirement of exclusion rests on grounds independent of deterrence. Of course unless the Court rejects deterrence as the primary rationale, the degree to which exclusion will deter must remain a primary consideration in decisions to suppress, therefore, the ALI tailors its recommendations around "what is constitutionally possible in the present state of the law," ALI Code § 290.2, *supra* note 120. Development of my argument has not been constrained by this consideration. The difference between present law and my theory is that the former gives the exclusionary rule much broader application than is required by the latter.

Criterion (3), whether but for the violation, the things seized would have been discovered, seems consistent with the requirements that in any deprivation of life, liberty or property, the forms of the "law of the land" be followed. If the things seized would have been discovered, notwithstanding the violation, it is difficult to see the violation as a part of that process by which the person is deprived of life, liberty or property. This, of course, does not mean that such violations should not be punished or compensated for in some other way, simply because the theory of due process does not require suppression. For useful discussion and criticism of amending the Federal Tort Claims Act, an apparent response to Burger's proposal in *Bivens,* see generally, *Gilligan, The Federal Tort Claims Act—An Alternative to the Exclusionary Rule,* 66 J. Crim. L. & C. 1 (1975). For discussion of an alternative of fining the governmental unit employing the errant police officers, see generally La Prade, *An Alternative to the Exclusionary Rule Presently Administed Under the Fourth Amendment,* 48 Conn. B. J. 100 (1974). For a helpful study of procedural rule-making, see generally Wilson and Alprin, *Controlling Police Conduct,* 36 L. and Contemp MP Prob. 488 (1971). For other useful studies treating rule-making, see generally K. Davis, Police Discretion (1976) Gowan, *Rule-Making and the Police,* 70 Mich, L. Rev. 659 (1972). The point to be made is this within the framework of the theory presented above, exclusion is not required if the things seized would have been discovered even had the violation not occurred.

Point (f) of the ALI's criteria also merits comment because it fits into the paper's theory of exclusion. Insofar as a violation appears to prejudice a party's ability to support his motion to suppress and thereby interferes with the party's ability to seek proceedings in accordance with the law of the land, the theory would require suppression; suppression would likewise seem to be required in instances in which violations extensively interfere with the party's ability to defend himself in the proceeding in which the things seized are sought to be offered in evidence against him. In the latter instance, the evidence seized unconstitutionally would seem to become a significant aspect of the proceedings by which the individual is deprived of life, liberty or property and would therefore require suppression under this article's theory.

124. 385 Mich. 276, 187 N.W.2d 870 (1971). See notes 112–14 *supra* and accompanying text.
125. 423 F.2d 974 (5th Cir. 1970). See notes 107–08 *supra* and accompanying text.
126. See notes 102–07 *supra* and accompanying text.

127. 423 F.2d 974. See notes 107–08 *supra* and accompanying text.
128. 385 Mich. 276, 187 N.W.2d 870. See notes 112–14 *supra* and accompanying text.
129. See Section II *supra*.
130. The interpretation of due process contained herein does not necessarily imply a total incorporationist theory of the due process clause of the fourteenth amendment. Since the fifth amendment due process clause relates to the national government and the fourteenth amendment due process clause relates to the states, the particular rights each guarantees to the individual need not be identical. That is, the rights which are a part of the law of the land that governs the relationship of the individual to the national government need not be identical to the rights that are a part of the law of the land which governs the relationship of the individual to state governments. It is not within the scope of this article to treat at length either the substantive constitutional law of search and seizure required by the fourth amendment or the problematic theory of incorporation. The mandate of the theory contained herein is simply this: whatever the content of these rights which are a part of the law of the land, substantial violations of these rights cannot be a part of the process by which an individual is deprived of life, liberty or property.
131. The standard of reasonableness is currently the same as it relates to search and seizure under both the fourth and fourteenth amendments, but the Court has emphasized that the demands of the federal system compel a distinction between evidence held inadmissible because of the Court's supervisory powers over federal courts and that held inadmissible because prohibited by the United States Constitution. Differences could conceivably arise in which conduct would constitute a substantial violation of the rules of evidence to be applied in federal criminal prosecutions but would not constitute a substantial violation of fourteenth amendment standards. Ker v. California, 374 U.S. 23, 31, 33 (1963).
132. ALI Code § 290.2 (2), *supra* note 120. For an argument similar to the one developed in this paper, see generally Wright, *Must the Criminal Go Free if the Constable Blunders?* 50 Tex. L. Rev. 736 (1972).
133. See note 123 *supra*.
134. Friendly, *The Bill of Rights as a Code of Criminal Procedure,* 53 Calif. L. Rev. 929, 953 (1965).
135. One suggestion of a means to rule on the context of constitutional rights absent the exclusionary rule is discussed by Oaks, *supra* note 24, at 704–06.
136. Friendly, *supra* note 134, at 952 n.117. Judge Friendly and others have suggested the possibility that the exclusionary rule could be maintained as it is now enforced if the constitutional law of search and seizure were made much less complex and reduced to rules more appropriate to a *constitution* than to a code of criminal procedure—rules which would also be more easily comprehensible to law enforcement officers. In the event this suggestion was to become an actuality and the substantive law of search and seizure were more modestly interpreted, applying the exclusionary rule to all constitutional violations would be much less subject to criticism. Given the unlikelihood of such an occurrence, however, my limiting of exclusion to instances of substantial constitutional violations accomplishes much the same objective in a manner which remains consistent with the principles of due process of law.
137. *See* notes 1, 2 *supra*.
138. This article has not addressed the difficult considerations relating to exclusion under other constitutional provisions, primarily the self-incrimination clause of the fifth amendment. Treatment of the fifth amendment question would require systematic treatment of matters necessitating another extended inquiry. It is appropriate to add, however, that certain of the arguments presented herein would apply to fifth amendment violations with even greater force, since certain fifth amendment violations may affect the credibility of confessions or other statements.

# The Fifth Amendment: Fox Hunters, Old Women, Hermits, and the Burger Court*

David M. O'Brien

There is no witness so dreadful, no accuser so terrible as the conscience that dwells in the heart of every man.

Polybius, *History,* Book 18, Section 43

## I. Introduction

Debate over the symbolic and practical value of the fifth amendment[1] waxes and wanes with constitutional interpretation. The present controversy was fostered by dire predictions that the "Burger Court"[2] would forge a "constitutional counter-revolution"[3] in the area of criminal procedure and, in particular, fifth amendment litigation. Indeed, by contrast to the Warren Court's "liberal construction,"[4] the Burger Court demonstrates a proclivity for strict construction of the amendment and a redefinition of the value of the privilege against self-incrimination.[5] Heretofore, the Burger Court's reconsideration of the principles and policies underlying the privilege led to retail rather than wholesale revision of the Warren Court's construction of the fifth amendment. Nevertheless, the Burger Court's strict construction and re-evaluation of the privilege against self-incrimination suggests a contraction in the fifth amendment's contours as shaped by the Warren Court.

The Burger Court's refusal to extend fifth amendment guarantees, moreover, has implications for the developing constitutional law of privacy. Ironically, whereas the Burger Court considerably broadened the scope of the Warren Court's enunciated constitutional right of privacy,[6] it has taken a dim view of "privacy" arguments for the privilege and consequently narrowed the contours of fifth amendment-protected privacy.[7]

This article discusses recent Burger Court decisions in terms of their continuity with and departure from established principles and patterns of judicial construction of the fifth amendment and protected privacy. It is not enough to rest with Dean Wigmore's observation that "[t]he history of the privilege does not settle the policy of the privilege . . . [and, moreover, there] is no agreement as to the policy of the privilege against self-incrimination."[8] A re-examination is all the more crucial since the history of and the principles and policies underlying the privilege guide constitutional interpretation.

*Notre Dame Lawyer* forum of original publication, 54 *Notre Dame Lawyer,* 26 (1978). Reprinted with permission. © by the *Notre Dame Lawyer,* University of Notre Dame.

*This article was written under a grant by the National Endowment for the Humanities.

A number of competing principles and policies justifying the adoption, extension, and contraction of the privilege have been frequently debated,[9] yet only three rationales seem fundamental. The "fox hunter's reason"[10] holds that the privilege is merely instrumental to guaranteeing a "fair" legal procedure, much as in a fox hunt certain rules give the fox a fair chance for its life. In contrast, the "old woman's reason"[11] holds that self-incrimination is "hard" for an individual; indeed, it poses perilous moral and legal consequences which violate an individual's conscience and ultimately deny his human dignity. Whereas both of these rationales may be traced to Jeremy Bentham,[12] the third rationale is of more recent vintage. Contemporary commentators argue that a privacy principle, or what might be termed the "hermit's reason," justifies the privilege.[13] The hermit's rationale for the privilege is that compelled confessions are serious invasions of privacy and, that such invasions of privacy are to be taken seriously. Each of these rationales has important consequences for the values and "validity attributed"[14] to the fifth amendment inasmuch as they promote differing principles and policies which shape the contours of the privilege and protected privacy. An analysis of each rationale clarifies the normative import of the fifth amendment and illuminates the Burger Court's reconsideration of the privilege and its applicability to claims of constitutionally protected privacy.

The following analysis seeks to elucidate judicial construction of the fifth amendment in order to show that the Burger Court's retrenchment constitutes a return to and extension of pre-Warren Court principles and policies of constitutional interpretation. The crucial issue in either the extension or contraction of the privilege's protection is what constitutes compulsion of self-incrimination. Examination of competing arguments for the fifth amendment focuses on three rationales—i.e., those of the fox hunter, old woman, and hermit—and their implications for determining the threshold requirement of compulsion of an individual's self-culpability.

A discussion of cases treating fifth amendment-protected privacy explicates the Burger Court's rejection of privacy arguments for the privilege. A further examination of cases dealing with private papers and documents, "required records," and the contexts and circumstances in which individuals may enjoy the benefits of the privilege, emphasizes the Burger Court's re-evaluation of the requirement of compulsion of self-incrimination, and concomitant reshaping of the contours of the fifth amendment. In terms of the three rationales for the privilege and in contrast to the Warren Court, Burger Court holdings indicate a rejection of the hermit's rationale, a re-evaluation of the old woman's rationale, and the tendency to tip the scales in favor of the fox hunter rather than the fox. The article concludes that the Burger Court is forging a narrow construction of the privilege's applicability, based upon both a re-evaluation of the rationales for and a literal interpretation of the fifth amendment, and, thereby, diminishing the utility of an important constitutional guarantee and safeguard for personal privacy.

## II. History and the Contours of the Fifth Amendment

### A. *Historical Background*

Notwithstanding Wigmore's orthodoxy that the privilege "is but a relic of controversies and dangers which have disappeared,"[15] the historical development of the privilege reflects the concern that "[m]an should be held by law to average law abidance, not to the utmost self-sacrifice."[16] The fifth amendment's provision that "[n]o person . . . shall be compelled in any criminal case to be a witness against himself" gave constitutional effect to the common law maxim: "Nemo tenetur prodere seipsum"— "No man is bound to betray (accuse) himself."[17] The maxim can be traced to John Lambert, an obdurate heretic, who in 1537, while chained to a stake, protested the inquisitorial practices of ecclesiastical judges.[18] Although the history of the maxim and its development into the contemporary privilege against self-incrimination has been well documented and debated,[19] not until the middle of the seventeenth century was the principle that "no man is bound to accuse himself" firmly established as a rule of evidence in English common law.[20] Yet, by the close of that century the principle as part of the common law tradition was incorporated into colonial legal systems.[21] As Dean Levy's careful study of the history of the fifth amendment concludes, "By 1776 . . . the principle [that a man is not bound to accuse himself] . . . was simply taken for granted and so deeply accepted that its constitutional expression had the mechanical quality of a self-evident truth needing no explanation."[22] The fifth amendment, like the fourth amendment, evolved in America out of the reception of the English common law and, in particular, its accusatorial system of criminal procedure.[23]

The common law maxim that "no man is bound to accuse himself" provided the historical basis for the constitutional right guaranteed by the fifth amendment. Still, the drafters of the Bill of Rights were apparently unsure of the precise scope of the common law maxim. Initially, George Mason, as author of the Virginia Declaration of Rights, urged the constitutionality of the common law rule of evidence as part of accepted accusatorial procedure:

> That in all capital or criminal prosecutions a man hath a right to demand the cause and nature of his accusation, to be confronted with the accusers and witnesses, to call for evidence in his favor, and to a speedy trial by an impartial jury of twelve men of his vicinage, without whose unanimous consent he cannot be found guilty; *nor can he be compelled to give evidence against himself;* that no man be deprived of his liberty, except by the law of the land or the judgment of his peers.[24]

Mason's formulation is not without ambiguity inasmuch as the guarantee appears within a list of enumerated rights of the accused and, consequently, fails to extend protection to anyone but the accused, nor in any proceeding other than a criminal prosecution. Moreover, since in seventeenth- and eighteen-century common law "the right applied to all stages of all equity and common-law proceedings and to all witnesses as well as to the parties,"[25] Mason's formulation provides "only a stunted version of the common" law maxim.[26]

By comparison, James Madison's draft of the fifth amendment provided a guarantee which embraced the broad scope of the traditional common law maxim:

> No person shall be subject, except in cases of impeachment, to more than one punishment or trial for the same offense; *nor shall be compelled to be a witness against himself;* nor be deprived of life, liberty, or property, without due process of law; nor be obliged to relinquish his property, where it may be necessary for public use, without just compensation.[27]

Madison's proposal broadly applied to civil and criminal proceedings, as well as to any stage or forum of the legal process, including both legislative and judicial inquiries. Indeed, because Madison's proposal apparently collapses the maxim "No man is bound to accuse himself" with the maxim "No man should be a witness in his own case"— "Nemo debet esse testis in propria causa"—his formulation would "apply to any testimony that fell short of making one vulnerable, but that nevertheless exposed him to public disgrace or obloquy, or other injury to name or reputation,"[28] and, moreover, would extend protection to third party witnesses in civil, criminal, or equity proceedings. In this regard, Madison's proposal transcended the guarantees of most state constitutions in order to embrace the broadest practices at common law.[29]

In committee, John Lawrence suggested that the clause constituted "a general declaration in some degree contrary to laws passed" and consequently should be "confined to criminal cases"; thereupon, the clause was amended without discussion and adopted unanimously.[30] Thus, we have the fifth amendment's present formulation, "No person shall . . . be compelled in any criminal case to be a witness against himself."

## B. *The Text and a Strict Construction*

The text of the fifth amendment indicates that the guarantee applies only "when the accused is *himself compelled* to act, either by testifying in court or producing documents."[31] Inclusion of the phrase "in any criminal case" literally limits the scope of the guarantee, precluding invocation of the right during police interrogations and by parties and witnesses in civil and equity suits as well as witnesses before non-judicial proceedings, such as grand jury investigations. While a strict construction definitively, albeit narrowly, defines the scope of the amendment's protection, it provides no clear guidance for determining what constitutes compulsion of an individual's self-accusation. Nevertheless, commentators have inferred that the amendment, literally applied, protects against compelled self-incrimination alone, and not self-accusation which leads to infamy or public disgrace at trial and at no other stage of criminal proceedings.[32] Accordingly, justifications for the privilege often center on the utility in preventing "the employment of a legal process to extract from the person's lips an admission of guilt,"[33] and protecting those suspected of crime from suffering the cruel and inhumane "trilemma of self-accusation, perjury, or contempt"[34] at trial.

Although historically the Supreme Court rejected such a strict construction of the amendment's scope,[35] the proclivity of modern jurists to refer to the amendment as conferring a *privilege against self-incrimination* imposes two restrictions that do not necessarily follow from a strict construction of the amendment.

First, the inference that the amendment grants only a *privilege* rather than a *right* has great jurisprudential significance. Privileges differ from rights: whereas privileges are granted and, hence, revocable by the government, rights are not granted nor do they derive from the government.[36] Rather, rights impose limitations on the exercise of governmental power, thereby defining the relationship between citizens and the government. To be sure, the practice of rights in America depends on judicial and legislative legitimization of claims to rights, but the government does not create those rights, it merely validates claims of rights in litigated or contested circumstances.[37] Therefore, "to speak of the 'privilege' against self-incrimination, degrades it, inadvertently, in comparison to other constitutional rights."[38] Provisions of the amendment confer the same constitutional status of protection against the exercise of governmental power as do other guarantees of the Bill of Rights.

Second, a literal reading and strict construction of the amendment does not perforce confine its protection only to "self-incrimination"— "a phrase that had never been used in the long history of its origins and development."[39] Since in criminal cases an individual's personal disclosures may expose him to civil liabilities or infamy, "[a] person can . . . be a witness against himself in ways that do not incriminate him."[40] As Levy observes:

> [T]o speak of a right against self-incrimination stunts the wider right not to give evidence against oneself. . . . The previous history of the right, both in England and America, proves that it was not bound by rigid definition. . . . The "right against self-incrimination" is a shorthand gloss of modern origin that implies a restriction not in the constitutional clause. The right not to be a witness against oneself imports a principle of wider reach, applicable at least in criminal cases, to the self-production of any adverse evidence, including evidence that made one the herald of his own infamy, thereby publicly disgracing him. The clause extended, in other words, to all the injurious as well as incriminating consequences of disclosures by witness or party.[41]

With a literal reading of the clause, then, the shorthand version of a privilege against self-incrimination appears unnecessarily to limit the scope of the fifth amendment.

A strict construction severely limits the contexts in which individuals may invoke the amendment and, in particular, the occasions on which individuals may legitimately claim fifth amendment-protected privacy. In other words, a strict construction promotes legitimization of privacy interests only when an individual is "compelled in any criminal case to be a witness against himself." The contours of fifth amendment-protected privacy, therefore, would be limited to the circumstances of an individual divulging personal information—not necessarily incriminating information—about his thoughts or engagements, under duress and compulsion of the government only in criminal cases.

The judicially fashioned contours of the fifth amendment and protected privacy, however, are broader than entailed by the logic of a literal reading of the amendment. As Justice Frankfurter once observed, "[T]he privilege against self-incrimination is a specific provision of which it is peculiarly true that 'a page of history is worth a volume of logic.' "[42] Both the history of the amendment and judicial interpretation have ensured broader protection than suggested by a literal reading of the fifth amendment.

## C. *The Supreme Court and the Scope of the Fifth Amendment*

The primary effect of the fifth amendment is that in criminal trials the accused cannot be compelled to take the witness stand and, moreover, it is improper for judges to comment on the failure of the accused to testify.[43] Witnesses must explicitly claim the right, otherwise they are considered to have tacitly waived it;[44] yet they do not make the final determination of the validity of their claims to exercise fifth amendment guarantees.[45] The Supreme Court has never accepted the historical principle that witnesses in civil suits may refuse to testify because of possible adverse affects on civil or proprietary interests, or because the result may be self-disgrace.[46] Even in criminal cases, the accused may refuse to answer only questions tantamount to admissions of guilt or inexorably leading to such evidence, but not where self-incrimination is "of an imaginary and unsubstantial character, having reference to some extraordinary and barely possible contingency, so improbable that no reasonable man would suffer it to influence his conduct."[47]

Although inclusion of the phrase "in any criminal case" in the fifth amendment literally limits the occasions when an individual may invoke his right against self-accusation to criminal trials, there exists compelling historical support that the framers bequeathed "a large and still growing principle."[48] As a matter of constitutional history, judicial policies tend to support the views that the fifth amendment's clause "is as broad as the mischief against which it seeks to guard."[49] The Supreme Court extended the contours of the amendment's applicability beyond criminal trials to grand jury proceedings[50] as well as legislative investigations,[51] and in some circumstances, to witnesses or parties in civil and criminal cases where truthful assertions might result in forfeiture, penalty, or criminal prosecution.[52] The Warren Court's landmark decision in *Miranda v. Arizona*[53] "expanded the right beyond all precedent, yet not beyond its historical spirit and purpose"[54] in extending the right to police interrogations at the time of arrest or in the station house. Thus, as a product of judicial decisions, the fifth amendment's protection extends from the time the inquiry "has begun to focus on a particular suspect"[55] through "custodial interrogation"[56] to the trial itself as well as other quasi-judicial and non-judicial proceedings.[57]

Judicial infidelity to the text of the constitution, however, is Janus-faced. Whereas constitutional interpretation broadened the scope of the fifth amendment's applicability in terms of the contexts in which an individual may invoke his right to remain silent, loose construction of the amendment also fostered policies which compromise fifth amendment protection.

Since 1896 the Supreme Court has upheld grants of immunity[58] on the assumption that although the amendment permits a witness "to refuse to disclose or expose him[self] to unfavorable comments," its primary function is only "to secure the witness against prosecution which might be aided directly or indirectly by his disclosure."[59] Consequently, an individual may be forced to forego the fifth amendment right to remain silent when offered immunity.[60] The practical value of the amendment was further restricted by the Burger Court's legitimization of limiting immunity grants—so-called "transactional immunity"[61]—to only "use" or "testimonial" immunity,[62] barring only use of disclosed information in criminal trials.[63] In addition to the policy of permitting grants of immunity to circumvent fifth amendment guarantees, the Burger Court continues to uphold so-called "implied consent" and "required record" statutes which impose upon privacy interests and may lead to self-incrimination.[64] Moreover, the Burger Court endorses the policy distinction by which the amendment protects individuals' evidence only of a "testimonial" or "communicative" nature but not "real" or "physical" evidence, such as blood tests or handwriting samples.[65]

The fifth amendment's guarantee, thus, has been circumscribed by judicial policies permitting grants of immunity, required records, and the distinction between real and testimonial evidence. The Burger Court promotes, but did not originate, these policies. Rather, the Burger Court's extension of these policies is based upon a reconsideration and re-evaluation of the jurisprudential basis of the privilege against self-incrimination.

The contraction or extension of the scope of the fifth amendment and protected privacy depends upon judicial construction of the purposes and policies behind the amendment. In *Murphy v. Waterfront Commission*[66] the Court perhaps most concisely elucidated the "complex of values" underlying the privilege against self-incrimination:

> It reflects many of our fundamental values and most noble aspirations: our unwillingness to subject those suspected of crime to the cruel trilemma of self-accusation, perjury, or contempt; our preference for an accusatorial rather than an inquisitorial system of criminal justice; our fear that self-incrimination will be elicited by inhumane treatment and abuses; our sense of fair play which dictates a "fair state-individual balance by requiring the government . . . in its contest with the individual to shoulder the entire load," . . . our respect for the inviolability of the human personality and of the right of each individual "to a private enclave where he may lead a private life." . . .; our distrust of self-deprecatory statements; and our realization that the privilege while "a shelter to the guilty," has often "a protection to the innocent."[67]

From this "complex of values,"[68] three basic rationales for the amendment may be discerned: (1) the necessity to maintain a responsible accusatorial system; (2) the desire to prevent cruel and inhumane treatment of individuals by forcing them into a "trilemma of self-accusation, perjury, or contempt"; and (3) the belief that compelled confessions are serious invasions of personal privacy. Significantly, each of these justifications for the fifth amendment implies different normative orientations toward the amendment and protection for personal privacy. The following section examines each of these rationales and their implications for judicial policies and construction of the privilege against self-incrimination and protected privacy.

### III.  The Rationales of a Fox Hunter, Old Woman, and a Hermit

#### A.  *The Fox Hunter's Reason*

The "fox hunter's reason" was Jeremy Bentham's phrase for the "preference for an accusatorial system rather than an inquisitorial system of criminal justice."[69] As Bentham characterizes the fox hunter's reason;

> [It] consists in introducing upon the carpet of legal procedure the ideal of *fairness,* in the sense in which the word is used by sportsmen. The fox is to have a fair chance for his life: he must have (so close is the analogy) what is called *law*: leave to run a certain length of way, for the express purpose of giving him a chance for escape.[70]

The fox hunter's rationale explicates the privilege against self-incrimination by drawing an analogy between a fox hunt and an accusatorial system of criminal justice. Just as in a fox hunt certain rules define permissible and impermissible ways by which fox hunters may capture the fox, so too rules of criminal procedure define an acceptable process for prosecuting suspects of criminal activity in an accusatorial system. Moreover, both the rules of the sport of fox hunting and rules of the adversary system of criminal prosecution are predicated upon the notion of fairness—fair treatment of the fox and the criminal suspect. The guarantee against self-accusation is justified as an "essential mainstay of our adversary system"[71] precisely because an accusatorial system requires fair treatment of suspects of criminal activity. The analogy between fox hunts and accusatorial systems, thus, illuminates the basis for and function of the fifth amendment. Significantly, the fox hunter's rationale, as further discussed below, implies that the privilege against self-incrimination can not be justified on its own merits. Instead the privilege is only a rule and policy objective of accusatorial systems.

In what sense is the privilege a policy objective? How does the privilege serve the ideal of justice as fair treatment in accusatorial systems? According to the fox hunter's rationale, "the essence [of accusatorial systems and, hence, the privilege] is the requirement that the State which proposes to convict and punish an individual produce the evidence against him by the independent labors of its officers, not by the simple, cruel expedient of forcing it from his own lips."[72] As the Warren Court reiterated in *Miranda v. Arizona:*

> [T]he constitutional foundations underlying the privilege is the respect a government—state or federal—must accord to the dignity and integrity of its citizens. To maintain a "fair state-individual balance," to require the government "to shoulder the entire load," . . . to respect the inviolability of the human personality, our accusatorial system of criminal justice demands that the government seeking to punish an individual produce the evidence against him by its own independent labours, rather than by cruel, simple expedient of compelling it from his own mouth.[73]

The guarantee against self-accusation is a policy objective of accusatorial systems because it functions as an instrument for securing and maintaining a "fair state-individual balance."

The normative import of the privilege therefore relates to its role in maintaining a relationship between the individual and the state aptly characterized as "equals meeting in battle."[74] As Abe Fortas observed:

> The principle that a man is not obliged to furnish the state with ammunition to use against him is basic to this conception. Equals, meeting in battle, owe no such duty to one another, regardless of the obligations that they may be under prior to battle. A sovereign state has the right to defend itself, and within the limits of accepted procedure, to punish infractions of the rules that govern its relationships with its sovereign individual to surrender or impair his right of self-defense.[75]

The fox hunter's rationale for the privilege, as Fortas explained, fundamentally derives from Hobbesian-Lockean precepts; "the privilege reflects the individual's attornment to the state and in a philosophical sense insists upon the equality of the individual and the state."[76] Since the primary value is a relationship of equality between the individual and the state—specifically, securing a "fair fight" while maintaining an idealized relationship comparable to Hobbes's "war of every man against every man"[77]— "the privilege against self-incrimination represents a basic adjustment of the power and rights of the individual and the state."[78] The privilege serves merely as a policy objective of accusatorial systems in which the government must provide compelling proof of an individual's culpability without compelling the individual into self-incrimination.

The normative significance of the privilege against self-incrimination, therefore, centers on its instrumental value for other ends—securing conditions for a "fair fight" and maintaining a "fair state-individual balance"—and not as an end-in-itself. Before discussing the implications for judicial policy-making, a brief examination of various arguments, which presuppose that the privilege has only instrumental value, further clarifies the fox hunter's rationale and illustrates its importance in contemporary discussions of the privilege against self-incrimination.

The fox hunter's rationale underlines several main arguments for the privilege found in the literature debating the value of the fifth amendment.[79] Foremost among the arguments is that historical abuses, exemplified by the Star Chamber, High Commission, and Inquisition, justify the adoption of the principle that "no man is bound to accuse himself" in securing a "fair fight" between the individual and the state in criminal prosecutions.[80] As Wigmore, no friend of the privilege, came to admit, "any system of administration which permits the prosecution to trust habitually to compulsory self-disclosure as a source of proof must itself suffer morally thereby."[81] A corollary argument urges the usefulness of the fifth amendment's guarantee in frustrating "bad laws" and "bad procedures" relating to government inquiries into citizens' political and religious beliefs.[82] Whether or not convincing, such arguments from history are designed to be persuasive since if individuals themselves are not permitted to limit governmental inquiries potentially serious abuses of power may result.[83] Notwithstanding a history of prosecutorial abuses, McNaughton observes that it would be foolish and inefficient to allow witnesses themselves in all instances to frustrate governmental inquiries.[84] Historical practices, moreover, do not settle the question of when and to what extent witnesses should be allowed to decide whether they should exercise their right to remain silent. Yet, absent an effective first amendment privilege,[85] the fifth amendment does provide a concededly blunt but "particularly effective [device for] frustrating belief probes"[86]—belief probes of the kind specialized in by the Star Chamber and, more recently, legislative committees during the McCarthy era.[87]

Additionally, albeit related to arguments from history, some commentators argue that the fifth amendment actually defines the practical limits of governmental power.[88] That is, a kind of "futility argument" urges that "truthful self-incriminating answers cannot be compelled, so why try?"[89] The merit of the futility argument, however, remains dubious as controversy rages over whether witnesses will resort to brinkmanship when testifying[90] (thereby giving advantage to the fox rather than the fox hunter) and, hence, whether other uses of the privilege can justify its prominence in accusatorial systems.

Other arguments for the privilege's utility indeed may be found in the literature. Supplementary arguments urge that the privilege protects innocent defendants from convicting themselves by bad performance on the witness stand;[91] third party witnesses are encouraged to appear and testify since they need not fear self-incrimination;[92] and, finally, as a consequence of the privilege, courts will not be burdened by false testimony.[93] These arguments corroborate a further argument that the guarantee against self-incrimination contributes to "respect for the legal process."[94] Respect for the legal process, however, may be only derivative[95] inasmuch as the amendment necessitates that the government conduct competent and independent investigations. Still, regardless of whether the fifth amendment directly or indirectly contributes to respect for the legal process, the import of the argument emphasizes again the interplay between the fifth amendment and the values of the accusatorial system.[96]

In identifying symbolic and practical uses of the privilege, the preceding arguments presuppose that the fifth amendment has only instrumental value and no intrinsic worth. Quite apart from the relative merits of each argument,[97] together the arguments underscore the significance of the fox hunter's rationale for and evaluation of the fifth amendment. What, then, are the implications of the fox hunter's rationale and the preceding arguments for judicial policies toward the fifth amendment?

If the fifth amendment is understood to have only instrumental value, then its scope and applicability must be narrowly drawn because "the argument from the need to maintain an accusatorial system would only apply where there was some danger of prosecution."[98] Consequently, where personal disclosures are not incriminating or where an individual receives immunity, claims under the amendment have no legitimacy. Grants of immunity are permissible and justifiable in accusatorial systems because immunity removes culpability for self-accusatory statements and, thus, leaves undisturbed the state-individual balance. The fair state-individual balance remains undisturbed, however, only in the sense that an individual is exculpable for accusatory self-disclosures. An individual's privacy interests are necessarily forfeited by grants of immunity, and furthermore, if an individual refuses to testify after being granted immunity from prosecution, he may be jailed for contempt.[99] As Robert McKay observes:

> Even though protection against certain harmful consequence is assured through a sufficient grant of immunity, the privacy interest is relinquished upon disclosure compelled in return for a grant of immunity. Moreover, there is no way to protect against the related hazard of damage to reputation. It is not easy to square the privacy interest (which arguably is) a prime purpose of the privilege with immunity statutes that require surrender of privacy.[100]

In other words, while under the fox hunter's rationale the individual and the state ostensibly remain on equal footing, the individual faces the prospect of protecting personal privacy only when self-disclosures are incriminating. He must forego privacy interests when personal disclosures are self-accusatory but not self-incriminating and is required to testify upon a grant of immunity regardless of privacy interests at the risk of being jailed for contempt for refusal. In sum, given the fox hunter's jurisprudential basis for the fifth amendment, personal privacy receives little or no consideration and protection. Privacy interests are tangential, to say the least, and receive limited recognition, at best, if the fifth amendment merely embodies a policy objective of accusatorial systems.

Still, more fundamentally, given the fox hunter's rationale, the fifth amendment confers only a privilege and not a right against self-accusation.[101] That is, the amendment may be extended or contracted depending upon judicial evaluations of its utility in different circumstances for maintaining an accusatorial system. This crucial implication of the fox hunter's rationale is well illustrated by Henry J. Friendly's argument:

> What is important is that on any view the Fifth Amendment does not forbid the *taking* of statements from a suspect; it forbids *compelling* them. That is what the words say, and history and policy unite to show that is what they meant. Rather than being a "right of silence," the right, or better the privilege [*sic*], is against being compelled to speak. This distinction is not mere semantics; it goes to the very core of the problem.[102]

As Friendly argues, the amendment's justification rests with its utility for prohibiting the government from compelling a person to be a witness against himself because only in compelling an individual does the government rupture the fair state-individual balance. The "very core of the problem" for judicial construction, therefore, becomes one of determining what constitutes personal compulsion.[103] Yet, governmental compulsion may be a matter of degree, dependent upon the circumstances of governmental inquiries.[104] Consequently, if the fifth amendment is justified only in terms of its utility and "compulsion is not a yes-or-no matter rather a continuum,"[105] then the privilege need not have the same contours in the police station as in the courtroom. Instead, the scope of the fifth amendment will vary with judicial evaluation of the degree of personal compulsion and the utility of the privilege relative to the maintenance of a fair state-individual balance.

Recent judicial efforts at line-drawing in evaluating the degree of governmental compulsion, moreover, indicate that the threshold requirement for effective exercise of the privilege is a demonstration of "genuine compulsion of testimony."[106] As the Burger Court, in *United States v. Washington,* reiterated:

> Absent some officially coerced self-accusation the Fifth Amendment privilege is not violated by even the most damning admissions. . . . The constitutional guarantee is only that the witness be not *compelled* to give self-incriminating testimony. The test is whether, considering the totality of the circumstances, the free will of the witness was overborne.[107]

Hence, not only are the legitimate occasions for invoking the privilege limited to where an individual makes self-incriminating disclosures, but moreover effective exercise of the privilege remains conditional upon a showing that the government exerted "genuine compulsion" in securing an individual's statements of self-culpability.

The fox hunter's rationale, when endorsed in judicial construction of the amendment, therefore, severely limits the scope of the privilege and its protection for personal privacy. Indeed, given an instrumental basis, the amendment provides only a relative constitutional guarantee. As a relative constitutional guarantee, the fifth amendment confers only a privilege against self-incrimination and not a right against self-accusation. As such, the privilege against self-incrimination is context-dependent, and its effective exercise turns upon judicial evaluation of the degree of compulsion rather than self-accusation per se.

### B. *An Old Woman's Reason*

Justice Douglas, dissenting in *Ullmann v. United States*,[108] urged the unconstitutionality of immunity grants on the grounds that the fifth amendment embodies more than an instrumental value and policy objective of our accusatorial system:

> The guarantee against self-incrimination contained in the Fifth Amendment is not only a protection against conviction and prosecution but a safeguard of conscience and human dignity and freedom of expression as well. . . . [T]he Framers put it well beyond the power of Congress to *compel* anyone to confess his crimes. *The evil to be guarded against was partly self-accusation under legal compulsion. But that was only a part of the evil. The conscience and dignity of man were also involved.*[109]

Justice Douglas' rejection of the fox hunter's narrow perspective on the fifth amendment and alternative interpretation embraced what Bentham termed "an old woman's reason"[110] for the privilege; namely, that a privilege against self-incrimination reflects the belief that it is cruel and inhumane to force a person to partake in his own undoing.

In Bentham's view, "[t]he essence of [the old woman's] reason is contained in the word *hard*: 'tis hard upon a man to be obliged to criminate himself.' "[111] Of course, Bentham had few kind words for the old woman's reason:

> Hard it is upon a man, it must be confessed, to be obliged to do anything that he does not like. That he should not much like to do what is meant by his criminating himself, is natural enough; for what it leads to, is, his being punished. What is not less hard upon him, is, that he should be punished. . . . Whatever hardship there is in a man's being punished, that, and no more, is there in his thus being made to criminate himself.[112]

According to Bentham, the old woman's rationale is, to borrow one of his favorite phrases, a bit of "nonsense on stilts," a mere pretense to reason, which if legally accepted "this plea of tenderness, this double-distilled and treble-refined sentimentality" would only serve the guilty and foster bad evidence.[113]

Notwithstanding Bentham's curt dismissal of the old woman's rationale, there exists considerable historical evidence that the rationale was an important jurisprudential basis for the development and establishment of a right against self-accusation.[114] In the late sixteenth century, for example, Cartwright and other Puritan leaders attacked the *ex officio* oath on the grounds that:

> Much more is it equall that a mans owne private faults should remayne private to God and him selfe till the Lord discover them. And in regard of this righte consider howe the Lord ordained witnesses where by the magistrate should seeke into the offences of his subjects and not by oathe rifle the secrets of theare hearts.[115]

Colonial common law practices and constitutional history demonstrate that a crucial basis for the fifth amendment was the belief that individuals should be protected "against physical compulsion and against the moral compulsion that an oath to a revengeful God commands of a pious soul."[116] As Zechariah Chafee observed, "Nothing else in the Constitution prevents government officials and policemen from exorting confessions from American citizens by torture and other kinds of physical brutality. . . ."[117]

While history supports both the fox hunter's and the old woman's rationale for the fifth amendment, the old woman's rationale, in contradistinction to the fox hunter's instrumental evaluation of the amendment, finds the fifth amendment's primary purpose in preventing the torture and inhumane treatment of individuals; a right against self-accusation respects the dignity of human beings. As David Louisell argues:

> [T]he best justification [for the fifth amendment] is simply this: It is essentially and inherently cruel to make a man an instrument of his own condemnation. The human tragedy having evinced as much cruelty as it has, any nurtured sentiment against sadism is indeed a welcome brake on human passion, a valued friend, not likely to be discarded for newer ones.[118]

In other words, the old woman's rationale, contrary to that of the fox hunter, recognizes that the fifth amendment embodies an end-in-itself, namely, respect for the moral dignity of the individual. Hence, the fifth amendment does not confer merely a privilege, as upon the fox hunter's rationale, but rather constitutionally denominates a right to remain silent.

According to the old woman's rationale, the significance of the fifth amendment does not depend on its instrumental role as a policy preference of accusatory systems, rather it lies simply in the constitutional recognition that human beings should be respected. Moreover, the old woman's rationale requires that we take rights seriously[119] and not dilute a constitutional guarantee by transposing a privilege against self-incrimination for a right against self-accusation. If the practice of rights and, in particular, the fifth amendment's guarantee is taken seriously, then "third degree" methods of interrogation, whether those employed by continental inquisitorial courts or modern grand juries and congressional investigating committees, are necessarily proscribed. So it is that the Court and its commentators[120] often justify the fifth amendment in terms of respect for the dignity and inviolability of the individual not only to foreclose browbeating, bullying, and other "barbaric practices,"[121] but also to preclude the trilemma of reluctant witnesses, i.e., forcing witnesses to *"choose among the three horns of the triceratops* (harmful disclosure, contempt, perjury)."[122] Reluctant witnesses must choose among the alternatives of *disclosure,* a "stultifying thing";[123] bringing *contempt* upon themselves by not testifying, an "unnatural act" of inflicting injury on oneself;[124] or *perjuring* themselves, which for religious persons also constitutes a sin against God.[125] By illuminating the perilous moral consequences of confronting and compelling an individual to testify against himself, such arguments support the right against self-accusation and underscore the significance of the old woman's rationale for the fifth amendment.

The old woman's rationale, however, not only cautions judicial construction of the fifth amendment to foreclose the possibility of third degree interrogations and confronting witnesses with a cruel trilemma of testifying, bringing themselves into contempt, or committing perjury, according to the old woman's rationale, the fifth amendment moreover extends protection to *any* claim against compulsory self-disclosure. Hence, the Court need not engage in line-drawing with regard to the degree of governmental compulsion or attempt to define "genuine compulsion of testimony."[126] Indeed, compelled disclosures, even on grants of immunity as Justice Douglas urged,[127] constitute inhumane treatment because individuals are forced to overcome aversions to self-condemnation in publicly testifying and, thereby, foregoing as well their privacy interests.

The old woman's rationale thus provides an alternative to the fox hunter's jurisprudential basis for the fifth amendment. The old woman's justification of the fifth amendment in terms of respect for the dignity and inviolability of the individual contrasts sharply with the fox hunter's instrumental evaluation and view of the fifth amendment as merely a policy objective of accusatory systems. Concomitantly, the implications of the old woman's rationale for judicial construction of the scope of the fifth amendment differ radically from those fostered by the fox hunter's rationale. Since the fifth amendment is interpreted to embody an end-in-itself, not merely an instrumental value, judicial interpretation must take seriously the notion of a right and in particular, a right against self-accusation.[128] It is therefore extraconstitutional to diminish the practical value of the fifth amendment by construing the amendment to confer a privilege against self-incrimination and not a right against self-accusation. If the fifth amendment does not confer a privilege but a right, then it is also wrong for Supreme Court Justices to fashion the contours of the amendment to different circumstances upon their construction of what constitutes "genuine compulsion of testimony"[129] or, in other instances, to allow the constitutional guarantee to be superceded by immunity grants. Furthermore, the old woman's rationale points to the ultimate dilemma which the fox hunter's rationale poses for constitutional interpretation: the fifth amendment is justified in terms of its instrumental value for securing and maintaining a fair state-individual balance; yet, judicial construction of the amendment's relative utility may lead to a narrow context-dependent privilege against self-incrimination, with its effective exercise turning on judicial evaluation of the degree of governmental compulsion on an individual, so that individuals, while criminally exculpable, still may face public disgrace, infamy, and self-condemnation, thus, dubiously remaining on an equal footing with the state.

Notwithstanding these arguments for and the moral appeal of the old woman's rationale, it too poses a paradox for constitutional interpretation of the fifth amendment. The old woman's rationale arguably "confronts the clear fact that the rule against self-incrimination is psychologically and morally unacceptable as a general governing principle in human relations."[130] Defenders of the fox hunter's rationale, such as Sidney Hook, often appeal to common sense in countering the old woman's moralism: "Let any sensible person ask himself whether he would hire a secretary, nurse, or even a sitter for his children, if she refused to reply to a question bearing upon the proper execution of her duties with a response equivalent to the privilege against self-incrimination."[131] Friendly reiterates the argument:

> No parent would teach such a doctrine to his children; the lesson parents preach is that a misdeed, even a serious one, will generally be forgiven; a failure to make a clean breast of it will not be. Every day people are being asked to explain their conduct to parents, employers, and teachers.[132]

The old woman's rationale indeed leads to paradox: on the one hand, the right against self-accusation is justified by its acknowledgement of the moral dignity and inviolability of the individual, and, on the other hand, the justification runs contrary to moral and social practices. In other words, an individual's non-disclosure would be morally acceptable and justifiable in legal proceedings but not in family affairs or social relationships.[133]

The paradox of the old woman's rationale, moreover, becomes more pressing with regard to claims of fifth amendment-protected privacy. The old woman's rationale, unlike the fox hunter's, assures extensive fifth amendment protection for privacy interests as derivative of the intrinsic worth of individuals. Claims to privacy or non-disclosure of personal thoughts or engagements have merit because of their derivation from, or association with, respect for the dignity of individuals, which itself requires that individuals not be forced to suffer the pain of self-accusation and condemnation.[134] Like the fox hunter's rationale, the old woman's rationale recognizes only the instrumental value of personal privacy, albeit for a different end: whereas the former rationale found validity in the utility of privacy interests when associated with an equilibrium between the individual and the state, the latter rationale recognizes personal privacy as an essential aspect of the dignity and conscience of individuals. Moreover, unlike the fox hunter's rationale, the old woman's rationale legitimates claims of protected privacy whenever and wherever individuals are compelled inhumanely and regardless of immunity from legal culpability to disclose personal information. Although fifth amendment-protected privacy under the old woman's rationale rests on moral principle and, hence, may not justifiably be forfeited by grants of immunity, protected privacy suffers the paradox of the old woman's rationale: non-disclosure of personal information which is self-accusatory or self-incriminating may not be legally compelled, but may be compelled, on ethical grounds, by an individual's lover, parents, friend, or employer.

### C. A Hermit's Reason

As an alternative to the rationales of the fox hunter and old woman, contemporary commentators have proposed that a privacy principle, or what might be termed the "hermit's rationale," serves as the jurisprudential basis for the fifth amendment. The hermit's rationale for the fifth amendment holds that compelled confessions are serious invasions of privacy and, furthermore, that invasions of privacy are to be taken seriously. To compel disclosure of personal information not only disturbs the fair state-individual balance and denies the dignity of man, but also diminishes the intrinsic worth of personal privacy.

For the hermit, the normative significance of individual privacy is an end-in-itself which attains constitutional expression and protection in the guarantee of the fifth amendment. As Leonard Ratner, some twenty years ago, urged:

> The privilege against self-incrimination is a constitutional facet of the right of privacy. The right of each individual to remain unmolested in the absence of independent evidence connecting him with the commission of a crime is but an aspect of the limitation which the privilege places upon the powers of the police. The privilege reflects the further principle, however, that a person's own knowledge of whether or not he has any connection with a criminal act is possible to him and should not be subjected to compulsory disclosure.[135]

That a privacy principle underlies the fifth amendment was increasingly acknowledged during the years of the Warren Court.[136] In particular, Justice Douglas urged the import of the value of privacy and its relation to the fifth amendment:

> Privacy involves the choice of the individual to disclose or to reveal what he believes, what he thinks, what he possesses. . . . That dual aspect of privacy means that the individual should have the freedom to select for himself the time and circumstances when he will share his secrets with others and decide the extent of that sharing. This is his prerogative, not the State's.[137]

Yet, if as Justice Douglas suggests, the fifth amendment constitutionally embodies a privacy principle, how is it that this principle has gained currency in only the last twenty years? Indeed, critics of the Supreme Court's acceptance of fifth amendment-protected privacy point out that the fox hunter's and old woman's rationales have historical support in the development of common and constitutional law, whereas privacy, let alone a right of privacy, was neither recognized in seventeenth- and eighteenth-century common law or given express recognition in the Bill of Rights.[138] Although not entirely persuasive, Judge Frank correctly countered such criticisms by observing that "[t]he critics of the Supreme Court, however, in their over-emphasis on the history of the Fifth Amendment, overlook the fact that a noble principle often transcends its origins, that creative misunderstandings account for some of our most cherished values and institutions. . . ."[139] Fortunately, Judge Frank, unlike Justice Douglas, further explicated the relationship between the fifth amendment and the value of personal privacy in countering supporters of the fox hunter's rationale and critics of the hermit's justification for the fifth amendment:

> They ignore the fact that the privilege—like the constitutional barrier to unreasonable searches, or the client's privilege against disclosure of his confidential disclosures to his lawyer—has, *inter alia,* an important "substantive" value, as a safeguard of the individual's "substantive" right of privacy, a right to a private enclave where he may lead a private life.[140]

Judge Frank thus makes explicit the import of and crucial difference between the rationales of the fox hunter and the hermit. Whereas the fox hunter views the fifth amendment as merely a procedural rule deriving its instrumental justification from its utility within an accusatorial system, the hermit's rationale justifies the fifth amendment in terms of a constitutional principle or right which fidelity to the Constitution requires that we take seriously.

In contrasting the fox hunter's and hermit's rationales, and cautioning the Court to take seriously the privacy justification, Judge Frank, like Ratner and Justice Douglas, does not indicate the implications of the hermit's rationale for judicial construction of the contours of the fifth amendment and protected privacy. Indeed, too often proponents of the hermit's rationale simply assert the normative significance of fifth amendment-protected privacy, but fail to articulate definite consequences for constitutional interpretation. Hence, there justifiably may be misgivings about "creative misunderstandings [which] account for some of our most cherished values and institutions"[141] when the nature of, and means for maintaining, those cherished values and institutions are not comprehended. Creative misunderstandings, no matter how "creative," lead only to further misunderstanding and confusion. The Warren Court's endorsement of a privacy rationale for the privilege, for example, ironically led to the denial of claims to fifth amendment-protected privacy. The Warren Court acknowledged that "the federal privilege against self-incrimination reflects the Constitution's concern for the essential values represented by 'our respect for the inviolability of human personality and of the right of each individual' to a private enclave where he may lead a private life"[142] only to deny the retroactivity of the no-comment rule in *Griffin v. California*.[143] Previously, the Court had employed a privacy rationale to deny the retroactivity of the exclusionary rule under the fourth amendment.[144] Acknowledgement of the import of a privacy rationale for the fifth amendment is not sufficient; instead a perspicuous view of the implications of the rationale for judicial construction is required.

Robert McKay, drawing from the Supreme Court's dicta concerning the interrelationship of the fourth and fifth amendments,[145] argues that a privacy principle underlies the fifth amendment's proscription of compelled self-disclosures:

> The limitation on searches and seizures prohibits only that which is "unreasonable," thus leaving the privacy of the home imperfectly secured in order to accommodate genuine necessities of the state. But the privacy of the mind, at least against the compulsion of self-accusation, is absolute. It is not sound as a modern expression of the original urge to protect freedom of conscience, that mind-freedom should be complete? Moreover, this respect of the fifth amendment appears as a logical corollary to the protections accorded to speech, press, and conscience in the first amendment.[146]

McKay's statement that "the privacy of the mind, at least against compulsion of self-accusation, is absolute" interpreted normatively is little more than bare assertion. It points, however, to a crucial implication of the hermit's rationale, namely, grants of immunity should not be permitted to supersede the strictures of the fifth amendment. McKay admits it is "not easy"— "impossible" is a more accurate adjective— "to square the privacy interest as a prime purpose of the privilege with immunity statutes that require surrender of privacy."[147] Nevertheless, the critical questions remain: what is the distinctive relationship between the fifth amendment, as opposed to the first and fourth amendments, to privacy interests?; and what are the criteria and consequences for judicial construction of the amendment?

McKay elaborated by discussing the connection between the guarantees of the first and fifth amendments:

> The First Amendment notion that no man may be compelled to worship or to speak in any particular way—or at all—may be regarded as an enlarged version of the more specific Fifth Amendment notion that no man shall be required to convict himself out of his own mouth.[148]

First amendment-protected privacy indeed may be broader i.e., the range of privacy interests which may be asserted under the amendment[149] than that guaranteed by the fifth amendment. Yet the first amendment literally only prohibits Congress from legislating on the establishment or free exercise of religion or otherwise "abridging the freedom of speech, or of the press; or the right of the people peaceably to assemble."[150] Strictly construed, the first amendment does not guarantee the privacy of what people profess or do; citizens may be required to make some disclosures. The fifth amendment does not simply guarantee a smaller version of the first amendment, rather it serves a significantly distinct function, namely, guaranteeing that individuals will not be compelled by the state to bear witness against themselves. McKay's argument for personal privacy, moreover, appears circular: a privacy rationale is asserted as justifying the fifth amendment, yet McKay argues from the amendment (or amendments) to the constitutional protection of personal privacy. Actually, McKay hedges his argument by concluding:

> In sum, from all the welter of reasons given in justification of the privilege against self-incrimination, it seems to me that only two have any probative force, and they are perhaps opposite sides of the same coin: (1) preservation of official morality, and (2) preservation of individual privacy.[151]

Thus, McKay appears to merge the rationales of the fox hunter and hermit.[152] In so doing, McKay emphasizes that the fifth amendment protects privacy interests associated with "the privacy of the mind," but fails to specify when and by what criteria individuals should be allowed to exercise the fifth amendment in order to protect their privacy interests.

Individuals may have a wide range of privacy claims co-extensive with their expectations and interests in limiting access by others, including the government, to their thoughts and engagements.[153] Consistent with this perspective that the fifth amendment safeguards "one's mental and emotional state including: personal thoughts, beliefs, ideas and information,"[154] Michael Dann endeavors to clarify the functions of the fourth and fifth amendments and their respective guarantees for personal privacy:

> [T]here are significant differences between the fourth and fifth amendment safeguards. The amendments differ in the general nature of the evidence prohibited. Unlike the fifth, the fourth amendment emphasizes protection against official intrusion into one's *physical,* as opposed to mental psychological, privacy. . . . Also, while the fourth amendment only prohibits, as a means by which the state can obtain evidence, "unreasonable" searches and seizures, the fifth absolutely prohibits the state from obtaining certain types of evidence against a person's will.[155]

Dann correctly stresses that the fourth amendment only limits governmental access to "reasonable" searches and seizures, and the fifth amendment provides an absolute bar to compelled incriminating personal disclosures. Dann, however, mistakenly finds that the amendments differ "in the general nature of the evidence prohibited." Dann's identification of privacy interests in "physical" seclusion with the fourth amendment's safeguards and "mental" privacy with the fifth amendment's guarantee bespeaks a false dichotomy between privacy interests associated with the respective amendments. Privacy is an existential condition of life which may be compromised by either causal access, intrusions which influence or causally affect individuals' engagements or future relationships, or interpretative access, intrusions which obtain information about individuals' thoughts and engagements.[156] Causal and interpretative access are analogous to, but not identical with, the so-called mind-body distinction since both forms of access are interdependent ways in which individuals' privacy may be compromised. The fourth amendment's regulation of governmental searches and seizures ostensibly provides a broad protection for individuals' interests in causal privacy—governmental intrusion upon and interference with individuals' "persons, houses, papers, and effects"—and interpretative privacy—governmental intrusions designed to gather information about individuals' engagements.[157] The fifth amendment's guarantee prohibits the government from compelling an individual to be a witness against himself by disclosing personal information, thereby protecting interpretative or informational privacy associated with self-accusatorial disclosures. In addition causal privacy is protected insofar as governmental demands for personal disclosures, no less than governmental intrusions into a person's "constitutionally protected area" under the fourth amendment, causally affect his engagements and future relationships.

The constitutionally significant difference between the fourth and fifth amendments, therefore, lies in their respective restrictions upon and regulation of the ways by which the government may obtain incriminating evidence and coterminously invade individuals' privacy. Dann's dichotomy between physical and mental privacy and two kinds of evidence protected under the amendments is too simple and therefore misleading. Differences between privacy interests protected under either amendment derive not from the kinds of evidence safeguarded, but rather from the distinctive ways in which the amendments define the manner by which the government may legitimately obtain access to individuals' lives in order to secure culpable evidence. Since the crucial difference between the fourth and fifth amendments relates not to the nature of the evidence sought, but to the manner by which the government may obtain evidence, judicial interpretation of the respective amendments' restrictions upon the exercise of governmental power becomes crucial for each amendment's substantive guarantees and safeguards for personal privacy.

Still, the hermit's rationale, and McKay's and Dann's arguments in particular, are subject to the criticism that "while the impact of claiming the privilege can *result* in the protection of certain aspects of one's privacy, privacy will not *explain* the Fifth Amendment privilege."[158] Similarly, Bernard Meltzer argues: "There is no coherent notion of privacy that *explains* the privilege: rather it is the privilege that produces a degree of privacy by insulating the suspect or defendant to produce oral or documentary evidence."[159] To be sure, personal privacy receives protection whenever claims asserted under the amendment are found legitimate; privacy and rights of privacy are not synonymous.[160] The fifth amendment, even when justified solely on the fox hunter's rationale, provides in some instances derivative protection for privacy interests.[161] What nevertheless remains obscure in such criticisms is the demand for an "explanation" of the fifth amendment in terms of privacy. Justifications differ from explanations:[162] the privacy rationale may provide compelling reasons for validating claims under the amendment, yet not explain the patterns of judicial construction and application of the amendment. Indeed, neither the fox hunter's nor the old woman's rationales provide explanations as such for the fifth amendment.

Perhaps what most perturbs critics of the privacy rationale is that every day individuals are compelled to disclose personal information about their thoughts and engagements, so why talk about privacy as a basis for the fifth amendment? In short, the hermit's rationale can be useful and comforting only for hermits. Judge Friendly's criticisms of the privacy rationale exemplify this view. Friendly finds that "to such extent as the privacy proponents offer any explanations of their thesis, they are disturbing in the last degree"[163] and assumes quick defeat of the rationale merely because testimonial compulsion and grants of immunity are part and parcel of our accusatorial system. In satisfaction, Friendly cites the Supreme Court's approval of Wigmore's observation: "For more than three centuries it has been recognized as a fundamental maxim that the public . . . has a right to everyman's evidence."[164] Fundamentally, Friendly revels in assuming that privacy must be absolute and therefore "the privacy theory . . . [must] lead to the absurd conclusion that the state cannot compel evidence from anybody."[165] Friendly nevertheless rejoices in the defeat of a straw man.

The hermit's rationale need not entail protection of every privacy claim under the fifth amendment. As Robert Gerstein argues:

> The right of privacy cannot be understood as embodying the rule that "privacy may be never violated." The alternative is to look at the right of privacy not as an absolute rule but as a principle which would establish privacy as a value of great significance, not to be interfered with lightly by governmental authority.[166]

Gerstein accepts Fried's analysis of privacy "as the *control* we have over information about ourselves,"[167] but departs from his view "that a man cannot (i.e., should not) be forced to make public information about himself. . . . Thereby his sense of control over what others know of him is significantly enhanced, even if other sources of the same information exist."[168] Gerstein suggests: "If the argument for privacy is made so broad as to sweep away tax returns, accident reports, and the capacity to compel testimony on personal matters in civil cases, for example, it must surely be rejected."[169] The privacy of individuals' thoughts and engagements has intrinsic worth, yet not every claim of privacy must be protected.

Gerstein, unlike McKay, Dann and Fried, furthermore endeavors to define the kinds of disclosures of personal information which should receive fifth amendment protection. Gerstein argues:

> I think we are dealing here with a special sort of information, a sort of information which it is particularly important for an individual to be able to control. . . . It is not the disclosure of the facts of the crime, but the mea culpa, the public admission of private judgement of self-condemnation, that seems to be of real concern.[170]

Gerstein's argument that the fifth amendment protects only against compelled disclosures of personal information which force an individual to make a judgement as to his own culpability leads back, however, to the paradox of the old woman's rationale.[171] Characteristically, Friendly overstates his counter argument:

> Far from being a moral doctrine, the privacy justification is about as immoral as one could imagine. To be sure, there may be offenses, for example, fornication and adultery, where the individual's right to be left alone may transcend the state's interest in solving them. . . . [Yet] can it be seriously argued that when a murder or rape or kidnapping has been committed, a citizen is morally justified in withholding his aid simply because he does not want to be bothered and prefers to remain in a "private enclave" from which the state has cause to believe he departed in order to do violence to another?[172]

Friendly's argument has merit and may prove convincing if one accepts his particular vision of the areas and extent to which the government should pursue the legal enforcement of public morality.[173] Nevertheless, Friendly concludes that the privacy argument is immoral only because he interprets the argument in an extreme form, namely, that privacy in legal and social practice entails an unqualified mutual noninterference among individuals.[174]

Contrary to Friendly, the hermit's rationale does not necessarily entail an ideal of unconditional noninterference among individuals. Instead, the privacy argument holds that the government should respect the moral autonomy of individuals. Therefore, governmental intrusions—intrusions whether in the form of searches and seizures or demands for self-disclosure—should be circumspect and limited.[175] The hermit's rationale, like that of the old woman, is based on moral principle and not, as the fox hunter's rationale, policy considerations.[176]

Notwithstanding the moral appeal of the hermit's rationale, privacy arguments provide ambiguous and incomplete guidance for the Court's determination of the contours of the fifth amendment. Failure to articulate independent standards for exercising the privilege suggests that the hermit's rationale may not usefully serve as the primary jurisprudential basis for the fifth amendment. Rather, the hermit's rationale may serve as an ancillary justification. It is not surprising that proponents of the hermit's rationale rely on other justifications for the privilege when fashioning their privacy arguments. McKay's argument, for example, combined the rationales of the fox hunter and the hermit so that the fifth amendment extends protection to claims of privacy while according consideration to the needs of law enforcement. In other words, the hermit's rationale serves to limit the extent to which policy considerations should control the application of the privilege. That is, there are good reasons under the fox hunter's evaluation for not limiting the effective exercise of the privilege to those contexts of third-degree interrogations which manifest "genuine compulsion of testimony."[177] Still, good reasons for extending the contours of the fifth amendment to one context, e.g., custodial interrogations, may not hold for another context, e.g., tax returns or accident reports. Gerstein's argument combining the hermit's and old woman's rationales, however, illustrates how the privacy argument may serve as an ancillary basis yet not entail absolute fifth amendment protection for personal privacy. The hermit's rationale, thus, as an independent unconditional basis for the fifth amendment proves unacceptable, but as an ancillary justification it may serve as a crucial consideration in judicial construction of the contours of the fifth amendment.

The preceding discussion suggests that the fox hunter's, old woman's, and hermit's rationales by themselves are insufficient in justifying the fifth amendment. While each rationale provides a significant analysis and justification for the fifth amendment, each neglects too much. Certainly, as Gerstein argues, "The case for allowing the privilege would be strongest when all of these purposes would be served by its application."[178] The import of the rationales for constitutional interpretation is nevertheless demonstrated by the fact as observed by Justice Harlan, that "[t]he Constitution contains no formulae within which we can calculate the areas . . . to which the privilege should extend, and [that] the Court has therefore been obliged to fashion for itself standards for the application of the privilege."[179] The following section shows that the Burger Court's treatment of the fifth amendment is predicated upon a re-evaluation of the principles and policies underlying the privilege. Specifically, it is argued that the Burger Court's treatment fosters a narrow construction of the privilege and diminishes protection of interests in personal privacy.

## IV. Principles, Policies, and the Burger Court's Construction of the Fifth Amendment

While a number of commentators observe that the Burger Court is evolving a narrow construction of the fifth amendment,[180] Jerold Israel maintains that "neither the record of the Court nor the tenor of its majority decisions, taken as a whole, really supports a broad movement towards restricting the protections afforded the accused."[181] To the contrary, the Burger Court's treatment of the fifth amendment in a number of areas collectively indicates a major re-evaluation and revision—revision, admittedly, on a retail rather than wholesale scale—of the fifth amendment and, in particular, a broad construction of the amendment as promoted by the Warren Court and, in recent years, in dissenting opinions of Justices Douglas,[182] Brennan,[183] and Marshall.[184] The Court's re-evaluation of the amendment, moreover, when explicated in terms of the preceding discussion of competing jurisprudential rationales, appears as a major revision in constitutional interpretation with wide-ranging significance for civil liberties and protected privacy under the fifth amendment.

The basic tenets of the Burger Court's treatment of the privilege stem from its view that "the fundamental purpose of the fifth amendment [is] the preservation of an adversary system of criminal justice."[185] Accordingly, the Burger Court's treatment of the fifth amendment may be expected to manifest, and thus be explicated in terms of, a jurisprudence comparable to that of the fox hunter's instrumental evaluation of the justification for the privilege.[186] The fox hunter's rationale, as earlier suggested, fosters an analysis of the privilege in terms of policy considerations of an accusatorial system. In contrast to the broad construction promoted by the old woman's and hermit's rationales which view the fifth amendment as denominating a constitutional principle or right,[187] an instrumental evaluation fosters a narrow construction. It limits the criteria for determining the constitutive elements of "personal compulsion" in terms of the degree of governmental pressure exerted on an individual to testify[188] and the kinds of evidence legitimately protected by the amendment,[189] as well as the circumstances or contexts for raising fifth amendment claims.[190]

The Burger Court's treatment and narrow construction of the privilege, furthermore, minimizes, if not rejects, the old woman's and hermit's rationales. Indeed, the Burger Court not only narrowly defines "personal compulsion" and the circumstances for invoking the privilege, but also adheres to a policy of extending fifth amendment protection only "to the person, not to information that may incriminate him."[191] Hence, in *Bellis v. United States*,[192] the Court validated a fifth amendment claim to quash a subpoena duces tecum propounded against an individual for production of private papers, but in *Couch v. United States*,[193] it refused to recognize any fifth amendment claim extending to a taxpayer's accountant, and subsequently, in *Fisher v. United States*,[194] further restricted invocation of the amendment by allowing Internal Revenue Service summons of an individual's attorney for third-party financial records prepared for the individual. The Court's narrow construction thus provides illiberal protection for personal privacy inasmuch as it holds that the fifth amendment "does not in any way protect expectations of privacy, but rather serves exclusively to prevent 'the state from compelling an individual to *personally* produce self-incriminating evidence.'"[195]

This section examines the basic tenets of the Burger Court's treatment and evolving narrow construction of the fifth amendment. More specifically, it discusses recent cases dealing with the Court's redefinition of "personal compulsion" and constitutionally protected privacy with regard to private papers, required records, and the contexts and circumstances in which individuals may claim the benefits of the privilege.

### A. *Personal Compulsion and Private Papers*

The Burger Court's jurisprudence and narrow construction of "the fundamental purpose of the fifth amendment [as] the preservation of an adversary system"[196] lead to a redefinition of the threshold requirement for exercising the privilege, namely, a demonstration of "genuine compulsion of testimony"[197] or "whether, considering the totality of the circumstances, the free will of the witness was overborne."[198] The implications and significance for the contours of the fifth amendment are well illustrated by the Burger Court's treatment of claims to fifth amendment-protected privacy with regard to private papers, documents, and business records.

To be sure, the Supreme Court long adhered to a distinction between individuals and corporations in applying fifth amendment guarantees so that only "natural" persons and not corporations could claim protection.[199] Moreover, since the amendment was viewed as establishing a personal right, it was often held that an individual must own or possess the records in order to assert a fifth amendment claim.[200] The Burger Court, however, has firmly established, on policy considerations, that "a party is privileged from producing . . . evidence, but not from its production."[201] Individuals may claim fifth amendment privacy interests and, for example, quash an administrative subpoena duces tecum requiring them to produce papers or documents in which they may have privacy interests.[202] They have, however, no legitimate expectations of privacy or fifth amendment claims against compulsion of testimony in papers held by a banking institution,[203] their accountants,[204] or their attorneys.[205]

In *Couch*, the petitioner was denied any reasonable expectation of privacy and claim under the fifth amendment to intervene when the Internal Revenue Service summoned petitioner's accountant for the petitioner's business records. The Court held that, "no Fourth or Fifth Amendment claim can prevail where, as in this case, there exists no legitimate expectation of privacy and no semblance of governmental compulsion against the person of the accused."[206] While the Court discussed concurrently rather than independently fourth and fifth amendment protections for privacy[207] and thereby collapsed the issues of reasonableness of individuals' expectations of privacy and governmental compulsion of personal disclosures, the Court noted, as an exception, that claims under the fifth amendment might be legitimate where individuals retained "constructive possession" of the materials, albeit held by a third party.[208] Although refusing to establish a *per se* rule to that effect and declining to specify the types of recognizable forms of constructive possession, the Court emphasized: "Possession bears the closest relationship to the personal compulsion forbidden by the fifth amendment. To tie the privilege against self-incrimination to a concept of ownership would be to draw a meaningless line."[209] The Burger Court thus appeared to overrule *sub silentio* earlier decisions regarding ownership as a prerequisite for fifth amendment claims where an individual retains possession of the papers or documents.[210] Indeed, citing *Perlman v. United States,*[211] the Court concluded that "[t]he criterion for Fifth Amendment immunity remains not the ownership of property, but the *'physical or moral compulsion exerted.'* "[212] The Court further stated:

> We do indeed believe that actual possession of documents bears the most significant relationship to Fifth Amendment protections against state compulsions upon the individual accused of crime. Yet situations may well arise where constructive possession is so clear or the relinquishment of possession is so temporary and insignificant as to leave the personal compulsion upon the accused substantially intact.[213]

In 1976, the Court proved it would not only strictly construe the requirement of compulsion of testimony, but also would narrowly interpret "constructive possession" of private papers. In *Fisher v. United States,*[214] taxpayers under investigation for possible civil or criminal liability under federal income tax laws obtained from their accountants documents related to their accountants' preparation of their tax returns, and they transferred the documents to their attorneys. Subsequently, the Internal Revenue Service served summonses on their attorneys, but they refused to comply. The Court, relying on *Couch,* held that individuals have no valid fifth amendment claims against their attorneys' production of such documents because "enforcement of the summons involved . . . would not 'compel' the taxpayer to do anything—and certainly would not compel him to be a 'witness' against himself."[215] The Court held that attorneys' production of papers was not constitutive of individuals' personal compulsion, nor do individuals retain constructive possession of such documents.

Individuals may have expectations of privacy in papers and documents held by their attorneys, but where individuals retain no constructive possession they have no legitimate claims under the fifth amendment. In *Fisher,* the Court thus reiterated its ruling in *United States v. Nobles* that the fifth amendment protects only against "compelled self-incrimination, not [the disclosure of] private information."[216] Moreover, Justice White, writing for the Court, emphasized its rejection of privacy arguments for the privilege:

> The Framers addressed the subject of personal privacy directly in the Fourth Amendment. They struck a balance so that when the State's reason to believe incriminating evidence will be found becomes sufficiently great, the invasion of privacy becomes justified and a warrant to search and seize will issue.

They did not seek in still another Amendment—the Fifth—to achieve a general protection of privacy but to deal with the more specific issue of compelled self-incrimination. . . . We cannot cut the Fifth Amendment completely loose from the moorings of its language, and make it serve as a general protection of privacy—a word not mentioned in its text and a concept directly addressed in the Fourth Amendment.[217]

*Fisher,* like *Couch,* underscores the Burger Court's narrow construction of the fifth amendment and its limited protection of personal privacy. Although the amendment literally suggests safeguards for individuals' privacy expectations in papers, at least where their production would constitutively force the individual to be a witness against himself,[218] the Burger Court's strict application of the amendment limits protection to only those situations where an individual orally divulges or produces written materials containing incriminating information. Hence, even where individuals have reasonable expectations of privacy in papers and turn those papers over to their legal agents, they do not retain constructive possession, and the forced production of the papers does not constitute compulsion prohibited by the fifth amendment. As Ritchie commented: "The Burger Court's analysis of the application of the privilege to documents and private writings not only reaffirms its literal interpretation of the privilege, but clearly indicates the extent to which that interpretation dilutes the privacy protection that the privilege could afford."[219]

The fifth amendment arguably does extend greater protection to personal privacy than the Burger Court's interpretation recognizes. *Couch* and *Fisher,* as Justice Brennan observes, "is but another step in the denigration of privacy principles settled nearly 100 years ago in *Boyd v. United States.*"[220] Indeed, the Court in the late nineteenth and early twentieth centuries extended the guarantees of both the fourth and fifth amendments to claims of personal privacy and thereby prohibited governmental access to vast amounts of personal information.[221] Historically, judicial interpretation of the fifth amendment paralleled in most instances the broad protection afforded by common law practices.[222] Hence, judicially enforced fifth amendment guarantees extended protection against compelled personal disclosures transcending that provided by a literal reading of the amendment.[223] *Boyd* thus stands as a watershed for a broad construction of the amendment. It recognized that the amendment guarantees a constitutional right, not simply a procedural rule, and that it extended to interests in personal privacy. Therefore, a liberal mandate existed for extending the fifth amendment not only to the defendant in criminal proceedings, but to witnesses in criminal, civil, grand jury, legislative and administrative proceedings.[224] As the Court reiterated in 1892, in *Counselman v. Hitchcock*: "[t]his provision must have a broad construction in favor of the right which it was intended to secure. . . . The privilege is not limited to criminal matters, but it is as broad as the mischief against which it seeks to guard."[225] The *Boyd*-fostered broad construction acknowledges that the fifth amendment may serve functions not suggested by a literal reading, yet logically related to the amendment's proscription of compelled personal disclosures because the amendment is construed to embody a constitutional principle or right. Consequently, the fifth amendment's protection should extend not only to defendants and witnesses when compelled to elicit incriminating personal information, but also where individuals have privacy interests in materials possessed by third parties and sought by administrative agencies.

Dissenters from the Burger Court's interpretation maintain, as did Justice Bradley in *Boyd,* that "the Fourth and Fifth Amendments delineate a 'sphere of privacy' which must be protected against governmental intrusion."[226] Indeed, dissenting in *Couch,* Justice Douglas parted with Justice Brennan, who held that as a precondition of evoking the fifth amendment, "reasonable steps" be taken by an individual to secure the privacy of materials not in his possession.[227] Douglas urged that a "Fifth Amendment claim [is] valid *even in absence of personal compulsion* so long as [the] accused has a reasonable expectation of privacy in articles subpoenaed."[228]

Justice Marshall's dissenting opinion in *Couch,* however, remains more helpful in understanding both the significance of the Burger Court's narrow analysis of the privilege and how a broad construction of the amendment could provide extensive safeguards for personal privacy. Justice Marshall began his dissent by reviewing alternative interpretations of *Boyd,* pointing out that the Burger Court's reliance on *Boyd* failed to focus "on the obvious concern of the case, the desire of the author of documents to keep them private."[229] Part of the Burger Court's difficulty in addressing the safeguards for privacy interests in private papers, Marshall suggested, derived from interpreting the interplay between the fourth and fifth amendments:

> The Fourth and Fifth Amendments do not speak to totally unrelated concerns. . . . Both involve aspects of a person's right to develop for himself a sphere of personal privacy. Where the amendments "run almost into each other," I would prohibit the Government from entering. The problem, as I see it, is to develop criteria for determining whether evidence sought by the Government lies within the sphere of activities that petitioner attempted to keep private.[230]

Thereupon, Justice Marshall proposed an analysis of fifth amendment-protected privacy similar to that of the fourth amendment formulated by Justice Harlan.[231]

Justice Marshall specified four criteria for analyzing claims to fifth amendment-protected privacy. The first criterion "is the nature of the evidence."[232] Justice Marshall observes that "[d]iaries and personal letters . . . lie at the heart of our sense of privacy" and should receive fifth amendment protection, whereas there exists no constitutional bar to the seizure of letters between co-conspirators of a crime.[233] Yet, where non-personal documents are not used in the furtherance of a crime, Justice Marshall would extend fifth amendment protection. The second consideration lies with the activities of the person to whom the papers were given, and the third, the purposes for which the papers are transferred. Finally, Justice Marshall urged the Court to "take into account the steps that the author took to ensure the privacy of the records."[234]

According to Justice Marshall, then, the reasonableness of individuals claims and expectations of informational privacy in papers and records under the fifth amendment becomes contingent on several factors: the nature of the documents (e.g., compare diaries and letters of extortion); what recipients of personal information do with it (e.g., compare attorneys' uses and trustees in a bankruptcy); the purposes of voluntarily relinquishing personal information to another (e.g., compare attorneys or accountants' use in preparation of individuals' tax liability with copies of documents for use in blackmailing); and the steps which individuals take to secure the privacy of their information (e.g., compare placing papers in a safe-deposit box for years with filing them in a business office or handing them over to an attorney).

Justice Marshall's analytical framework for fifth amendment-protected privacy bears a family resemblance to *Boyd's* broad construction of constitutionally protected privacy. Justice Marshall's analysis, like *Boyd* and its progeny, provides extensive protection for personal privacy commensurate with the contexts and expectations of privacy, upon a consideration of the government's need for evidence of criminal activity and the right of individuals to define for themselves a "zone" of privacy, i.e., to place limits on their disclosures and access by others to personal information and engagements. Moreover, the government would be prohibited from circumventing and, thereby, nullifying the fifth amendment's guarantee "by finding a way [e.g., as with administrative summons to third parties] to obtain the documents without requiring the owner to take them in hand and personally present them to the government agents."[235]

By contrast to a broad construction of the fifth amendment based upon the recognition that it guarantees a constitutional right extending some protection to privacy interests, recent Burger Court decisions significantly limit the amendment's protection. To be sure, the Burger Court's treatment is not without precedent.[236] Instead, the Court appears to consider as controlling only those cases which support its re-evaluation of the jurisprudential basis for the fifth amendment and protected privacy by "disregarding the testimonial nature of private papers and drawing an artificial distinction between speech and writing: the privilege prohibits compelling a person to *speak* and incriminate himself but it does not prohibit compelled revelation of *written* thoughts."[237] In other words, the Court confines fifth amendment protection to situations in which an individual is compelled to disclose incriminating information orally or by personally relinquishing private papers or documents. As the Court, in *Andresen v. Maryland,* reiterated, "unless incriminating testimony is 'compelled,' any invasion of privacy is outside the scope of the Fifth Amendment's protection. . . ."[238]

### B. *Personal Compulsion and Compelled Disclosures*

As an exception to the broad contours of the fifth amendment fostered by *Boyd* and its progeny[239] in the late nineteenth and early twentieth centuries, a doctrine of "required records" which precluded the privilege's protection for personal disclosures developed. In this area, the Burger Court's decisions appear consistent with the prevailing historical trend in constitutional interpretation. Indeed, the Court's treatment extends the doctrine so as to more strictly define the nature of personal compulsion and thereby, contract the scope of the fifth amendment.

Dicta in *Wilson v. United States*[240] first suggested that the fifth amendment had no applicability where recordkeeping was required by law in order to provide information for governmental regulation. The doctrine of required records, however, was not fully developed until 1948 in *Shapiro v. United States.*[241] *Shapiro* held that records required to be kept under the regulatory power of Congress had "public aspects," and thus, personal information contained therein was not subject to fifth amendment protection. Twenty years later, in *Grosso v. United States,* the Court clarified the doctrine:

> The premises of the doctrine, as it is described in *Shapiro,* are evidently three: first, the purpose of the United States's inquiry must be essentially regulatory; second, information is to be obtained by requiring the preservation of records of a kind which the regulated party has customarily kept; and third, the records themselves must have assumed "public aspects" which render at least analogous to public documents.[242]

The broad doctrine espoused in *Shapiro* was subsequently supported in *California v. Byers*,[243] where a plurality upheld California's "hit-and-run" statute requiring a driver of a motor vehicle involved in an accident to stop at the scene and give his or her name and address. The Court observed that "the disclosure of inherently illegal activity is inherently risky. . . . But disclosures with respect to automobile accidents simply do not entail the kind of substantial risk of self-incrimination involved in [serious criminal cases]. Furthermore, the statutory purpose is noncriminal and self-reporting is indispensable to its fulfillment."[244]

The Burger Court thereby severely limited fifth amendment safeguards for personal privacy by denying protection for custodians of records[245] and by upholding the government's requiring of statements concerning criminal activity, e.g., as with reporting and registration requirements.[246] Accordingly, many of the Court's commentators found the required records doctrine to "swallow the privilege whole in relation to written documents"[247] and, thereupon, diminish the constitutional protection afforded personal privacy. As McKay observed, "A government that can roam at will through all records that it may demand to inspect because it may demand that they be kept is not a government that is bound to respect individual privacy."[248]

Certainly, privacy arguments for the privilege can be taken too far; privacy interests can justifiably be invalidated by interests in securing and maintaining civil order, e.g., as with accident reports.[249] The Burger Court's policy preference regarding the fifth amendment, however, demonstrates a proclivity to dismiss all privacy interests when construing the nature of personal compulsion with regard to required records. Consider, for example, recent decisions construing the effective exercise of the privilege with regard to compelled personal disclosures required in filing tax returns.[250]

Personal income tax returns have long been held to be required records since the Internal Revenue Service's requirements are derived from the government's taxing power.[251] In 1927, in *United States v. Sullivan*,[252] the Court established that the fifth amendment is not a defense against prosecution for failing to file an income tax return. Several years later, the problem posed by illegal income earners and reporting requirements of filing tax returns was again raised in *Murdock v. United States*[253] where a taxpayer filed a return claiming certain deductions but refused to answer on fifth amendment grounds Internal Revenue Service questions concerning the deductions; whereupon, he was prosecuted for willful failure to supply the necessary information. The Supreme Court reversed the district court's dismissal of the indictment[254] and subsequently held that even though Murdock's previous claim was invalid, a "good faith" claim of the privilege would negate any willfulness of failure to supply information and bar conviction.[255] Nevertheless, pursuant to *Sullivan*, the government's taxing power appears paramount, outweighing any individual's claim to privacy interests in non-disclosure of financial information.[256]

During the Warren Court, however, some limitations were imposed upon statutes relating to record keeping and required registration.[257] In particular, the Warren Court recognized that obligations of illegal income earners to register and pay occupational and wagering excise taxes created "real and appreciable" hazards of self-incrimination. This is significant since part of the Internal Revenue Service's statutory scheme requires it to disclose information to federal and state law enforcement officers. In *Marchetti v. United States*,[258] the Court struck down a statute requiring gamblers to register and to submit monthly information concerning their wagering activities, holding that failure to supply wagering information was justified under the fifth amendment since the information was not customarily kept, the reports had no "public records" aspects, and moreover, the requirements were directed at a "select group inherently suspect of criminal activities."[259] In dicta, noting the necessity of a broad construction of the privilege and protected privacy, the Court remarked that "[t]he Government's anxiety to obtain information known to a private individual does not without more render that information public; if it did, no room would remain for the application of the constitutional privilege."[260]

By contrast, the Burger Court's treatment appears to strictly and literally interpret the nature of personal compulsion and disregard the forfeiture of privacy interests in compelled disclosures required by filing tax returns. Justice Brennan, dissenting in *Beckwith v. United States*,[261] observed that the Court's analysis fails to recognize that the "practical compulsion to respond to questions about [an individual's] tax returns is comparable to the psychological pressures described in *Miranda*."[262] Justice Brennan's criticisms of the Court's narrow construction of personal compulsion is well illustrated by its 1976 decision in *Garner v. United States*.[263] In *Garner,* the Court held that a taxpayer earning illegal income and not desirous of exposure to criminal charges for failure to file a tax return must claim the privilege against self-incrimination on his tax return. If, however, incriminating information is disclosed on the return and the privilege is not asserted, then the taxpayer forfeits his or her expectations of privacy and in any future criminal case may not exercise the fifth amendment guarantee.

*Garner* epitomizes the Burger Court's literal construction of personal compulsion and how it circumscribes fifth amendment-protected privacy. Garner, in filing his federal income tax returns, reported his occupation as a "professional gambler." Subsequently, Garner was indicted for conspiracy involving the use of interstate transportation and communications facilities to "fix" sporting contests and transmit bets. At trial, in order to establish Garner's guilt, the government not only introduced testimony of his co-conspirators and telephone toll records, but also his tax returns. Garner's objections were overruled and he was eventually convicted. Before the Supreme Court, Garner first relied upon *Miranda* in arguing that his failure to claim the privilege against self-incrimination on his tax returns was not a knowing and intelligent waiver. The Court, however, observed that he had prepared his tax returns in the leisure and privacy of his home and, therefore, the *Miranda* safeguards developed in the context of custodial situations were not applicable. The Court emphasized that "unless a witness objects, a government ordinarily may assume that its compulsory processes are not eliciting testimony that [the individual] deems to be incriminating."[264] Second, Garner relied on *Mackey v. United States*,[265] in which the Court held that *Marchetti* and *Grosso* were non-retroactive, arguing that his post-disclosure claim provided sufficient protection for his disclosures on his tax returns. Here, Garner's argument failed insofar as Mackey's returns had been directed at persons "inherently suspect of criminal activities," whereas his own were directed towards the general public.

Significantly, the Court disregarded the fact that Garner's disclosures, made for one purpose, i.e., filing his income tax return, were being used by the government for another purpose, i.e., in a criminal prosecution. Indeed, the Court presumes that such governmental uses of personal information do not threaten the fair state-individual balance reflected in an accusatorial system. "Only the witness knows whether the apparently innocent disclosure sought may incriminate him, and the burden appropriately lies with him to make a timely assertion of the privilege. If, instead, he discloses the information sought, any incriminations properly are viewed as not compelled."[266] *Garner,* thus, underscores other Burger Court rulings strictly construing the requirement of personal compulsion necessary for effective exercise of the privilege. In *United States v. Kordel,*[267] the Court held that a witness under compulsion to make disclosures who reveals incriminating information instead of claiming fifth amendment protection loses the privilege's benefits, and in *Schneckcloth v. Bustamonte*[268] the Court ruled that individuals may also "lose the benefit of the privilege without making a knowing and intelligent waiver."[269]

The Burger Court's narrow construction severely contracts the scope of the fifth amendment-protected privacy and, in particular, diminishes the practical value of the privilege and individuals' privacy interests in financial matters. More specifically, an irrebuttable presumption exists requiring taxpayers to make basic disclosures fundamental to neutral reporting requirements. Only an individual or a group suspected of criminal engagements may not be required to supply information relating to those engagements. Protection of individuals' privacy interests in financial disclosures by claims under the fifth amendment will not bar prosecution, but conviction will not follow, regardless whether the claim is valid, if it was asserted in "good faith." If, however, incriminating information is disclosed on a tax return and the privilege is not raised, then the taxpayer forfeits his or her expectations of privacy and in any future criminal prosecution may not rely on the amendment.

### C. *Contexts and Circumstances of Personal Compulsion*

Concomitant with evolving a narrow construction of personal compulsion, the Burger Court's treatment of the fifth amendment restricts the contexts and circumstances in which individuals may enjoy the benefits of the privilege. Notwithstanding prosecutorial anticipation and civil libertarian trepidation that *Miranda* would be overturned, the Burger Court has not departed from the Warren Court's premise in *Miranda,* namely, that "interrogation of persons suspected or accused of crime contains inherently compelling pressures which work to undermine the individual's will to resist and to compel him to speak where he would not otherwise do so freely."[270] Instead, the Burger Court appears to be re-evaluating the necessity of full *Miranda* warnings[271] in every situation and, by distinguishing *Miranda* requirements (as mere "prophylactic rules"[272]) from the fifth amendment's constitutional guarantee, sharply defining the contexts and circumstances which require that individuals be given *Miranda* warnings or enjoy fifth amendment protection.

Prior to *Miranda,* courts permitted individuals at trial to claim fifth amendment protection and prohibit the introduction of self-incriminating statements obtained through police interrogation only upon showing "a totality of circumstances evidencing an involuntary . . . admission of guilt."[273] Five members of the Warren Court, however, enlarged the scope of the fifth amendment's protection upon the recognition that "[t]he privilege against self-incrimination protects the individual from being compelled to incriminate himself in any manner; it does not distinguish degrees of incrimination."[274] As Ritchie observes, "In *Miranda,* the Warren Court rejected the argument that society's need for interrogation outweighs the privilege; it indicated that the right to be free from compulsion could not be abridged."[275] Indeed, the Court reasoned that the fifth amendment's justification in terms of maintaining a fair state-individual balance requires the government "to shoulder the entire load"[276] in proving an individual's culpability.

Whereas the Warren Court's evaluation and broad construction fostered procedural safeguards in order to ensure the practical value of individuals' rights under the fifth amendment, the Burger Court's policy orientation and narrow construction[277] finds *Miranda* a "procedural [as distinguished from constitutional] ruling,"[278] and thus permits prosecutorial use of an individual's incriminating statements made without the benefit of full *Miranda* warnings[279] or a "knowing and intelligent"[280] waiver of fifth amendment protection. In *Michigan v. Tucker,*[281] the Court emphasized that the "protective guidelines" of *Miranda* were designed to "supplement" the privilege, and "these procedural safeguards were not themselves rights protected by the Constitution but were instead measures to ensure that the right against compulsory self-incrimination was protected."[282] Hence, both because the Burger Court narrowly construes personal compulsion and views *Miranda* requirements as not constitutionally mandated, but only procedural safeguards based on policy considerations, law enforcement has considerable flexibility in prosecuting individuals on the basis of their incriminating statements since deviations from *Miranda* will not necessarily offend the fifth amendment.

Accordingly, in *Harris v. New York,*[283] the Court held that statements, inadmissible against the defendant in the prosecution's case because of the failure to satisfy the procedural safeguards required by *Miranda,* may, if their trustworthiness satisfies legal standards, be used for impeachment of the defendant's trial testimony. In dissent, Justice Brennan argued that *Miranda* had settled the issue, reiterating its holding that "statements merely intended to be exculpatory by the defendant are often *used to impeach his testimony at trial. . . . These statements are incriminating in any meaningful sense of the word and may not be used without the full warnings and effective waiver required for any other statement.'"*[284] Chief Justice Burger, for the five-member majority, however, was apparently more concerned that "[t]he shield provided by *Miranda* [would] be perverted into a license to use perjury by way of a defense, free from the risk of confrontation with prior inconsistent utterances."[285] In *Oregon v. Hass,*[286] the Court extended *Harris* to permit the defendant's impeachment by use of statements obtained while he was in police custody and after he had requested a lawyer but before the lawyer was present. The Court further diminished the safeguards required by *Miranda* in *Michigan v. Tucker,*[287] ruling that the fifth amendment was not violated by the prosecution's use of testimony of a witness discovered as the result of the defendant's statements to police given without *Miranda* warnings. Again, in the following year, in *Michigan v. Mosley*,[288] the Court upheld police interrogation, after a two-hour interval, of an individual who had earlier exercised his right to remain silent. In *Miranda*, the majority held:

> Once warnings have been given, the subsequent procedure is clear. If the individual indicates in any manner, at any time prior to or during questioning, that he wishes to remain silent, the interrogation must cease. At this point he has shown that he intends to exercise his Fifth Amendment privilege; any statement taken after the person invokes his privilege cannot be other than the product of compulsion, subtle or otherwise. Without the right to cut off questioning, the setting of in-custody interrogation operates on the individual to overcome free choice in producing a statement after the privilege has been once invoked.[289]

The Burger Court, however, over the dissenters' objection that "*Miranda* established a virtually irrebuttable presumption of compulsion . . . and that presumption stands strongest where, as in this case, a suspect, having initially determined to remain silent, is subsequently brought to confess his crime,"[290] construed the critical *Miranda* safeguard at issue to require only that police "scrupulously honored" a person's "right to cut off questioning."[291] Notwithstanding the view of some of the Court's commentators, such as Jerold Israel, that "*Tucker, Mathiason,* and perhaps even *Mosley* did not significantly detract from the basic *Miranda* ruling,"[292] Justice Brennan candidly observed that *Mosley* "virtually empties *Miranda* of principle, for plainly the decision encourages police asked to cease interrogation to continue the suspect's detention until the police station's coercive atmosphere does its work and the suspect responds to resumed questioning."[293]

That the Burger Court's construction of the contours of the privilege's protection entails significant erosion of *Miranda* safeguards is underscored by its 1977 *per curiam* ruling in *Oregon v. Mathiason*.[294] In *Mathiason*, the suspect, a parolee, following a police request, voluntarily went to the police station where, even though he admitted committing a crime, he was informed that he was not under arrest and allowed to leave after the questioning. The Court rejected the Oregon Supreme Court's opinion excluding the confession as having "read *Miranda* too broadly,"[295] and, over Justice Marshall's contention in dissent that coercive elements were "so pervasive"[296] as to require *Miranda* warnings, concluded that the suspect was not in "custody" in the police station and, hence, *Miranda* warnings were not required.

Although the Burger Court has not overturned *Miranda per se*, it has significantly diluted the practical value of *Miranda's* procedural requirements and the feasibility of fifth amendment protection by permitting in *Harris* and *Hass* prosecutorial use of individuals' self-accusatorial statements and, in *Tucker, Mosley,* and *Mathiason,* by sanctioning considerable flexibility in police interrogation of criminal suspects.[297] The Burger Court departs from *Miranda* in part because, as with its treatment of the exclusionary rule and the fourth amendment,[298] it views *Miranda's* requirements as procedural rules based on policy and not constitutional principle. More fundamentally, the Court permits departures from *Miranda* because it promotes a strict construction of the privilege and demonstration of personal compulsion necessary for enjoying the privilege's benefits. The Warren Court's broad interpretation of the fifth

amendment led to an extension of the benefits of the privilege against self-incrimination and imposition of *Miranda* safeguards not only to station house interrogations but to any context of "questioning initiated by law enforcement officers after a person has been taken into custody or otherwise deprived of his freedom of action in any significant way."[299] By contrast, the Burger Court's strict construction of the nature of personal compulsion promotes the privilege's protection only when "considering the totality of the circumstances, the free will of the witness is overborne."[300] The Court's treatment thus signifies a retrenchment to pre-*Miranda* rulings so that the fifth amendment protects against only police interrogations in contexts in which the "totality of circumstances evidenc[es] an involuntary . . . admission of guilt."[301] As Ritchie comments, "the Court has taken too literally the maxim that the privilege protects the accused from being convicted on evidence forced 'out of his mouth,' "[302] and, therefore, has rendered insignificant the psychological pressures that bear upon individuals in police custody, or without full *Miranda* warnings, or a knowing and intelligent waiver of their rights, or after renewed questioning following lengthy periods of detention.

The Burger Court's strict construction, moreover, fosters not only retrenchment in fifth amendment protection for individuals in contexts of custodial interrogation, but also the refusal to extend the contours of the privilege to non-custodial interviews and questioning.

In *Beckwith v. United States,*[303] the Court considered the issue whether Internal Revenue Service special agents, investigating criminal income tax violations, must give *Miranda* warnings in non-custodial interviews with taxpayers. Two Internal Revenue Service special agents visited Beckwith in a private residence in order to question him about his income tax liability and, before beginning their questions, gave him the standard Internal Revenue Service warning that they could not compel him to answer or submit any incriminating information, rather than informing him that he had a right to remain silent.[304] While Chief Justice Burger, for the majority, agreed that in such instances the taxpayer is already the "focus" of a criminal investigation, he construed *Miranda* to safeguard only against the compulsion inherent in custodial interrogations, as distinguished from non-custodial interviews as in *Beckwith.*[305] Narrow construction of the nature of personal compulsion thus allowed the Court to avoid serious consideration whether, in dissenting Justice Brennan's words, "[i]nterrogation under conditions that have the *practical consequence* of compelling the taxpayer to make disclosures, and interrogation in 'custody' having the same consequences, are . . . peas from the same pod."[306] Hence, in *Beckwith,* as in *Garner,*[307] the Court limited the contours of the privilege's protection by its narrow construction of personal compulsion and *Miranda's* procedural safeguards; it emphasized that "[p]roof that some kind of warnings were given or that none were given would be relevant evidence only on the issue of whether the questioning was in fact coercive."[308]

The Court continued to confine sharply the contours of fifth amendment protection by further underlining the distinction between custodial and non-custodial interrogations in *United States v. Mandujano,*[309] *United States v. Washington,*[310] and *United States v. Wong.*[311] In *Mandujano,* Chief Justice Burger, for the Court, held that the fifth amendment does not require suppression in a perjury prosecution of false statements made to a grand jury by an individual who was not given *Miranda* warnings

when called to testify, even though he was a "putative" or "virtual" defendant. Chief Justice Burger emphasized that individuals have an absolute right to decline to answer questions during an in-custody police interrogation, but before a grand jury (a non-custodial context) have an absolute duty to answer all questions because of their obligation imposed by taking an oath to testify.[312] Notwithstanding the import of privacy arguments for the privilege's protection in such contexts, the Court added that, "[n]or can [the privilege] be invoked simply to protect the witness's interests in privacy. Ordinarily, of course, a witness has no right of privacy before the grand jury."[313]

In *Washington,* an individual suspected with others of possible theft was subpoenaed to appear as a witness before a grand jury. While given a series of warnings, including the warning that he had the right to remain silent, he was not informed in advance of his testimony that he was a potential defendant in danger of indictment and, subsequently, was indicted for theft. Chief Justice Burger, writing for the majority, observed that the fifth amendment privilege extends to grand jury proceedings, but does not require suppression of an individual's incriminating testimony unless it was obtained by "genuine compulsion."[314] Again reiterating the Court's narrow construction of personal compulsion and fifth amendment protection, Chief Justice Burger emphasized "the need for showing overbearing compulsion as a prerequisite to a Fifth Amendment violation."[315] Thus, *Washington,* as *Tucker, Garner, Beckwith,* and *Mandujano,* reaffirmed the Court's strict construction of the protection and benefits of the fifth amendment. "The constitutional guarantee is only that the witness not be *compelled* to give self-incriminating testimony. The test is whether considering the totality of the circumstances the free will of the witness was overborne."[316]

## V. Conclusion

The Burger Court's treatment of claims to fifth amendment protection, with regard to private papers, required records, and the application of *Miranda* requirements to custodial and non-custodial interrogations, indicates the proclivity toward strict construction and narrowing of the contours of the fifth amendment. While prosecutors, police, and conservatives may rejoice in the Burger Court's "law and order"[317] policy orientation, civil libertarians may find consolation because the Court has not overturned *Miranda,* rather only engaged in retrenchment from the liberal jurisprudence[318] of the Warren Court.

Civil libertarians, moreover, could perhaps applaud the Burger Court's efforts to return to a strict construction of the fifth amendment guarantee. Unfortunately, the Burger Court's strict construction appears to be the result of its law and order policy orientation towards the privilege against self-incrimination, rather than an attempt to reconstruct a right against self-accusation upon a literal reading of the amendment's guarantee that, "[n]o person shall . . . be compelled in any criminal case to be a witness against himself."[319] The Court's strict construction fails to foster a literal interpretation; this is exemplified by the Court's refusal to consider the consequences of compelled personal disclosures in *Couch, Fisher, Andresen,* and *Garner,* as well as the practical ways in which an individual may be compelled to be a "witness against

himself." Instead, the Court's strict construction, e.g., in *Harris, Tucker, Mosley, Mathiason, Beckwith, Mandujano,* and *Washington* appears only to lead to a literal interpretation of personal compulsion and, hence, the opportunity to circumscribe fifth amendment protection.

The Burger Court's contraction of the benefits and protection of the fifth amendment guarantee, furthermore, reflects a fundamental reconsideration and re-evaluation of the amendment's jurisprudential basis. *Schultz, Couch, Fisher, Nobles,* and *Andresen* underscore the Burger Court's rejection of privacy arguments for the privilege.[320] In contrast to the Warren Court's extension of the contours of fifth amendment-protected privacy,[321] the Burger Court's strict construction protects only "compelled self-incrimination, not [the disclosure of] private information,"[322] so that "unless incriminating testimony is 'compelled,' any invasion of privacy is outside the scope of the Fifth Amendment."[323] The diminishing utility of the fifth amendment guarantee for claims to constitutionally protected privacy in the Burger Court's analysis is further promoted by its re-evaluation of the merits of the old woman's rationale[324] and concomitant literal interpretation of personal compulsion requiring a "showing [of] overbearing compulsion as a prerequisite to a Fifth Amendment violation."[325] Thus, the Burger Court focuses primarily on what was termed the fox hunter's rationale[326] for the privilege against self-incrimination, namely, its role in "the preservation of an adversary system of criminal justice."[327] Indeed, the Burger Court's law and order policy orientation accords, if not prompts, its focus on the fox hunter's instrumental evaluation of and justification for the privilege. The Burger Court's treatment of the fifth amendment guarantee, hence, not surprisingly circumscribes protection for personal disclosures with respect to private papers[328] and required records,[329] condones both police practices that deviate from and thereby dilute *Miranda* and the prosecutorial use of individuals' incriminating statements which result from such police practices,[330] as well as tolerates "police trickery" in obtaining individuals' self-accusatorial statements.[331] Civil libertarians, therefore, may well applaud the Burger Court's endeavor to return to a strict construction of the Constitution but lament that its law and order policy orientation fosters a fundamental jurisprudential shift and contraction in the contours of the fifth amendment and protected privacy.

### Notes

1. The amendment provides: "No person . . . shall be compelled in any criminal case to be a witness against himself. . . ." U.S. CONST. amend. V.
2. The article adopts the conventional characterization of the "Burger Court" so as to refer to those decisions since the appointment of Warren Burger as Chief Justice on June 23, 1969. The designation of "Burger Court" decisions is appropriate because since the appointment of Chief Justice Burger the Court's composition has changed—President Nixon appointed Harry A. Blackmun in 1970 and Lewis F. Powell and William H. Rehnquist in 1971; and, in 1975, President Ford appointed John Paul Stevens to the Court—with the consequence that recent appointees constitute a majority which has demonstrated a proclivity for re-evaluating and redefining the contours of the fifth amendment. For discussions of the Burger Court or, alternatively termed the "Nixon Court," see S. WASBY, *Continuity and Change: From the Warren Court to the Burger Court* (1977); Abraham, *Of Myths, Motives, Motivations, and Morality: Some Observations on the Burger Court's Record on Civil Rights and Liberties,* 52 Notre Dame Law. 77 (1977).
3. *See generally* R. Funston, *Constitutional Counterrevolution?* (1977).

4. Chief Justice Earl Warren urged the necessity of a liberal construction of the fifth amendment in *Quinn* v. *United States,* 349 U.S. 155, 162 (1955), stating: "A liberal construction is particularly warranted in a prosecution of a witness for a refusal to answer, the presumption of innocence accorded a defendant in a criminal trial. To apply the privilege narrowly or begrudgingly—to treat it as an historical relic, at most to be tolerated—is to ignore its development and purpose."

5. The Burger Court has limited the privilege's applicability and protection in both pre-trial and trial contexts. *See Garner* v. *United States,* 424 U.S. 648 (1976); *Michigan* v. *Mosley,* 423 U.S. 96 (1975); *Brown* v. *Illinois,* 422 U.S. 590 (1975); *Michigan* v. *Tucker,* 417 U.S. 433 (1974); *Schneckcloth* v. *Bustamonte,* 412 U.S. 218 (1976); *United States* v. *Dionisio,* 410 U.S. 1 (1972); *Kastigar* v. *United States,* 406 U.S. 441 (1972); *Harris* v. *New York,* 401 U.S. 222 (1971); *Williams* v. *Florida,* 399 U.S. 79 (1970).

While the Burger Court has not overruled *Miranda,* it refuses to extend *Miranda* requirements not only with regard to police interrogations but also administrative and grand jury investigations. *See United States* v. *Wong,* 431 U.S. 174 (1977); *United States* v. *Washington,* 431 U.S. 181 (1977); *United States* v. *Mandujano,* 435 U.S. 564 (1976); *Beckwith* v. *United States,* 425 U.S. 341 (1976).

The diminishing constitutional significance of the fifth amendment is underscored by a series of holdings on the privilege's inapplicability to required records and private papers or documents. *See Andresen* v. *Maryland,* 427 U.S. 463 (1976); *Fisher* v. *United States,* 425 U.S. 391 (1976); *United States* v. *Nobles,* 422 U.S. 225 (1975); *California Bankers Ass'n* v. *Shultz,* 416 U.S. 21 (1974); *Couch* v. *United States,* 409 U.S. 322 (1973); *California* v. *Byers,* 402 U.S. 424 (1971).

6. The Warren Court in a herculean exercise of judicial power constitutionally denominated a right of privacy in *Griswold* v. *Connecticut,* 381 U.S. 479 (1965), when striking down a statute which prohibited the use of contraceptives by married couples. The Burger Court, in a series of cases manifesting extra-judicial activism, extended the right of privacy to an unmarried woman's use of contraceptives. *Eisenstadt* v. *Baird,* 405 U.S. 438 (1972); a woman's decision to have an abortion, *Roe* v. *Wade,* 410 U.S. 113 (1976), and *Doe* v. *Bolton,* 410 U.S. 179 (1973); and held unconstitutional a statute which required a husband's consent before a wife could secure an abortion. *Planned Parenthood of Central Missouri* v. *Danforth,* 428 U.S. 52 (1976); as well as suggested that parents may not exercise an absolute veto over abortions for unmarried daughters under eighteen, *Bellotti* v. *Baird,* 428 U.S. 132 (1976).

7. *See* 425 U.S. 564: 427 U.S. 463: 425 U.S. at 400–01: 422 U.S. at 233 n.7; *United States* v. *Calandra,* 414 U.S. 338, 353 (1974); 409 U.S. at 331; 416 U.S. 21; 402 U.S. 424.

8. 8 J. Wigmore, *Evidence* § 2251 (McNaughton ed. 1961).

9. For discussions of competing principles and policies of the privilege, see: Ellis, *A Comment on the Testimonial Privilege of the Fifth Amendment,* 55 Iowa L. Rev. 829 (1970): Friendly, *The Fifth Amendment Tomorrow: The Case for Constitutional Change,* 37 Cin. L. Rev. 671 (1968): McNaughton, *The Privilege Against Self-Incrimination,* 51 *J. Crim. L., Criminology, Police Sci.* 138 (1960); Sowle, *The Privilege Against Self-Incrimination: Principles and Trends,* 51 *J. Crim. L. Criminology, Police Sci.* 131 (1960).

10. *See* 5 J. Bentham, *A Rationale of Judicial Evidence* 238–39 (1827). The "fox hunter's reason" is discussed in text accompanying note 70 *infra.*

11. *See* 5 J. Bentham, *supra* note 10, at 230–38. The "old woman's reason" is discussed in text accompanying note 108 *infra.*

12. *See* 5 J. Bentham, *supra* note 10.

13. The Supreme Court affirmatively asserted a privacy rationale for the privilege in a number of cases; *see Miranda* v. *Arizona,* 384 U.S. 436, 460 (1966); *Tehan* v. *Shott,* 382 U.S. 406, 416 (1966); 381 U.S. at 484; *Murphy* v. *Waterfront Commission,* 387 U.S. 52, 55 (1964); *United States* v. *White,* 322 U.S. 694, 698 (1944); *Feldman* v. *United States,* 322 U.S. 487, 489–490 (1940); *Boyd* v. *United States,* 116 U.S. 616, 630 (1886). A number of the Court's commentators urge that a privacy principle underlies the privilege. *See* Dann, *The Fifth Amendment Privilege against Self-Incrimination: Extorting Physical Evidence from a Suspect,* 43 S. Calif. L. Rev. 597, 601–602 (1970); Fried, *Privacy,* 77 Yale L. J. 475, 488–489 (1968); Gerstein, *Privacy and Self-Incrimination,* 80 Ethics 87 (1970); McKay,

*Self-Incrimination and the New Privacy, The Supreme Court Review* 209 (P. Kurland ed. 1967); Ratner, *The Consequences of Exercising the Privilege against Self-Incrimination,* 24 U. Chi. L. Rev. 472, 487 (1957). Privacy arguments for the privilege are examined in text accompanying note 134 *infra.*

14. Prior to his appointment to the Supreme Court, Chief Justice Burger expressed his doubts about the practical feasibility and validity of the privilege: "I am no longer sure that the Fifth Amendment concept in its present form and as presently applied and interpreted [*i.e.,.e.,* by the Warren Court], has all the validity attributed to it." McDonald, *A Center Report: Criminal Justice,* 1 *The Center Magazine* 69–77 (Nov. 1968).

15. Wigmore, *Nemo Tenetur Seipsum Prodere,* 5 Harv. L. Rev. 71 (1892).

16. Silving, *The Oath* (pts. 1–2), 68 Yale L. J. 1329, 1527 (1959).

17. *See generally L. Levy, The Origins of the Fifth Amendment* 3 (1968); Corwin, *The Supreme Court's Construction of the Self-Incrimination Clause,* 29 Mich. L. Rev. 1 (1930) 8 J. Wigmore, *supra* note 8, § 2251, at 295; Wigmore, *supra* note 15.

18. *The Answers of John Lambert to the Forty-Five Articles,* 5 *The Acts and Monuments of John Foxe: A New and Complete Edition* 184 (Rev. Stephen Cahely ed.).

19. *See generally* L. Levy, *supra* note 17; 8 Wigmore, *supra* note 8, at § 2251; Silving, *supra* note 16.

20. *See* L. Levy, *supra* note 17, at 333–400.

21. Six of the original thirteen states (Maryland, 1776; North Carolina, 1776; Pennsylvania, 1776; Virginia, 1776; Massachusetts, 1780; New Hampshire, 1784) included the principle in their constitutions or Bill of Rights, and in the remaining states the principle was recognized by their courts. *See generally* Pittman, *The Colonial and Constitutional History of the Privilege against Self-Incrimination in America,* 21 Va. L. Rev. 763 (1935).

22. L. Levy, *supra* note 17, at 430.

23. For discussions of the historical basis of the fifth amendment in the evolution of the Anglo-American accusatorial system, see: L. Levy, *supra* note 17, at 333: 8 J. Wigmore, *supra* note 8 at § 2250; Pittman, *supra* note 21. For discussions of the interplay between the fourth and fifth amendments, see Note, *Formalism, Legal Realism, and Constitutionally Protected Privacy under the Fourth and Fifth Amendments,* 90 Harv. L. Rev. 945 (1977).

24. Section 8, Virginia Declaration of Rights, *reprinted in* 7 F. Thorpe, *The Federal and State Constitutions, Colonial Charters, and Other Organic Laws* 3813 (1909). Even while the privilege was only a rule of evidence, the Supreme Court has stated: "The right of an accused person to refuse to testify, which had been in England merely a role of evidence, was so important to our forefathers that they raised it to the dignity of a constitutional enactment, and it has been recognized as 'one of the most valuable prerogatives of the citizen.' " *Slochower* v. *Board of Education,* 350 U.S. 551, 557 (1956). *See also Brown* v. *Walker,* 161 U.S. 591, 610 (1896); 349 U.S. at 161–62.

25. L. Levy, *supra* note 17, at 407.

26. *Id.*

27. *Id.* at 422.

28. *Id.* at 243–44.

29. *See generally* Pittman, *supra* note 21.

30. Amendments reported by the House Select Committee, July 28, 1789, are printed in 5 *Documentary History of the Constitution of the United States of America* 1786–1870 at 186–189, quoted and discussed by Levy, *supra* note 17, at 424–425.

31. Comment, *The Protection of Privacy by the Privilege Against Self-Incrimination: A Doctrine Laid to Rest?* 59 Iowa L. Rev. 1336, 1343 (1974).

32. *See* L. Mayers, *Shall We Amend the Fifth Amendment?* (1959); Mayers, *The Federal Witness's Privilege Against Self-Incrimination,* 4 *Am. J. Legal History* 107 (1960); Corwin, *supra* note 17.

33. 8 J. Wigmore, *supra* note 8, § 2251, at 378.

34. 8 J. Wigmore, *supra* note 8, § 2251, at 316. *Murphy* v. *Waterfront Commission of New York,* 378 U.S. 52, 55 (1964).

35. *See generally* Levy, 84 *J. of Pol.* 1 (1969), and text accompanying note 43 *infra.*

36. For the classic analysis of rights, liberties, powers, privileges, and immunities, see: W. Hohfeld, *Fundamental Legal Conceptions* (1919). *See also* J. Feinberg, *Social Philosophy* (1973); McCloskey, *Rights—Some Conceptual Issues,* 54 *Austl. J. of Phil.* 99 (1976).

37. *See generally* R. Flathman, *The Practice of Rights* (1976).
38. Levy, *supra* note 35, at 3 n.9.
39. Levy, *supra* note 17, at 427.
40. *Id.*
41. *Id.* at 425–427.
42. *Ullmann* v. *United States*, 350 U.S. 422, 438 (1956).
43. *Garrity* v. *New Jersey*, 385 U.S. 493 (1967); *Spevack* v. *Klein*, 385 U.S. 511 (1967); *Griffin* v. *California*, 380 U.S. 609, 614 (1965).
44. 402 U.S. 424; *Rogers* v. *United States*, 340 U.S. 367, 370 (1951); *United States* v. *Monia*, 317 U.S. 434, 437 (1943).
45. 402 U.S. at 432, 435; *Mackey* v. *United States*, 401 U.S. 667, 704–705 (1971); *Hoffman* v. *United States*, 341 U.S. 479, 486 (1951); *Mason* v. *United States*, 244 U.S. 362, 365 (1917).
46. *Hale* v. *Henkel*, 201 U.S. 43 (1906); 161 U.S. 591.
47. *Emspak* v. *United States*, 349 U.S. 190 (1955), quoting *The Queen* v. *Boyles*, 1 B & S 311, 330–331 (1861).
48. Levy, *supra* note 35, at 19.
49. *Counselman* v. *Hitchcock*, 142 U.S. 547, 562 (1892).
50. *See Lefkowitz* v. *Cunningham*, 429 U.S. 893 (1977); 402 U.S. at 437; *United States* v. *Kordel*, 397 U.S. 1, 6 (1970); *McCarthy* v. *Arndstein*, 266 U.S. 34 (1924); 161 U.S. 591 (1896); 142 U.S. at 563; 116 U.S. 616 (1886); *Marbury* v. *Madison*, 5 U.S. 137 (1863).
51. *See, Watkins* v. *United States*, 354 U.S. 178, 195–196 (1957); *Bart* v. *United States*, 349 U.S. 219 (1955); 349 U.S. 190; 349 U.S. 155; 266 U.S. at 40; 142 U.S. at 563–564.
52. *See* 266 U.S. 34; 5 U.S. 137.
53. 384 U.S. 436.
54. Levy, *supra* note 35, at 38.
55. *Escobedo* v. *Illinois*, 378 U.S. 478, 490 (1964).
56. 384 U.S. at 444.
57. *See Miranda* v. *Arizona*, 384 U.S. 436 (1966) (police interrogations); *Emspak* v. *United States*, 349 U.S. 190 (1955); *Quinn* v. *United States*, 349 U.S. 155 (1955) (legislative classifications); *McCarthy* v. *Arndstein*, 266 U.S. 34 (1924) (civil proceedings); *ICC* v. *Brimson*, 154 U.S. 447 (1894) (administrative investigations); *Counselman* v. *Hitchcock*, 142 U.S. 547 (1892) (grand jury proceedings).
58. 161 U.S. 591.
59. *Id.* at 631.
60. In *Ullman* v. *United States*, 350 U.S. 422 (1956), the Court stated that grants of immunity "need only remove those sanctions which generate the fear of justifying invocation of the privilege" but not protect against infamy or disgrace. *Id.* at 431. *See also United States* v. *Wilson*, 421 U.S. 309 (1975); 406 U.S. 441; 161 U.S. at 631.
61. *See* 397 U.S. 1 (1970); 161 U.S. 591.
62. *Kastigar* v. *United States*, 406 U.S. at 444 (upheld "use" or "testimonial" immunity as authorized by the Organized Crime Control Act of 1970). *See also Zicarelli* v. *New Jersey Investigation Comm'n*, 406 U.S. 472 (1972).
63. *See* 406 U.S. at 462 (Douglas, J., dissenting).
64. For pre-Burger cases see *Marchetti* v. *United States*, 390 U.S. 39 (1968); *Costello* v. *United States*, 383 U.S. 942 (1966); *Lewis* v. *United States*, 348 U.S. 922 (1966); *Communist Party of the United States* v. *Subversive Activities Control Board*, 367 U.S. 1 (1961); *United States* v. *Kahringer*, 345 U.S. 22 (1953); *Shapiro* v. *United States*, 335 U.S. 1 (1948).
65. *United States* v. *Dionisio*, 410 U.S. 1, 5–7 (1973) (voice samples); *United States* v. *Wade*, 388 U.S. 218, 221–23 (1967) (compelled police lineups); *Gilbert* v. *California*, 388 U.S. 263, 265–67 (1967) (handwriting samples); *Schmerber* v. *California*, 384 U.S. 757, 760–65 (1966) (compulsory blood samples).
66. 378 U.S. 52.
67. *Id.* at 55. 350 U.S. at 426–29; 161 U.S. at 638–39.
68. 378 U.S. at 55.
69. *Id.*

70. 5 J. Bentham, *supra* note 10, at 238–39.
71. 384 U.S. at 460.
72. *Culombe* v. *Connecticut*, 367 U.S. 568, 581–82 (1961). In *Rogers* v. *Richmond*, 565 U.S. 534 (1961), the Court stated that, "ours is an accusatorial and not an inquisitorial system— a system in which the State must establish guilt by evidence independently and freely secured and may not by coercion prove its charge against an accused out of his own mouth." *Id.* at 541. *See also* 431 U.S. 181; 427 U.S. at 484 (Brennan, J., dissenting).
73. 384 U.S. at 460 (citations omitted).
74. *See* 5 J. Bentham, *supra* note 10, at 305. *See also* Meltzer, *Required Records, the McCarran Act, and the Privilege Against Self-Incrimination*, 13 U. Chi. L. Rev. 687 (1950, 1951) and Fortas, *The Fifth Amendment: Nemo Tenetur Prodere Seipsum*, 25 Clev. B. A. J. 95 (1954).
75. Fortas, *supra* note 74, at 98–99.
76. Fortas, *supra* note 74, at 95. *See also* 378 U.S. at 489; 384 U.S. at 459–60.
77. *See* T. Hobbes, *Leviathan* 108 (H. Schneider ed. 1958).
78. Fortas, *supra* note 74, at 97.
79. For a survey of arguments offered in support of the fifth amendment, *see generally* McNaughton, *supra* note 9, and Sowle, *supra* note 9. McNaughton concludes: The privilege, like the screw driver, is used for all sorts of reasons, most of them having little or no relation to its purpose. The significant purposes of the privilege remaining . . . are two: (1) The first is to remove the right to an answer in the hard cases of instances where compulsion might lead to inhumanity, the principal inhumanity being abusive tactics by a zealous questioner. (2) The second is to comply with the prevailing ethic that the individual is sovereign and that proper rules of battle between government and individual require that the individual not be bothered for less than good reason and not be conscripted by his opponent to defeat himself. McNaughton, *supra* note 9, at 150–151 (emphasis in original) (footnotes omitted).
80. *See* L. Levy, *supra* note 17, at 266–330; 8 J. Wigmore, *supra* note 8, § 2250, at 267–295.
81. 8 J. Wigmore, *supra* note 8, § 2251, at 296 n.1. By contrast in 1892, Wigmore wrote disparagingly of the privilege: "As to its intrinsic merits, then, may we not express the general opinion in this way, that the privilege is not needed by the innocent, and that the only question can be how far the guilty are entitled to it?" Wigmore, *supra* note 15, at 86.
82. *See* McNaughton, *supra* note 9, at 145; *see also* E. Griswold, *The Fifth Amendment Today* 7–9, 61, 75 (1955); Kalven, *Invoking the Fifth Amendment: Some Legal and Impractical Considerations*, 9 Bull. Atom. Scientists 181, 182–183 (1953).
83. *See* Meltzer, *supra* note 74, at 639–99, 701.
84. McNaughton, *supra* note 9, at 143.
85. *See generally* O. J. Rogge, *The First and the Fifth* (1960).
86. McNaughton, *supra* note 9, at 146.
87. *See Barenblatt* v. *United States*, 360 U.S. 109 (1959); *Watkins* v. *United States*, 354 U.S. 178 (1957); *Sweezy* v. *New Hampshire*, 354 U.S. 234 (1957).
88. *See generally* Meltzer, *supra* note 74.
89. McNaughton, *supra* note 9, at 143.
90. *Id.*
91. *See Wilson* v. *United States*, 149 U.S. 60, 66 (1893); Meltzer, *supra* note 74.
92. *See* Meltzer, *supra* note 74; Wigmore, *supra* note 15.
93. *See* Meltzer, *supra* note 74; Ratner, *supra* note 13, at 484, 487–489.
94. *See* 384 U.S. at 459–460; 378 U.S. at 589. *See also* 8 J. Wigmore, *supra* note 8, § 2250, at 309; Fortas, *supra* note 74, at 97; McNaughton, *supra* note 9, at 144 n.34.
95. For a discussion of arguments that the privilege only derivatively or per se contributes to respect for the legal process *see* McNaughton, *supra* note 9, at 144 n. 34.
96. *See generally* Z. Chafee, *The Blessings of Liberty* 186–190 (1956); 8 J. Wigmore, *supra* note 8, § 2251, at 312; Meltzer, *supra* note 74. For discussions of accusatorial systems see: H. Packer, *The Limits of the Criminal Sanction* 149–70 (1968); Damaska, *Evidentiary Barriers to Conviction and Two Models of Criminal Procedure: A Comparative Study*, 121 U. Penn. L. Rev. 506 (1972–1973); Griffiths, *Ideology in Criminal Procedure or A "Third" Model of the Criminal Process*, 79 Yale L. J. 359 (1970).

97. The relative merits of each of the preceding arguments has been debated in the literature; for a survey and brief discussion of the merits of each argument *see,* 8 J. Wigmore, *supra* note 8, at § 2251; McNaughton, *supra* note 9; Sowle, *supra* note 9.
98. Gerstein, *supra* note 13, at 88.
99. 412 U.S. 309.
100. McKay, *supra* note 13, at 230.
101. *See* text accompanying note 36 *supra.*
102. H. Friendly, *Benchmarks* 271 (1967).
103. *Id.* at 271–75.
104. *Id.* at 271–76. For the Burger Court's treatment of the issue of governmental compulsion in determining effective exercise of the privilege in different contexts see 431 U.S. 181; 427 U.S. 463; 425 U.S. 341; 424 U.S. at 654–655; 417 U.S. at 440; 412 U.S. at 222–227, 235–240, 246–247; 401 U.S. at 226. Compare discussions by the Warren Court in 384 U.S. at 479, 480; 378 U.S. 478; 378 U.S. at 8; 365 U.S. 534.
105. H. Friendly, *supra* note 102, at 275.
106. 417 U.S. at 440.
107. 431 U.S. 181. In *Garner* v. *United States,* 424 U.S. 648 (1976), the Burger Court quoted approvingly *United States* v. *Monia,* 317 U.S. 424 (1943), to support its narrow construction of the fifth amendment: "The Amendment speaks of compulsion. It does not preclude a witness from testifying voluntarily in matters which may incriminate him. If therefore, he desires the protection of the privilege, he must claim it or he will not be considered to have been compelled within the meaning of the Amendment." 424 U.S. at 654–655. The Court added that the witness may also "lose the benefit of the privilege without making a knowing and intelligent waiver." *Id.* at 654 n.9. *See also* 412 U.S. at 222–27, 235–40, 246–47; 427 U.S. 463.
108. 350 U.S. 422.
109. *Id.* at 445–46 (second emphasis added).
110. 5 J. Bentham, *supra* note 10, at 230.
111. *Id.* at 230.
112. *Id.* at 231.
113. *Id.* at 231–38.
114. *See generally* L. Levy, *supra* note 17; 8 J. Wigmore, *supra* note 8, at § 2250.
115. L. Levy, *supra* note 17, at 177.
116. Pittman, *supra* note 21, at 783 (emphasis added).
117. Z. Chafee, *supra* note 96, at 188.
118. Louisell, *Criminal Discovery and Self-Incrimination,* 53 Calif. L. Rev. 89, 95 (1965).
119. *See generally* R. Dworkin, *Taking Rights Seriously* 184–205 (1977): R. Fiathman, *The Practice of Rights* (1976).
120. *See Palko* v. *Connecticut,* 302 U.S. 319, 325–326 (1937) (Cardozo, J.); *Murphy* v. *Waterfront Comm.,* 378 U.S. 52, 55 (1964); 5 J. Bentham, *supra* note 10, Griswold, *The Right to Be Let Alone,* 55 Nw. L. Rev. 216, 221 (1960); L. Griswold, *supra* note 82; Mayers, *supra* note 32.
121. *See generally* 5 J. Bentham, *supra* note 10; Griswold, *supra* note 120; Mayers, *supra* note 32; McNaughton, *supra* note 9, at 147.
122. McNaughton, *supra* note 9, at 147.
123. *Id.*
124. *See also* Griswold, *supra* note 120; Meltzner, *supra* note 74; McNaughton, *supra* note 9, at 148.
125. *See generally* Silving, *supra* note 16. As Fortas argues *"Mea culpa* belongs to a man and his God. It is a plea that cannot be extracted from free men by human authority." *See* Fortas, *supra* note 74, at 100.
126. 417 U.S. at 440. *See* text accompanying note 105 *supra.*
127. 350 U.S. at 440 (Douglas J., dissenting).
128. *See* text accompanying note 35 *supra.*
129. 417 U.S. at 440.

130. Louisell, *supra* note 118, at 95.
131. S. Hook, *Common Sense and the Fifth Amendment* 73 (1963).
132. Friendly, *supra* note 9, at 73.
133. A similar paradox arises with pleas of mental insanity. At times, defendants plead criminal insanity at trial and, consequently, are not held responsible nor punishable for their actions as part of their treatment. *See generally* H. Fingarette, *The Meaning of Criminal Insanity* (1972); R. Laing, *The Divided Self* (1965).
134. *See* text accompanying note 169 *infra*.
135. Ratner, *supra* note 9, at 488–89.
136. *See* 384 U.S. at 460; 381 U.S. at 484; 382 U.S. at 416; 378 U.S. at 55. *See also* 322 U.S. at 698; 322 U.S. at 489–90; 116 U.S. at 630.
137. *Warden* v. *Hayden*, 387 U.S. 294, 323 (1967).
138. *See generally* Dworkin, *The Common Law Protection of Privacy*, 2 U. Tasmania L. Rev. 418 (1967); O'Connor, *The Right to Privacy in Historical Perspective*, 53 Mass. L. Q. 101 (1968); Warren and Brandeis, *The Right of Privacy*, 4 Harv. L. Rev. 193 (1890). *But see* Pratt, *The Warren and Brandeis Argument for a Right to Privacy*, Pub. L. (1975).
139. *United States* v. *Grunewald*, 233 F.2d 556 (2d Cir. 1956), *rev'd*, 351 U.S. 391 (1957).
140. *Id.* àt 581–82 (Frank, J., dissenting).
141. *Id.*
142. 382 U.S. at 446.
143. 380 U.S. at 614.
144. *Linkletter* v. *Walker*, 381 U.S. 618 (1965).
145. *See* 387 U.S. at 302–303; *Mapp* v. *Ohio*, 367 U.S. 643, 656–57 (1961); *Cohen* v. *Hurley*, 366 U.S. 117, 154 (1961); 322 U.S. at 489–90; *Gouled* v. *United States*, 255 U.S. 298, 311 (1921); *Weeks* v. *United States*, 232 U.S. 383, 391–95 (1916); *Bram* v. *United States*, 168 U.S. 532, 543–44 (1897); 116 U.S. at 633.
146. McKay, *Book Review*, 35 N.Y.U.L. Rev. 1097, 1100–1101 (1969).
147. McKay, *supra* note 13, at 212.
148. *Id.* at 230.
149. The Supreme Court has acknowledged a connection between personal privacy and the first amendment in a number of areas of litigation. For example, in the area of associational privacy see: *Williams* v. *Rhodes*, 393 U.S. 23 (1968); *Watkins* v. *United States*, 354 U.S. 178 (1957); 354 U.S. 234; *Terry* v. *Adams*, 343 U.S. 461 (1953); *Communications Ass'n* v. *Douds*, 339 U.S. 382 (1950). *A. F. of L.* v. *American Sash Co.*, 335 U.S. 538 (1949); *Everson* v. *Board of Education*, 330 U.S. 1 (1947); *Smith* v. *Allwright*, 321 U.S. 649 (1944); *West Virginia State Board of Education* v. *Barnette*, 319 U.S. 62 (1943); *Cantwell* v. *Connecticut*, 310 U.S. 296 (1940); (recognizing a right of associational privacy for religious associations); *Whitney* v. *California*, 274 U.S. 357 (1927) (acknowledging associational privacy with regard to forming and joining political parties). *Gilbert* v. *Minnesota*, 254 U.S. 326, 335 (1920) (Brandeis, J., dissenting). *See also Louisiana* v. *NAACP*, 366 U.S. 293, 296 (1961); *Bates* v. *City of Little Rock*, 361 U.S. 516, 523 (1960); *Shelton* v. *Tucker*, 364 U.S. 479, 485–486 (1960); *NAACP* v. *Alabama*, 357 U.S. 449, 462 (1958). The Court also recognized first amendment privacy interests with respect to the possession of pornography and obscenity in one's home, *Stanley* v. *Georgia*, 294 U.S. 557, 564 (1969); and against mailers of sexually provocative materials, *Rowan* v. *United States Post Office Dept.*, 397 U.S. 728 (1970); but rejected privacy claims to possess obscene materials outside the home. *See United States* v. *12 200-Ft. Reels of Super 8mm. Film*, 413 U.S. 123 (1973); *Paris Adult Theatre I.* v. *Slaton*, 413 U.S. 49 (1973); *United States* v. *Thirty-Seven Photographs*, 402 U.S. 363 (1971); *United States* v. *Reidel*, 402 U.S. 351 (1971). In two other areas of first amendment litigation, however, the Court avoided claims to protected privacy; first, in the context of governmental surveillance, *Laird* v. *Tatum*, 408 U.S. 1 (1972); and *United States* v. *United States District Court*, 407 U.S. 297 (1972); and second, in the area of invasion of privacy by the media. *Cox Broadcasting Corp.* v. *Cohn*, 420 U.S. 469 (1975); *Cantrell* v. *Forest City Publishing Company*, 419 U.S. 425 (1974); *Time, Inc.* v. *Hill*, 385 U.S. 374 (1967). *See also Paul* v. *Davis* 424 U.S. 645 (1976), and *Time* v. *Firestone*, 424 U.S. 448 (1976).

150. U.S. Const. amend. I. *See generally* W. Berns, *The First Amendment and the Future of American Democracy* (1976).
151. McKay, *supra* note 13, at 213–14.
152. Erwin Griswold, in articulating his version of a privacy rationale for the fifth amendment, also collapses the privacy argument with that basing the privilege on its instrumental role in accusatorial systems and utility for maintaining the "distribution of power" between the state and individual. *See* Griswold, *supra* note 120, at 221, 224–25.
153. For the author's analysis of privacy and its legal protection, see O'Brien, *Privacy and the Right of Access: Purposes and Paradoxes of Information Control,* 30 Ad. L. Rev. 45, 62–82 (1978).
154. Dann, *supra* note 13, at 611.
155. *Id.* at 602.
156. For an elaboration of this analysis, see O'Brien, *supra* note 153, at 75–79. *See also* Garrett, *The Nature of Privacy,* 18 *Philosophy Today* 263 (1974).
157. *See generally* O'Brien, *Reasonable Expectations of Privacy: Principles and Policies of Fourth Amendment-Protected Privacy,* New England L. Rev. (June 1978).
158. Comment, *Papers, Privacy, and the Fourth and Fifth Amendments: A Constitutional Analysis,* 69 Nw. L. Rev. 626, 630–31 (1974).
159. Meltzer, *supra* note 74, at 687 (emphasis added).
160. *See* O'Brien, *supra* note 153, at 75–76.
161. *See* text accompanying notes 99 and 133 *supra.*
162. *See generally* Austin, *A Plea for Excuses,* reprinted in *J. Austin Philosophical Papers* (1970); *The Philosophy of History* (P. Gardiner ed. 1974).
163. Friendly, *supra* note 9, at 683.
164. *Id.* at 689 n.90.
165. *Id.* at 689.
166. Gerstein, *supra* note 13, at 89.
167. Fried, *supra* note 13, at 482. For a critique of Fried's analysis of privacy see O'Brien, *supra* note 153, at 71–73.
168. Fried, *supra* note 13, at 488.
169. Gerstein, *supra* note 13, at 89.
170. *Id.* at 90–91.
171. *See* text accompanying note 130 *supra.*
172. Friendly, *supra* note 9, at 689. *But see* Ellis, *Vox Populi v. Suprema Lex: A Comment on the Testimonial Privilege of the Fifth Amendment,* 55 Iowa L. Rev. 829 (1970).
173. For discussions of the limits of legal enforcement of morality, see A. Bickel, *The Morality of Consent* 1–25 (1975); Lord Denlin, *The Enforcement of Morality;* Fuller, *Positivism and Fidelity to the Law—A Reply to Professor Hart,* 71 Harv. L. Rev. 630 (1958); H. L. A. Hart, *Solidarity and the Enforcement of Morality,* 35 U. Chi. L. Rev. 1 (1967); H. L. A. Hart, *Positivism and the Separation of Laws and Morals,* 71 Harv. L. Rev. 593 (1958).
174. *See generally* McCloskey, *A Critique of the Ideal of Privacy,* 74 Mind 483 (1965).
175. In other words, the privacy argument attempts to make explicit what remains implicit in our "liberal regime"; namely, that by design the legal parchment of the United States Constitution and Bill of Rights consecrated the founding principle of limited government—which implies that both the governors and the governed are subject to the rule of law and "that governmental powers stop short of certain intrusions into the personal life of the citizen." Emerson, *Nine Justices in Search of a Doctrine,* 64 Mich. L. Rev. 219, 299 (1965). "Liberal regime" refers not only to the legal parchment of our Constitution but also the sources and way of life in America. The "liberal regime" has been defined as "the regime devoted to the principle that the purpose of government is the securing of the equal right of every individual to pursue happiness as he understands it." T. Pangle, *Montesquieu's Philosophy of Liberalism* 1 (1973). *See also* J. Cropsey, *Political Philosophy and the Issues of Politics* 1–15 (1977); L. Strauss, *Natural Right and History* 135–38 (1953).
176. For a discussion of the difference between arguments from policy and principle, see Dworkin, *supra* note 119, at 14–80.
177. 417 U.S. at 440.
178. Gerstein, *supra* note 13, at 88.
179. 385 U.S. at 522 (Harlan, J., dissenting).

180. *See generally* Higgins, *Business Records and the Fifth Amendment Right Against Self-Incrimination,* 38 Ohio St. L. Rev. 351 (1977); Ritchie, *Compulsion That Violates the Fifth Amendment: The Burger Court's Definition,* 61 Minn. L. Rev. 383 (1977); Note, *Formalism, Legal Realism, and Constitutionally Protected Privacy under the Fourth and Fifth Amendments,* 90 Harv. L. Rev. 945 (1977); Comment, *The Protection of Privacy by the Privilege Against Self-Incrimination: A Doctrine Laid to Rest?* 59 Iowa L. Rev. 1336 (1974).

181. Israel, *Criminal Procedure, The Burger Court and the Legacy of the Warren Court,* 75 Mich. L. Rev. 1319, 1425 (1977).

182. *See, e.g.,* 409 U.S. at 338–44 (Douglas, J., dissenting).

183. *See, e.g.,* 427 U.S. at 484–94 (Brennan, J., dissenting).

184. *See, e.g.,* 409 U.S. at 344–51 (Marshall, J., dissenting).

185. 424 U.S. at 655.

186. *See* text accompanying note 70 *supra.*

187. *See* text accompanying notes 119 and 135 *supra.*

188. *See* text accompanying notes 238 and 315 *infra.*

189. *See* text accompanying notes 196–238 *infra.*

190. *See* text accompanying notes 266–316 *infra.*

191. 409 U.S. at 328.

192. *Bellis* v. *United States,* 417 U.S. 85 (1974).

193. 409 U.S. 322.

194. *Fisher* v. *United States,* 425 U.S. 391 (1976).

195. Comment, Iowa L. Rev., *supra* note 180, at 1339.

196. 424 U.S. at 655.

197. 417 U.S. at 440.

198. 431 U.S. at 188.

199. *See Bellis* v. *United States,* 417 U.S. 85 (1974); *McPaul* v. *United States,* 364 U.S. 372 (1960); *United States* v. *Fleishman,* 339 U.S. 349 (1950); *Oklahoma Press Publishing Co.* v. *Walling,* 327 U.S. 186 (1946); *United States* v. *White,* 323 U.S. 694, 701 (1944); *Wilson* v. *United States,* 221 U.S. 361 (1911); 201 U.S. 43. In *Bellis,* the Burger Court reiterated: "These decisions . . . reflect the Court's consistent view that the privilege against self-incrimination should be limited to its historic function of protecting only the natural individual from compulsory incrimination through his own testimony or personal records." 417 U.S. at 91–92 (quoting 322 U.S. at 701).

200. *See* Note, *"Books and Records and the Privilege against Self-Incrimination."* 33 Brooklyn L. Rev. 70, 71 (1966); *see also Johnson* v. *United States,* 228 U.S. 457 (1913).

201. 228 U.S. at 458 (quoted approvingly in 427 U.S. at 473).

202. *Compare* 417 U.S. 85 *with* 409 U.S. 322 *and California Bankers Association* v. *Schultz,* 416 U.S. 21 (1973); *United States* v. *Miller,* 425 U.S. 435 (1976); *Fisher* v. *United States,* 425 U.S. 391 (1976).

203. 416 U.S. 21.

204. 409 U.S. 322.

205. 425 U.S. 391; *see also* 425 U.S. 435.

206. 409 U.S. at 336.

207. The Burger Court, however, rejects the so-called "convergence theory" of the fourth and fifth amendments in protecting personal privacy. In *Andresen* v. *Maryland,* 427 U.S. 463, 472 (1976), the Court identified Boyd v. United States, 116 U.S. 616 (1886) with the convergence theory of the amendment. In dicta in *Boyd,* the Court observed that the fourth and fifth amendments "run almost into each other" and, thereupon, concluded that, "We have been unable to perceive that . . . the seizure of a man's private books and papers to be used in evidence against him is substantially different from compelling him to be a witness against himself." *Id.* at 633. *Boyd's* finding that the amendments were complementary not in the sense of adjacent guarantees but in the sense of independently demarcated and alternative guarantees, which at times are contiguous in providing overlapping and intersecting protection for personal privacy, thus promoted a broad construction of the fifth amendment and protected privacy based on the nature of the materials and not, as with the Burger Court's analysis, upon the manner or degree of governmental compulsion exerted

on the individual. *See* 378 U.S. 52; 367 U.S. at 656–57; 366 U.S. at 154; *Davis* v. *United States,* 328 U.S. 582 (1946); 322 U.S. at 489–90; *Gambino* v. *United States,* 275 U.S. 310 (1927); *Agnello* v. *United States,* 269 U.S. 20 (1925); 255 U.S. 298; 232 U.S. at 391–95; 168 U.S. at 543–44.

208. 409 U.S. at 333.
209. *Id.* at 331.
210. *See, e.g.,* 322 U.S. 694.
211. *Perlman* v. *United States,* 247 U.S. 7 (1918).
212. 409 U.S. at 336 (quoting 247 U.S. at 15 (emphasis added).
213. 409 U.S. at 336–37.
214. 425 U.S. 391.
215. *Id.* at 398 (quoting *Hale* v. *Henkel,* 201 U.S. 43, 69–70 (1906) (emphasis in original).
216. 422 U.S. at 233 n.7. *See also* 427 U.S. 463.
217. 425 U.S. at 400–01.
218. *See* text accompanying note 41 *supra.*
219. Ritchie, *supra* note 180, at 393.
220. 425 U.S. at 414 (Brennan, J., dissenting).
221. *See* cases cited in note 207 *supra.*
222. *See* text accompanying notes 43–57 *supra.*
223. Compare text accompanying notes 31 and 43 *supra.*
224. *See* cases cited in note 57 *supra.*
225. 142 U.S. at 562.
226. 409 U.S. at 339–40 (Douglas, J., dissenting).
227. *Id.* at 337 (Brennan, J., concurring).
228. *Id.* at 343–44 (Douglas, J., dissenting).
229. *Id.* at 346 (Marshall, J., dissenting).
230. *Id.* at 349–50 (Marshall, J., dissenting).
231. Katz v. United States, 389 U.S. 347, 360–61 (1967) (Harlan, J., concurring).
232. 409 U.S. at 350 (Marshall, J., dissenting).
233. *Id.*
234. *Id.* at 350–51 (Marshall, J., dissenting).
235. *Id.* at 337 (Brennan, J., dissenting).
236. Throughout the twentieth century a number of decisions rejected the broad view of the fifth amendment fostered and promoted by *Boyd* and its progeny. *See* 327 U.S. 186; 322 U.S. at 701; 228 U.S. at 458; 221 U.S. 361; 201 U.S. at 72, 74. Compare cases cited in note 207 *supra.*
237. In *Fisher,* 425 U.S. at 405–14, the Burger Court actually extended the doctrine that the fifth amendment protects only "testimonial" and not real or physical evidence. The Court reasoned that since the accountant's workpapers were not the taxpayer's, they did not constitute testimonial declarations nor did their seizure constitute personal compulsion of the taxpayer: rather the written documents were analogous to blood, handwriting, and voice samples previously held admissible. *See* 410 U.S. at 8; 402 U.S. at 433–34; 388 U.S. at 221–23; 388 U.S. 266; 384 U.S. 263; *Holt* v. *United States,* 218 U.S. 245 (1910).
238. 427 U.S. at 477. *Andresen* supplements *Couch* and *Fisher* by dealing with an element of personal compulsion not previously addressed. The Court held that the fifth amendment provides no protection against a search warrant for business records otherwise immune from subpoena, thereby, further confining the construction of personal compulsion and the privilege protection.
239. *See* note 221 *supra.*
240. 221 U.S. at 380.
241. 335 U.S. at 32–36.
242. *Grosso* v. *United States,* 390 U.S. 62, 67–68 (1968).
243. 402 U.S. 424.
244. *Id.* at 431.
245. *See* 427 U.S. 463; 425 U.S. 391; 409 U.S. 322; 416 U.S. 21.

246. *See Lewis* v. *United States*, 348 U.S. 419 (1955); *United States* v. *Kahriger*, 345 U.S. 22 (1953). *But see* 390 U.S. 62; *Marchetti* v. *United States*, 590 U.S. 39 (1968); *Albertson* v. *Subversives Activities Control Board*, 682 U.S. 70 (1965).
247. McKay *supra* note 13, at 217.
248. *Id.*
249. *See* 402 U.S. 424; text accompanying note 165 *supra.*
250. *See* 424 U.S. 648; text accompanying note 263 *infra.*
251. *See United States* v. *Sullivan*, 274 U.S. 259, 262–64 (1927).
252. *Id.*
253. *United States* v. *Murdock*, 284 U.S. 141 (1961).
254. *Id.*
255. *Id.* at 148–51.
256. 345 U.S. 22.
257. *See Haves* v. *United States* 390 U.S. 89 (1968); 391 U.S. 39, 45 U.S. 22 (holding that gamblers are not protected from required registration).
258. 390 U.S. at 47.
259. 390 U.S. 39.
260. *Id.* at 57.
261. 425 U.S. 341.
262. *Id.* at 349–50 (Brennan, J., dissenting).
263. 424 U.S. 648.
264. *Id.* at 655.
265. 401 U.S. 667.
266. 424 U.S. at 655.
267. 397 U.S. 1.
268. 412 U.S. 218.
269. *Id.* at 222–27, 235–40, 246–47.
270. 384 U.S. at 467.
271. *Miranda* v. *Arizona*, 384 U.S. 436 (1966), held that in order to safeguard the fifth amendment privilege, an individual in custody must, prior to interrogation, be clearly informed that he has the right to remain silent, and that anything he says will be used against him in court; he must be clearly informed that he has the right to consult with a lawyer, to have the lawyer with him during interrogation, and that, if he is indigent, a lawyer will be appointed to represent him. *Id.* at 467–73.
272. *See* cases cited in 412 U.S. at 53.
273. 373 U.S. at 514.
274. 384 U.S. at 476.
275. Ritchie, *supra* note 180, at 414. *See also* 384 U.S. at 479–80.
276. 384 U.S. at 460 (quoting 8 Wigmore, *supra* note 8, at 347).
277. In *Miranda* v. *Arizona*, the Court observed that "our contemplation cannot be only of what has been but of what might be. Under any other rule a constitution would indeed be as easy of application as it would have little value and be converted by precedent into impotent and lifeless formulas. Rights declared in words might be lost in reality. And this has been recognized. The meaning and vitality of the Constitution have developed against narrow and restrictive construction." 384 U.S. at 443. *See also* 217 U.S. at 379.
278. 430 U.S. at 438 (Blackmun, J., dissenting).
279. *See, e.g., Oregon* v. *Mathiason*, 429 U.S. 492 (1977); 423 U.S. 96; *Oregon* v. *Hass*, 420 U.S. 714 (1975); 417 U.S. 433; 404 U.S. 222. *See Doyle* v. *Ohio*, 426 U.S. 610 (1976) (held that due process precludes use of defendant's silence at time of arrest, after receiving Miranda warnings, to impeach his exculpatory testimony offered for the first time at trial).
280. *See, e.g.*, 412 U.S. 218. *See also* 431 U.S. 174.
281. 417 U.S. 433.
282. *Id.* at 443–44.
283. 401 U.S. 222.
284. *Id.* at 230. (Brennan, J., dissenting) (emphasis added).
285. 401 U.S. at 227. *See also* 431 U.S. at 178; 425 U.S. at 577, 585; 424 U.S. at 657–58; *United States* v. *Knox*, 396 U.S. 77 (1969); *Glickstein* v. *United States*, 222 U.S. 139, 142 (1911).

286. 420 U.S. 714.
287. 417 U.S. 433.
288. 423 U.S. 96.
289. 384 U.S. at 473–74 (footnote omitted).
290. 423 U.S. at 114 (Brennan, J., dissenting).
291. *Id.* at 104.
292. Israel, *supra* note 181, at 1375. By contrast Ritchie argues that, "In both *Harris* and *Tucker,* the Court seems to be reasoning that a statement must be involuntary before its use will contravene the fifth amendment guarantee. This appears to be an outright rejection of *Miranda's* finding that the compulsion inherent in custodial interrogation violates the privilege. The *Miranda* safeguards were necessary in order to dispel the inherent compulsion: in *Harris* and *Tucker,* the Court found no compulsion even though *Miranda* safeguards were disregarded." *See* note 180 *supra.*
293. 423 U.S. at 112, 118.
294. 429 U.S. 492.
295. *Id.* at 496.
296. *Id.* at 498 n.6. (Marshall, J., dissenting).
297. *But see* 460 U.S. 387.
298. *See, e.g.,* 46 U.S.L.W. 4229 (1978); 428 U.S. at 458–59; 428 U.S. 465, 414 U.S. at 348; 403 U.S. at 414–15 (Burger, C.J., dissenting); 394 U.S. at 174–75.
299. 384 U.S. at 444. *See also* 391 U.S. 324; 391 U.S. 1.
300. 431 U.S. at 188.
301. 373 U.S. at 514.
302. Ritchie, *supra* note 180, at 397 (quoting 378 U.S. at 8).
303. 425 U.S. 341.
304. The Internal Revenue Service agents read Beckwith the following warning: "Under the fifth amendment to the Constitution of the United States, I cannot compel you to answer any questions or to submit any information if such answers or information might tend to incriminate you in any way. I also advise you that anything you say and any information which you submit may be used against you in any criminal proceeding which may be undertaken. I advise you further that you may, if you wish, seek the assistance of an attorney before responding." 425 U.S. at 344. Compare the requirements specified in 384 U.S. 436.
305. 425 U.S. at 345–46.
306. 425 U.S. at 348.
307. 424 U.S. 648. *See* text accompanying note 264 *supra.*
308. 425 U.S. at 350 (emphasis added).
309. 425 U.S. 564.
310. 431 U.S. 181.
311. 431 U.S. 174. *See also* 415 U.S. 269 (held that admission of defendant's false exculpatory statements, made to secure free counsel, as evidence of his knowledge that deposits in a "Totten trust" bank account were incriminating, and as evidence of willfulness in making the statements before a grand jury with knowledge of their falsity, did not violate the privilege against self-incrimination).
312. 425 U.S. 564. Chief Justice Burger's argument dismisses without consideration the old woman's rationale for the privilege. *See* text accompanying note 108 *supra.* On the relation of the privilege to the oath to tell the truth, *see generally* Silving, *supra* note 16.
313. 425 U.S. at 572–73 (quoting 414 U.S. at 353).
314. 431 U.S. at 187 (quoting 417 U.S. at 440).
315. 431 U.S. at 190.
316. *Id.* at 189.
317. *See generally* Levy, *Against the Law* (1974); Mason, *The Burger Court in Historical Perspective,* 89 *Pol. Sci. Q.* 27 (1974); Stephens, *The Burger Court: New Dimensions in Criminal Justice,* 60 Geo. L. J. 249 (1971).
318. *See* W. Murphy & C. Pritchett, *Courts, Judges and Politics* 661–62 (2d ed. 1974).
319. *See* text accompanying note 35 *supra.*
320. *See* text accompanying notes 191–95, 202–19, 236–38, 245–48, 312 *supra.*

321. *See* text accompanying notes 136–37, 142, 214–35, 258–60 *supra*.
322. 422 U.S. at 233 n.7.
323. 427 U.S. at 477.
324. *See* text accompanying note 108 *supra*.
325. 97 S. Ct. at 1820.
326. *See* text accompanying note 69 *supra*.
327. 424 U.S. at 655.
328. *See* text accompanying notes 194–201 *supra*.
329. *See* text accompanying notes 239–68 *supra*.
330. *See* text accompanying notes 270–316 *supra*.
331. *See, e.g., Oregon v. Mathiason*, 97 S. Ct. 711 (1977) (police falsely told defendant that his fingerprints were found at scene of the burglary); *Michigan v. Mosley*, 423 U.S. 96 (1975) (police falsely told defendant that a co-defendant had confessed to participation in a homicide but had named the defendant as the one who had shot the victim); *Frazier v. Cupp*, 394 U.S. 731 (1969) (police falsely told defendant that they had arrested defendant's alibi witness who had confessed to participation in the crime).

---

# Representation and Republican Government: Contemporary Court Variations on the Founders' Theme*

Ralph A. Rossum

In his dissenting opinion in *Baker v. Carr*, Mr. Justice Felix Frankfurter observed with characteristic perspicacity:

> What is this question of legislative apportionment? Appellants invoke the right to vote and have their votes counted. But they are permitted to vote and their votes are counted. They go to the polls, they cast their ballots, they send their representative to the state councils. Their complaint is simply that the representatives are not sufficiently numerous or powerful—in short, that Tennessee has adopted a basis of representation with which they are dissatisfied. *Talk of "debasement" or "dilution" is circular talk. One cannot speak of "debasement" or "dilution" of the value of a vote until there is first defined a standard of reference as to what a vote should be worth.* What is actually asked of the Court in this case is to choose among *competing bases of representation*— ultimately, really, among *competing theories of political philosophy*—in order to establish an appropriate frame of government for the State of Tennessee and thereby for all States of the Union.[1]

Justice Frankfurter admonished the Court to examine the underlying "theories of political philosophy" on which competing schemes of representation are based. His admonition has gone unheeded. This paper is an attempt to explore the consequences of this unwillingness or inability on the part of the contemporary Court (and especially

Reprinted with permission from the *American Journal of Jurisprudence*, © 1978.

*Revised version of a paper prepared for delivery at the 1976 Annual Meeting of the American Political Science Association in Chicago.

the Warren Court) to address these broader issues and to define "a standard of reference as to what a vote should be worth."² It focuses on three major reapportionment cases: *Gray v. Sanders,*³ *Wesberry v. Sanders,*⁴ and *Reynolds v. Sims.*⁵ There are two reasons for selecting these particular cases. To begin with, they constitute the first substantive rulings by the Court on representation and apportionment after its holding in *Baker* that such questions are, in fact, justiciable. Furthermore, they offer the Court's most comprehensive discussion to date of the nature and meaning of representation. Subsequent decisions of both the Warren and Burger Courts have simply built upon, but have never reexamined the premises of, these seminal cases.

*Gray v. Sanders* held that Georgia's county-unit system of primary elections to state-wide offices violated the Equal Protection Clause of the Fourteenth Amendment. This system was somewhat analagous to the federal electoral college. Unit votes were allocated among the counties in such a manner that the eight largest counties had six unit votes each, the next 30 had four unit votes each, and the remaining 121 counties had two unit votes each. The candidate for nomination who received the most popular votes in a primary was awarded the unit votes for that county. The practical consequence of this system was that the vote of a citizen counted less and less as the population of his county increased. In fact, a combination of the units from the counties with the smallest populations gave counties having only one-third of the total state population a clear majority of county votes.

Justice Douglas wrote the opinion of the eight-member majority.⁶ He began by dismissing the analogy of the federal electoral college as not only inapposite but also unpersuasive.⁷ After all, he insisted, "the electoral college was designed by men who did not want the election of the President to be left to the people."⁸ Moreover, he continued, the concept of "we the people" under the Constitution "visualizes no preferred class of voters but equality among those who meet the basic qualifications." "Every voter is equal to every other voter in his State."⁹ Gaining momentum, Justice Douglas further declared that "the conception of political equality from the Declaration of Independence, to Lincoln's Gettysburg Address, to the Fifteenth, Seventeenth, and Nineteenth Amendments can mean only one thing—one person, one vote."¹⁰ Applying this conception to the factual setting in *Gray,* he concluded:

> Once the geographical unit for which a representative is to be chosen is designated, all who participate in the election are to have an equal vote—whatever their race, whatever their sex, whatever their occupation, whatever their income, and wherever their home may be in that geographical unit. This is required by the Equal Protection Clause of the Fourteenth Amendment.¹¹

In *Wesberry v. Sanders,* the Court extended the one person, one vote principle to Congressional elections. The Georgia district in which the City of Atlanta was located had a 1960 population of 823,680, as compared with the average of 394,312 for all ten Georgia districts. Justice Black held for a six-member majority that such a disparity in the population of Congressional districts was contrary to the Constitutional requirements of Article I, Section 2, that representatives in Congress be chosen "by the people of the several States,"[12] which, Black continued, "means that as nearly as is practicable one man's vote in a Congressional election is to be worth as much as another's."[13] Black reviewed the history of the adoption and ratification of the Constitution and concluded, among other things, that:

> It would defeat the principle solemnly embodied in the Great Compromise— equal representation in the House for equal numbers of people—for us to hold that, within the States, legislatures may draw the lines of congressional districts in such a way as to give some voters a greater voice in choosing a Congressman than others. The House of Representatives, the Convention agreed, was to represent the people as individuals, and on the basis of complete equality for each voter.[14]

In *Reynolds v. Sims,* the Court built on *Gray* and *Wesberry*[15] and made "one man, one vote" the Constitutional rule for apportioning both houses of a bicameral state legislature. Chief Justice Warren wrote the majority opinion. He argued that in a republican government, "legislators represent people, not trees or acres. Legislators are elected by voters, not farms or cities or economic interests."[16] In essence, representative government is "self-government through the medium of elected representatives." Moreover, "each and every citizen has an inalienable right to full and effective participation in the political process of his State's legislative bodies."[17] Since most citizens can achieve this participation only as qualified voters through the election of legislators to represent them, Chief Justice Warren went on to declare that "full and effective participation by all citizens in state government requires that each citizen have an equally effective voice in the election of members of his state legislature. Modern and viable state government needs, and the Constitution demands, no less."[18]

A great deal of the sloppy legal craftsmanship[19] for which the Warren Court became famous is to be found in these three decisions. Thus, consider generally the way in which the Court's majorities in each of these cases persist in using the simplistic and utterly meaningless slogan of one man-one vote.[20] The question of permitting certain voters the opportunity to vote two, five, or ten times was never raised in any of the litigation. Rather, to paraphrase Justice Frankfurter's comments in *Baker,* the central question in all of these cases was how much was the voter's one vote worth. Talk of one man, one vote never met this question and simply added to doctrinal confusion.

Further obfuscation results from the Court's emphasis on "equal representation for equal numbers of people." In the winner-take-all system of electing legislators employed in the United States, there is simply no such thing as "equal representation." By its very nature, it discriminates by rejecting the will of the minority voters. Legislators tend to represent the interests of the majority coalition that elects them, not the total population of their district. "Equal representation for equal numbers of people" can be achieved only through the adoption of some system of proportionate representation. The Court, however, has failed to recognize this[21] and continues to assume that "equal representation" can be realized merely by equalizing the population among districts. As a consequence, it has come to void apportionment plans on the basis of simple arithmetic arguments, with no demonstration of representational purpose or actual discrimination. Other examples of analytical laxness and intellectual incoherence are also present. Given the restraints of space, a single instance from each case must suffice.

Turning first to *Gray,* Justice Douglas' insistence that "the conception of political equality from the Declaration of Independence, to Lincoln's Gettysburg Address, to the Fifteenth, Seventeenth, and Nineteenth Amendments can mean only one thing—one person, one vote," comes perhaps most immediately to mind. As Alexander Bickel has pointed out, this sentence is notable "for its references to documents not commonly taken as having legal effect."[22] Moreover, Douglas' interpretation of at least one of these documents is curious, indeed. Far from requiring a representative government based on the principle of one man, one vote, the Declaration of Independence is perfectly compatible with the idea of constitutional monarchy.[23] Otherwise, it would not have been necessary for Jefferson to submit facts to a "candid world" to prove that the British king was guilty of a "long train of abuses and usurpations." It would have been sufficient for him merely to say that monarchy in itself is illegitimate. As Martin Diamond observes, the Declaration charges George III to be "unfit to be the ruler of a free people" not because he was a king, but "because he was a *tyrannical* king. Had the British monarchy continued to secure the colonists their rights, as it had prior to the long train of abuses, the colonists would not have been entitled to rebel. It was only the fact, according to the Declaration, that George III had become a tyrannical king that supplied the warrant for revolution."[24]

The Declaration of Independence is, quite simply, neutral on the question of forms of government. Any form of government is legitimate so long as it secures equal freedom and is "instituted" by the "consent of the governed." Justice Douglas to the contrary, this need not require democracy and certainly not one man, one vote. The Declaration does not state that consent is the means by which the government is to operate. It says only that consent is necessary to institute the government, i.e., to establish it. By this standard, limited monarchy such as existed in 18th century Great Britain is a wholly legitimate form, as it, too, was based on consent. As Sir William Blackstone declared in his *Commentaries on the Laws of England,* the crown possesses its power "by the general consent of the people, the evidence of which general consent is long and immemorial usage."[25]

Whether Justice Black's opinion in *Wesberry* is stronger analytically, more craftsmanlike, and less manipulative of its materials than Douglas' in *Gray* need not concern us here. It is not, however, without its failings. Thus, Black examines the records of the Federal Convention of 1787, the subsequent state constitutional ratifying conventions, and *The Federalist,* and concludes on the basis of that examination that "those who framed the Constitution meant" that "as nearly as practicable one man's vote in a congressional election is to be worth as much as another's."[26] In support of his position, he quotes extensively from *Federalist* No. 57:

> Who are to be the electors of the federal representatives? Not the rich more than the poor; not the learned more than the ignorant; not the haughty heirs of distinguished names, more than the humble sons of obscure and unpropitious fortune. The electors are to be the great body of the people of the United States.[27]

For Justice Black, the meaning of this passage is clear: "Readers surely could have fairly taken this to mean, 'one person, one vote.' "[28] However, as Justice Harlan points out with devastating effectiveness, Black's entire discussion is based on a confusion of two distinct issues: direct election of representatives within the states and the apportionment of representatives among the states.[29] All the historical evidence which Black introduces merely establishes the latter, which, of course, was not the question at bar, but leaves altogether unresolved the former, i.e., the very point of contention. Black's confusion in large part results from his misreading of the meaning of the Great Compromise. As Harlan points out: "The Great Compromise concerned representation *of the States* in the Congress. In all of the discussion surrounding the basis of representation of the House and all the discussion whether Representatives should be elected by the legislatures or the people of the States, there is nothing which suggests even remotely that the delegates had in mind the problem of districting within a State."[30] And, as if he had not already inflicted enough damage to Black's argument, Harlan proceeds to remind him of the following observation in *Federalist* No. 54: "It is a fundamental principle of the proposed Constitution, that as the aggregate number of representatives allotted to the several States, is to be determined by the federal rule founded on the aggregate number of inhabitants, *so the right of choosing this allotted number in each state is to be exercised by such part of the inhabitants, as the State itself may designate.*"[31]

The analytical failings of Chief Justice Warren's opinion in *Reynolds* are no less apparent. Consider, for example, Warren's declaration that "each and every citizen has an *inalienable right* to full and effective participation in the political processes of his State's legislative bodies."[32] Confusion abounds in this statement. An inalienable right is a right that cannot be taken from someone—it is a natural right. In the state of nature, however, there are no nations, no states, and most assuredly, no legislative bodies. Nations, states, and legislatures are artificial constructs, the creations of man. What Warren in effect is arguing here is that men have a natural right to full and effective participation in a conventional arrangement. The absurdity of this speaks for itself.[33]

What is of greater moment, however, than the poor legal craftsmanship which these decisions exhibit is the total refusal on the part of the Court to heed Justice Frankfurter's admonition and examine the underlying philosophic issues present in these cases. The questions of representation and apportionment are fundamentally shaped by "competing theories of political philosophy."[34] They are, as Justice Fortas would later state in *Avery v. Midland County,* "admittedly complex and subtle" and are to be governed by "substance, not shibboleth."[35] The Court, however, has refused to take up these questions;[36] it has been content to engage in shibboleth and to apply the simplistic formula of one man, one vote. By so doing, however, the Court has simply vindicated Justice Fortas' assessment that "Constitutional commandments are not surgical instruments. They have a tendency to hack deeply—to amputate."[37] The Court has "hacked deeply," indeed, and amputated much of the philosophical complexity and subtlety that surrounded these questions during the Constitutional Convention and the subsequent ratification process. In the hands of the contemporary Court, representation has been reduced to a slogan—one man, one vote. It is as if the Court had reduced a rich and intricate orchestral composition to a simplistic children's round, which can be sung over and over again in every state, regardless of circumstances. By so doing, however, it has deprived the public of much that it needs to hear if representative government is to be understood and if the Founders' contribution is to be appreciated.

To begin with, the Warren Court's one man, one vote formulation totally dismisses what had been for the Founders and what had remained until *Gray, Wesberry,* and *Reynolds* a vital and very much unresolved question: viz., on what is representation to be based—population, wealth, or a combination of the two?[38] For the Court, there was no question. As Chief Justice Warren stressed in *Reynolds,* "population is" not only "the starting point for consideration" but also "the controlling criterion for judgment in legislative apportionment controversies."[39] Yet, this potentially conflicts with other statements in *Reynolds.* After all, as the Chief Justice declared, "Legislators are elected by voters, not farms or cities or economic interests"—or, as he also should have added, by nonvoters, i.e., by the entire population. Warren speaks of "residents, or citizens, or voters" interchangeably, as if apportionment on any one of these three bases would result in complete voter equality.[40] However, this blurring of distinct meanings is acceptable only if the ratio of voters to the total population or citizen population or both is constant throughout the state. If no such uniform ratio exists, Warren's language also comes into conflict with Justice Douglas' pronouncement in *Gray* that "all who participate in the election are to have an equal vote."[41]

Ample evidence was available to the Court to establish that widely varying ratios were, in fact, prevalent within many states, and that, as a consequence, the use of any population base broader than actual voters would simply magnify the electoral power of the voter who happens to live in a district where relatively large numbers of nonvoters reside. Thus, for example, in the 1962 Congressional elections in Missouri, the actual number of voters per 100 adult inhabitants ranged from 7.75 in Pulaski County to 44.41 in Camden County—a ratio over 5.7 to 1. If one were to implement the Court's directives in *Reynolds* and construct districts that were precisely equal in population, the result would be to give each vote cast in Pulaski County 5.7 times the weight of each vote cast in Camden County.[42] The same difficulty attends reapportionment on the basis of the registered voter population. In assembly elections in New York in 1960, the actual number of voters per 100 registrants ranged from 51.8 in Sullivan County to 95.6 in Delaware County. If assemblymen had been apportioned precisely according to registration, one ballot in Sullivan would have had almost twice the weight of one in Delaware.[43] Chief Justice Warren and the Court's majority, however, chose to ignore this evidence. By so doing, a serious question is raised. If they are willing to allow certain factors to affect the complete ballot equality of voters (for example, nonvoters), why are they not willing to allow other factors such as wealth, geography, and historical subdivisions? This is a question which the Court's own opinion poses but which it is incapable of answering. It is also a question which the Founders, through their more comprehensive view of the concept of representation, were never obliged to confront.

The Founders were genuinely committed to republican government. The genius of the American people required no less.[44] Republican government was defined by Madison in *Federalist* no. 39 as one "which derives all its powers directly or indirectly from the great body of people; and is administered by persons holding their offices during pleasure, for a limited period, or during good behavior. It is *essential* to such a government, that it be derived from the great body of the society, not from an inconsiderable proportion, or favored class of it."[45] In contrast with pure democracy, in which "citizens . . . assemble and administer the government in person," in republican government, a "scheme of representation takes place."[46] What was to be included in this "scheme of representation"? The Virginia Plan, introduced early in the Federal Convention, provides some insight into the Founders' thinking on this question.

The Virginia Plan proposed, among other things, "that the rights of suffrage in the National Legislature ought to be proportioned to the Quotas of contribution, or to the number of free inhabitants, as one or the other rule may seem best in different cases."[47] Representation based on population alone was not proposed, and when debate on this resolution arose on May 30 and June 11, it focused primarily on the "free inhabitants" clause—raising as it did the sensitive question of slavery. Consensus was finally achieved for a revised resolution "that the right of suffrage . . . in the National Legislature ought not to be according to the rule established in the Articles of Confederation, but according to some equitable ratio of representation."[48] Clearly, the Convention was much more convinced of the propriety of proportional representation than of the basis on which this representation should be proportioned.

A considerable number of delegates to the Convention saw wealth as altogether deserving of representation. Gouverneur Morris of Pennsylvania was perhaps the most articulate spokesman for this position. He argued that "property ought to be taken into the estimate [of apportionment] as well as the number of inhabitants." As he explained it:

> Life and liberty were generally said to be of more value, than property. An accurate view of the matter would nevertheless prove that property was the main object of society. The savage State was more favorable to liberty than the Civilized; and sufficiently so to life. It was preferred by all men who had not acquired a taste for property; it was only renounced for the sake of property which could only be secured by the restraints of regular Government. These ideas might appear to some new, but they were nevertheless just. If property then was the main object of Government certainly it ought to be one measure of the influence due to those who were to be affected by the Government.[49]

Rufus King of Massachusetts agreed. He stressed that "the number of inhabitants was not the proper index of ability and wealth; but property was the primary object of Society; and that in fixing a ratio this ought not to be excluded from the estimate."[50] Few went so far as Pierce Butler of South Carolina, who, as Madison's Notes have it, "contended strenuously that property was *the only just measure of representation.* This was the great object of government: the great cause of war, and the great means of carrying it on."[51] Rather, most agreed "that Representation ought to be in the Combined ratio of number of Inhabitants and of wealth, and not of either singly."[52] A typical formulation of this position was that the House of Representatives ought to represent numbers and that the Senate ought to represent wealth.[53]

For many, however, wealth was an altogether "impracticable rule" for apportionment.[54] To begin with, the wealth of a state—both actual and potential—was extremely difficult to measure. As Benjamin Franklin observed, it was this difficulty in "ascertaining the importance of each colony" that led the Continental Congress on September 6, 1774, to give each colony or province one vote.[55] Ironically, this same difficulty now led many delegates at the Philadelphia Convention to favor a proportional representation simply on the basis of numbers. Apportionment on the basis of wealth also raised other problems. Thus, even more than apportionment on the basis of population, it raised the explosive slavery issue.[56] The Convention was reluctant to "admit in the Constitution the idea that there could be property in men."[57] However, if wealth were to be the basis of representation, the Southern States would have insisted on it. Thus, for many of the delegates, it was preferable to base representation on population, where a slave could at least be considered as three-fifths of a man, than on property, where he would never be more than another man's chattel.

The difficulties raised by a "scheme of representation" based on wealth simply rendered it "impracticable." The Convention ultimately concluded that representation would have to be on the basis of numbers alone, and on June 13, deleted from the Virginia Plan all references to apportionment according to wealth. By so doing, however, the Convention did not intend to disparage the importance of wealth or property. Rather, it simply chose to accept George Mason's formulation "that numbers of inhabitants; though not always a precise standard of wealth was sufficiently so for every substantial purpose."[58] Of course, this would not be the case in every situation. However, as James Madison declared to his colleagues, "in the United States, it was sufficiently so for the object in contemplation. Although their climate varied considerably, yet the Governments, the laws, and the manners of all were nearly the same, and the intercourse between different parts perfectly free; population, industry, arts, and the value of labor, would constantly tend to equalize themselves."[59] In short, population was to serve as a "proxy indicator" for wealth and property. *Federalist* No. 54 was to state as much: since "it is agreed on all sides, that numbers are the best scale of wealth and taxation, . . . they are the only proper scale of representation."[60] Although Justice Black quotes this very passage in *Wesberry*, he never appreciates its implications. As a consequence, he and his judicial brethren proceed to bestow full constitutional protection upon what the Founders regarded as merely a "measure" or indicator of their more comprehensive understanding of representation.

The Court's one man, one vote decisions have not only depreciated the Founders' concern with questions of the proper basis of representation but have also misconstrued the purposes for which the Founders promoted and perfected representation.[61] For the Founders, representation made it possible for republican government to exist over an extended territory.[62] This was their great "discovery." Prior to this time, representation was understood in terms of its affinity to self-government.[63] According to this view (a view, it should be mentioned, which was held by many of the Anti-Federalists), individual liberty was best secured when the government remained close to the people where it could operate "mildly and systematically" and with a minimum of coercion.[64] To reduce government to an affair of persuasion, however, required a small territory and a relatively homogeneous people. Otherwise, the people would not feel a sufficient kinship with their governors; neither would they easily identify their individual interests with the common interest. As the Anti-Federalist Brutus remarked: "In a republic, the manners, sentiments, and interests of the people should be similar. If this be not the case, there will be a constant clashing of opinions; and the representatives of one part will be continually striving against those of the other."[65]

Those skeptical of the Founders' expectations for representation adhered to what might be called the "concentric circles" argument[66]—that human "affections are commonly weak in proportion to the distance or diffuseness of the object."[67] They contended that the laws of a free government must rest on the confidence of the people and operate gently. If they are to be "executed on free principles," they can never extend in influence very far from the "centre" where the benefits of the government induce the people to support it voluntarily.[68] This acceptance of the "concentric circles" argument required them, in turn, to favor a small republic. Only in a small republic would the "ties of acquaintance, habit, and fortune, be sufficient to allow a free people to form their own government and laws and so administer them "as to create a confidence in, and respect for, the laws; and thereby induce the sensible and virtuous part of the community to declare in favor of the laws, and to support them without an expensive military force."[69] A large and extended republic, they feared, could never provide more than a "shadow of representation."[70] It would lack the "fellow feelings" and similar sentiments necessary to win the confidence and voluntary attachments of the people. Persuasion would fail; military force would emerge.[71] Inevitably, freedom would give way to aristocratic domination.

The Founders abandoned this view and argued instead that representation was to be understood, not in terms of its affinity to self-government, but in terms of popular election.[72] Of all the Founders, James Wilson's thinking on this question was perhaps most influential. He declared unequivocally that "the right of representation is conferred by the act of electing."[73] Suffrage was to assume primary importance in the Founders' new science of representation: the old emphasis on small size, civic virtue, and closeness was irrelevant. Voting became for the Founders "an act of the first political consequence;" in fact, they considered it the very heart of representation.[74] By so doing, they combined in their understanding of representation both the mode of filling offices and the source of political authority. Concerning the mode of filling offices, representation meant popular election. Concerning the source of political authority, it meant that the original source of authority—i.e., sovereignty—lies in the people. Thus, representation for the Founders included both the principle of popular sovereignty and the principle of popular election to office.

With this understanding of representation, a large republic became feasible. Edmund Randolph stressed this point in the Virginia Ratifying Convention, "No extent of Earth seems to be too great. . . . The principles of representation and responsibility may pervade a large as well as small territory."[75] As a consequence, the extended republic established by the Constitution could be rendered secure. After all, it was broadly based on the representative principle, with its foundation solidly resting on popular sovereignty and its superstructure—capable of being raised to a "considerable altitude"—supported by popular election.[76]

For the Founders, then, representation was identified with popular election. Together, they helped to justify the creation of a large and "comprehensive Federal Republic."[77] This linking of representation to suffrage, has, however, contributed greatly to the Warren Court's efforts to make the former as personal a right as the latter. It has, for the most part, disregarded any consideration of the ends for which the Founders promoted and perfected representation and has focused instead on the process of election and the mechanisms of apportionment. Its efforts to provide every citizen with the "inalienable right to full and effective participation" by requiring that "each citizen have an equally effective voice in the election of members of his state legislature" have ultimately led to some rather bizarre consequences. *Whitcomb v. Chavis* is an excellent case in point.[78] In *Whitcomb*, the supporters of losing candidates in multi-member districts petitioned the Court for redress, claiming that since their candidates had been defeated, they had been deprived of their right to "full and effective participation in the political processes" of their state legislatures. A tolerant Justice White was forced to explain to them certain elementary political realities:

> As our system has it, one candidate wins, the others lose. Arguably, the losing candidates' supporters are without representation since the men they voted for have been defeated; arguably they have been denied equal protection of the laws since they have no legislative voice of their own. This is true of both single-member and multi-member districts. *But we have not yet deemed it a denial of equal protection to deny legislative seats to losing candidates.*

The Warren Court's complete identification of representation with election can in large part be attributed to the Founders' efforts so to redefine representation and republican government that they would no longer require small size, civic virtue, and homogeneity of customs and manners. Its one man, one vote decisions, however, have been much more sensitive to questions concerning the processes of popular election than to the purposes of representation. To return to the musical analogy introduced earlier, the Court has been able to pick out the melody of the Founders' composition on representation with much greater facility than its harmony and counter-melody. By keying only on election and apportionment, it has failed to perceive altogether such nonimitative contrapuntal elements in the Founders' score as reflective versus refining representation, quantitative versus qualitative majority rule, and indirect versus direct political questions. Each of these elements must be briefly explored.

The Founders redefined representation so as to equate it with popular election. Although that ends the matter for the Court, it did not for the Founders. Depending upon institutional arrangements, elected representatives can operate in two fundamentally different and contradictory ways: they can either reflect the sentiments and feelings of the people, or refine and improve upon their views. They can provide for likeness or competence. John Adams in his "Thoughts on Government" reflected well the tension that can exist between these two strains of thought. He argued that representatives should be "of the most wise and good" while at the same time maintaining that they should be "in miniature an exact portrait of the people at large. [They] should think, feel, reason, and act like them."[79] Adams nowhere attempted to reconcile this tension between the requirements of deputation to the "wise and good" (i.e., the best) and the requirements of reflection of the whole. But, while Adams provides no ultimate reconciliation of the problem, he does provide its classic formulation, viz., men finally must choose between reflective and refining representation.

Those at the Founding who favored reflective representation argued that the legislature should be an exact miniature of the people, containing spokesmen for all classes, all groups, all interests, and all opinions in the community. As Brutus argued:

> The very term, representative, implies that the person or body chosen for this purpose should resemble those who appoint them—a representation of the people of America, if it be a true one, must be like the people. It ought to be so constituted, that a person, who is a stranger to the country, might be able to form a just idea of their character, by knowing that of their representatives. They are the sign—the people are the thing signified.[80]

In other words, representation would be complete only if it collected "the interests, feelings, opinions, and views of the people . . . [in the same] manner as they would be were the people are assembled."[81]

This view of representation, however, was open to certain objections. To begin with, it required a numerous legislature and, hence, a small republic. Moreover, as R. R. Livingston queried in the New York Ratifying Convention: "What, shall the unjust, the selfish, the unsocial feelings be represented? Shall the vices, the infirmities, the passions of the people be represented?"[82] As a consequence, most of the Founders favored a policy of refinement in which the men who are chosen "represent only the elevated thoughts that are current in the community and the generous propensities that prompt its noblest actions rather than the petty passions that disturb or the vices that disgrace it."[83] This refinement was achieved in two ways. First, the extended republic itself contributed to the improvement of the character of representation. As James Madison stressed in *Federalist* No. 10:

> As each Representative will be chosen by a greater number of citizens in a large than in a small Republic, it will be more difficult for unworthy candidates to practice with success the vicious arts, by which elections are too often carried; and the suffrages of the people being more free, will be more likely to centre on men who possess the most attractive merit, and the most diffusive and established characters.[84]

Second, popular appointments were to be refined through the process of "successive filtrations."[85] Thus, the founders provided for indirect election of the Senate and the President. As John Rutledge explained: "An election by the Legislature would be more refined than an election immediately by the people: and would be more likely to correspond with the sense of the whole community."[86] They did not, however, wish to see this "pushed too far." With Madison, they "thought too that the great fabric to be raised would be more stable and durable if it would rest on the solid foundation of the people themselves, than if it should stand merely on the pillars of the Legislatures."[87] Thus, the Founders sought to provide for both reflective and refining representation—for enough popular influence for republican safety and enough refinement and competence for good administration. They were sensitive to the need for both kinds of representation and the strengths that each could provide—a sensitivity sorely lacking in the Warren Court's one man, one vote formulation and in its desire to insure that every legislative body faithfully reflects the political "complexion" of the society.[88]

The Warren Court's insensitivity to questions of refinement is part and parcel of a broader problem—its lack of understanding of the distinction between quantitative and qualitative majority rule. In *Reynolds*, for example, Chief Justice Warren argued simply that the majority shall rule. "To conclude differently, and sanction minority control of state legislative bodies, would appear to deny majority rights in a way that far surpasses any possible denial of minority rights that might otherwise be thought to result."[89] This statement is interesting in two respects. First, it states the problem simply in terms of majority rule versus minority rule. Once it establishes that the majority shall rule, however, it is altogether devoid of instruction on the question of which majority. Must the Court accept tyrannical or oppressive or racist majorities with as much equanimity as decent and public-regarding majorities? Since the Court is more concerned that the majority shall rule than that it shall rule well, apparently so. Second, Chief Justice Warren's statement is also interesting in that it completely dismisses what for Madison and the Founders was the "great difficulty" in framing governments "to be administered by men over men": "You must first enable the government to controul the governed; and in the next place, oblige it to controul itself." The Founders' response to this difficulty was two-fold: "A dependence on the people is no doubt the primary controul on the government; but experience has taught mankind the necessity of auxiliary precautions."[90] The Court, in its one man, one vote decisions, has chosen to disregard the Founders' counsel and to rely exclusively on "a dependence on the people." The majority is to rule, and, as the Court held in *Lucas v. Colorado General Assembly,* even the majority itself cannot deprive itself of the right to rule as a majority.[91] It has discounted completely the importance of such "auxiliary precautions" as separation of power and bicameralism, federalism, and even judicial review in protecting the majority from their "temporary delusions" and in promoting qualitative as opposed to simply quantitative majority rule.[92] Alexander Bickel has speculated on the tragic but ironic consequences that are likely to eventuate from this course of action. "Majoritarianism is heady stuff. It is, in truth, a tide flowing with the swiftness of a slogan—whether popular sovereignty, as in the past, or one man, one vote, as in the Warren Court's formulation. The tide is apt to sweep over all institutions seeking its level everywhere. . . . The tide could well engulf the Court itself also."[93] After all, if the majority cannot deprive itself of the right to rule as a majority, on what possible grounds can the Court hope to restrain it? Why should the Court be allowed to stand as the only locus of power countervailing that of the majority, and why should it, "by reliance on the majoritarian principle," forbid all others what it can reach?[94]

At bottom, the Court's difficulties with reflective versus refining representation and quantitative versus qualitative majority rule can be traced to its emphasis on indirect as opposed to direct political questions. In this respect, the Court simply reflects the modern dispensation, wherein questions of representation and consent have come to replace what Bertrand de Jouvenal and Harvey C. Mansfield, Jr., call the more "direct political questions" of the goodness or badness of governmental actions.[95] The direct political question, Is this law or government decent, good, or useful? has been obscured or forgotten in the modern dispensation's preoccupation with the question, Is this law or government truly representative, i.e., has it in some manner received the consent of the majority? The Court, then, has replaced the question of goodness with the question of legitimacy. It has subordinated the quality of the policy to the quantity of consent. This is in striking contrast with the understanding of the Founders, who insisted that "the prudent enquiry in all cases, ought surely to be not so much *from whom* the advice comes as whether the advice be *good.*"[96] The Founders generally understood that insuring the right of consent is less problematic than insuring the wisdom of those consenting. Accordingly, they sought to design institutions which would secure the same results as this elusive wisdom would have provided. For the Court, as for the modern dispensation, the concern is different. Institutions must be so modified as to provide the people's representatives with good title to rule, not to insure that they rule well. As a consequence, the Court's attention has been diverted from the worth of policy to its formulation, from the uses of power to its legitimatization through consent. This preoccupation with legitimacy and representation, however, has contributed greatly to our present crisis in public authority, wherein, as

Theodore J. Lowi has pointed out, we face the "spectacular paradox" of a Constitution which is almost totally democratized but whose government is increasingly felt to be illegitimate.[97] This is a strange consequence, indeed, for a Court which set out to enhance the public's commitment to American democracy by insuring that every citizen have the opportunity for "full and effective participation" in its political processes.

This paper has attempted to explore some of the consequences of the Court's failure to heed Justice Frankfurter's admonition and address itself to the "competing theories of political philosophy" that underlie the question of representation. The consequences, which should be apparent by now, are rather alarming. The reapportionment cases raise not only practical questions concerning the process of representation, but also philosophical questions concerning its basis and purpose. They touch upon issues that are "admittedly complex and subtle." Through a careful examination of these questions and of the answers which the Founders initially gave to them, the Court could have served as a "republican school master" and educated the American citizenry on the problems as well as the promise of representative government. It chose, however, to avoid these questions and to engage in the shibboleth of one man, one vote. By so doing, it has helped to impoverish, not to educate.

It was suggested earlier in this paper that the Warren Court reduced the Founders' composition on representation to something like a simple children's round which it has repeated over and over again in all the States. In retrospect, that assessment of the Court's variations on the Founders' theme may have been too generous. At a time when the prospects for representative government are growing increasingly dim, both at home and abroad, and when the American citizenry is becoming ever more apprehensive of the future of the Republic, the Court continues to skirt these fundamental issues.[98] Through its one man, one vote slogan, it has apparently impoverished itself no less than the public. At this unhappy juncture, perhaps the Court should be seen as reducing these complex philosophic questions to something we can whistle in the dark.[99]

### Notes

1. *Baker v. Carr*, 369 U.S. 186, 299–300 (1962). Mr. Justice Frankfurter dissenting. Emphasis added.
2. This paper does not explore the political (i.e., partisan consequences of reapportionment, see Ward Elliott, *The Rise of Guardian Democracy* (Cambridge: Harvard University Press, 1974); nor does it explore the policy consequences of one man, one vote, see Roger Harrison and Robert Crew, "The Effects of Reapportionment on State Public Policy Outputs," *Law and Society Review*, Vol. VIII (February, 1973, and Thomas R. Dye, *Politics in States and Communities* (Englewood Cliffs, N.J.: Prentice-Hall, Inc., 1973), pp. 131–135.
3. 372 U.S. 368 (1963).
4. 376 U.S. 1 (1974).
5. 377 U.S. 533 (1964).
6. Only Mr. Justice Harlan dissented.
7. 372 U.S. at 378.
8. *Ibid.*, p. 376. The distinction between immediate and mediate election by the people, which the Founders were anxious to preserve, is completely obliterated by Justice Douglas. See, for example, Max Farrand, *The Records of the Federal Convention of 1787* (New Haven: Yale University Press, 1937), II, 56. (Hereafter cited as Farrand.)
9. 372 U.S. at 380.
10. *Ibid.*, p. 381.

11. *Ibid.,* p. 379.

12. "The House of Representatives shall be composed of Members chosen every second Year by the People of the several States, and the Electors in each State shall have the Qualifications requisite for Electors of the most numerous Branch of the State Legislature."

13. 376 U.S. 7–8.

14. *Ibid.,* p. 14.

15. See 377 U.S. at 560.

16. *Ibid.,* p. 562. Reiterating this theme later in his opinion, Chief Justice Warren declared: "Citizens, not history or economic interests, cast votes. Considerations of area alone provide an insufficient justification for deviations from the equal-population principle. Again, people, not land or trees or pastures, vote." *Ibid.,* p. 380.

17. *Ibid.,* p. 565.

18. *Ibid.*

19. For a further discussion of this question of judicial craftsmanship, see Alexander M. Bickel, *The Supreme Court and the Idea of Progress* (New York: Harper & Row, Publishers, Inc., 1970), pp. 45, 81–100, and Walter F. Murphy, *Congress and the Court* (Chicago: University of Chicago Press, 1962), pp. 120–121, 266.

20. Anthony Lewis appears to be responsible for the coining of this catchy but empty surrogate for thought. Lewis's summary of the Twentieth Century Fund's conference on legislative reapportionment on June 15, 1962, bore the title of *One Man-One Vote.* See Ruth C. Silva, "One Man, One Vote and the Population Base," *Representation and Misrepresentation,* ed. Robert A. Goldwin (Chicago: Rand McNally and Co., 1968), pp. 54–55. See also Richard C. Cortner, *The Apportionment Cases* (New York: W.W. Norton & Company, 1970), pp. 206–207.

21. See, however, *Whitcomb v. Chavis,* 403 U.S. 124 (1971).

22. Bickel, *The Supreme Court and the Idea of Progress,* p. 13.

23. See Paul Eidelberg, *A Discourse on Statesmanship: The Design and Transformation of the American Polity* (Urbana: University of Illinois Press, 1974), p. 447.

24. Martin Diamond, *The Revolution of Sober Expectations* (Washington, D.C.: American Enterprise Institute for Public Policy Research, 1974), p. 7. Emphasis in the original.

25. Sir William Blackstone, *Commentaries on the Laws of England,* I. p. 190.

26. 376 U.S. at 8.

27. Alexander Hamilton, James Madison and John Jay, *The Federalist,* ed. Jacob E. Cooke (New York: The World Publishing Co., 1961), p. 385. All references to *The Federalist* are to this edition.

28. 376 U.S. at 18.

29. *Ibid.,* p. 26. Mr. Justice Harlan dissenting.

30. *Ibid.,* pp. 31–32. Emphasis in the original. As the late Professor Alfred H. Kelly would subsequently affirm: "To put the matter bluntly, Mr. Justice Black, in order to prove his point, mangled constitutional history. The quotations from the debates of the Convention on which he builds—Mason, Madison, Wilson, Patterson, Franklin, Sherman, C.C. Pinckney, and so on—are all real enough, but they have to do with the great debate in the Convention between the proponents of state equality in the legislature and the advocates of what Madison called 'proportionate representation' as between the states. They have nothing at all to do with the question of representation within the states." Alfred H. Kelly, "Clio and the Court: An Illicit Love Affair," *Supreme Court Review* (1965), pp. 135–136. See also Charles A. Miller, *The Supreme Court and the Uses of History* (New York: Simon and Schuster, 1969), pp. 131–135.

31. *The Federalist,* No. 54, p. 369. Emphasis added.

32. 377 U.S. at 565. Emphasis added.

33. Warren's position is not unlike that recently taken by the United Nations General Assembly when it declared that the Palestinian people have an inalienable right to nationhood.

34. 369 U.S. at 300. Mr. Justice Frankfurter dissenting.

35. 390 U.S. 474 (1968). Mr. Justice Fortas dissenting.

36. Although this paper focuses principally on the Warren Court, the Burger Court has shown no greater interest in exploring the philosophic issues underlying questions of representation. See, for example, Gordon E. Baker, "One Man, One Vote, and 'Political Fairness'—or, How

the Burger Court Found Happiness by Rediscovering *Reynolds v. Sims*," 23 *Emory Law Journal* (Summer, 1974), pp. 701–723. As the title suggests, this happiness has been achieved not by responding to Justice Frankfurter's invitation to explore the broader questions on which representation and apportionment depend but rather by adopting and following a policy of "political fairness" which, as Justice Byron White stressed in the 1973 decision of *Gaffney v. Cummings*, aims "at a rough scheme of proportional representation of the two major political parties." 412 U.S. 735, 738 (1973).

37. *Avery v. Midland County*, 390 U.S. at 497 (1968). Mr. Justice Fortas dissenting.

38. See Justice Harlan's excellent discussion of this question in *Reynolds v. Sims*, 377 U.S. at 622–623.

39. 377 U.S. at 533. See also *Wesberry*, where Justice Black quoted from *The Federalist*. Numbers . . . are the only proper scale of representation." No. 54 p. 368. This statement, however, occurs in the context of a discussion on the Three-fifths Compromise. Since it was never the purpose of this compromise to permit slaves actually to vote (If it had been, the court would doubtless have been forced to coin the phrase, one slave, three-fifths vote.), Justice Black's reliance on this quotation is obviously misplaced.

40. See 377 U.S. at 577.

41. 372 U.S. at 379. To the extent it conflicts with the language of Justice Douglas, it seems to support that of Justice Brennan, who in *Kirkpatrick v. Preisler* declared, "There may be a question whether distribution of congressional seats except according to total population can ever be permissible under Article I, Section 2." 394 U.S. 526, 534 (1969).

42. Appellants' Reply Brief, *Kirkpatrick v. Preisler*, 394 U.S. 526 (1969), at 4–5. These figures do not appear to be unique to the 1962 congressional elections. Thus, in 1964, only 10.99 per cent of the total population of Pulaski County voted in contrast with 53.59 per cent of the total population of Camden County; likewise, in 1966, only 5.96 per cent of the population voted in Pulaski County while 44.41 per cent exercised their right of suffrage in Camden County. Neither are these figures unique to the State of Missouri. Thus, in the 1968 congressional elections, four years after *Reynolds* and the massive reapportionment that followed in its wake, only 23.7 per cent of the total population of California's 38th Congressional District voted in contrast with 66.0 per cent of the total population of California's 35th District—a ratio of almost 2.8 to 1. The results in Illinois were almost identical: only 23.0 per cent of Illinois' 7th Congressional District voted while 61.5 per cent of those in Illinois' 13th District did—a ratio of 2.7 to 1. In New York, they were even more dramatic: 15.8 per cent of the total population of its 14th District voted in contrast with 55.7 per cent of its 39th District—a staggering ratio of over 3.5 to 1.

43. Silva, "One Man, One Vote and the Population Base," p. 60. See also Terry B. O'Rourke, *Reapportionment: Law, Politics, Computers* (Washington, D.C.: American Enterprise Institute for Public Policy Research, 1972), p. 19. "Disparities among the number of voters in districts apportioned according to the equal population standard frequently defeat the Court's avowed intention that all votes be weighted equally. For example, in 1969, the number of registered voters in California Assembly districts ranged from a low of 43,439 to a high of 160,547."

44. See, for example, the comments of John Dickinson: "A limited monarchy he considered as one of the best governments in the world. It was not certain that the same blessings were derivable from any other form. It was certain that equal blessings have never yet been derived from any of the Republican form. A limited monarchy, however, was out of the question. The spirit of the time—the state of our affairs, forbade the experiment, if it were desirable." Farrand, I, 87. James Mason's sentiments were similar: "Notwithstanding the oppressions and injustice experienced among us from democracy: the genius of the people is in favor of it, and the genius of the people must be consulted." *Ibid.*, p. 101. See also pp. 66 and 153.

45. *The Federalist*, No. 39 p. 251. Emphasis in the original.

46. *Ibid.*, No. 10, pp. 61–62.

47. Farrand, I, 20. Here, too, it must be stressed that the Founders' discussion focused on representation as between the states and had nothing at all to do with the question of districting within the states.

48. *Ibid.*, pp. 30, 196–200.

49. *Ibid.*, p. 533.

50. *Ibid.*, p. 541.

51. *Ibid.,* p. 542. Emphasis added.

52. The words are those of Elbridge Gerry of Massachusetts. Farrand, I, 541. As Gouverneur Morris acknowledged, "property ought to have its weight; but not all the weight." *Ibid.,* p. 567.

53. See Charles Cotesworth Pinckney, Farrand, I, 401: General Charles Pinckney, *Ibid.,* p. 426; and Abraham Baldwin, *Ibid.,* p. 470.

54. See James Wilson, Farrand, I, 583; and Charles Cotesworth Pinckney, *Ibid.,* p. 542.

55. *Ibid.,* p. 200.

56. After all, slaves were a very valuable form of property. As Forrest McDonald points out, "the 596 slaves owned by the four delegates from South Carolina were probably worth half again as much as the total public security holdings of all the other members. The slaves and farmlands owned by the delegates from Virginia and Maryland were worth far more than the mercantile, banking, and manufacturing property owned by all the other delegates." Forrest McDonald, *We The People: The Economic Origins of the Constitution* (Chicago: University of Chicago Press, 1958), p. 92.

57. The words are James Madison's. Farrand, II, 417.

58. Farrand, I, 579. For other members of the Convention who expressed similar sentiments, see Roger Sherman, *Ibid.,* p. 582; Nathaniel Ghorum, *Ibid.,* p. 587; William Johnson, *Ibid.,* p. 593; and James Wilson, *Ibid.,* p. 605.

59. Farrand, I, 585.

60. *The Federalist,* No. 54, p. 368.

61. The Founders did not claim to have discovered the principle of representation. As *Federalist* No. 14 observed, "Europe has the credit of discovering this great mechanical power in government, by the simple agency of which, the will of the largest political body may be concentered, and its force directed to any object, which the public good requires." They did, however, as the subsequent discussion will establish, "claim the merit of making the discovery the basis of unmixed and extensive republics." *The Federalist,* No. 14, p. 84.

62. See *The Federalist,* No. 14. For a sensitive discussion of this understanding of representation, see Murray Dry, "Representation and Republican Government in the American Founding," (unpublished Ph.D. dissertation, Department of Political Science, University of Chicago, 1970).

63. Dry, pp. 204–206. See also Gordon Wood, *The Creation of the American Republic* (Chapel Hill: University of North Carolina Press, 1969), p. 447.

64. "Additional Letters of the Federal Farmer," in *Empire and Nation,* ed. Forrest McDonald (Englewood Cliffs, N.J.: Prentice-Hall, Inc., 1962), p. 137.

65. "Brutus," No. 1, in *The Complete Anti-Federalist,* ed. Herbert J. Storing (Chicago: University of Chicago Press, forthcoming).

66. This argument is perhaps most closely identified with George Clinton, who writing as Cato observed that the principles that bind mankind together "are, in their exercise, like a pebble cast on the calm surface of a river—the circles begin in the center, and are small, active, and forcible, but as they depart from that point, they lose their force, and vanish into calmness. The strongest principle of union resides within our domestic walls. The ties of the parent exceed that of any other; as we depart from home, the next general principle of union is amongst citizens of the same state, where acquaintance, habits, and fortunes, nourish affection, and attachment; enlarge the circle still further, and, as citizens of different states, though we acknowledge the same national denomination, we lose in the ties of acquaintance, habits and fortunes, and thus by degrees we lessen in our attachments, till, at length, we no more than acknowledge a sameness of species." George Clinton, "The Letters of Cato," *Essays on the Constitution of the United States,* ed. Paul Leicester Ford (Brooklyn, N.Y.: Historical Printing Club, 1892), p. 259. (Hereafter cited as *Essays*).

67. *The Federalist,* No. 17, p. 107.

68. "Letters of the Federal Farmer," *Pamphlets on the Constitution of the United States,* ed. Paul Leicester Ford (Brooklyn, N.Y.: Historical Printing Club, 1888), p. 290. (Hereafter cited as *Pamphlets.*) See also James Winthrop, "The Letters of Agrippa," *Essays,* p. 54.

69. "The Letters of Cato," *Essays,* p. 259. See also "Letters of the Federal Farmer," *Pamphlets,* p. 294.

70. "Additional Letters of the Federal Farmer," *Empire and Nation,* p. 168.
71. "Brutus," No. 1.
72. *The Federalist,* No. 57, p. 384. "The elective mode of obtaining rulers is the characteristic policy of republican government."
73. James Wilson, *The Works of James Wilson,* ed. Robert Green McCloskey (Cambridge, Mass.: Harvard University Press, 1967), p. 364.
74. *Ibid.,* pp. 786, 788, and 405.
75. Jonathan Elliot (ed.), *The Debates in the Several State Conventions on the Adoption of the Federal Constitution as Recommended by the General Convention at Philadelphia in 1787* (Philadelphia: J.B. Lippincott and Company, 1863), III, p. 85. (Hereafter cited as Elliot.)
76. James Wilson, Farrand, I, 49. See also James Wilson's comments in the Pennsylvania Ratifying Convention, John Bach McMaster and Frederick D. Stone (eds.), *Pennsylvania and the Federal Constitution* (Lancaster, Pennsylvania: The Historical Society of Pennsylvania, 1888), pp. 222–223.
77. The expression is James Wilson's. See McMaster and Stone, p. 225.
78. 403 U.S. 124 (1971).
79. John Adams, *The Political Writings of John Adams,* ed. George A. Peck, Jr. (Indianapolis: Bobbs-Merrill Co., Inc., 1954), p. 86. James Wilson reflects much the same tension. In the Federal Convention, he declared that the government "ought to possess not only 1st. the *force* but 2ndly, the *mind or sense* of the people at large. The Legislature ought to be the most exact transcript of the whole Society." Farrand, I, 132. Emphasis in the original. Yet, in the Pennsylvania Ratifying Convention, he admitted that it was of more consequence to have representatives who are able "to know the true interest of the people than their faces." McMaster and Stone, *Pennsylvania and the Federal Constitution,* p. 336. Likewise, in his law lectures delivered at the University of Pennsylvania in 1791, he taught that the citizens have a duty to entrust the management of government to "the wisest and best citizens." *The Works of James Wilson,* pp. 157, 778.
80. "Brutus," No. 3.
81. "Additional Letters of the Federal Farmer," *Empire and Nation,* p. 114.
82. Elliot, II, pp. 275–276.
83. Alexis de Tocqueville, *Democracy in America,* ed. Phillips Bradley (New York: Random House, 1945), I, p. 212.
84. *The Federalist,* No. 10, p. 63.
85. James Madison, Farrand, I, 50.
86. *Ibid.,* p. 359. See also John Dickinson, *Ibid.,* p. 136; Elbridge Gerry, *Ibid.,* p. 152; and Edmund Randolph, *Ibid.,* p. 218.
87. Farrand, I, 50.
88. *Reynolds v. Sims,* 377 U.S. at 567.
89. 377 U.S. at 565.
90. *The Federalist,* No. 51, p. 349.
91. 377 U.S. 713 (1964).
92. For an excellent discussion of the ways by which these "auxiliary precautions" can be used as "temporary barriers to popular ineptitude," see Martin Diamond, "Conservatives, Liberals, and the Constitution," in *Left, Right and Center,* ed. Robert A. Goldwin (Chicago: Rand McNally and Company, 1967), pp. 60–86.
93. Bickel, *The Supreme Court and the Idea of Progress,* pp. 111–112.
94. *Ibid.,* p. 115. Although Chief Justice Warren declares in *Reynolds* that "our constitutional system amply provides for the protection of minorities by means other than giving them majority control of state legislatures," (377 U.S. at 566) it should be apparent that the Court's own language helps to undermine these very same constitutional protections.
95. Bertrand de Jouvenal, *Sovereignty: An Inquiry into the Nature of the Political Good* (Chicago: University of Chicago Press, 1957), pp. 3, 4, and 6; Harvey C. Mansfield, Jr., "Hobbes and the Science of Indirect Government," LXV *American Political Science Review* 1 (March, 1971), pp. 97–98.
96. *The Federalist,* No. 40, p. 267. Emphasis in the original.

97. Theodore J. Lowi, *The End of Liberalism* (New York: W.W. Norton, 1969), p. 68.
98. See note 35, *supra*.
99. As Alexander Bickel declared more than a decade ago: "Until the Supreme Court succeeds in working out some principle of representation which, instead of distorting the past and oversimplifying the present, takes some account of all the objectives that properly play a role in the construction of deliberate, representative institutions—until then it is not possible to rejoice that the federal courts will have the last word in apportion[ment]." Alexander Bickel, *Politics and the Warren Court* (New York: Harper & Row, 1965), p. 195.

---

## Some Post-*Bakke*-and-*Weber* Reflections on "Reverse Discrimination"

Henry J. Abraham

### I

So much has been said, written, and emoted concerning the subject of "reverse discrimination" that it represents a veritably frustrating experience to endeavor to come to grips with it in a nonredundant, nonbanal, non-breast-beating manner. The difficulty is compounded by the all too pervasive substitution of passion for reason on the wrenching issue—one that, admittedly, invites passion. Indeed, passion informed not an insignificant number of the record filings of the 120 briefs *amicii curiae* in the first central "reverse discrimination" case of *Regents of the University of California v. Allan Bakke*,[1] in which oral argument was presented to the Supreme Court of the United States in mid-October 1977. It took place in a sardinelike packed Court chamber, with more than 200 putative spectators waiting in line all night in the hope of perhaps hearing one three-minute segment of that potential bellweather decision—toward which the court, in an unusual action, called for the filing of supplementary briefs by all parties concerned two weeks later in order to argue specifically the *statutory* question(s), involved in the application of Title VI of the Civil Rights Act of 1964. Passion similarly governed the denouement of the second major "reverse discrimination" case, *United Steel Workers and Kaiser Aluminum and Chemical Corporation v. Weber*,[2] which the Court decided in June 1979, almost exactly one year after the *Bakke* holding. And passion, however comprehensible emotionally, has clouded the arguments and contentions of even the most cerebral professional as well as lay observers of the "reverse discrimination" issue, the resolution of which may well constitute a watershed in this particularly crucial aspect of the race syndrome, of what Gunnar Myrdal more than three decades ago so pointedly titled "The American Dilemma."

In the hope of avoiding an abject surrender to the aforementioned passion(s), I shall do my best to discuss the matter in a rational basis while pledging to strive to eschew what Headmaster Stanley Bosworth of St. Ann's Episcopal School in Brooklyn so tellingly, if perhaps a mite expansively, identified as "the piety, puritanism, and

Reprinted with permission of Henry J. Abraham and the *University of Richmond Law Review*.

guilt that have combined to stir the worst semantic confusion" conceivable[3] in this emotion-charged policy spectrum. It would thus be helpful to try to identify at the outset what we are, or *should be*, talking about in any attempted analysis of the constellation of "reverse discrimination" and what we *should not be* talking about. To do that, it is necessary to find what the concept *means*. "I only want to know what the words mean," once commented Mr. Justice Oliver Wendell Holmes, Jr., the judicial philosopher of our age; but he freely admitted, with E. M. Forster, that there is "wine in words." A lot of wine and other rather less consumable liquids have been poured into the notion, into the alleged meaning, of "reverse discrimination."

## II

Stipulating the audience of these ruminations to be educated, intelligent human beings, who read, see and/or hear the news that informs our *vie quotidienne,* I am comfortable in assuming a basic familiarity with the issues involved. I also am aware that and, I daresay, without exception, any reader will have strong feelings on the matter. So do I. We would not be human if we did not; while they operate on a host of levels and are triggered at vastly diverse moments, we all have consciences. Stipulating these facets, I should first endeavor to make clear what "reverse discrimination" is *not*: (1) It is *not* action, be it in the governmental or private sector, designed to remedy the absence of proper and needed educational preparation or training by special, albeit costly, primary and/or secondary school level preparatory programs or occupational skill development, such as "Head Start," "Upward Bound," etc., always provided that access to these programs is not bottomed on race but on educational, and/or economic need be it cerebral or manual. (2) It is *not* the utilization of special classes or supplemental tutoring or training, regardless of the costs involved (assuming, of course, that these have been properly authorized and appropriated) on any level of the educational or training process, from the very pre-nursery school bottom to the very top of the professional training ladder. (3) It is of course *not* the scrupulous exhortation and enforcement of absolute standards of non-discrimination on the basis of race, sex, religion, nationality, and also now age (at least up to 70, with certain exceptions, some of which will be discontinued by 1982). (4) It is *not* the above-the-table special recruiting and utilization efforts which, *pace* poo-pooing by leaders of some of the recipient groups involved, are not only pressed vigorously, but have been and are being pushed and pressed on a scale that would make a Bear Bryant and Knute Rockne smile a knowing well-done smile. (5) It is *not* even an admission or personnel officer's judgment that, along with sundry other criteria, he or she may take into account an individual applicant's racial religious, gender, or other characteristics as a "plus"—to use Mr. Justice Powell's *Bakke* term—but only if that applicant can demonstrate the presence of demonstrable explicit or implicit merit in terms of ability and/or genuine promise. For I shall again and again insist that *the* overriding criterion, *the* central consideration, must in the final analysis be present or arguably potential merit. It must thus be merit and ability, not necessarily based exclusively upon past performance, but upon a mature, experienced judgment that merit and ability are in effect in the total picture either by their presence or by their fairly confident predictability. These five aforementioned "nots", which are all aspects of the concept of "affirmative action"—are naturally not an exhaustive enumeration. Yet they are illustrative of common practices that, in my view, do *not* constitute "reverse discrimination"—always provided that they remain appropriately canalized within proper legal and constitutional bounds—for they give life to the basic American right of equality of *opportunity*. One of the major problems, alas, is that militant pro-"reverse discrimination" advocates insist on substituting a requirement of equality of *result* for the requirement of equality of *opportunity*—a requirement based on the dangerous notion of statistical group parity, in which the focal point becomes the group rather than the individual.

This brings me to the necessary look at a quintet of what "reverse discrimination" *is*: (1) It *is,* above all, what in the final analysis, the *Bakke* and *Weber* cases fundamentally were all about, namely the setting aside of quotas—be they rigid or quasi-rigid—i.e., the adoption of a *numerous clausus,* on behalf of the admission or recruitment or training or employment or promotion of groups identified and classified by racial, sexual, religious, age, or nationality characteristics. For these are characteristics that are, or should be, proscribed on both legal and constitutional grounds, because they are *non-sequiturs* on the fronts of individual merit and ability and are, or certainly should be, regarded as being an insult to the dignity and intelligence of the quota recipients. "Our Constitution is color-blind," thundered Mr. Justice John Marshall Harlan in lonely dissent in the famous, or infamous, case of *Plessy* v. *Ferguson* in 1896, "and neither knows nor tolerates classes among citizens."[4] His dissent, which became the guiding star of the Court's unanimous holding in the monumental and seminal 1954 ruling in *Brown* v. *Board of Education of Topeka, Kansas,*[5] now prompts us to ask the question whether, as the proponents of "reverse discrimination" urge, the "Constitution must be color-conscious in order to be color-blind?"[6] But to continue what "reverse discrimination" is, it *is* (2) the slanting of what should be neutral, pertinent, and appropriate threshold and other qualification examinations and/or requirements; double-standards in grading and rating; double-standards in attendance and disciplinary requirements. It *is* (3) the dishonest semanticism of what are called *goals* or *guidelines,* that the bureaucracy has simply pronounced legal and/ or constitutional on the alleged grounds that they differ from rigid quotas, which admittedly would be presumably illegal and/or unconstitutional. Fully supported by Mr. Justice Powell's dismissal of them in the *Bakke* decision as a "semantic distinction" which is "beside the point,"[7] I submit that this distinction is as unworkable as it is dishonest—in the absence of, to use a favorite Department of Health, Education and Welfare, Department of Labor, and O.E.E.O. term, "good faith" vis-a-vis the far-reaching efforts of affected educational institutions and employers to function under the concept of "goals" or "guidelines." But while going to enormous lengths to deny any equation of "goals" or "guidelines" with "quotas," the largely unchecked enforcement personnel of the three aforementioned powerful and well-funded agencies of the federal government—personnel that, certainly in the realm of the administration of higher education, often lacks the one-would-think essential experience and background—in effect *require* quotas while talking "goals" or "guidelines." Indeed, within hours, if not minutes of the *Bakke* decision, for example, Eleanor Holmes Norton, the aggressive head of the O.E.E.O., announced that the Supreme Court holding would make no difference, whatever, in the agency's established policies! Thus, there is extant an eager presumption of a lack of a good faith effort against the background-imposition of rigid compliance quotas, based upon frequently irrelevant group statistics, statistics that are demonstrably declared to be *ultra vires* by Title VII, Sec. 703(j) of the Civil Rights Act of 1964. (4) Reverse discrimination *is* such a statutory provision—one recently challenged and declared unconstitutional by U.S. District Court Judge A. Andrew Hauk,[8] and then upheld by U.S. District Court Judge Daniel J. Snyder, Jr., who was affirmed by the United States Court of Appeals for the Third Circuit[9]—as that mandated under the Public Works Employment Act of 1977. Under that Act, Congress enacted a rigid requirement that 10 per cent of all public works contracts designed to stimulate employment go to minority business enterprises. How does this law identify such enterprises? They are, according to its terms, private businesses that are at least half-owned by members of a minority group or publicly held businesses in which minority group members control a majority of the stock. And who are these statutorily recognized minorities? They are, says the Act, "Blacks, Orientals, Indians, Eskimos, Aleuts," and what is termed "the Spanish-speaking." At issue, in what has quickly come to be known as the "1977 Ten Per Cent Set-Aside Quota Law," are thousands of construction jobs and billions of dollars worth of Government contracts. But when the U.S. Supreme Court initially had the case before it a few days after the Bakke decision came down, it ducked the problem on the ground that the award involved had already been consummated and the money expended, the issue thus being moot.[10] However, the Court has since agreed to reexamine it with its docketing of the potentially seminal case of *Fullilove* v. *Kreps*,[11] for which oral argument is scheduled for the 1979-80 term. And reverse discrimination is (5) the widely advanced notion, a favorite of officials at the very highest levels of all branches of our contemporary Administration that, somehow, two wrongs make a right; that the children must pay for the sins of their fathers by self-destructive actions; that, in the words of Mr. Chief Justice Burger's dissenting opinion in the pro-reverse discrimination *Franks* decision in 1976, "of 'robbing Peter to pay Paul.'"[12]

### III

It is, of course, the latter issue—one I suggested as my fifth illustration of what "reverse discrimination" *is*—that lies at the heart of the matter. To put it simply, but not oversimplifiedly, it is the desire, the perceived duty, the moral imperative, of compensating for the grievous and shameful history of racial and collateral discrimination in America's past. That discrimination is a fact of history which no fair person can deny and the reappearance of which no decent or fair person would sanction, let alone welcome. America's record since the end of World War II, and especially since the *Brown* decision, is a living testament to the far-reaching, indeed exhilarating, ameliorations that have taken place, and are continuing to take place, on the civil rights front. This is a fact of life amply documented and progressively demonstrated, and I need not do so here. (I have tried to do it in my *Freedom and the Court,* now in its third edition,[13] which—ironically in view of my stance on "reverse discrimination" encountered difficulties in certain parts of the country as recently as a decade or so ago because of its allegedly excessive liberality on the race issue. I presume it all depends, to utilize Al Smith's felicitous phrase, "whose ox is being gored"—and at which moment in history.) Anyone who denies the very real progress cum atonement that has taken place, and is continuing to take place, in both the public and the private sector is either a fool, dishonest, or does so for political purposes—and the largest numbers fall into that latter category. American society today is absolutely committed to the fullest measure of egalitarianism under our Constitution, mandated in our basic document by the "due process" clause of Amendments Five and Fourteen and the latter's "equal protection of the laws" clause as well as in a plethora of legislation. But that Constitution, in the very same Amendments, safeguards liberty as well as equality—a somber reminder that rights and privileges are not one-dimensional.

It is on the frontiers of that line between equality and liberty that so much of the "reverse discrimination" controversy, both in its public and private manifestations, has become embattled. It is here that the insistent, often strident, calls for compensatory, preferential, "reverse discrimination" action are issued—and, more often than not, they issue from a frighteningly profound guilt complex, a guilt complex that has become so pervasive as to brush aside as irrelevant on the altar of atonement even constitutional, let alone legal, barriers—witness, for example, the opinions by Justices Brennan and Blackmun in both the *Bakke* and *Weber* rulings. To cite just one or two cases in point: One argument that veritably laces the pro-"reverse discrimination" arguments of the briefs[14] in *Bakke* and *Weber,* especially those by the American Civil Liberties Union, the Association of American University Professors, Harvard University, Stanford University, the University of Pennsylvania, Columbia University, and the NAACP, among others, is that the injustices of the past justify, indeed demand, a "temporary use of affirmative action including class-based hiring preferences and admission goals" in favor of racial minorities. In other words, the record of the past creates the catalyst cum mandate for the imposition of quotas like the 16 places out of 100 admittedly set aside by the Medical School of the University of California at Davis for the "special" admission of members of certain minority groups.[15] What the school did is entirely straightforward and clear: it *did* establish a quota; it *did* practice discrimination; it *did* deny admission to a fully qualified white applicant, Allan Bakke, on racial grounds—which, as Mr. Justice Stevens's stern opinion for himself and his colleagues Burger, Stewart, and Rhenquist, makes clear, is clearly forbidden by the plain language of Title VI of the Civil Rights Act of 1964. The University had justified its action on the grounds of redress for past racial discrimination (the University, incidentally, had *never* practiced discrimination—and had, and has, never been accused of such until it denied Allan Bakke's admission); on the need for compensatory action; and a commitment to "genuine equal opportunity." In the responsive, apposite words of a widely-distributed statement by the Committee on Academic Nondiscrimination and Integrity:

> Just as no one truly dedicated to civil liberties would contemplate a 'temporary' suspension of, say, the right to counsel or the right to a fair trial as a means of dealing with a crime wave, so no one truly dedicated to equality of opportunity should contemplate a 'temporary' suspension of equal rights of individuals in order to achieve the goal of greater representation. The temporary all too often becomes the permanent. It is not the ultimate ends we proclaim but the temporary means we use which determine the actual future.[16]

In *Weber,* the central issue was a similar type of quota arrangement, although it governed employment rather than education: The Steelworkers and the Kaiser Corporation, under contemporary pressure by government agencies to engage in "affirmative action," had devised a plan that "reserves for black employees 50% of the openings in an in-plant craft training program until the percentage of black craft workers in the plant is commensurate with the percentage of blacks in the local labor force."[17] Both the U.S. District Court[18] and the U.S. Court of Appeals[19] has ruled that the plan clearly violated Title VII, Sec. 703, of the Civil Rights Act of 1964, which *specifically* outlaws racial discrimination in employment because of "race, color, religion, sex, or national origin."[20] But while admitting the presence of the plain statutory proscription, Mr. Justice Brennan in effect sanctioned its violation on the basis of the *spirit* of the law rather than its letter.[21]

A related, although somewhat different justification advanced on the altar of redressing past wrongs by temporarily—or perhaps not so temporarily?—winking at legal and constitutional barriers, one I prefer to call the "I am not really pregnant, just a little bit," approach to the problem, is illustrated by Ronald Dworkin, Professor of Jurisprudence at Oxford University, in his following 1977 defense of the use of racial criteria in connection with the well-known 1974 Washington Law School "reverse discrimination" case of *De Funis* v. *Odegaard:*[22]

> Racial criteria are not necessarily the right standards for deciding which applicants should be accepted by law schools for example. But neither are intellectual criteria, nor indeed, any other set of criteria. [Sic!] The fairness—and constitutionality—of any admissions program must be tested in the same way. It is justified if it serves a proper policy that respects the right of all members of the community to be treated as equals, but not otherwise. . . . We must take care not to use the Equal Protection of the Laws Clause of the Fourteenth Amendment to cheat ourselves of equality.[23]

Which, of course, is exactly what he in effect counsels here—in addition to the inequality of "reverse discrimination." In other words, the desired end justifies the means—no matter what the Constitution may command! We have here another patent illustration of the guilt complex syndrome which, not content with equal justice under law and equality of opportunity, insists upon, in Harvard Law Professor Raoul Berger's characterization, the attainment of "justice at any cost."[24] Yet it represents the gravamen of the concurring opinions in *Bakke* by Justices Brennan, Marshall, and Blackmun; the controlling holding in the *Weber* case via the pen of Mr. Justice Brennan; and that of the concurring opinion therein by his colleague Blackmun.

Along with a good many others who consider themselves bona fide civil libertarians and are certifiable champions of civil rights, who decades ago fought the good fight for equal justice and non-discrimination—when fighting it was far more fraught with professional and personal risks than it is now—I confess, however, that I do not have a guilt complex on that issue. Myself a sometime victim of discrimination, of prejudice, and of the *numerus clausus,* i.e. of quotas, I know that two wrongs not one right make; that any so-called "temporary suspension" of constitutional rights, is a cancer upon constitutionalism; that there is no such thing as being a little bit pregnant. Because of our religious persuasion my parental family and I were exiled from, and a number of members of our family were exterminated by, a land where our ancestors had lived for 500 years. As relatively recently as 1952, I was told quite frankly by an administrator at a major Northern University—one of the first proudly to carry the *anti*-Allan Bakke banner twenty-five years later—that I could not be promoted then because "we have already promoted one Jew this year." To which he added, and he was wholly sincere, "no personal offense meant." Happily, those times are gone—and I, for one, will not support their return on the altar of siren-like calls for atonement for past wrongs, etched in socio-constitutional rationalizations and manifestations of preferential treatment, compensatory standards, and quotas that are based on criteria and considerations other than those of fundamental merit, of ability, of equality of opportunity, and of equality before the law.

## IV

There is one other matter cum issue that must be addressed as a complement to my exhortation of the legal process, the necessity of playing the proverbial judicio-governmental societal game according to its rules. That, of course, is the role of the judiciary in interpreting the Constitution and the laws passed (and executive actions taken) under its constellation. The line between judicial "judging" and "lawmaking" is of course an extremely delicate and vexatious one: what represents "judicial activism" to some represents "judicial restraint" to others, and vice versa. All too often an observer's judgments correspond to the answer to the question "whose ox is gored?" Jurists are human, as we all are, yet they unlike laymen, are presumed to be professionally qualified to render objective judgment on the meaning, range, and extent of constitutionally and statutorily sanctioned or interdicted governmental authority and exercise of power. To be sure, in Mr. Justice Cardozo's memorable phrase from his seminal *The Nature of the Judicial Process*, "it is not easy to stand aloof" when one deals with so controversial a policy matter as the resort to discrimination as a cure for discrimination, for, as that great jurist and sensitive human being put it so poignantly, "[t]he great tides and currents which engulf the rest of men, do not. . .pass [even] the judges idly by."[25] And they assuredly have not done so—notwithstanding what would appear to be some crystal clear statutory, and some relatively clear constitutional, commands. *Au contraire,* these commands have served jurists as well as legislators and mere citizens as justifications and/or rationalizations along the pathways of coming to grips with the issue in settling fashion in either political, or socio-economic, or philosophical, or statutory, or, in the final analysis, judicially constructed terms.

But there are demonstrable limits to subjectivity and result orientation, even when these are viewed against the notion of an obligation to heed, as Mr. Justice Holmes put it, "the felt necessities of the time."[26] One of these limits is the ascertainable intent of lawmakers in enacting legislation. *De minimis,* courts have an absolute basic obligation to examine *statutory* language and *legislative intent* as evidenced by the printed record—and the "reverse discrimination" field is no exception. Admittedly, the *constitutional* ground is considerably less clear: for the very verbiage and concept of "equal protection" (and, for that matter, "due process of law") defy finite or categorical definition—regrettably all-too-often depending upon the eye of the beholder or the subject and object of the aforementioned ox-goring. Yet even on constitutional *qua* constitutional grounds it is difficult to deny the verity of Mr. Justice Powell's point in his majority opinion in the 1978 *Bakke* case when he noted that: "The guarantee of equal protection cannot mean one thing when applied to one individual and something else when applied to a person of another color. If both are not accorded the same protection, then it is not equal."[27]

Be that as it may, one who attempts to be a dispassionate commentator need not reach, as in effect the Court customarily tried very hard not to read, the constitutional issue (here the Fourteenth Amendment's equal protection of the laws clause). For if words mean anything, the basic statute involved, namely the 1964 Civil Rights Act's Title VII, would indeed seem to be crystal clear in *proscribing* the kind of racial quotas that the United States District Court and the United States Circuit Court found to have violated Brian Weber's rights, for example, but which, on appeal, the highest court of the land *upheld* in its 5:2 decision.[28] The controlling opinion, written by Mr. Justice Brennan, acknowledged the statutory, the linguistic command, but he and his four supporters found approbative warrant in the law's "spirit" rather than in its letter. For the law's Section 703 (a) makes it unlawful for an employer to classify his employees "in any way which would deprive or tend to deprive any individual of employment opportunities or otherwise adversely effect his status as an employee, because of such individual's race, color, religion, sex, or national origin." And, perhaps even more tellingly, Section 703 (j) provides that the Act's language is not to be interpreted "to require any employer . . . to grant preferential treatment to any individual or to any group because of the race . . . of such individual or group" to correct a racial imbalance in the employer's work force. Further to buttress historical and factual documentation on statutory grounds that the authors of the Civil Rights Act were demonstrably opposed to racial quotas, one need only take a glance at the voluminous, indeed repeated, documentation to that extent in the *Congressional Record* during the debates that led to the passage of the 1964 Civil Rights Act. Thus, the latter's successful Senate floor leader, Senator Hubert Humphrey (D.-Minn.), in responding to concerns voiced by doubting colleagues, vigorously and consistently gave assurance that no racial quotas or racial work force statistics would be employable under the law. In one exchange with his colleague William Robertson (D.-Va.), he made the following offer: "If the Senator can find in Title VII . . . any language which provides that an employer will have to hire on the basis of percentage or quota related to color . . . I will start eating the pages one after another, because it is not in there."[29]

It is difficult, indeed, it is in fact impossible, to argue with the facts of the statute's language or with Congressional intent: Mr. Justice Brennan's opinion attempted to vitiate those facts by (1) seizing upon the allegation that the joint Steelworkers—Kaiser Corporation agreement to hire one black for every white trainee was not *required* but was *voluntary;* and (2) that, in any event, the program would expire upon reaching statistical workforce-by-race availability-in-the-community parity. One need not embrace the angry and sarcastic language of Mr. Justice Rhenquist's dissenting opinion to support his documented contentions that, as to (1) anyone with any knowledge of the course of affirmative action programs knows that they are patently Government-*required;* and that, as to (2), S (j) of Section 703—quoted above—(a) forbids such a program and (b) the notion that it would prove to be "temporary" is either naive or "Houdini"-like. Whatever one's personal views on the underlying issue, whatever one's sympathies, the Rhenquist dissent, as Professor Philip B. Kurland of the University of Chicago School of Law put it, is simply unanswerable in terms of statutory construction and Congressional intent.

To a very considerable degree it was not the Rhenquist dissent, but that by Mr. Chief Justice Burger, which comes to the heart of the matter if one wishes to abide by the imperatives of the governmental framework under which we live. For he points to the salient fact that: "The Court reaches a result I would be inclined to vote for were I a member of Congress considering a proposed amendment of Title VII. I cannot join the Court's judgment, however, because it is contrary to the explicit language of the statute and arrived at by means wholly incompatible with long-established principles of separation of powers. Under the guise of 'statutory construction,' the Court effectively rewrites Title VII to achieve what it regards as a desirable result. It 'amends' the statute to do precisely what both its sponsors and its opponents agreed the statute was *not* intended to do."

There *is no* response to the Chief Justice's admonition—for it assesses accurately the obligations accruing under our system's separation of powers and the attendant roles of the three branches. In brief, and calling a spade a spade, the Court *legislated*—a function in this instance demonstrably reserved to the Legislature (Congress). The elusive line between "judging" and "legislating" is, to repeat, of course, a monumentally difficult one to draw in a great many instances, and it represents *the* basic issue of controversy in the exercise of judicial power. But there is *no* controversy in the present instance: Congress spoke and wrote with uncharacteristic clarity! Nonetheless, a majority of five Supreme Court Justices, given the nature of the public policy issue at hand, would neither listen nor read accurately.

## V

A concluding word on the desirability of "reverse discrimination" per se. I hope I have demonstrated what I regard as its tenets; what it *is*, and what it is *not*. Whether or not one agrees with that position, and regardless of how one perceives or reads the inherent statutory and constitutional issues, what of the merits of the proposition of racial, or sexual, or religious, or nationality quotas, or by whatever other noun they may be perfumed? It is not easy to do for me—as my students and colleagues would testify—but I will endeavor to be brief: I shall call as my star witness upon someone whose credentials on the libertarian front are indisputably impeccable, Mr. Justice William O. Douglas. In his dissenting opinion in *De Funis* v. *Odegaard,* after finding that Marco De Funis had been rejected by the University of Washington School of Law "solely on account of his race,"[30] Douglas lectured at length on that classification, styling it at the outset as introducing "a capricious and irrelevant factor working an invidious discrimination,"[31] and insisting that the Constitution and the laws of our land demand that each application for admission must be considered in "a racially neutral way,"[32] a phrase he italicized and one, incidentally, quoted with approval by Mr. Justice Powell in *Bakke.* "Minorities in our midst who are to serve actively in our public affairs," he went on, "should be chosen on talent and character alone, not on cultural orientation or leanings."[33] Warmly he cautioned that there is no constitutional right for any race to be preferred. . . . A De Funis who is white is entitled to no advantage by reason of that fact nor is he subject to any disability, no matter his race or color. Whatever his race, he had a constitutional right to have his application considered on its individual merits in a racially neutral manner. . . . So far as race is concerned, any state sponsored preference of one race over another in that competition is in my view 'invidious' and violative of the Equal Protection Clause.[34]

Mr. Justice Douglas concluded on a note that, for me, hits the essence of the entire issue: "The Equal Protection Clause," he insisted

commands the elimination of racial barriers, not their creation in order to satisfy our theory as to how society ought to be organized. The purpose of the University of Washington cannot be to produce Black lawyers for Blacks, Polish lawyers for Poles, Jewish lawyers for Jews, Irish lawyers for the Irish. It should be to produce good lawyers for Americans. . . .[35]

That, I submit in all humility, is the sine qua non of the matter. It is my fervent hope, though far from a confident expectation—especially given the unsatisfactory, multi-faceted, evasion-inviting response given by the Court in *Bakke*—that we will still, at this late hour, resolve to heed the now retired Justice's admonition and substitute for "lawyers" whatever educational, occupational, or professional noun may be appropriate in given circumstances in the justly egalitarian strivings of all Americans, regardless of race, sex, creed, nationality, or religion, for a dignified, happy, prosperous, and free life, blessed by a resolute commitment to and acquiescence in equal justice under law—which is as the cement of society.

### Notes

1. 38 U.S. 265 (1978).
2. 99S. Ct. 2721 (1979).
3. *The New York Times,* October 29, 1977, "Letters" page.
4. 163 U.S. 537, at 562.
5. 347 U.S. 483.
6. See Mr. Chief Justice Hale's dissenting opinion in *De Funis* v. *Odegaard,* 507 P. 2d 1169 (Wash. 1973), at 1189. (Italics added.)
7. *Regents of the University of California* v. *Allan Bakke,* 57 LEd. 2d 750, at 770.
8. *Associated General Contractors of California* v. *Kreps,* 441 F. Supp. 955 (Ca., 1977).
9. *Contractors Association of Western Pennsylvania* v. *Kreps,* 441 F. Supp. 936 (Pa., 1977).
10. *Kreps* v. *Associated General Contractors of California,* 57 LEd 2d 1153 (1978).
11. *Fullilove* v. *Kreps,* 584 F.2d 600 (1979).
12. *Franks* v. *Bowman Transportation Co.,* 44 LW 4356, at 4366.
13. (New York: Oxford University Press, 1977).
14. E.g., *Bakke* Brief of the American Association of University Professors, *amicus curiae,* by Matthew W. Finkin, Attorney.
15. *Regents of the University of California* v. *Bakke,* 57 LEd 2d 750, at 750.
16. Statement dated December 26, 1977.
17. 99 S. Ct. 2721, *op. cit.,* fn. 2, at 2724, Brennan, J., opinion of the Court.
18. 415 F. Supp. 761 (1976).
19. 563 F.2d 216 (1978).
20. 42 U.S.C.A. §2000e-2 (a, d, j)
21. *Op. cit.,* fn. 17, at 2726–7. (Italics added.)

22. 417 U.S. 623 (1974).
23. Ronald Dworkin, "De Funis v. Sweatt," in Cohen, Nagel, and Scanlon, *Equality and Preferential Treatment* (Princeton: Princeton University Press, 1977), p. 82.
24. *Government by Judiciary: The Transformation of the Fourteenth Amendment* (Cambridge: Harvard University Press, 1977).
25. (New Haven: Yale University Press, 1921), p. 168.
26. *The Common Law* (Boston: Little, Brown, 1881), p. 1.
27. *Regents of the University of California v. Bakke,* 438 U.S. 265, Powell, Jr., opinion for the Court.
28. *Op. cit.,* fns. 2 and 17.
29. 110 *Congressional Record,* 7420 (1964).
30. 42 LW 4584 (1974).
31. Ibid.
32. Ibid.
33. Ibid., at 4585.
34. Ibid.
35. Ibid., at 4586.

---

# Democracy, Liberty, and Equality

Alexis de Tocqueville

The first and most intense passion that is produced by equality of condition is, I need hardly say, the love of that equality. My readers will therefore not be surprised that I speak of this feeling before all others.

Everybody has remarked that in our time, and especially in France, this passion for equality is every day gaining ground in the human heart. It has been said a hundred times that our contemporaries are far more ardently and tenaciously attached to equality than to freedom; but as I do not find that the causes of the fact have been sufficiently analyzed, I shall endeavor to point them out.

It is possible to imagine an extreme point at which freedom and equality would meet and blend. Let us suppose that all the people take a part in the government, and that each one of them has an equal right to take a part in it. As no one is different from his fellows, none can exercise a tyrannical power; men will be perfectly free because they are all entirely equal; and they will all be perfectly equal because they are entirely free. To this ideal state democratic nations tend. This is the only complete form that equality can assume upon earth; but there are a thousand others which, without being equally perfect, are not less cherished by those nations.

The principle of equality may be established in civil society without prevailing in the political world. There may be equal rights of indulging in the same pleasures, of entering the same professions, of frequenting the same places; in a word, of living in the same manner and seeking wealth by the same means, although all men do not take an equal share in the government. A kind of equality may even be established in

From *Democracy in America*, Volumes I and II, by Alexis de Tocqueville, translated by Henry Reeve, revised by Francis Bowen, and edited by Philips Bradley. Copyright 1945 and renewed 1973 by Alfred A. Knopf, Inc. Reprinted by permission of Alfred A. Knopf.

the political world though there should be no political freedom there. A man may be the equal of all his countrymen save one, who is the master of all without distinction and who selects equally from among them all the agents of his power. Several other combinations might be easily imagined by which very great equality would be united to institutions more or less free or even to institutions wholly without freedom.

Although men cannot become absolutely equal unless they are entirely free, and consequently equality, pushed to its furthest extent, may be confounded with freedom, yet there is good reason for distinguishing the one from the other. The taste which men have for liberty and that which they feel for equality are, in fact, two different things; and I am not afraid to add that among democratic nations they are two unequal things.

Upon close inspection it will be seen that there is in every age some peculiar and preponderant fact with which all others are connected; this fact almost always gives birth to some pregnant idea or some ruling passion, which attracts to itself and bears away in its course all the feelings and opinions of the time; it is like a great stream towards which each of the neighboring rivulets seems to flow.

Freedom has appeared in the world at different times and under various forms; it has not been exclusively bound to any social condition, and it is not confined to democracies. Freedom cannot, therefore, form the distinguishing characteristic of democratic ages. The peculiar and preponderant fact that marks those ages as its own is the equality of condition; the ruling passion of men in those periods is the love of this equality. Do not ask what singular charm the men of democratic ages find in being equal, or what special reasons they may have for clinging so tenaciously to equality rather than to the other advantages that society holds out to them: equality is the distinguishing characteristic of the age they live in; that of itself is enough to explain that they prefer it to all the rest.

But independently of this reason there are several others which will at all times habitually lead men to prefer equality to freedom.

If a people could ever succeed in destroying, or even in diminishing, the equality that prevails in its own body, they could do so only by long and laborious efforts. Their social condition must be modified, their laws abolished, their opinions superseded, their habits changed, their manners corrupted. But political liberty is more easily lost; to neglect to hold it fast is to allow it to escape. Therefore not only do men cling to equality because it is dear to them; they also adhere to it because they think it will last forever.

That political freedom in its excesses may compromise the tranquillity, the property, the lives of individuals is obvious even to narrow and unthinking minds. On the contrary, none but attentive and clear-sighted men perceive the perils with which equality threatens us, and they commonly avoid pointing them out. They know that the calamities they apprehend are remote and flatter themselves that they will only fall upon future generations, for which the present generation takes but little thought. The evils that freedom sometimes brings with it are immediate; they are apparent to all, and all are more or less affected by them. The evils that extreme equality may produce are slowly disclosed; they creep gradually into the social frame; they are seen only at intervals; and at the moment at which they become most violent, habit already causes them to be no longer felt.

The advantages that freedom brings are shown only by the lapse of time, and it is always easy to mistake the cause in which they originate. The advantages of equality are immediate, and they may always be traced from their source.

Political liberty bestows exalted pleasures from time to time upon a certain number of citizens. Equality every day confers a number of small enjoyments on every man. The charms of equality are every instant felt and are within the reach of all; the noblest hearts are not insensible to them, and the most vulgar souls exult in them. The passion that equality creates must therefore be at once strong and general. Men cannot enjoy political liberty unpurchased by some sacrifices, and they never obtain it without great exertions. But the pleasures of equality are self-proffered; each of the petty incidents of life seems to occasion them, and in order to taste them, nothing is required but to live.

Democratic nations are at all times fond of equality, but there are certain epochs at which the passion they entertain for it swells to the height of fury. This occurs at the moment when the old social system, long menaced, is overthrown after a severe internal struggle, and the barriers of rank are at length thrown down. At such times men pounce upon equality as their booty, and they cling to it as to some precious treasure which they fear to lose. The passion for equality penetrates on every side into men's hearts, expands there, and fills them entirely. Tell them not that by this blind surrender of themselves to an exclusive passion they risk their dearest interests; they are deaf. Show them not freedom escaping from their grasp while they are looking another way; they are blind, or rather they can discern but one object to be desired in the universe.

What I have said is applicable to all democratic nations; what I am about to say concerns the French alone. Among most modern nations, and especially among all those of the continent of Europe, the taste and the idea of freedom began to exist and to be developed only at the time when social conditions were tending to equality and as a consequence of that very equality. Absolute kings were the most efficient levelers of ranks among their subjects. Among these nations equality preceded freedom; equality was therefore a fact of some standing when freedom was still a novelty; the one had already created customs, opinions, and lwas belonging to it when the other, alone and for the first time, came into actual existence. Thus the latter was still only an affair of opinion and of taste while the former had already crept into the habits of the people, possessed itself of their manners, and given a particular turn to the smallest actions in their lives. Can it be wondered at that the men of our own time prefer the one to the other?

I think that democratic communities have a natural taste for freedom; left to themselves, they will seek it, cherish it, and view any privation of it with regret. But for equality their passion is ardent, insatiable, incessant, invincible; they call for equality in freedom; and if they cannot obtain that, they still call for equality in slavery. They will endure poverty, servitude, barbarism, but they will not endure aristocracy.

This is true at all times, and especially in our own day. All men and all powers seeking to cope with this irresistible passion will be overthrown and destroyed by it. In our age freedom cannot be established without it, and despotism itself cannot reign without its support.

* * *

I have shown how it is that in ages of equality every man seeks for his opinions within himself; I am now to show how it is that in the same ages all his feelings are turned towards himself alone. *Individualism* is a novel expression, to which a novel idea has given birth. Our fathers were only acquainted with *egoisme* (selfishness). Selfishness is a passionate and exaggerated love of self, which leads a man to connect everything with himself and to prefer himself to everything in the world. Individualism is a mature and calm feeling, which disposes each member of the community to sever himself from the mass of his fellows and to draw apart with his family and his friends, so that after he has thus formed a little circle of his own, he willingly leaves society at large to itself. Selfishness originates in blind instinct; individualism proceeds from erroneous judgment more than from depraved feelings; it originates as much in deficiencies of mind as in perversity of heart.

Selfishness blights the germ of all virtue; individualism, at first, only saps the virtues of public life; but in the long run it attacks and destroys all others and is at length absorbed in downright selfishness. Selfishness is a vice as old as the world, which does not belong to one form of society more than to another; individualism is of democratic origin, and it threatens to spread in the same ratio as the equality of condition.

Among aristocratic nations, as families remain for centuries in the same condition, often on the same spot, all generations become, as it were, contemporaneous. A man almost always knows his forefathers and respects them; he thinks he already sees his remote descendants and he loves them. He willingly imposes duties on himself towards the former and the latter, and he will frequently sacrifice his personal gratifications to those who went before and to those who will come after him. Aristocratic institutions, moreover, have the effect of closely binding every man to several of his fellow citizens. As the classes of an aristocratic people are strongly marked and permanent, each of them is regarded by its own members as a sort of lesser country, more tangible and more cherished than the country at large. As in aristocratic communities all the citizens occupy fixed positions, one above another, the result is that each of them always sees a man above himself whose patronage is necessary to him, and below himself another man whose co-operation he may claim. Men living in aristocratic ages are therefore almost always closely attached to something placed out of their own sphere, and they are often disposed to forget themselves. It is true that in these ages the notion of human fellowship is faint and that men seldom think of sacrificing themselves for mankind; but they often sacrifice themselves for other men. In democratic times, on the contrary, when the duties of each individual to the race are much more clear, devoted service to any one man becomes more rare; the bond of human affection is extended, but it is relaxed.

Among democratic nations new families are constantly springing up, others are constantly falling away, and all that remain change their condition; the woof of time is every instant broken and the track of generations effaced. Those who went before are soon forgotten; of those who will come after, no one has any idea: the interest of man is confined to those in close propinquity to himself. As each class gradually approaches others and mingles with them, its members become undifferentiated and lose their class identity for each other. Aristocracy had made a chain of all the members of the community, from the peasant to the king; democracy breaks that chain and severs every link of it.

As social conditions become more equal, the number of persons increases who, although they are neither rich nor powerful enough to exercise any great influence over their fellows, have nevertheless acquired or retained sufficient education and fortune to satisfy their own wants. They owe nothing to any man, they expect nothing from any man; they acquire the habit of always considering themselves as standing alone, and they are apt to imagine that their whole destiny is in their own hands.

Thus not only does democracy make every man forget his ancestors, but it hides his descendants and separates his contemporaries from him; it throws him back forever upon himself alone and threatens in the end to confine him entirely within the solitude of his own heart.

* * *

The period when the construction of democratic society upon the ruins of an aristocracy has just been completed is especially that at which this isolation of men from one another and the selfishness resulting from it most forcibly strike the observer. Democratic communities not only contain a large number of independent citizens, but are constantly filled with men who, having entered but yesterday upon their independent condition, are intoxicated with their new power. They entertain a presumptuous confidence in their own strength, and as they do not suppose that they can henceforward ever have occasion to claim the assistance of their fellow creatures, they do not scruple to show that they care for nobody but themselves.

An aristocracy seldom yields without a protracted struggle, in the course of which implacable animosities are kindled between the different classes of society. These passions survive the victory, and traces of them may be observed in the midst of the democratic confusion that ensues. Those members of the community who were at the top of the late gradations of rank cannot immediately forget their former greatness; they will long regard themselves as aliens in the midst of the newly composed society. They look upon all those whom this state of society has made their equals as oppressors, whose destiny can excite no sympathy; they have lost sight of their former equals and feel no longer bound to their fate by a common interest; each of them, standing aloof, thinks that he is reduced to care for himself alone. Those, on the contrary, who were formerly at the foot of the social scale and who have been brought up to the common level by a sudden revolution cannot enjoy their newly acquired independence without secret uneasiness; and if they meet with some of their former superiors on the same footing as themselves, they stand aloof from them with an expression of triumph and fear.

It is, then, commonly at the outset of democratic society that citizens are most disposed to live apart. Democracy leads men not to draw near to their fellow creatures; but democratic revolutions lead them to shun each other and perpetuate in a state of equality the animosities that the state of inequality created.

The great advantage of the Americans is that they have arrived at a state of democracy without having to endure a democratic revolution, and that they are born equal instead of becoming so.

* * *

Despotism, which by its nature is suspicious, sees in the separation among men the surest guarantee of its continuance, and it usually makes every effort to keep them separate. No vice of the human heart is so acceptable to it as selfishness: a despot easily forgives his subjects for not loving him, provided they do not love one another. He does not ask them to assist him in governing the state; it is enough that they do not aspire to govern it themselves. He stigmatizes as turbulent and unruly spirits those who would combine their exertions to promote the prosperity of the community; and, perverting the natural meaning of words, he applauds as good citizens those who have no sympathy for any but themselves.

Thus the vices which despotism produces are precisely those which equality fosters. These two things perniciously complete and assist each other. Equality places men side by side, unconnected by any common tie; despotism raises barriers to keep them asunder; the former predisposes them not to consider their fellow creatures, the latter makes general indifference a sort of public virtue.

Despotism, then, which is at all times dangerous, is more particularly to be feared in democratic ages. It is easy to see that in those same ages men stand most in need of freedom. When the members of a community are forced to attend to public affairs, they are necessarily drawn from the circle of their own interests and snatched at times from self-observation. As soon as a man begins to treat of public affairs in public, he begins to perceive that he is not so independent of his fellow men as he had at first imagined, and that in order to obtain their support he must often lend them his co-operation.

When the public govern, there is no man who does not feel the value of public goodwill or who does not endeavor to court it by drawing to himself the esteem and affection of those among whom he is to live. Many of the passions which congeal and keep asunder human hearts are then obliged to retire and hide below the surface. Pride must be dissembled; disdain dares not break out; selfishness fears its own self. Under a free government, as most public offices are elective, the men whose elevated minds or aspiring hopes are too closely circumscribed in private life constantly feel that they cannot do without the people who surround them. Men learn at such times to think of their fellow men from ambitious motives; and they frequently find it, in a manner, their interest to forget themselves.

I may here be met by an objection derived from electioneering intrigues, the meanness of candidates, and the calumnies of their opponents. These are occasions of enmity which occur the oftener the more frequent elections become. Such evils are doubtless great, but they are transient; whereas the benefits that attend them remain. The desire of being elected may lead some men for a time to violent hostility; but this same desire leads all men in the long run to support each other; and if it happens that an election accidentally severs two friends, the electoral system brings a multitude of citizens permanently together who would otherwise always have remained unknown to one another. Freedom produces private animosities, but despotism gives birth to general indifference.

The Americans have combated by free institutions the tendency of equality to keep men asunder, and they have subdued it. The legislators of America did not suppose that a general representation of the whole nation would suffice to ward off a disorder at once so natural to the frame of democratic society and so fatal; they also thought that it would be well to infuse political life into each portion of the territory in order to multiply to an infinite extent opportunities of acting in concert for all the members of the community and to make them constantly feel their mutual dependence. The plan was a wise one. The general affairs of a country engage the attention only of leading politicians, who assemble from time to time in the same places; and as they often lose sight of each other afterwards, no lasting ties are established between them. But if the object be to have the local affairs of a district conducted by the men who reside there, the same persons are always in contact, and they are, in a manner, forced to be acquainted and to adapt themselves to one another.

It is difficult to draw a man out of his own circle to interest him in the destiny of the state, because he does not clearly understand what influence the destiny of the state can have upon his own lot. But if it is proposed to make a road cross the end of his estate, he will see at a glance that there is a connection between this small public affair and his greatest private affairs; and he will discover, without its being shown to him, the close tie that unites private to general interest. Thus far more may be done by entrusting to the citizens the administration of minor affairs than by surrendering to them the control of important ones, towards interesting them in the public welfare and convincing them that they constantly stand in need of one another in order to provide for it. A brilliant achievement may win for you the favor of a people at one stroke; but to earn the love and respect of the population that surrounds you, a long succession of little services rendered and of obscure good deeds, a constant habit of kindness, and an established reputation for disinterestedness will be required. Local freedom, then, which leads a great number of citizens to value the affection of their neighbors and of their kindred, perpetually brings men together and forces them to help one another in spite of the propensities that sever them.

In the United States the more opulent citizens take great care not to stand aloof from the people; on the contrary, they constantly keep on easy terms with the lower classes: they listen to them, they speak to them every day. They know that the rich in democracies always stand in need of the poor, and that in democratic times you attach a poor man to you more by your manner than by benefits conferred. The magnitude of such benefits, which sets off the difference of condition, causes a secret irritation to those who reap advantage from them, but the charm of simplicity of manners is almost irresistible, affability carries men away, and even want of polish is not always displeasing. This truth does not take root at once in the minds of the rich. They generally resist it as long as the democratic revolution lasts, and they do not acknowledge it immediately after that revolution is accomplished. They are very ready to do good to the people, but they still choose to keep them at arm's length; they think that is sufficient, but they are mistaken. They might spend fortunes thus without warming the hearts of the population around them; that population does not ask them for the sacrifice of their money, but of their pride.

It would seem as if every imagination in the United States were upon the stretch to invent means of increasing the wealth and satisfying the wants of the public. The best-informed inhabitants of each district constantly use their information to discover new truths that may augment the general prosperity; and if they have made any such discoveries, they eagerly surrender them to the mass of the people.

When the vices and weaknesses frequently exhibited by those who govern in America are closely examined, the prosperity of the people occasions, but improperly occasions, surprise. Elected magistrates do not make the American democracy flourish; it flourishes because the magistrates are elective.

It would be unjust to suppose that the patriotism and the zeal that every American displays for the welfare of his fellow citizens are wholly insincere. Although private interest directs the greater part of human actions in the United States as well as elsewhere, it does not regulate them all. I must say that I have often seen Americans make great and real sacrifices to the public welfare; and I have noticed a hundred instances in which they hardly ever failed to lend faithful support to one another. The free institutions which the inhabitants of the United States possess, and the political rights of which they make so much use, remind every citizen, and in a thousand ways, that he lives in society. They every instant impress upon his mind the notion that it is the duty as well as the interest of men to make themselves useful to their fellow creatures; and as he sees no particular ground of animosity to them, since he is never either their master or their slave, his heart readily leans to the side of kindness. Men attend to the interests of the public, first by necessity, afterwards by choice; what was intentional becomes an instinct, and by dint of working for the good of one's fellow citizens, the habit and the taste for serving them are at length acquired.

Many people in France consider equality of condition as one evil and political freedom as a second. When they are obliged to yield to the former, they strive at least to escape from the latter. But I contend that in order to combat the evils which equality may produce, there is only one effectual remedy; namely, political freedom.

\* \* \*

I had remarked during my stay in the United States that a democratic state of society, similar to that of the Americans, might offer singular facilities for the establishment of despotism; and I perceived, upon my return to Europe, how much use had already been made, by most of our rulers, of the notions, the sentiments, and the wants created by this same social condition, for the purpose of extending the circle of their power. This led me to think that the nations of Christendom would perhaps eventually undergo some oppression like that which hung over several of the nations of the ancient world.

A more accurate examination of the subject, and five years of further meditation, have not diminished my fears, but have changed their object.

No sovereign ever lived in former ages so absolute or so powerful as to undertake to administer by his own agency, and without the assistance of intermediate powers, all the parts of a great empire; none ever attempted to subject all his subjects indiscriminately to strict uniformity of regulation and personally to tutor and direct every member of the community. The notion of such an undertaking never occurred to the human mind; and if any man had conceived it, the want of information, the imperfection of the administrative system, and, above all, the natural obstacles caused by the inequality of conditions would speedily have checked the execution of so vast a design.

When the Roman emperors were at the height of their power, the different nations of the empire still preserved usages and customs of great diversity; although they were subject to the same monarch, most of the provinces were separatley administered; they abounded in powerful and active municipalities; and although the whole government of the empire was centered in the hands of the Emperor alone and he always remained, in case of need, the supreme arbiter in all matters, yet the details of social life and private occupations lay for the most part beyond his control. The emperors possessed, it is true, an immense and unchecked power, which allowed them to gratify all their whimsical tastes and to employ for that purpose the whole strength of the state. They frequently abused that power arbitrarily to deprive their subjects of property or of life; their tyranny was extremely onerous to the few, but it did not reach the many; it was confined to some few main objects and neglected the rest; it was violent, but its range was limited.

It would seem that if despotism were to be established among the democratic nations of our days, it might assume a different character; it would be more extensive and more mild; it would degrade men without tormenting them. I do not question that, in an age of instruction and equality like our own, sovereigns might more easily succeed in collecting all political power into their own hands and might interfere more habitually and decidedly with the circle of private interests than any sovereign of antiquity could ever do. But this same principle of equality which facilitates despotism tempers its rigor. We have seen how the customs of society become more humane and gentle in proportion as men become more equal and alike. When no member of the community has much power or much wealth, tyranny is, as it were, without opportunities and a field of action. As all fortunes are scanty, the passions of men are naturally circumscribed, their imagination limited, their pleasures simple. This universal moderation moderates the sovereign himself and checks within certain limits the inordinate stretch of his desires.

Independently of these reasons, drawn from the nature of the state of society itself, I might add many others arising from causes beyond my subject; but I shall keep within the limits I have laid down.

Democratic governments may become violent and even cruel at certain periods of extreme effervescence or of great danger, but these crises will be rare and brief. When I consider the petty passions of our contemporaries, the mildness of their manners, the extent of their education, the purity of their religion, the gentleness of their morality, their regular and industrious habits, and the restraint which they almost all observe in their vices no less than in their virtues, I have no fear that they will meet with tyrants in their rulers, but rather with guardians.

I think, then, that the species of oppression by which democratic nations are menaced is unlike anything that ever before existed in the world; our contemporaries will find no prototype of it in their memories. I seek in vain for an expression that will accurately convey the whole of the idea I have formed of it; the old words *despotism* and *tyranny* are inappropriate: the thing itself is new, and since I cannot name, I must attempt to define it.

I seek to trace the novel features under which despotism may appear in the world. The first thing that strikes the observation is an innumerable multitude of men, all equal and alike, incessantly endeavoring to procure the petty and paltry pleasures with which they glut their lives. Each of them, living apart, is as a stranger to the fate of all the rest; his children and his private friends constitute to him the whole of mankind. As for the rest of his fellow citizens, he is close to them, but he does not see them; he touches them, but he does not feel them; he exists only in himself and for himself alone; and if his kindred still remain to him, he may be said at any rate to have lost his country.

Above this race of men stands an immense and tutelary power which takes upon itself alone to secure their gratifications and to watch over their fate. That power is absolute, minute, regular, provident, and mild. It would be like the authority of a parent if, like that authority, its object was to prepare men for manhood; but it seeks, on the contrary, to keep them in perpetual childhood: it is well content that the people should rejoice, provided they think of nothing but rejoicing. For their happiness such a government willingly labors, but it chooses to be the sole agent and the only arbiter of that happiness; it provides for their security, foresees and supplies their necessities, facilitates their pleasures, manages their principal concerns, directs their industry, regulates the descent of property, and subdivides their inheritances: what remains, but to spare them all the care of thinking and all the trouble of living?

Thus it every day renders the exercise of the free agency of man less useful and less frequent; it circumscribes the will within a narrower range and gradually robs a man of all the uses of himself. The principle of equality has prepared men for these things, it has predisposed men to endure them and often to look on them as benefits.

After having thus successively taken each member of the community in its powerful grasp and fashioned him at will, the supreme power then extends its arm over the whole community. It covers the surface of society with a network of small complicated rules, minute and uniform, through which the most original minds and the most energetic characters cannot penetrate, to rise above the crowd. The will of man is not shattered, but softened, bent, and guided; men are seldom forced by it to act, but they are constantly restrained from acting. Such a power does not destroy, but it prevents existence; it does not tyrannize, but it compresses, enervates, extinguishes, and stupefies a people, till each nation is reduced to nothing better than a flock of timid and industrious animals, of which the government is the shepherd.

I have always thought that servitude of the regular, quiet, and gentle kind which I have just described might be combined more easily than is commonly believed with some of the outward forms of freedom, and that it might even establish itself under the wing of the sovereignty of the people.

Our contemporaries are constantly excited by two conflicting passions: they want to be led, and they wish to remain free. As they cannot destroy either the one or the other of these contrary propensities, they strive to satisfy them both at once. They devise a sole, tutelary, and all-powerful form of government, but elected by the people. They combine the principle of centralization and that of popular sovereignty; this gives them a respite: they console themselves for being in tutelage by the reflection that they have chosen their own guardians. Every man allows himself to be put in leading-strings, because he sees that it is not a person or a class of persons, but the people at large who hold the end of his chain.

By this system the people shake off their state of dependence just long enough to select their master and then relapse into it again. A great many persons at the present day are quite contented with this sort of compromise between administrative despotism and the sovereignty of the people; and they think they have done enough for the protection of individual freedom when they have surrendered it to the power of the nation at large. This does not satisfy me: the nature of him I am to obey signifies less to me than the fact of extorted obedience.

I do not deny, however, that a constitution of this kind appears to me to be infinitely preferable to one which, after having concentrated all the powers of government, should vest them in the hands of an irresponsible person or body of persons. Of all the forms that democratic despotism could assume, the latter would assuredly be the worst.

When the sovereign is elective, or narrowly watched by a legislature which is really elective and independent, the oppression that he exercises over individuals is sometimes greater, but it is always less degrading; because every man, when he is oppressed and disarmed, may still imagine that, while he yields obedience, it is to himself he yields it, and that it is to one of his own inclinations that all the rest give way. In like manner, I can understand that when the sovereign represents the nation and is dependent upon the people, the rights and the power of which every citizen is deprived serve not only the head of the state, but the state itself; and that private persons derive some return from the sacrifice of their independence which they have made to the public. To create a representation of the people in every centralized country is, therefore, to diminish the evil that extreme centralization may produce, but not to get rid of it.

I admit that, by this means, room is left for the intervention of individuals in the more important affairs; but it is not the less suppressed in the smaller and more private ones. It must not be forgotten that it is especially dangerous to enslave men in the minor details of life. For my own part, I should be inclined to think freedom less necessary in great things than in little ones, if it were possible to be secure of the one without possessing the other.

Subjection in minor affairs breaks out every day and is felt by the whole community indiscriminately. It does not drive men to resistance, but it crosses them at every turn, till they are led to surrender the exercise of their own will. Thus their spirit is gradually broken and their character enervated; whereas that obedience which is exacted on a few important but rare occasions only exhibits servitude at certain intervals and throws the burden of it upon a small number of men. It is in vain to summon a people who have been rendered so dependent on the central power to choose from time to time the representatives of that power; this rare and brief exercise of their free choice, however important it may be, will not prevent them from gradually losing the faculties of thinking, feeling, and acting for themselves, and thus gradually falling below the level of humanity.

I add that they will soon become incapable of exercising the great and only privilege which remains to them. The democratic nations that have introduced freedom into their political constitution at the very time when they were augmenting the despotism of their administrative constitution have been led into strange paradoxes. To manage those minor affairs in which good sense is all that is wanted, the people are held to be unequal to the task; but when the government of the country is at stake, the people are invested with immense powers; they are alternately made the playthings of their ruler, and his masters, more than kings and less than men. After having exhausted all the different modes of election without finding one to suit their purpose, they are still amazed and still bent on seeking further; as if the evil they notice did not originate in the constitution of the country far more than in that of the electoral body.

It is indeed difficult to conceive how men who have entirely given up the habit of self-government should succeed in making a proper choice of those by whom they are to be governed; and no one will ever believe that a liberal, wise, and energetic government can spring from the suffrages of a subservient people.

A constitution republican in its head and ultra-monarchical in all its other parts has always appeared to me to be a shortlived monster. The vices of rulers and the ineptitude of the people would speedily bring about its ruin; and the nation, weary of its representatives and of itself, would create freer institutions or soon return to stretch itself at the feet of a single master.

I believe that it is easier to establish an absolute and despotic government among a people in which the conditions of society are equal than among any other; and I think that if such a government were once established among such a people, it not only would oppress men, but would eventually strip each of them of several of the highest qualities of humanity. Despotism, therefore, appears to me peculiarly to be dreaded in democratic times. I should have loved freedom, I believe, at all times, but in the time in which we live I am ready to worship it.

On the other hand, I am persuaded that all who attempt, in the ages upon which we are entering, to base freedom upon aristocratic privilege will fail; that all who attempt to draw and to retain authority within a single class will fail. At the present day no ruler is skillful or strong enough to found a despotism by re-establishing permanent distinctions of rank among his subjects; no legislator is wise or powerful enough to preserve free institutions if he does not take equality for his first principle and his watchword. All of our contemporaries who would establish or secure the independence and the dignity of their fellow men must show themselves the friends of equality; and the only worthy means of showing themselves as such is to be so: upon this depends the success of their holy enterprise. Thus the question is not how to reconstruct aristocratic society, but how to make liberty proceed out of that democratic state of society in which God has placed us.

These two truths appear to me simple, clear, and fertile in consequences; and they naturally lead me to consider what kind of free government can be established among a people in which social conditions are equal.

It results from the very constitution of democratic nations and from their necessities that the power of government among them must be more uniform, more centralized, more extensive, more searching, and more efficient than in other countries. Society at large is naturally stronger and more active, the individual more subordinate and weak; the former does more, the latter less; and this is inevitably the case.

It is not, therefore, to be expected that the range of private independence will ever be so extensive in democratic as in aristocratic countries; nor is this to be desired; for among aristocratic nations the mass is often sacrificed to the individual, and the prosperity of the greater number to the greatness of the few. It is both necessary and desirable that the government of a democratic people should be active and powerful; and our object should not be to render it weak or indolent, but solely to prevent it from abusing its aptitude and its strength.

The circumstances which most contributed to secure the independence of private persons in aristocratic ages was that the supreme power did not affect to take upon itself alone the government and administration of the community. Those functions were necessarily partially left to the members of the aristocracy; so that, as the supreme power was always divided, it never weighed with its whole weight and in the same manner on each individual.

Not only did the government not perform everything by its immediate agency, but as most of the agents who discharged its duties derived their power, not from the state, but from the circumstance of their birth, they were not perpetually under its control. The government could not make or unmake them in an instant, at pleasure or bend them in strict uniformity to its slightest caprice; this was an additional guarantee of private independence.

I readily admit that recourse cannot be had to the same means at the present time, but I discover certain democratic expedients that may be substituted for them. Instead of vesting in the government alone all the administrative powers which guilds and nobles have been deprived, a portion of them may be entrusted to secondary public bodies temporarily composed of private citizens: thus the liberty of private persons will be more secure, and their equality will not be diminished.

The Americans, who care less for words than the French, still designate by the name of County the largest of their administrative districts; but the duties of the count or lord-lieutenant are in part performed by a provincial assembly.

At a period of equality like our own, it would be unjust and unreasonable to institute hereditary officers; but there is nothing to prevent us from substituting elective public officers to a certain extent. Election is a democratic expedient, which ensures the independence of the public officer in relation to the government as much as hereditary rank can ensure it among aristocratic nations, and even more so.

Aristocratic countries abound in wealthy and influential persons who are competent to provide for themselves and who cannot be easily or secretly oppressed; such persons restrain a government within general habits of moderation and reserve. I am well aware that democratic countries contain no such persons naturally, but something analogous to them may be created by artificial means. I firmly believe that an aristocracy cannot again be founded in the world, but I think that private citizens, by combining together, may constitute bodies of great wealth, influence, and strength, corresponding to the persons of an aristocracy. By this means many of the greatest political advantages of aristocracy would be obtained without its injustice or its dangers. An association for political, commercial, or manufacturing purposes, or even for those of science and literature, is a powerful and enlightened member of the community, which cannot be disposed of at pleasure or oppressed without remonstrance, and which, by defending its own rights against the encroachments of the government, saves the common liberties of the country.

In periods of aristocracy every man is always bound so closely to many of his fellow citizens that he cannot be assailed without their coming to his assistance. In ages of equality every man naturally stands alone; he has no hereditary friends whose cooperation he may demand, no class upon whose sympathy he may rely; he is easily got rid of, and he is trampled on with impunity. At the present time an oppressed member of the community has therefore only one method of self-defense: he may appeal to the whole nation, and if the whole nation is deaf to his complaint, he may appeal to mankind. The only means he has of making this appeal is by the press. Thus the liberty of the press is infinitely more valuable among democratic nations than among all others; it is the only cure for the evils that equality may produce. Equality sets men apart and weakens them; but the press places a powerful weapon within every man's reach, which the weakest and loneliest of them all may use. Equality deprives a man of the support of his connections, but the press enables him to summon all his fellow countrymen and all his fellow men to his assistance. Printing has accelerated the progress of equality, and it is also one of its best correctives.

I think that men living in aristocracies may, strictly speaking do without the liberty of the press; but such is not the case with those who live in democratic countries. To protect their personal independence I do not trust to great political assemblies, to parliamentary privilege, or to the assertion of popular sovereignty. All these things may, to a certain extent, be reconciled with personal servitude. But that servitude cannot be complete if the press is free; the press is the chief democratic instrument of freedom.

Something analogous may be said of the judicial power. It is a part of the essence of judicial power to attend to private interests and to fix itself with predilection on minute objects submitted to its observation. Another essential quality of judicial power is never to volunteer its assistance to the oppressed, but always to be at the disposal of the humblest of those who solicit it; their complaint, however feeble they may themselves be, will force itself upon the ear of justice and claim redress, for this is inherent in the very constitution of courts of justice.

A power of this kind is therefore peculiarly adapted to the wants of freedom, at a time when the eye and finger of the government are constantly intruding into the minutest details of human actions, and when private persons are at once too weak to protect themselves and too much isolated for them to reckon upon the assistance of their fellows. The strength of the courts of law has always been the greatest security that can be offered to personal independence; but this is more especially the case in democratic ages. Private rights and interests are in constant danger if the judicial power does not grow more extensive and stronger to keep pace with the growing equality of conditions.

Equality awakens in men several propensities extremely dangerous to freedom, to which the attention of the legislator ought constantly be directed. I shall only remind the reader of the most important among them.

Men living in democratic ages do not readily comprehend the utility of forms: they feel an instinctive contempt for them, I have elsewhere shown for what reasons. Forms excite their contempt and often their hatred; as they commonly aspire to none but ready and present gratifications, they rush onwards to the object of their desires, and the slightest delay exasperates them. This same temper, carried with them into political life, renders them hostile to forms, which perpetually retard or attest them in some of their projects.

Yet this objection which the men of democracies make to forms is the very thing which renders forms so useful to freedom; for their chief merit is to serve as a barrier between the strong and the weak, the ruler and the people, to retard the one and give the other time to look about him. Forms become more necessary in proportion as the government becomes more active and more powerful, while private persons are becoming more indolent and more feeble. Thus democratic nations naturally stand more in need of forms than other nations, and they naturally respect them less. This deserves most serious attention.

Nothing is more pitiful than the arrogant disdain of most of our contemporaries for questions of form, for the smallest questions of form have acquired in our time an importance which they never had before; many of the greatest interests of mankind depend upon them. I think that if the statesmen of aristocratic ages could sometimes despise forms with impunity and frequently rise above them, the statesmen to whom the government of nations is now confided ought to treat the very least among them with respect and not neglect them without imperious necessity. In aristocracies the observance of forms was superstitious; among us they ought to be kept up with a deliberate and enlightened deference.

Another tendency which is extremely natural to democratic nations and extremely dangerous is that which leads them to despise and undervalue the rights of private persons. The attachment that men feel to a right and the respect that they display for it are generally proportioned to its importance or to the length of time during which they have enjoyed it. The rights of private persons among democratic nations are commonly of small importance, of recent growth, and extremely precarious; the consequence is that they are often sacrificed without regret and almost always violated without remorse.

But it happens that, at the same period and among the same nations in which men conceive a natural contempt for the rights of private persons, the rights of society at large are naturally extended and consolidated; in other words, men become less attached to private rights just when it is most necessary to retain and defend what little remains of them. It is therefore most especially in the present democratic times, that the true friends of the liberty and the greatness of man ought constantly to be on the alert to prevent the power of government from lightly sacrificing the private rights of individuals to the general execution of its designs. At such times no citizen is so obscure that it is not very dangerous to allow him to be oppressed; no private rights are so unimportant that they can be surrendered with impunity to the caprices of a government. The reason is plain: if the private right of an individual is violated at a time when the human mind is fully impressed with the importance and the sanctity of such rights, the injury done is confined to the individual whose right is infringed; but to violate such a right at the present day is deeply to corrupt the manners of the nation and to put the whole community in jeopardy, because the very notion of this kind of right constantly tends among us to be impaired and lost.

There are certain habits, certain notions, and certain vices which are peculiar to a state of revolution and which a protracted revolution cannot fail to create and to propagate, whatever, in other respects, are its character, its purpose, and the scene on which it takes place. When any nation has, within a short space of time, repeatedly varied its rulers, its opinions, and its laws, the men of whom it is composed eventually contract a taste for change and grow accustomed to see all changes effected by sudden violence. Thus they naturally conceive a contempt for forms which daily prove ineffectual; and they do not support without impatience the dominion of rules which they have so often seen infringed.

As the ordinary notions of equity and morality no longer suffice to explain and justify all the innovations daily begotten by a revolution, the principle of public utility is called in, the doctrine of political necessity is conjured up, and men accustom themselves to sacrifice private interests without scruple and to trample on the rights of individuals in order more speedily to accomplish any public purpose.

These habits and notions, which I shall call revolutionary because all revolutions produce them, occur in aristocracies just as much as among democratic nations; but among the former they are often less powerful and always less lasting, because there they meet with habits, notions, defects, and impediments that counteract them. They consequently disappear as soon as the revolution is terminated, and the nation reverts to its former political courses. This is not always the case in democratic countries, in which it is ever to be feared that revolutionary tendencies, becoming more gentle and more regular, without entirely disappearing from society, will be gradually transformed into habits of subjection to the administrative authority of the government. I know of no countries in which revolutions are more dangerous than in democratic countries, because, independently of the accidental and transient evils that must always attend them, they may always create some evils that are permanent and unending.

I believe that there are such things as justifiable resistance and legitimate rebellion; I do not therefore assert as an absolute proposition that the men of democratic ages ought never to make revolutions; but I think that they have especial reason to hesitate before they embark on them and that it is far better to endure many grievances in their present condition than to have recourse to so perilous a remedy.

I shall conclude with one general idea, which comprises not only all the particular ideas that have been expressed in the present chapter, but also most of those of which it is the object of this book to treat. In the ages of aristocracy which preceded our own, there were private persons of great power and a social authority of extreme weakness. The outline of society itself was not easily discernible and was constantly confounded with the different powers by which the community was ruled. The principle efforts of the men of those times were required to strengthen, aggrandize, and secure the supreme power; and, on the other hand, to circumscribe individual independence within narrower limits and to subject private interests to the interests of the public. Other perils and other cares await the men of our age. Among the greater part of modern nations the government, whatever may be its origin, its constitution, or its name, has become almost omnipotent, and private persons are falling more and more into the lowest stage of weakness and dependence.

In olden society everything was different; unity and uniformity were nowhere to be met with. In modern society everything threatens to become so much alike that the peculiar characteristics of each individual will soon be entirely lost in the general aspect of the world. Our forefathers were always prone to make an improper use of the notion that private rights ought to be respected; and we are naturally prone, on the other hand, to exaggerate the idea that the interest of a private individual ought always to bend to the interest of the many.

The political world is metamorphosed; new remedies must henceforth be sought for new disorders. To lay down extensive but distinct and settled limits to the action of the government; to confer certain rights on private persons, and to secure to them the undisputed enjoyment of those rights; to enable individual man to maintain whatever independence, strength, and original power he still possesses; to raise him by the side of society at large, and uphold him in that position; these appear to me the main objects of legislators in the ages upon which we are now entering.

It would seem as if the rulers of our time sought only to use men in order to make things great; I wish that they would try a little more to make great men; that they would set less value on the work and more upon the workman; that they would never forget that a nation cannot long remain strong when every man belonging to it is individually weak; and that no form or combination of social polity has yet been devised to make an energetic people out of a community of pusillanimous and enfeebled citizens.

I trace among our contemporaries two contrary notions which are equally injurious. One set of men can perceive nothing in the principle of equality but the anarchical tendencies that it engenders; they dread their own free agency, they fear themselves. Other thinkers, less numerous but more enlightened, take a different view: beside that track which starts from the principle of equality to terminate in anarchy, they have at last discovered the road that seems to lead men to inevitable servitude. They shape their souls beforehand to this necessary condition; and, despairing of remaining free, they already do obeisance in their hearts to the master who is soon to appear. The former abandon freedom because they think it cangerous; the latter, because they hold it to be impossible.

If I had entertained the latter conviction, I should not have written this book, but I should have confined myself to deploring in secret the destiny of mankind. I have sought to point out the dangers to which the principle of equality exposes the independence of man, because I firmly believe that these dangers are the most formidable as well as the least foreseen of all those which futurity holds in store, but I do not think that they are insurmountable.

The men who live in the democratic ages upon which we are entering have naturally a taste for independence; they are naturally impatient of regulation, and they are wearied by the permanence even of the condition they themselves prefer. They are fond of power, but they are prone to despise and hate those who wield it, and they easily elude its grasp by their own mobility and insignificance.

These propensities will always manifest themselves, because they originate in the groundwork of society, which will undergo no change; for a long time they will prevent the establishment of any despotism, and they will furnish fresh weapons to each succeeding generation that struggles in favor of the liberty of mankind. Let us, then, look forward to the future with that salutary fear which makes men keep watch and ward for freedom, not with that faint and idle terror which depresses and enervates the heart.

* * *

Before finally closing the subject that I have now discussed, I should like to take a parting survey of all the different characteristics of modern society and appreciate at last the general influence to be exercised by the principle of equality upon the fate of mankind; but I am stopped by the difficulty of the task, and, in presence of so great a theme, my sight is troubled and my reason fails.

The society of the modern world, which I have sought to delineate and which I seek to judge, has but just come into existence. Time has not yet shaped it into perfect form; the great revolution by which it was created is not yet over; and amid the occurrences of our time it is almost impossible to discern what will pass away with the revolution itself and what will survive its close. The world that is rising into existence is still half encumberd by the remains of the world that is waning into decay; and amid the vast perplexity of human affairs none can say how much of ancient institutions and former customs will remain or how much will completely disappear.

Although the revolution that is taking place in the social condition, the laws, the opinions, and the feelings of men is still very far from being terminated, yet its results already admit of no comparison with anything that the world has ever before witnessed. I go back from age to age up to the remotest antiquity, but I find no parallel to what is occurring before my eyes; as the past has ceased to throw its light upon the future, the mind of man wanders in obscurity.

Nevertheless, in the midst of a prospect so wide, so novel, and so confused, some of the more prominent characteristics may already be discerned and pointed out. The good things and the evils of life are more equally distributed in the world: great wealth tends to disappear, the number of small fortunes to increase; desires and gratifications are multiplied, but extraordinary prosperity and irremediable penury are alike unknown. The sentiment of ambitio universal, but the scope of ambition is seldom vast. Each individual stands apart in solitary weakness, but society at large is active, provident, and powerful; the performances of private persons are insignificant, those of the state immense.

There is little energy of character, but customs are mild and laws humane. If there are few instances of exalted heroism or of virtues of the highest, brightest, and purest temper, men's habits are regular, violence is rare, and cruelty almost unknown. Human existence becomes longer and property more secure; life is not adorned with brilliant trophies, but it is extremely easy and tranquil. Few pleasures are either very refined or very coarse, and highly polished manners are as uncommon as great brutality of tastes. Neither men of great learning nor extremely ignorant communities are to be met with; genius becomes more rare, information more diffused. The human mind is impelled by the small efforts of all mankind combined together, not by the strenuous activity of a few men. There is less perfection, but more abundance, in all the productions of the arts. The ties of race, of rank, and of country are relaxed; the great bond of humanity is strengthened.

If I endeavor to find out the most general and most prominent of all these different characteristics, I perceive that what is taking place in men's fortunes manifests itself under a thousand other forms. Almost all extremes are softened or blunted: all that was most prominent is superseded by some middle term, at once less lofty and less low, less brilliant and less obscure, than what before existed in the world.

When I survey this countless multitude of beings, shaped in each other's likeness, amid whom nothing rises and nothing falls, the sight of such universal uniformity saddens and chills me and I am tempted to regret that state of society which has ceased to be. When the world was full of men of great importance and extreme insignificance, of great wealth and extreme poverty, of great learning and extreme ignorance, I turned aside from the latter to fix my observation on the former alone, who gratified my sympathies. But I admit that this gratification arose from my own weakness; it is because I am unable to see at once all that is around me that I am allowed thus to select and separate the objects of my predilection from among so many others. Such is not the case with that Almighty and Eternal Being whose gaze necessarily includes the whole of created things and who surveys distinctly, though all at once, mankind and man.

We may naturally believe that it is not the singular prosperity of the few, but the greater well-being of all that is most pleasing in the sight of the Creator and Preserver of men. What appears to me to be man's decline is, to His eye, advancement; what afflicts me is acceptable to Him. A state of equality is perhaps less elevated, but it is more just: and its justice constitutes its greatness and its beauty. I would strive, then, to raise myself to this point of the divine contemplation and thence to view and to judge the concerns of men.

No man on the earth can as yet affirm, absolutely and generally that the new state of the world is better than its former one; but it is already easy to perceive that this state is different. Some vices and some virtues were so inherent in the constitution of an aristocratic nation and are so opposite to the character of a modern people that they can never be infused into it; some good tendencies and some bad propensities which were unknown to the former are natural to the latter; some ideas suggest themselves spontaneously to the imagination of the one which are utterly repugnant to the mind of the other. They are like two distinct orders of human beings, each of which has its own merits and defects, its own advantages and its own evils. Care must therefore be taken not to judge the state of society that is now coming into by notions derived from a state of society that no longer exists; for as these states of society are exceedingly different in their structure, they cannot be submitted to a just or fair comparison. It would be scarcely more reasonable to require of our contemporaries the peculiar virtues which originated in the social condition of their forefathers, since that social condition is itself fallen and has drawn into one promiscuous ruin the good and the evil that belonged to it.

But as yet these things are imperfectly understood. I find that a great number of my contemporaries undertake to make a selection from among the institutions, the opinions, and the ideas that originated in the aristocratic constitution of society as it was; a portion of these elements they would willingly relinquish, but they would keep the remainder and transplant them into their new world. I feat that such men are wasting their time and their strength in virtuous but unprofitable efforts. The object is, not to retain the peculiar advantages which the inequality of conditions bestows upon mankind, but to secure the new benefits which equality may supply. We have not to seek to make ourselves like our progenitors, but to strive to work out that species of greatness and happiness which is our own.

For myself, who now look back from this extreme limit of my task and discover from afar, but at once, the various objects which have attracted my more attentive investigation upon my way, I am full of apprehensions and of hopes. I perceive mighty dangers which it is possible to ward off, mighty evils which may be avoided or alleviated; and I cling with a firmer hold to the belief that for democratic nations to be virtuous and prosperous, they require but to will it.

I am aware that many of my contemporaries maintain that nations are never their own masters here below, and that they necessarily obey some insurmountable and unintelligent power, arising from anterior events, from their race, or from the soil and climate of their country. Such principles are false and cowardly; such principles can never produce aught but feeble men and pusillanimous nations. Providence has not created mankind entirely independent or entirely free. It is true that around every man a fatal circle is traced beyond which he cannot pass; but within the wide verge of that circle he is powerful and free; as it is with man, so with communities. The nations of our time cannot prevent the conditions of men from becoming equal, but it depends upon themselves whether the principle of equality is to lead them to servitude or freedom, to knowledge or barbarism, to prosperity or wretchedness.

# Epilogue

> Let every American, every lover of liberty, every well wisher to his posterity, swear by the blood of the Revolution, never to violate in the least particular, the laws of the country; and never to tolerate their violation by others. As the patriots of seventy-six did to the support of the Declaration of Independence, so to the support of the Constitution and Laws, let every American pledge his life, his property, and his sacred honor.
>
> *Abraham Lincoln*

---

## The Perpetuation of Our Political Institutions

Abraham Lincoln

As a subject for the remarks of the evening, the perpetuation of our political institutions is selected.

In the great journal of things happening under the sun, we, the American People, find our account running, under date of the nineteenth century of the Christian era. We find ourselves in the peaceful possession, of the fairest portion of the earth, as regards extent of territory, fertility of soil, and salubrity of climate. We find ourselves under the government of a system of political institutions, conducing more essentially to the ends of civil and religious liberty, than any of which the history of former times tell us. We, when mounting the stage of existence, found ourselves the legal inheritors of these fundamental blessings. We toiled not in the acquirement or establishment of them—they are a legacy bequeathed us, by a *once* hardy, brave, and patriotic, but *now* lamented and departed race of ancestors. Their's was the task (and nobly they performed it) to possess themselves, and through themselves, us, of this goodly land; and to uprear upon its hills and its valleys, a political edifice of liberty and equal rights; 'tis ours only, to transmit these, the former, unprofaned by the foot of an invader; the latter, undecayed by the lapse of time, and untorn by usurpation—to the latest generation that fate shall permit the world to know. This task of gratitude to our fathers, justice to ourselves, duty to posterity, and love for our species in general, all imperatively require us faithfully to perform.

How, then, shall we perform it? At what point shall we expect the approach of danger? By what means shall we fortify against it? Shall we expect some transatlantic military giant, to step the Ocean, and crush us at a blow? Never! All the armies of Europe, Asia and Africa combined with all the treasure of the earth (our own excepted) in their military chest; with a Buonaparte for a commander, could not by force, take a drink from the Ohio, or make a track on the Blue Ridge, in a trial of a thousand years.

Address before the Young Men's Lyceum of Springfield, Illinois, January 27, 1838.

At what point then is the approach of danger to be expected? I answer, if it ever reach us, it must spring up amongst us. It cannot come from abroad. If destruction be our lot, we must ourselves be its author and finisher. As a nation of freemen, we must live through all time, or die by suicide.

I hope I am over wary; but if I am not, there is even now, something of ill-omen amongst us. I mean the increasing disregard for law which pervades the country; the growing disposition to substitute the wild and furious passions, in lieu of the sober judgement of Courts; and the worse than savage mobs, for the executive ministers of justice. This disposition is awfully fearful in any community; and that it now exists in ours, though grating to our feelings to admit, it would be a violation of truth, and an insult to our intelligence, to deny. Accounts of outrages committed by mobs, form the every-day news of the times. They have pervaded the country, from New England to Louisiana;—they are neither peculiar to the eternal snows of the former, nor the burning suns of the latter;—they are not the creature of climate—neither are they confined to the slaveholding, or the non-slaveholding States. Alike, they spring up among the pleasure hunting masters of Southern slaves, and the order loving citizens of the land of steady habits. Whatever, then, their cause may be, it is common to the whole country.

It would be tedious, as well as useless, to recount the horrors of all of them. Those happening in the State of Mississippi, and at St. Louis, are, perhaps, the most dangerous in example, and revolting to humanity. In the Mississippi case, they first commenced by hanging the regular gamblers: a set of men, certainly not following for a livelihood, a very useful, or very honest occupation; but one which, so far from being forbidden by the laws, was actually licensed by an act of the Legislature, passed but a single year before. Next, negroes, suspected of conspiring to raise an insurrection, were caught up and hanged in all parts of the State: then, white men, supposed to be leagued with the negroes; and finally, strangers, from neighboring States, going thither on business, were, in many instances, subjected to the same fate. Thus went on this process of hanging, from gamblers to negroes, from negroes to white citizens, and from these to strangers; till, dead men were seen literally dangling from the boughs of trees upon every road side; and in numbers almost sufficient, to rival the native Spanish moss of the country, as a drapery of the forest.

Turn, then, to that horror-striking scene at St. Louis. A single victim was only sacrificed there. His story is very short; and is, perhaps, the most highly tragic, of any thing of its length, that has ever been witnessed in real life. A mulatto man, by the name of McIntosh, was seized in the street, dragged to the suburbs of the city, chained to a tree, and actually burned to death; and all within a single hour from the time he had been a freeman, attending to his own business, and at peace with the world.

Such are the effects of mob law; and such are the scenes, becoming more and more frequent in this land so lately famed for love of law and order; and the stories of which, have even now grown too familiar, to attract any thing more, than an idle remark.

But you are, perhaps, ready to ask, "What has this to do with the perpetuation of our political institutions?" I answer, it has much to do with it. Its direct consequences are, comparatively speaking, but a small evil; and much of its danger consists, in the proneness of our minds to regard its direct, as its only consequences. Abstractly considered, the hanging of the gamblers at Vicksburg, was of but little consequence. They constitute a portion of population, that is worse than useless in any community; and their death, if no pernicious example be set by it, is never matter of reasonable regret with any one. If they were annually swept, from the stage of existence, by the plague or small pox, honest men would, perhaps, be much profited, by the operation. Similar too, is the correct reasoning, in regard to the burning of the negro at St. Louis. He had forfeited his life, by the perpetration of an outrageous murder, upon one of the most worthy and respectable citizens of the city; and had he not died as he did, he must have died by the sentence of the law, in a very short time afterwards. As to him alone, it was as well the way it was, as it could otherwise have been. But the example in either case was fearful. When men take it in their heads today, to hang gamblers, or burn murderers, they should recollect, that, in the confusion usually attending such transactions, they will be as likely to hang or burn some one, who is neither a gambler nor a murderer as one who is; and that, acting upon the example they set, the mob of tomorrow, may, and probably will, hang or burn some of them, by the very same mistake. And not only so; the innocent, those who have ever set their faces against violations of law in every shape, alike with the guilty, fall victims to the ravages of mob law; and thus it goes on, step by step, till all the walls erected for the defence of the persons and property of individuals, are trodden down, and disregarded. But all this even, is not the full extent of the evil. By such examples, by instances of the perpetrators of such acts going unpunished, the lawless in spirit, are encouraged to become lawless in practice; and having been used to no restraint, but dread of punishment, they thus become absolutely unrestrained. Having ever regarded Government as their deadliest bane, they make a jubilee of the suspension of its operations; and pray for nothing so much, as its total annihilation. While, on the other hand, good men, men who love tranquility, who desire to abide by the laws, and enjoy their benefits, who would gladly spill their blood in defence of their country; seeing their property destroyed; their families insulted, and their lives endangered; their persons injured; and seeing nothing in prospect that forebodes a change for the better; become tired of, and disgusted with, a Government that offers them no protection; and not much averse to a change in which they imagine they have nothing to lose. Thus, then, by the operation of this mobocratic spirit, which all must admit, is now abroad in the land, the strongest bulwark of any Government, and particularly of those constituted like ours, may effectually be broken down and destroyed—I mean the *attachment* of the People. Whenever this effect shall be produced among us; whenever the vicious portion of population shall be permitted to gather in bands of hundreds and thousands, and burn churches, ravage and rob provision stores, throw printing presses into rivers, shoot editors, and hang and burn obnoxious persons at pleasure, and with impunity; depend on it, this Government cannot last. By such things, the feelings of the best citizens will become more or less alienated from it; and thus it will be left without friends, or with too few, and those few too weak, to make their friendship effectual. At such a time and under such circumstances, men of sufficient talent and ambition will not be wanting to seize the opportunity, strike the blow, and overturn that fair fabric, which for the last half century, has been the fondest hope, of the lovers of freedom, throughout the world.

I know the American People are *much* attached to their Government—I know they would suffer *much* for its sake;—I know they would endure evils long and patiently, before they would ever think of exchanging it for another. Yet, notwithstanding all this, if the laws be continually despised and disregarded, if their rights to be secure in their persons and property, are held by no better tenure than the caprice of a mob, the alienation of their affections from the Government is the natural consequence; and to that, sooner or later, it must come.

Here then, is one point at which danger may be expected.

The question recurs "how shall we fortify against it?" The answer is simple. Let every American, every lover of liberty, every well wisher to his posterity, swear by the blood of the Revolution, never to violate in the least particular, the laws of the country; and never to tolerate their violation by others. As the patriots of seventy-six did to the support of the Declaration of Independence, so to the support of the Constitution and Laws, let every American pledge his life, his property, and his sacred honor; let every man remember that to violate the law, is to trample on the blood of his father, and to tear the character of his own, and his children's liberty. Let the reverence for the laws, be breathed by every American mother, to the lisping babe, that prattles on her lap—let it be taught in schools, in seminaries, and in colleges;— let it be written in Primmers, spelling books, and in Almanacs;—let it be preached from the pulpit, proclaimed in legislative halls, and enforced in courts of justice. And, in short, let it become the *political religion* of the nation; and let the old and the young, the rich and the poor, the grave and the gay, of all sexes and tongues, and colors and conditions, sacrifice unceasingly upon its altars.

While ever a state of feeling, such as this, shall universally, or even, very generally prevail throughout the nation, vain will be every effort, and fruitless every attempt, to subvert our national freedom.

When I so pressingly urge a strict observance of all the laws, let me not be understood as saying there are no bad laws, nor that grievances may not arise, for the redress of which, no legal provisions have been made. I mean to say no such thing. But I do mean to say, that, although bad laws, if they exist, should be repealed as soon as possible, still while they continue in force, for the sake of example, they should be religiously observed. So also in unprovided cases. If such arise, let proper legal provisions be made for them with the least possible delay; but, till then, let them if not too intolerable, be borne with.

There is no grievance that is a fit object of redress by mob law. In any case that arises, as for instance, the promulgation of abolitionism, one of two positions is necessarily true; that is, the thing is right within itself, and therefore deserves the protection of all law and all good citizens; or, it is wrong, and therefore proper to be prohibited by legal enactments; and in neither case, is the interposition of mob law, either necessary, justifiable, or excusable.

But, it may be asked, why suppose danger to our political institutions? Have we not preserved them for more than fifty years? And why may we not for fifty times as long?

We hope there is no *sufficient* reason. We hope all dangers may be overcome; but to conclude that no danger may ever arise, would itself be extremely dangerous. There are now, and will hereafter be, many causes, dangerous in their tendency, which have not existed heretofore; and which are not too insignificant to merit attention. That our government should have been maintained in its original form from its establishment until now, is not much to be wondered at. It had many props to support it through that period, which now are decayed, and crumbled away. Through that period, it was felt by all, to be an undecided experiment; now, it is understood to be a successful one. Then, all that sought celebrity and fame, and distinction, expected to find them in the success of that experiment. Their *all* was staked upon it:—their destiny was *inseparably* linked with it. Their ambition aspired to display before an admiring world, a practical demonstration of the truth of a proposition, which had hitherto been considered, at best no better, than problematical; namely, *the capability of a people to govern themselves.* If they succeeded, they were to be immortalized; their names were to be transferred to counties and cities, and rivers and mountains; and to be revered and sung, and toasted through all time. If they failed, they were to be called knaves and fools, and fanatics for a fleeting hour; then to sink and be forgotten. They succeeded. The experiment is successful; and thousands have won their deathless names in making it so. But the game is caught; and I believe it is true, that with the catching, end the pleasures of the chase. This field of glory is harvested, and the crop is already appropriated. But new reapers will arise, and *they,* too, will seek a field. It is to deny, what the history of the world tells us is true, to suppose that men of ambition and talents will not continue to spring up amongst us. And, when they do, they will as naturally seek the gratification of their ruling passion, as others have *so* done before them. The question then, is, can that gratification be found in supporting and maintaining an edifice that has been erected by others? Most certainly it cannot. Many great and good men sufficiently qualified for any task they should undertake, may ever be found, whose ambition would aspire to nothing beyond a seat in Congress, a gubernatorial or a presidential chair; *but such belong not to the family of the lion, or the tribe of the eagle.* What! think you these places would satisfy an Alexander, a Caesar, or a Napoleon? Never! Towering genius disdains a beaten path. It seeks regions hitherto unexplored. It sees *no distinction* in adding story to story, upon the monuments of fame, erected to the memory of others. It *denies* that it is glory enough to serve under any chief. It *scorns* to tread in the footsteps of *any* predecessor, however illustrious. It thirsts and burns for distinction; and, if possible, it will have it, whether at the expense of emancipating slaves, or enslaving freemen. It is unreasonable then to expect, that some man possessed of the loftiest genius, coupled with ambition sufficient to push it to its utmost stretch, will at some time, spring up among us? And when such a one does, it will require the people to be united with each other, attached to the government and laws, and generally intelligent to successfully frustrate his designs.

Distinction will be his paramount object; and although he would as willingly, perhaps more so, acquire it by doing good as harm; yet, that opportunity being past, and nothing left to be done in the way of building up, he would set boldly to the task of pulling down.

Here then, is a probable case, highly dangerous, and such a one as could not have well existed heretofore.

Another reason which *once was*; but which, to the same extent, is *now no more,* has done much in maintaining our institutions thus far. I mean the powerful influence which the interesting scenes of the revolution had upon the *passions* of the people as distinguished from their judgment. By this influence, the jealousy, envy, and avarice, incident to our nature, and so common to a state of peace, prosperity, and conscious strength, were, for the time, in a great measure smothered and rendered inactive; while the deep rooted principles of *hate*, and the powerful motive of *revenge*, instead of being turned against each other, were directed exclusively against the British nation. And thus, from the force of circumstances, the basest principles of our nature, were either made to lie dormant, or to become the active agents in the advancement of the noblest of causes—that of establishing and maintaining civil and religious liberty.

But this state of feeling *must fade, is fading, has faded,* with the circumstances that produced it.

I do not mean to say, that the scenes of the revolution *are now* or *ever will be* entirely forgotten; but that like everything else, they must fade upon the memory of the world, and grow more and more dim by the lapse of time. In history, we hope, they will be read of, and recounted, so long as the bible shall be read;—but even granting that they will, their influence *cannot be* what it heretofore has been. Even then, they *cannot be* so universally known, nor so vividly felt, as they were by the generation just gone to rest. At the close of that struggle, nearly every adult male had been a participator in some of its scenes. The consequence was, that of those scenes, in the form of a husband, a father, a son, or a brother, a *living history* was to be found in every family—a history bearing the indubitable testimonies of its own authenticity, in the limbs mangled, in the scars of wounds received, in the midst of the very scenes related—a history, too, that could be read and understood alike by all, the wise and the ignorant, the learned and the unlearned. But *those* histories are gone. They *can* be read no more forever. They *were* a fortress of strength; but, what invading foemen could *never do,* the silent artillery of time *has done*; the levelling of its walls. They are gone. They *were* a forest of giant oaks; but the all-resistless hurricane has swept over them, and left only, here and there, a lonely trunk, despoiled of its verdure, shorn of its foliage; unshading and unshaded, to murmur in a few more gentle breezes, and to combat with its mutilated limbs, a few more ruder storms, then to sink, and be no more.

They *were* the pillars of the temple of liberty; and now, that they have crumbled away, that temple must fall, unless we, their descendants, supply their places with other pillars, hewn from the solid quarry of sober reason. Passion has helped us; but can do so no more. It will in future be our enemy. Reason, cold, calculating, unimpassioned reason, must furnish all the materials for our future support and defence. Let those materials be moulded into *general intelligence, sound morality* and, in particular, *a reverence for the constitution and laws*; and, that we improved to the last; that we remained free to the last; that we revered his name to the last; that, during his long sleep, we permitted no hostile foot to pass over or desecrate his resting place; shall be that which to learn the last trump shall awaken our WASHINGTON.

Upon these let the proud fabric of freedom rest, as the rock of its basis; and as truly as has been said of the only greater institution, *"the gates of hell shall not prevail against it."*